THE HUNDRED YEARS

VOLUME II

Trial by Fire

A succession of catastrophes in the middle years of the fourteenth century brought France to the brink of destruction. The bankruptcy of the French state and a bitter civil war within the Royal Family were followed by the defeat and capture of the King of France by the Black Prince at Poitiers. A peasant revolt and a violent revolution in Paris completed the tragedy. In a humiliating treaty of partition France ceded more than a third of its territory to Edward III of England. Not for sixty years would the English again come so close to total victory.

Yet the theme of this volume is not destruction, but survival. France's great cities, provincial towns and rural communities resisted where its leaders failed. They withstood the sustained savagery of the soldiers and the free companies of brigands to undo most of Edward Ill's work in the following generation. England's triumphs proved to be brittle and short lived.

Based on a wide range of contemporary sources, both printed and unprinted, and coloured by a lively historical imagination, *Trial by Fire* is the absorbing continuation of Jonathan Sumption's 'immensely impressive history' (*Daily Telegraph*).

Jonathan Sumption was a History fellow of Magdalen College, Oxford, until 1975. He is a QC practising at the commercial bar and is the author of *Pilgrimage* and *The Albigensian Crusade.* The other volumes in his account of the Hundred Years War, *Trial by Battle*, *Divided Houses*, and *Cursed Kings*, are also published by Faber & Faber.

by the same author

PILGRIMAGE: An Image of Medieval Religion
THE ALBIGENSIAN CRUSADE
THE HUNDRED YEARS WAR Volume I: Trial by Battle
THE HUNDRED YEARS WAR Volume III: Divided Houses
THE HUNDRED YEARS WAR Volume IV: Cursed Kings

THE HUNDRED YEARS WAR

JONATHAN SUMPTION

VOLUME II
Trial by Fire

faber and faber

First published in 1999
by Faber and Faber Ltd
Bloomsbury House
74–77 Great Russell Street
London WC1B 3DA

This paperback edition first published in 2001

Photoset by Parker Typesetting Service, Leicester
Printed and bound by CPI Group (UK) Ltd, Croydon, CR0 4YY

A CIP record for this book
is available from the British Library

ISBN 978-0-571-20737-4

To Bernard

Contents

Maps and Plans

In the text

Preface

At most times, war has been the principal collective enterprise of mankind. It has given human societies their identities. It has shaped their institutions, and provided the ultimate test of their solidity. This volume tells the story of a prolonged crisis in the affairs of France, the richest and most advanced society of late medieval Europe, which had in a real sense been formed by war and in the 1350s was almost destroyed by it. The strain of continual invasion, the financial and economic problems of defence, the shock of a grave and unexpected defeat in battle, combined for a brief period to bring the French state to the verge of extinction and to dissolve bonds of civil society which men had taken for granted for more than a century. As at similar crises in the history of France, in 1792 and 1870, these events were accompanied by savage recriminations among Frenchmen: venomous argument in elected assemblies; an unsuccessful revolution in Paris and another among the peasant communities of the north.

The main theme of this volume, however, is not destruction but survival. Stable communities are remarkably resilient in the face of catastrophe. The cities and rural communities of France survived, damaged and impoverished but intact, to undo most of Edward III's work in the following generation. There is no symmetry in war, and although France was defeated, England was not victorious. The English achieved a brief and flattering peace, which lasted for just nine years in the 1360s. They did this not by sustained military pressure, but by capturing the King of France, John II, who was able to impose it on his subjects. Englishmen and Gascons caused immense destruction in the territory of France, but they conquered very little of it. They crashed like great waves over the country, then ebbed away. They lacked the administrative and financial resources to impose a thorough-going occupation, something that only the police states of the nineteenth and twentieth centuries have been able to achieve, and then only for short periods.

These events were recorded by those who lived through them in some of the most vivid narratives to survive from the medieval period. As the English chronicle tradition faded, the French one came into its own. Pierre d'Orgement (or whoever else wrote the continuation of the *Grandes chroniques de France*) lived through the Parisian revolution of Étienne Marcel as one of the Dauphin's entourage, and described it in language which loses nothing by its laconic, passionless style. Jean de Venette witnessed the same events as a resident of the city. The Castilian chronicler Ayala had served both rivals for his country's crown and commanded a division in the disastrous battle of Nájera. The Northumberland chronicler Thomas Gray of Heton fought in Scotland and the poet Chaucer in France.

For all their literary qualities, however, these sources need to be approached with the same caution which one brings to reading newspaper accounts of modern wars. Those who work daily in the law courts will know how fallible even eye-witnesses can be. To write the history of the fourteenth century from Froissart's elegant but muddled and inaccurate chronicle, as some nineteenth-century historians tried to do, would be absurd. One might as well use Shakespeare, or indeed Donizetti. The present volume is based primarily on the record sources, printed and unprinted, of England, Scotland and France, and on those of the Papacy and the Spanish kingdoms. Some of these convey the atmosphere of these appalling years with as much dramatic intensity as the most colourful chronicles. The French chancery registers, for example, in which ordinary Frenchmen confessed their misdeeds to the state in order to be pardoned, provide countless miniature autobiographies in which the war can be seen through the eyes of its lesser actors and victims.

In these and other respects, the principles on which this history is written were explained in the preface to the first volume, published in 1990, and have not changed.

J.P.C.S.
Greenwich
April 1998

CHAPTER I

The Truce of Calais Problems of Victory 1347–1349

The rain fell in England throughout the summer of 1348 as, amid a landscape of mud and flattened grain, men celebrated a decade of war and three years of victory. In a succession of opulent tournaments in the spring at Reading, Bury St. Edmunds, Lincoln and Eltham, teams of horsemen dressed in bulky padded armour and huge decorated pot-helmets rode into the lists to fight each other with blunt lances according to the stylised convention of lawyers, heralds and romancers. At Lichfield, where one of the most splendid of these pageants was held at the beginning of May, the King, disguised in the armour of one of his household knights, entered the lists with his companions dressed in uniform blue and white, their horses covered in blue velvet, gold plate and silk. Twenty-eight ladies of the court assisted them in the procession, wearing extravagant fancy dress of the same colours. Nearly 300 more watched among the supporters from the boundaries, peering at the spectacle through the eye-slits of fantastic decorated masks. 'Thus did they squander their wealth and deck out their bodies with the trappings of frippery, buffoonery and lust . . .,' an unfriendly observer wrote; 'not one of the men whom they were serving seemed to realise that their victories were a gift from the God of all bounty, the true benefactor of the chivalry of England.'[1]

Perhaps they did not. When, at Windsor some six weeks later, Edward III's court celebrated the churching of the Queen after the birth of her sixth son, the tournament teams included all the most famous of the King's prisoners of war: the Count of Eu, Constable of France, carried off the prize; the lord of Tancarville, Chamberlain of Normandy who, like the Constable, had been captured at Caen as he tried to halt the advance of the English army through Normandy in July 1346; there was a handful of the survivors of the terrible slaughter of the French army at Crécy, a month later; David II, King of Scotland, taken at Neville's Cross as the largest Scottish army to invade England for many years dispersed and fled around him; and Charles of Blois, claimant of

Brittany, one of the ablest and most persistent enemies of the English cause, who had surrendered in the last moments of the battle of la Roche Derrien in June 1347. At the beginning of August 1348, Edward III endowed the chapel of St. George at Windsor to house his newly founded order of chivalry, the Order of the Garter, that 'most noble brotherhood' which proved to be the only enduring monument of this brief moment of hubris.[2]

Beyond his realm Edward's reputation had never been higher. After years in which his campaigns had failed, his continental alliances had fallen apart, his debts had mounted and his pretensions had come to seem increasingly absurd, men watched in astonishment as the King overwhelmed the foremost military power of Europe. Petrarch was to proclaim the transformation of the English from the 'most timid of all the uncouth races' into the supreme warriors of Europe. The protagonists in a German civil war offered Edward the Crown of Germany, which he had the good sense to refuse. The King of Castile, whose realm had moved in the orbit of France for more than a century, betrothed his heir to Edward's daughter Joan. Alfonso's ambassadors were pointed out among the courtiers attending Edward's great tournament at Lincoln in April 1348. Princes and noblemen of France, Germany and the Low Countries laid their disputes before him as, once, their forebears had laid them before Edward I at the height of his fame.[3]

Some of these men believed that Edward III had only to press his advantages in order to achieve complete victory. Yet, between the truce of Calais in September 1347 and the autumn of 1355, a period of eight years, the English King fought no major campaign on the continent. He clung on to what he held. His commanders fought off raids and launched others of their own. He watched as the war became a formless mêlée fought between small forces of half-disciplined soldiers and punctuated by ill-observed truces. The reason was lack of money, the perennial problem which had limited all his enterprises. Walter Chiriton, the London financier whose syndicate had paid most of the cost of the siege of Calais, crashed in April 1349, a victim of the King's duplicity and of his own dishonesty and greed. Edward's ministers turned to more orthodox methods of public finance as much from necessity as conviction. The debt generated by the campaigns of the mid-1340s was gradually paid off, a process which was still continuing well into the next decade. Chiriton's affairs were wound up over a period of two years by his creditors and guarantors. The revenues of the customs had been mortgaged to Chiriton years before. Edward did not recover control of them until the summer of 1351. The seedy expedients of the past were perforce abandoned in favour of ordinary parliamentary taxation. Yet Parliament could be demanding. The King had to submit to compromises some of which radically affected the way in which the war had hitherto been managed. There were two assemblies in the early months of 1348, in January and April, and on both occasions fierce protests were heard about the financial practices of Edward's government and the methods by which troops had been recruited and ships and supplies requisitioned. Some promises of amendment were made and largely kept. The final outcome was the grant of a single parliamentary subsidy for each of the next three years. In January 1352 this was renewed for a further three years. These subsidies were nominally raised for the renewed prosecution of the war. But in practice they were spent on the defence of past gains, the discharge of past debts and the daily expenses of government. The reality was that the first ten years of war had consumed eighteen years' worth of war taxation and ordinary government revenue. It would be several years before England was in a position to resume the war on any scale.[4]

Behind this unaccustomed financial prudence lay Edward III's growing awareness of the limits of his realm's resources and the difficulty of maintaining public support for a war without end. Many of Edward's subjects had supposed that his victories at Crécy and Calais meant the end of war taxation. When the collectors continued to go about their work as if nothing had happened, some of them encountered serious resistance. For the King, the recovery of his just rights in France was a point of honour as well as political ambition. It was supported by the great majority of the higher nobility, many of whom profited mightily by it. Yet the expenditure of so much effort and money, the abandonment of the conquest of Scotland and the sufferings of the coasts and harbours of southern England was a high price, not self-evidently justified in anyone else's eyes. 'All that I win through wit, he wastes through pride,' said the monks and moralists to those 'grave men of arms, bold squires of blood, bowmen many' in *Winner and Waster,* an acerbic satire written in 1352.[5]

Honi soit qui mal y pense. The phrase, which was coined in about 1348, is more likely to have referred to Edward's war aims and their critics than to any lady's garter. Yet those aims were as enigmatic as his famous motto. All that can be said with confidence is that his ambitions were smaller than his claims. Edward had claimed the Crown of France since 1340, but whenever he was strong enough to bargain with his adversary on something like equal terms he was always ready to trade his claim for territory. How much territory depended on the military situation of the moment. The least that Edward was ever willing to accept was the whole of the duchy of Aquitaine as it had stood on the death of his grandfather in 1307. This meant not only the Bordelais, the Landes and the valley of the Adour and its tributaries, but also Saintonge, southern Périgord and the Agenais. If he could get it he wanted more: Quercy and the Rouergue; Poitou; the Limousin, which Edward I had briefly won and lost at the end of the thirteenth century; the provinces of Anjou and Maine in the western Loire; Brittany; even Normandy; in fact the whole tract of western France which the Angevin dynasty had ruled at the height of its power in the twelfth century. Moreover, the status of this territory was at least as important as its extent. Whatever Edward gained had to be held in free sovereignty, quit of the residual obligations to the French Crown which even the Angevins had acknowledged. This much is clear from the hints that Edward's ambassadors had let slip in the interminable and frustrating diplomatic conferences in the papal palace at Avignon in 1344 and from the loud assertions of Henry of Lancaster in the same place ten years later.

Even in the aftermath of Edward's greatest victories, in 1346 and 1356, it is unlikely that he expected to be King of France. The claim to the French throne was a bargaining counter, a device for achieving a satisfactory settlement when the time was right, and a means of causing embarrassment to the Valois Kings. Edward was enough of a realist to know this. But he also knew that he could not admit it. To acknowledge that his royal title was no more than the prelude to crude horse-trading would have destroyed its practical value. So the King said nothing, refusing to disclose what he wanted except at moments when it seemed attainable. The disasters of the 1330s had taught him patience, and experience brought him a better understanding of his enemies than they ever had of him. He rarely negotiated from a position of weakness, always preferring to temporise, to wait for another year, another campaign, another ally. He took refuge in truces, preserving his conquests, gaining time, gathering his limited resources for a better day.

In France, the failures of the past decade had been received with incomprehension, frustration and finally with unconcealed fury. When the Estates-General opened in Paris on 30 November 1347, the purpose of the meeting was to canvass opinion as to how the war should be prosecuted and to prepare the ground for further heavy taxation to pay for it. But when Philip VI's ministers had made their opening speeches and the assembled representatives withdrew to consider their opinions among themselves, there were 'loud mutterings' and angry proposals for reforming the government. They hardly troubled to hide their feelings behind the courtly convention which attributed a king's every error to his advisers. They blamed the King himself.

> First, great Lord [said the representatives of the towns], you must take stock of the quality of the advice which you have been given in the conduct of your wars, and understand how by listening to it you have lost everything and gained nothing . . . You know how strong your forces were, what fine armies you led to Buirenfosse, Thun-l'Évêque, Bouvines and Aiguillon, and so many other places. Each time you marched out to sustain your honour with huge bodies of troops raised at vast expense, then conceded craven truces and marched gingerly away again. And this although the enemy was out-numbered and standing in the midst of your realm.

They reminded the King of the way in which he had been out-manoeuvred outside the walls of Paris in 1346, when the English army had crossed the Seine and bolted northward. They lectured him about the folly of exhausting his army on the forced marches through Picardy which had ended on the battlefield of Crécy. They protested about the great burdens which they had borne, the fines, the duties and the taxes which they had paid and which had come to so little.[6] Some of them may have shared the opinion which had been widely held in the immediate aftermath of the battle, which extended the blame to the whole nobility of France. What were these well-born, professional soldiers doing breaking the bridges of the Seine in the face of Edward III's army (a normally respectful chronicler asked) instead of marching across them to challenge the enemy in the field?[7] For his part, the French King, ageing, obese, world-weary, gradually withdrew from the active management of affairs, leaving them in the hands of his heir John, Duke of Normandy, and a handful of favoured military commanders and ministers who struggled to bring order and economy to the overblown bureaucracy and undisciplined finances of the French state.

Public opinion is apt to blame defeat on folly and weakness of will. The main demand of the Estates-General of December 1347 was that there should be no more half measures in the conduct of the war. They objected to the truces, which they characterised as shameful and cowardly, and to the over-cautious generalship of Philip VI, who had always refused to run risks except on the day of Crécy. The truce which had been agreed between the two Kings outside Calais was due to expire on 8 July 1348. The Estates-General wanted a large army raised in 1348 and an invasion of England mounted across the Channel. 'In this way and in no other will you be able to stop the war,' they said; 'and to this end we shall gladly place our bodies and our wealth at your disposal.' Armed with this promise the French government's commissioners descended on the local communities of the kingdom in the early months of the year 1348 to agree the form and value of their contributions. Almost all of them agreed to pay the cost of a given number of soldiers, which was probably assessed in rough proportion to the number of households. The government had been struggling to impose a system of this kind since 1345 in the face of the pressures of war and the recalcitrance of local politicians. The shock of defeat loosened purse-strings now. The promises of the communities of France must have amounted to more than 2,500,000 *livres*. This was more than the largest subsidy receipt for any earlier year of the war. The repair and equipment of a large fleet of ships was already in hand in January. In March, the royal *baillis* and seneschals began to assess towns and villages for infantry service. By this time the French government's preparations were far enough advanced for accurate intelligence about them to have reached England.[8]

The celebrations of the English and the revenge of the French were interrupted by an unexpected natural disaster. Bubonic plague, which had been endemic in the east for centuries, appeared in Genoa and Sicily in the autumn of 1347. The plague was spread by rats and their parasites. It was carried in ships and their cargoes and along the trade routes of the Mediterranean and western Europe. In winter, it was succeeded by pneumonic plague, a still more virulent form which developed when infected parasites attacked victims with an existing pneumonic infection. In this form, it was spread by exhalation and transmitted rapidly from man to man along the roads and crowded city streets of medieval Europe. During the winter of 1347–8 the plague was reported in southern France. Beginning in the ports of Narbonne, Marseille and Montpellier, it spread north up the valley of the Rhone and west into Gascony where populations weakened by war, floods and harvest failure succumbed in thousands. The epidemic was viewed with distant horror in the north when pilgrims, travellers and seamen brought the news. With them came the disease itself. It reached Rouen at the end of June 1348, when the first Mediterranean galleys arrived in the river port. Burgundy was affected in July. The first outbreak in the Île de France was reported at Roissy, whence it reached Paris in August or September. The epidemic waned with the onset of winter but in the spring of 1349 it spread with fresh vigour through northern France, and in cities such as Paris and Reims reached its greatest intensity in the summer of that year before gradually dying out in 1350.

The epidemic of 1347–50 was the greatest demographic catastrophe which Europe has suffered in its recorded history. Although statistical precision is impossible and records are sparse and inconsistent, the most plausible estimates suggest that a third of the population of western Europe died. The worst affected regions of France were in the south. The principal towns of Provence and Languedoc lost over half their population, some of them rather more. At Perpignan, the mortality may have been as high as 70 per cent. The cardinals fled from Avignon, leaving behind them a city in which half the houses were tenanted by corpses. Anecdotal evidence suggests a similar level of mortality in Bordeaux. In the northern provinces of France the mortality was somewhat lower. The best estimates which can be made suggest that Paris and Reims each lost about a quarter of its inhabitants, and they were probably typical of the larger towns. In the country, the mortality is likely to have been less, and some areas escaped altogether. The psychological shock is hard for modern minds to capture. In the graphic phrase of the poet Guillaume de Machaut, who lived through the epidemic, death 'leapt from its cage', attacking its victims suddenly, indiscriminately. Fatalism and despair took hold among populations confronted by the daily spectacle of blackened bodies tipped into vast open pits in improvised cemeteries: a disaster which they did not understand and could neither avoid nor control. In the Low Countries, great processions of flagellant penitents began to appear in the streets of the main towns. Death, corruption, repentance, became increasingly insistent themes of an age of war in which life was cheap and brief.[9]

The plague reached England a little later than France. The first recorded case was in Melcombe (Dorset) in early July 1348. By August it had reached Bristol, by November London. A meeting of Parliament which had been summoned for January 1349 was postponed and then cancelled. The law courts were closed. Ministers and officials fled from Westminster and the King withdrew to Langley. In the course of 1349, the epidemic spread through the Midlands and North. The level of mortality was significantly higher than it was in France. This may have been because pneumonic plague, which was transmitted more rapidly and was almost always fatal, was a more important factor in the colder climate of England. But whatever the reason, the evidence, which is patchy, suggests that in rural areas of southern England and the Midlands, between 40 per cent and 50 per cent of the population died. The mortality in the towns can only be guessed, for there is hardly any evidence apart from the hyperbole of the chroniclers. It must have been even higher.[10]

The Black Death might have been expected to have a significant impact on the war. In May 1348, after desultory negotiations with the Papacy and the court of France had proceeded all winter without result, Edward III proposed that the truce of Calais should be extended on account of the epidemic in southern France, which was then at its height. Since the English King had made no plans for a campaign in 1348 and probably could not afford one, this was a cheap concession. Philip VI was more equivocal. Although he discreetly abandoned the plans to invade England, which the Estates-General had foisted on him in the previous year, Philip did make a serious attempt to resume the war in July and August. The failure of this attempt was probably due in large measure to the plague. Ministers dispersed. Their subordinates sickened or died. The operations of government were disrupted. The collection of tax revenues was seriously hampered and in parts of the country stopped altogether. The tax contributions agreed with the local communities at the beginning of the year had now to be radically reduced. Languedoc, which had been among the first provinces to be visited by the epidemic, was particularly badly affected. Several of its cities found themselves unable to collect anything at all.[11] These difficulties go some way to explain why the French not only abandoned their more ambitious projects for 1348 but made no attempt to undertake any major campaign until well into the following year.

In the longer term the consequences are more difficult to assess.

The plague had very little effect on the recruitment of soldiers in either country. It certainly made some walled towns more difficult to defend. The main burden of keeping watch and manning the walls always fell on the inhabitants, and a drastic reduction of their numbers was bound to put severe strains on the survivors. In most places, however, the gaps must have been quickly filled by refugees from the devastated open villages around. At one stage there was concern about the effect of the epidemic on the recruitment of field armies. Edward III certainly anticipated difficulties in this direction, and it would be surprising if the same thought had not occurred to his rival.[12] In the event the difficulties never materialised. The professional fighting class, the noblemen and gentlemen who supplied the bulk of the men-at-arms, suffered less than any other group from the Black Death. They were better nourished and clothed and lived in cleaner houses, away from the large cities. The plague was a 'great respecter of princes, knights and judges' according to the Parisian doctor Simon of Couvin. His opinion was widely shared among those contemporary observers who thought about the matter, and in England is supported by reasonably reliable statistical evidence. Even among the classes which were more severely affected, the plague of 1348–50 struck disproportionately against the very young and the very old, so that it was probably not until the 1360s and 1370s that its full impact was experienced by recruiting officers. Foot soldiers and archers may have become more difficult to find. But the difficulties seem to have been overcome. The army with which Edward III entered France in 1359 was larger than any previous army of invasion except for the one which had besieged Calais in the summer of 1347. The proportion of archers and foot soldiers in its ranks was roughly comparable. There is some evidence of a fall in the proportion of archers and foot soldiers in French armies of the 1350s, but it is more likely to reflect the changing tactical ideas of French commanders than anything else. The relationship between population and the size of armies was distant and uncertain before the age of universal conscription, and in medieval societies the proportion of the population which fought in organised military units was always very small. The main constraints on the size of armies remained the financial resources and organisational skills of governments and, in England, the availability of shipping.[13]

By far the most significant consequence of the epidemic was its impact on the financial resources of the French Crown. The high mortality of the years 1347–50 caused serious financial difficulty for those in France who lived on agricultural rents. As demand for land and food fell and as labour became scarce and expensive, landowners found their incomes severely squeezed. This directly affected the Crown, which was a considerable landowner. But the Crown was also affected indirectly, as the disaster reduced the taxable capacity of the nobility and the Church who were the main financiers of the war effort, and of very many towns and villages of the French provinces. The tax contributions agreed with the local communities at the beginning of 1348 had represented one of the most promising developments for many years in the difficult fiscal history of France. By the following year it was clear that the plague had destroyed it. There was a determined attempt in the early 1350s to switch the emphasis to sales taxes, and to compensate for the shrinking tax base by greatly increasing the rate. In other circumstances, the attempt might have succeeded. But it foundered, like other experiments which followed, on the growing resistance of taxpayers and on the practical impossiblility of overcoming it in the middle of a mounting political crisis.

By comparison England, although it experienced even higher mortality than France, suffered less from difficulties of this kind. Population pressure and land hunger had been particularly intense in England before the Black Death. In most parts of the country tenants seem to have been found for vacant land quite quickly even from a much reduced population. After some difficult years in the early 1350s, rents held up reasonably well. Edward III's officials proved adept at resolving such difficulties as remained. They had the advantage of a more efficient system of assessment and collection than their adversaries did. Moreover, except on the marches of Scotland, they did not have to cope with the problems of war damage and political dissolution. In England as in France large subsidies were granted to the Crown at the beginning of 1348, a tenth and fifteenth, year on year for three years. But in England they were collected. The government continued to use the pre-plague assessments of each community regardless of its reduced population. It persistently rejected petitions for an abatement on account of the plague, instead increasing the number of collectors and arming them with fierce additional powers. Consequently, although collection was somewhat delayed by administrative dislocation and by the astonishingly high mortality among the collectors themselves, some 89 per cent of the assessment was eventually brought in.[14] The contrast with France could not have been more complete. In both countries the plague heightened social tensions, as prices rose and as the Church and the nobility struggled to hold down wages and the government to collect taxes. France paid the price of these tensions during the violent urban and rural revolutions of the 1350s. But in England the exceptionally close solidarity between the government and the nobility and gentry of the provinces enabled them to exercise a higher degree of social control over the mass of the population and to defer the reckoning for more than two decades.

Edward III's strategic position in France in 1348 depended on his control of a number of enclaves in the western provinces of the kingdom. His subjects were firmly installed at three points on the Atlantic coast: at Calais, in southern Brittany and along the coast of Gascony from Bordeaux to Bayonne. In addition, Edward was acknowledged as King of France by the revolutionary committees which controlled the county of Flanders, including the important North Sea port of Sluys. None of these possessions, however, was secure. Their defence gave rise to a variety of political, financial and logistical problems, all of which underlined the essential unimportance of battles as a means of achieving anything of long-term significance.

Flanders, which had never been occupied by the English King's armies or governed by his officials, was the weakest part of Edward's Atlantic empire, for his possession of it depended on an unstable oligarchy over which he had no direct control. It was now nearly nine years since the uprising of the industrial towns of Flanders had deposed the Count and replaced his government by a committee of the leading towns, dominated by the commercial oligarchy of Ghent. For most of that period the government of the towns had pursued a policy of alliance with England. They had recognised Edward III as King of France in 1340 and intervened in his campaigns on the northern frontier with large bodies of soldiers. This policy had been justified by the need to preserve the supplies of English wool for the cloth industry on which the greater towns depended. But it had been costly. Flemish goods had been periodically excluded from their French markets. The county had lain for long periods under a papal interdict. Many Flemings had lost their lives in successive ill-fated campaigns devised by their leaders. In strictly political terms too, the price had been high. The defence of Flanders against constant French raids and the formation of large and more or less cohesive armies to assist the campaigns of Edward III, had been achieved only because Ghent had exercised an increasingly irksome dictatorship over the rest of the county. In the summer of 1348 there was widespread unrest among the smaller towns of Flanders. They had never gained much from the English alliance, and their own cloth industries had been ruthlessly contained in the commercial interests of Ghent. A growing band of Flemish exiles in France fanned the discontent. The eighteen-year-old Count, Louis de Mâle, had passed most of his teens in exile at the French court. He was determined not to pass the rest of his life there as his father had done. He watched his opportunities with some skill. In the summer of 1348 he formed a small army from among the exiles around him and moved from France to the duchy of Brabant.[15] Far away in Avignon, the diplomats were still haggling over the terms for extending the truce. Philip VI stalled their progress.[16]

In July, the truce was allowed to expire. A large body of French troops arrived at Saint-Omer and Aire-sur-la-Lys to cut off the rebellious Flemings from their English ally. These places were close to the boundary of Flanders and only twenty-five miles from the English garrison at Calais. The commanders of the army were two men who knew the King's mind well. Charles of Spain, still only twenty-two years old, was an ambitious politician and an ingenious and aggressive military commander in high favour of the French court. Geoffrey de Charny, an older man, was a Burgundian who had fought for Philip VI since the earliest campaigns of the war and had borne the *Oriflamme* in the army which had failed to relieve Calais in 1347. He was much admired in his day as a soldier of exemplary courage and as an arbiter on points of chivalry. He was also a man of strong personal piety, a founder of monasteries and the first recorded owner of the famous relic now known as the Holy Shroud of Turin. An English chronicler who rarely praised any Frenchman called Geoffrey de Charny 'a man filled with the experience of years, gifted with profound wisdom and the spirit of adventure, by common repute a knight more skilled in the art of war than any man in France.' He was given exceptional powers over civil and military officials in the marches of Calais and Flanders and virtually unfettered discretion in his use of them. Yet his first attempts were dogged by the same ill fortune and bureaucratic inertia which had defeated his predecessors. On 14 August 1348, as the French marched out of Saint-Omer toward Calais they were driven back by torrential rainstorms, the worst summer rains in living memory. At the end of August they tried again, approaching Calais by the south and occupying Coulogne, a small village on a island of firm ground less than three miles from the town. Here Geoffrey built an improvised fort protected by ditches and earthworks, and set about diverting the streams which fed the harbour of Calais and supplied fresh water to the town. Then, lunging north-west towards Marcq, Geoffrey cut the causeway from Calais to Gravelines by which victuals and equipment reached the town. This short campaign caused grave concern in Calais. But it proved impossible to follow it up. It had been intended to deploy a much larger French army on the march of Calais in the autumn. Troops had been summoned to muster at Amiens on 1 September. The facts are obscure, but the summons seems to have been a complete failure. The plague, which had now reached the Seine at Rouen and Paris and was spreading across the plain of Champagne, was probably the main reason. But disorder and penury in the principal departments of the French government may have been another. The Count of Eu, Constable of France, who was a prisoner of war in England, offered to act as an intermediary between the two governments, and Philip eventually authorised him to agree a truce. This well-liked, urbane French nobleman, the champion of Edward's tournaments and confidant of several of his courtiers, was already moving to the equivocal position between England and France which cost him his life three years later. On 5 September 1348 a short truce was agreed by the Count of Eu and the Earl of Lancaster in London, for a period of six weeks. They agreed that within that period a distinguished band of prelates and noblemen from each realm would come to Boulogne and Calais to negotiate something more permanent.[17]

While the two governments prepared the instructions of their ambassadors, the communal governments of Flanders collapsed. The men of Alost in the eastern part of the county were the first to rise in rebellion against the rule of Ghent. In July they expelled the agents of the great town and called on the Count to come to their aid. The men of Ghent reacted as they had done before. They sent an armed force to impose their will on the recalcitrant town. But this time Alost was reinforced by supporters of the Count who came across the border from Brabant to support them. They confronted the Ghent militia outside the gates and put them to flight. On 29 August 1348 Louis de Mâle issued a manifesto promising an amnesty for the offences of the past and appealing to the Flemings to come to his aid. It was addressed to the men of Bruges, the ancient seat of the Counts of Flanders where Louis' family had many friends. But it was widely read throughout Flanders and it made a great impression among the enemies of Ghent. At about the same time, the Count crossed the border from Brabant and entered Alost. In one town after another the agents of Ghent were ousted and its supporters proscribed or expelled.

The councillors of Ghent were immovable. They raised a huge army within their walls and sent it to attack Louis de Mâle at Alost. The councillors of Bruges, in spite of the deep divisions within their town, raised a second army to reinforce them. Both armies failed completely. On 14 September 1348 Louis de Mâle came out of Alost to parley with the men of Ghent. He addressed them as friends. He told them that he was their lawful ruler. He promised to pardon them for all their rebellions and to restore their ancient laws and customs as they had stood before the restoration of his father in 1329. In the encampment of the army of Ghent angry argument broke out and some fighting, a microcosm of the disputes which divided every community of Flanders. The weavers and fullers were determined to maintain the English alliance which they believed to be fundamental to their economic survival. But the lesser trades, the seamen, the butchers, the fishmongers and others wanted to go over to the Count. Then, as the marshals succeeded in restoring discipline, the news arrived that the army of Bruges, which was on its way to join them, had mutinied, murdered its officers and declared for Louis de Mâle. The men of Ghent were afraid that their line of retreat would be cut off by the spreading revolt. They withdrew. Louis de Mâle conducted a triumphant march through eastern Flanders. Dendermonde, Grammont and Oudenarde opened their gates to him. Courtrai expelled its garrison of Ghent militiamen and English mercenaries.

On 17 September 1348 the Count arrived outside the gates of Bruges. The town was in a state of extreme tension. The cloth workers dominated the council and may still have commanded the support of most citizens. But they were overawed by the inhabitants of the outlying district (the *franc*), large numbers of whom had arrived in the town during the past few days. They had the gates opened, and allowed the Count to march in triumph through the town. Giles Coudenbroek, the leader of the cloth workers, who had dominated Bruges during the rule of Ghent, was arrested and sent as a prisoner to Oudenarde. His fellow councillors were expelled. Coudenbroek's supporters attempted a counter-attack a few days later. They invaded the market square and the Halle with drawn swords. But they were put down by force and many of them were killed.

Only Ghent and Ypres now stood out for the cause of the revolution of 1339 and the English alliance. The leaders of the cloth workers of Ghent knew that having controlled Flanders for so long they could expect no favours from Louis de Mâle. A great number of their allies who had been expelled from other towns arrived to swell their ranks and stiffen their resolve. They were joined soon afterwards by the town militia which returned, humiliated, from the débâcle at Alost. Vigourous measures were taken to ensure that the town was not betrayed from within, as Bruges had been. Potential supporters of the Count were identified, then rounded up and murdered. Their goods were seized and their houses sacked and burned. The councils of Ghent

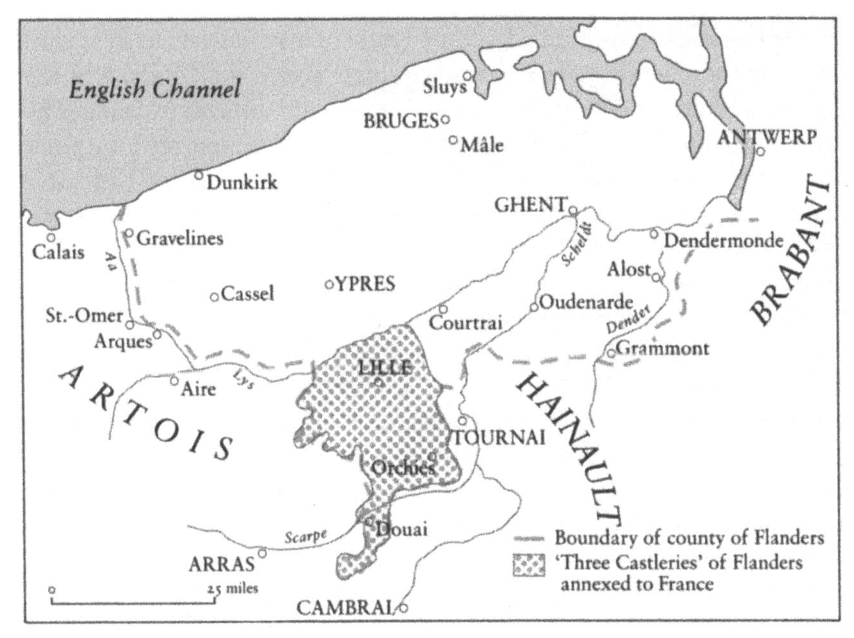

1 Flanders, 1348

and Ypres urgently appealed to the King of England for help. They sent messengers both to Edward III in England and to his officers in Calais. But Louis de Mâle was already gathering his strength around Ypres and along the roads and waterways west of Ghent. At the end of October 1348 Louis' ally the Duke of Brabant entered Flanders with a fresh army and encamped by the River Scheldt twenty miles east of Ghent at Dendermonde. Both towns were now completely blockaded.[18]

Regular couriers brought the news of these events to Edward III. Their messages must have made unpleasant reading. The English King's bargaining position in the coming negotiations with France was poor enough as it was. He did his best to extract the maximum advantage from the situation while it still remained fluid, but it was not much. On 28 September 1348 Henry of Lancaster and Bishop Bateman of Norwich crossed the Channel to Calais to negotiate an extension of the truce with France. Lancaster brought with him not only the usual diplomatic procurations but extensive powers to take action in Edward's name in Flanders and a small army, more than 400 strong. In the first few days of October 1348 fresh troops were summoned to reinforce him and ships were urgently emptied of their cargoes in order to carry more men and horses to Calais.[19]

The French King appointed a commission of his ministers to treat with the English. They installed themselves high above the Channel in the castle of Boulogne and engaged in protracted and difficult exchanges by messenger with their opposite numbers in Calais. The main sticking point was Geoffrey de Charny's new fort at Coulogne. Henry of Lancaster insisted that there would be no truce until it was demolished. In England, Edward III did his best to maintain the pressure. On 22 October 1348 he announced that an army would sail from Sandwich within the next ten days and that he would take command of it in person. Bishops throughout the realm were ordered to have prayers said for the success of his venture. In the last few days of October the King set out with much ceremony for the coast. These announcements must have contained a large element of bluff. Edward already realised that there was nothing that he could do for the Flemings. Early in November 1348 a delegation of twelve dignitaries from Ghent and Ypres arrived in England to make a final appeal for help. He told them that he could not afford to intervene unless they paid all his expenses, which they were in no position to do. The English King did not say that the regime of Ghent was doomed and that they would do well to make the best arrangements they could with the Count, but he must have thought it. The news of Edward's response was received with consternation in Ghent. 'Lord help us!', the crowd wailed; 'our leaders are fools and we are dupes.'[20] In the second week of November 1348 the French gave way on the fort of Coulogne and agreed to demolish it. On the 13th the two sides met in plenary session in the patch of open ground north of Guines which was to serve for many years as the traditional meeting place of the ambassadors of the two realms, and there they settled a fresh truce to last until 1 September 1349. By the terms of the truce the English agreed that they would do nothing to undermine the loyalty of Philip VI's 'party' in Flanders.[21]

Louis de Mâle had already begun to follow the sinuous course between England and France which enabled him to survive for more than thirty years in control of his unruly principality. He knew that there were powerful interests in Flanders which were steadfastly opposed to the interests of France. Some of them had never forgiven the French annexation of the three castleries of Lille, Douai and Orchies in southern Flanders which had truncated the Walloon regions of the county more than forty years before. Others, still powerful in the towns, remained economically dependent upon Edward III's realm and passionately opposed to anything which severed the county's links with it in the service of French foreign policy. Louis had already begun to distance himself from his French patrons within days of his recovery of Bruges. At some personal risk he had paid off all his French troops, who were no more popular with his subjects now than they had been in the time of his father.[22] Like the men of Ghent and Ypres, Louis also sent his agents to wait upon Edward III and the Earl of Lancaster. They negotiated two remarkable treaties with Edward's councillors in the course of a series of meetings at Calais and Dunkirk in November 1348. Early drafts were being discussed while the Anglo-French conferences were still in progress. The first treaty, which was concerned with the internal government of Flanders, was no more than a solemn acknowledgement of the *fait accompli* which Louis de Mâle had achieved since the end of August. The essential point was that although Louis remained a vassal of Philip VI he promised to live in peace with Edward III and to allow his subjects to go on recognising Edward III as King of France, as many of them had sworn to do. The juridical consequences of this untidy compromise were ignored, and perhaps did not matter. The French government was probably consulted and may even have tolerated it. But they were certainly not consulted about the second treaty, which was negotiated in great secrecy and never published. This document began by reciting the 'great wrongs' which successive Kings of France had done to Flanders in the time of Louis' forebears. This was a reference to the lost provinces of the south. Louis promised that before the expiry of the truce with France he would deliver an ultimatum to the French King. He was to demand the return to Flanders of the three castleries, together with most of the county of Artois, which had been separated from Flanders for more than a century. If this demand was refused, as it was bound to be, Louis undertook to renounce his homage to Philip VI not later than 22 September 1349, and to enter into a military alliance with Edward III. On about 15 November 1348 Edward arrived in person at Calais. A few days later, on 4 December, he met Louis de Mâle at Dunkirk and the two men sealed the treaties with their privy seals. The English King must have congratulated his ambassadors. If Louis had performed his promises the double treaty of Dunkirk would have been a considerable diplomatic coup.[23]

The main advantage of the treaties to Louis de Mâle was that in return for a few face-saving concessions Edward III abandoned Ghent and Ypres to their fate. Their representatives had been present at Dunkirk and had agreed to be bound by the terms of the public treaty.[24] One of those terms was that they should surrender to the Count and acknowledge his authority. Louis gave the rebellious towns two weeks. Ypres, which was starved by the blockade and suffering terribly from the plague, surrendered before the deadline expired. An attempt by some cloth workers to mount a counter-revolution was easily put down. In Ghent, however, the fanatics took control as soon as the news of the treaty arrived. An angry mob assembled, led by the weavers and by die-hards expelled from other towns. They took over the centre of the town, around the Friday Market where Edward III had been proclaimed King of France nine years before, and turned it into an armed camp. They sacked the abbeys of St. Bavo and St. Peter. They attacked the mansions of the rich mercantile families who were thought to favour surrender. When the parish of St. Peter, a crowded quarter enclosed by canals and waterways in the southern part of the town, resolved to submit to the Count, the mob fought their way through the streets lighting fires as they went. On 7 January 1349, Louis de Mâle announced an amnesty for everyone who withdrew from the town and submitted to his officers before sunset on the following day. Thousands of men and women made their way through the gates into the open fields outside to take up his offer. Inside the town, the survivors fell to quarrelling among themselves. Some sent messages into the Count's camp offering negotiations; others dug themselves in for the last battle. It came three days later on 13 January 1349. A thousand heavily armed men of the Count's army fought their way from the gates through the open places in the centre of Ghent. The defenders were scattered. Some of them were cut down in the streets. Some drowned in the Scheldt. Hardly any escaped alive. The captain of the weavers was found by a search party hiding in an oven in a nearby house. They hacked off his limbs, then dragged him into a public square to finish him off. In Ghent, as in Bruges and Ypres, the power of the cloth workers was broken. Their guilds were suppressed. Their leaders were proscribed. Thus ended in recrimination and bloodshed the revolution of 1339.[25]

When, in 1345, the communal governments of Flanders had last been threatened with extinction by popular unrest and political machination, Edward III had diverted an army and a fleet to the Zwyn and had broked a settlement in person from the cabin of his flagship. The English King's financial difficulties were not the only reason for his relative passivity during the final crisis of 1348. It reflected a radical change in the strategic and diplomatic outlook of his ministers, due mainly to the occupation of Calais in the previous year. No longer was it necessary to spend tens of thousands of pounds in propping up the unstable coalitions of urban Flanders and earning the capricious goodwill of the Duke of Brabant, in order to be able to use their territories as a landing ground and marshalling area for armies and their ports for the warehousing of vast quantities of stores. For more than two centuries, it was Calais which was to be the 'bolt and key to open our way to France'.[26]

Throughout that period Calais was critical to England's military enterprises. Amphibious warfare remained an extremely undeveloped art in fourteenth-century Europe. It was virtually impossible to land an army on a defended coast. The French never tried it. Edward III did so only once, in Normandy in 1346, when he succeeded more by luck than judgment. Calais not only gave the English safe access to the continent. Its possession largely resolved one of the most difficult logistical problems which they had encountered in the first decade of the war, namely the carriage of large armies across the sea on merchant ships. England, with its long, indented coastline and its many harbours, had a large merchant marine, but by continental standards the ships were relatively small. They were designed for carrying bulky cargoes, such as wool. They had deep holds and short, narrow decks. In wartime, when the ships were constantly in danger of attack and there were no friendly harbours to put into at night, they needed double and sometimes even treble crews in order to work shifts. There was therefore little space for passengers. During the first decade of the war the average English merchantman of, say, sixty tons burden could not carry more than about ten soldiers with their horses, equipment and stores in addition to its crew of twenty-five. Horses, which were heavy and awkward and had to be lifted in and out of the holds on hoists, posed special difficulties. As a result, in 1338, 350 ships and nearly 12,000 crewmen had been required to carry an army of just 4,400 men to Antwerp. Some of the ships did two round trips. For the army of Normandy in 1346, which numbered about 7,000 or 8,000 men, no less than 750 ships had to be found. These huge fleets took at least four months to assemble and called for truly prodigious expenditure of money and bureaucratic sweat. Requisitioning on the scale required caused severe economic disruption in the coastal communities of England and contributed to a noticeable decline in the size of the English merchant marine. The achievement of 1346 could probably not have been repeated.[27]

After 1347 it did not need to be. Sandwich, a rich and populous town with a fine natural harbour protected by the Goodwin Sands, became the main port of embarkation for Calais. The short passage could be done with single crews in a few hours. With a secure base on the French side, the troops no longer had to be ready to fight as soon as they landed. They could be ferried across the Channel in relays, a few hundred at a time, using relatively small numbers of ships. Stores could be accumulated in the warehouses of the town over weeks and months beforehand. Horses, carts and siege engines could be brought over on barges. For Edward III's great mounted raid into Picardy in 1355, about 3,000 men were transported to Calais over a period of four or five weeks using a fleet of twenty-five large vessels. By comparison about 300 ships were needed to carry the rather smaller army which the Prince of Wales led to Gascony in the same year.[28]

Until 1360 Edward III treated Calais as part of France. He ruled it in right of the French Crown and heard appeals from its courts in that capacity. The civil government of Calais was based on the laws and customs in force there before the English occupation. The constitution of the town was only very gradually changed, and some of the civic offices continued to be filled by Frenchmen, including Eustache de Saint-Pierre, one of the 'burghers' who had surrendered the keys to the English King in August 1347. But within a very short time Calais became an English colony. Edward III expelled almost all the French inhabitants on the day he took possession and began to resettle it with his own countrymen. Calais was an uninviting place in wartime. Around the market place and St. Nicholas' church a hybrid community grew up, of English traders, seamen and innkeepers, Flemish immigrants, rootless journeymen and soldiers of fortune from every nation. A number of Londoners settled there, tempted by generous grants of property and privileges. Most of the inhabitants, however, were soldiers. The town was an armed camp, the headquarters of a military district containing the greatest permanent concentration of troops in Europe. For many years its sole *raison d'être* was the service of its enormous garrison.[29]

The territory which the English controlled was never limited to Calais itself. Beyond the walls a group of outlying forts and castles controlled the approaches to the town and marked out the limits of the English 'pale', a land of marsh and shifting streams and abandoned villages, a bleak no man's land which was for many years the scene of continual raids and counter-raids. Shortly after Calais surrendered in August 1347, the English had occupied Marcq and Oye, two villages by the shore east of the town on the road to Gravelines, where they built improvised defences out of wooden palisades and wine barrels filled with rubble. Sangatte on the west side of the town was seized, apparently without opposition, in 1349 and temporary fortifications were constructed there too. All of these forts were replaced in the following years by permanent stone castles.[30] During the early 1350s the English garrisons gradually pushed the boundary of the pale outwards, acquiring a formidable ring of fortresses linked by causeways and water channels.

The senior royal officer in the pale was the Captain of Calais, who was sometimes a great nobleman, more commonly an experienced professional soldier drawn from the royal household. He commanded the garrison of the town and appointed the constables of Calais castle and of the outlying forts. All of these men were answerable to him. The Captain was also responsible for a growing military administration. The Treasurer, usually a senior Exchequer or Chancery clerk from Westminster, was responsible for the finances of the garrison. The Receiver was in charge of stores and supplies. A Marshal was concerned with military discipline and a Bailiff with the civil administration of the town. All of these officers presided over bureaucratic departments of their own. The garrison's numbers varied with the political situation, with the enthusiasm of individual Captains and with the exigencies of the King's finances. When John Beauchamp took over as Captain in 1356 its nominal strength, including his own retinue, was just under 1,400 men. About 400 of these were men-at-arms, the rest mostly archers and auxiliaries. Beauchamp, however, was appointed at a time of acute tension and the garrison's strength was usually rather less than this, about 1,200. Most of the men were retainers of the more senior officers and volunteers recruited in England. But there was also a fair number of Flemish, German and Italian mercenaries some of whom served for long periods and were endowed with houses in the town. The garrison had to provide most of its own services and maintained a large core of workmen on its permanent strength. Beauchamp's garrison included no less than 220 masons, carpenters and miscellaneous tradesmen and journeymen, not to speak of boatmen, engineers and artillerymen, gatekeepers, storemen, grooms, stablemen and farriers, cobblers, tailors, rope-makers, trumpeters, messengers and spies, day watchmen and night watchmen, clerks and chaplains.[31] The distinction between combatants and non-combatants in this warlike society was never very precise. Tradesmen on the garrison's strength often had to work in dangerous conditions and were expected to carry arms and to fight when called on. The inhabitants of the town not only carried arms but served watches and fought at the walls and gates under the Captain's orders. Some of them joined his periodic raids into French territory. Although very little is known about the civil population of Calais in the mid-fourteenth century it is probable that from the combined strength of town and garrison the Captain could count on more than 2,000 fighting men.[32]

Supplying this extraordinary military community was an elaborate operation. The troops and horses of the garrison consumed victuals and fodder daily in great quantity, and more had to be stored for a siege or a sudden *chevauchée* into the hinterland. In addition the Prince of Wales and probably other prominent English commanders kept supplies and equipment permanently stored in the town in case they had to reinforce it at short notice. The continual work of construction and repair required regular supplies of timber, building stone and lime. Bows and arrows, stones, spears and lances were needed. Carts and wagons, barges and beasts of burden were imported to distribute stores through the town and among the outlying garrisons of the pale. All this had to be obtained from elsewhere and most of it from England. The barren marsh around Calais produced almost nothing. Flanders, the only other source of supply, could not be relied upon, particularly after the counter-revolution of 1348. The garrison depended mainly on the regular requisitioning of supplies in the south-eastern counties of England, particularly Essex and Kent. These operations were at first confided to sheriffs or other royal officials. But in the course of the 1350s they were taken over by great merchants in London and the east coast ports, a fresh opportunity for enterprising war financiers. Some of them, like the Lynn grocer and former customs farmer John Wesenham, made large profits by it. None of this was popular with the public but, as the King's ministers pointed out when the Commons objected, it was unavoidable if Calais was to be held. And there was general agreement as long as the war continued that Calais ought to be held. In the 1390s John of Gaunt, looking back on half a century of effort, might tell Parliament that 'Calais grieved more England and did more hurt thereto than profit, for the great expenses about the keeping thereof.' Few men agreed with him.[33]

Perhaps they would have done if they had known how expensive Calais really was. There were periodical attempts to make the town contribute something to its own defence. But it had virtually no resources of its own. Its inhabitants lived on the garrison, and on travellers crossing the Channel from England, who were required by law to pass through it. The townsmen enjoyed generous commercial privileges in England and there were periodical attempts to make them more generous. A year after the occupation of the town there was a short-lived project for making Calais a compulsory staple port for exports of English cloth, tin and lead. But in wartime conditions none of these ventures could make the community of Calais into a self-supporting economy.[34] The Treasurer's officials collected modest amounts from tolls charged on people entering and leaving the town and from duties on their goods. Fees for use of the public mills and fines levied by the marshals and bailiffs brought in a little more. A mint was established soon after the conquest and the Treasurer regularly made a profit of about 10 per cent by coining bullion sent from England to pay the wages of the garrison. But these sums, however energetically collected, made a paltry contribution to the enormous cost of defending the town against the French. Between January 1348 and February 1361, a period of some thirteen years in which the garrison was almost continuously on a war footing, the English government spent £183,786 on the defence of Calais, 85 per cent of which was met by direct payments from the Exchequer at Westminster. This represented an average of nearly £14,000 per year, by far the largest recurring item of war expenditure in the English government's budget. It was almost as much as the Constables of Bordeaux spent on the defence and administration of the entire duchy of Aquitaine over the same period, and they financed at least half their expenditure from local sources.[35]

If anything, the Treasurer's accounts, from which these figures are taken, understated the burden, for they did not include the increased expenditure on the royal fleet which became necessary once the English held territory on both sides of the Channel. Although the French had suffered terrible losses at sea during the 1340s they were still a naval power to be reckoned with, and their principal maritime towns, Boulogne, Dieppe and Rouen, were only a few hours sailing time from Calais. The security of the English garrison depended on the effective control of the Channel not just in a few weeks of exertion around the King's great expeditions, but throughout the fair weather months from May to October, year after year. In the first two or three years after the capture of Calais the Captains of the town maintained a small navy of their own. This included an oared galley under the command of an Italian adventurer called Aimeric of Pavia, which was stationed in the harbour, and at least four large armed sailing ships which were employed in running supplies, money, messages and troops to and fro across the Channel.[36] This arrangement seems to have come to an end at the beginning of the 1350s when the King carried out a major programme of acquisition and reorganisation. In 1345 he had possessed about twelve sailing ships stationed in various ports of southern and eastern England. By the summer of 1351 his fleet had increased by gift, purchase or capture to twenty-five, and at least five more were acquired between 1352 and 1355. The crewing records suggest that these were substantial vessels, generally more than 100 tons burden and in some cases more than 200. They had permanent masters who commanded them at sea and were responsible for their upkeep when they were laid up. But they were manned by temporary crews, who were recruited when they were required by press-gangs in the coastal towns. Most of the ships were based at the Tower of London where a growing department presided over by the Clerk of the King's Ships was charged with the expensive business of keeping them repaired, caulked and rigged, and storing weapons and victuals for their crews. A few of the King's ships were used for supplying the beleaguered garrison of Berwick-on-Tweed. But most of them were stationed for the summer months at Sandwich, Calais and Winchelsea, where they were used to patrol the Channel, to escort men and cargoes, and to enforce on ships English and foreign the King's high-handed claims to the sovereignty of the narrow seas.[37]

The cost of the garrison at Calais and of the fleet which served it were symptomatic of the growing importance of overheads in Edward III's war budget: expenditure which steadily drained the Exchequer whether fighting was in progress or not, conserving past gains without bringing the King any closer to achieving his ambitions. The occupation of territory was prodigiously expensive and unproductive and, as the English expanded their reach inland from the Atlantic seaboard of France, the cost of keeping their conquests strangled all their more aggressive enterprises. Those who had assumed, in the aftermath of the battle of Crécy, that Edward could now dictate his terms had seriously misunderstood the realities of the war and the tremendous force of inertia which any conqueror must overcome. As the glow of Crécy faded it became apparent how little had really changed.

Edward III was resigned to these truths in the march of Calais, and perhaps even in Aquitaine. He had also toyed briefly with the idea of a permanent occupation of the Cotentin, only to abandon it soon after landing there in July 1346. But it was in Brittany that his dilemma was most acute. Edward's officers had controlled much of the duchy of Brittany since 1342, when English soldiers first landed there to turn a vicious civil war to their own advantage. Six years later, the political situation was as promising as it had ever been. The rival claimants to the duchy were John de Montfort, an eight-year-old child who was being brought up in England as Edward's ward; and Charles of Blois, who had fought for it with persistence and some success for five years until he was wounded and captured at the disastrous battle of la Roche-Derrien in June 1347.

After the battle of la Roche-Derrien, Philip VI had appointed Amaury de Craon, head of one of the great families of western France, as 'guardian' of the duchy, a title which he held until 1349. Amaury was an able soldier who did a great deal to restore the French position in eastern Brittany and succeeded in averting the complete collapse of the party of Blois. But the truth was that the French government had lost interest in Brittany. Amaury had no successor, and for the next few years the French King's policy consisted in launching brief and irregular raids into the duchy from the neighbouring provinces of Anjou, Maine and Normandy. These were usually diversions designed to tie down English forces in Brittany while more important operations occurred elsewhere. Organised opposition to the English in Brittany was led by Charles' wife, Jeanne de Penthièvre, and by the viscounts of Rohan. It was their territories in the north and centre of the peninsula which were the main source of resistance to English rule.

The Rohans were consistent and inflexible in their hostility to the foreigner. Jeanne was more equivocal. Her view was that her husband's party would fall apart without him and that if his cause was to survive some arrangement would have to be made with Edward III. So, within a few weeks of his capture, she proposed a treaty of ransom and a marriage alliance to the English King, and sent her ambassadors to press her cause in England. It is not clear why these negotiations came to nothing, but quite likely that they foundered on the opposition of Philip VI and of the Pope, Clement VI. Clement was a staunch defender of French interests and his consent was required for any marriage between spouses within the prohibited degrees of affinity.[38] So, for several years, Jeanne was condemned to continue the struggle with few resources and no assistance from outside, if only in order to conserve what bargaining power she had. For the time being she and her allies held on to Rennes and Nantes, the two great cities of the French-speaking east, to the march lands by the eastern border, the Rohan lands of the central highlands around Josselin and Pontivy, and to her own inheritance, the great appanage of Penthièvre which gave her control of the whole north coast from Pontorson, Dol and Dinan in the east to Morlaix in the west. Outside these regions the party of Blois held only isolated places: Quimper in the south-west of the peninsula, and the handful of castles belonging to adherents who were still loyal.[39] Their main strategic difficulty was the same as that of the English in Gascony in the 1330s. The passive defence of scattered castles could delay defeat but it could not achieve victory. There was no reserve of strength behind these garrisons and no one who could assemble a field army to take the offensive.

Except for the region of Quimper, the English and their Breton allies held the whole of the coastal areas of the west and south including the four major fortress-towns of Brest, Hennebont, Ploermel and Vannes, together with the Guérande peninsula north of the Loire and the Bay of Bourgneuf south of it. The main centres of the English administration were Vannes and Brest. Vannes was the seat of the English King's Lieutenants in the province, where they had their council, their financial administration, an important mint and, from 1351, a court of appeal for the whole territory. Brest, which mattered more to the English government than any other place in Brittany, was in the process of being transformed from a modest fishing village to a great fortress and the centre of the semi-autonomous military district. The captain of Brest, who was answerable directly to the King, controlled most of the western cape of Brittany including the outlying harbours of Saint-Matthieu and le Conquet and the islands of Ushant and Tristan.[40]

Edward's interest in this vulnerable and anarchic province of his French kingdom was strictly determined by geography and money. Brittany was not a convenient point of entry into France. There were few good harbours on the north coast and none of them was in English hands. An army going to the duchy would therefore have to reach it as Edward himself had done in 1342, by the long and hazardous route around the Ushant reef. What mattered in Edward's eyes was not so much to hold on to this barren property as to deny possession to the French. In an age when ships navigated from cape to cape, a powerful French presence in western Brittany would have severed communications between England and Bordeaux and made the defence of Gascony exceptionally difficult. One way of preventing this misfortune would have been to maintain a large army of occupation at the expense of the

Exchequer more or less indefinitely, as Edward was already doing in the march of Calais. But he was not willing and probably not able to do this. Instead, Brittany was administered between 1347 and 1358 by a succession of military entrepreneurs to whom Edward abandoned control of the occupied areas together with the revenues of the dukes of Brittany within them and most of the profits of war.[41]

In 1348 Edward had two Lieutenants in the duchy, both of whom operated as more or less independent contractors. Sir Thomas Dagworth, a resourceful and intelligent soldier who had governed the province in various capacities for most of the past six years, was responsible for the whole of the peninsula. A disreputable Breton adventurer called Raoul de Caours was responsible for the territory between the Loire and the Sèvre at Niort much of which, although it was geographically part of Poitou, had belonged for many years to the dukes of Brittany . Raoul was paid a lump sum of 1,500 *écus* and was promised an income of £1,000 a year from any lands that he should conquer, but otherwise his function, as Edward's officials characteristically expressed it, was to 'serve the lord King at his own expense without asking him for anything'. Both Lieutenants operated with very limited forces. Dagworth retained about 500 men. Raoul de Caours had about 300. Numbers could sometimes be made up with the aid of Breton noblemen allied to the English cause and independent captains operating in the duchy under loose bonds of allegiance to Edward III. But even so, Dagworth was able to collect only 300 men-at-arms and 400 archers to fight the greatest battle of his career at la Roche-Derrien in 1347. Dagworth's successors were generally rather worse off than he was. Few of them had his force of personality or his wealth and reputation, and some encountered serious difficulty in recruiting troops in England. Dagworth himself had been obliged to employ a fair number of Flemish and German mercenaries. His successors took a growing proportion of adventurers and ruffians: outlaws, escaped jailbirds, convicted rapists and murderers. As one of them observed, they were 'neither knights nor squires but worthless fellows', men without loyalties or standards who would not serve a moment longer than their twelve pence a day and forty marks a year.[42]

The great problem of the English Lieutenants in Brittany was that the revenues of the dukes, from which they were expected to meet the cost of its defence, did not exist. There had never been a satisfactory system of general taxation in Brittany even before the civil war, and the English were in no position to introduce one. The lucrative sale of *brefs de la mer*, which conferred immunity from the Duke's right to seize wreck washed up on the rocky Breton foreshore, had been appropriated by the King's officers in Bordeaux and granted out to favoured friends. The Duke's hereditary lands produced nothing in the anarchic conditions of the 1340s and 1350s. It is true that a great deal of land was confiscated from enemies, but only to be granted out at once to friends. The royal clerk who was sent out in 1345 to administer the revenues of the duchy reported that there were none.[43] Soldiers serving Brittany had to live off the land, at first by simple freebooting, but eventually by a system of institutionalised plundering known as 'ransoms of the country' or *patis*. *Patis* were essentially payments of protection money levied by garrison troops for leaving the inhabitants of a district alone and, when necessary, for defending them against other plunderers. Every garrison commander marked out his ransom district. Villages within marching range of his men were assessed for as much as could be extracted without driving the inhabitants away, in cash if possible, but otherwise in victuals, stone, timber, nails, labour or whatever else the inhabitants could supply. Arrears were collected by force, sometimes with considerable brutality.[44] Some captains made considerable sums out of *patis* even in the 1340s when the system was still relatively undeveloped. A Dutch soldier of fortune calling himself Croquard was one of the first to become rich by this means. He had begun his career as a page-boy, and Froissart recorded that when he visited his native Holland he was still treated as one. But in Brittany he was briefly a great figure fighting on equal terms with some of the most famous knights of the day. When he died (in a riding accident) he was reckoned to have 40,000 *écus* and a stable of thirty or forty war-horses. The stories of such men no doubt grew in the telling. But they drew many ambitious young adventurers to find death or riches in the snake-pit of Brittany.[45]

The practice of ransoming districts relieved the Lieutenants' administration of the burden of paying for the lesser garrisons. But it raised nothing for their treasury. Moreover, in the border areas it was politically very damaging. Garrisons lodged in distant frontier forts were small groups of men surrounded by a hostile or indifferent population. They were oppressed by boredom, prone to sudden outbursts of capricious brutality which drove the inhabitants into the arms of the enemy. Many Bretons must have felt like the peasants of northern Brittany who turned up with sticks and stones to support Charles of Blois when he came to besiege the English garrison of la Roche-Derrien in 1347.[46]

The taking of *patis* had another more insidious consequence which the English did not immediately appreciate. It made it impossible for the King's Lieutenants to control their subordinates, with the result that the conduct of the war gradually passed out of their hands. In the four major towns under English control the garrisons were drawn for the most part from retained troops of the Lieutenant or of the Captain of Brest. Their pay was often in arrears and they tended to make good the deficiency by thieving. But they were at least under the Lieutenants' orders. The same was true in castles garrisoned by his officers, as his contracts with them usually stipulated. The smaller towns, however, and most of the inland castles had not been captured by the efforts of the King or his Lieutenants but by the private enterprise of their captains; and, although these men acknowledged the residual authority of the King's government, they regarded their castles as their own and their right to exact *patis* from the surrounding district as absolute. In war, as an English soldier once declared before the Parlement of Paris, 'it is lawful for the subjects of one side to acquire the property of the subjects of the other by force of arms and to treat it as their own.' No one demurred, and in point of law he was right. And if he was right then so was the Captain of Lesneven who refused to admit the Lieutenant (then the Earl of Northampton) in 1345. The Lieutenant wanted to transfer the castle to another. But the Captain wanted to 'tax his men and tenants in corn and money'. *Patis* were lawful spoil of war. They belonged to the conqueror.[47]

It was generally assumed that in moments of great danger men like these would join the army of the Lieutenants with their men, if only for self-preservation. But this was not assured. The brothers de Spinefort, who were the castellans of Hennebont, defied Sir Thomas Dagworth during the campaign of la Roche-Derrien and then held it against him by force until he took the place by assault and hanged them. This was an extreme case but it was not unique. Early in 1352 Dagworth's successor Walter Bentley composed a long and careful memorandum for the King's Council in which he pointed out that because the frontier captains paid themselves and their troops, he had no real control over them. They were fighting *pour leur singulier profit*. When they had exhausted one area they abandoned the castle and moved on to another. They took extended holidays in France to relieve their boredom, buying safe-conducts from the French King's officers and spending money extravagantly. In times of danger they were often reluctant to venture their gains and their lives in battle. The response of the Council to

Bentley's memorandum was that the situation was 'dangerous', even 'scandalous'. Garrisons in major towns, they said, should be no larger than necessary and should be regularly paid. Soldiers taking a castle should be entitled to its contents as spoil of war but the castle itself should belong to the King, and his Lieutenant should entrust it to a reliable captain who would obey his orders and give security for his good conduct. No garrison troops should wander about without leave plundering the country. Most of this was entirely unrealistic because the Council was not willing to provide the resources which would have been required. The truth is that they did not much mind. Provided that the sea-lanes were kept around the western cape, Brittany was low in their priorities.[48]

Bentley knew what he was talking about, for he had been a poacher before he became a gamekeeper, and in many ways his career exemplified the vices and ambitions of the men he was complaining about. He was a Yorkshire knight who had fought in Scotland in the 1330s and in France since 1339. After disgracing himself in an unruly incident at the royal court at Westminster he had arrived in Brittany in 1342, probably in the retinue of the Earl of Northampton. Like others of his kind he struck out on his own when the cause of Blois weakened and failed in the middle of the 1340s. He formed his own band and led it with reckless valour in a succession of small-scale adventures. By 1346 he had acquired at least two castles in western Brittany, including the island fortress of Tristan in the Bay of Douarnenez where his officers exacted valuable tolls from passing ships.[49]

Bentley was a very competent soldier but his greatest gains were not made by conquest. He made them by marrying a rich Breton dowager, Jeanne de Belleville, dame de Clisson, and creating a more or less autonomous military territory out of her lands. Other men also tried to build their fortunes by marrying into the Breton nobility and entering into their disputes. Some of them succeeded even better than he did. Roger David (or Davey), who seems to have come from Wiltshire, began his career as a squire in the retinue of Sir Thomas Dagworth. By 1346 he was already commanding a band of twelve archers. At the beginning of the 1350s he was captain of Quimperlé on the south coast of Brittany. He also occupied the small castle of Quimerch in Finistère. But the real foundation of David's fortune was his marriage to Jeanne de Rostrenen, dowager Viscountess of Rohan, some time before February 1352. It is not difficult to understand why these elderly ladies were drawn to their younger, foreign husbands. In the anarchic conditions of mid-fourteenth

2 Brittany: principal garrisons, 1347–1355

century Brittany they needed a champion to hold their own against acquisitive sons and brothers and enemies among their own people. Jeanne de Rostrenen, whose first husband had been killed by the English at la Roche-Derrien claimed a third of the viscounty of Rohan as her dower in addition to the substantial domains in central Brittany which she had inherited from her parents. In February 1352 she and Roger David received from the English Lieutenant the grant of Guémenée-sur-Scorff, a town on the south-western edge of the Rohan viscounty which was close to the disputed territories and became David's base of operation. Very soon after this, David suffered a setback. He was captured by his enemies and made to promise that he would surrender all the towns under his command (but not the castles) in lieu of his ransom. Fortunately for his future career he was prevented by the Lieutenant from performing this agreement, and by methods which are not recorded he recovered both his liberty and his property. By the end of 1353 he had taken Pestivien, within fifteen miles of Jeanne de Penthièvre's capital at Guingamp. Rather later, probably in 1354, he took Trogoff, whose formidable fortress stood across the road from Guingamp to Morlaix. By the middle of the 1350s Roger David was a considerable power in northern and western Brittany.[50]

Such men found their own followers with more or less success according to their reputations. Many of them built up coherent gangs of men who had known each other in England. Thomas Bentley, who commanded one of the dame de Clisson's castles in Bas-Poitou, was probably Walter's brother. Roger David fought with his nephew Nicholas. Hugh Calveley, a minor landowner from Cheshire, formed a company of fifteen men-at-arms from his relations, neighbours and friends to fight with him in Brittany. Bands like his had a courage and *esprit de corps* formed in one of the most violent communities of provincial England. Calveley's was almost certainly responsible for the capture of the great fortress of Bécherel which was taken by escalade in 1350. From here his men caused mayhem in the north-east of Brittany for several years. They went on, their numbers swollen by fresh drafts from Cheshire, to fight under Calveley in most of the major campaigns in France and Spain for the next two decades. Calveley himself became a rich man, who mingled with kings and princes and married an Aragonese princess. A generation before, it would have been an unimaginable destiny for a man of his origins.[51]

Yet even Calveley's fortune was eclipsed by that of another Cheshire man, Robert Knolles, a taciturn professional soldier who was destined to become the most feared English captain of his generation. Not much is known about Knolles' origins, but contemporaries are agreed that he was a man of base extraction. His family were 'poor and undistinguished yeomen' according to one. He probably began his military career as an archer, which admittedly meant more in Cheshire than it did elsewhere, but not much more. By 1352 Knolles controlled an impressive array of castles and lordships on the eastern march of Brittany. They included Fougeray, some twenty-five miles south of Rennes; Gravelle, directly east of it on the borders of Brittany and Maine; and, rather later, Chateaublanc, south-east of the city on the road from Redon. These powerful fortresses represented a serious threat to the security of Rennes, one of the principal walled cities of Jeanne de Penthièvre's allegiance.[52]

The exact circumstances in which places like these were captured are hardly ever recorded, but they cannot have involved great movements of troops. Most of them were taken by stealth by small groups of men. This was what the war in Brittany was like: shapeless campaigns of skirmishes, ambushes and escalades at night, fought between men whom only accident or condition placed on one side rather than the other. The balladist Cuvelier's story of the young Bertrand du Guesclin tricking his way into the castle of Fougeray with thirty partisans disguised as wood-cutters bowed beneath the weight of their bundles is evocative, even though it is apocryphal. On the other hand the famous verse account of the battle of the Thirty, however much it may be embroidered in detail, describes an incident which really happened. The leading protagonists in this affair were Jean de Beaumanoir and an Englishman who was called 'Bramborc' by the French and may have been called Robert of Bamborough in fact. Jean de Beaumanoir was the brother-in-law of the Viscount de Rohan and commanded the garrison of the Viscount's principal castle at Josselin. 'Bramborc' was the English captain of Ploermel, eight miles away. According to Jean le Bel (who had met some of the protagonists) Beaumanoir challenged 'Bramborc' to an arranged battle between three chosen champions of each side. The Englishman dismissed that as a 'game of chance':

> I will tell you what we shall do. Choose twenty or thirty companions from your garrison and I shall choose the same number from mine. Then we shall meet on good ground where no one can disturb us, and let no man on either side give aid or comfort to the combatants.

The teams were in fact selected from several places in Brittany and the

English side included almost all the great figures of the occupying army, among them Calveley, Knolles and John Dagworth (nephew of the great Lieutenant) as well as a number of Bretons and Germans in their service. They met half way between the two castles on 26 March 1351 and fought according to exact rules fixed by agreement at a preliminary conference of the commanders. There was no limitation on the weapons to be used, which included maces and battle-axes. But there were agreed starting signals, referees and truces for taking refreshments and dressing wounds. The battle was fought for several hours and resulted in a complete victory for Beaumanoir's team. There were heavy casualties on both sides. The French lost six of their number. The English lost more, including 'Bramborc' himself. All the English survivors were captured 'for it would have been wrong to flee'. These so-called 'hastiludes', fought out in enclosed lists like tournaments but *à outrance* with real weapons, were not unheard of before. In 1338 Henry of Lancaster had fought twenty-a-side against the Scots beneath the walls of Berwick. The event had lasted three days and two Englishmen had been killed in it. Similar arranged battles had been suggested during Edward III's campaigns in France in 1340 and 1346, when the political stakes were greater, but they had been refused mainly for that reason. Between the minor figures, however, who had only their personal reputations to win or lose, they were much commoner, particularly after 1350. Two years after the battle of the Thirty another arranged battle was fought under very similar conditions on the march of Gascony in which seventeen of the French team of twenty were killed and most of the survivors on both sides were wounded. As feats of arms these were famous affairs. The battle of the Thirty inspired a long heroic poem which was translated into several dialects and made celebrities of the victors. When Froissart ate at the table of Charles V of France in 1373, one of his fellow guests was 'honoured above all others' because he could still display the wounds which he had received when he had fought as a young man among the Thirty. But such encounters, although they indulged the joy of fighting, the hope of profit and the lust for fame, decided nothing and served no real purpose of war. There were some, as even Froissart conceded, who accused the participants of crude showing off.[53] Incidents like the battle of the Thirty were, however, evocative for another reason. They were symptoms of a war fought without strategic discipline or central control, by captains who were answerable only to themselves. It was Brittany rather than Calais which became the model for territories invaded by the English and their allies. And, as the bonds of civil society broke down under the pressure of war in one province after another, men trained in the school of Brittany were to be foremost among the plunderers of France.

The campaigns of the Earl of Lancaster in the south-west had greatly extended the limits of the duchy of Aquitaine to the east and north. The English King's garrisons now held the valley of the Garonne as far as Aiguillon, the Dordogne as far as Lalinde, and the Adour to Saint-Sever. They also controlled most of the northern shore of the Gironde. These regions were subject to more or less effective administration by officers of Edward III or his principal vassals. Beyond them Edward's government controlled territory extending in streaks and patches through Saintonge, the Agenais and southern Périgord. But there was no regular frontier anywhere and no one had any very precise notion of how extensive the duchy was. In 1354, on the eve of a major diplomatic conference, Edward III's ministers at Westminster confessed that they did not know where the limits of the King's territory lay or even whether they included Angoumois or Quercy. Two years later, when they were contemplating another conference, an expert had to be sent to Bordeaux to find out.[54] In practice possession was the law and was all that mattered to the King's officers on the spot. But there were few regions in which they did not have to jockey for advantage with those of the King of France. In 1347 the French still held le Mas d'Agenais and Marmande in the midst of the English garrisons of the Garonne. In the Dordogne valley there were still French strongholds between Bordeaux and Bergerac, including the important bridge-town of Sainte-Foy. Each side had friends and allies within the territory nominally controlled by the other. Events were dictated by small groups of men facing each other across short distances, and the war followed a logic of its own driven by local interests and local rivalries, barely affected by the interests or objectives of governments.

The English King's chief representative in the duchy was the Seneschal, who was responsible for the whole administration and defence of the duchy. He was a considerable figure, with extensive powers of patronage and wide discretions which, if only because of the distance from Westminster and the slowness of communications, were subject to minimal supervision. His importance was reflected in his salary, at £500 sterling a year one of the highest in the service of the Crown.[55] After a succession of brief and unsatisfactory appointments, Sir John Cheverston held this office for most of the 1350s. He was very typical of the kind of man who served as Seneschal in Gascony: a west-country knight of no great importance in his own country, but a competent administrator, an energetic soldier, and a skilful manipulator of the jealous and violent nobility of the south-west and the handful of privileged towns on which the survival of the English duchy had always depended. The other principal officers of the Gascon government were the Constable of Bordeaux, who was responsible for finance; and the mayor of Bordeaux, who presided over the affairs of the duchy's principal city. All of these great officers, in this period, were appointed by the King of England and all of them were Englishmen. Nevertheless, the government of Gascony was not a government of Englishmen. It was overwhelmingly Gascon. Its stability depended chiefly on the two major cities of the duchy, Bordeaux and Bayonne, and on perhaps two dozen great Gascon families whose clients and kinsmen were distributed throughout the duchy. The Seneschal was required, and in any event wise, to consult the Council of Gascony, on which many of them were represented. Beneath the handful of officials who addressed each other in English, corresponded with the King's ministers in Latin, maintained attorneys at Westminster and had tombs and chantries made ready for themselves in the English provinces, there was the mass of lesser functionaries: judges, officials, provosts and *jurats*, garrison commanders. Theirs was the face of government to most Gascons. One or two of them may have been Englishmen who, like the long-serving Seneschal of the Landes, Thomas Hampton, had made their lives in the region. But almost all of them were local men.

After a long period in which the Seneschal had been obliged to fight off large French armies with a handful of static garrisons and virtually no field army, the defence of the duchy had been completely reorganised at the end of the 1340s by the Earl of Lancaster and by a number of his officers who remained behind after the Earl had returned to England. A deliberate attempt was made to avoid tying down excessive numbers of men in garrison duties in fixed locations, many of which were far away from the real threat. In times of danger small mobile field forces were recruited at short notice to carry out specific military objectives: to defend a castle, to raise a siege, to carry out a raid. They served for limited periods, rarely more than two months, and then disbanded. Some of these men were drawn from the permanent garrisons. Most of them belonged to the retinues of Gascon lords drawn from a limited area close to Bordeaux: the Bordelais, the Bazadais, the Landes. Their companies were quite unlike the retinues with which the Gascon nobility had traditionally gone to war, large and formless hordes of armed men generally fighting on foot. A typical company was between ten and sixty strong. It usually consisted entirely of cavalrymen and mounted infantry. Like the retinues which fought in English armies, they acquired with experience the courage and discipline of friends fighting together. The total military capacity of the duchy must be a matter of conjecture. The partial records which survive suggest that task forces could number anything between sixty men belonging to one or two companies and a thousand men belonging to several dozen.[56] But larger forces could certainly be collected for major military operations, by allowing a longer time for recruitment and drawing on a larger geographical area. In 1352 just under 3,800 men were retained by the nobility of the duchy to serve under the Earl of Stafford, in addition to the men whom Stafford had brought with him from England. They comprised:

Bannerets and knights	144
Other men-at-arms	1,117
Mounted infantry	1,328
Mounted archers	30
Foot soldiers	1,096

This is the only large Gascon army of the period for which anything like a complete record survives. But it was probably fairly typical for both size and composition of what the duchy could produce for a great occasion, at any rate before the arrival of the Prince of Wales transformed the situation in the mid-1350s.[57]

It was not, however, the occasional field operations or *grandes chevauchées* like Stafford's which accounted for the high cost of defending Gascony, but the overheads, and in particular the number and size of its permanent garrisons. The main difference between Gascony and Brittany was that Edward III's officers there were a government, not a force of occupation. The King never forgot that he and his forebears had been dukes of Aquitaine for two centuries, and he recognised obligations to his subjects there which would have seemed excessively scrupulous to his officers in Brittany. But the cost of government in wartime was high. In the major towns and a small number of strategically important castles, the garrisons were commanded by castellans appointed by the King, the Seneschal or the Earl of Lancaster. A much larger number of garrisons was recruited by the lord of the place which they were defending and served under him. But in either case the men's wages were paid (eventually) by the King. It was a heavy burden. In the early 1350s the Constable of Bordeaux was paying the garrisons of more than sixty towns and castles. Some of these garrisons were small standing armies: 120 men at Mauléon on the Pyrenean march, 95 at Rochefort at the opposite extremity of the duchy on the Charente, no less than 250 at Bergerac on the Dordogne.[58]

These arrangements were cheaper than the less effective system based on large and immobile bodies of local troops which Oliver Ingham had operated as Seneschal before 1344. But they were not cheap, and they rapidly exhausted the revenues of the duchy. The lands and revenues of the King in Gascony were treated as a source of patronage, not revenue. They were habitually granted out to Gascon noblemen to reward past services and to buy loyalty. In wartime it would have been dangerous to do anything else. But the result was that the whole of the Earl of Lancaster's enormous conquests in the Bazadais, the Agenais, Périgord and Saintonge were granted out almost at once, and the extended territory of the duchy had to be defended with the revenues of the original heartlands. This meant the profits of the mints at Bordeaux and Dax, the customs levied on the traffic of the Gironde, and a number of miscellaneous fees and charges. All of these revenues were suffering in the late 1340s from plague, economic depression and war. For the first decade of the war Edward III's ministers had struggled, with mixed results, to uphold the traditional axiom of English policy that Gascony should finance itself. No one paid even lip service to this principle now. Between 1348 and 1361 more than half of the expenditure of the ducal administration in Bordeaux had to be financed by the English Exchequer.[59]

In those parts of the duchy where the Seneschals and their subordinates employed paid garrisons and exercised effective administrative control, indiscriminate plundering by local troops was rare and the taking of *patis* almost unknown. The neighbouring provinces of the south-west were a different matter. They were still, at least nominally, under French control and they suffered from constant raids by small bands of Gascon soldiers. The raiding had begun with the occupation of isolated castles and small walled towns and villages. But as the first pioneers learned how weak and how rich these provinces were, they became bolder, and others followed in their path. Between the campaigns of the Earl of Lancaster in the mid-1340s and the final collapse of French civil government some twelve years later, the raiders and their garrisons spread over large parts of southern and central France. This creeping occupation, spreading outward from the epicentre in Gascony to one French province after another, was almost entirely the work of independent captains operating for their own account.

One of the earliest and most notorious examples was the occupation of the castle of Blanzac, south of Angoulême. Blanzac had been captured by the Seneschal Oliver Ingham in 1342 in an ordinary operation of war. But when the army moved on, one of the captains serving in it, Guillaume Pons de Pommiers, took over the place for his own account with a garrison which he paid out of his own pocket for more than sixteen years. Within a short time of its capture travellers in the district reported that in spite of the truce which was then in force the garrison had 'smashed, stolen or burned' everything within marching distance. This was still relatively uncommon, even shocking, in 1343. But it became the common experience of every province of France.[60] The government in Bordeaux gave its tacit approval to the conquests of such men, and it paid the wages of a small number of particularly important independent garrisons. Sometimes, its records refer to them as belonging to 'our party'. But for most of these men party was a matter of symbols and sometimes of convenience. They were their own masters and they recruited and paid their own troops. They made their profits by systematically denuding the country of grain and cattle, by looting churches and by exacting ransoms and *patis* just as the independent captains of Brittany did. They were Edward III's subjects and some of them had close connections with his officials in Bordeaux. But they were generally indifferent to his larger political designs and to the pacts and truces of his Seneschal. They too were fighting *pour leur singulier profit*.

The independent garrisons were called *routiers* by French officials (from the French word *route*, meaning company). Their victims usually called them 'English'. But the truth is that except during the great expeditions of the Earl of Lancaster and the Prince of Wales, there were very few Englishmen in south-western France in the mid-fourteenth century, and those were almost all employed in administrative duties in Bordeaux or in the principal border fortresses. The captains of the independent companies were almost always Gascons or, in some cases, Béarnais. The same was true of their men. For many of these men, war was an economic necessity. They lived in a region with few natural resources, on the tiny parcels of land to which their families' holdings had been reduced by generations of partition. They took naturally to the mercenary traditions of a province which had for centuries furnished soldiers for other men's battles, and where private warfare was endemic. The wars of Edward III, which made some of the richest agricultural provinces of France fair game for determined plunderers, was a golden opportunity for the impoverished nobility of Gascony, which they seized with both hands. But there was also a real relish for the way of life of these small, errant companies of soldiers who inflicted such terrible hardships on France in the course of the fourteenth century. Years later, at the French court, the historian Froissart heard Arnaud-Amanieu d'Albret reminiscing about the golden years of the mid-fourteenth century, when he had commanded his own company in south-western France. Every day they had came upon some rich prize, some merchant of Toulouse, Condom, la Réole or Bergerac, 'dont nous estoufions nos superfluitez et jolietez'. His companion laughed. 'There's the Gascon way of life for you,' he said: 'living by other men's misfortunes.'[61]

Périgord was among the first provinces of the south-west to suffer extensive destruction at the hands of independent raiders. This beautiful and varied province traversed by the broad basin of the Dordogne and, further north, by the steeper valleys of the Isle and the Dronne and their tributaries, included some of the most fertile and populous parts of south-western France. When the Earl of Lancaster left at the end of 1346 the English were firmly in control of the southern part of the province, where they had taken possession of most of the walled towns and *bastides* of the Dordogne valley as far as Lalinde and Molières. From their bases in the Dordogne valley English and Gascon raiders penetrated year by year further into the centre and north of the province. Nearly two thirds of the enormous Anglo-Gascon garrison of Bergerac were mounted men. This was a force designed for raiding, not for passive defence, and indeed within a few years the ambitious castellan of Bergerac, an Englishman called William Darampton, had captured a clutch of castles for his own account lying north of the town, towards Périgueux. Augier de Montaut, another aggressive empire builder, was a local lord who operated in the valley of the Isle. This man's driving motive was a virulent and long-standing vendetta against the Count of Périgord who was the main pillar of the French Crown in the region. His principal garrison, at Mussidan, was maintained like Darampton's at the expense of Edward III.[62]

For the next fifteen years the provincial capital, Périgueux, a rich commercial and ecclesiastical city at the centre of a knot of road and

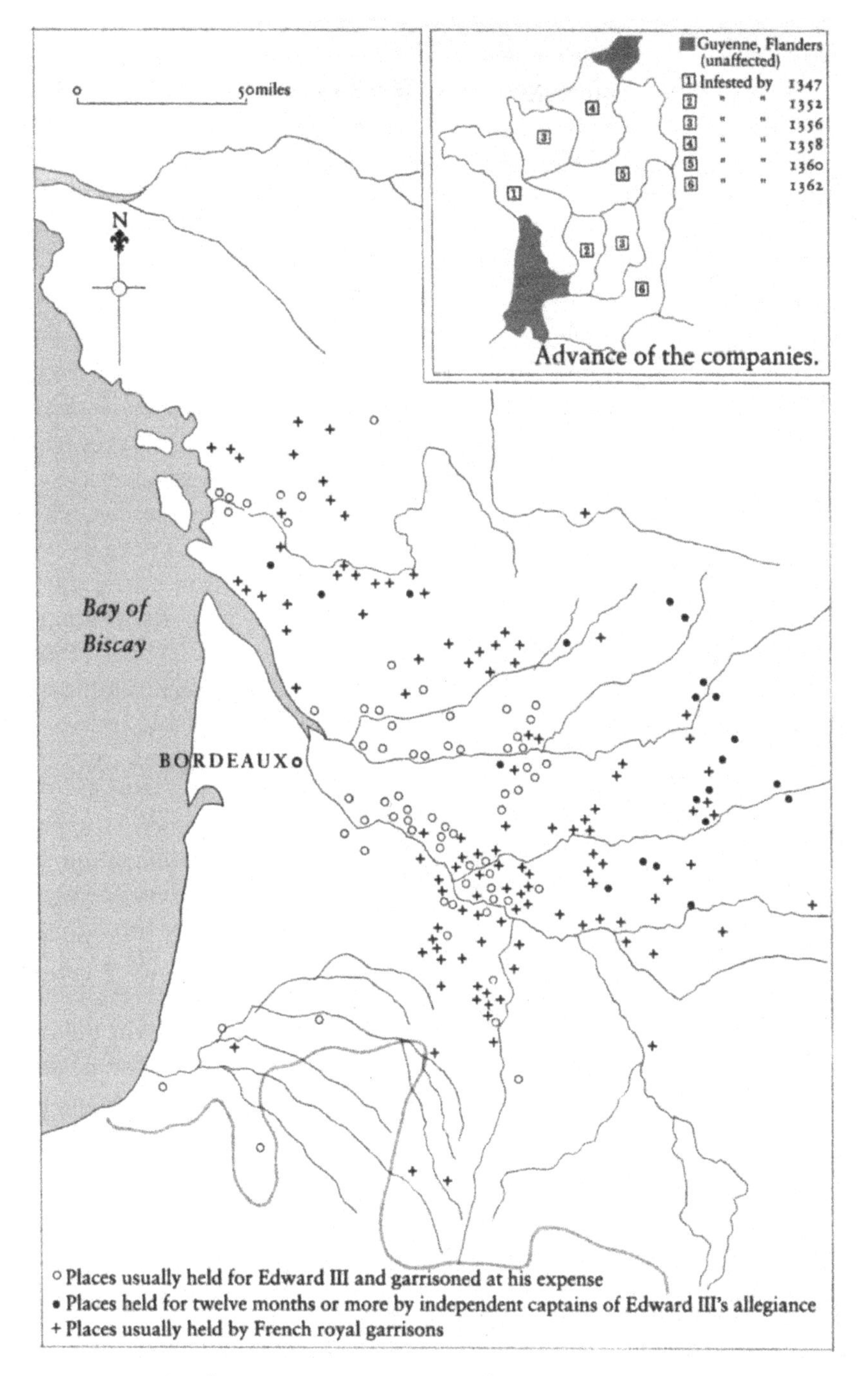

3 South-western France: Principal garrisons, 1348–55

river lines, found itself surrounded by hostile garrisons. A handful of them were paid by the Constable of Bordeaux and commanded by reliable captains who were more or less amenable to the orders of the Seneschals. The rest, although they flew the English King's banner and nailed his arms above their gates, were fighting for themselves and lived entirely from their spoils. The awkward, dilapidated walls of Périgueux's double town were not made for such a crisis and the shrunken population was incapable of manning their whole length. 1347 was a terrible year in Périgueux. The harvest had failed the previous autumn and soldiers and bandits blocked the roads, preventing supplies from reaching the city from further afield. Torrential rain flooded the lower part of the city and carried away a section of the walls. The streets were filled with starving and penniless refugees from the surrounding region. The accounts of the town clerk give a vivid impression of life within the beleaguered city. On Shrove Tuesday, when food was traditionally distributed to the poor, the crush of beggars was so intense that eight people were suffocated. At Whitsun nearly 3,000 rations were handed out. Enemy garrisons raided up to the gates, looting and burning the suburbs and outlying villages. They killed those who were caught unawares or carried them off for ransom, mutilating those who could not pay. Masons working on the walls and outworks abandoned their materials and fled as soldiers were sighted from the towers and the great bells of St. Front sounded the alarm. The inhabitants lived in constant fear of dark nights and traitors. Strangers found wandering by the moat were seized as spies and branded on the forehead with the *fleur de lys*. At the end of July 1347, when persistent rumours of treason were circulating, mounted patrols rode through the streets after dark holding burning torches into the pitch black night. The citizens of a relatively large town like Périgueux were certainly not helpless in the face of enemy raiders. They formed their own militia, which attacked the garrisons around them with ferocious courage and occasional success. The enemy garrisons at Saint-Privat and Saint-Astier were captured in June 1347. The prisoners were brought into Périgueux to be hanged from the main gates and towers of the city as a warning to their fellows. But these were ephemeral triumphs. The raiders had no difficulty in recruiting fresh men, and occupied new redoubts as soon as they had been expelled from the old. Within two years of its capture, Saint-Astier was once more in the hands of the Anglo-Gascons.[63]

Poitou suffered almost as much damage as Périgueux from the depredations of the single garrison of Lusignan, a sombre illustration of what a small but organised force of men could do. Lusignan was a powerfully built fortress dating from the twelfth century, sited on a promontory over the River Vonne, twelve miles from Poitiers. It had been occupied by the Earl of Lancaster in September 1346 during his famous raid in the province. When the Earl had withdrawn, he had left a garrison there under the command of a well known nobleman of the Bordelais, Bertrand de Montferrand and two of his brothers. Bertrand commanded 500 men in wartime and 300 in time of truce, for which he was paid a lump sum from the Exchequer at Westminster. Many of his troops, particularly among the infantry, were recruited from the new underworld of military journeymen: misfits and outcasts, criminals and fugitives from justice, impoverished adventurers from other parts of France or from foreign countries, as well as local men from the town of Lusignan and its surrounding district, who joined in the violence for a share of the loot or to pursue their private quarrels with their neighbours. Guyon Pévrier from Cosne-sur-Loire in the Nivernais was wanted for two murders, a forgery and many thefts when he enlisted in the garrison of Lusignan. He had his equivalents in almost every Anglo-Gascon garrison operating beyond the boundaries of the duchy. A renegade monk and a penniless squire from the Auvergne, companions in arms hiring themselves out to one garrison commander after another; a teenager from Normandy who took to 'evil ways and following the great companies' and whose father boxed his ears so hard that he died: the records of the French royal Chancery and Parlement are filled with the obscure, usually brief lives of men like these.[64]

Between 1346 and 1350 the garrison of Lusignan laid waste fifty-two parishes, destroyed ten monasteries and launched devastating raids against towns and castles throughout south-western Poitou. At one stage they also occupied the castle of Faye, just south Saint-Maixent, extending their range well into the valleys of the Sèvre. The French King's representatives could do little to stop them. Poitiers, the provincial capital, was put on a permanent war footing. Garrisons were installed at Niort, Saint-Maixent, Parthenay and Montreuil-Bonnin. All trade with the enemy was forbidden in the hope of destroying the market for looted goods. In May 1347 an attempt was even made to surprise the castle and take it by storm, but the attacking force was ambushed as it approach and retreated in humiliating disorder.[65]

When the truce of Calais was made in September 1347 the consuls of Périgueux, like many towns of France, had a transcript made for their use. But they soon discovered that the truce made virtually no difference to their situation. When the English reduced the number and size of the garrisons in their pay, as they generally did in time of truce, redundant soldiers were released to wander through the region and join up with any independent captain who could offer them work. The garrison of Lusignan, although they were in the English King's pay, fought on as if nothing had changed. The French endeavoured to contain the raids by maintaining small mobile field forces in the frontier provinces, which intervened on the fire-fighting principle when and where they were required. The system was very similar to the one operated by the English seneschals of Gascony after the reforms of the Earl of Lancaster or the wardens of the march operated in the Scottish borderlands. These forces, rarely more than a few hundred strong, were drawn from the retainers and clients of the royal captain in the region, from the royal garrisons under his command and occasionally from the citizens of the larger towns. They were thinly spread. A local captain like Thibault de Barbazan, for example, was expected to keep the peace between 1348 and 1352 across the whole eastern march between the valleys of the Garonne and the Adour, with a cavalry force of 300 or 400 men based at Condom and twelve garrisons spread out across the region. At the beginning of the 1350s, the Béarnais nobleman Bertrand d'Espagne had to defend the whole march of Quercy and southern Périgord on the same lines. They were rapidly overwhelmed by the scale and range of the Gascon raids.[66]

The root of the problem, as always, was want of money and the traditional suspicions of the provincial communities of France for the central government and its officers. Taxpayers were still notoriously reluctant to pay taxes in time of truce, however fragile the military situation. When, early in 1348, the communities of the Toulousain were commanded to send their representatives to discuss war taxation with the King's commissioners, the men of Villelongue (one of the taxing districts of the province) expressed their fervent support for the King's cause and voted an adequate grant of money to sustain it. But the terms were that the first instalment was to be held by stakeholders, to be released to the war treasurers only when the current truce had failed. If the King should make a new truce or extend the old, collection was to cease at once.[67] This attitude was beginning to disappear in northern France, where the tradition of royal government was older and men were adjusting to a state of permanent war. But the provinces of the south-west, with their long-standing distrust of public authorities, clung obdurately to the ancient prejudice that war taxes were for fighting wars and not for preparing to fight them. This made it exceptionally difficult for the French to fight a defensive war against dispersed and undirected enemies who could choose their time and place to violate the truce. Organised resistance was tardy and inefficient. The French commanders could redress the position only by conducting major field operations designed to forestall the enterprises of the English before they happened or to retaliate with overwhelming force afterwards. Fourteenth-century truces were fragile. Over-reaction, too early or too late, usually destroyed them in the end.

Legal convention had little to contribute. The practice was for each government to nominate two or four 'conservators' in each province whose function was to hear complaints about breaches of the truce and to deal jointly with those responsible for them. But it was not always easy to discover who was responsible or to decide on which side of this formless war his allegiance lay. If the conservators disagreed, as they frequently did, the law sanctioned self-help. The aggrieved party was entitled to decide for himself who was at fault and to take reprisals. Within a short time the process of reprisal and counter-reprisal was indistinguishable from war. In the months which followed the truce of Calais, the English Seneschal of Gascony passed much of his time touring trouble spots on the march of the duchy with a large armed escort, conferring with French officials and with the conservators of either side. He achieved very little for his pains. Those who hoped to live in peace were well advised to make their own private arrangements with their adversaries as if the agreements of their rulers had never been made. The Count of Périgueux and the Countess of Angoulême both made private agreements with the Seneschal of Gascony in the early months of 1348.[68] By May 1348 the truce had failed entirely at several points along the south-western march. Armies were being recruited in Bordeaux and Toulouse. Another was assembling in Saintonge, where the French King's agents were preparing in the utmost secrecy to attack the garrison of Saint-Jean d'Angély. In Poitou, Floton de Revel, one of the French King's more energetic ministers, confronted the garrison of Lusignan in June 1348 at Chenay on the banks of the Sèvre Niortaise. According to his own account he inflicted 'much damage' on them.[69]

The activities of garrison troops like those of Blanzac, Mussidan or Lusignan brought home to the inhabitants of the south-western provinces how vulnerable small towns were to very small bands of practised brigands. Only the largest and most significant towns had garrisons, and even in those the main burden of keeping watch and manning the walls fell on the inhabitants. Their numbers had often been reduced by plague and flight. Their walls usually dated from the twelfth century, the last period in which the region had suffered from persistent warfare. In most places the defences followed an irregular course around the circuit of the town, with sharp angles and blind corners. Gaps pierced for paths, chicken runs and houses were hastily blocked up with rubble. The watchman's view was liable to be obstructed by suburban buildings and vegetation, while access to the walls from within could be difficult and slow, as the lanes were narrow and blocked by carts, animals and rubbish. Moonless nights held special perils for such places. One incident caused a great stir in the region. In May 1347, a small band of Gascon adventurers acting on their own initiative succeeded in capturing the *bastide* of Domme, which contained one of the main French mints of the south-west. The raiders carried off a large quantity of bullion and coin. They left a garrison which resisted all attempts to dislodge it and terrorised the rest of the district for about a year. Yet Domme was a well fortified town, sited in what should have been an impregnable position.[70]

The captors of Domme had climbed the escarpment overlooking the Dordogne on which the town was built. But the usual method of entering a walled town was by 'escalade', a simpler and less dramatic technique which consisted of creeping up on a town at night from two directions at once and placing ladders against dark corners of the walls.

> They spy out a walled castle for a day or two beforehand [wrote the northern chronicler Jean le Bel]; then, collecting together a group of thirty or forty brigands, they approach it from one side and then from another. At the break of day they burst in and set fire to a house, making so much noise that the inhabitants think that there must be 1,000 men-at-arms among them and flee in all directions. Then they break into the houses and loot them before departing loaded with spoil.

In the nature of things escalade was a method for irregulars, or 'brigands' as Jean le Bel called them. It depended on surprise and on the paralysing effect of boredom and exhaustion among the watch. The regular armies of the lieutenants and seneschals could rarely hope to achieve as much. Their recruitment was too public, their movements too well advertised. This was why, in spite of its simplicity, escalade was regarded at the end of the 1340s as a new and dangerous peril. In March 1349 the English Seneschal of Gascony ordered that full war rates should henceforth be paid to garrison troops serving in frontier towns, even in time of truce. He gave as the reason the threat from ladder parties attacking from two sides at once under cover of darkness. The same vigilance, the same alarms, the same violence were common now to peace and war. The difference between the two became a matter of diplomatic convention, the starting point for further conferences whose outcome was irrelevant in most parts of France.[71]

Even after the truce of Calais had been renewed by the ambassadors of the two Kings in November 1348, it remained a dead letter in the south-west. The independent companies continued their plundering of Saintonge, Angoumois, Poitou and Périgord. From Périgord they extended their reach through the river valleys into the high Limousin plateau, a sparsely inhabited region of shepherds and cattle farmers, of isolated villages and castles and rich churches where Edward III's armies had never been and his officers in Bordeaux maintained no garrisons. The occupation of large parts of the Limousin by armed bands was in some ways the classic illustration of their methods. The origin of the cancer was Nontron, a small walled town on the borders of Limousin and Périgord. Nontron had been occupied in 1345 by a disaffected relative of the Count of Périgord who had formed an alliance of convenience with the English. He had used the town as a base for raids in northern Périgord and had successfully resisted every attempt to dislodge him. In the summer of 1346 the place had been briefly and unsuccessfully besieged by troops of the Duke of Normandy. An attempt to buy out the garrison failed obscurely three years later. By then the raiders of Nontron had already planted several clones. Fifteen miles north-east of the town lay the castle of Montbrun, a bone of contention among competing members of a local noble family. One of them made common cause with some members of the garrison of Nontron. He seized the castle keep of Montbrun, expelled its occupants, and invited in the Anglo-Gascons to help him hold it. The incoming soldiers demolished the curtain walls of the castle and reinforced the keep, to make it defensible by a small number of men. Then they made it a base for raiding in the western Limousin. Not long after this incident, another disaffected Limousin nobleman captured the thirteenth-century castle of Aixe, which dominated the crossing of the River Vienne a few miles downstream from Limoges. His motive was a grudge against the French King's officials, who had condemned his elder brother for treason and confiscated the family's possessions. He too declared himself for Edward III and, when the French King's Lieutenant laid siege to the castle, he turned to the Anglo-Gascons for help. The skilful exploitation of local divisions and grievances and the occupation of small, isolated castles were both hallmarks of the independent captains in the days before they learned to recruit armies several thousand strong.[72]

In the Limousin the leading light among them was a famous adventurer at the outset of his career: Jean de Gasnoye *alias* Jean de Sault, who called himself the 'Bascon de Mareuil'. He was a squire from Sault-de-Navailles in Béarn. His pseudonym was probably derived from the castle of Mareuil near Nontron, which was occupied by Gascon companies at about this time and may have been under his command. The Bascon de Mareuil was the earliest of the great captains of companies to achieve more than local notoriety. By the beginning of the 1350s he already enjoyed a reputation for carrying out bold enterprises, often over great distances. He disported himself, says Jean le Bel, like a 'great lord, richly dressed and mounted' and rode into the lists with a moor's head crest above his jousting helmet. The Bascon fought under English colours and the government in Bordeaux acknowledged him as 'one of our party'. But so far as can be discovered he never took their pay. He lived on plunder, on ransoms and on *patis*. At some time in 1348 the Bascon de Mareuil and thirty companions captured by escalade the small castle of Comborn north of Brive. The lord of Comborn, a former royal captain of the province, was surprised in his bed. He was to pass some five years in captivity before he finally agreed to ransom himself for the enormous sum of 20,000 *écus*. The castle, which was well sited on a narrow spur of rock in the gorge of the Vezère, became a base from which raiding parties could range over the whole of southern Limousin.[73] The Bishop of Limoges and the officers of the King of France struggled to create a ring fence around this new enemy, putting garrisons into nearby castles which were strong enough to be defended and demolishing those which were not. They achieved almost nothing. Into the disorder created by the companies of Nontron and Comborn sprang fresh bands drawn by the prospect of profit in more or less virgin territory. Within the next two or three years a new headquarters was opened up at Excideuil, whence a fresh web of garrisoned houses and forts was laid across the western march of the Limousin. Excideuil, with its great double-towered keep and extensive walls was a more formidable fortress than any which the Gascons had so far occupied in the region. That they could contemplate holding such a place at all shows how great their strength had now become.[74]

*

In March 1349 the ambassadors of England and France assembled once more on the traditional meeting ground outside Guines to discuss proposals for a permanent peace, a charade to which they had committed themselves on the previous occasion. After six weeks of fruitless discussion they dispersed again at the beginning of May. In Paris, the government was paralysed. The plague was at its height. The Duke of Burgundy died in April. The Queen, the Duchess of Normandy and the Chancellor of the realm all succumbed in the following months. Officials and clerks sickened or fled. The King's Council left the capital in June. Philip himself wandered without his Chancery about Brie and the Gâtinais, accompanied by a handful of clerks and servants. Although the truce still had several months to run and had been solemnly extended until May 1350, the war in the south-west continued with unabated ferocity. In the Agenais and southern Périgord a succession of cat-fights led to bruises and reprisals. Tonneins was captured by the French and recaptured by the Anglo-Gascons. Port-Sainte-Marie was captured by Gascon partisans who gained admittance by a trick. This was a humiliating loss for the French. Port-Sainte-Marie was the main river port used for supplying their field armies in the lower Garonne.[75] The French King's officers retaliated at several points along the march, and as the diplomats put their seals to the new truce there were already at least three sieges in progress there. The troops of three southern seneschalsies were encamped outside Montcuq, a castle on the remote march of Quercy and the Agenais, which a troop of Gascons had occupied during the winter. Another force was besieging Saint-Astier in the valley of the Isle. Further north, the Seneschal of Poitou had collected a sizeable army of local men and laid siege to the Anglo-Gascon garrison of Lusignan.

The English Seneschal of Gascony at this stage was Thomas Cook, a competent soldier who had served as marshal of the Earl of Lancaster's army in the famous campaigns of 1345 and 1346. Cook raised two substantial task forces at great speed. Stephen Cusington, another of Lancaster's protégés, was sent west into the Dordogne valley with one of them. The other, about 500 strong, marched north at the end of May with Cook himself to confront the Poitevins outside Lusignan. The outcome went a long way to vindicate the new English strategy of using small mounted task forces under experienced commanders. Cusington was unable to save Saint-Astier which was taken by storm, the sixth time in less than a decade that this small market town had changed hands by violence. But he baulked an attempt by the French to follow up their victory by attacking Bergerac, the eastern bastion of the English in the valley of the Dordogne. Cook's army had a more eventful passage. About twenty miles from Lusignan, by the village of Limalonges, they were ambushed by the army which the Poitevins had raised for the siege of Lusignan. The Gascons dismounted after the fashion of the English and took up a position on rising ground. The Poitevins, who outnumbered them by about three to one, rode around their flank, invaded their baggage park where the horses were tethered, and then charged Cook's army from the rear. They had not yet learned the lessons of Morlaix, Auberoche and Crécy. The first two lines of French cavalry were impaled on the embedded lances of the Gascons and suffered terrible casualties. The third stood immobile in its starting position watching their opportunities until nightfall, when they made off. The Poitevins had lost about 300 dead and many more captured. Among the prisoners was that elegant paladin Jean de Boucicaut, *moult preudhomme et de grand savoir*, whose restless courage and misjudgments were to cost him several long spells in English prisons.[76]

There was worse to follow. On the way south one of the Gascon captains detached his company from the rest of the Seneschal's army and captured the castle of Taillebourg. This great fortress, dominating the main crossing of the Charente north of Saintes, was the principal surviving stronghold of the French in Saintonge. In Saintes itself a plot was uncovered to surrender the town to the enemy, and as panic gripped the inhabitants hurried arrangements had to be made to reinforce them. The English responded by reinforcing their own garrisons. It was not until the beginning of August 1349 that the local representatives of the two governments in the south-west agreed to enforce the truce, some three months after it had been made and just as the King's Council in Paris emerged from its lethargy and decided to repudiate it.[77]

CHAPTER II

Return to Arms 1349–1352

The French decision to repudiate the truce was made at the beginning of August 1349. The reasons are not recorded. But there can be little doubt that the depredations of the Anglo-Gascons in the south-west was the main one. The scale and range of their operations were now so great and the creeping occupation of new territory so extensive that without a counter-attack on a large scale several provinces were likely to become ungovernable. The situation in Saintonge was particularly grave. The loss of Taillebourg and the plot to betray Saintes were sombre warnings. There was a serious danger that the English would take control of la Rochelle, the only significant port at the French King's disposal south of the Loire.

The timing of the French ministers' decision was no doubt due mainly to the loss of Taillebourg in early June, but it must also have owed something to the fact that they had money in their coffers. The tax collection campaign of 1348 had been a disaster. But what the government failed to collect in tax revenue was more than made up by that perennial source of windfall revenue, the manipulation of the coinage. This was now much more than an occasional expedient. It was a regular instrument of financial management. A small committee of the royal Council directed the regular rise and fall of the silver value of current coin, keeping the mints working and coinage profits flowing in. The operation was supervised by two ingenious experts, Jean Poilevillain, Parisian timber merchant and bullion dealer, and Nicholas Braque, a royal official with a persistent reputation for corruption and long experience of coinage operations. The proportion of the nominal value of the coinage which the Crown took in charges and profit rose to nearly 30 per cent, the highest level since the King's accession. The treasury day-books for the second half of 1349 (an isolated survival) testify to the success of the system. They suggest that the French government was running a substantial budget surplus during this period, which was entirely due to phenomenally high receipts from the mints. They contributed two thirds of the government's revenues from all sources.[1]

Although the idea must have been mooted for some weeks beforehand, the final decision seems to have been made by the King's secret Council at a meeting at Vincennes. Those present included Philip VI himself, Hugh d'Arcy Bishop of Laon and Jean de Nesle, lord of Offémont, his two most influential counsellors both of whom were intimately involved in the King's dealings with England.[2] The execution of the decision was confided to Jean's son Guy de Nesle. The career of this ambitious young soldier was a sign of the cliquishness of Philip VI's government as well as of the eclipse of more famous names at the battle of Crécy. Still only twenty-two years old, Guy had fought in every great campaign since 1345 and had been a marshal for a year. On 9 August 1349 he was appointed captain-general in Saintonge. His authority was subsequently extended to Poitou, Angoumois, Périgord and Limousin, in fact the whole of western France from Loire to the Garonne. His army, which was recruited at great speed from every province of France except Normandy and Languedoc, was the strongest which the French had raised since 1347.[3] The plan which was eventually devised was to form two independent forces out of it. One, under Guy's own command, was to invade northern Saintonge and reconquer the valley of the Charente. The other would invade Bas-Poitou, the region comprising the northern Vendée and the south shore of the Loire estuary.

While the French ministers gathered their forces, their agents recruited a fleet of fighting ships and crews in the Castilian ports of the Bay of Biscay. Edward III's daughter Joan Plantagenet had died of the plague at Bordeaux on her way to Spain to marry the heir to the throne of Castile. Her death closed a brief and promising chapter in Castile's relations with England which had opened with the marriage treaty of 1348. It allowed time for second thoughts in the Spanish kingdom about a treaty which represented a radical break with Castile's traditional foreign policy and had been controversial ever since it was made. Moreover, it coincided with a renewed outbreak of the long-standing vendetta between the seamen of Bayonne and those of the Biscay ports of Castile. In the late summer of 1348, only a few weeks after Joan's death, an English ship carrying the new Constable of Bordeaux and victuals for the garrisons of Gascony was attacked by a ship of Santander, the *Santa Maria*, fitted out for war and filled with soldiers. The two ships engaged in a running battle for several hours before the *Santa Maria* was boarded and brought into Bayonne.

Castilian seamen sought out allies in the ports of France and early in 1349 a joint squadron of Norman and Castilian vessels was cruising off the Atlantic coast attacking English ships in the mouth of the Seine. French diplomacy assiduously widened the breach. In July 1349, a month before Guy de Nesle began to recruit his army, Philip VI settled his accounts for the Castilian mercenary fleet which he had hired in 1347 but never used, an old bone of contention. Immediately afterwards, a flotilla of Castilian ships was fitted out to fight in support of Guy de Nesle.[4]

When the news of Guy de Nesle's appointment reached the plague-ridden community at Westminster, about three weeks after it had been made, it caused great alarm. Edward III was in no position to pay for a major campaign nor to organise one in the short time available. There was a flurry of activity. On 28 August, the King instructed four lawyers to enquire into breaches of the truce. On the same day he reappointed Henry of Lancaster as his Lieutenant in Gascony and began to make to arrangements for him to sail for Bordeaux as soon as possible.[5] A few days after this, two of Edward III's officers in Calais were sent to the Count of Flanders to call on him to perform the obligations which he had undertaken in secret at Dunkirk the year before. According to the letter of the treaty Louis de Mâle was due to issue very shortly an ultimatum demanding the surrender by Philip VI of the three castleries of Walloon Flanders, the prelude to making war on him. But the treaty was worthless. The French King appears to have found out about it in April, when a visit of Geoffrey de Charny to the court of Flanders coincided with the indiscreet arrival of ambassadors from England. Geoffrey had delivered a vigorous protest and produced a copy of the Count's oath of fealty to remind him of his obligations. Louis de Mâle had many obligations, not all of them consistent. But he had no intention of being drawn into the crossfire between England and France in the way that had cost his father his county. It is not clear what answer he gave to the English emissaries who reached him in September, or to another embassy which was sent out from England in the following month. But when the time came, he did not stir.[6]

The main defence of the English possessions in Saintonge was a line of walled towns and castles which had been captured and garrisoned by the Earl of Lancaster in the autumn of 1346: Rochefort, Soubise, Tonnay-Charente, Tonnay-Boutonne and Saint-Jean-d'Angély. Between them these places held the valley of the River Boutonne and the whole of the lower valley the Charente to the sea. Although the fortresses of northern

Saintonge represented the northern bastions of the duchy of Aquitaine, the English regarded them as falling beyond its boundaries, the germ of future expansion in western France. Their special status was reflected in the fact that they were not placed under the authority of the Seneschal of Gascony but fell under the direct control of the Edward III's ministers in England, who appointed their captains and supplied and manned them by sea directly from England.[7] When Guy de Nesle invaded Saintonge in September 1349 with the advance guard of his army, Tonnay-Boutonne, the most northerly of these places, was captured almost immediately. On about 25 September 1349 the French army laid siege to Tonnay-Charente, a small walled town on the Charente which in better times had been a prosperous wine port. Tonnay-Charente was by no means the largest of the garrisons of the English in the region, but it was the key to their position there. It was the highest point of the Charente which was navigable by ocean-going ships, and was the point from which victuals and other supplies were distributed by river barge to the other garrisons. If the place had fallen Saint-Jean-d'Angély, twenty miles upstream, would probably have become untenable. The French constructed elaborate siege works around the town. They brought in the Castilian ships to complete its investment from the river. They sank blockships in the river. They undermined the walls and tried to carry them by assault. The defences of Tonnay-Charente were old and weak and the English had done little to improve them since taking possession. Nevertheless the place held out. After several fruitless and uncomfortable months Guy de Nesle's army was still there, enduring the cold winds blowing across the coastal marsh.[8]

The other French army, which invaded Bas-Poitou at about the same time, succeeded better. The region around the Bay of Bourgneuf and along the south bank of the lower Loire was a land of flat scrub and marsh, sparse and infertile, on which a surprisingly large population eked out a living from smallholdings of vines and grain. Its economic value lay in its salines, the richest of western Europe, from which the markets of England, northern France and the Low Countries were for the most part supplied. It was also of great strategic importance to the English, for it gave them a foothold south of the Loire from which to attempt one day the junction of their territories in Brittany and Gascony, an ambition which had long been dear to Edward III's heart. But Bas-Poitou remained for most of the fourteenth century a region of ambiguous loyalties which the English, always the prisoners of local politics and fickle allies, never securely occupied. Real power in the region was shared between two great noble families, those of Retz and Clisson. The lord of Retz in 1349 was a baby whose lands were administered by his guardian, Fulk de Laval. He was a local nobleman who had once, briefly, been a supporter of John de Montfort but had never aligned himself with the English. Fulk was remembered by a younger contemporary as a showy dresser who wore corsets so tight that they made him ill. But he deserves a better memorial than this, for he was an able soldier, the archetype of the loyal, energetic local potentate who had always provided the sinew of the defence of the French provinces. He controlled three important fortresses in Bas-Poitou, at Princé, Machecoul and Saint-Etienne-de-Mermorte, all of which were garrisoned at the expense of Philip VI. The Clisson family was for the moment wholly in the camp of the English. Olivier de Clisson, the head of the house, had been executed in Paris in 1343 for intriguing with Edward III and all of his lands had been confiscated. But his widow, the formidable and bellicose Jeanne de Belleville, had succeeded in remaining in occupation of much of it with the help of English soldiers. In 1349 the English had garrisons on the islands of Noirmoutier and Bouin (both of which were real islands in the fourteenth century) and at la Barre, Beauvoir, Chauvet and Prigny in the Bay of Bourgneuf, as well as a group of fortresses in the lordship of Belleville on the march of Poitou to the south-east. Most of these places belonged to Jeanne de Belleville.[9]

Edward III's officers should have been well placed to resist a French attack. Unfortunately they were divided by a bitter feud between two ambitious men: the Lieutenant in Bas-Poitou, Raoul de Caours, and the English fortune-hunter Walter Bentley. Bentley had married Jeanne de Belleville at some time in 1348 or early 1349 and immediately began to take control of her castles in the Bay of Bourgneuf. Raoul objected, as well he might. One of the terms of his appointment had been that he should have the disposal of all that he occupied. He claimed that these castles were his by right of conquest. By June 1349 relations between the two men were so bad that they were on the verge of armed combat. Raoul de Caours darkly contemplated treachery. He secretly approached Fulk de Laval and two other local magnates, offering to change his allegiance and to deliver up all the Clisson fortresses in the Bay of Bourgneuf. His terms were that he should be allowed to hold them and their salines under the King of France, and that he should be paid 10,000 *écus* for the arrears of his soldiers' wages. This arrangement was agreed by the three Frenchmen and was eventually ratified by

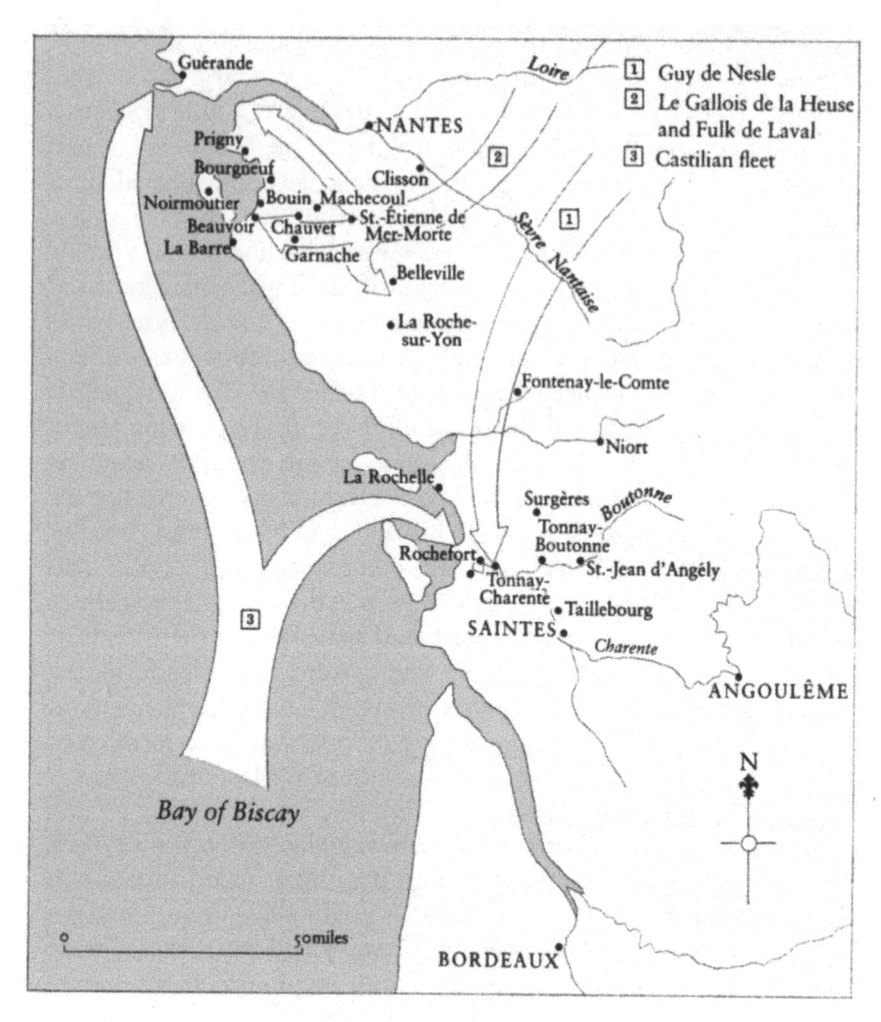

4 French invasion of Saintonge and Bas-Poitou, September 1349–February 1350

the King of France. But it was never put into effect, because in a final attempt to resolve the quarrel Edward III took the castles into his own hands before Raoul had time to carry out his bargain. Their garrisons, which included a fair number of Englishmen, remained loyal. Rather later, word of Raoul's treachery seems to have reached the English. In October Edward removed him from his lieutenancy and granted all the disputed lordships and castles to Walter Bentley and his wife.[10]

By the time that this order reached Brittany it no longer mattered. The

French arrived in Bas-Poitou at the end of September 1349 with an army and a fleet of forty-four French and Castilian vessels. The command had been given to Guillaume 'le Gallois' de la Heuse, an experienced soldier with a reputation for reckless bravado who had recently returned to France after passing two years as a prisoner of war in England. Within three months he had swept the English away. Beauvoir was captured by assault at the beginning of October. Garnache and Chauvet followed in quick succession. The garrison of Prigny made a stand beneath the walls, but they were defeated and the castle taken. Fulk de Laval was then given the task of reducing the islands with the aid of the fleet and an army of his allies and retainers. Noirmoutiers and Bouin were both captured. During November Fulk's men were raiding the coast of the Guérande peninsula north of the Loire, attacking coastal settlements and picking off English merchant ships sheltering in the harbours. There was a small sea battle off Guérande in which about a dozen English merchantmen laden with wine were overwhelmed by the Spanish seamen. All their crews were killed and their hulls and cargoes were carried off to be sold as prize in Flanders. While this was happening la Heuse himself turned south and invaded the dower lands of Jeanne de Belleville. The town of Belleville and its outlying forts were overrun so swiftly that by the end of the year they were all in French hands and their English captains were facing accusations of treason at home.[11]

An odder fate awaited Raoul de Caours, the man who had wanted to commit treason but had not acted fast enough. He had his revenge against the English in the following year, when he gathered 120 partisans of Blois and ambushed Sir Thomas Dagworth on the forest road from Auray to Vannes. Dagworth had only a small escort with him. Although he defended himself with ferocity, fighting on even after he had been badly wounded and blinded in one eye, they ran him through and killed him. This happened on 20 July 1350. It was not quite the end of Raoul's career. He clung to his ambition to build himself a great lordship in the Bay of Bourgneuf long after he had lost the means of achieving it. Early in 1351 he was making extravagant claims for his influence in the English-occupied towns of Brittany, promising the French King to procure the surrender of almost every one of them if he were restored to his castles in Bas-Poitou. A few months later he was found trying to recover Beauvoir-sur-Mer from its French garrison with the aid of a group of Montfortists. Later that year, Raoul was living on the island of Noirmoutiers when it was raided by Breton pirates and was carried off. He is never heard of again.[12]

The Earl of Lancaster arrived in Bordeaux at the beginning of November 1349, when the rout in Bas-Poitou was almost over. He must have come within sight of the French and Castilian ships on his passage south. He brought very few troops with him from England, barely 160 of his own retainers and perhaps as many more raised by his companions. Waiting for him in the city was a small army of Gascons, probably no more than a few hundred strong.[13] The Earl made no attempt to relieve Tonnay-Charente or to interfere with French operations further north. The probability is that he was too short of men, in particular archers, to contemplate a pitched battle with the army of Guy de Nesle. Instead, after a pause of a few days, he cast out in an unexpected direction, marching out of Bordeaux down the south bank of the Garonne.

The Anglo-Gascons swept through the Agenais, hardly pausing to collect the surrenders which were pressed on them by panic-stricken towns and villages in their path. At the beginning of December they invaded Languedoc. Villages and barns were burned for twenty-five miles around as his army passed by. Forty-two towns and castles were captured, most of them without striking a blow for their defence. Terror and destruction were not simply the incidental consequences of Lancaster's campaign. They were essential to his purpose. He wanted to force the French to sue for the renewal of the truce before their armies in western France did irreparable damage to Edward III's positions there. With the small strength at his disposal, he believed that this could best be achieved by a rapid *chevauchée* through undefended territory elsewhere.[14] Perhaps he was right. Languedoc was vulnerable. There had been only one previous attack on the province by an Anglo-Gascon army, by Oliver Ingham in 1339, which had not come to much. The inhabitants of its towns were not rebuilding their walls, reorganising their watches or laying in stores, as those of the western provinces had learned to do. The French, who had expected Lancaster to land in northern France, had made no preparations at all to fight in Languedoc. Philip VI's representative there was an elderly caretaker, Guillaume de Flavacourt, Archbishop of Auch, who had intermittently exercised the functions of royal Lieutenant for a number of years. He was an able enough administrator but no general, and he was almost entirely bereft of troops.[15] In the second week of December 1349, the Earl of Lancaster lunged towards Toulouse.

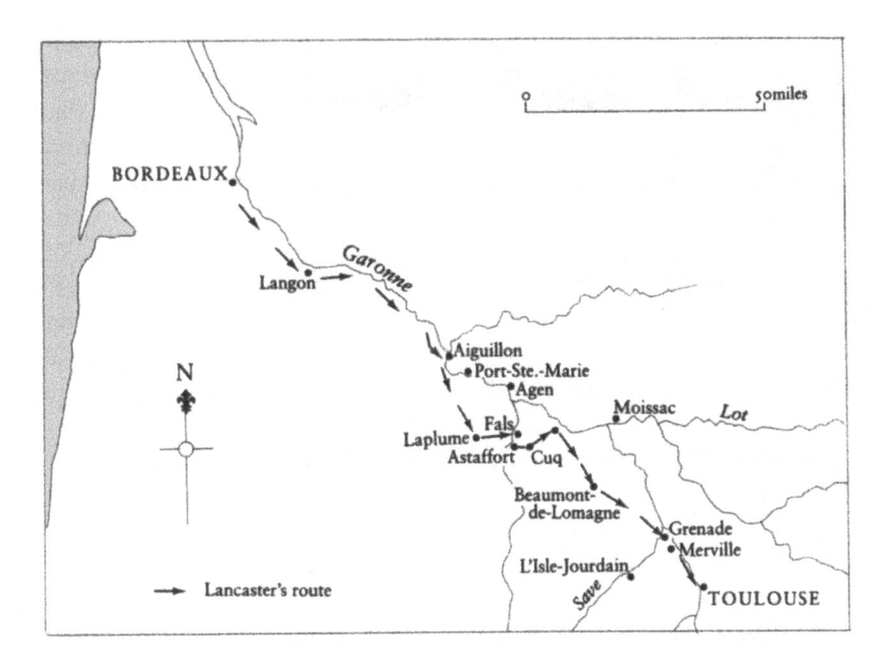

5 Henry of Lancaster's raid in Languedoc, December 1349

Toulouse was one of the great commercial cities of the south. Its population of about 20,000 souls, perhaps two thirds of what it had been before the plague, marked it out as one of the largest provincial cities in France. Its four bridges over the Garonne, its fine red-brick houses, churches and public buildings, its spreading suburbs all proclaimed the city's past prosperity. Only the walls, which were the main monument of civic pride in other French cities, had been neglected. They had been partly demolished at the end of the Albigensian crusade more than a century before, and they still had long gaps and stretches of useless, crumbling masonry. An expensive campaign of reconstruction, begun four years earlier, had so far made little progress. But the city had one of the best organised municipal governments of the region. The consuls and the Lieutenant (who was in Toulouse) summoned help from the nobility of Languedoc. They organised the inhabitants into military units and sent demolition parties out towards the approaching army of the Earl of Lancaster to break the bridges in his path. On about 14 December 1349, while Lancaster was still some way from the city, he was persuaded by the emissaries of Guillaume de Flavacourt to agree to a temporary cease-fire. The ostensible object of this was to enable an arranged battle to be fought on 19 December at L'Isle-Jourdain, a small town on the river Save twenty miles east of Toulouse. It is unlikely that Lancaster took this challenge very seriously, but he may well have hoped to negotiate a general truce. If so, he was disappointed. No negotiations of any value occurred and no French army appeared at L'Isle-Jourdain on the appointed day. There was nothing that Lancaster could do except to burn the suburbs and villages on the north and west side of the city.[16] Strong French forces, too strong for his army, were by now gathering around him. The Count of Armagnac recruited 3,000 men in the course of December, most of whom probably came from his own lands in the Rouergue. The men of Languedoc summoned by the Lieutenant were due to appear in Toulouse on 1 January 1350. Before anything came of these laborious preparations the Earl of Lancaster had withdrawn from the province. By 30 December 1349 he was back in the duchy.[17]

His brief and violent enterprise had achieved almost nothing. Of the towns which he had captured, a few received permanent garrisons. Most of these were in the southern Agenais where they rounded out the territory which the Anglo-Gascons already held. At least one important garrison was lodged in the heart of Languedoc, at Beaumont-de-Lomagne, thirty-five miles north-west of Toulouse, where it might serve as another Lusignan. But the French government was not panicked into a premature truce. On the contrary, when Lancaster retreated to the west, they moved the mustering point of the army of Languedoc from Toulouse to Moissac on the borders of Agenais. Early in the new year Jacques de Bourbon, Count of la Marche was sent urgently from the north to take command of it.[18]

The French might have shown greater interest in discussing a truce if they had not had larger designs in the north. Towards the end of 1349 Geoffrey de Charny devised a plan to recapture Calais. The plan depended upon the co-operation of an Italian mercenary, Aimeric of Pavia, who had served in the garrison of Calais under both French and English masters and was currently Edward III's galley-master there. Aimeric commanded one of the gate-towers of the citadel on the western side of the town. He agreed to admit Geoffrey de Charny's troops into the citadel at night. For this, he was promised an enormous bribe, 20,000 *écus* according to one report. Italians, said Froissart, were 'by nature covetous'. It is uncertain whether Aimeric really intended to betray Edward III or whether he always planned to double-cross the

French. There is, however, no doubt about what he in fact did. He reported the plot to the King. Edward received the news at his manor of Havering on Christmas Eve. He assembled a small army with great speed and secrecy among his household troops and from the retainers of the Prince of Wales and the Earl of March, who were with him. About a week later they crossed the Channel with the King by night and lodged in the citadel of Calais.

Geoffrey de Charny did not know that his plans had been discovered and had no idea that Edward III was in the town. He gathered his men in secret at Saint-Omer. The size of his army may be judged by the number of great men among them. Apart from Geoffrey himself, there were Eustache de Ribbemont who was the French military governor in the march of Flanders, and all the other commanders of the border: Charles de Montmorency, Oudard de Renti and Moreau de Fiennes. They had about 1,500 men-at-arms and 4,000 infantry according to reasonably reliable contemporary reports. During the night of 1 January 1350 Geoffrey de Charny approached Calais by the south-west. Before dawn on the 2nd, he drew up his men in lines on the wet sand between the gate-tower and the sea. In front of them, at the foot of the tower, the gate was seen to be open; the drawbridge over the moat was down and the portcullis up. Aimeric of Pavia came out to meet them. There was a long conference with the French commanders. As the tide began to come in and the sky grew lighter, the troops became restive and suspicious. Eventually Aimeric was given the first instalment of the bribe and handed over his son as a hostage for his good conduct. A group of French scouts then went forward to the end of the bridge to satisfy themselves that all was well. Soon after Aimeric had disappeared into the castle, the French royal standard appeared above one of the towers and the banners of Geoffrey de Charny and his companions above the others. The leading companies, enough to take possession of the tower, rushed across the wooden bridge through the gate. But once they were inside, the drawbridge was raised, the portcullis brought down and trumpets sounded from the walls. The French standards promptly disappeared from the towers. When the French soldiers penetrated into the space between the inner and outer walls of the castle, they were set upon by sixty knights lying in wait for them. All were captured.

Their companions, waiting for the signal on the beach, could see what had happened. The familiar cry of 'Trahi!' was heard. Much of the French army panicked and fled. Charles of Montmorency, a former Marshal, who had already gained a reputation for cowardice at Crécy, was the first to escape. Those who stood firm, less than half the original force, were hastily drawn up in battle order by Geoffrey de Charny. Edward III had been waiting inside the south gate of the town with his household troops and a large part of the garrison, including 250 archers. When the English trumpets sounded from the citadel they issued forth and attacked the French lines crying 'Edward! St. George!' At the same moment, the Prince of Wales, with the rest of the troops, sortied from the sea-gate on the northern side and, moving along the sand below the town wall, fell on Geoffrey de Charny's army from the other side. It was a rout. More than 200 French men-at-arms were killed by arrow or in hand-to-hand fighting. About thirty others were captured. The rest fled across the sands into the treacherous marsh where many of them were drowned.[19]

The prisoners included three of the principal commanders: Geoffrey de Charny himself, Eustache de Ribbemont and Oudart de Renti. The English released Eustache on parole on the same day in order to ensure that Philip VI had an eye-witness account of the disaster that had befallen his men. He later crossed to England to surrender to his captors. Geoffrey de Charny, who had been badly wounded in the fight, was held at Calais for a short time, then brought to London as a prisoner for the second time in his career. Eventually, in about July 1351, he paid a high price for his liberty. Most of his companions were released on parole during the next year and ransomed themselves in due course. Those who had escaped generally preferred to keep a tight-lipped silence about what they had done on that day. As for Aimeric de Pavia, he kept his money and, two days after the battle, took leave of absence to join the flow of pilgrims going to Rome for the Jubilee Year. His son was taken back to the French castle of Guines, but his fate is not recorded.[20]

Philip VI's government was already in disarray when the news of this disaster reached him. The King was in declining health. His relations with his heir, John Duke of Normandy, which had been tense for several years, were further embittered in January 1350 by a family quarrel, the result of Philip's sudden remarriage to a much younger woman. Within the King's counsels and in the upper reaches of the civil service, the Duke of Normandy's friends and protégés jostled for power with the representatives of an older establishment. Their arguments were masked by the discretion of the participants and by the formality of the surviving documents. But the opportunism and abrupt changes of policy which characterised the last months of Philip's reign were almost certainly the result.

There was at least one influential strand of opinion which wanted to resume negotiations with the English. When Jacques de Bourbon arrived at Moissac on about 22 February 1350 to take command of the army of Languedoc he opened negotiations with the Earl of Lancaster almost at once. Two papal legates, who had been sent into Gascony when news of Lancaster's expedition reached Avignon, acted as mediators. Within a few days a temporary truce was agreed, in order to enable a new diplomatic conference to be convened. It was for a very short period, until 12 April 1350, and was initially limited to Languedoc and the neighbouring provinces in which Jacques de Bourbon was Lieutenant. But shortly afterwards, probably about the beginning of April, it was prolonged and extended to the whole of France. The armies dispersed. Henry of Lancaster sailed for England. On 9 April 1350 Guy de Nesle paid off his army, after unsuccessfully besieging Tonnay-Charente for more than six months. The pavilions were erected once more at the traditional meeting ground of the diplomats by the castle of Guines. The plenipotentiaries gathered there in the course of May 1350: two papal nuncios, the Bishop of Norwich and his colleagues, and Philip's principal ministers the lord of Offémont, the Bishop of Laon and the Abbot of Saint-Denis .[21]

The new conference, the third since the original truce of Calais had been sealed in September 1347, marked the complete severance between the work of the diplomats and that of the soldiers. During February 1350 Edward III's Council resolved upon a major continental expedition under the King's command, the first since 1346. It is unlikely that the English King's finances were equal to the effort, but his ministers showed every sign of serious intent. The requisitioning of ships began early in March and the recruitment of soldiers about a month later. Stores were laid in. A sailing date was fixed, in June.[22] For his part, Philip VI informed his officers that he had no confidence in the current truce or in the outcome of the negotiations, and instructed them to prepare for war in any event. On 22 February 1350 Philip VI sent two agents to Bruges to pay 20,000 florins to the agents of the King of Castile for the continued use of his subjects' ships. The Spanish vessels, which had wintered at Sluys, were mobilised during March and in early April were lying off the east coast of England. South of the Channel, a French fleet struggled into existence at Leure in the mouth of the Seine and all over Normandy troops were being recruited to man it. The main army was summoned to meet at Amiens in June 1350.[23] These bustling, public preparations for war were by now the routine preliminaries of any significant diplomatic occasion. Neither side could expect to get much at the conference table unless its threat to make war was taken seriously.

In the south-west, however, bluff was not enough. Without waiting for the conference to begin or the truce to end, the Count of Armagnac launched a rapid and highly effective campaign to recover the places garrisoned by Henry of Lancaster during his brief raid of the previous year. In the course of May and June 1350, while the diplomats were gathering at Guines and Calais, he retook every one of them. The whole of the south bank of the Garonne upstream of Aiguillon was reoccupied in Philip VI's name with the exception of Port-Sainte-Marie, where an enormous Anglo-Gascon garrison obstinately held out, surrounded by French forts on every side. Although Armagnac was quite capable of doing all this on his own initiative there is no doubt that he was acting on the instructions of Philip VI's ministers. His campaign was being financed by a fierce assault on the taxpayers of Languedoc, conducted by two special commissioners sent from Paris. Other agents of Philip's government were busy in Milan, Genoa and Marseille recruiting crossbowmen to reinforce his army during the summer.[24] Armagnac had just declared his intention of carrying the war onto the north bank of the Garonne when it was announced that the ambassadors at Guines had finally agreed a fresh truce to last for just over a year, until August 1351. The agreement had been made on 13 June 1350 in an atmosphere of anger and distrust reflected in the elaborate provisions for its enforcement. One of its terms required an oath to be sworn not only by the principal ministers but also by leading field commanders and captains of garrisons on each side.[25]

The news of the truce, perhaps because it was so unexpected, was received with great joy by ordinary people in France and with relief by the English government. Bishop Bateman of Norwich sent two men-at-arms post-haste to carry the news into Bas-Poitou and Gascony and take the pressure off Edward's forces there. In the south-west, clerks copied out the terms many times for distribution to garrisons and field commanders. The Count of Armagnac halted his campaign on the Garonne and Edward III abandoned his plans to invade France. But the minor commanders, the independent captains and the dispossessed victims of every French or English campaign were less easy to control. Self-help was too deeply ingrained in the ways of the fourteenth century, and a rash of violent incidents occurred within days of the announcement of the truce. Indeed, one of Bateman's messengers was lynched as he passed through Tours on his way south.[26] The Anglo-Gascons were responsible for the most spectacular incidents. During the late summer of 1350 there was a succession of attacks by English partisans on French towns of the Dordogne valley. They included some significant places: Sainte-Foy-la-Grande, Villefranche-de-Périgord and Domme (again), all of which were captured by escalade in the second half of July. Villefranche was retaken within a month by the local French Seneschal. The captors of Domme held out on their crag over the river for some seven months until it too was recaptured and they were hanged from trees like common footpads. The Bordeaux government probably had nothing to do with either of these ventures. Sainte-Foy was a different matter. It was the only significant French garrison town on the Dordogne downstream of Bergerac and its capture brought the whole navigable section of the river under English control. Élie de Pommiers, the man responsible for the deed, was acting on his own initiative, but his family were prominent in the Bordelais and some of them were close to the Edward III's Council there. After a decent interval the town was annexed to the King's domain; the Constable of Bordeaux indemnified Élie for his expenses and paid the wages of his garrison.[27]

A more extraordinary incident occurred in northern Poitou. On 24 June 1350, within eleven days of the truce, the Bascon de Mareuil captured Loudun with a mixed band of Gascons, Englishmen and French and German adventurers, many of whom seem to have been recruited from the garrison of Lusignan. Loudun lay just south of the Loire, surrounded by its walls and overshadowed by an immense twelfth-century keep. It was fifty miles north of Lusignan and about 140 miles from the Bascon's base in the southern Limousin. Once he was in possession he began to exact *patis* from the surrounding villages, to kidnap local merchants and noblemen for their ransoms, and to steal and burn over an expanding area of Poitou and Touraine. The rapid breakdown of public order tempted every kind of adventurer, criminal and rowdy to add his own contribution. Local gangs took to touring the villages of the region demanding ransoms and *patis* in feigned Gascon accents.[28] It is possible that the Bascon de Mareuil did not know about the truce when he took Loudun, but if so he must have discovered very soon afterwards. Nevertheless, he defied the French to expel him. They responded with vigour. One of the Marshals, Edward de Beaujeu, formed an army by withdrawing garrison troops from the march of Calais. To these were added 2,000 mercenaries from Italy and Provence who had originally been intended for the army of the Count of Armagnac on the Garonne. Beaujeu laid siege to Loudun at about the beginning of August 1350. Towards the end of the month, after they had beaten off a succession of fierce assaults, the Anglo-Gascons surrendered on terms and abandoned the town to the French. While Beaujeu attacked the Bascon de Mareuil in Loudun, another French army finally dealt with Lusignan. It happened remarkably quickly. Guy, lord of Mortemer, the deputy Seneschal of Poitou, arrived outside Lusignan at the end of July with an army recruited in the region and a siege train brought from Poitiers. The lower town was taken by storm almost at once. Its church was turned into a fortress and siege works were constructed around the castle. The castellan held out for some weeks, but he eventually accepted terms while he was still strong enough to demand them. Before the autumn was out, the Anglo-Gascons had left.[29]

The truce entirely failed to halt the war at sea. Although the Castilians had been named in it, their seamen had their own quarrels with the subjects of Edward III and saw no reason to observe the King of France's truce. There were still about forty large Castilian vessels based at the Flemish port of Sluys in the summer of 1350. Their decks were built up for fighting at sea, and their crews were reinforced by several hundred armed Flemings out for loot and adventure. They launched a ferocious offensive in the crowded lanes across the North Sea, which continued regardless of the truce. These events brought panic to the south and east coast harbours of England, reminiscent of the worst period of the French naval offensive of the 1330s. In July men were arrayed for coastguard duty for the first time in several years. In August a mass of requisitioned ships, fitted out for war service with raised wooden castles fore and aft, gathered off the Kent coast at Sandwich. There they were filled with men-at-arms, and squadrons were distributed among a more famous group of captains than had fought in one place since the siege of Calais.[30] They included the King himself, the Prince of Wales, Henry of Lancaster, and the Earls of Northampton and Warwick.

On the evening of 29 August 1350 there was a great battle at sea off Winchelsea. The Castilian ships were passing south through the Channel, making for home laden with cargoes bought in Flanders. As they passed Dungeness they were intercepted by the English fleet. About twenty-four Spanish ships were engaged by about twice that number of their enemies'. The Castilians were famous for the great size of their sailing ships, which towered over the English cogs 'like castles to cottages', as the chronicler wrote. Their height enabled them to pour missiles from crossbows and catapults onto the crowded decks of the English vessels below. The English suffered very heavy casualties before they could get close enough to board. But once the Spanish ships had been hooked with chains and grappling irons and boarded from rope ladders, the English encountered little effective resistance. The Castilians and Flemings were cut down with swords and axes and the wounded and dead thrown overboard. Very few were thought worth taking alive for their ransoms. By nightfall, when the battle ended, most of the Castilian ships engaged in it had been captured and their crews were dead. It was one of the last important naval battles in which sailing ships were drawn up like armies on land and soldiers fought each other directly from the decks. It was also the rare case of a successful interception at sea, which in an age without effective methods of naval reconnaissance was achieved more often by luck than judgment.[31]

The English claimed a victory, as perhaps they were entitled to. But it was an incomplete victory, bought at a heavy price. By all accounts their losses had been terrible, and Froissart may have been right in saying that Edward's own ship was so badly damaged that it almost sank. Moreover, the battle failed to eliminate the threat to English shipping. Not all of the Castilian ships which fought in it were captured. Some escaped at nightfall and others, which had been lying out to sea waiting for the moment to join in, made off as well. These ships joined forces in the next few days with a number of French vessels from the ports of Normandy and Picardy. They hovered off the east coast of England for several weeks before withdrawing northward to pass another winter at Sluys. The mere presence of the Castilians in northern waters for another year continued to cause immeasurable damage to England's commerce. It was necessary for the English to initiate a convoy system for merchant vessels crossing the North Sea. The annual wine fleet which sailed from Plymouth to Bordeaux in October had to be provided with a large complement of soldiers and an escort of ships fitted out for war. Measures such as these were expensive and economically burdensome. They used up scarce shipping space. They caused long delays. The convoy fees (which paid for the hire of warships and the wages of troops) were high. The insecurity of the Atlantic sea routes and the cost of defence were the main reason for the sharp fall in the Gascon wine trade during these years and a corresponding rise in the cost of wine in England. Six months after the battle of Winchelsea the Channel was still closed to English shipping by enemy ships lying off the coast. When, in April 1351, Andrew Offord, one of Edward III's principal Chancery clerks, tried to cross from Dover to Calais to meet the ambassadors of the Count of Flanders, he could find no one willing to take him. He ordered the Mayor and Bailiff of Dover and the lieutenant constable of the castle to provide him with a ship and crew. They replied that they would not do it 'even if the King were here himself.' Offord eventually got to Calais in a rowing boat.[32]

On 22 August 1350 Philip VI of France died in the Benedictine abbey of Coulombs in the valley of the Eure. The end of his wretched reign was overshadowed by plague, divisions and defeat. All that can be said is that worse was to follow in the time of his successor. Aged thirty-one at his accession, John Duke of Normandy was a man of impressive physical appearance but rather delicate health. In public he cut the figure which men expected of a King. He was gracious. He was showy. He was a competent knight and lacked nothing for courage, as those who saw him on the battlefield of Poitiers could testify. But as a ruler he was a man of limited intelligence and mediocre talents. The new King inherited most of his father's faults and few of his virtues. Although not secretive and conspiratorial, as Philip had been, he showed most of the other symptoms of his family's chronic and habitual insecurity. He was intensely suspicious of potential enemies and unremitting in his hatred of real ones. He was obstinate and petulant, without his father's astuteness in judging men. There was much truth in Froissart's judgment on him, that he took a view too quickly and clung to it too long: *léger à enformer et dur à ôter une opinion.*[33] Yet at the crises of his reign, when there was little guidance to be had from convention or prejudice, John could be remarkably impulsive and inconsistent. He struck out wildly against those whom he conceived to be working against him. He allowed short-lived moods of bitterness and resentment to take control of policy for brief but disastrous periods, before he reverted to a more measured assessment of his problems. Almost nothing is known about the deliberations among the King's entourage except what can be inferred from events. But it seems clear that John was drawn to strong characters. His own more malleable personality was easily overborne by skilful talkers and calculating friends. They pressed their opinions on him with the determination of men who had learned to despise him. This was certainly part of the reason for the perplexing drifts and turns of

French policy in the 1350s, as decisions waited on the shifting of factions and coalitions on the royal Council.

The new King's advisers were for the most part survivors of his father's day: Simon Bucy, the authoritarian President of the Parlement of Paris, a rich self-made lawyer whose unbending loyalty and tremendous diligence earned him an influential place in the counsels of the first two Valois; Guillaume Flote, the former Chancellor, another efficient political technician; Hugh d'Arcy, Bishop of Laon, negotiator of successive truces with the English, who was shortly to become Archbishop of Reims; and, when he eventually returned from captivity in the summer of 1351, the great paladin Geoffrey de Charny. They were gradually joined by other, younger men who owed their advancement to the friendship of the King. The most dependable of them was Pierre de la Forêt, an able, rather colourless ecclesiastical lawyer who had been the head of John's administration for several years before his accession. He became Chancellor of France and eventually Archbishop of Rouen. The ambitious Renaud Chauvel, another career administrator, became the chief officer of the Chambre des Comptes and in due course Bishop of Chalons. Like many weak men, John II found it difficult to work closely with those who were not his friends. But some of his choices aroused acrimonious controversy, particularly outside the close circle of the court. It was not that they were fools or sluggards. On the contrary, most of them were able men who worked hard in the Crown's interest as they perceived it. But they were undoubtedly cronies, and from a distance their loyalty looked like self-serving. Most of them were conspicuously richer by the middle of the decade than they had been at the beginning. Simon Bucy, whose father had been a humble legal clerk, was showered with gifts of money and land, and acquired much more from the fees and retainers of litigants and petitioners. Every Parisian must have known about Bucy's magnificent suburban properties and his great urban estate by the gates of the abbey of St. Germain-des-Près, where the rue de Buci still runs today. Robert de Lorris, who became John's Chamberlain, was an even more skilful accumulator than Bucy. This intelligent and ambitious politician of humble origins (his father had been a Paris innkeeper) had risen through the King's bureaucracy to become Philip VI's private secretary. In this job he showed himself to be an exceptionally skilful negotiator who successfully handled some of the darker dealings between the French Crown and the Papacy, including the arrangements by which Clement VI became one of the principal financiers of the

French war effort. Disgraced in the purge of the civil service which followed the battle of Crécy, Robert renounced his orders, became a knight and then, after a brief period of obscurity, re-emerged as one of John's confidants when he was Duke of Normandy. Within three years of the King's accession he was the proprietor of great landed estates in Picardy and the Île de France, including the palatial domain of Ermenonville by the road to Soissons. Both of his sons were engaged to marry daughters of the ancient nobility. Fortunes on this scale were rare, but they were conspicuous, and the careers which produced them probably seemed more typical than they really were.[34]

Of all John's companions in the early years of his reign by far the most prominent, and the most enviable, was Charles of La Cerda, who was known as Charles of Spain. But for the misfortunes of his grandfather, Charles' family would have been kings and princes of Castile instead of impoverished exiles in France, dependent on their wits and on the generosity of the Crown. So he was certainly not a base-born parvenu. Moreover, he was exceptionally able. He had commanded on the Calais front in 1348, at the age of twenty-two, and had already shown himself to be one of the better soldiers in the King's service as well as a shrewd diplomat. But Charles had compensating faults. He was intensely and obviously ambitious; he was covetous; he was showy and conceited; he was arrogant to rivals and bullying to subordinates; he pushed his protégés in the royal service, and excluded those of others. These qualities made him many enemies. It is possible that John had been behind Charles of Spain's rapid promotion even before his accession to the throne. There was no doubt about Charles' favoured position after it. The Italian Chronicler Matteo Villani, who was well informed about events at the French Court, reported that John loved him with a 'special love'. The King had 'no God but him' was how an embittered rival put it.[35]

Generosity was a virtue of kings and John II was certainly not the first King of France to distribute largesse openly to his servants and friends. But it is probably true that he did so on a more reckless scale than his immediate predecessors. When, years later, his financial officers were taxed with this by their enemies, they did not deny it. Their defence was that they were unable to prevent it. When they urged economy the King ignored them, they complained. When they queried particular grants he insisted. The fault, they said, lay in John's natural generosity. He was *si très débonnaires et si très larges*. But behind this generosity, John's servants could see his abiding insecurity, his intense desire to be sure of those around him when there were others beyond the circle who hated or despised him. 'He could never bring himself to say No, because of the danger in which he stood on account of the war'.[36] They might have added that measured against the immensity of the French government's financial problems in the 1350s, the King's grants to his dependents were a comparatively minor factor. The real objection to them was always political and came mainly from those who were left out. Fourteenth-century governments depended on a delicate balance of patronage and loyalty which was too easily destroyed by such possessive friendships, and men quickly lost confidence in a ruler whom they believed to be controlled by others in their own interest.

At first, the accession of John II brought the optimism of all beginnings and even the new King's extravagance was an asset. After his coronation at Reims, he made his formal entry into Paris on 17 October 1350 surrounded by dukes, counts and princes of his realm and rode to Notre-Dame through streets decked with streamers and filled with crowds of citizens dressed in the colours of their trade.[37] John was to be a Parisian King as none of his predecessors had been for half a century. Philip VI had disliked the city. He preferred the manors and hunting lodges of the Île de France, and when official business required his presence in the capital he transacted as much of it as he could from the calm distance of Vincennes. But John made his home in the Hôtel de Nesle, the rambling thirteenth-century mansion on the left bank of the Seine, and in the royal apartments and gardens of the *Cité*, where he was more visible to his subjects as well as more vulnerable to their anger. After the dour ways of the court of Philip VI the new reign brought all the free-spending display which characterised aristocratic life in the aftermath of the Black Death: heavy banquets and tremendous festivities; elaborate music and dancing; ornate courtesy and loud hospitality; the exhibition of status and wealth in fashionably tailored costumes of bright colours, worn with jewellery so excessive that the Emperor Charles IV, who had been brought up in France, once rebuked the King's heir in public for his 'pompous clothing'.[38]

The first incident to darken his reign occurred only a month after the King's entry into Paris, on 16 November 1350. Raoul de Brienne, Count of Eu and Constable of France, who had recently arrived on parole from England to raise money for his ransom, was arrested by the King's order and summarily convicted of 'great and evil treasons'. On the following morning he was executed at dawn in the courtyard of the Hôtel de Nesle. Although the evidence against him was said to have been overwhelming and the Count to have admitted his guilt, his crime was never disclosed. The official silence encouraged wild and scurrilous theories. The real explanation did not emerge until some eighteen months later in the course of venomous exchanges at the court of Avignon between the ambassadors of England and France. Edward III had demanded a prodigious ransom from the Constable, reputed to be 80,000 gold *écus*. After five years in captivity, and with no prospect of raising such a sum from his own resources, Raoul had been persuaded to deliver up the county and castle of Guines (which he owned) to the English King in lieu of payment. Guines was in the middle of the war zone at the edge of the march of Calais. It was a revealing transaction. Guines was worth very little to the Constable. But to Edward III it was the gate to Picardy and Artois. Its sale was a straightforward real estate transaction, an ancient aristocratic attitude in keeping with the character of a war that made prisoners into merchandise of their captors. But the lawyers thought otherwise. They believed that Raoul had higher obligations, and John II regarded him as a traitor.[39]

Whichever of them was right, the sudden fall of such a great noblemen created a sensation in France. It was widely believed that John II's severity had been encouraged by Charles of Spain, and these rumours seemed to be confirmed when Charles replaced him as Constable at the beginning of the following year. He thereby became the senior military officer of the Crown at the age of twenty-four. John showered favours upon the new Constable. In December 1350 he granted him the whole of the county of Angoulême in a charter prefaced by gushing tributes to great men in general and Charles in particular. This was followed by a lavish succession of royal grants of land which Charles proceeded to round out by the most unscrupulous and high-handed methods. For the next three years, until his violent death in January 1354, Charles of Spain was to be the dominant influence in the direction of the war.[40]

Except for the egregious Jean Poilevillain, who remained in charge of coinage operations until 1356, it is not possible to identify the men behind the increasingly aggressive administration of the new King's financial affairs. It is clear that John had decided at the outset that he would have to deal with the structural deficit which had addled the conduct of the war for most of the reign of his father. Philip VI's government had experienced a sharp increase in the cost of warfare during the 1340s, to which it had only gradually become reconciled. Philip's problem had been essentially the same as Edward III's, namely the very high cost of static defence. The great campaigns of the war might supply the framework of its history and they struck the imagination of contemporaries, but their cost was dwarfed by the cost of defending territory, expenditure which had to be met winter and summer, year in year out, even if nothing was happening. In the early 1340s, when the Gascons were in retreat and the English King had no footholds in the north, the French had been able to wind down their operations almost entirely during periods of truce and in winter. Ten years later they found themselves having to maintain large permanent garrisons in southern and central France and in eastern Brittany, as well as a standing army on the march of Calais. Moreover, there was an urgent need to increase the wages paid for war service. In a time of rapid wage inflation, even the special rates (or *grands gages*) paid by Philip VI on major campaigns were not attractive enough to draw recruits in the numbers required. Philip's marshals had encountered serious difficulties in finding soldiers during the last three years of his reign. For service on the march of Calais, which was demanding yet boring and unglamorous, they had to pay about a third more than the *grands gages*, and in April 1351 John II was obliged to accept that in future these rates would apply generally for war service throughout France.[41] By then a large increase in the revenues of the Crown had become essential, merely to enable the French to stand still, let alone to mount major offensive campaigns.

Jean Poilevillain's contribution to curing the deficit was to be even more significant in the new reign than it had been in the old. In the first four years after John II's accession, coinage values rose and fell at approximately six-monthly intervals, causing serious economic disruption and great agony to the owners of landed estates and the wealthier businessmen, but bringing considerable revenues into the treasury. For some of this period the *monnayage* (or difference between the intrinsic and nominal value of the coinage) ran at well over 40 per cent. But experience suggested that revenues from the mints, however expertly managed, were vulnerable and insecure and it was obvious that they were unpopular. In the first few months of John's reign there was therefore a relentless campaign to increase the rate and frequency of taxes and to improve the efficiency of their collection. In December 1350 the King travelled to Avignon to pay his respects to Clement VI, the most overtly francophile of all the fourteenth-century Popes. As well as being the largest of the French government's creditors, he held the key to the taxation of the French Church. Clement, who had granted Philip

VI a tenth of the revenues of the Church year on year throughout the 1340s, was now persuaded to extend the grant up to the first half of the year 1354. A third of the sum collected was earmarked for the repayment of his past loans, but the rest of it was destined for the defence of the realm. In the new year the government embarked on a prolonged series of negotiations with the communities of France. The King presided in person over the Estates of Languedoc, which opened in Montpellier on 8 January 1351. The representatives of the rest of the realm met in Paris five weeks later on 16 February 1351 under the eyes of John's ministers. The Paris assembly was persuaded to agree in principle that a sales tax of 6d. in the pound was 'least onerous to our people and most suitable for our needs', as John later put it. This was half as much again as the rate at which taxes had been levied during the 1340s. The outcome of the assembly at Montpellier is not recorded but judging by subsequent events the southerners seemed to have agreed to a tax levied at 20 *s.p.* per hearth or 8d. in the pound on sales. These were exceptionally high rates. The hearth tax rate was 25 per cent more than the Crown had ever demanded before. Moreover, it was assessed on each community according to the pre-plague figure for the number of households. It is fair to say that since few of the representatives at either assembly had power to bind their constituents, their views were no more than impressive propaganda. The final result was rather variable, and it took a long time to achieve. But the surviving fragments of information suggest that very large sums were collected. Almost all the provinces of France agreed to pay at the rates which the Crown had demanded. John's ministers had the advantage of a new reign, fresh beginnings, unreasoned optimism. Experience and perhaps the example of Edward III had taught them the value of managing public opinion, which they did with persistence and skill. The new taxes of 1351 established conventional rates, and provincial assemblies meeting year after year by and large adhered to them until the catastrophes of the mid-1350s finally engulfed the whole machinery of collection.[42]

The sharp increase in the burden of taxation at the outset of John II's reign, coming as it did on top of his increasingly ruthless manipulation of the coinage and the underlying economic problems following the Black Death, caused severe strains in many parts of France as well as a tendency to look jealously on any expenditure of the Crown which could not be justified in strictly military terms. The representatives of the Norman towns, meeting at Pont-Audemer in March 1351, assented to the higher rates of taxation with 'obedience, love and loyalty', but not before they had pointed out how onerous the burden was when it was accompanied by 'war, plague, the burning of fields and towns, the murder of their people, the destruction of their trade, the alteration of the coinage, the requisitioning of their goods, the harassments of countless mercenary troopers and so-called general officers, and the levies imposed on many of our towns (such as Rouen) which are already paying for their own walls and citadels.' As if to echo these words, when John II's commissioners arrived in Rouen to enforce the collection of the tax, an angry mob threw over the counters of the collectors and flung their chests on the ground. The incident sparked off a brief rebellion which was put down with much violence. In August 1351 twenty-three of the ringleaders were hanged. There were few incidents as serious as this, but there was a good deal of passive resistance, and as time went on it tended to increase.[43]

In the spring of 1351 Charles of Spain was appointed as John II's Lieutenant in the whole of western France between the Loire and the Dordogne. In practice, he was probably responsible for the main decisions affecting the conduct of the war in Languedoc as well, and in the following year his lieutenancy was formally extended from the Dordogne to the Mediterranean and the Pyrenees. In his time there was a significant change in the direction of French strategy in the south-west, away from the valley of the Garonne which had been the principal theatre of the war in the past fifteen years, and towards the great coastal plain of Saintonge and the neighbouring provinces of the west. To some extent, Charles was guided in this by his own self-interest. Unless the French could restore their position in Saintonge there was little prospect of his ever effectively possessing the adjacent county of Angoulême which John II had granted to him at the beginning of the year. Anglo-Gascon raiders had roamed freely through the Angoumois for several years and occupied a number of castles on the marches towards Saintonge and Périgord. Charles' predecessor (Joan of Navarre) had made agreements with the English Seneschal of Gascony which more or less connived in their activities.[44] But the main factor in French strategic thinking at this time was the growing realisation of their leaders that if the advances of the Anglo-Gascons north of the Gironde continued, they presaged the occupation of the whole Atlantic coast of France from Bayonne to Mont-Saint-Michel. The French had been concerned about this for some time, certainly since 1349. In the larger pattern of the war, the change in the geographical priorities of the French had another and perhaps greater significance. The wearing succession of campaigns which they had waged in the Garonne valley in the 1330s and 1340s had had as their ultimate object the capture of Bordeaux and the expulsion of the English from Gascony. Philip VI had always perceived his Lieutenants as executing the decree of forfeiture which his court had pronounced against Edward III in 1337. They had failed because of the great strength of Bordeaux itself, and because the dense rash of castles held by the English and their allies in the Agenais strangled their lines of communication and prevented them from supplying their armies further west. No one even pretended that Gascony could be conquered from Saintonge. The Gironde was too formidable an obstacle, as the French commanders were well aware. Their decision to concentrate their efforts in the 1350s on the coastal provinces of the west marked the practical abandonment of the attempt to expel the English from the south-west and their acceptance, however reluctant, that the great object was now to limit the expansion of the English and their Gascon vassals into other parts of France.

The truce of June 1350, which had failed almost as soon as it had been proclaimed, was in law a personal contract between Edward III and Philip VI. Its legal status was rather uncertain once the King who made it was dead. John and Charles of Spain were content to let the uncertainty continue. The French King evaded Edward's requests for the confirmation of the truce and when, in December 1350, he travelled south, he left his representatives to confer with the English ambassadors outside Guines and to put off any final decision. As the plenipotentiaries went away empty handed, Charles of Spain's preparations for a new campaign in western France proceeded with vigour. He wanted a trial of strength to mark the beginning of the new reign.[45]

The main target of the Constable's campaign was Saint-Jean-d'Angély, which was a walled town on the river Boutonne, the westernmost of the line of fortresses which defended the English possessions in Saintonge. It was also the closest major English fortress to Charles' county of Angoulême. Saint-Jean-d'Angély had once been a rich town. But it had suffered serious damage at the time of its capture by the Earl of Lancaster in 1346. During the English occupation it had been deserted by many of its inhabitants, impoverished by heavy taxation, ransoms and the devastation of the surrounding countryside from which they had once drawn their trade. The place had become a military encampment, a small-scale Calais. With up to 600 men on its payroll, the garrison was the second largest in English-occupied France.

Moreover, like many of the border garrisons of northern Saintonge it was largely recruited in England, fed from stores shipped from English ports, and paid directly from the English Exchequer. But in 1351 the garrison was far below its nominal strength. The walls of the town were old and ruinous. And the defenders, who must have been coming to the end of their winter stores, were low on victuals.[46] The French operation was conducted by Guy de Nesle, whose last military enterprise had been the unsuccessful siege of Tonnay-Charente in the previous year. He arrived outside the town in February with the advance guard of the army, about 1,500 men. By the end of March they had captured the bridge over the Boutonne and had built two forts on the roads leading south, to hold off any relief force.[47]

The Seneschal of Gascony, Sir John Cheverston, had only recently arrived in the duchy from England. In a very short space of time, he organised a relief force. At the end of March 1351 Cheverston and the son of the lord of Albret marched north from the Gironde. They brought with them several hundred men and a large train of supplies which they hoped to force through the French lines into the beleaguered town. When Guy de Nesle learned about their movements on 31 March, Cheverston and Albret were near Saintes, making for the bridge over the Charente at Taillebourg. Leaving a screen of troops behind him to contain the garrison of the town, Guy marched south through the night and positioned himself between the approaching forces of the Seneschal and the bridge. The two armies met on the following morning, 1 April 1351, some three miles from Saintes outside the village of Saint-Georges. Guy de Nesle borrowed the battle tactics of the English, an interesting and original development. He drew up most of his men on foot on rising ground, except for small cavalry forces which he placed at the wings. There was a short violent mêlée in which the French were completely defeated. It is not clear what went wrong, but it seems that before Guy de Nesle could join battle with the enemy in front of him he was attacked from the rear by another Anglo-Gascon force, some 300 or 400 strong, which had been brought together from the English garrisons of Taillebourg and Tonnay-Charente further north. A large number of French knights were captured including Guy de Nesle himself and his deputy, Arnoul d'Audrehem, captain of Angoulême. The survivors, several hundred of them, retreated in confusion along the road to Saintes and shut themselves in the town. For the English it was a famous and profitable victory. It was also a tribute to the flexibility of their military organisation, the effectiveness of their scouting and the initiative of their commanders. But it achieved virtually nothing. The lord of Caupenne, who commanded the garrison at Taillebourg, took 250 men and succeeded in entering Saint-Jean-d'Angély with them a few days after the battle. This was probably achieved by going the long way round and approaching the town from the north. But with the French firmly dug in across the southern approaches to the town it was hopeless to try to get the stores through. So Cheverston and Albret returned to Bordeaux taking their army and their wagon train with them. The captured French commanders were ransomed at great speed. Guy de Nesle's ransom was paid in part within three weeks of his capture and he was released on parole. Arnoul d'Audrehem was free by the end of the month. Their captors wanted their profits. The French army around Saint-Jean-d'Angély was quickly reinforced and new siege works were built. In May Charles of Spain arrived to direct the siege in person.[48]

While the blockade of Saint-Jean-d'Angély intensified, the French took advantage of the disarray of their adversaries to mount subsidiary campaigns elsewhere. Towards the end of April a group of men led by a minor lord of the district, Arnaud de Cervole, captured the huge fortress of the Archbishops of Bordeaux at Montravel outside Castillon. It was the first recorded military enterprise of a man with a famous career before him who, as the 'Archpriest', became one the most feared *routier* captains of his age. His own role in the capture of Montravel passed almost unnoticed at the time, but it was a considerable stroke even so. This place, with its double circuit of walls, its great moat and its commanding position on the north bank of the Dordogne was the gate of Périgord. Its possession enabled the French commanders in the region to block river communications between Bordeaux and Bergerac, which they had not been in a position to do since they had lost Sainte-Foy the year before. The Count of Périgord promptly took possession of the place and garrisoned it for the King's account. The English King's officers in Bordeaux were dismayed. They laid siege to Montravel at once with a considerable force. But they were unable to recover it, and the French remained in possession for another five years.[49] These events were the signal for a rash of significant desertions in the lower Dordogne, which must have reminded old hands in Bordeaux of the worst days before the campaigns of the Earl of Lancaster. Raymond de Fronsac, one of the great lords of southern Saintonge, came over in June 1351. Gaillard de Durfort, the colourful ex-priest whose vast clan controlled several dozen castles and *bastides* in the Agenais and southern Périgord, was finally bought over by Charles of Spain in the following year after a long period of havering and backsliding. The guiding motive in each case was a feud with other noblemen of Edward III's obedience. But the fall of Montravel, which seemed to presage major French advances in the region where their interests lay, was probably the last straw for these calculating trimmers. They thought that they knew which way the tide was moving. So did some important towns. Bazas, one of the principal acquisitions of the Earl of Lancaster, had to be urgently reinforced from Bordeaux in order to stop its citizens surrendering it to the French.[50]

In June, Jean de Melun, Count of Tancarville, an influential soldier and courtier close to the King, was sent into Brittany to harass English positions in the peninsula and to pin down English troops there. His army was formed mainly from the retainers of Breton noblemen of the party of Blois. It was probably fairly small, and its achievements were not impressive. The main operation was the siege of Ploermel which was the largest English garrison in central Brittany and a thorn in the side of the viscounts of Rohan. But although the French constructed elaborate siege works and manned them against the English for several weeks, they made no progress at all. Walter Bentley showed himself to be an aggressive strategist and talented commander, very much in the mould of his predecessor Sir Thomas Dagworth. Instead of trying to relieve the town or sheltering in his coastal strongholds, as the French had perhaps expected, Bentley collected troops from the garrisons under his command and launched a noisy diversionary raid into the neighbouring provinces of France. In the second half of August he invaded Maine and sacked the town of Chateau-Gontier. Then, turning south, he occupied Varades on the Loire. Bentley's raid caused terror among the inhabitants of the lower Loire, who had so far seen very little fighting, and consternation among the French commanders in western France. Jean de Melun was forced to abandon the siege of Ploermel. At the beginning of September he was urgently collecting reinforcements in order to fight a defensive campaign on the lower Loire.[51]

Bentley's minor triumph was the only bright point in what had otherwise been a summer of unrelieved gloom for Edward III and his ministers. They could not afford a great continental expedition on the scale of 1346. The only way of relieving the pressure on their possessions in Saintonge was to mount violent raids against more vulnerable parts of France in the hope of forcing a truce on the French King. It was the strategy which had failed in 1349, and it failed again in 1351.

The more important operations were all conducted from Calais. The garrison of the town was reinforced in March, and at the end of that month Henry of Lancaster (now a duke) arrived with a large retinue of soldiers and diplomats to direct operations.[52] Intense efforts were made to draw in the Count of Flanders who was still, nominally, an ally of the English King. But Louis de Mâle had no intention of becoming involved. He had already decided that there was more to fear from John II than from Edward III. He had declined to attend the French King's coronation at Reims because he would have been required to homage there. But he had attended the new King's *joyeuse entrée* into Paris and he had stood by while the Castilian galleys had used his ports as bases for damaging raids against the English coast. When Edward's agents called on him yet again to observe the promises which he had made in the secret treaty of Dunkirk, Louis avoided giving a direct answer. Early in April, English troops commanded by the Captain of Calais and that old adventurer Walter Mauny launched a cattle-rustling raid deep into northern France. For a time the town's stores were filled with carcasses of beef, pork and mutton, and meat was sold in the market for next to nothing. In the middle of the month, a second, much larger raid was led by the Duke of Lancaster himself. Lancaster marched south and attempted to surprise Boulogne. He was beaten off by the garrison. He then attacked Étaples, equally unsuccessfully, and turned inland towards Fauquemberque, Thérouanne and Saint-Omer. The population of Thérouanne had learned wisdom since the days when they had confronted an English army in the open fields. They took refuge in their citadel, from which they hurled missiles down on the invaders, inflicting heavy casualties. The French garrisons of the march stayed within their walls as Lancaster swept by. The main achievement of this brief enterprise was the burning of many farms and suburban houses, the collection of an impressive quantity of booty, and the destruction of 120 ships lying in French harbours. But it was not enough to draw Louis de Mâle into the war on Edward's side. Louis' representatives in Calais suggested that their master might fight for Edward III if a sufficiently large subsidy was paid to him. But while the English agents returned to England for instructions, the Count prepared to receive the ambassadors of the King of France.[53]

The third English raid, which was launched at the beginning of June 1351, was a disaster. This time the commander was John Beauchamp, the younger son of the Earl of Warwick. He was a hardened soldier who had carried the King's standard at the battle of Crécy and had just been appointed Captain of Calais. Beauchamp's raid began uneventfully. He left Calais by night, followed by 600 mounted troops, most of the strength of the garrison, and struck east towards Saint-Omer. Unfortunately for him, the French had greatly increased their forces on the march after the first English *chevauchées* in the spring. Reinforcements had been pouring into Compiègne since the second half of May. As Beachamp's raiding force made their way back with their spoil, they were harassed at every stage by troops of Edward de Beaujeu, the French commander of the march. On 8 June 1351 the English were cornered in a bend of the river not far from Ardres and forced to fight a battle on open ground on very unequal terms. They had to defend themselves with swords and axes, for their archers had used almost all their arrows. Beaujeu was killed at the beginning of the battle as he led the French attack across the trenches which the English had dug around their lines. But the dead commander's brother shouted out his war cry, 'Beaujeu!', and his followers renewed the assault. They were soon afterwards joined by fresh men from the French garrison of Saint-Omer. The English were overwhelmed. Almost all of the survivors, including Beauchamp himself, were captured.[54] For a few days Calais was held by less than half its usual garrison, a source of grave concern in England when the news arrived there. William Clinton, Earl of Huntingdon, was immediately appointed acting Captain of Calais and crossed the Channel at the end of the month with twenty-nine ships and a mixed force of men-at-arms and archers, about 230 men in all, who had been scratched together in less than a fortnight. Edward III announced that he would follow with a new army. Recruitment of men began in Wales and southern England on 15 June 1351. As for Louis de Mâle, the Duke of Lancaster was sent to plead personally with the evasive Count. He was empowered to offer him a marriage alliance and a (rather ungenerous) subsidy if he would agree to launch an immediate attack on the French towns of the northern march.[55]

While the English rattled their swords, Bishop Bateman, accompanied by the Earl of Huntingdon, returned to the pavilions outside Guines to meet the councillors of the King of France and propose yet another truce. The conference opened on 7 July 1351. It made little progress. The French knew that while their troops were still besieging Saint-Jean-d'Angély Edward III needed a truce much more than they did. They would concede nothing more than a brief cease-fire, limited to the march of Calais. Bateman left for London on 18 July to get further instructions. During the next fortnight the English bargaining position collapsed. Without waiting for the Duke of Lancaster to come, Louis de Mâle travelled to France and met the French King at Fontainebleu. There, on 14 July 1351, he concluded a treaty which settled all their differences. Louis formally renounced his claims to the lost castleries of Walloon Flanders, in return for which he was promised a large cash grant and armed assistance if Flanders should be invaded by the English. The Count abandoned the English alliance. He undertook never allow English forces to operate on his territory. He promised to serve in French armies like a loyal subject of the Crown. There was an element of hypocrisy on both sides, for John II never paid the money and Louis de Mâle never served in his armies. But this was little comfort to the English, who had finally lost their only continental ally and had to watch impotently as their surviving friends in the Flemish towns were proscribed and banished.[56]

In London, Bateman received his instructions at the Tower on 27 July. He left for Calais a week later. It must have been shortly after his arrival that he learned that the garrison of Saint-Jean-d'Angély had capitulated. They had already eked out their rations for much longer than expected and could hold on no longer. On 5 August 1351 they agreed a conditional surrender with the officers of Charles of Spain. The terms conspicuously saved their honour. There was to be a cease-fire until 31 August. During this period the garrison undertook not to receive any victuals into the town or to do anything to improve the fixed defences. But they were to be at liberty to summon help, and if a relieving army should appear between 25 and 31 August there was to be an arranged battle on ground staked out in advance by two knights from each side. Gentlemen serving in the garrison (but no others) would be allowed to pass through the French lines to fight with the relieving army. But if the town was not relieved, the garrison would deliver it up to the French on the last day of the month and march away with their lives and liberty and all the goods that they could carry.[57]

Although the terms for renewing the truce had been agreed between the diplomats at Guines by the end of August, the French King's representatives refused to seal them until Saint-Jean-d'Angély had surrendered. John II travelled south with his entourage to be present in person. By 29 August his tents were set up before the walls. Two days later, on the appointed date, he took possession of the town. The Gascon commander, Raymond of Caupenne, marched away with his men. On 11 September 1351, when the news from Saint-Jean-d'Angély was confirmed, a truce for one year was formally sealed outside Guines. The armies dispersed. Jean de Melun paid off his troops, and Charles of Spain paid off some of his. Walter Bentley abandoned Varades and returned to Brittany. The English reinforcements in Calais went home, and the Duke of Lancaster departed to fight the heathen in eastern Germany and Poland, taking a large crowd of English knights with him. John II enjoyed his victory. In the military history of his reign, this proved to be the high point. But it bankrupted him. On 26 September 1351, after long deliberations in the Council in Paris, the King suspended payment of almost all royal debts for the duration of the truce.[58]

Although the new truce was more or less observed in the north of France there was not even a pretence of enforcing it in the south, where both governments had long ago abandoned hope of controlling their subordinates. The result was a continuous guerrilla war, interrupted by periodic *chevauchées* by heavily armed companies of raiders. Charles of Spain was the leading spirit in this half-war. He was still a long way from achieving his ambitions in the region. Many of the French companies who had taken part in the siege of Saint-Jean-d'Angély stayed in his service after the town had fallen and, in spite of the truce, they occupied themselves during the autumn in harassing the surviving English garrisons of northern Saintonge.[59] Further south, on the borders of Gascony and Angoumois, Charles' subordinates continued their efforts to round out his county as if nothing had happened outside Guines. At the beginning of November, they made a bold attempt to recapture the bridge-town of Sainte-Foy. This was not the private adventure of a few brigands. The men responsible were well known as friends and protégés of the Constable. They included Friquet de Fricamps, a Norman knight who had been appointed captain of the King's troops in Angoumois at the beginning of October; and the future marshals, Jean de Clermont and Jean de Boucicaut. Several hundred of their men gathered covertly in the woods around Sainte-Foy and tried to capture the place by escalade. The attempt failed. But although the raiders were driven off, the Constable of Bordeaux, John Charnels, who had been sent to reinforce the place, suffered the humiliation of being taken prisoner during a rash sortie from the gates.[60]

The English for their part returned to the irregular war as soon as the regular one had been suspended. In the autumn of 1351, while Friquet de Fricamps and his companions were mopping up places on the southern edge of Angoumois, organised companies of Gascon free-booters began a sustained assault on the province of Quercy. The invasion of Quercy is in its own way as revealing as the earlier invasions of Périgord and the Limousin. Quercy was a poorer and more sparsely populated province than its neighbours on the west. Cahors, the provincial capital, was known to Dante as the city of usurers, but its great days had passed even in his time. There was a small number of modest towns and rich monastic churches. Elsewhere, patches of fertility in the depths of the valleys were separated by large expanses of dense forest and harsh, rocky upland. It was not until the end of the 1340s that the war began to penetrate this region. Belaye, a castle on the south bank of the Lot, had been occupied for several years by Raymond-Bernard de Durfort, a nobleman from the neighbouring province of the Agenais who used it to pursue a long-standing personal vendetta with the Bishops of Cahors. Raymond-Bernard held it for three years in the English King's name, between 1345 and 1348, but Edward's interest in Quercy was so limited that he allowed it to be surrendered in a private deal with the Bishop. In 1347, at Christmas-time, the Gascons occupied Belcastel, a castle on the south bank of the Dordogne, close to the prosperous market town of Martel and the great pilgrimage church of Rocamadour. They successfully resisted every attempt to dislodge them. They withstood a siege of several weeks. They accepted money to go away, then stayed. They were still in occupation eighteen months after their first arrival. The occupation of Belcastel was the first really serious incursion by the Gascons in Quercy, but it was not as serious as another incident which occurred at the end of 1348. In December a much larger Gascon company captured Montcuq, a powerful twelfth-century keep on the march towards the Agenais near the *bastide* town of Lauzerte. It required a siege of several weeks by the combined forces of Quercy, Périgord and the Agenais to dislodge these men in the following summer. By now, local noblemen were already being drawn into the skein of factions and alliances which had divided the Agenais for years. The Anglo-Gascons quickly acquired confederates there: men of easy violence like the lord of Pestillac whose family fought out their ancient quarrels against the *bastide* of Moncabrier from their great twelfth-century castle above the valley of the Lot. Gascon adventurers were already serving here by 1350 and fighting his battles in the plain. Further north, in the valley of the Dordogne, the local enemies of the abbey of Souillac raided and burnt its domains with the assistance of Gascons from the west. Incidents like these were classic examples of the way in which the irregular war fed on ancient quarrels as it spread outwards from the duchy like a contagious disease.[61]

6 Quercy: Anglo-Gascon garrisons, 1351–2

For a time they remained marginal and strictly local affairs, confined for the most part to the western marches of the province. The decisive moment came in December 1351, a week before Christmas, when a large company of Gascons captured Saint-Antonin, a walled town at the opposite extremity of Quercy. The inhabitants of Saint-Antonin hardly thought themselves at risk, and had no proper system of organised watches. The invaders pillaged the town and then garrisoned it as a base for fresh raids in Quercy and the neighbouring provinces of Rouergue and the Albigeois. This spectacular stroke was the work of Jean de

Grailly, 'Captal' de Buch, a young man at the threshold of a famous military career. 'No knight was more celebrated in all Gascony' was what Froissart would one day write about him, 'and none was more feared by the French for the audacity of his deeds.' Jean de Grailly belonged to one of the most influential noble dynasties of the Bordelais. His grandfather was one of the founding members of the Order of the Garter and his wife was a daughter of the lord of Albret. His family had been a pillar of the English war effort from the outset. Such a man was far too close to the English administration in Bordeaux for his acts to be repudiated even if the inclination had been there.[62]

Where he led the way, lesser fortune-hunters quickly followed. In the spring of 1352 the companies of marauders came in waves up the valleys of the Lot and the Dordogne, spreading out along the minor rivers and over the *causses* of Martel, Gramat and Limogne. In most places only the baldest outline of the facts is known, pieced together from the pay records of garrisons and the evidence given to a papal commission of enquiry many years later. But the story of one region, in the north-west corner of the province, can be followed in the accounts and minute-books of the town clerk of Martel, a moving survival, stained by water and partly eaten by rats, which conveys something of what it meant to live in a small town in Quercy under constant siege by distant, unseen enemies: letters filled with fear arriving from other towns; bands of armed men seen passing by the walls and barred gates of the town and through the forest roads of the nearby *causse*; panic-stricken warnings sent on to other places in their path; delegates sent to plead for help from the viscount of Turenne, from the Seneschal of Quercy, from the Pope, from whoever else would listen; hurriedly improvised meetings of towns and barons of the region; weapons distributed among the inhabitants; men sent to buy artillery in Toulouse; suburbs abandoned by their populations, now quartered in cramped, rent-controlled lodgings within the walls; money raised to ransom prominent citizens seized by armed men; tradesmen setting up their benches on the walls so that they could keep watch as they worked; desperate labour on the walls and ditches; and always the ever-present fear of surprise and the suspicion of treachery within. The brigands arrived in the vicinity of Martel in the spring of 1352. In about October they occupied Souillac, ten miles away on the north bank of the Dordogne. With its compact ramparts and its great Benedictine abbey, Souillac was a valuable prize and a fine base from which to despoil the rich basin of fertile land which the monks and their tenants had reclaimed from the marsh over two centuries. The Seneschal of Quercy raised an army in the province to confront them. But he was defeated in the field and his men put to flight. The companies occupying Souillac took about six months to exhaust the district. Then, instead of penetrating further afield they offered to surrender possession of the place to the representatives of the province in return for 5,000 *écus*. The men of Martel took the initiative in organising the response. They arranged a meeting of the principal towns of Quercy at Figeac in January 1353, which agreed to accept the brigands' offer. The money was raised by assessments on their communities, who found it by borrowing and by taxing their inhabitants. Martel alone raised a fifth of the amount. It was one of the earliest recorded examples of a variety of ransom known as *rachat* (or *videment*), which became one of the simplest and most productive methods employed by the companies to loot large areas of the country. By the time the Anglo-Gascons left the region of Souillac, their compatriots had spread all over the rest of Quercy, inflicting damage so severe that half a century later the inhabitants remembered this time as the beginning of their miseries.[63]

In November 1351 the King of France founded a new order of chivalry, the Order of the Star. John's order, whose full title was 'Company of Knights of Notre-Dame de la Noble-Maison', was no doubt in some degree inspired by Edward III's Order of the Garter. But it was larger, more lavish in its conception, and more showy in its celebrations, a conscious attempt to regenerate the demoralised and impoverished nobility of France and to fire them with something of the enthusiasm for the war which the English King had achieved among the nobility of his own country. In his charter of endowment John II looked back to a golden age of French chivalry when French knights had been celebrated throughout Europe for their strength and courage and kings of France had been better served. Now, for want of training, experience and inclination and 'other causes which one knows not', the descendants of these men had sunk into a life of lethargy, idleness and private pleasure. The French King may or may not have believed in this superficial and inaccurate vision, but there is no doubt that many of his subjects did. The knights of the new order, 500 strong, swore to give the King loyal advice, to serve no others, and to fight for him until they were killed or captured, never retreating. Every year, on the eve of the feast of the Assumption, the whole order was to assemble for an annual chapter and a banquet at which the most valiant heroes of the past year, three princes, three bannerets and three knights bachelor, would be seated at the table of honour before all the others. In an oblique reference to the recriminations which had followed the battle of Crécy, the charter of foundation declared that any member who left the field of battle dishonourably should be suspended from the order and his shield turned face inward in the chapter house. The King established his new foundation at the 'Noble-Maison' of Saint-Ouen, a great manor house on the road from Paris to Saint-Denis which had once belonged to his grandfather, that fine model of French chivalry Charles of Valois. He founded a college of canons there (not unlike Saint George's Windsor) and endowed it with lands and goods confiscated from convicted traitors. Here, on 6 January 1352 a magnificent inaugural ceremony was attended by all the most prominent soldiers of the realm. The knights, dressed in robes of red and white, trimmed with fur, and wearing uniform signet rings, processed through the great hall of the manor. The walls had been festooned with specially made tapestries and decked with the painted shields of the first members. The floors were laid with velvet cloth. The knights dined off gold plate. 'Yet immediately afterwards,' a contemporary wrote, 'the light of the Star was dimmed and horribly eclipsed.'[64]

While these tremendous ceremonies were in progress at Saint-Ouen, the English captured Guines, one of the strongest defensive positions of the French on the march of Calais. Guines was a small town at the edge of an expanse of desolate swamp, six miles south of Calais, which was dominated by a large castle and a convent of Benedictine nuns. It was the main French fortress of the region after Boulogne and Saint-Omer, as well as the main prison used to house English prisoners of war. It was taken shortly before dawn on 6 January 1352 by a small band of men recruited in the streets of Calais by an English squire called John Dancaster. Dancaster was an obscure soldier of fortune from Lincolnshire who had taken service in the garrison of Calais after being banished for various acts of violence in England. His was a very typical history. According to English accounts he had studied the defences of Guines while working in a labour gang during a brief spell as a prisoner of war there. He and his men blacked their armour and crossed the moat under cover of darkness by walking over a transverse wall just below the water level. Then they placed scaling ladders against the wall and climbed silently over the parapets. The captain of the castle was away attending the inaugural feast of the Order of the Star. Some of the garrison were playing dice or chess in the hall. Others were asleep in bed. The sentries were sluggish. The English knifed them and threw their bodies over the wall. Then they invaded the keep, killing anyone in their way. They released the prisoners of war and with their aid took over the rest of the castle. The defenders were rounded up and expelled through the main gate. On the following morning the French commander in the sector sent two knights to parley with Dancaster from beneath the wall. They demanded to know in whose name he was holding the castle. But Dancaster would not answer them. So, they sent a small group of emissaries to remonstrate with Edward III in England. These men arrived at the Palace of Westminster, apparently without waiting for a safe-conduct, on 15 January 1352.

The capture of Guines put the English in an extremely awkward position and for some time they were unsure whether to disown or exploit it. It was a gross violation of the truce, but at the same time an acquisition of incalculable value for the defence of Calais, since it controlled the main waterway and one of the main roads leading to the town. When the French agents came before him, Edward III's first instinct was to appease their anger and preserve the truce which had cost him so much diplomatic and military effort in the previous year. He denied that the deed had been done by his authority, which was probably true. He provided the Frenchmen with a letter ordering any subject of his who might be holding the castle to surrender it at once to its rightful owner. But during the next few days, he began to change his mind. As it happened, Parliament had been summoned to meet in January 1352. The first effective session occurred on 17 January, only two days after Edward's audience with the French agents. The opening address was delivered by the Chief Justice, Sir William Shareshull. It was extremely bellicose. The King of France, Shareshull said, had dishonoured his oath and violated the truce in Brittany, in Gascony and at sea. The Lords and Commons were invited to advise the King what should be done in this extremity. Three days later, on 20 January, before they had come to any conclusions, they were summoned together again to hear another harangue, this time from Edward's Chamberlain, Bartholomew Burghersh. Burghersh was even more passionate against the French than Shareshull had been. He accused John II of plotting against England 'with all the subtlety and cunning that he or his counsellors possess'. He added violence in the march of Calais to the catalogue of John's crimes against the truce. It was evident that in the past few days Edward and his ministers had decided to keep Guines and brace themselves for the inevitable resumption of the war. Parliament duly gave them the advice they wanted to hear. A fresh subsidy was voted for each of the next three years to counter the 'malice of the enemies of the realm'. On 29 January 1352 the Captain of Calais sent fifty-five men to take possession of Guines from John Dancaster and hold it in the name of Edward III. A few days after this, the English King pardoned all Dancaster's crimes and rewarded him for his pains.[65]

The French were outraged. The deputy of the captain of Guines, who had been one of those pushed out of the gate on the night of the capture of the castle, was arrested and accused of taking a bribe to let the English in. Although the accusation was almost certainly false he was drawn and quartered in the market square of Saint-Omer.[66] In Paris John II's ministers contemplated their depleted coffers and schemes of revenge. The truce of September 1351 had had the usual consequence of reducing the flow of tax revenues, at any rate in the north where it had been more or less observed. Coinage manipulation was the only resource available to the government at short notice. On 22 January 1352, a special session of the French King's Council, attended by the Treasurers, met in Paris and resolved upon a revaluation of the coinage and a sharp increase in the *monnayage*. For several weeks, as the mints turned out the new coins, the gross margin taken by the government was no less than 44 per cent, one of the highest levels ever attained. These measures hit wage-earners hard, and they were exceptionally unpopular in spite of the battery of exchange and price controls which accompanied them. But they brought an immediate flood of cash into the King's coffers.[67] Since John's debts were not, at this stage, being paid and plans for significant non-military expenditure were being shelved at whatever political cost, it became possible to contemplate reopening the war at least for a short period. The main decisions were made in February 1352. They involved the creation of no less than three separate armies, in Brittany, Saintonge and the march of Calais.

One of the first casualties of these decisions was Charles of Blois, the claimant of Brittany. After passing more than four years in captivity in Vannes and London, Charles had been released on parole in the autumn of 1351 and had visited Paris to mix with the unfamiliar courtiers and ministers of a new reign and to raise money for the payment of his ransom. He had not the least prospect of buying his liberty from his own resources, which had never been very great and were seriously depleted as a result of his efforts over the past decade to gain the duchy of Brittany. But he had found an active champion in Charles of Spain. While Charles of Blois was at the French court, the favourite was betrothed to his daughter. A little later, John II was persuaded to mark this happy event by undertaking to pay Charles of Blois' ransom himself. But Charles was as unlucky in his timing as in so much else. He returned to Calais in the spring of 1352 and reached agreement with Edward III's agents to pay a ransom of 400,000 *écus*, the cost of a short campaign. But the first instalment was due almost immediately, and John II could not pay it. So, at the beginning of May 1352, Charles had to surrender to his bail and return to the Tower of London.[68]

The fighting began in Brittany at the end of March 1352, while Charles of Blois was still haggling with his captors at Calais. Baldo Doria, continuing his family's ten-year tradition of service to the house of Blois and sporting the title of 'Admiral of Brittany', led the advance guard up the main inland road. He occupied Redon in the last few days of the month, expelling the English garrison. The main body of the army of Brittany assembled at Rennes in the course of April and May under the command of Guy de Nesle. Most of these men were recruited in Brittany itself, and in Normandy and the Loire provinces nearby. The army of Saintonge was also recruited locally, in Saintonge itself and in Poitou. They assembled at the beginning of April at Saint-Jean-d'Angély and Saintes under the command of three local captains, and laid siege shortly afterwards to the great English fortress of Taillebourg on the Charente. The main effort, however, was reserved for the march of Calais, where the French bent all their energies to the recovery of Guines. Geoffrey de Charny was reappointed as Captain of the march and assembled, largely from the existing garrisons of the region, an army of 1,500 men-at-arms and 3,000 infantry including a large contingent of Italian bowmen. In May he laid siege to Guines.[69]

The English government's finances had only just been restored to a state of perilous balance when they were burdened with this fresh crisis. They were certainly not equal to the strain of a major continental war. Edward III's officers in France were left to cling on as best they could while modest reinforcements were found for them. Priority was given to the defence of Gascony and Saintonge, where the English had been under severe pressure for almost a year. In the first week of February 1352, while Parliament was still sitting, it was decided to send a small expeditionary force to Bordeaux under the command of Ralph Stafford. In the following months, Stafford was raised to the dignity of an Earl and appointed royal Lieutenant in the duchy. Walter Bentley, the Lieutenant in Brittany, was in England when Guy de Nesle began his invasion of the peninsula. He was promised a special subsidy of £2,400 and allowed to recruit men in the west country to reinforce his strength. Both men had the utmost difficulty in reaching their destinations. Flemish privateers had been cruising off the south coast of England since the beginning of the year. In March, they were joined by French galleys and armed merchantmen from the French Channel ports, who stationed themselves off the Isle of Wight waiting for the English ships to emerge. The port of embarkation was changed from Southampton to Fowey and back again. In April 1352 a determined attempt was made to draw off the French ships by fitting out a small fleet in the mouth of the Thames and raiding down the coast of Picardy and Normandy. It was a failure. Stafford and Bentley were still waiting impotently by the Solent in July.[70]

In spite of the small scale and disorganised beginnings of the English response, the French offensive of 1352 was a humiliating failure, the worst strategic reverse which they had suffered since 1347. The greatest disappointment was their failure to recapture Guines. The castle was defended by a relatively small number of men, 115 soldiers and a handful of artificers and assistants under the command of one of Edward III's household knights, Thomas Hogshaw.[71] But it was a powerfully constructed place surrounded by moats or marsh on every side except towards the town, where it was defended by a massive barbican. It was almost inaccessible by land but relatively easy to supply from Calais by water. When Geoffrey de Charny arrived, he occupied the town without difficulty. He took over the convent which stood opposite the main gate of the castle, which he renamed 'la Bastide' and began to convert into an independent fortress from which the castle could be battered into submission. The convent buildings were surrounded by a stockade of felled trees. They were then armed with springalds and canon and guarded by hundreds of soldiers. Behind the stockade men laboured to crenellate the bell-tower and the strengthen the outer walls.

The English were concerned about the scale of Geoffrey de Charny's operations and the progress of his works at Guines, more perhaps than they need have been. During the last week of May Edward's ministers decided to throw financial caution to the winds and issued orders for the recruitment of a large expeditionary force, at least 6,000 strong. All the ports of the south and east coasts were combed for ships to carry them to Calais. During June and July the town of Guines and the islands of firm ground north of it became the site of savage and continual fighting as the garrison of the castle launched sorties against the Bastide and raiding parties were sent out from Calais to help them. The English, who were usually heavily outnumbered, got the worst of most of these encounters. But they needed only to succeed once in order to set back Charny's work by several weeks. In the middle of July, an exceptionally strong raiding party left Calais, comprising not only a large part of the permanent garrison but several ship-loads of reinforcements who had embarked in England a few days earlier and landed secretly in Calais by night. They made their way across the marsh under cover of darkness and fell upon the French army encamped around Guines, killing large numbers of them. They also succeeded in burning part of the newly constructed defences of the Bastide. Edward III's cumbrous preparations to invade northern France in force were still far from complete when Geoffrey de Charny decided that the castle could not be taken. A few days after the English raid he abandoned the siege, leaving a garrison to hold the Bastide but the castle still in the hands of the enemy.[72]

Before dispersing his men to their garrisons, Geoffrey de Charny had one final act of vengeance to perform. He marched swiftly across the marsh roads to Fretun, a small hamlet three miles south-west of Calais at the foot of the heights of Sangatte, where the English had just finished building a new tower. The commander of this small outpost was Aimeric of Pavia, the man who had double-crossed Geoffrey the year before. When Geoffrey arrived without warning on 25 July 1352, he captured the tower and overwhelmed the garrison. Aimeric was carried off in triumph to Saint-Omer where an enormous crowd watched him tortured with red hot irons and dismembered with an meat-axe.[73]

Guy de Nesle's army of Brittany fared worse. They reoccupied the old French siege works around Ploermel and resumed the siege of the town which Jean de Melun had been forced to abandon the year before. Early in May 1352, they laid siege to the fortress of Robert Knolles at Fougeray. They constructed the usual *bastides* and works around the castle. Then, leaving a small force to contain the garrison, they withdrew to pass the months of June and July idly encamped in different parts of the plain of western Brittany, waiting for the English to intervene.[74]

Walter Bentley did not succeed in leaving England until the very end of July 1352, when he eventually sailed from Fowey. He had managed to extract from the Treasury only two thirds of the promised subsidy, and had raised less than half the number of men he had planned, 160 archers and perhaps about the same number of men-at-arms.[75] The rest of his army was waiting for him on his arrival. French sources estimated Bentley's total strength at 1,500 men, which was probably about twice the true figure. But he made up in boldness and speed what he lacked in numbers. Within a week of his landing in Brittany Bentley had relieved both Ploermel and Fougeray, dispersing the light French forces positioned around them before Guy de Nesle could do anything to stop him. The French army, most of which had been stationed around Rennes, marched hurriedly south, reaching Malestroit on 11 August 1352. Three days later, on 14 August, their scouts found the English army encamped by a stream near the castle of Brembili, about half a mile east of the village of Mauron. Guy de Nesle came up with the main body of the French army in the early evening. By this time Bentley had been able to draw up his men in battle order, the men-at-arms in a line along the crest of a hill with a hedgerow at their backs, the archers placed slightly forward at the wings. It was the classic English battle plan. But Bentley's men were on open ground, unprotected by woods, trenches or field works, and they were greatly outnumbered. Guy de Nesle regarded their position as hopeless and sent a messenger to invite them to surrender. It was, perhaps, a matter of form. Bentley refused.

The French plan was to disperse Bentley's archers with cavalry. Then, borrowing from English battle practice, as the French were learning to do, they intended to attack the English line on foot, overwhelming them by force of numbers. It very nearly succeeded. The lord of Hangest, who was in command of the cavalry, charged the archers at one wing of the English army. Their formations had no protection on the flank and they were ill equipped for close combat. Once the French horsemen had penetrated their ranks, many of them turned and fled from the field. The rest of the French army, led by dismounted men-at-arms, fought their way up the slope through the long grass towards the English centre, forcing them back until they were pinned against the hedgerow behind them. The English fought with ferocity, but until the end of the battle they seemed certain to be defeated. Then, two large groups of French soldiers were seen to fall back. One of them was the retinue of Jean de Beaumanoir, the hero of the battle of the Thirty. A little later, the rest began to withdraw down the hill. Shortly, the whole French army broke and scattered.

It was a costly victory. Bentley himself was wounded. His troops suffered heavy casualties, aggravated by Bentley's decision after the battle to have thirty archers beheaded for deserting the field. So serious was his position in the aftermath of the battle that it was necessary to send urgently to England for fresh drafts to make good the gaps in the garrisons of southern Brittany. However, the losses of the French were worse and, among the Bretons, catastrophic. One hundred and sixty prisoners were taken alive, including forty-five knights. When the victors counted the dead they found 500 men-at-arms in coat armour. Among them was the French commander, Guy de Nesle, killed at the age of twenty-five; Alain, viscount de Rohan, the most prominent nobleman of Brittany, the second of his line within five years to be killed in battle fighting against the English; and a mass of Breton noblemen whose names read like a roll call of the party of Blois. The corpses of eighty-nine knights of John II's Order of the Star were found among the dead, surrounded by those of their squires and retainers. They had not retreated.[76]

Ralph Stafford was almost as badly delayed as Bentley. For all the effort that went into finding ships and crews for his men, only thirty-three English ships and eight galleys of Bayonne were available by the end of June. Nearly 380 men (some two thirds of them archers) were eventually crammed into these vessels in the first week of July, together with a handful of servants and Exchequer clerks, as many victuals as could be carried in the bottoms of the holds, and more than £5,000 in cash. Many of the men had to leave their horses behind.[77]

The delay caused much anxiety to the English administration in Bordeaux. Indeed it is possible that they would have been better off if Stafford's expedition had never been conceived. For when the French ministers had made their plans back in March they had not reckoned on fighting a campaign in the Garonne valley and had made no arrangements for reinforcing their troops there. But early in May, when they learned about Stafford's intentions, they appointed Amaury de Craon as the King's Lieutenant in Languedoc and sent him urgently to the south-west to organise its defence. Amaury was an efficient commander who had made a considerable reputation for himself in Brittany and Poitou. He arrived in the province within three weeks of his appointment and put garrisons into several dozen towns and castles of the south-western march. Then, seeing that Stafford had not arrived, he went onto the offensive. A fresh subsidy was extracted from the communities of the south. Troops were recruited throughout Languedoc, Rouergue and the French-controlled parts of Périgord and the Agenais, and were sent to muster at Moissac. On 24 June 1352, Amaury opened his campaign. He marched down the Garonne valley and set up his campaign headquarters at Agen at the end of the month.

From there his troops fanned out through the southern Agenais, attacking English garrisons. The main detachment was placed under the command of Charles of Navarre, the King's young cousin, and ordered to besiege Port-Sainte-Marie, an important harbour on the north bank of the Garonne. In spite of the presence of a large garrison, and in spite of a bold attempt by the English Seneschal to lead a relief force from Bordeaux, the French rapidly captured the bridge. The town was untenable after that, and it surrendered at the beginning of July 1352.[78] While all this was happening, a large army of Gascons, some 3,800 strong waited idly in Bordeaux for the Earl of Stafford to arrive.

When, eventually, Stafford did arrive, on 21 July 1352, he moved quickly. The whole army marched immediately up the Garonne valley, leaving the galleys of Bayonne to follow behind with victuals and supplies. On 15 August 1352, the feast of the Assumption, Stafford arrived outside Agen. Within the town, panic gripped the citizens. Their walls were still incomplete on the western side, near the banks of the Garonne, and the new suburb of Bezat was exposed. The gap was swiftly closed with wooden barricades and building material taken from the half-finished works of the bridge. Every adult man was called out to man the walls. But neither side was really prepared for the encounter. Amaury de Craon was in the town with a large number of French men-at-arms but not, as he conceived, enough to confront Stafford's army in battle. He had sent for help from other French commanders in the south as soon as the news of the Earl's landing had reached him, and Charles of Spain, Arnoul d'Audrehem and the Count of Armagnac were all said to be on their way. Stafford, on the other hand, although he commanded a large army, was extremely short of archers. He was not in a position to fight off a relief force. What was more, the boats bringing his supplies from Bordeaux were unable to get further upstream than Marmande, where a powerful French garrison still controlled the passage of the Garonne. A few days after his arrival before Agen, the French attempted a sortie from the town. There was a brief, violent mêlée in the fields below the walls, in which they were defeated with heavy losses. The prisoners included Jean de Boucicaut and no less than seven knights of the Star. Boucicaut, who had already been a prisoner of war once, was sold to Edward III and shipped to England, where he remained a prisoner for three years before he was able to raise the steep ransom demanded of him. This minor victory enabled Stafford to withdraw with honour but little else before the end of August 1352.[79] As the Earl marched back with his army in the direction from which he had come, the French commanders in Saintonge and Angoumois launched a ferocious counter-attack in the valley of the Dordogne. By the time Stafford reached Bordeaux, in the first week of September 1352, there was serious concern about the safety of Bergerac as well as the great fortress of the lord of Albret at Moncuq nearby.[80]

Stafford's next enterprise went some way to justify his expedition and to redeem his reputation as a strategist. On 17 September 1352 the Lieutenant and the lord of Albret suddenly appeared outside the French garrison town of Blaye and carried it by assault. This remarkable and unexpected stroke avenged one of the worst humiliations of the opening years of the war when, in 1339, the French had taken Blaye from beneath the noses of the English. Its recapture brought the whole of the north shore of the Gironde under English control except for the mouth of the estuary, where the French continued to hold on to Royan and Talmont. The Anglo-Gascons then divided their forces. The lord of Albret and the Constable of Bordeaux took about 1,000 men to relieve Bergerac and Moncuq. Stafford himself went north with the rest of the army and scattered the French troops who had been besieging the fortress of Taillebourg since April.[81]

About three months after his arrival in the duchy Stafford returned to England with the autumn wine fleet. As for Amaury de Craon, he disbanded his army on 24 September 1352 and left the province a few days later.[82] But although the armies had dispersed and the lieutenants and their marshals, general officers and paymasters had gone, irregular companies of Anglo-Gascon troops redoubled their efforts during the autumn and winter months. At about the beginning of October 1352 a group of Gascon adventurers seized Lafrançaise, a small thirteenth-century *bastide* occupying an incomparable strategic position on a steep escarpment 300 feet above the river Tarn. The men responsible for this deed cannot be identified, but the probability is that they came from the garrison of the Captal de Buch at Saint-Antonin, some forty miles away to the east. From Lafrançaise the English were able to paralyse river communications in the region and block the important road from Montauban to Moissac. The event caused pandemonium in Languedoc and an unparalleled burst of fortification and tax gathering. An emergency meeting of representatives of the towns of Languedoc was called by the *capitouls* of Toulouse. They resolved to send a messenger post-haste to the King to explain the danger of their situation. Toulouse itself was only about a day's march from Lafrançaise. But it was relatively well-placed to defend itself. It was populous and well organised and it had learned a good deal from the experiences of 1339, 1345 and 1349. Moreover, powerful reinforcements were brought into the city by the Count of Foix within days of the news breaking. Other southern towns were less fortunate. At Albi the cathedral quarter on the western edge of the town was defended by modern walls, by the fortified palace of the Bishops, and by the half-built mass of the great brick cathedral of Ste.-Cecile. But the rest of the town was weak. In spite of the expenditure of 30,000 *livres* on repairs over the past six years the defences still consisted mainly of rubble ramparts with old-fashioned square towers and dangerous gaps. There was no permanent garrison. The citizens screamed for help. They were 'virtually unwalled and undefended', they said.

From Paris, John II contemplated the humiliating and disorderly series of defeats which his commanders had suffered since the beginning of the year, and wrote reassuring letters to the cities of Languedoc. He appointed the Seneschal of Toulouse as his acting Lieutenant in the province. He promised to send them a better Lieutenant in due course. He said that he would come in person if necessary.[83] But John's eyes were fixed on the northern provinces, on the Channel and on the defence of his capital. Although the English King had abandoned his plans to invade France almost as soon as he had conceived them in a moment panic in May, John's intelligence about what was happening in England was irregular and inaccurate. He remained convinced until well into the autumn that an enormous English army was about to cross the sea. Troops summoned from all over northern France had assembled at Compiègne during September. Subsidiary armies, recruited in the eastern provinces and from the francophone territories beyond the Rhone and the Meuse, were summoned to other mustering points, at Troyes, Saint-Quentin, Maçon and Dijon.[84]

Even after Edward III's phantom army had faded away, the tension generated by the affair of Guines continued to preoccupy John's ministers. They knew now how unreliable truces were and how vulnerable even major garrisoned fortresses in good repair could be in the face of a surprise attack by night. When, on 1 October 1352, Geoffrey de Charny handed over command of the march of Calais to his successor, the whole of the north-west plain of Artois had become an armed camp perpetually on the eve of battle. The English had pushed out the limits of their enclave from the walls of Calais until they controlled most of the marshes and waterways which served as its

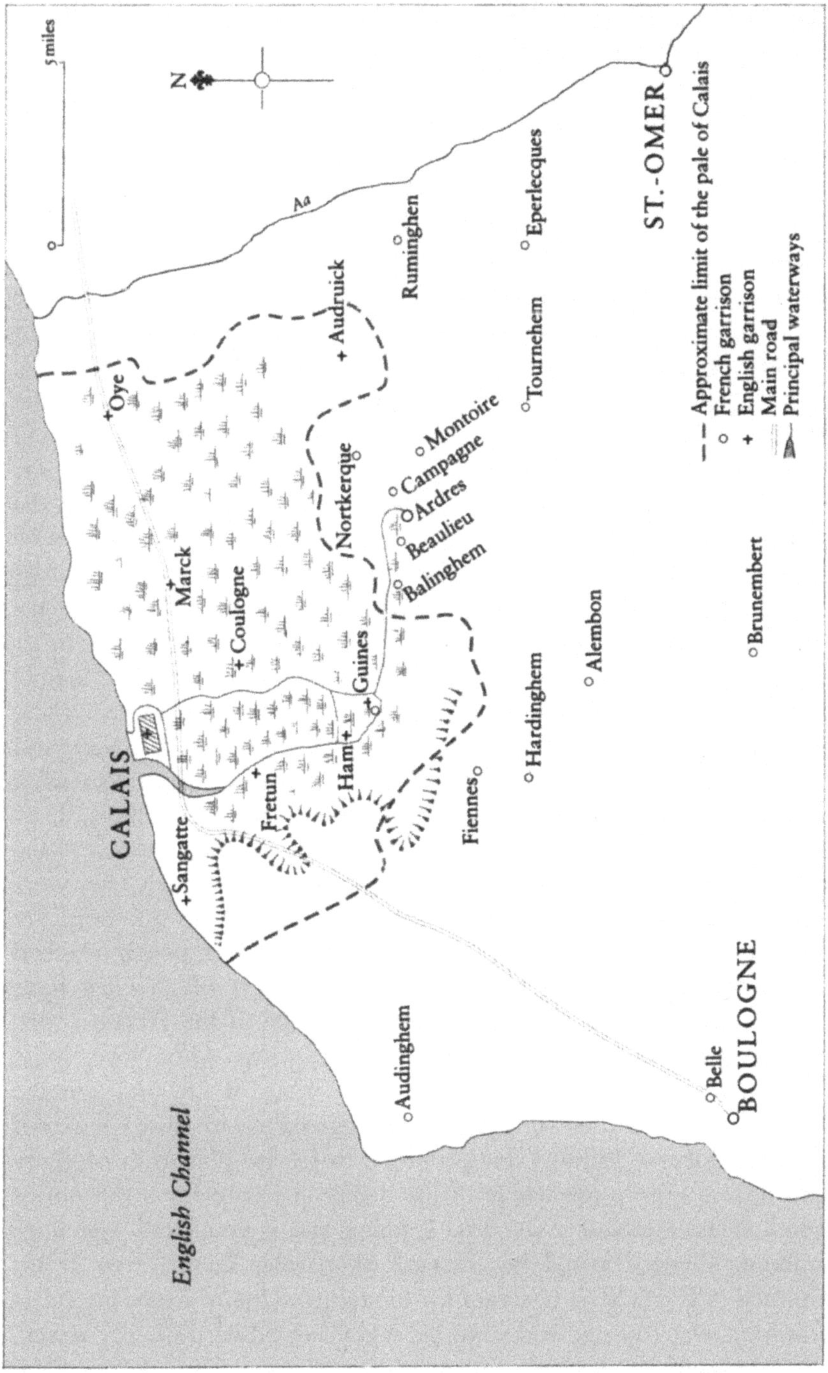

7 The march of Calais, 1352

natural line of defence. Their outlying forts had become formidably strong and efficiently supplied. On their side, the French had found themselves defending a deep front extending from Saint-Omer to Boulogne. Between these anchor-towns with their vast garrisons and stores, the countryside had been abandoned by most of its inhabitants as men shut themselves behind the walls of the towns and soldiers took over every defensible structure: church towers, barns, stone farm houses and manors, water-mills, and improvised forts hastily constructed at bridges and crossroads. At the end of the year 1352, the French were maintaining, at crippling cost, more than sixty garrisons on the march of Calais alone.[85]

A more potent symptom of failure of the French offensive was the abandonment of John II by most of his supporters in Brittany, including even Charles of Blois. When the news of the battle of Mauron was brought to Charles in the Tower of London, he reacted with the melancholy resignation for which he was already famous: 'Blessed be God,' he said, 'for the fortune that he grants us.' His wife was less inclined to trust in providence. She now determined to procure his release and restoration on whatever terms she could make, with or without the assistance of the King of France. In November 1352, Jeanne de Penthièvre presided over an assembly representing all the remaining territories under her control: eleven towns, twenty-three lay barons and sixteen ecclesiastics. They resolved to revive the old project of a marriage alliance between the houses of Plantagenet and Blois. They sent a delegation to England which was led by two of the heroes of the battle of the Thirty, Jean de Beaumanoir and Yves Charruel. They were men whose loyalty to the cause of France was beyond question. Yet when they arrived in England in the new year they swiftly reached agreement with Edward III's councillors on terms which must have caused consternation when they became known at the French court. The document opened by announcing that there would be 'love, unity, peace and perpetual alliance' between the King of England and the house of Blois and their subjects. Edward agreed to recognise Charles of Blois as Duke of Brittany. He promised to release him from captivity and restore him to the whole of the duchy in return for a ransom of 300,000 *écus* (about £50,000). Pending the payment of this huge amount, Charles would be released on parole, leaving two of his children in England as hostages for his return. One of them, his eldest son John, was to be betrothed to a daughter of Edward III. There were careful provisions for the further conduct of the war. The substance of it was that Brittany would henceforth be neutral, closed to the armies of both sides unless it was attacked by the French, in which case Charles and Edward would join together in an offensive and defensive alliance against the aggressor. Edward III might have insisted on being recognised as King of France, which would have been a formidable problem for so upright an individual as Charles of Blois. But Edward did not insist, and the matter was passed over in silence. As for the young John de Montfort, whose cause was thus summarily abandoned by his guardian, he was to be compensated by the grant of his family's ancient domains in the Guérande peninsula and by a pension from the Breton treasury. These terms, which were sealed in the Palace of Westminster on 1 March 1353, were agreed on behalf of the communities of Brittany. But it is scarcely conceivable that Charles had not approved them personally. In the short period in which they remained in force, they marked the nadir of John II's fortunes in western France until, shortly, yet worse misfortunes befell him.[86]

CHAPTER III

The King of Navarre

1352–1355

The humiliating outcome of the campaigns of 1352 marked a turning point in John II's unhappy reign. Two years after his accession the optimism and freshness of outlook was gone. 'Be it known', declared the Abbot of St.-Remi of Reims, when selling a property to a draper of the city, 'that since we are burdened by the taxes, tenths and other exactions continually imposed on us, and by the dead weight of our debts and the devaluation of the coin in which we receive our rents, we do hereby sell . . .'[1] He spoke for a large part of the debt-burdened nobility of the realm, many of whom had to suffer not only taxation and devaluation but the hazards and expense of fighting in the King's army, the heavy cost of horses and equipment, the crushing burden of their ransoms, the frustration of wages unpaid and promises of pensions and grants dishonoured. There had been murmurs of discontent from such men before, after the stalemates of 1340 and 1342, and the disasters of Crécy and Calais. In the mid-1350s they began to turn against the government with venomous incomprehension and in some cases with violence.

There were many among the higher nobility and the Church, and some at the heart of the royal administration, who were inclined to blame the misfortunes of France on the defects of her institutions, on the corruption of the civil service and on the excessive power of a weak monarch and the dishonesty of his powerful friends. Some of these themes enjoyed a wider appeal in mid-fourteenth-century France: among the champions of the liberties of France's ancient provinces, among radical spirits in the larger cities, among theorists and moralisers of the universities and, eventually, among the half-directed mobs looking for men to blame for poverty and defeat. All of the fissiparous tendencies of French society, which had been contained by a century and a half of intensive government, began to re-emerge as the monarchy lost its confidence and its prestige, the pretence of power which had for so long been a substitute for the reality. During the following years these disparate groups, representing very different political positions and opposing economic interests, gradually formed themselves into a more coherent opposition. Its leader was an unstable and impulsive young man of demonic energy and ambition and erratic flashes of genius: Charles 'the Bad', Count of Évreux and King of Navarre.[2]

Charles of Navarre was only twenty years old in 1352, but he was already laden with the grievances of the past. He was the son of Philip, Count of Évreux, first cousin of the late King, and Joan of Navarre, the only child of Louis X. He was therefore born of the *fleur de lys* on both sides, as he was apt to point out, and on one view ranked higher in the royal family of France than either John II or Edward III. Yet Charles was an outsider. His mother had been elbowed from the throne after the death of Louis X, the first assertion of the so-called Salic Law which excluded women from the royal succession. Joan had been the heiress to a splendid landed inheritance from her parents, including the kingdom of Navarre and the immense county of Champagne, one of the great fiefs of medieval France covering the greater part of six modern *départements*. The Salic Law had no application to fiefs, which could unquestionably be inherited or transmitted by women. But her uncle, Philip V, deprived her of almost everything. The young princess, who was a small child at the time of these events, was promised compensation in cash. But it was a comparatively paltry sum and it was never paid. When, early in the reign of Philip VI, her claims were pressed and finally settled, she recovered Navarre but was obliged to renounce her rights in Champagne in exchange for the county of Angoulême, the small territory of Mortain in southern Normandy, and some cash. Angoulême was a poor substitute for Champagne. Its revenues proved to be disappointing and they were progressively reduced by the war in the south-west. Shortly before Joan died in 1349 she abandoned it in exchange for some scattered lordships in Normandy and the Île de France. These territories, together with his father's county of Évreux, the kingdom of Navarre and the ill-defined right of a prince of the royal blood to participate in the government of the French state, constituted the shrunken inheritance to which Charles of Navarre succeeded.[3]

The possession of Navarre by a prince of the House of France was a historical oddity. Navarre was a tiny independent kingdom occupying an important strategic position across the western passes of the Pyrenees. Wedged between Castile and Aragon to the south, its territory extended over the north face of the Pyrenees beyond Saint-Jean-Pied-de-

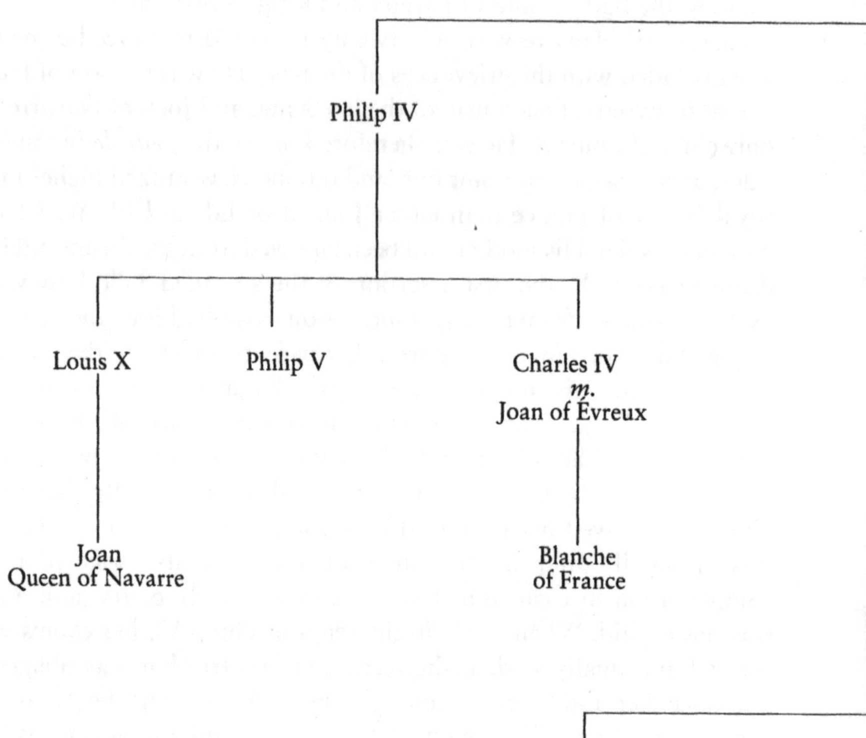

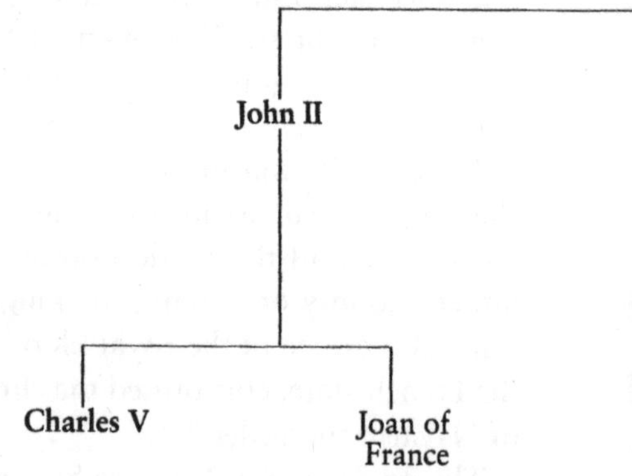

8 Houses of Valois and Évreux

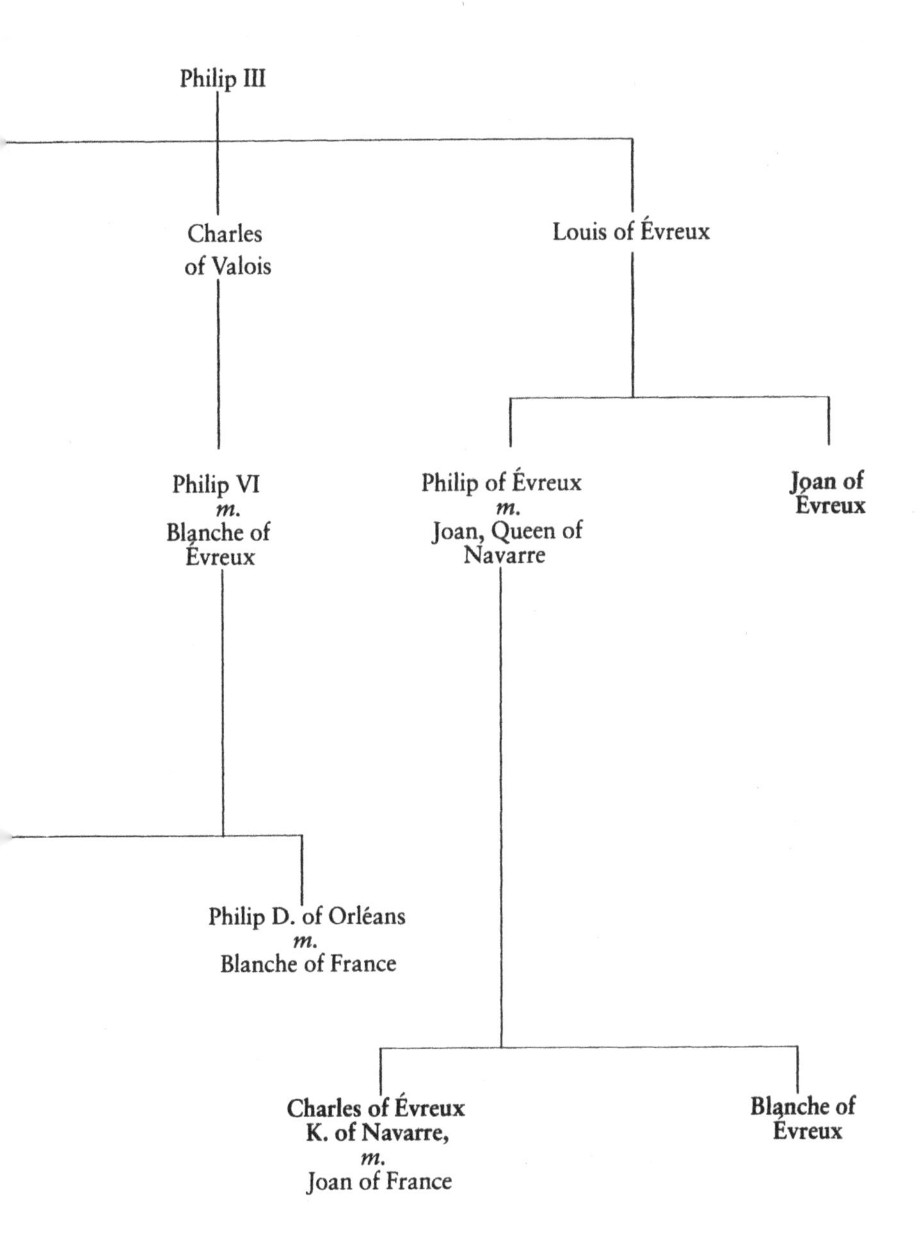
Philip III
Charles of Valois
Louis of Évreux
Philip VI *m.* Blanche of Évreux
Philip of Évreux *m.* Joan, Queen of Navarre
Joan of Évreux
Philip D. of Orléans *m.* Blanche of France
Charles of Évreux K. of Navarre, *m.* Joan of France
Blanche of Évreux

Port to within ten miles of Bayonne. The kingdom had ancient connections with France. French and Gascon immigrants had populated its monasteries and towns since the eleventh century and filled the hostels along the pilgrimage route to Santiago, which was still called the *camino francès*. Politically, it had been a client state of France since the thirteenth century, when the play of dynastic marriage and succession had brought it first into the hands of the Counts of Champagne and then into those of the Capetians. The first French rulers of Navarre had been rather distant figures. They had come to Pamplona to be crowned and displayed to their people in the streets of the city, held aloft on a buckler by the *ricos-hombres*. Sometimes their corpses had returned to be buried in the Cathedral. But except on these grand occasions they had rarely visited Navarre. The kingdom had been governed by small groups of Navarrese councillors supervised by officials sent from France. During the 1330s, however, this began to change. As the kings of the dynasty of Évreux became estranged from their cousins of France, they became more interested in Navarre. Joan of Navarre and her husband stayed there for long periods, holding court at Pamplona, Estella, Tudela and Olite. Their principal agent in the kingdom, Philip of Melun, Archdeacon of Sens, began to reconstruct the administration and embarked upon a programme of irrigation and road building. Navarre had some advantages for an ambitious dynastic politician intent on meddling in the affairs of France. It was remote and easily held against an invader, as Charlemagne had discovered at Roncevalles. There were modest tax revenues which could be swollen in short periods of intense effort by grants from the *Cortes* of the kingdom. The mountain regions of the north were bleak and poor, inhabited (as a French traveller had once written) by 'savage men subsisting on savage land'. In the south of the kingdom the basin of the River Ebro and its tributaries was warm and fertile, growing wheat, vines, olives and almonds. There were small mines of lead and copper, and a nascent metal-working industry at Olite making weapons and armour. But by far the most important resource of Navarre was its manpower. The kingdom was extremely densely populated. Tax records, kept in the methodical manner of its French masters, suggest that it must have had at least 50,000 households on the eve of the Black Death, which implies a population between 200,000 and 250,000. Like most of the Pyrenean regions of France, Navarre had suffered particularly heavily in the epidemic. It may have lost as many as two thirds of its inhabitants.[4] But even after the plague, the land could only intermittently support its people. Emigration was a long-standing tradition. Like Wales and Scotland, Béarn and Savoy, those other overpopulated mountain states at the outer margins of the war, its sparse hills produced large numbers of savage, poorly armed and covetous infantrymen to fight in other men's wars and greedy and ambitious mercenary captains to lead them.

Joan of Navarre died, probably from the plague, in October 1349 at the castle of Conflans outside Paris. She was buried in the choir of the abbey of Saint-Denis, by the tomb of her father Louis X, surrounded by the effigies of her kinsmen whom she had hated. Her last years, which had been passed almost entirely in Navarre, had been overshadowed by the continuing dispute with her relations about her inheritance, and by the war with England, on which she had taken an increasingly independent line, making her own arrangements with the English King's representatives in Bordeaux without regard to the interests or wishes of the King of France. Her son Charles briefly visited Navarre in the summer of the following year to be crowned, and to organise the affairs of his kingdom.[5] But apart from this period and a few fleeting visits, the whole of the first twelve years of his reign was spent in France.

When Charles of Navarre returned to France in July 1351 he received a number of military commands of the sort commonly conferred on the younger members of the royal family. He served briefly as royal Lieutenant in Languedoc in the quiet summer of 1351. When he returned to Languedoc in the more demanding circumstances of the following year, he was obliged to serve under Amaury de Craon. But he commanded the army which captured Port-Sainte-Marie on the Garonne in July 1352 and, a few weeks later, the troops which had gathered to defend the coast of Picardy at the height of the invasion scare. Charles, however, was never a great soldier or even an enthusiastic one. His talent was for politics. He was a man of magnetic personality with a charisma that impressed enemies as well as friends. A hostile contemporary described him as a 'small man with a lively wit, a penetrating eye, and an easy, unaffected eloquence; his astonishing shrewdness and extraordinary charm enabled him to find supporters as no other prince of the blood could do, not just among the common people but among men of substance and power.' Charles was utterly unscrupulous in the pursuit of his ambitions. At court, he made good use of his connections. His sister Blanche, a famous beauty, had married Philip VI at the end of his life. His aunt, Joan of Évreux, was the widow of that other elderly bridegroom King Charles IV. These two formidable and conspiratorial dowagers were powerful figures in the inward-looking and much inter-married world of John II's court. The young King of Navarre was in high favour there, and at the outset his admirers included the King. On 12 February 1352 Charles married John II's daughter Joan in the beautiful royal manor of Vivier-en-Brie whose ruins can still be seen east of Paris. It was a magnificent occasion. The King, his brother the Duke of Orléans, his four sons and all their retinue appeared clothed in uniform robes of blue and red. Charles was still a minor. But John marked the occasion by solemnly pronouncing him to be of age.

Charles of Navarre was admitted to the inner circle of the Valois family. But he knew that he had no real power, and he resented it the more for seeing power exercised so close at hand. He did not sit in the inner councils of the state. His fortune did not stand comparison with that of the princes around him or even of that triumphant interloper Charles of Spain. He possessed the scattered lordships which his mother had held at the time of her death, and he was entitled to the pension which she had been granted but rarely paid in partial compensation for the loss of Champagne. On 18 January 1352, some three weeks before his marriage, the King had promised to pay him all the arrears of the pension, amounting to 60,000 *livres* as well as a dowry of 100,000 gold *écus*. These sums were never paid. The English had occupied Guines a few days before John's promises were made, and Charles' marriage took place amid the bustle of preparations for war. They consumed every penny which John's treasurers could find. Charles of Navarre, like Charles of Blois and countless other hopeful pensioners, petitioners and clients of the Crown, found that the King's resources were not equal to his promises. The King of Navarre was not even allowed possession of all the domains which were by rights his own and which ought to have been released to him on his majority.[6]

At an early stage Charles of Navarre conceived an intense hatred of Charles of Spain. The original reason for the quarrel was the grant of the county of Angoulême to the favourite at the end of 1350. Angoulême had belonged to Charles of Navarre's mother, and although she had surrendered it willingly enough when Philip VI had offered her alternative domains in the north, Philip and his successor had hung on to the most valuable of those domains. In October 1352 John II formally confirmed the grant of Angoulême to the Constable. He probably did this because the King of Navarre had challenged it. As Charles saw it his rival had 'disinherited' him. Certainly the contrast between the austere economies of the Chambre des Comptes and the indulgence shown to the Constable was complete and public. During the winter of 1352–3 when the King of Navarre was unable to obtain either the land or the money which was due to him, the flow of grants to Charles of Spain continued unabated, his influence over the King undiminished. Charles of Navarre was not alone in his resentment. As time went on the Constable became increasingly overbearing in his manner and unscrupulous in his methods. One nobleman, Regnault de Précigny, who entered into a very unequal exchange of properties with the Constable in October 1352, later gave evidence that he had been locked in Charles' castle of Niort and told that the King insisted on the transaction; unless he submitted he would be taken to Paris and put in the Châtelet. It is not always easy to distinguish the truth from the embellishments of disappointed men. But this story was plausible or it would not have been told. At the time, Regnault said, Charles of Spain was 'feared and hated, and no one would raise his voice against him.' The Constable did nothing to appease these feelings. He was tactless and arrogant, and curtly dismissive of those who crossed him. For the King of Navarre, with his ambition, his supreme confidence in his own abilities and his intense pride of lineage, this was unspeakably mortifying.[7]

The first signs of a Navarrese 'party' begin to appear early in 1353 when Charles, in spite of the poverty of his landed endowment, began to use his name and his charm to build up a power-base in southern Normandy, around his father's county of Évreux. Normandy was a province with a large aristocracy, where the grievances of great landowners and devalued noblemen had a special resonance. John, Count of Harcourt, the head of one of the most prominent noble families of Normandy became the foremost of Charles' supporters. He was an old-fashioned believer in the autonomy of his province and the evils of taxation, in some ways resembling his uncle who had rebelled against the Philip VI for much the same reasons and fought in Edward III's army at Crécy. Other noblemen of Normandy appeared in growing numbers at Charles of Navarre's court at Évreux and spoke up for his cause elsewhere. Their motives were probably much the same as Harcourt's. Some of them may also have been friends and dependents of the Count of Eu, one of the great men of the province whose summary execution in 1350 was still held against the King and his favourite. Others were disappointed suitors, the rank and file of most palace revolutions, who resented their own financial difficulties the more for seeing other men prosper at the expense of the state. But there were also more thoughtful men whose motives were less self-interested and who were closer to the heart of the royal administration. They were frustrated by the slow rhythms and obstructive ways of the Parisian bureaucracy, repelled by what they saw as the degeneration of royal government and the self-serving ways of its principal ministers. Although their attitude to the King was initially respectful and correct, it became increasingly difficult for them to reserve their criticisms for his councillors. There was a growing tide of opinion in the civil service, the higher aristocracy and the Church that the King was unfit to govern in a time of crisis. Jean de Meulan, Bishop of Paris, a distinguished and widely respected man who had been brought into the royal Council in the autumn of 1351 to bring some order to the King's finances; his nephew Amaury, a hitherto loyal councillor who had served John II since his accession and Philip VI before him; Guillaume Bertrand, Bishop of Beauvais, another Norman on John's Council, whose brother had been a Marshal under Philip VI; Jean de Picquigny, a great nobleman of Picardy, royal governor of Artois, hereditary vidâme of Amiens, enormously rich and well-connected, the sort of territorial magnate who ought to have been among the King's natural allies but had experienced defeat too often. The King of Navarre's skill in drawing together malcontents of such complex and disparate motives is the real measure of his genius.[8]

The most enigmatic of these men, Robert le Coq, Bishop of Laon, was ultimately to emerge as the leading radical behind the Navarrese revolution. Robert, like so many of John's servants, was a self-made man of modest origins. He had entered the royal service in the last years of the reign of Philip VI after a successful career as an advocate in the Parlement and had recently, in October 1352, become Bishop of Laon. He was the senior judicial officer of John's household. He had served as John's permanent representative of the papal court in Avignon for more than a year. He had sat intermittently in John II's secret Council from the outset of the reign. But none of this was enough. What Robert le Coq wanted was to be Chancellor of France, the second office of the realm after that of Constable. Robert was a sinuous and quarrelsome schemer with a waspish tongue. Yet resentment and ambition were not his only motives, and in spite the accusations of his enemies (which are the main sources for his early career) he was neither corrupt nor wholly unprincipled. He hesitated a long time before deserting John II and attaching himself to Charles of Navarre. When he did so, he brought to Charles' circle an austere attachment to honest administration and the purposeful, clear-sighted logic of a fanatic. The main point that he had in common with the King of Navarre was his loathing of Charles of Spain, whose influence he envied and resented and whom he believed to have obstructed his career by patronising one of his rivals. A 'useless bastard' was what Robert called him behind his back.[9]

At the moment when John II's administration was beginning to fall apart in jealous acrimony and bickering, he lost one of his most valuable allies. Pope Clement VI died at Avignon on 6 December 1352. His body was carried up the valley of the Rhone, through country still untouched by war, to be laid to rest in the magnificent choir of the abbey of la Chaise-Dieu, where he had been brought up as an oblate. Smooth and princely, intelligent and devious, Clement had been wedded to the cause of France, whose war effort he had at one stage financed out of his own pocket and whose diplomatic interests he had always put first. His successor was a very different sort of man. Etienne Aubert, who was elected on 18 December 1352, took the name Innocent VI. He came from the Limousin. As a Cardinal he had been one of the two legates who had laboured fruitlessly to stop the war between 1345 and 1348. He had met Edward III at Lisieux on his march through Normandy. He had been with Philip VI in the aftermath of the battle of Crécy and in the last days of the siege of Calais. He knew better than most Cardinals what the war was like. By training Innocent was a lawyer, like his predecessor. But he had none of his predecessor's incisiveness. He was an old man at the time of his election, gouty and infirm. In spite of his gaunt appearance and austere manner, he was impressionable, indecisive and vacillating. Perhaps his only merit as a peacemaker, apart from his patent honesty, was that he was less partisan than Clement had been. 'Although we were born in France', he once wrote to the Duke of Lancaster, 'and although for that and other reasons we hold the realm of France in special affection, yet in working for peace we have put aside our private prejudices and tried to serve the interests of everyone.'[10]

The responsibility for restarting the negotiations in 1353 belonged not to Innocent himself but to another more subtle ecclesiastical politician, Guy of Boulogne, Cardinal of Porto. Guy of Boulogne was the son of Robert, Count of Boulogne and Mary of Flanders and, as such, he belonged to one of the greatest noble families of France. Because of his parentage and his talents he had enjoyed an extremely rapid ascent through the hierarchy of the Church, becoming successively papal chaplain, Archbishop of Lyon, and a Cardinal in 1342 before he was thirty. He was already one of the more influential members of the college of Cardinals when the accession of John II brought him fresh prospects of power. His brother, Jean de Boulogne, was a close friend of the new King; his niece, Jeanne de Boulogne was John's queen. In the summer of 1352, during the last months of the reign of Pope Clement VI, Guy of Boulogne set out for the court of France on a personal mission, conducted without any official status and at his own expense, to bring about a reconciliation between the two belligerents.[11]

As a peacemaker Guy of Boulogne had one advantage, and perhaps only one. He had thought more carefully about the origins of the war than most of the conciliators who had tried over the years to end it, and he was less inclined to see the solution in simple, moral terms. He could see that outright victory was beyond the reach of either side. And since almost all the fighting occurred in France, continued stalemate was infinitely more damaging to France than it was to England. It was plain that no peace could be had on anything like the terms which the French had proposed at previous diplomatic conferences. There would have to be a political compromise and it would have to involve major territorial concessions by the King of France. A few of John II's advisers were already inching towards the same conclusion. Unfortunately, although Guy of Boulogne perceived the solution, he was supremely ill-suited for achieving it. For although he was clever and affable, he was also vain and politically insensitive. Moreover, he was too close to one of the principal protagonists. In Paris he warmed to Charles of Navarre as many others had done. In a court tense with rivalries and ill-feeling, he chose to work through his friends, relations and connections, oblivious of the fact that in the eyes of their enemies he was branding himself as a partisan. Above all, Guy of Boulogne was a Frenchman, closely associated with the royal family of France. Indeed, he was admitted to the secret Council of the King shortly after his arrival and took an active part in its deliberations for most of the following year.[12] The English knew this and they were always very guarded in their dealings with him. This may have been unfair, for Guy genuinely wanted to go down in history as the man who brought an end to the Anglo-French war. But it was hardly surprising.

At the beginning of December 1352 Henry of Lancaster arrived in Paris with a large retinue of English knights to fight a duel against Otto, Duke of Brunswick. Henry had accused the Duke of trying to capture him while he passed through Germany on the way back from his crusade in Prussia. Otto had responded by accusing Henry of slander. In the event the duel was never fought. Although the two combatants rode into the lists in the Pré-aux-Clercs in the presence of the King of France and a great crowd of noblemen and onlookers, John imposed a settlement on them before they joined battle. But Henry of Lancaster's time was not wasted. John II received him at the Louvre before the affair in the Pré-aux-Clercs, and entertained him at a magnificent reception afterwards. Guy of Boulogne had a long interview with the Duke and a number of the English King's councillors who were with him, including Reginald Cobham and the Chamberlain, Bartholomew Burghersh. At this meeting, the Cardinal disclosed his plans for a fresh diplomatic conference under his own chairmanship early in the new year. The Englishmen had no authority to agree to such a thing, but they seemed well disposed towards peace, or so Guy reported to Innocent VI when, shortly afterwards, he was called back to Avignon for the coronation of the new Pope. The Duke of Lancaster evidently made a strong impression on Guy of Boulogne, who was perhaps less cautious than he should have been in the face of Henry's charm and professions of goodwill. The outcome was that the English agreed to meet the Cardinal and the councillors of the French King at the traditional meeting place outside Guines in March 1353.[13]

In the north of France, where the troops of both sides were under the direct control of their governments and conformed more or less to their orders, it was possible to keep the peace while the laborious diplomatic preliminaries began. The problems lay in the south-west, where the English King's officials were no longer in control of the fighting and the French were unwilling to disarm themselves in the hope of getting an illusory peace. Anglo-Gascon irregulars continued to attack remote churches, castles and towns, and some less remote ones such as Surgères, a powerful fortress in the north of Saintonge only twenty miles from la Rochelle, which was captured by escalade one night in January 1353. This coup threatened to destroy the commerce of France's only significant Biscay port. The French King's ministers were bound to respond. They sent Louis of Harcourt to the region as royal captain. He was busy recruiting troops throughout February and March 1353. At the opposite end of the southern theatre, in Languedoc, decisions were made locally, not by ministers in Paris. The communities of the district of Beaucaire (and probably other districts as well) had promised a subsidy of 10 *s.t.* per hearth to finance a campaign against the Anglo-Gascon garrisons of Lafrançaise and Saint-Antonin in

Quercy. An impressive army, recruited largely by the initiative of the municipality of Toulouse, had been besieging the enemy garrison of Lafrançaise since early November 1352 under the direction of the local Seneschal and the Counts of Comminges and Foix. The bastide fell in the middle of January 1353 while the English were still considering their response to the Cardinal of Boulogne's proposal.[14]

Not long before the new year, John II decided to appoint a new Lieutenant in Languedoc. John, Count of Armagnac, whose jurisdiction covered the whole of the Gascon march from the River Dordogne to the Pyrenees, was the richest magnate of the south-west. His vast and concentrated domains in Rouergue and along the south-eastern march of the English duchy produced for him a substantial income and very considerable numbers of soldiers as well as conferring a natural authority on their owner. Armagnac had governed his dominions since his fifteenth year and he was exceptionally experienced in the ways of the region. He was destined to remain continuously in office for five years and to dominate the affairs of the south-west for twenty. It is true that he was not a great commander of armies. But he was an excellent administrator and negotiator. He was also a man of fierce independence of mind who did not tolerate insubordination from below or interference from above. His previous lieutenancy, in 1346–7, had been an unhappy affair, his efforts marred by want of funds and by constant disputes with his masters in Paris, punctuated by periodic threats of resignation. He had a freer hand under John II. This was partly, no doubt, because of the declining importance of Languedoc in the King's strategic notions. But John's government was also more pliable than his father's, more inclined to delegate and increasingly distracted by the awful catastrophes occurring in the north of the realm. One consequence of Armagnac's appointment was therefore that the King's officers in Languedoc became increasingly independent in their conduct of the war there.[15]

The new Lieutenant was assisted by another less celebrated but in his own way equally remarkable figure, Bertrand de Pibrac, prior of the Parisian monastery of St.-Martin-des-Champs. Bertrand had been concerned on and off with the finances of the southern provinces since the early 1340s when he had first served as a commissioner for enforcing the *gabelle*. In January 1352 he had been reappointed with instructions to press on the inhabitants of the south the perils in which they stood and to extract money from them by every available method.

It was largely due to his efforts that the inhabitants of Languedoc were gradually becoming reconciled to regular war taxation and that the province became more or less self-sufficient financially. With self-sufficiency came a considerable measure of autonomy and practical independence of control from Paris. Not only did the Estates of Languedoc and the communities of the south vote their own grants of taxation, as they had always done, but they tended to impose increasingly stringent conditions designed to ensure that local revenues were spent on the defence of the region and not elsewhere. When, in the days of Philip VI, this idea had been pressed by the abrasive Bishop of Rodez, Gilbert of Cantobre, the Crown had contested it with vigour. The Bishop's domains had been confiscated by royal officials. But his views became the orthodoxy of the 1350s. This was not at all unwelcome to the Count of Armagnac. Attempts to requisition funds in the hands of local receivers and treasurers for use elsewhere, or to assign revenues to third parties, met with his unrelenting opposition.

> My friends, [he wrote to the officers of the Chambre des Comptes, who had tried to appropriate the revenues of the southern mints] I will have you know that whatever orders may come from the north, for as long as I remain Lieutenant here not one penny from the mints will be spent on anything other than the war in Gascony, and anyone who acts on such orders will be answerable for it to me. So if you want your orders obeyed you had better make sure that your next letter of that kind includes a clause removing me from my office.[16]

Within days of taking up his duties at the beginning of the year 1353 Armagnac had thrown himself into the war in the south-west. Taking over from the Counts of Comminges and Foix, he gathered a fresh army at Castelsarrasin in January 1353 to deal with the Anglo-Gascons at Saint-Antonin. On 3 February he laid siege to the town.[17]

The representatives of England and France gathered outside Guines in the presence of the Cardinal of Boulogne at the beginning of March. It is unlikely that the English were authorised to agree to anything more than a truce and perhaps to engage in preliminary discussions of a peace. But the status of their principal ambassadors showed that they took the occasion seriously. Simon of Islip, once keeper of Edward III's privy seal, had been Archbishop of Canterbury for two years. Bishop Bateman of Norwich, who had attended every important diplomatic occasion since the ill-fated Avignon conference of 1344, was by now the most experienced diplomat in Edward's service. The Duke of Lancaster and Michael Northburgh, the current keeper of the privy seal, were probably closer to the English King's counsels than any men living. For their part, the French sent an embassy which was a microcosm of the divisions and jealousies within John II's government. Pierre de la Forêt, Archbishop of Rouen, John's long-standing Chancellor was its leading member. There were also Charles of Spain and Robert le Coq, who had hardly a civil thought for each other; the Chamberlain, that acquisitive parvenu Robert de Lorris; the disaffected Guillaume Bertrand, Bishop of Beauvais and the equivocal Jean de Boulogne. Unfortunately almost nothing is known about their discussions except that they were brief and evidently hampered by lack of preparation on both sides. What is clear is that the French made some proposals which were promising enough not to be dismissed out of hand. These must have involved significant territorial concessions to Edward III. They may also have conceded the English King's long-standing demands that whatever he held in France should be held in full sovereignty and not as a vassal of the French Crown. After several sessions it was agreed that because of 'shortage of time and other reasons' it would be necessary to adjourn the conference until 19 May 1353 and to sign a short truce in the meantime. Some attempt was made to ensure that the truce was better observed than its predecessors. The leading ambassadors, including Charles of Spain and the Duke of Lancaster, swore personally that any infringement on their side would be rectified within fourteen days; otherwise they would surrender themselves as prisoners to their enemy. This document was sealed on 10 March 1353. As soon as a copy could be made, a Gascon knight in the garrison of Calais was sent post-haste to Saint-Antonin to carry the news to the Count of Armagnac before the town was forced to surrender.[18]

The news of the truce reached the Count in the third week of March 1353. It was an extremely inconvenient moment. The siege of the town had been in progress for six weeks. Reinforcements had been summoned from distant provinces. Bertrand de Pibrac was presiding over an assembly of the Estates of Languedoc in the little town of Najac a few miles away from the siege in the heart of the region menaced by the Captal de Buch's garrison. Although the Estates had already voted subsidies at the end of the previous year to clear the Gascons from the Rouergue and Quercy, they were persuaded to make new and onerous contributions, payable in April, May and June. But it was a condition of the grant that the proceeds were to be spent on the campaign, and that collection should be suspended immediately if there was a truce. Once again the French had to face the perennial problem that taxpayers lowered their guard in time of truce while the enemy could choose his moment for breaking it. The Count of Armagnac reluctantly complied with the terms agreed at Guines and lifted the siege of Saint-Antonin.[19]

The Duke of Lancaster and his companions returned from Guines to England shortly before Easter, which fell this year on 24 March 1353. Secrecy was hard to achieve in the open halls of medieval courts. Within a month John II was receiving reports from England that Edward III had been unimpressed by his ministers' proposals at Guines and intended to break off further negotiations.[20] Then, at the beginning of May 1353, a letter arrived in Paris from the English ambassadors, explaining that there would be some delay. Edward, they said, had called an enlarged meeting of his Council to consider the proposals which had been made at Guines. Unfortunately, many of those summoned had been ill or unable to attend at short notice, and it had been necessary to put off the meeting until 16 May. It would not therefore be possible for the conference to reconvene on 19 May. They suggested that it should reopen on 25 June instead. This message caused consternation in France, where a meeting of the ambassadors and the principal ministers of the King was summoned to consider it. What happened next is difficult to discover. It is, however, reasonably clear that the proposals made at Guines (whatever they were) had been found highly unpalatable to some people about the court of France. The fact that the King and at least a substantial part of his Council had been persuaded to go along with them was a tribute to the Cardinal's political skills. But there was now a serious danger that the truce would dry up tax revenues and paralyse the French military effort while proposals for peace would lead nowhere. Some of those present at the meeting openly accused Edward III of bad faith. The outcome was a venomous dispute among John II's advisers, followed by an announcement that the French would not attend on the adjourned date which the English ambassadors had suggested. They said nothing about what (if any) date would be acceptable to them, but Guy of Boulogne was very pessimistic. He believed that the French government was no longer willing to participate in his peace conference on whatever date might be found for it. His gloom was entirely justified. The French proclaimed the *arrière-ban* in Normandy on 8 May.[21] They repudiated the truce almost immediately in Saintonge and within six weeks in Languedoc as well.

As Constable, Charles of Spain was responsible for executing these decisions. But it is likely that they also represented his personal preference. He had always been anxious to prosecute the war as vigorously as the government's resources would allow. Shortly after these events several long-standing members of John II's Council withdrew, in some cases permanently. They included Robert le Coq and Guillaume Bertrand, Bishop of Beauvais, both of whom had been among the ambassadors at Guines. There were other councillors who remained at their posts but, like these two, would in due course emerge as allies and advisers of the King of Navarre. Charles of Navarre himself was inscrutable. On 12 May 1353 he celebrated Whitsun with the King, who showered him with gifts. But on the 16th he wrote from Paris to his lieutenants in Pamplona ordering them to send him thirty Navarrese cavalry and 300 infantry to reinforce his garrisons in southern Normandy. This was followed in the next few weeks by demands for several hundred more.[22]

The accusations of bad faith which were levelled against Edward III in Paris were not far from the truth. The conference at Guines and the imminent deadline set for its resumption had forced him to formulate his war aims more precisely, and to discuss them more openly. When Edward's ministers came to recount these events to the Great Council which met in the autumn, they set out the King's ambitions with bleak precision. He wanted to be restored to possession of every part of the duchy of Aquitaine which had ever been held by his ancestors. This meant Saintonge, Angoumois, Poitou, Périgord, the Limousin, Quercy and the Rouergue. In the north he wanted Brittany, Normandy and Flanders and the restoration of the small county of Ponthieu which he had owned before the outbreak of the war. All of these territories were to be his in full sovereignty. In return, he was willing to make a permanent peace and to renounce his claim to the Crown of France. Edward was admittedly prepared to negotiate about Normandy, and in practice probably about Flanders and Brittany as well, but not about any of the other provinces nor about the principle of full sovereignty.[23] He must have known these were unattainable ambitions in 1353. They went far beyond anything that the French can have contemplated at Guines in March and beyond anything that Edward's strategic position in France could justify. He had therefore attempted to withdraw from the Cardinal's conference without openly repudiating it and without losing the benefit of the truce.

The English King might have been more candid with Guy of Boulogne if he had trusted him. But he did not. He thought that the Cardinal was far too close to the French court to serve as mediator. The fact that Guy's elder brother had been among the French ambassadors at Guines spoke for itself. Edward sent his confessor, a Dominican friar called John Woodruff, to Avignon to explain his mind informally to the Pope. He hoped that Innocent might be persuaded to sound out the French King and to discover how much room there was for compromise. Woodruff travelled discreetly through France and arrived in the papal city some time in June 1353. Innocent VI received him, as was his habit during the hot Rhone summers, in his private palace at Villeneuve on the opposite side of the river, away from the din and smell of Avignon, among the cool and spacious mansions of the French Cardinals and the massive fortifications of the French Kings. He listened as the messenger outlined Edward III's proposals for the dismemberment of France. He gave Woodruff no encouragement, but he suppressed his displeasure and forwarded the substance of Edward's message to the King of France for his observations. Sensing part at least of the problem, Innocent also sent Raymond Pelegrini, an Italian curial official who had once served as papal nuncio and collector in England, to make discreet enquiries of Edward III about whether some other mediator would be more acceptable than the Cardinal of Boulogne.

In July 1353 the Pope was able to discuss these matters privately with a more satisfactory messenger than Woodruff, William of Whittleseye. He was Archbishop Islip's nephew and may actually have been with him at Guines. He came to find out how the French King had reacted to Edward's proposals. Innocent replied that it was too soon to expect any reaction, but that he could hardly expect it to be favourable when it came. He pressed the new emissary for his views on how to proceed. Whittleseye mentioned the misgivings which existed in England about the impartiality of the Cardinal of Boulogne. Innocent answered that Guy was a man of such high birth, stature and merit that although one must expect him in the circumstances to love the King of France better than his rival, in this matter only the public interest weighed with him. The Englishman tactfully admitted that this was so. But, he said, Edward had made up his mind on the point and was not going to change it. 'By this conversation', Innocent wrote to Guy of Boulogne, 'you may see how suspicious the English are and how difficult you will find it to bring these negotiations to a successful conclusion without compromising your honour.'[24]

In the southern provinces of John II's kingdom, these deliberations had already been overtaken by events in the field. At the beginning of May

1353 Louis of Harcourt laid siege to Surgères, the fortress-town of northern Saintonge which English raiders had seized earlier in the year. His troops captured the hospital priory of St. Giles in the eastern suburbs of the town and transformed it into a great bastide blocking the road south. In Quercy, the Count of Armagnac had been able to maintain the tensions around him in spite of the truce. Although he had had to lift the siege of Saint-Antonin at the beginning of March, the subsidies voted by the Estates of Languedoc at Najac were collected anyway, and a heavy-handed campaign of recruitment continued throughout April, May and June. When the consuls of Uzès refused to supply crossbowmen, citing the truce among other excuses, Armagnac's commissioners had them all arrested. The Count's army eventually assembled in the last week of June 1353. A few days later he laid siege to Saint-Antonin for the second time. At some stage his men also invested the small castle of Feneyrols on the north bank of the Aveyron some five miles upstream, where the Gascons had established a subsidiary garrison.[25]

In July, as Armagnac was digging himself in around Saint-Antonin and Feneyrols, the French opened a third front in the Limousin. The dioceses of Limoges and Périgueux, which had been among the first to be overrun by *routiers* at the end of the 1340s, had been the scene of regular police campaigns since then. In the autumn of 1352 Arnoul d'Audrehem, the ablest commander among Charles of Spain's protégés, had waged a highly successful campaign against the Anglo-Gascon garrisons of the region, capturing both Nontron and Montbrun, the two places from which the cancer had spread. In July 1353 Arnoul attacked the main surviving Anglo-Gascon stronghold in the Limousin at Comborn. Comborn was the headquarters of the Bascon de Mareuil and by now accommodated a very large garrison. They came out and fought a fierce battle with Audrehem's men outside the main gate of the castle, in which they inflicted heavy losses on the enemy and almost captured their commander. But once they were surrounded and the besiegers dug in around them, it was only a matter of time before the place fell. At the beginning of August 1353 the garrison surrendered on terms. Even then they exacted a heavy price, reported to be 30,000 *écus*, for going away and promising not to raid in the Limousin any more.[26] Even in his moment of triumph a local commander like Arnoul d'Audrehem must have felt that he was rolling the stone of Sisyphus. The disorder was now too general to be dealt with simply by capturing castles. Although the activities of the Anglo-Gascon bands in the Limousin diminished after the fall Comborn, they were too well-rooted in the region to disappear. Excideuil became the headquarters of those who stayed behind. Their range was greatly extended, and towns many miles from the nearest enemy garrison could still find themselves attacked without warning at night, as the small market town of Uzerche did on 30 June 1354. Uzerche was a compact walled town built over a steep spur of land by the River Vezère. It should have been relatively easy to defend. But 'murderers and robbers calling themselves English' came with ladders while the guards were asleep. They climbed over the wall, attacked the gate-keepers from behind and killed them. Then they opened the gates for their fellows. On a Monday night they burnt down the buildings around the public square and plundered the richer houses. On the Tuesday they attacked the monastery, where many of the inhabitants had taken refuge, but failed to capture it. On the Wednesday they burned the whole quarter of the town by the river bridge and then withdrew leaving the streets strewn with corpses including thirty-two of their own number.[27] It was a minor but characteristic incident.

The difficulties of the Limousin were no different from those of other vulnerable provinces of southern and central France. Bands of men fighting under a conveniently loose allegiance to Edward III shifted from place to place, exhausting one district, then turning on another. 'Murderers and robbers calling themselves English' continued to control much of the open country and rode freely through what they did not control. The villages and smaller towns, without garrisons or ramparts to defend them, threw in their lot with the enemy for their own protection while the great towns and cities found themselves isolated within their walls. The town of Agen could stand for many such places. It was an important administrative centre and the main forward base of the French Lieutenants in the Garonne valley. Although its walls were incomplete, it had a considerable royal garrison at most times and it never fell to the English in spite of many attempts. Nevertheless, it depended on the *plat pays* around them for its livelihood, and could not survive in a state of continual half-siege. Agen was in great difficulties in the early 1350s. Most of the villages and castles around it were in the hands of the enemy. The roads were impassable. Men could not harvest their vines without a large armed guard. The municipality could not afford to send a delegation of three men to Paris to describe their predicament to the King without passing a hat around the other towns of the region. Périgueux, which had no royal garrison until 1355, had been in a state of almost permanent siege for several years, as armed bands of Anglo-Gascon soldiers occupied not only castles but mills, barns, manors and church towers for miles about. There were fourteen enemy garrisons in the immediate vicinity of the town according to a petition which the consuls of the town addressed to the King. As a result, the citizens could no longer import the food that they needed for their own tables, let alone to stock their shops and markets. Their suburban gardens, farms and vineyards lay abandoned and uncultivated. Ancient enemies joined hands with newer and more distant ones. In the summer of 1353, the Count of Périgord, who was John II's foremost ally in the province, saw the chance to revive the long-standing vendetta of his family with the citizens of Périgueux. He prowled about the walls threatening violence and destruction, supported by hired companies of soldiers recruited from the partisans of both sides. The problems of Périgueux were reflected in the number of its inhabitants. The city and *bourg*, which had held nearly 2,500 households in the 1330s, had barely 800 in the middle of the 1350s. Although plague contributed something to this fall, the Black Death had been relatively mild in Périgueux. The main cause was the war. The men of Agen and Périgueux regarded their fate as an uncommon catastrophe, but the truth was that John II's ministers were receiving similar tales of indigence and distress all the time.[28]

As the French provincial administration disintegrated and even great walled cities looked vulnerable, Edward III's Council in Bordeaux began to take a greater interest in these regions, which they had hitherto left to freebooters to roam in as they pleased. Comborn, although it had originally been captured in a private venture of the Bascon de Mareuil, was defended at the end by a garrison which included Élie de Pommiers, Arnaud Amanieu d'Albret and several companies from the Bordelais. These were men closely associated with the ducal government who had played a prominent part in the defence of English strongholds in the Dordogne valley. Not long after the castle surrendered, Élie de Pommiers was appointed as Edward III's Seneschal in the three provinces of Périgord, Limousin and Quercy, the first time for nearly thirty years that the English government thought it worth having such an officer.[29]

Although the truce made at Guines in March 1353 had been a dead letter since May, on 26 July the English and French ambassadors duly met in Paris and went through the motions of extending it until November. No one could afford to disarm themselves, and the sieges of Surgères and Saint-Antonin continued as if nothing had happened. The fighting degenerated into an unconnected series of local wars fought by local commanders and settled by cease-fire agreements negotiated on the spot. At the end of September 1353 the garrison of Saint-Antonin finally abandoned the place to the Count of Armagnac and marched away under the protection of a safe-conduct. Surgères fell to the French in November. Shortly afterwards Louis of Harcourt met the English Seneschal at Libourne and agreed a local truce for Saintonge which was more or less observed. All across the march of Gascony walled towns and castles in the obedience of the French made their own arrangements with English commanders, paying what money they could afford in order to be left in peace during the autumn harvest. After exhaustion and winter had brought the campaigns to an end the ambassadors of the two realms gathered once more at Guines. On 3 December 1353 they extended the truce until the end of April 1354. They agreed to meet again in March. That was all.[30]

In Paris John II's ministers found their efforts to contain the spreading disorder hindered by financial crisis and administrative paralysis, and by growing divisions among themselves. Charles of Navarre withdrew to his domains in Normandy during the summer in order to complete his military plans. By the end of the year he had at least 600 Navarrese troops crammed into his castles at Évreux, Meulan and Mantes. He was also recruiting within France. A number of disaffected noblemen, gang leaders and soldiers of fortune had joined him. One of them was none other than the Bascon de Mareuil, captor of Comborn and Loudun. Another was Rabigot Dury, who was to become famous at the end of the 1350s as the ravager of Champagne and the Île de France, and was probably an Englishman. Messengers passed between Évreux and Navarre engaged in what Charles' officials laconically called 'difficult and secret matters'. How secret Charles' plans really were is difficult to say. He was very candid with his retainers. 'I want your help against a man with whom I have a quarrel,' he told the French captain of Caen as they rode after hares in the fields by the Eure. Rumours of Charles' activities had evidently reached England by the autumn. The Duke of Lancaster wrote to him suggesting that he might look to him for support if he needed it. In France, tensions were high. Everyone knew that the King of Navarre was planning some stroke against the government of John II. It was even thought that he might be about to make war in Burgundy, in alliance with the King of England and the rebellious nobility of Franche-Comté. Garrisons were being reinforced to meet this threat in December. In Paris there were signs of a belated attempt to placate the King's hot-headed young son-in-law. Robert le Coq returned to the Council at the end of the year. So did some of Charles' other friends. But the King of Navarre had already decided upon his course.[31]

Shortly before Christmas 1353 Charles and his younger brother Philip went to Paris, where the King was due to celebrate the festival with his friends including Charles of Spain. They told their confederates before they left that they intended to pick a quarrel. When the two brothers arrived, they exchanged 'gross insults' with the Constable in the presence of the King. Philip of Navarre was an impulsive and reckless young man of easy violence, unlike his more calculating elder brother. He advanced on the Constable with a dagger. John gripped Philip's arm and separated them. 'How then, good cousin,' John said; 'would you draw weapons in my chamber?' About a fortnight later, on 7 January 1354, Charles of Spain was travelling unescorted through southern Normandy with Jean de Melun, Count of Tancarville. They stopped for the night at an inn in l'Aigle, a small town on the River Risle not far from the King of Navarre's principal residence at Évreux. Soon after dawn on 8 January, the inn was surrounded by armed men. Philip of Navarre went in with John, Count of Harcourt, the Bascon de Mareuil, Rabigot Dury and a band of Norman squires and Navarrese soldiers. They burst into the Constable's room with lighted torches and found him naked in his bed. 'Charles of Spain,' the Prince of Navarre said; 'I am Philip, son of a King, whom you have foully slandered.' According to one account, Charles fell on his knees and begged for Philip's mercy. He promised him his weight in gold. He said that he would abandon all his lands and leave the realm never to return. But the Bascon de Mareuil and Rabigot Dury set upon him with four troopers and plunged their swords into him. When, later in the day, the Countess of Alencon sent her servants out from Verneuil to bury the body, they found eighty wounds in it.[32]

At the time of the murder the King of Navarre was outside the town in the fields by the road from Verneuil with a large company of Norman noblemen and Navarrese troops. 'It is done!', the Bascon de Marueil shouted, as he rode out towards them from the gate. The news must have come as a shock to some of Charles' companions, for he had been putting it about that the plan was to take the Constable alive. He adeptly turned their dismay to his advantage. Gathering his followers around him in the fields he told them that they were all accomplices now. But they could defend themselves together. For his part, he would accept no pardon from the King unless they were all included. After these hurried exchanges, Charles rode back to the castle of Évreux. Here he was joined by many of the leading men of the province: the Count of Harcourt; Harcourt's brother Louis who had recently commanded the armies of John II in Saintonge; his uncle Godfrey, the old conspirator; the lords of Hambye and Graville and their retainers; the King's former councillor Amaury de Meulan; and many others. Even if this was not the 'whole nobility of Normandy' as Charles boasted a few days afterwards, it was a substantial part of it, including many men whom John II might have expected to find on his own side at such a moment.[33]

Charles of Navarre made no attempt to conceal his own role in the murder or to pass off responsibility on anyone else. During the following week messengers left Évreux with letters addressed to the University of Paris, the Pope, several foreign princes, all the councillors of the King of France and the principal towns of his realm, asking for their support. 'Know then', he wrote, 'that. . . it was I who ordered the death of Charles of Spain. . . If the King is angered by what I have done, then I am sorry. But I say that when he has reflected on it a while he should rejoice at being rid of such evil counsel.' He said that he had been moved by the great evils which Charles of Spain had brought upon the realm and by the calumnies which the Constable had directed against himself and his closest kinsmen. He had acted for the 'common good of the realm', and he called upon the communities of France to support him in his endeavour. Charles was arrogant, but he was also shrewd and well advised. These letters would not have been written unless there was a solid groundswell of support for his actions. At the French court the distress of the King and the horror of his ministers paralysed the work of the government. John himself did not utter a word for four days after the news arrived. Then, on 13 January 1354, when he had recovered his composure, he sent a deputation consisting of the Count of Vendôme, Geoffrey de Charny and Robert de Lorris to attend on the King of Navarre at Évreux and hear his version of events. Charles' answer was defiant. 'I was there,' he said; 'I had it done.'[34]

Within a few days of the Constable's death Charles of Navarre had made contact with the English. He addressed his first letters to Henry of Lancaster, whom he had met in Paris in the previous year. Writing on 10 January 1354 Charles related with chilling candour the death of his rival and the reasons which had led him to order it. He explained the grave peril in which he now stood from the Constable's allies and dependents and from the vengeance from the King of France. In such an extremity, he said, he was learning to recognise his true friends, 'and especially you in whom I have the greatest confidence'. He enclosed a letter to Edward III and another to the Prince of Wales, which the Duke was asked to forward to them if he judged it appropriate. What Charles wanted was that the English King should send men-at-arms and archers urgently to Calais and Guines, where they could hold themselves ready to come to his aid when he gave the word. Failing that, he wanted troops placed at his disposal from the garrisons of Brittany. A week later, on 18 January 1354, Charles renewed his appeal with fresh urgency. He reported the mission of the Count of Vendôme. He told the Duke that he was receiving news from well-placed sympathisers in Paris. This was probably a reference to Robert de Lorris, the King's conspiratorial Chamberlain, who owed almost everything to John's favour but found it convenient in an unstable world to keep in with his enemies as well. From this source he had learned that the King was planning a military campaign to seize him and his domains. Charles professed to have no doubt about the outcome. Every Norman nobleman would live and die beside him, he said.[35]

In spite of their urgent tone and oleaginous professions of friendship, these were tricky letters. If Charles of Navarre had really wanted the English to send troops into Normandy he would have approached them earlier, and he would have asked for them to be sent at once, not held in readiness on the marches of Calais and Brittany. His real purpose was to increase the pressure on his father-in-law so as to get a better settlement. This basic ambiguity in the King of Navarre's position persisted throughout the long and chequered history of his dealings with the English. Charles was a prince of France. His claims to lands and dignities were pressed with persistence and sometimes with violence. But they were pressed in the course of what remained for all its acidity a family quarrel. In the last resort it could never be in his interest to destroy the house of Valois or to dismember France in the cause of England, and it was only in brief moments of intense frustration that he can ever seriously have contemplated such a thing. Besides, Charles never forgot that if the King of England had a good claim to the crown of France then he himself had a better one. His brother Philip learned to fight alongside the English and to serve their interests as if they were his own. But Philip was a rasher spirit and a less astute politician. For Charles himself, the English were tactical allies to be used in moments of need but never to be served.

Much of this might have been read between the lines of Charles' letters to Henry of Lancaster. But Henry took them at face value. He saw in the King of Navarre what Edward III had once seen in Robert of Artois, in John de Montfort and in the urban oligarchies of Flanders. Charles' messengers found the Duke of Lancaster in Brabant, where he was engaged in the tortuous resolution of a family quarrel among the ruling families of Hainault and Holland. Henry could see the opportunities in France's new troubles. But there was very little that he could do, and nothing quickly. His plan, when the immediate business was done, was to travel on to the court of Savoy to make trouble for France along her eastern border. He had only a small diplomatic retinue with him and a handful of his household troops. Moreover, his authority to commit the English government was very limited. The truce was still in force and Lancaster had sworn personally to observe it. So he forwarded the King of Navarre's letters to England. Then he sent one of his servants, Walter Bintree, to Évreux to explain his difficulties to the King of Navarre and to reassure him that in spite of the deliberate pace of events his request was being taken seriously. Bintree was to tell Charles that the Duke would be at Bruges on 7 or 8 February 1354. It was essential that he should send someone there with full powers to negotiate on his behalf. When the Duke of Lancaster received Charles' second appeal for help, a few days after Bintree had left, he redoubled his efforts to obtain a quick decision from Westminster. It would be necessary for him to return to England, he wrote back to Charles on 26 January 1354, which he would do as soon as he had been able to discuss the situation with Charles' agents in Bruges. This need not cause delay. He could return to Calais in less time than it would take to send troops there. Meanwhile Charles should on no account trust the 'fair words' which would doubtless be proffered by his enemies in order to disarm him.[36]

In England Edward III had papers prepared at great speed enlarging the Duke of Lancaster's powers so as to allow him to conclude an alliance with the King of Navarre. Michael Northburgh, the keeper of Edward's privy seal, prepared a draft which indicated what kind of treaty the King's councillors had in mind. This document, which referred to the principals by code names, showed what illusions had been generated at Westminster by the prospect of a fresh civil war in France. What was proposed was nothing less than a partition of the realm between Edward III and Charles of Navarre. Edward would promise to mount a seaborne invasion of Normandy. There, he would join forces with the King of Navarre, march on Paris, and have himself crowned King of France at Reims. As for Charles, he would receive as his reward the whole of Normandy, Brie and Champagne, and in the south virtually all of Languedoc together with a lump sum payment from the French treasury of 100,000 *écus*.[37]

Early in February 1354, two groups of emissaries from Évreux made their way by separate routes to Flanders. As soon as they reached Bruges, the leaders of the delegation, Thomas de Ladit, Chancellor of Navarre, and the Norman knight Friquet de Fricamps, were conducted to the Duke of Lancaster's presence in his lodgings at the port of Damme. More than two years later, when Friquet was under interrogation in the Châtelet, he described the scene which followed. Henry of Lancaster gave them a magnificent meal. He told them about his plans to travel on to Savoy, and pointed out a Savoyard knight in his entourage who was to accompany him. He expatiated on how much John II had loved Charles of Spain, how terrible would be his revenge and how much Charles stood in need of England's help. He told Friquet de Fricamps that he would make him 'as good an Englishman as he had previously been a Frenchman'. Perhaps Friquet did not reply (as he claimed to have done) that he could 'never serve the King of England'. But there is little doubt that Charles' ambassadors had come to receive promises and not to give them. They encouraged Lancaster to carry on his preparations, but they refused to be drawn into any formal commitment of their own. The Duke urged them to return with him to England to draw up plans with Edward's ministers. He drew Thomas de Ladit aside and spoke to him privately in a window opening. But he could not persuade him to come. At the end of the meeting Lancaster gave the two men a document in which he gave his personal undertaking to fight for Charles against anyone except Edward III himself and the Prince of Wales. The Duke could not commit his master, he explained, but he was sure that Edward would be willing to send 200 men-at-arms and 500 archers if they were needed. The emissaries listened, and withdrew.[38]

In fact Edward was preparing to raise an even larger army. Orders had already been given to recruit 500 men-at-arms and a 1,000 archers in England. Since no commissions of array were issued in the counties, these must have been drawn entirely from the royal household and the retinues of the nobility. A general requisition of merchant shipping was ordered in all ports from Lynn to Plymouth on 1 February 1354, as soon as Lancaster's report was received in England. On 18 February

1354 the King's ships were mobilised. The plan was to gather the whole armada together at Southampton in time to sail for Normandy early in March. This was an ambitious timetable. But the English ministers were plainly serious about it. At about the beginning of March Henry of Lancaster returned to London to take control of the preparations in person.[39]

While his representatives flirted inconclusively with the Duke of Lancaster at Bruges, the King of Navarre was already listening to 'fair words' from the agents of John II. It is not clear how much the French King knew about Charles' dealings with the Duke of Lancaster, but it is hardly conceivable that Charles had not let him know somehow or other. For whatever reason John moved in less than a month from schemes of violent revenge to abject surrender. This was in part the work of those two indulgent ladies, Charles' aunt the dowager Queen Joan and his sister the dowager Queen Blanche. But there is every reason to believe that the man who was chiefly responsible for the King's change of heart was the Cardinal of Boulogne. Guy had been drawn to the young King of Navarre and his friends during his long stay at the French court. He had no doubt identified the dead Constable as the main opponent of peace within the French government. But his strongest motive was to save the peace conference which he had convened with so much difficulty the year before and whose continuance was the main purpose of his presence in northern France. At the time of the Constable's murder, the delegates were due to meet again either at Guines in March or at Avignon in late April. Negotiations to fix the venue and the agenda were continuing as the dramas of l'Aigle and Évreux unfolded. In Avignon the Pope received Charles of Navarre's personal physician, and responded with remarkable complaisance to his account of the murder of the Constable. He was sorry to learn that the Constable's behaviour had caused offence, he wrote to Charles; he hoped that the young Prince would now conduct himself with that humility and discretion which became his high birth. To John II he counselled patience and restraint. Innocent's motives, and very probably his words, were those of the Cardinal of Boulogne.[40]

Weakened by the loss of his closest friend and adviser, brought under intense pressure by the Church, and guided by councillors several of whom were in league with the King of Navarre, John II resolved to make peace with his son-in-law. On 8 February 1354 he appointed the Cardinal of Boulogne and the Duke of Bourbon as his commissioners and empowered them to offer Charles everything that he wanted.

Immediately after their appointment these two men set out from Paris down the valley of the Seine to negotiate with the King of Navarre in his great castle at Mantes. They were accompanied by a throng of courtiers and ministers including Robert le Coq and Robert de Lorris, who sympathized with Charles of Navarre more strongly than they cared to admit. They were joined at Mantes by the two dowager Queens. Their high rank allowed them to be quite open about their sympathies: in their eyes Charles could do little wrong.

In the midst of the discussions the King of Navarre found time to write to Henry of Lancaster. He addressed him 'as a son to a father', and offered him soothing half-truths about what was happening. The talks were dragging on, he said. The King's councillors were being very difficult, and his commanders were putting men-at-arms into all the castles of the region around. Henry was urged to press on with the preparations for his campaign but to put back his arrival in France by a few days to allow the conference at Mantes to come to an end. Within a fortnight the Duke would be receiving news in London which he would find most reassuring. The truth was that with instructions as wide as he had and sympathies as strong, Guy of Boulogne had no difficulty in reaching agreement with the King of Navarre. By 22 February 1354 a treaty was concluded which met all of Charles' objectives and made him a considerable territorial power in northern France. Charles surrendered the paltry compensation which his mother had received for the county of Angoulême, and accepted instead the county of Beaumont-le-Roger, Breteuil and Conches, the viscounty of Pont-Audemer and the whole of the Cotentin peninsula in addition to the towns of Mantes, Meulan and Évreux which he already held by inheritance from his father. These provisions gave the King of Navarre a concentrated domain extending across much of Lower Normandy which he was to hold 'as nobly' as the Duke of Normandy himself, with his own courts and administration. Charles' new territories were strategically situated between France's capital and her main foreign enemy. They also generated a substantial income, nominally 37,000 *livres* a year, in practice probably not much less. When added to the resources of Navarre it was enough to finance private war on a considerable scale. The French King promised that in due course he would make a further grant of land representing the magnificent dowry which he had promised when Charles had married his daughter. As for the murder at l'Aigle, letters of remission were promised pardoning Charles himself, his brothers and all his confederates for the death of the Constable.

According to one source Charles of Navarre promised to endow numerous chapels at which masses would be said for the repose of the Constable's soul. But if this is so, the promise was made informally and then forgotten.[41]

What John II really thought about the behaviour of his son-in-law is difficult to say, for he kept it to himself. On 4 March 1354 there was a curious and tense reconciliation between the two men in the Great Chamber of the Parlement in Paris. The whole royal Council was present as well as several peers of France and the Cardinal of Boulogne. The King, who had had to send his son Louis of Anjou to Évreux as a hostage for Charles' safety, listened in silence as the King of Navarre asked to be pardoned for the murder of the Constable even though he had had 'good and just cause to do the deed, which cause he would declare to the King then and there, or at some other time as he might prefer'. It was left to the two dowager Queens, Joan and Blanche, to beg the King for his mercy and promise that Charles would henceforth bear himself as a loyal vassal. The words of pardon were pronounced by the Cardinal. He delivered a short address pointing out that Charles was of John's blood, his vassal, his son-in-law and a peer of his realm, and that although never a man so close to the throne had done such a deed, yet he had done it by unworthy counsel and deserved to be forgiven. When the Cardinal had finished the King and his court rose from their seats without a word and left.[42]

Charles of Navarre had already written to pass on the glad news to Henry of Lancaster and Edward III. The two Queens had laboured mightily for a reconciliation, he explained, and the King of France had been most reasonable. The resulting agreement had been highly satisfactory. And, while Charles was grateful for the assistance which the English had offered, they must now cut off their enterprise. 'We would not wish that any violence should be done on our account.' Besides, he added, all the ports of Normandy had now been filled with troops, ships and supplies, especially those where the French King's ministers considered that the English were likely to attempt a landing. By the time Henry of Lancaster received this message, the news that he had been duped had already been broken to him by the Cardinal of Boulogne. The hole by which Henry had planned to enter France had been sealed, the Cardinal had written. Henry did not trouble to conceal his irritation. He was 'astounded', he wrote to Charles of Navarre, that he should reach agreement with the King of France so soon after appealing to him for troops, and could only hope that when his hour of need came he would find other friends as willing to help him as Henry had been. To Guy of Boulogne Lancaster wrote a bitter little letter. There were 'other holes which you cannot block for all your clever ways', he said. Perhaps, the Cardinal replied with gloating sarcasm, the Duke of Lancaster would be just as fortunate in his allies if he ever took it into his head to murder one of the closest friends of Edward III: he should try it one day.[43]

The treaty of Mantes was a grave embarrassment for the English. But it did not alter the essential strategic predicament of the French government, which was severely overstretched financially and no longer capable of governing the southern and western provinces of the realm. In one sense the fiasco strengthened England's hand. It tilted the balance in the French King's Council in favour of those who were prepared to make peace even at the price of large sacrifices of territory. Ever since the first discussions of such a compromise, at Guines in March 1353, those most closely associated with it had been the friends of Charles of Navarre. Once John II was persuaded to reach an accommodation with him, their influence grew mightily. It was these men who joined the French King's embassy as it made its way across the marsh of Guines to meet the English at the traditional meeting place north of the town: Robert le Coq, and the Chamberlain Robert de Lorris, equivocal politicians who had both been at Mantes; Guillaume Bertrand, Bishop of Beauvais; and two minor lay councillors, the lords of Roucy and Châtillon, all trimmers of uncertain allegiance. Only the president of the embassy, John II's long-standing Chancellor Pierre de la Forêt, was unambiguously loyal to him.

Although the conference did not formally open until the beginning of April 1354 it is clear that intense negotiations were already in progress during the last ten days of March. By the time the formal sessions began, the ambassadors had already reached agreement on the principle of exchanging Edward III's claim to the Crown of France for territory. On 30 March 1354 at Westminster Edward formally empowered his representatives to agree to this. Only the extent of the territory to be ceded remained in dispute. On 6 April 1354, in the presence of the Cardinal of Boulogne, the diplomats sealed two agreements. The first was an extension of the truce for a year, until 1 April 1355. This was fairly uncontroversial. The second was a permanent treaty of peace. By this remarkable document the French agreed to transfer to Edward III in full sovereignty the whole of the duchy of Aquitaine as it existed in

1323 on the eve of the war of Saint-Sardos, together with Poitou and the Limousin, and the Loire provinces of Maine, Anjou and Touraine: in summary, the whole of western France south of Normandy, with the exception of the duchy of Brittany. In addition Edward III was to retain the town and district of Calais. Edward for his part agreed to make peace and to renounce his claim to be King of France. The terms were to be published by the Pope at Avignon on 1 October 1354 in the presence of the ambassadors of the two realms, who were thereupon to make the solemn and public renunciations of rights and territories for which the treaty provided. Any dispute which might arise as to the precise extent of the territories ceded was to be settled by arbitration before the Pope (acting in his private capacity) before the end of the year.[44]

Although he refrained from saying so too loudly, Edward III was delighted by the outcome of the conference. In the middle of May, as Parliament was concluding its business at Westminster and preparing to disperse, Edward's Chamberlain Bartholomew Burghersh called the lords and Commons before him in the Palace of Westminster. He did not tell them what had been agreed at Guines. But he had said that there was 'every hope, God willing, of a lasting and honourable peace', and he asked them to approve whatever terms might be agreeable to the King and the Lords. 'And with one voice,' the clerk recorded, 'the Commons answered Yes! Yes!.' The King even tried to bring forward the date fixed for the meeting at Avignon, at which the treaty was to be confirmed. An advance party left London for the papal city on 20 May 1354, soon after Parliament had given its approval. Arrangements were made for 'prelates and barons' to follow via Bordeaux at the end of June, more than three months before the appointed date. Preparations for their departure were made with so much bustle that the Cardinal of Boulogne protested that the English were in danger of letting the secret out.[45]

While Edward III contained his impatience, his ministers went to great lengths to ensure that the truce was observed and that the achievements of his ambassadors were not spoiled by the rash acts of a few soldiers and brigands. All reprisals against French property at sea were absolutely forbidden. The march of Calais fell silent. A promising campaign in Saintonge was halted on 20 April 1354, within a few days of proclamation of the truce in the region. Exceptional measures were taken to enforce discipline on the garrison commanders of the south-west. During the summer John Streatley, the Constable of Bordeaux, and Bertrand de Montferrand, the former captain of Lusignan and despoiler of Poitou, toured the border areas exacting solemn undertakings to observe the truce and paying money to local commanders who were willing to give penal bonds for their good behaviour. It is not clear what steps were taken beyond the border areas, but there can be no doubt that some were. For although there were some minor incidents (such as the attack on Uzerche in June 1354), by and large even the independent castellans operating in Quercy, Périgord and the Limousin were brought under a brief and tenuous measure of control never achieved before or after.[46]

Brittany looked at one point as it might present a more serious obstacle to peace. The English Lieutenants' difficulties in controlling the garrisons there dwarfed even those of the Seneschal of Gascony. They had come to a head only a few months earlier when Edward III, having made an extremely advantageous treaty with Charles of Blois found himself quite unable to implement it in the face of opposition from the independent garrisons operating in the province. Since the terms provided for a general restitution of property to those who had owned it before the civil war, they were threatened with the loss of their conquests and their livelihood. John Avenel, the rather ineffectual Lieutenant whom Edward sent out to the duchy in April 1353, found his orders disregarded even when they were supported by explicit commands from the King. Foremost among the recalcitrants was Avenel's immediate predecessor Walter Bentley. He held several castles in his own right, including the important island fortress of Tristan in the Bay of Douarnenez, and he would not surrender any of them. Bentley himself made the mistake of going to England to argue his case before the King, as a result of which he was arrested and incarcerated in the Tower of London. The other captains simply sat tight and breathed defiance. In July 1353 the Council considered the situation with a group of Breton noblemen and officials, but there was nothing that they could do about it except send a commissioner to Brittany to talk to the captains and ask their 'causes and reasons'. The circumstances did not augur well for Edward's ability to make a lasting peace, even on terms that suited him.[47]

Before long Charles of Blois, who had returned to the duchy on parole, lost patience. In September, some men of his entourage surprised the castle of Tristan in the west of the peninsula and slaughtered the English garrison which was holding it. Charles' own role in this incident was obscure, but Edward may not have taken too much trouble to investigate it. He was grateful for an excuse to abandon a treaty which had become an embarrassment. Charles of Blois returned to custody in England.[48] In November, it was decided to relieve Avenel and replace him with the redoubtable Sir Thomas Holland. In the following year the King began to confirm the title of some of the principal English captains. Even Bentley was eventually released from prison and allowed to resume his acquisitive career.[49]

It was only a matter of time before the problems of Brittany spilled over into the rest of western France. Throughout the conference at Guines there was fierce fighting in the north-east corner of the duchy between the French Marshal, Arnoul d'Audrehem, and Hugh Calveley's garrison at Bécherel. The sequence of attack and counter-attack proved extremely difficult to stop when the truce was made. On 10 April 1354, four days after it was sealed, there was a bloody encounter between the dismounted cavalry of each side near the great castle of the lords of Tinténiac at Montmuran in which Calveley himself was captured and his men suffered heavy losses. According to tradition Bertrand du Guesclin, the hero of a later and more fortunate generation of French soldiers, received his knighthood at this battle. At almost the same moment Sir Thomas Holland arrived in the duchy to take up his appointment, bringing with him a large retinue of fresh troops. Holland had been firmly instructed to observe the truce. But he was an aggressive commander who had won a famous reputation at Caen and Crécy. He was almost immediately drawn into Calveley's war. Faced with the prospect that the English positions around Bécherel might fall, Holland hired the services of Martin Henriquez, the Navarrese captain who commanded Charles of Navarre's troops in Normandy. Martin had time on his hands now that his master had made peace with the King of France. So he marched with Holland into north-eastern Brittany, and in May invaded Lower Normandy, burning part of the suburbs of Caen and Bayeux. It was not until June that this self-contained campaign was brought to an end and the chivalry of both sides turned to fighting each other in the lists in a succession of spectacular and lethal tournaments on the marches of Normandy.[50]

The terms of the treaty of Guines were kept secret for several months after it was made. It is not hard to see why. The treaty conceded substantially all the war aims of Edward III as he had outlined them to the English Parliament in the previous year. Only Normandy, which he had admitted was negotiable, was missing from the list of provinces to be ceded to him. Indeed if the treaty had ever been ratified, it would have given the English King more than he was able to get in 1360, when the King of France was his prisoner, his troops had ravaged every province of the realm, and his army had been within sight of the walls of Paris. The French King's ministers knew as well as anyone how controversial such a bargain would be once the news broke. Guy of Boulogne, for whom it represented the culmination of eight months of labouring in the barren vineyard of Anglo-French diplomacy, believed that its premature disclosure would be 'more dangerous to the cause of peace than anything in world'.[51] The Cardinal's fears about the controversy which the treaty would arouse were quickly justified.

The Count of Armagnac emerged at an early stage as a potential opponent. He had never had much sympathy for the peacemakers and compromisers on John II's Council. He had also made elaborate preparations for a summer campaign in the south-west. Guy of Boulogne, who was apprehensive about what Armagnac would do if left to himself, took it upon himself to summon him to Paris to receive his orders from the King in person, an act of officious meddling which caused a certain amount of resentment among ministers. John's orders, which in the end were delivered by messenger, were to observe the truce provided that the English did.[52] In the event Armagnac neither came to Paris nor observed the truce. In May 1354 he embarked on a campaign of raids and sieges in the Agenais which would have aroused more protest if it had achieved anything. The Count's troops sat outside Aiguillon for almost a month until they were driven off by Sir John Cheverston. He took a force of mounted troops from the Bordelais round by the north and threatened the French army from the rear. Armagnac seems to have withdrawn rather than risk battle. Towards the end of June the Count attacked Lusignan-Grand on the north bank of the Garonne, but failed to take it. An attempt to capture Madaillan ended in humiliating chaos, when the Italian bowmen and the French infantry in his army fell out and fought a pitched battle against each other under the astonished eyes of the garrison. The solitary successes of this campaign were the extremely expensive acquisition of Beauville and some neighbouring castles on the borders of Agenais and Quercy. Their garrisons were bought over, but they drove a hard bargain. Armagnac eventually had to pay them 20,000 *écus*.[53]

In the middle of April 1354, a few days after the treaty of Guines had been made, the French King summoned an assembly of the principal noblemen and towns of the realm, which must have met at about the end of May. It is not clear how much they were told or what they advised, but the King was probably no more candid with them than Edward III had been with Parliament. The gyrations of French policy are wrapped in embarrassed and conspiratorial silence. By the end of the summer, however, opinion was clearly hardening against the treaty. In August, there was a decisive shift within the royal Council, but only the public symptoms of it are known. John, Count of Harcourt, and his brother and uncle, who had been the leading supporters of Charles of Navarre among the nobility of Normandy, came to make their peace with the King. They apparently told him the whole story of the planning of the Constable's murder. They implicated several of the King's closest counsellors. These included men who had been intimately involved in advising the King and in negotiating the treaties of Mantes and Guines. According to more or less informed gossip at court, Robert de Lorris had known in advance of the plot against the Constable. He had also disclosed to Charles of Navarre the deliberations of the King's Council after it had happened. Robert fled to Avignon within a few days of the Harcourts' revelations and took refuge at the papal court. Guy of Boulogne was probably accused of nothing more than over-indulgence of the King of Navarre and his supporters, but he too withdrew from court in disgrace at about the end of August and made for Avignon some days afterwards. Robert le Coq was not accused of anything, but he had been as closely associated as anyone with the diplomacy of the past six months. He left the Council at about the same time. He was probably dismissed. In the reaction which followed the King of France seems to have concluded that both the treaty of Mantes with Charles of Navarre and the treaty of Guines with Edward III had both been the work of disloyal schemers working against his interests. His instinct was encouraged by the survivors on his Council. They included several men who had been present on both occasions, but none who cared to acknowledge their part. At some point in the autumn, probably in early September, the King and his advisers secretly resolved to repudiate both treaties.[54]

While these eruptions were in progress in Paris, an enormous English embassy began to leave for Avignon. Michael Northburgh left with the first group and a great quantity of muniments and baggage on 29 August 1354. Four senior members of Edward III's Council in Bordeaux travelled directly from Gascony, including the lord of Albret. On 4 October 1354 Bishop Bateman followed with the next party. The last of the ambassadors to leave were the most important of them, the Duke of Lancaster and the Earl of Arundel. On 31 October 1354 the royal Council met in the private chapel of the palace of Westminster to draw up their instructions. The two noblemen were commanded to inform the Pope that Edward would renounce his claim to the Crown of France provided that the treaty which his representatives had agreed at Guines was confirmed and that satisfactory arrangements were made about the precise boundaries of the territory which the French were to cede. This was evidently thought to be the only potential source of controversy. There was some concern about the provinces of Angoumois and Quercy, which had not been specifically mentioned at Guines and might, on one view, be thought to lie outside the limits of the old duchy of Aquitaine. Since these provinces were important for the defence of the duchy, the ambassadors were to press hard for their inclusion among the ceded territories, but not so hard as to imperil the whole treaty. They were also to claim Normandy but only, it seems, for the purpose of giving it up in exchange for concessions elsewhere. In the last resort, if they could not reach agreement with the French ambassadors about the precise metes and bounds of the ceded territories, they were to leave them to the adjudication of the Pope. Edward was anxious to consolidate his advantages. If possible the whole business was to be completed by April 1355. In the last week of November 1354 Lancaster and Arundel crossed the Channel to Calais accompanied by an army of soldiers, servants and clerks, 500 horsemen all told, in addition to the escorts sent by the King of France to see to the observance of their safe-conducts. As they made their magnificent way across France the political situation was transformed.[55]

The first signs of the French Council's more aggressive policy were already emerging in the south-west. Jean de Clermont, who had succeeded Guy de Nesle as a Marshal, was appointed as John II's Lieutenant in the western provinces between the Loire and Dordogne. Clermont was a practised courtier, one of a generation of French commanders who readily found common interests with Englishmen of their own class. Here was a man who, the year before, could make a private visit to England to pursue a ransom and be splendidly entertained at Westminster by Edward III and his ministers while French armies fought Edward's subjects in Saintonge and the Rouergue. He had 'polite society in the palm of his hand', according to the Knight of la Tour Landry. But he was a soldier of very limited talent. At the end of that month he invaded the English-occupied territory on the north shore of the Gironde and attacked the important garrison towns of Libourne and Saint-Emilion. This enterprise came to nothing. But not long afterwards the English delegation at Avignon began to receive reports of a substantial build-up of troops in the French garrisons of the south-west march. They were the prelude to more menacing operations.[56]

Relations between the King of Navarre and his father-in-law became progressively cooler, and by October broke down altogether. Charles believed that the King was planning to arrest him. Since he had many well-placed friends to tell him what was happening at court, he was probably right about this. He sent one of his confidential servants to Avignon to ask the Pope to intercede for him in Paris and, when that made no difference, he resolved to go to Avignon himself. He left at the beginning of November and, after making an erratic path through the French provinces to evade the King's agents, he arrived in the papal city in the first ten days of December 1354. Charles may have calculated that the French King would not dare to attack him while he was at the papal court, particularly when he was so well-placed to intrigue with Edward III's agents there. If so, he underestimated John's new-found resolution. At the end of November 1354 the French King pronounced the forfeiture of all Charles of Navarre's domains in France. He gave as his reason Charles' departure from the realm without leave. Troops were sent into Normandy at once to take possession of the confiscated lands. The King travelled to Caen to supervise the operation himself. Most places surrendered without striking a blow, as they were commanded to do. Only six held out for the King of Navarre: Évreux and Pont-Audemer, and the citadels of Cherbourg, Avranches, Gavray and Mortain in the Cotentin peninsula. They were all garrisoned by Navarrese troops who cared nothing for the authority of the King of France and were immovable in the face of his officers. They declared that they would answer to no one but their master.[57]

The Duke of Lancaster and the Earl of Arundel arrived at Avignon with their company shortly after Christmas 1354. They were met two miles from the city by an impressive delegation of cardinals, bishops and officials. A ceremonial cortège of 200 riders led by thirty-two fully caparisoned horses escorted them across the great stone bridge over the Rhone, watched by a throng so great that the bridge had been impassable all day. But when Lancaster and his companions reached their lodgings in the city, they found the rest of the English embassy despondent and demoralised. William Bateman was dying. Although he had been in the papal city for about two months and Michael Northburgh for nearly three, they had been able to transact virtually no diplomatic business. No ambassadors had arrived from the King of France and no explanation had been offered for the delay. The English agents drew their own conclusions from scraps of information reaching them from the retinues of the French Cardinals and fugitives from the north, magnified by the rumour and gossip of the papal city. The King of Navarre had been received by Innocent VI on his arrival in the presence of the whole College of Cardinals and had dined privately with the Pope at least twice. He was reported to be hiding in the palace of one of the French cardinals, where he was engaged in long consultations with Guy of Boulogne and Robert de Lorris. The transactions of England and France seemed to have receded into the background. 'They say that some of those who were previously concerned in these negotiations are not so much in favour with their King as they once were,' one of the English agents reported to Edward III at the end of December; 'for which reason the rest have found their interest in making peace much diminished.'[58]

In Paris John II passed much of the month of January and the early part of February closeted with his military advisers: the Constable Jacques de Bourbon, the two Marshals Arnoul d'Audrehem and Jean de Clermont, and the Count of Armagnac. They began to plan the resumption of the war on a large scale. There was to be a sustained campaign against the English in Gascony during the summer. The rest of Charles of Navarre's lands in Normandy were to be occupied. And an ambitious new venture was planned in Scotland. The Duke of Lancaster's instructions, drawn up at Westminster in confident ignorance three months before, were a dead letter.[59]

The embassy of the King of France finally arrived in Avignon in about the middle of January 1355. Its leading members were the Chancellor Pierre de la Forêt and the Duke of Bourbon (elder brother of the Constable). They had nothing to offer. As soon as the conference opened the English called on their opponents to ratify the treaty of Guines. They were supported by the Cardinal of Boulogne, who confirmed the terms of the treaty and related the promises which both parties had made to ratify it at Avignon. But the French would have none of this. They rejected outright the idea that Aquitaine or any other province occupied by the English could be held in full sovereignty. The King of France, they said, had no right to authorise the dismemberment of the kingdom, which he had sworn at his coronation to preserve. The English replied that the rights claimed by the French Crown in Aquitaine had been the source of bitter contention and constant warfare for many years and that no peace worth the name was possible while these rights subsisted. If the coronation oath was an obstacle, then the solution was a papal dispensation. There was no possibility of reconciling such uncompromising positions even if the instructions of the ambassadors had been looser than they were. The conference limped on for about a month. The Duke of Lancaster kept open house at his lodgings, entertaining the Cardinals and officials of the papal court with great magnificence and getting through 100 barrels of wine and several thousand pounds in expenses. In the strongly pro-French atmosphere of the papal city, there was no doubt something to be said for such an emphatic assertion of England's presence. 'Truly,' men said, 'the world cannot produce his equal.' But there was no peace.[60]

The King of Navarre hovered conspiratorially about the fringes of the conference, extracting what advantage he could from the situation. He pretended to leave Avignon with much pomp and bustle soon after the French ambassadors arrived. But when he had gone a short distance from the city he stopped and returned secretly by night to an apartment in the palace of Guy of Boulogne. Here, for about two weeks, Charles engaged in a series of clandestine discussions with the Duke of Lancaster. The French ministers did not discover what had happened until, more than a year later, the details were extracted by torture from one of the King of Navarre's retainers. The two men agreed that Charles would make open war on the King of France in alliance with the English. The detailed strategy would be worked out later. The essential points were that Charles would return as soon as possible to Navarre to raise an army. He would embark with his men from a Gascon port in the summer and return to Normandy by sea. Henry of Lancaster would raise a second army in England. The two commanders were then to join forces in the Cotentin peninsula and conduct a joint invasion of Normandy. The whole of this arrangement was subject to Edward III's approval and would need to be confirmed by a formal treaty of alliance. Henry agreed to meet the King of Navarre in the Channel Islands immediately before his army landed in Normandy to seal the document and make the final arrangements. But he had learned to be wary of Charles' fickleness. He extracted from him a solemn oath that the English would not be double-crossed as they had been last time.[61]

In the cavernous halls of the papal palace nearby, the forms of diplomatic exchange were finally exhausted towards the end of February. The English were much embittered against the French, whom they accused of dishonesty; and against the Pope, who had complaisantly let them get away with it. The most that the Pope could induce the parties to accept was an extension of the truce for just three months, from 1 April to 24 June 1355. Innocent hoped that the pause might allow some compromise to emerge. But the truth was that both governments needed the time in order to complete their military preparations. The conference ended with a brutal reassertion by the Duke of Lancaster of Edward III's claim to the Crown of France and a complete rejection of any arrangement which left him with the obligations of a vassal for the territory he held there. Lancaster then left Avignon with his suite and returned to England.[62]

CHAPTER IV

Scotland and Languedoc 1355–1356

Scotland, once the dominant factor in Edward III's political calculations, had almost been forgotten by 1355. The Scottish campaign in the north of England in 1346, which had been designed to relieve the pressure on France in the early stages of the siege of Calais, was the last occasion on which the 'auld alliance' had threatened Edward's rear, and at the battle of Neville's Cross, which brought it to a bloody close, the English seemed at last to have achieved the elusive final victory which they had sought for half a century. It was not only that the largest Scottish army to invade England for several decades had been dispersed and put to flight. The King, David II, had been taken prisoner and transported to London. More than fifty barons of Scotland, almost all the leaders of the nation and most of its experienced soldiers, had been killed or captured. Within a year, the English had reoccupied the border sheriffdoms of Berwick, Roxburgh, Peebles and Dumfries, a swathe of territory across the southern lowlands. Edward Balliol, the puppet whom Edward III had recognised as King of the rest of Scotland since 1334, returned with Edward's troops and installed himself on the Isle of Hestan off the Galloway coast, in a region where his family had been great lords for generations and where his name still counted for something. Here, in constant danger from Scottish raids, protected by English men-at-arms and supplied with victuals by the English Sheriff of Cumberland, Balliol maintained his diminutive court and his pretensions to dominion over all Scotland from the Firth of Clyde to the Northern Isles.[1]

Most prisoners of fourteenth-century wars could expect to be promptly released against indentures for the payment of their ransoms, regardless of the political advantages of keeping them. But the English King made an exception for the Scots. Although the law held them to be the private property of their captors, Edward required them to be delivered into his own custody and held in his castles. None was to be ransomed or paroled without the leave of his Council. Edward intended if he could to disable the Scottish nation for a generation. It was a popular policy in England. The Parliament which met at Westminster at the beginning of April 1348 made it a condition of the grant of a tax that the leaders of the Scots, especially David II and the Knight of Liddesdale, should on no account be released. When, a few days later, a deputation came from Scotland to argue the point with the King's Council at Westminster, they were told that David Bruce had been caught burning and killing in England like a common freebooter and had no right to invoke the laws of war to ransom himself. Edward would have been willing enough to release David as part of a wider settlement with the Scots, and virtually said so. But the ambassadors' instructions did not extend that far.[2]

The government of Scotland, so far as there was one, was in the hands of Robert, the hereditary Stewart of the kingdom, who had been elected as Guardian in the aftermath of the disaster of Neville's Cross. He had been the obvious choice. He was the King's nephew and heir presumptive. He had been Guardian before, during the exile of David II in Normandy in the 1330s. With his extensive domains in western Scotland he was the most powerful nobleman of the realm. But Robert was a mediocrity, who had fled from Neville's Cross at the crucial moment of the battle. His control of events was always tenuous. Some sense of direction was supplied by the Stewart's adjutants: William Laundels, Bishop of St. Andrews, an old friend of the King who had probably shared his exile abroad; and Sir Robert Erskine, a knight from Renfrewshire, who became Chamberlain of Scotland and the main director of Scotland's foreign policy. They were able men. But their task was not easy. Consistency was hard to achieve in a world overshadowed by the jealous squabbles of local warlords and gang leaders, and by the halting fortunes of the King of France.[3] Scotland was comprised in the truce of Calais as one of the 'allies and associates' of France, with the characteristic caveat that the French should not be answerable if the Scots declined to be bound. But the Scots, demoralised and exhausted and without effective leadership, were in no position to make war even if they had wished to. In the following years, they tacitly consented to the successive truces which the French made on their behalf. And when these failed their captains on the border made local bargains of their own.[4]

The English dominated the border region from a small number of powerful garrisoned fortresses: Berwick, Wark, Norham and Roxburgh on the Tweed; and the great castle of the Bohuns at Lochmaben which controlled the routes into Dumfriesshire and western Scotland. Behind

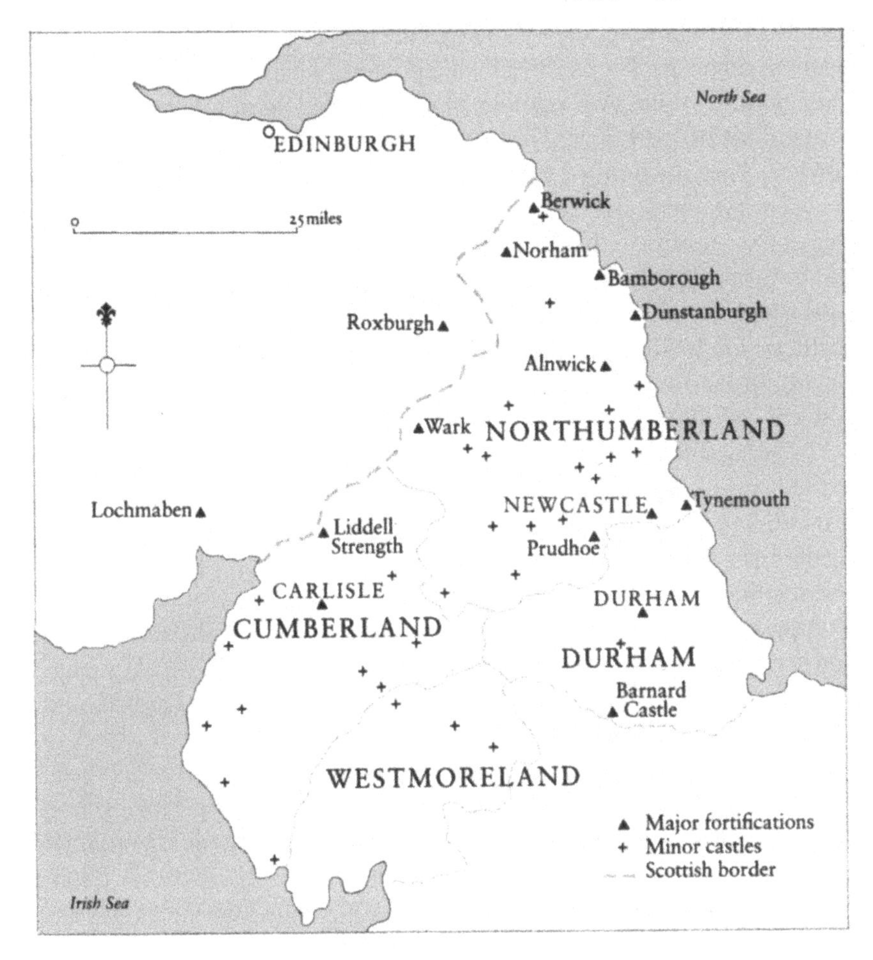

9 The Scottish border, 1346–1356

the border lay the walled city of Carlisle and the impressive castles of Northumberland: the coastal fortress of Bamburgh and the Percy stronghold at Alnwick, which was almost entirely rebuilt in this period. Edward III never visited the region and rarely sent any of the great captains of his court. The defence of the north was left entirely to local men. The main responsibility rested with the Wardens of the March. These great officers, who had been regularly appointed since the end of the thirteenth century, were for practical purposes independent military governors in the two districts into which the border region was divided: the western march, comprising Cumberland and Westmoreland, and the eastern march in Northumberland. They were always members of the great northern families: Percy and Neville in the east; Clifford, Lucy and Dacre in the west. They enjoyed wide powers, which tended to increase. They manned their own castles, which included some of the principal strongholds of the north. They controlled the King's garrisons in their districts. They maintained what amounted to standing armies from their kinsmen, retainers, dependants and friends. They could array all adult men in the counties in their charge to serve without pay against the Scots, and in moments of grave crisis could call on the men of Yorkshire and Lancashire as well. It was the beginning of the long process by which the northern aristocracy was to become an almost independent political community, at once the shield of England and the major threat to its political stability.[5]

The Scots still held the whole of the valley of the Clyde, Stirling Castle at the head of the Firth of Forth, and the fortress-towns of Edinburgh and Dunbar. Between these strongholds and the English fortresses of the border lay a broad swathe of ungoverned territory where loose bands of undisciplined Scottish warriors hid in the dense forests, killing and robbing indiscriminately. Until he was captured at Neville's Cross the leader of the guerrilla bands of the border had been William Douglas, known as the 'Knight of Liddesdale', 'scourge of the English and rampart of the Scots'. Douglas had been the Scots' most effective guerrilla leader since the days of William Wallace. His capture had been a great misfortune for the Scottish cause in the Lowlands. However, at the end of the 1340s another William Douglas appeared. He was the head of his famous family, the nephew and heir of 'Good Sir James Douglas', one of the great heroes of the war of independence against Edward I. William lord of Douglas had passed most of his life in France before returning to his native land in his early twenties, not long after the disaster of Neville's Cross. He found part of his inheritance appropriated by the Knight of Liddesdale (who was his godfather) and the rest occupied by the English. Douglas learned to hate the Knight of Liddesdale. But he slipped naturally into the great guerrilla leader's role, harassing the English garrisons of Berwick and Roxburgh and firmly establishing himself in the Douglas heartlands of the central march.[6]

Writing to Edward III, one of his captains of the border gave a graphic account of the routine of arson, cattle rustling and murder which had already reduced most of the region to a green desert:

Earl Patrick [of Dunbar] and the Earl of Sutherland invaded England on 28 June and pillaged the country to within two leagues of Bamburgh, taking at least 2,000 animals and many prisoners. When they had collected up their booty and burned the land around they marched back towards their base at Dunbar. They had got only about 4 leagues beyond the border when they were cut off by a company of our men from Roxburgh who dismounted and attacked them on the march. The Scots were soundly thrashed, more than half their number killed or captured, and all the prisoners and animals that they had taken in England were recovered. The two earls escaped only with great difficulty.

While this was happening, the King's correspondent added, another Scottish guerrilla band made an attempt on Roxburgh itself.

Alexander Ramsey hid himself with 200 men-at-arms just two leagues from the town. All our company had just sat down to eat in our quarters. Suddenly they burst out of the woods and appeared outside the town. They would have burned it down if we had not driven them off and left many of them dead on the ground. As it was they retreated empty-handed. My company's horses were too tired to follow them. But of the three brothers, John, Thomas and Henry Kerr, who are the worst adversaries I have ever met with among the men of the forest or the bands of William Douglas, John is now slain, killed by a blow from one of my men which penetrated his leather and went right through his body. The other two are my prisoners in the castle ward.[7]

The atmosphere of continual half war would have been recognised by any garrison commander in Brittany, Saintonge or the march of Calais.

So the secular decline of the northern economy continued. Arable land retreated as men turned to sheep and cattle, which required less manpower and could be removed into the high ground and forests at the first sign of danger. Around the greater towns and castles, war and wall-building and dealing in captured goods became the main pillars of the local economy. Berwick, which had once been the chief commercial town of southern Scotland, became the Calais of the north, a walled encampment on the north side of the Tweed surrounded by ungoverned wasteland. The Scots cut off the road north and raided up to the gates. Victuals had to be found for the garrison in England and carried round the coast in heavily armed ships. Reports reaching Westminster suggested that the inhabitants of the town were gradually abandoning what trade they had and giving the place up to the soldiers.[8]

The Wardens of the Marches could not pacify the border, but they could contain its problems and prevent them from troubling the rest of the kingdom. That was good enough for the King's ministers at Westminster. The menace from Scotland had addled the English war effort in France for years before the battle of Neville's Cross. It had forced the government to divide England at the Trent, reserving the tax revenues and manpower of the northern counties for defence against the Scots. More significant, even if less direct, was the effect which the threat from Scotland had had on public opinion, which had been taught by half a century of border warfare to hate and fear the Scots and to exaggerate beyond recognition their power to harm the English kingdom. Before Neville's Cross there had been many Englishmen who found it hard to accept the expenditure of so much money and effort in France while a threat from Scotland subsisted. The English government was liberated from much of this pressure for almost a decade after the battle. The reservation of the revenues of the north came to an end in 1349.[9] And, although the manpower of Cumberland, Westmoreland and Northumberland continued in practice to be placed at the disposal of the Wardens of the March, Lancashire, Yorkshire and the north Midlands now began to contribute growing numbers of men to England's armies and garrisons in France.

Captured in battle at the age of twenty-two, David II was destined to spend a decade of his life in English prisons, much of it in the bleak apartments of the Tower of London which he shared with other Scottish and French prisoners of state. His rank, and the fact that he was Edward III's brother-in-law, ensured that he was comfortably accommodated and honourably treated. But he had no prospect of being released until Edward III had obtained a settlement with the Scottish kingdom. What kind of settlement Edward had in mind became apparent from the demands which he pressed on David and a succession of delegations from Scotland. The northern kingdom was to become a fief of the English Crown, whose kings would do homage to Edward and his successors and serve in their armies in France. All the 'disinherited' Englishmen who had received grants in Scotland in the time of Edward I and Edward II were to be restored to the lands from which Robert Bruce had expelled them. And if David (who was still childless) were to die without issue, Edward III or one of his sons was to succeed him. As security for all of this the English King required the surrender of all the castles and walled towns of Scotland. These undiplomatic demands would have removed the Stewart's claim to succeed to the throne and disinherited much of the Scottish nobility. There was not the slightest prospect of their being accepted in Scotland.

Edward III must have known this, and in private he was more accommodating. The difficulty, as Edward was to discover when he captured the King of France, was that the power of fourteenth-century kings depended too much on their personality, and on the skein of friendships and unspoken bargains by which they influenced events without commanding them. In captivity David II quickly lost his status and influence in Scotland. Although messages were continually carried to and fro by his chaplain, physician and domestic servants, the Scottish King's interests diverged ever more obviously from those of his subjects. David was desperate to be released on almost any terms. For the most part, the Scots were uninterested in any settlement that they could not afford, and were much more reluctant than he was to compromise the historic independence of their realm. Nothing had been achieved by the summer of 1350, when David II send a plea for help to the Pope. He felt devoid of bargaining counters, he said, and abandoned by the King of France in whose cause he had launched the disastrous invasion of 1346. He begged Clement VI to intercede for him with King Philip in order to ensure that his fate was not forgotten in the French government's negotiations with England. The Knight of Liddesdale was even more desperate than David was. He had built up his fortune from small beginnings by usurping the domains of his godson and by brutality at the expense of his rivals. He knew that the young lord of Douglas was undoing him in his absence. The Pope duly wrote to Philip. But before the letter could be dealt with in Paris, the French King was dead. Philip's son had other preoccupations and perhaps other strategic notions. In spite of several ambitious attempts, the French had never been able to bring effective aid to the Scots. The 'auld alliance' must have seemed a spent force after Neville's Cross.[10]

At the end of 1350 Edward III made a new proposal. David, he suggested, could be released, all the English castles in southern Scotland returned to the Scots, and peace restored between the two realms in exchange for a ransom of £40,000 and a promise by David and the whole community of Scotland that one of Edward's younger sons would succeed him if he died childless. It was a cunningly judged offer. David must have approved it in advance, or it would hardly have been made. And, although it was anathema to the Stewart, who would lose his hopes of the succession, it offered the Scots much of what they wanted: peace and security, and a guarantee that the English and Scottish thrones would remain separate. Edward dropped his previous demands for homage. As for Edward Balliol, he could be discarded. A document was prepared. Edward's Council agreed it informally with 'certain men of Scotland'. But rather than negotiate the details with another difficult and obstructive Scottish delegation with insufficient powers, Edward III had it carried to the Scots by the Knight of Liddesdale himself. Douglas was released on parole for the purpose. He returned to Scotland and put the plan before a council of the prelates and barons at Scone early in the new year. The outcome of the debate is not recorded, but Edward's proposal was evidently not rejected out of hand. In April 1351 an important diplomatic conference was held in the abbey town of Hexham in Northumberland. The English King was represented by the Earl of Northampton and by the chief barons of the border, Henry Percy and Ralph Neville; the communities of Scotland by Robert Erskine and William Laundels with three others. The Knight of Liddesdale was there in person. Balliol had already delivered his protests to Edward III, and sent his agents to represent him at the conference. Nobody paid much attention to them. After a few days, the conference was adjourned and reconvened at Newcastle in July. The eventual outcome, a draft treaty, satisfied the Scottish ambassadors, but they could only agree it subject to the approval of the Parliament of Scotland. It was therefore resolved that David II, like the Knight of Liddesdale before him, would be released on parole for long enough to reason with his subjects in person.[11]

In February 1352 David was temporarily released in exchange for an impressive band of hostages: the Stewart's elder son, the heirs of 6 earls and barons of Scotland and no less than 100 Scottish knights. Escorted by 200 cavalry, he made his way through the desolated lowlands into his realm. At the end of February 1351 David was at Scone, where another Scottish assembly had assembled to consider the treaty. They rejected it. According to an English chronicler, they responded 'with one voice' that they were willing to ransom their King but would never subject their country to the English. David completely failed to persuade them that Edward III's proposal left the independence of Scotland intact. There was a brief period of uncertainty, while the principal actors decided what to do next. The English King had certainly hoped that David would refuse to take no for an answer. He had even discussed with the Knight of Liddesdale a plan to suppress the opposition by force, if necessary with the aid of the English garrisons of the border. But either David's supporters were too timid or David himself would have no truck with it. At the beginning of April 1352 the Scottish king surrendered at Berwick to Sir John Coupland, the man whose teeth he had knocked out at Neville's Cross. In May he was back in the Tower of London.[12]

For the Knight of Liddesdale the failure of the treaty was unspeakably bitter. It left him to face the prospect of indefinite incarceration in London, while the last remnants of his power in the lowlands fell to his godson. He refused to accept the verdict of Scone. When he returned to London he made a private treaty with Edward III. On 17 July 1352 the Knight swore on the Gospels to serve Edward III against all men anywhere 'save for the Scots in Scotland unless he chooses.' Edward for his part released him from captivity without ransom and confirmed him in possession of the great thirteenth-century castle of Hermitage under Caldcleugh Head and the lordship of Liddesdale around it, old Douglas territory still largely controlled by the English. But if Edward hoped that the Knight of Liddesdale would raise a civil war in Scotland, he was disappointed. The Knight settled quietly in Liddesdale. Then, about a year after his return to the country, he was ambushed and killed while hunting in the forest of Ettrick by retainers of the younger Douglas. Thus were avenged the grievances of a decade and the foundations laid of a lowland empire feared by English and Scottish Kings alike.[13]

The King of France and his ministers followed Edward III's long-drawn dealings with the Scots as best they could. But although they were quite well informed about events in London and south-eastern England, the French had very little intelligence about anything that happened in the north. Their best source of information was probably the small Scottish merchant community at Bruges, which was the main entrepôt for the trade of the east coast ports of Scotland. The news of the conferences of Hexham and Newcastle did not reach Paris until after they had ended. Too late, John II addressed a florid plea to the 'prelates, barons, magnates and noblemen of the community of the realm of Scotland', urging them to stand by the alliance with France and to fight the common enemy. The messengers who carried these letters to Scotland added their own exhortations. But there is no evidence that they had any impact. The most that John could promise by way of help was a comfortable exile in France for those who were defeated. On 8 August 1352, at the height of the French campaigns in Brittany and the Garonne Valley, John wrote another letter to the Scots imploring them to reject the proposed treaty with England, six months after they had done so for their own reasons. He had great confidence, he said, in their loyalty to the French alliance and their constancy in the face of adversity. The truth was that John had nothing to offer to the Scots. After the truce of Guines in March 1353, which had raised short-lived hopes of peace at the French court, the French King wrote to William

Laundels, whom he had probably known during the exile of the Scottish King in Normandy in the 1330s. He declared that Scotland held a special place in his affections and that his mind dwelt as much on the well-being of its inhabitants as on that of his own people. He assured Laundels that proper provision would be made for the security of Scotland in any treaty of peace. He sent agents to other Scots magnates with the same message. When, a year later, John's ambassadors made another truce with the English at Guines, Scotland was included in it and the King wrote asking them to observe it. But in the secret treaty which was made at the same time, the Scots were not mentioned.[14]

The Scots cannot have known the details of the secret treaty of Guines. But they drew the right conclusions from what had happened. In July 1354, after several months of intermittent negotiation, they finally agreed to ransom their King. The sum promised was 90,000 marks. It was agreed that although the ransom was payable by instalments over a period of nine years, David II should be released at once on parole in exchange for the heirs of twenty of the most prominent lay magnates of Scotland. The Scottish ambassadors agreed no alteration in the status of the Crown and they made no final peace. But they knew that by the laws of war, David could not wage war in England while he was Edward III's prisoner on parole. The treaty provided that a truce would be declared, which was to last until the final instalment of the ransom had been paid. If it had been implemented, it would have marked the practical withdrawal of Scotland from the French alliance.[15]

The French were well aware of this. It was their intervention which wrecked the treaty. It was in August 1354, a month after the conference of Newcastle, that John II's Council turned decisively against the treaty of Guines. Although the Scots duly ratified the ransom agreement in early October, difficulties and delays began almost immediately afterwards. At the outset these may have been attributable to the real problems of raising the first instalment of the ransom in an impoverished country gravely damaged by war. But by the end of the year it was evident that the French had persuaded the Scots to repudiate their agreement with Edward III and to reopen the war. In order to do this it was necessary to promise them armed assistance and, almost certainly, money. The circumstances are shrouded in obscurity. On 5 and 11 January 1355, there were two meetings of the French Royal Council in Paris, attended by Yon de Garencières, the Chamberlain of the Dauphin's household, and one of the few Frenchmen with first hand experience of the affairs of Scotland. Twenty years before, in the winter of 1335–6, he had taken a small contingent of French troops to Aberdeen, the advance guard of a great French army which never came. John II now appointed him as his Lieutenant in Scotland and put him in command of a small expeditionary force.[16]

By February 1355, when the first instalment of David II's ransom was due to be paid, it had become clear in England that the treaty was a dead letter. Large raiding parties were reported to be gathering in the Lowlands. At the end of the month, all the northern counties of England were placed on a war footing. David II was removed from the keep at Newcastle, where he was waiting for his release, and brought back south. He was taken to Odiham, a grim thirteenth-century fortress by the main road from London to Winchester, which belonged to Queen Philippa. She had planted an enclosed garden there, with ornamental hedges and covered seats, a lace cuff on a mailed fist. The Scottish King was received there on 7 March 1355. Yon de Garencières had been given his final orders and letters of appointment at Saint-Denis two days earlier. On 16 March he left with his company of sixty men, including two native Scots, all 'elite knights with famous and valiant squires'.[17]

The Duke of Lancaster arrived back in England on 28 March 1355, having travelled through France as fast as his dignity would allow.[18] He was followed within days by two emissaries of Innocent VI sent hot foot after him to limit the damage done in the acrimonious closing days of the Pope's diplomatic conference. The principal of the new legation, Androin de la Roche, was a Benedictine monk from Burgundy, who had been Abbot of Cluny for the past four years. He may have realised the hopelessness of his first mission when he was appointed. But if he did not, his eyes were soon opened. In the middle of April 1355 he appeared with his colleague at a meeting of the Great Council in the Palace of Westminster. He presented a proposal to extend the current truce to allow further negotiations to occur. Unusually, the King answered him in person. The French, he said, had often arranged for papal legations to come before him to propose truces. They invariably repudiated them as soon as it suited them. He was willing to consult his Council about the latest proposal, but his own inclination was to reject it. He would return his formal answer in due course. As the legates made their way back down the Dover road, the Council resolved to reopen the war with simultaneous campaigns in Normandy and Gascony.[19]

To command the army of Gascony, the King appointed his eldest son,

Edward of Woodstock, Prince of Wales. The 'Black Prince' (as he became known in the following century) was 24 years old in 1355, and was receiving his first independent command. It would be interesting to know more about this remarkable man, who was destined to be an even greater soldier than his father. A man who could inspire extravagant loyalty among his friends and subordinates and who married late in life for love must have been more than the cardboard figure described by the chroniclers of his day. But his personality is almost completely concealed behind their conventional praise. He was physically impressive, extravagantly generous with money and favour, self-assured, impatient of difficulty or opposition. That much can be deduced from his acts. The young prince already had some experience of war. He had fought at Caen and Crécy in 1346 and endured the long siege of Calais. He had commanded part of the army which defeated Geoffrey de Charny beneath the walls of Calais in January 1350, and one of the squadrons which had fought against the Castilians off Winchelsea later in the same year. But in all of these adventures he had been overshadowed by his father and by Henry of Lancaster, Edward's chief of staff and principal captain. The Prince was intensely ambitious to win his own fame. According to his own account he 'prayed the King to let him be the first to cross the sea.' So, it was proposed to raise an expeditionary army of 800 men-at-arms and 1,400 mounted archers to fight under his command. More than half of these men were retained by the Prince himself.[20] But he was also assigned as his companions some exceptionally experienced soldiers with ample resources of their own: the Earl of Suffolk, who was the head of the Prince's council; the Earl of Oxford, who had commanded the Prince's division at Crécy; the Earl of Warwick, Sir Reginald Cobham and Sir James Audley, all men whose military careers went back to the beginning of the war. No less than nine of the Prince's companions were Knights of the Garter or were admitted to the order later.

The French ministers, who received regular reports from travellers and spies, can hardly have failed to notice the brouha which surrounded the Prince's expedition. The tremendous bureaucratic preliminaries began in the second half of April 1355 as soon as the Great Council had dispersed. The Prince and his companions recruited men all over England. Ships were requisitioned in every maritime county. Stores of wine and victuals were accumulated in great quantities at the ports, and in the estuaries of Dartmouth and Fowey. Ramps and hurdles for loading and stowing horses were ordered in Hampshire and throughout the West Country. Green and white cloth was bought in bulk wherever it could be found in order to make the particoloured tunics and hats of the Prince's Cheshire archers. By the beginning of June 1355 the scale on which the Prince and his companions were buying supplies had caused steep price rises among victuallers and armourers. The date of embarkation was fixed for the beginning of July. It was eventually decided that the Prince and the greater part of his army would leave from Plymouth, whose great sheltered harbour was becoming the normal port of embarkation for Brittany and Gascony; the rest would sail with the Earls of Suffolk and Warwick from Southampton. The whole fleet should be in Bordeaux by the end of the month.[21]

The English government was more discreet about its plans to invade Normandy with Charles of Navarre. No grandiloquent announcements appeared. No requests were made for prayers. No breath of it appeared in the instructions given to those who were to requisition ships or purchase supplies. Thirty-eight large ships were collected for Lancaster's use. Of these, twenty-three came from the King's growing fleet of ships of war. Another was bought in Flanders. The rest seem to have been quietly detached from the armada which was being requisitioned for the Prince of Wales. During June all of these vessels were moored off Edward III's mansion at Rotherhithe on the Surrey shore of the Thames, where their streamers in the colours of the Duke of Lancaster could be plainly seen by all passing river traffic. In order to prevent reports from reaching France, it was necessary to stop merchant ships in the port of London from leaving for foreign destinations throughout June and the first part of July. Judging by the size and number of the ships there must have been about 1,200 troops assigned to the expedition. They were 'picked men', according to Robert of Avesbury. They included, in addition to Lancaster himself, the Earls of Northampton, Stafford and March and many of the golden youth of the English nobility, who were taking part in their first important military enterprise. Among them was the King's sixteen-year-old son Lionel.[22]

For the past eight years Edward III had fought a succession of local campaigns, largely defensive in purpose, and rarely involving more than a few hundred men. The greatest of them, Stafford's expedition to Gascony in 1352, had involved little more than 4,000 men of whom less than 400 were sent out from England. Stafford's had been the classic limited raid, a *chevauchée* lasting less than three months and costing under £12,000.[23] The Prince's expeditionary force of 1355 was a larger and more costly affair but its scale was still modest by comparison with the hosts of the 1330s and 1340s. Like Stafford's army it was very much a personal enterprise of the participants. The Welsh archers were conscripted in the traditional way by commissioners of array. But the rest were contract troops. The Prince and the principal magnates who accompanied him entered into indentures with the King, in which they agreed to raise specified numbers of troops in return for wages, expenses and other emoluments. Increasingly, the companies which these contractors agreed to raise were mixed companies, comprising not only men-at-arms, but the appropriate proportion of archers and even, in some cases, specialists such as miners, carpenters, farriers and the like. The retainers of the great men of the army performed their obligations by entering into very similar instruments with lesser men, and so on down to the smallest units of the army, a knight with his squire and page. Because of the political problems of conscription this was now the normal method of raising English armies. The war may have been justified by essentially public interests, but its operations were becoming a largely private enterprise.[24]

By now the terms of service followed a more or less standard form. The indentures provided for the payment of war wages according to the number of days served, with an advance at the outset. For long service, the advance was usually generous: in the Prince's case, half a year's wages. In addition, retainers were entitled to be compensated for horses lost on the campaign, according to a valuation made by the marshal's officers when the retainer presented himself for service. In accordance with a practice which had begun in the middle of the 1340s, captains of companies also received a recruitment bonus known as a *regard*. The usual rate was 100 marks per quarter for every thirty men-at-arms recruited, but for particularly onerous services or highly valued captains, a double *regard* was sometimes paid. The division of the spoils of war was elaborately regulated, either in the indenture or, in the absence of any express agreement, by tradition. The enemy's king or the commander of his army were reserved for the King or the Prince, who paid a discretionary reward to the captor. Other prisoners, and booty taken in conquered territory, were shared between the King (or whoever was ultimately paying the wage-bill) and the men. The usual rule at this time was that the captain took half the profits of field service and a third of those made in garrison service.

These arrangements made English contract armies of the 1350s into elaborate business ventures, in which wages, *regards* and the speculative chances of war served as potent recruiting agents. A famous captain like Sir John Chandos, one of the prince's retainers in 1355, could make considerable sums out of *regards*, not to speak of the spoils of war. He was not born to great wealth, but made his fortune by his skills as a commander and military administrator. He attracted a large following by his reputation as a soldier and the prospect of honour and profit which service in his company offered. In the next major expeditionary army to leave England's shores, in 1359, he commanded a retinue equal to that of the lesser earls. Money was the main engine of Chandos' enterprise just as it was for most of his followers. Yet there was a great deal more to contract service than money. These groups of men developed an *esprit de corps* which contributed much to the fighting quality of English armies. Retinues marched and fought together as a unit. Many of them signed up for service with the same retinue in one campaign after another. They were kinsmen, clients, neighbours and friends of those who led them, men who were used to coming together in peacetime to witness documents, acting as each others' sureties in the county court and defending each others' interests in their communities at home: a miniature of English provincial society projected onto the battlefields of France. There is a revealing story about Ralph, Earl of Stafford, leading his retinue to fight in France some years after this, when he was an old man. One of his retainers, Robert Swynnerton, had recently married his granddaughter, a valuable match which the Earl had a large part in arranging. As they passed along the roads of Kent, Stafford enquired of Swynnerton whether he had performed all the terms of his marriage contract. On receiving an unsatisfactory answer, he had Swynnerton escorted home by two members of his council. They were to see to it that he did his duty by his family before he was allowed to join the campaign.[25]

The money required to pay fleets and armies, however recruited, had to be found. During the summer, the Prince of Wales spent £19,500 on advances of war wages and *regards* and another £3,330 on shipping before he even arrived at Plymouth. By the time he sailed it is likely that his army had consumed the equivalent of a year's parliamentary taxation. The cost of Lancaster's expedition to Normandy is more difficult to quantify, but it must have been substantial. In the next financial year, which began at the end of September 1355, at least £110,000 was spent on military operations, more than half of it on the Prince's army in Gascony.[26] Edward III's ability to finance expenditure on this scale at a time when his rival was travailing in the gravest financial crisis of the war, was the most important single explanation for his achievement in the next half-decade.

To some extent it was due to the efficient collection of Parliamentary taxes, the traditional source of war finance. The success of the three-year subsidy of 1348–51, collected on the morrow of the Black Death, had been remarkable enough. The results of the next three-year grant, which was collected between 1352 and 1354, were even better. About 95% of the theoretical yield was brought in, even though the assessments dated from before the epidemic and had to be collected from a shrunken population. In the longer term, however, the great object of Edward's ministers was to reduce their reliance on Parliamentary taxes. The political cost of direct taxation year upon year to pay for a war without end was high. Substitutes such as purveyance and judicial fines by which the King had tried to ease his financial predicaments in the past were no better. Edward's ministers were well aware that without public support, or at any rate tolerance, the war could not be fought at all. It was said of William Edington, Bishop of Winchester and successively Treasurer of the Exchequer and Chancellor, that he was 'always striving to protect the commons from extortionate demands and heavy taxation'. No one would have said that about Archbishop Stratford in the 1330s and 1340s or the rebarbative Chief Justice Shareshull, whose commissions of trailbaston and periodical provincial tours of the King's Bench had contributed so much to the coffers of the King and the Prince of Wales in the early 1350s.[27]

Edington was mainly responsible for Edward III's ability to finance the war in the second half of the 1350s. He was a career administrator, a Wiltshire man of obscure origins who had come to the notice of Bishop Orleton of Salisbury as a young man and entered the government's service in the 1330s as a Chancery clerk. He had served for four years as Keeper of the Wardrobe (the King's personal financial office) and then taken over control of the Exchequer in 1345 at the nadir of its fortunes. Here he showed himself to be an officer of relentless efficiency and uncompromising personal integrity. He centralised the direction of the government's finances in the Exchequer, and put an end to the independence of the numerous offices which had been used to appropriate royal revenue directly during the period of hand-to-mouth expedients which the King had favoured before. Personalities are hard to distinguish behind the anonymity of the royal accounts. However, it seems to have been Edington who was mainly responsible for the successful liquidation of most of great burden of royal debt which

Edward had allowed to accumulate in the first decade of the war. It was he who devised in conjunction with various syndicates of London and provincial bankers the schemes for buying up dishonoured royal debt at ten or fifteen per cent of their nominal value, which produced an orgy of financial speculation at the close of the 1340s but enabled the government to cast off the millstones of the past. And he was certainly responsible for the rapid reconstruction of the English public finances in the following decade.

Edington's greatest service was the transformation of the customs system which, from being a useful but secondary source of revenue, became the main engine of English war finance and briefly enabled Edward III to do without direct taxation altogether. It is difficult to know how much of this remarkable feat was due to accident and how much to design. Between the autumn of 1352 and the following summer there had been a radical reorganisation of the highly regulated English export trade. Sales for export, which had previously been concentrated by law in the 'staples' of Antwerp and Bruges, were now required to be transacted in a small number of designated staple towns in England itself, where foreign merchants were invited to resort for their supplies. Indeed, for a period of about four years, Englishmen were actually forbidden to export wool. These measures were taken for a variety of reasons, not all of them good ones. They included the high cost of carrying English cargoes in armed convoys across the North Sea and Edward III's deteriorating relations with the rulers of Flanders and Brabant. But their main object was to boost the export trade by making English markets more attractive to foreign traders, and particularly to the wholesalers and financiers of Italy and the Low Countries who dominated the continental traffic in wool and cloth. Foreign merchants, moreover, had the great merit in the government's eyes of being assessable to duties at a higher rate. These changes were accompanied by a sustained onslaught against corruption and smuggling, those ancient and endemic problems of the customs service. The stream of peremptory summonses and regulations issuing from Westminster, the interrogation of obscure weighmen and harbourmasters before committees of the King's Council, the sight of Edington inspecting confiscated cargoes of smuggled wool in Westminster Hall, these are all evocative incidents of thorough government by which the English war effort was being sustained in its third decade. But Edward III's servants were lucky as well as skilful. For the middle years of the decade marked the beginning of a brief boom in the economy of western Europe from which only France, torn apart by war and civil disorder, failed to benefit. In England there was a surge of exports the like of which had not been seen for decades. According to a well-informed chronicler, the general belief at the time of the Parliament of November 1355 (when the customs were extended for another six years) was that wool exports were running at 100,000 sacks per year and yielding £250,000 in customs revenue. The true figures, although much smaller, were still remarkable enough by historical standards. Between 1346 and 1351 the customs had been farmed out for just £50,000 a year. In the next two years, when royal officials resumed control, they did not even make this much. But in 1353–4, the first full year of the new system, the customs yielded £113,420, and the average over the next six years was more than £83,000, the approximate equivalent of two parliamentary subsidies every year. Although much of this revenue was assigned to Edward's captains and contractors in order to pay for war expenditure, a good deal of it was retained in the form of cash balances which could be used to finance campaigns at short notice. This was one reason why the English King was able in the 1350s to send quite substantial expeditionary forces to intervene in France at crucial times and places without the agonising delays which had obstructed such adventures before. Two hundred years later the ministers of a Tudor King would commission transcripts of the customs accounts of 1353–4 in order to discover how it had been done, and in the seventeenth century the enemies of Charles I would use them to make pointed comparisons of medieval efficiency and modern corruption.[28]

During the spring of 1355, when the English government's strategic choices for the summer were being made, the main preoccupation of John II and his ministers was the destruction of Charles of Navarre. In February, Charles had been summoned to answer for his offences in Paris. He was given two months to comply, until the middle of April. But large plans were already in hand for occupying the errant prince's remaining possessions in Normandy. Rouen was filled with the hubbub of preparations for war. The arsenal throbbed with the noise of shipwrights and armourers. The French admirals planned to put ten large galleys and eight oared barges in service by May, the largest war fleet which they had found from their own resources since 1340. Baldo Doria, the great Genoese war contractor, now almost permanently settled in France, and his long-standing rival Rainier Grimaldi of Monaco were commissioned to find 6,000 oarsmen and crossbowmen in Italy and Provence. They began to arrive in April. The Estates of Normandy met to consider ways and means of financing simultaneous operations on land. In the middle of April they granted a subsidy equal to the cost of 2,000 men-at-arms, payable over three months in June, July and August.[29]

The man charged, at least nominally, with the command of these operations was the King's heir, the Dauphin Charles, who was appointed as his Lieutenant in Normandy at the end of March 1355. The Dauphin was then an impressionable young man of 17 with little political judgment and no military experience. He was probably the only person who could convincingly represent the King in this independent-minded province. But his authority was fragile. Charles of Navarre's garrisons and officials remained in control of much of Lower Normandy. In these regions not only were the Dauphin's tax farmers unable to collect the new subsidy, but the King of Navarre's collectors took it instead and paid it into his treasury. The Dauphin was surrounded by the leaders of the Norman aristocracy. But there were many who, like the former royal councillor Amaury de Meulan, brought their companies to the Dauphin's army but maintained covert contact with the agents King of Navarre. Others stayed away altogether.[30]

In Paris the confident bustle concealed deepening anxieties among John II's ministers, and early symptoms of another change of policy. The government had to cover several fronts at once with limited forces and as yet no reliable information about the enemy's plans. It was true that such fighting as had occurred had been on a small scale. But it had gone badly. There had been a serious incident at Guines on the march of Calais, where the French had been clinging for three years to the *bastide* which they had constructed in the convent at the castle gate. The English captain of the castle suddenly attacked this place at about the beginning of May, burnt the outworks and installed his own garrison. In the south-west the Count of Armagnac and the Marshal de Clermont were engaged in needling raids into the duchy of Aquitaine, Armagnac south of the Dordogne in the Agenais, Clermont north of it in Saintonge and Angoumois. Both men suffered a succession of embarrassing reverses. Clermont was unable to stop the English Seneschal, Sir John Cheverston, from capturing the important town and fortified abbey of Guîtres after a siege of several weeks in April and May. Armagnac failed to capture Castelmoron, an important English-held bridge-town on the Lot which he attacked in May, and failed again before Lesignan, further south in the valley of the Garonne. For the second time in less than a year he laid siege to Aiguillon, the double town at the confluence of the Lot and the Garonne. But Sir John Cheverston, who had had advance warning of the Count's plans, had stuffed the town with stores and reinforcements. The siege was abandoned early in June after about six weeks.[31]

There had been high hopes in Paris of a diversionary raid in Edward III's rear from Scotland. But these had already begun to fade. When Yon de Garencières landed in Scotland towards the end of April 1355, he found the Scots reluctant, their government disorganised and unready, and their army non-existent. Yon had come laden with money, which he liberally distributed to prominent Scottish noblemen. But it took several weeks of bargaining to persuade them to embark on another risky and dangerous enterprise against the English. Even then they would do so only when the current truce had expired and in return for a large subsidy, payable in gold in advance. Inevitably, this took some time to arrange. Meanwhile Yon's men kicked their heels and the advantage of surprise was lost. Edward III's ministers knew about the French presence in Scotland by the beginning of June. They took immediate measures to defend the border. But they were measures on a modest scale, confined to the northern counties, and they involved only minimal disruption of the two expeditions in preparation in the south.[32]

Charles of Navarre was at Pamplona. He was supervising the final arrangements for the expedition to Normandy, which he was due to undertake jointly with the Duke of Lancaster. Lancaster's Chamberlain, Simon Simeon, was at his side, representing the Duke's interests at the Navarrese court, watching for the ever-expected signs of backsliding and treachery. On the surface all was well. Charles had retained more than seventy prominent Navarrese noblemen for the campaign. Between them, these men had raised companies with a combined strength of more than 1,700. Considering that there were already 600 Navarrese soldiers in Normandy and that the Cortes of Navarre had been unable to offer more than 30,000 Navarrese pounds by way of subsidy, this was an impressive achievement. Most of the men must have been serving without wages, on promises of spoil. Spoil was certainly the main motive of their leader, Martin Henriquez de Lacarra, hereditary *alferez* (standard-bearer) of the kingdom. Henriquez, although still in his early twenties, had already commanded the King of Navarre's troops in Normandy in 1353 and 1354, acquiring a taste for the war of ambush and escalade and the habit of working with the English which had proved to be highly profitable to him.[33]

By May 1355, Charles was ready. He sent Simon Simeon and a Norman retainer of his called Colin Doublet to England with letters informing the Duke of Lancaster of his plans. Charles intended, he said, to sail to Cherbourg, where the harbour was still controlled by his officers. There he would call on the King of France to deliver up the castles and domains seized from him in the previous autumn. Charles declared himself ready to serve the Duke of Lancaster with all his strength. But of course, he added ominously, John II might offer him an acceptable agreement, in which case it would be unnecessary for the Duke to mount the joint invasion of Normandy which they had planned together in Avignon.[34]

When did Charles of Navarre decide to double-cross the King of England again? It had always been clear that his real object was to work a reconciliation with his father-in-law, if he could do it on acceptable terms, and that the noise of war which surrounded him was merely directed to getting them. The English are unlikely to have been under any illusions about this. Their plans depended on the continuing obduracy of the two men. This assumption was becoming increasingly shaky. Charles of Navarre did not appear in answer to John II's summons. But he was most anxious that his excuses should be known. He pleaded delays by the messengers carrying the details of his arrangements. He said that he was engaged in pressing business at the court of Castile. He certainly did not hurl defiance at his antagonist. In Paris, he was declared in default. Three summonses were required before he could be condemned in his absence. He was immediately sent another which required his attendance in May. The slow procedures of the Parlement brought Charles precious time. As always, he had well placed sympathisers at court, including several on the royal Council. Some of the French King's ministers had always had doubts about the wisdom of confronting the King of Navarre at a time when France was preparing to resist a renewed onslaught from England. As the news came in of French reverses and English plans in the making, these doubts intensified. The Chancellor, the two dowager Queens and the Duke of Bourbon were profoundly shocked by the spectacle of discord and civil war at the heart of the royal family and were quite unable to see the dispute in purely political terms. They all lobbied on his behalf. Their efforts were regularly reported to Charles' officials in the citadel of Évreux and by them to Charles himself in Pamplona. By the middle of May 1355 panic took hold among the growing number in Paris who regarded the present situation as a catastrophe. On 15th, Charles failed to answer to his second summons. At about the same time rumours began to reach Paris of his agreements with the English. The details were still very unclear. The French ministers do not seem to have known yet about the Duke of Lancaster's plan to join forces with him in Normandy. They believed that the English would probably invade Picardy from Calais while Charles of Navarre made a separate landing in the Cotentin. It was a natural enough assumption, and incidents like the attack on the convent of Guines must have encouraged it.[35]

On 17 May 1355 John II went to the abbey of Saint-Denis, the custodian of the *Oriflamme*, the great war standard of France. There he proclaimed the *ban* and the *arrière-ban* and summoned his army to assemble on the Somme at Amiens.[36] Two days later, on the 19th, the two dowager Queens came before the King in Paris. It was the first of a succession of highly charged meetings in which they tried to persuade the King to pardon his son-in-law and restore his confiscated land. They spoke (as they told Charles) 'as graciously as possible.' Moreover, it was plain that they spoke for a large body of the higher nobility and for a growing number of John's councillors. These included John's brother, Philip Duke of Orléans, the Constable Jacques de Bourbon, his brother the Duke of Bourbon, the Chancellor Pierre de la Forêt, Guillaume de Melun Archbishop of Sens and his brother Jean de Melun Count of Tancarville, all of them amongst the most influential noblemen of John's court. Only the lawyers and administrators, those great representatives of the authoritarian tradition, were conspicuously absent. At the end of May, two emissaries arrived from the Count of Foix, bearing a letter from their master asking for an adjournment of the King's summons against Charles of Navarre. They also brought another from Charles himself, written in the most conciliatory tone which he could contrive. On 31 May, John II gave way. He insisted that Charles would have to surrender for a nominal period the six places which he still held in the Cotentin and Lower Normandy. But when that had been done, he would be pardoned and all his lands would be restored to him. John wrote to his son-in-law on 1 June, rather cagily accepting his professions of loyalty and offering him a safe conduct to come to Paris with 200 men-at-arms. The dowager Queens and Charles' allies on the Council wrote more forceful letters. The safe conduct, they said, allowed him to come by land or sea and would undoubtedly be honoured in either case. 'But for your own safety, and to allay suspicion of your plans, you should come by land.'[37]

It took at least eight days in the mid-fourteenth century for a team of mounted messengers to get from Paris to Pamplona. By the time that the French King's letters reached the Navarrese capital Charles had left. He crossed the pass of Roncevalles in the middle of May 1355 and mustered his army at la Bastide Clairence, a small river port in the foothills of the Pyrenees at the northern extremity of his dominions. Early in June the Navarrese marched into Edward III's duchy of Aquitaine and embarked on ships which had been made read for them in the harbour of Capbreton, north of Bayonne. The ships were mostly Castilian vessels which had been hired over the past few weeks and collected at Fuentarrabia just over the border. But there were also five large vessels of Bayonne and one of Bordeaux, made available by the Seneschal of Gascony.[38]

When on 4 June 1355 the news reached Paris, it caused consternation at the French court. Perhaps all that effort to soften and obstruct a petulant prince had been in vain. From Rouen, the Dauphin called on every available man-at-arms to be ready to defend his own district. In the last fortnight of June his troops began to gather around the provincial capital. Two armies were formed. One, under the command of the Admiral of France, was made responsible for the defence of the Chef de Caux, north of the estuary of the Seine. The other, larger force was placed under the command of the Constable and stationed at Caen across the road which led east from the Cotentin peninsula to Rouen and the Île de France. In Paris, a commission of three conciliators was appointed to go into the Cotentin to meet the King of Navarre as soon as he landed and to explain to him the government's change of heart. The Constable, the Count of Tancarville and Geoffrey de Charny were the men charged with this delicate mission. Geoffrey was an elder statesman above partisan loyalties. The other two were declared advocates of compromise. Shortly, that great trimmer Robert de Lorris was added to their number. 'They will say such things to you as will satisfy you,' the two dowager Queens wrote to Charles of Navarre.[39]

On 5 July 1355 the Navarrese fleet arrived at Cherbourg. In the castle, Charles of Navarre found Colin Doublet waiting for him with news of the build-up of troops in southern England and a letter from the Duke of Lancaster redolent with suspicion and distrust. Lancaster said that he had made all his arrangements to come to Charles' aid. But he warned Charles not to deceive him by trading concessions with the King of France. A day or two later, a messenger arrived from Geoffrey de Charny announcing his mission and asking for a safe conduct for himself and his colleagues. Charles moved his headquarters to

Valognes, close to the beaches where Edward III had landed in 1346. Here he appointed three ambassadors of his own to deal with the King of France's commissioners: two French knights of his retinue and Martin Henriquez.[40]

On 10 July 1355 Henry of Lancaster's fleet sailed from Rotherhithe. Unfortunately it made very slow progress. As the ships passed Greenwich, a strong headwind blew up. After tacking for several days they got no further than Sandwich, where they were forced to lie at anchor for more than a month.[41] The respite was extremely welcome to Charles of Navarre. He desperately needed time to complete his negotiations with the French court before the arrival of an English army forced his hand. It was common ground throughout the negotiations that Charles would recover his domains. But the parties found plenty of other bones of contention and passed most of August in snarling over them. Charles wanted better security for the restoration of his castles, once he had delivered them up, than John was willing to offer. He also wanted to hold his domains as an appanage, free of the jurisdiction of the Parlement of Paris, the same ancient problem which had brought the Kings of England to open war with the Valois dynasty. These altercations were eventually resolved by concessions on both sides. But not before the negotiations had come to the verge of failure and John's ministers in Paris had begun to brace themselves for a bloody civil war.[42]

At Calais, another gathering of ambassadors, French and English, went through the forms of negotiation, haggling about terms for extending a truce which had already expired and which neither side intended to observe except for immediate tactical reasons. The Chancellor of France and the Duke of Bourbon demanded redress for the incident at the *bastide* of Guines. They called for the surrender of the Duke of Lancaster and the Earl of Arundel who had personally guaranteed the observance of the last truce. The Bishop of London and his two colleagues responded with evasion and temporising, and with counter-accusations of their own.[43]

As the negotiators passed between Valognes, Caen, Paris and Calais the English and French commanders warily eyed each others' movements. The French admiral sent two ships to cruise off the south coast of England collecting information about concentrations of troops and stores. The English, for their part, received accurate reports about the mobilisation of the French galley fleet in the Seine estuary. The Duke of Lancaster sent Simon Simeon to Cherbourg, ostensibly to confer with the King of Navarre, in fact to gather information about the activities of

Charles' diplomats and the dispositions of the French and Navarrese armies in Normandy.[44]

In the middle of August 1355 Lancaster's fleet began to tack laboriously round the Kent coast in the face of high seas and terrible storms. They did not reach Portsmouth until the end of the month. There the Duke received the reports which his spies had brought back from Normandy. They told him that Charles of Navarre had agreed terms with the King of France. They reported on the build-up of French troops along the Norman coast. In their opinion the French and Navarrese were now working together to trap the English army when it landed. 'Thus was the King of England deceived,' said Jean le Bel. At the beginning of September 1355, Edward III cancelled the expedition.[45]

The reports of the spies were in fact premature. John II did not give his commissioners their final instructions until 30 August. But the English had correctly divined how events were moving. The treaty between Charles of Navarre and the King of France was formally sealed at Valognes on 10 September 1355. It was designed to resolve all the disputes of the past three years, and between more reasonable individuals than Charles and his father-in-law, it might have done so. Seven walled towns and castles in Normandy which were occupied by Charles of Navarre's garrisons were to be nominally surrendered to the Constable of France. He would be entitled to appoint a captain to command them, but the Navarrese garrisons were to remain in possession to ensure that Charles was not tricked. The King of Navarre for his part promised that he would come before John II at a formal audience to ask his pardon, before receiving the disputed castles back of John's grace. He was also to recover possession of all his other domains and compensation for the damage which had been done to them while they had been in the King's possession. An untidy compromise was reached on the subject of Charles' financial claims and the dowry of his wife. His demand for freedom from the appellate jurisdiction of the royal courts was rejected. But in spite of these minor disappointments, the King of Navarre had substantially achieved his object. He had restored himself to the position he had held before the confiscation of his possessions in the previous autumn, and he had done so without letting the English into Normandy. Edward III had been baulked. On about 17 September 1355 Charles rode to the Dauphin's headquarters at the castle of Vaudreuil, on the south bank of the Seine. Here, in the sumptuous painted apartments laid out by John II, the two men passed several days together. On 24 September Charles duly appeared before the King in the great hall of the Louvre in Paris. Once again, it fell to the dowager Queens to make his excuses and to Charles to receive his pardon, declaring to the assembled courtiers as he did so that he had 'done nothing against the King that a loyal vassal might not properly do.'[46]

When Charles of Navarre changed sides, Edward III was left with a difficult strategic problem. The Prince of Wales sailed from Plymouth on 9 September 1355, two months late.[47] Since his expedition had been intended to form the southern front of a combined invasion of France from north and south, much of its strategic purpose had disappeared. Edward's own army was now idly encamped around Portsmouth, while his enemies had a much larger one in north-western France which they were free, if they chose, to use against the Prince's forces in the south. In the first two weeks of September Edward's ministers were engaged in a feverish search for ways of keeping John II's army in the north. To this end they devised an ambitious plan to mount simultaneous campaigns in Brittany and Picardy in what remained of the year's campaigning weather.

The Breton arm of this pincer movement depended mainly on the Navarrese garrisons of lower Normandy and the army which Charles had brought with him to Cherbourg. These men had come to loot. They became increasingly restive and undisciplined as Charles' delicate, diplomatic balancing act continued. Some of them had already embarked on localised pillaging expeditions of their own. In the last few days before the treaty of Valognes was sealed, Martin Henriquez opened negotiations for his own account with Edward III, just as he had done at a similar moment in 1354. He agreed to bring 1,750 Navarrese troops into the service of the English King. Another Navarrese captain, Pedro Remirez, promised to contribute a further 250 men. This was substantially all of Charles' army in Normandy. The King of Navarre, who remained on the most cordial terms with Henriquez, must have connived at this arrangement. But he had probably had no choice. He did not dare send his army back to Navarre even had he had the shipping available to do so. The only alternative would have been to pay them. So, on 7 September 1355, Henriquez received a cash advance of £1,200 from the English Treasury, representing a month's service, and agreed to join forces with the English commanders on the march of Brittany. On the same day it was decided at Westminster that the Duke of Lancaster would be sent out to take command of the Anglo-

Navarrese army there. He was appointed as Edward III's Lieutenant in Brittany and throughout western France. Twenty-five ships remaining from the fleet gathered to invade Normandy were put at his disposal in Southampton. This suggests an expeditionary force of 400 or 500 mounted men at the most.[48]

The northern arm of the pincer was to be a brief but powerful mounted raid through Picardy led by the King himself. Edward expected to embark for Calais in early October and to be back a month later. On 12 September 1355 criers went through the streets of London summoning men who had been stood down from the Normandy campaign to report for duty at Sandwich by the 29th. A rapid and extremely effective recruitment campaign added to their numbers in the course of the next four or five weeks. Noblemen across central and southern England were pressed to contribute their retinues. A large force of archers said to be 500 strong was raised in London. Letters were despatched to friends and retainers of the King in the Low Countries and Germany, summoning their companies to Calais as quickly as they could get there.[49]

These plans, involving simultaneous campaigns by three English armies in France, proved to be too ambitious. But the threat may have been as effective as the reality. 'I will have it known throughout France that I shall invade the country, do battle with King John and destroy everything in my path,' Edward was quoted in France as saying. The French garrisons along the march of Calais were reinforced and several thousand troops were assembled on the Somme at Amiens in the first few days of October. Many of these troops had been transferred from the Dauphin's command in Normandy. As a result, plans which were being made in Paris to send the Dauphin to the south-west to confront the Prince of Wales had to be abandoned. On 9 October 1355, John II received the *Oriflamme* at Saint-Denis for the second time in a year. The English King had achieved his strategic object before striking a blow in anger.[50]

At Westminster, Edward responded to the French King's new dispositions in the middle of October. He reinforced his own army in very similar fashion, by postponing the Duke of Lancaster's expedition to Brittany until the following spring and transferring the men and ships gathered at Southampton to the army of Picardy. Fresh reinforcements were obtained from the north of England. At the end of September 1355, after several months of extreme tension on the border, the Scots had concluded a truce of nine months with the English King's representatives in the north. As a result, several hundred men had been released for service in France. They included the retinues of Percy and Neville, the first time that these great barons of the border had fought overseas since the beginning of the war; and the private army, 280 strong, of that magnificent and worldly ecclesiastical warrior Thomas Hatfield, Bishop of Durham. In addition, although the border garrisons were supposed to be maintained at normal strength, a number of garrison troops took advantage of the situation to join the King's *chevauchée* without leave and enjoy a more glamorous and lucrative form of warfare under the King's eye.[51]

Two weeks before the Scots agreed to the truce, the agents of the French Treasury had delivered the subsidy which they had required as the price of invading England. The money, 40,000 gold *écus*, was handed over to their representatives in Bruges: Walter Wardlaw, a Scottish theologian at the University of Paris who occasionally represented his country's interests in France; and two merchants, including the famous Perth businessman, John Mercer. These three men carried the money to Scotland, together with the arrears of wages and expenses due to Yon de Garencières and his men. They must have arrived at about the beginning of October. Within a few days the Scots repudiated the truce and opened their campaign. They swiftly overran the English-occupied regions of the eastern Lowlands and crossed the Tweed near the great English border fortress at Norham. Then they marched into Northumberland burning everything in sight. Their army was relatively small. It consisted of the lowland gangs of the lord of Douglas, the retainers and allies of Patrick Earl of March and the garrison of his castle at Dunbar as well as Yon de Garencières' sixty men, no more than 2,000 men in all and probably less. But they encountered no organised opposition except from the garrison of Norham. On 10 October 1355 the constable of Norham, Thomas Gray, tried to intercept the Franco-Scottish force with fifty men of his garrison and some hurriedly recruited local levies. At Nesbit, a small village 15 miles south of Berwick-on-Tweed, Gray was ambushed. Although he fought (by his own account) with 'wonderful courage' and inflicted heavy casualties on the enemy, his scratch army was routed and he himself was captured and sent a prisoner to Scotland. Gray's *Scalacronica*, an eclectic, highly personal account in French of the wars of his time was begun and largely completed during his captivity in Edinburgh castle.[52]

The first news of the Scottish invasion of Northumberland reached

Edward III on about 20 October, some ten days after it had begun. He was at Sandwich, supervising the final arrangements to invade Picardy. A large part of his army had already crossed the Channel, and the rest were in the process of boarding their ships. Yon de Garencières' timing was accidental but perfect. However, there was no sign that Edward was unduly concerned. He ordered the arraying of troops in every county north of the Trent. He sent Ralph Neville, who was with him in Kent, back to the north to take command of them. Then he returned briefly to Westminster to confer with his Council about the defence of the north. Having done this he left the details to them. On 28 October 1355 he returned to Sandwich and boarded his ship for Calais. Barges were ordered to be ready to bring back his horses and baggage by 11 November. The opening of Parliament, which would require his presence at Westminster, was postponed until the 23rd. Edward evidently intended to be away for no more than about three weeks.[53]

On 2 November 1355 the English army marched out of Calais. Edward had with him his sons, John of Gaunt and Lionel of Antwerp, who were taking part in their first military campaign, and most of the great captains who had led his armies in two decades of warfare: Henry of Lancaster, the Earls of Northampton and Stafford, and Walter Mauny. With them rode a force of about 5,000 men, including about 1,000 men of the Calais garrison and another 1,000 raised in the Low Countries and Germany by old companions-in-arms such as Henry of Flanders. They marched along the south-west road towards Saint-Omer. Then they turned south towards Amiens. At Thérouanne, Edward III's company was met by Jean de Boucicaut. Boucicaut was the King's prisoner, who was in France on parole to find his ransom. He was not therefore permitted to fight. But he was able to survey the strength of the English army and report on it to the French commanders. Edward allowed him to pass freely through the lines, believing that his reports would impress the enemy. But Boucicaut took a different view. He thought that Edward had a 'fine force, but not as strong as I would have expected.' This was no doubt what he told John II. John's own army was not much more impressive. Arnoul d'Audrehem, one of the Marshals, was stationed at Saint-Omer with about 300 men. Around the pale of Calais, troops had been concentrated in all the stronger towns and castles: Boulogne, Hesdin, Montreuil, Ardres and Aire. The main body of the French host was still gathering at Amiens. The King had set up his headquarters in the Benedictine Abbey of St. Fuscien, south of the city, where he contemplated the disappointing results of a month of intensive

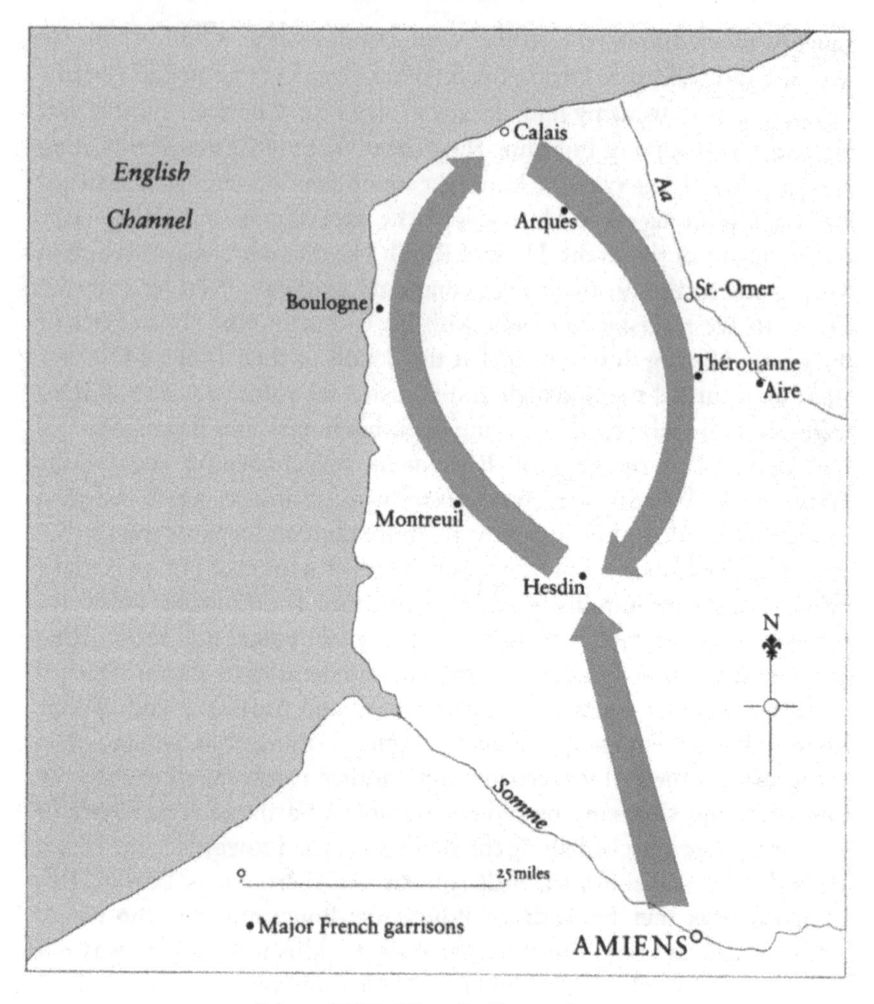

10 Edward III in Picardy, November 1355

recruitment. John had an adequate force of cavalry, including the troops of the Dauphin and the retinue of the newly reconciled King of Navarre. But although the *arrière-ban* was proclaimed throughout the provinces of the north as soon as the English landed, and reminders were sent out in increasingly menacing and hysterical terms to officials of the northern provinces, infantry contingents arrived late and in small numbers.[54]

Unwilling to confront the English in battle with the forces available to him, King John adopted a scorched earth policy. As the English advanced south, small detachments of French troops retreated before them, destroying or removing stores and crops in their path. On 5 or 6

November Edward III's army reached Hesdin. They broke into the famous park of Hesdin Castle, laid out by the eleventh-century counts of Flanders in the days when their territory extended to the southern limits of Artois. Edward passed about three days here. His men were already becoming uncomfortable. They had nothing to drink 'except water', and were running low on victuals. There had not been time to arrange a proper supply train for the army before its departure, and the burned ground of Picardy had yielded almost nothing. The two Kings warily followed each other's movements over the next few days. Neither was confident enough of his strength to risk battle. On about 8 November, the French army marched north out of Amiens towards the enemy. The English retreated towards Boulogne, the only direction in which the French had not wasted the land. John II followed them at a cautious distance. On 11 November, Edward III re-entered the pale of Calais. The French marched in a wide arc around the march and arrived at Saint-Omer soon afterwards.

The shadow-boxing continued for a little while longer. On the following morning, 12 November 1355, the principal French commanders, the Constable Jacques de Bourbon, and the Marshal Arnoul d'Audrehem, proposed an arranged battle: single combat between the two Kings in person, perhaps accompanied by their sons and selected champions from among the nobility. These artificial and invariably abortive proposals were by now familiar to those who had fought in France in 1339, 1340 and 1346. As always when great reputations and valuable propaganda were at stake, each side blamed the other for refusing. The most plausible and best informed account was that of Jean le Bel. According to him, the Duke of Lancaster broke off the discussions, saying that the English army had waited three days at Hesdin when John II could have had his battle, but it was now too late. The first English companies were already embarking for England. Edward III landed in Kent that very day.[55] Three days later, on 15 November, the French King paid off his army at Saint-Omer and left.[56] The campaign had achieved almost nothing. Its chief importance lay in the events which unfolded elsewhere while the two Kings were distracted in Picardy. As Edward III set foot in England, he received the news 'toute chaude' that in his absence the Scots and the French had captured Berwick-on-Tweed.

It had happened ten days before, on the night of 6 November 1355. The men responsible were Patrick Earl of March, one of the leaders of the Nesbit raid in October, and Thomas Stewart, Earl of Angus, a young man who, like Douglas, had been brought up at the exiled Scottish court in France in the 1330s and had recently returned to his native land. They collected together a small force of Scots and the French troops of Yon de Garencières' tiny army. After six days of preparations, these men arrived in the Tweed in small boats under cover of darkness and put scaling ladders against the wall of the lower town. The defences of Berwick were in reasonably good repair. But the length and irregular circuit of the walls, pierced by nineteen towers and four gateways, made it a difficult place to guard. The captain of the town, the Northumbrian baron William Lord Greystoke, was one of those who had deserted his post without leave to fight with Edward III in France. So, when the attackers came over the wall just before dawn, there was only a handful of men on watch. The garrison was roused by the alarm. They fought a rearguard action through the streets of the town. The rest of the population rose from their beds and fled into the castle. Within a few minutes the Scots were running amok through the streets looting any building in their way and heading towards the castle.[57]

Berwick castle lay on the west side of the town, separated from it by a moat and a bridge. It was defended by a large garrison, swollen by men-at-arms and refugees from the town. They were reinforced within a few hours by fresh men brought by John Coupland from Roxburgh. But even in the best conditions the castle was vulnerable, sited on low ground and overlooked by the town walls. When Robert Bruce had captured the town of Berwick in 1318, it had taken him just five days to reduce it. In 1355 the Scots laid siege to it immediately. Shortly afterwards, Robert Stewart the Guardian arrived to take command in person. A succession of assault parties was thrown against the defences in the hope of taking the place before reinforcements could arrive from southern England. The Douglas Tower, which defended the eastern approach to the bridge, quickly fell to them. From here, they began to dig mines towards the main walls.[58]

After John II had left Saint-Omer he too found that grave events had happened behind his back. The Prince of Wales had invaded Languedoc virtually unopposed and wreaked havoc across a great tract of south-western France extending from the Atlantic to the Mediterranean. The French King received the first rumours, quickly followed by fuller written reports, on the road to Paris. 'It is not unknown in war,' he reflected in a letter to the inhabitants of Montpellier, 'for the one side to experience a reverse and then to rise up and overwhelm their conquerors.'[59] Was it the English he was thinking of or the French?

The Prince of Wales had arrived in the Gironde on 20 September 1355 after a passage of ten days from Plymouth. On the day after his arrival the King's letters patent appointing him as Lieutenant in the duchy were read out in the cathedral of Bordeaux before a great crowd of officials, ecclesiastical dignitaries and spectators. Immediately after the ceremony in the cathedral, the Prince met leading members of the Gascon nobility at an enlarged meeting of his council. Not all of them were strangers. The Albrets had been regular visitors at the court of Edward III. Jean de Grailly was a fellow member of the Order of the Garter, and his son the Captal de Buch had travelled with the Prince from England. Like Henry of Lancaster in 1345, the Prince resolved to launch a major *chevauchée* as early as possible, before the weather deteriorated and before the French had a chance to organise their defence. No one had expected him to move so quickly.

All those present agreed that the target should be the lands of the Count of Armagnac. Armagnac was the representative of the King of France in the region and the main threat to the security of Gascony. Moreover he had recently found a winning streak after the humiliations of the spring. Instead of throwing himself against the well-defended English strongholds of the march, he had begun to copy the strategy of the English, launching a succession of raids deep into the heartlands of the duchy. The first of these raids had occurred back in April during the siege of Aiguillon. On that occasion, Armagnac had penetrated deep into the Bazadais and the eastern Bordelais, pulling up vines and destroying villages and suburbs. Learning from his success, he had invaded the Bazadais again at the end of August. Then, unexpectedly lunging south towards the valley of the Adour, he had ravaged the Landes and the districts of Saint-Sever and Bayonne, pursued by the English Seneschal with as many troops as he had been able to gather at short notice. These raids inflicted great distress on the inhabitants of the duchy, who found themselves experiencing for the first time in many years the harrowing insecurity and physical destruction which was the ordinary lot of Périgord, Limousin and Quercy. The Prince was 'inflamed with anger' when the Count's deeds were described to him.[60]

About two weeks passed during which horses and stores were unloaded from the ships, men and beasts were rested. An advance depot was set up at Saint-Macaire, about thirty miles up the Garonne. Then, on 5 October 1355, the army left Bordeaux. Its total strength is a matter of informed guesswork. The Prince had brought about 2,200 fighting men with him from England. The Gascon nobility, which provided nearly 4,000 men for the *chevauchée* of the Earl of Stafford in 1352, cannot have done less for the Prince of Wales. On that footing he must have had between 6,000 and 8,000 men under his command, an army roughly comparable with the one which had fought under Edward III at Crécy. They marched up the south bank of the Garonne as far as Langon, then turned south through the city of Bazas and across the vast marshy plain of the eastern Landes towards the county of Armagnac. On 12 October 1355 the army reached the limits of the duchy of Aquitaine just north of Labastide d'Armagnac, a walled new town lying across the Bordeaux road. New knights were made among the squires of the army and the banners of the commanders, which were kept rolled up in friendly territory, were unfurled. The Prince ordered his troops in the traditional fashion in three columns. This enabled the army to march across a broad front, which made foraging easier and destruction more extensive. It also allowed them to come quickly together in something like battle order if they were attacked. They advanced in parallel lines and began burning: crops, woodland, villages and isolated farms and houses. Within hours their presence was signalled by a huge pall of smoke and a ring of fire extending for many miles around. Three substantial places were burned on the first day of the invasion. The large fortified village of Monclar burned so fiercely that the Prince had to withdraw into the fields to escape from the heat. For the next eleven days, from 13 to 23 October, the Anglo-Gascons marched through Armagnac. The county extended over a green undulating landscape of low hills and shallow valleys, densely scattered with ancient castles, fortified hill villages and occasional *bastides*: 'a noble, rich and beautiful region', thought the anonymous diarist who followed the Prince's column on its march. The walls of these places had been put up quickly and cheaply long ago. They were good for keeping out bandits and wild animals, but little more. The Prince's army burned a broad track across the province, destroying every place in their path except Montesquieu and Mirande, which were too strongly defended; and the small town of Bassoue, which was spared by the Prince's order because it belonged to the Church. 'We have wasted and destroyed this region,' the Prince reported home, '. . . which has given great satisfaction to the subjects of our Lord the King.'[61]

The eastern extremity of Armagnac was marked by the valley of the River Gers. When the Prince's army reached it they did not pause as perhaps some of them had expected to. They pressed on eastward, an arduous trek across the steep, dry valleys of Astarac and Comminges

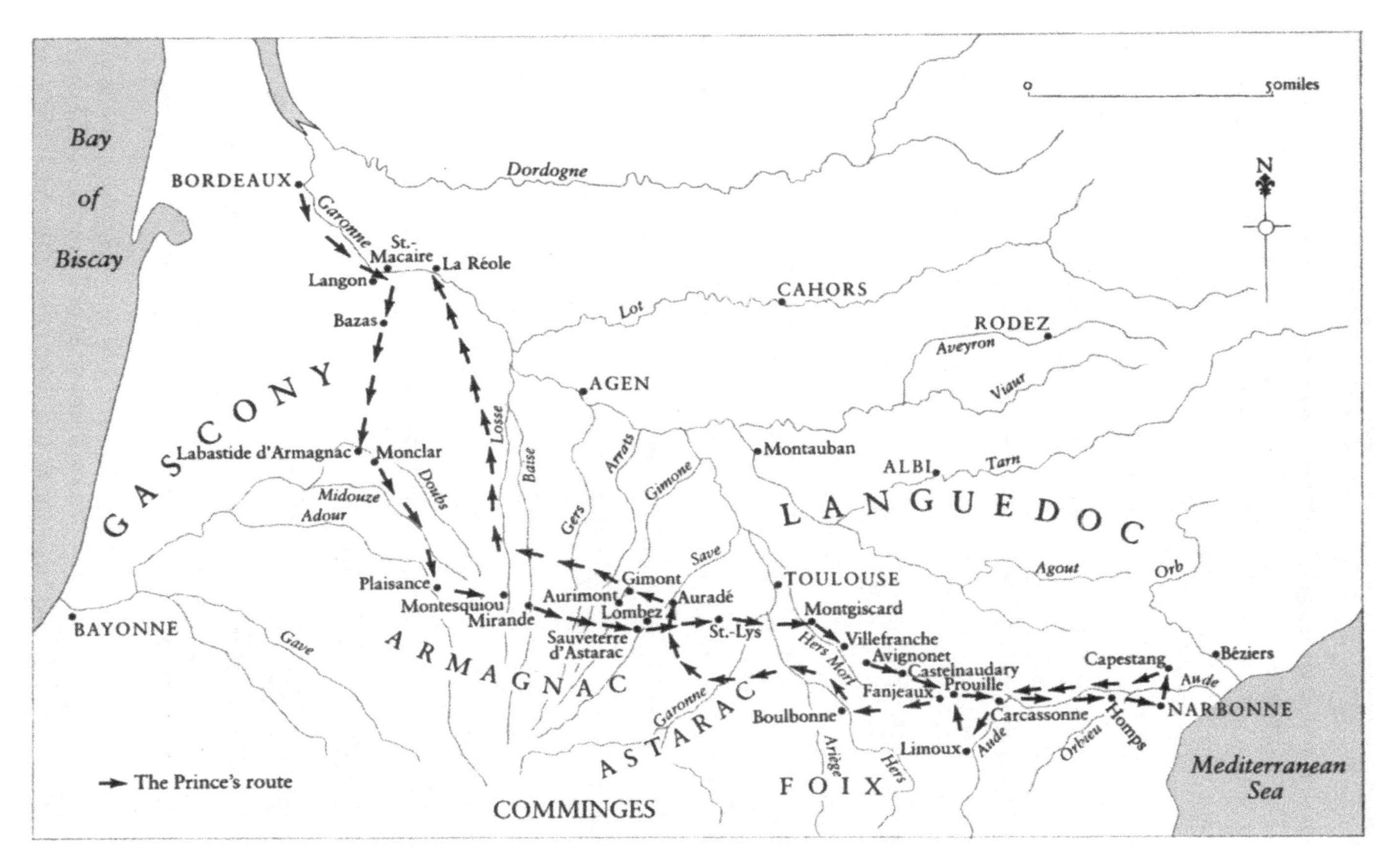

11 The Prince of Wales in Languedoc, October–December 1355

within sight of the crests of the Pyrenees. The villagers fled before them, abandoning the newly gathered harvest in their barns and storehouses. It was not even necessary for the invaders to send out forage parties. The pattern was monotonously regular. The larger, better manned towns such as Sauveterre d'Astarac and Lombez were left alone. The rest were occupied without opposition, then plundered, destroyed and abandoned.[62]

French defensive operations were conducted by a quarrelsome triumvirate consisting of the Count of Armagnac, the Marshal de Clermont and the Constable Jacques de Bourbon. Armagnac commanded an army of local troops which had been urgently summoned into being as soon as the Prince had arrived in Bordeaux. Clermont had brought his men down from north of the Dordogne. The Constable was no doubt accompanied by some northern retinues. Rather more substantial reinforcements had been expected to arrive with the Dauphin until they were diverted to Picardy. But even without them, according to the French King's information, the number of troops at the disposal of his commanders in the south-west comfortably exceeded the Prince's strength. The problem lay in the Count of Armagnac's strategy of avoiding battle at all costs, which he had consistently followed in the south-west in order to avoid a repetition of the disasters of Bergerac, Auberoche and Crécy. If this policy made sense against the modest forces of Sir John Cheverston, then it plainly made even better sense against the Prince of Wales, with his larger numbers and his considerable force of English longbowmen. Armagnac therefore limited himself to defending the principal towns and castles and the major river crossings. This was inglorious and demoralising in the eyes of the population of Languedoc and it was the source of much tension between Armagnac and the Constable. Even this largely passive scheme of defence might have produced better results if the Prince had mounted his raid by the Garonne Valley, as he had been expected to do, instead of further south. Armagnac was at Agen when the Prince left Bordeaux. While the Anglo-Gascons burnt their away across his domains, he and his two colleagues were marching south to the regional capital of Toulouse. There they shut themselves in and braced themselves for a siege, stopping gaps in the defences and breaking the bridges on all the main approaches to the city.[63]

On the evening of 26 October 1355, the Prince was reported at Saint-Lys, a small town about 15 miles south-west of Toulouse. The French commanders assumed that he would now either turn back home or attack the city. This was a plausible enough assumption. But the Prince did neither of these things. On 28 October he crossed both the Garonne ('swift, rocky and terrifying', according to the diarist) and the Ariège ('even more dangerous') within twelve hours. The rivers were forded at places where horses had never crossed before. None of them was guarded. Once he had reached the east bank of the Ariège, the Prince turned north to within a few miles of the walls of Toulouse as if to attack them. The Constable hurriedly left for Montauban to hold the crossings of the Tarn and the Garonne and to obstruct any attempt to invest the city from both sides. But the Prince had no intention of passing the winter in a long siege of a major city like Toulouse. Instead, he struck east towards the Mediterranean, leaving the French forces behind him.[64]

The great plain of the Toulousain, already in the fourteenth century the granary of southern France, extended as far as the eye could see on either side of the old Roman road to Narbonne. The towns along the route had suffered badly from the economic misfortunes of the past few years, and most of them had also lost a large part of their population in the plague. But they still lived well on grain and cloth and on the commerce of one of the great crossroads of southern Europe, where the routes of Aquitaine, Catalonia and the Rhone Valley met. One of the 'fattest lands in the world', Froissart called it. Most of the towns of the region stood on low-lying ground, behind rudimentary walls of clay and brick surviving from the wars of an earlier generation. No serious measures had been taken to strengthen them for many years. The Prince's troops encountered no opposition. They became bolder and began to attack the larger, richer and stronger towns which they had previously passed by.

When the English arrived, they spread out around the town and their assault parties began to throw themselves against the walls. Their archers were formed up in divisions and fired volleys of arrows so dense that the defenders could no longer hold their positions on the walls. Then the assault parties pressed their advantage and poured across the defences to capture the place. There was tremendous slaughter and violence. The whole town was infested by the invaders. It was sacked and pillaged and everything in it carried off. The English did not bother with mere bales of cloth when there was so much gold plate and coin to be taken. When they had captured a townsman or a peasant they demanded ransom from him and if he would not pay they left him mutilated. Then they abandoned the town, burning and ruinous, its citadel demolished and its walls thrown down.

Froissart's conventional images might have described any of the market towns which the Anglo-Gascons burned on their march: Montgiscard, Villefranche, Avignonet, Castelnaudary. The English were astonished by the ease of their advance. 'Every day,' the Prince wrote to his father's chief minister in England, 'our divisions captured towns, castles, fortresses.'[65]

On Tuesday 3 November 1355 the army arrived before Carcassonne, one of the principal towns of Languedoc and a major administrative and ecclesiastical centre. The distant view of the city profoundly impressed the English. It was 'larger, stronger and more beautiful than York', Sir John Wingfield thought. One man even compared it with London. Carcassonne was really two towns. On a rocky platform overlooking the Aude from the east stood the *cité*, a vast fortress-town with a double circuit of walls pierced by a powerful citadel and fortified gateways and towers. This imposing defensive system was a monument of insecure government. It had been reconstructed in the course of the thirteenth century to serve as one of the main bastions of the Crown in a province where it had only recently assumed control. On the opposite side of the river, towards Toulouse, lay the *bourg*, a modern town which had grown up since the middle of the thirteenth century. Most of the inhabitants and virtually all the wealth of the town were concentrated there. It had a large garrison, including much of the nobility of the outlying region. But it was unwalled and virtually indefensible. When the English arrived, the population withdrew together with their defenders into the *cité*, leaving the enemy to take possession without opposition. They helped themselves to everything which the inhabitants had been too late or too slow to take with them. They drank themselves insensible on Muscat wine, the sweet wine for which Frontignan and Rivesaltes were already becoming known. The citizens obtained a short truce. They sent a delegation out from the *cité* to parley with the Prince. They offered him a prodigious sum to be left alone. But this kind of bargain, however commonplace with subordinate commanders, was hardly ever accepted by Edward III or his son. They had to observe the fiction that their enemies were rebellious subjects. The Prince told the delegates that he had come for 'justice, not money.' He demanded surrender. They refused. On 6 November 1355, after passing three days in the *bourg*, the troops went through the place systematically firing the houses. Then they withdrew through the burning streets to the fields outside to watch the conflagration. No attempt was made on the defences of the *cité*.[66]

The roads east from Carcassonne passed through the flat sandy basin of the lower Aude, a 'tedious journey' the diarist thought, done in foul conditions, driving rain and mud underfoot. They reached Narbonne on 8 November 1355. Narbonne was a city with a famous past, now in steep decline. The Aude had shifted its course to the north. Rival ports, Montpellier and Aigues-Mortes, had encroached on its trade. The great gothic choir of the cathedral of St. Just had been completed six years before. But the rest of it was never built. Narbonne was another double city. The *cité*, the ecclesiastical and administrative centre, was a walled and garrisoned fortress. The *bourg*, on the opposite side of the river, contained the commercial and industrial quarters and most of the richer residential areas. Like Carcassonne's, it was virtually open. Not long before, its walls had been reported to be incomplete and collapsing for want of repair, and although plans had been made to rebuild them and some preliminary demolitions had been carried out, very little had been done. The invaders found the *bourg* deserted and occupied it without resistance.

As the army set about looting the mansions of the *bourg*, the Prince himself lodged in the Carmelite convent. There he received a messenger sent to him by two emissaries of the Pope. They had come, they said, to negotiate a truce and desired a safe conduct to the Prince's presence. They were treated with the utmost disdain. The messenger was kept waiting for two days. Then he was sent back with a direction that since Edward III had now crossed the Channel with his army, they should address themselves to him.

The Prince, however, was beginning to encounter more serious tests of his self-confidence. His men had marched nearly 300 miles from home and had come within sight of the Mediterranean. They could never remain too long in one place without running short of victuals. The rain had swollen the streams across the flats around Narbonne and reduced the whole plain to a bog where marching was difficult and fresh water could not be had. There were probably enough supplies for the moment in Narbonne. But the town was becoming increasingly difficult for the English to hold. The garrison of the *cité* bombarded the *bourg* day and night with catapults, causing heavy casualties among the invaders. When, on 10 November, they began to shoot burning arrows into the wooden houses, the Anglo-Gascons decided to withdraw. They retreated through the burning streets. As they did so, they were pursued by angry mobs of townsmen who swarmed after them across the bridges from the *cité*, attacking stragglers and smashing some of the

Prince's wagons. It was the first significant resistance that he had encountered.[67]

There were signs of more to come. French prisoners brought into the English camp were reporting that the French commanders had now gathered their forces west of Narbonne. In fact, although the Prince did not know it, the Count of Armagnac and the Constable de Bourbon were less than fifteen miles away from him at the bridge-town of Homps on the Aude. They seemed to be trying to cut off the invaders' retreat and force them to battle on their own terms. The Prince held a council of war. It was decided to retreat towards home. At first the plan was to outmarch the French army by the north. The Anglo-Gascons moved up the Domitian Way towards Béziers. But they found their route blocked by troops brought down from the Rhone Valley by the Seneschal of Beaucaire. Runners sent ahead by the Prince to test the defences of Béziers found the town filled with men-at-arms. The English army passed the night of 11 November near the castle of Capestang, which was about half-way between Béziers and the Count of Armagnac's encampment at Homps. On the following day they turned east towards Armagnac. They expected to have to fight. Ambitious squires came forward to be knighted on the eve of battle. But there was no battle. On the following day the French army was found to have withdrawn west towards Toulouse. The Prince followed them as far as Carcassonne. Then he struck out south into undefended territory towards the county of Foix.[68]

The plan now was to pass well south of Toulouse, leaving the largest possible distance between the two armies. The Prince's army split into two units and smashed their way across the Razès. On 15 November, the captains of the army passed Sunday at the famous Dominican foundation of Prouille. While they were being received as lay brothers into the community, the rest of the army burned four towns within twelve hours. They included the great cloth town of Limoux on the Aude and the hill town of Fanjeaux, which thus achieved a brief moment of fame for the first time since it had served as the holy city of Catharism a century and a half before. There was no irony in the contrast. The men at Prouille were commanding an army at war, and fought with the efficient brutality with which wars had always been fought. Like Froissart, men pitied their victims and admired their chivalry in the same breath.[69]

On 17 November 1355 there was a significant encounter between the Prince and the Count of Foix in the Cistercian abbey of Boulbonne. The

Count, Gaston Phoebus, was twenty-four years old, the same age as the Prince himself. He was a flamboyant young man, charming, humourous and learned, the future author of a manual on hunting and another on the art of prayer. He ruled the two concentrated principalities of Foix and Béarn on the north face of the Pyrenees. Although these territories were not as extensive of those of John of Armagnac, Gaston Phoebus was after John the most powerful feudatory of the south-west. His allegiance was valuable. But it was also increasingly uncertain. Gaston's father had been the main pillar of the French Crown in the region for the first three years of the war, and had remained consistently faithful to the house of Valois for the rest of his life. But after the death of the old count, in 1343, there were signs of a change of sentiment. One reason was the ambition of the new count to throw off his dependence on the Kings of France and become a sovereign prince, at least in his dominions of Béarn whose precise legal status had always been rather unclear. In September 1347, when the fall of Calais had reduced the prestige of the French Crown to its lowest point for many years, Gaston Phoebus announced to the King of France's representative that he considered Béarn to be held of 'no man on earth but of God alone.' The Frenchman was so astonished that he called for a notary to take down the Count's words verbatim. There was, however, another more potent emotion in Gaston Phoebus' breast. That was his intense jealousy of the Count of Armagnac and his resentment of Armagnac's growing influence in south-western France. The vendetta of the Counts of Armagnac and Foix was very ancient. It dated back to the previous century when they had first become rivals in the rich territory along the foothills of the western Pyrenees. So, as the government in Paris became more dependent on the energy and loyalty of John of Armagnac, the position of the Count of Foix became ever more ambiguous. Although Gaston Phoebus continued to acknowledge that he was a vassal of the French King for the county of Foix, he did almost nothing for his sovereign. Apart from a brief period in 1351 and 1352 when he took part in some minor campaigns in the Garonne Valley, he evaded every request for military assistance and refrained from doing anything against the English. When, at the end of 1352, John II reappointed the Count of Armagnac as his Lieutenant in Languedoc, Gaston promptly withdrew from all French military operations in the region. Worse, although the new Lieutenant had his hands full in dealing with English incursions in the Aveyron and the Tarn Valleys, Gaston invaded his lands with more than 2,000 men and did a great deal of damage there.[70]

Like many territorial noblemen who quarrelled with the government, Gaston Phoebus found a natural ally in Charles of Navarre. He had much in common with that polished conspirator. He was a near neighbour. He was married to his sister. His ambitions, like Charles's, were blocked by the King's friends. So, although the Count of Foix cannot by now have had much credit to draw on at the French court, it was he who spoke for the King of Navarre's interests in the spring of 1355 when Charles was trying to work his way back into royal favour. It was only a matter of time before Gaston made approaches to the English as Charles had done. There had already been overt signs of sympathy. The Count's bastard brother and close collaborator, Arnaud-Guilhem, did homage to Edward III in England in the summer of 1355. When later in that year the Prince of Wales invaded Languedoc, Gaston allowed his subjects to serve in the Prince's army. The Prince for his part issued orders strictly forbidding the plundering of any of the Count's property. Whatever tacit arrangements existed were confirmed at Gaston's meeting with the Prince at Boulbonne. The Count of Foix did not formally become an ally of the English. But he moved gradually into their orbit, offering them discreet co-operation when it was needed, and providing a perennial source of menace in John of Armagnac's rear.[71]

The march back from the Mediterranean to the Atlantic was an exhausting trek by an army which had left the elation of conquest behind them. The Prince took a southerly route, which avoided the French army but meant travelling over steep hillsides and stony tracks. It rained incessantly. And as the streams filled with mud, food and fresh water became hard to find. At one point wine was being given to the horses. The days shortened and the nights grew cold. Most of the men had to sleep outside without tents or blankets. There were few towns to pillage and those were well defended or belonged to the Count of Foix. On 17 and 18 November the army repeated its feat of three weeks before, crossing the Ariège and the Garonne in single file over a period of thirty-six hours although both rivers were swollen by autumn rains, to the 'stupor' of the inhabitants of the region.[72]

John of Armagnac's men harassed stragglers, scouts and foragers. But they did not attack the main body of the Prince's army while it was at its most vulnerable. It was not until the Prince's army had passed the Ariège that any serious attempt was made to cut him off. By now the resentment and frustration which Armagnac's passivity had provoked in the people of Languedoc had spread to the Lieutenant's headquarters in Toulouse. The Constable, Jacques de Bourbon, was impatient for action. His relations with the Count of Armagnac had become so bad that news of their quarrels reached the English on their march. On about 18 November 1355 the French army marched south-west from Toulouse. Their plan seems to have been to stop the Prince on the river Save, a fast running river which would be difficult for them to ford. If so it was a humiliating failure. When the Prince was within fifteen miles of the river, his scouts found the French army approaching in five columns in battle order some miles ahead. There was a violent skirmish between an isolated detachment of French troops and an English reconnaissance force, in which the French suffered heavy casualties and more than thirty of them were captured. Armagnac halted his advance immediately. Instead he decided to retreat across the Save at Lombez. At night the two armies watched each other's camp fires across the river. Then, on 21 November, Armagnac broke the bridges over the river and withdrew towards the north. Early on the 22nd, the Prince's men repaired the bridge at Auradé and crossed over. They caught up with Armagnac's rearguard near the small town of Aurimont on the river Gimone and pursued them down the river valley as far as Gimont. Gimont was a walled town with a bridge. For a few hours it seemed that Armagnac's army were going to make a stand there. On the 23rd, before dawn, the Anglo-Gascons drew themselves up in battle order on the hills south of the town. But when the sun rose they found that the French army had folded their tents and stolen away in the night. They had left only a garrison to hold the town. The Prince crossed the Gimone a few miles further south without opposition and resumed his march. On 28 November 1355 the army re-entered the duchy. Most of the Gascons and Béarnais were paid off. The English refurled their banners.[73]

The Prince was highly satisfied with the campaign. A great quantity of booty had been brought back from Languedoc, enough to fill about a 1,000 carts according to reports. The ransoms of French prisoners were collected gradually over the following months as contracts were enforced and promissory notes were cashed. Many of the Prince's followers became rich men.[74] The military value of the enterprise was more questionable. No battles had been won, no territory conquered, and no castles garrisoned. But the Anglo-Gascons had destroyed about 500 villages lying in a band about 200 miles long by forty miles wide across southern France. They had ruined at least a dozen walled towns and the trading and residential quarters of three major cities. The damage to the economy of the south-west was very serious. The English were well aware that wars were fought with money and they understood perfectly the economic consequences of what they were doing. The Prince's clerks examined the tax records in captured towns and interrogated functionaries whom they found there. They concluded that in the Toulousain, the Carcassès and the Narbonnais they had destroyed communities with a combined taxable capacity of 400,000 *écus*. Carcassonne, Limoux and the smaller towns nearby alone accounted for 100,000 *écus* of tax revenue and the wages of 2,000 men-at-arms. Not only was the taxable capacity of these places much reduced, but what was left of it had now to be appropriated to reconstruction, wall building and local defence, leaving very little to finance field operations. At the end of October 1355, as the Prince was circumventing Armagnac's army south of Toulouse, the town council of Millau met 120 miles away in the heart of Rouergue to resolve upon the reconstruction of its walls, a great collective enterprise which took many years and consumed most of the available tax revenues of the town throughout that period. Similar decisions were being made throughout Languedoc in the last few weeks of 1355. A fresh campaign of wall-building began at Narbonne. The initial surveys were undertaken within ten days of the Prince's departure and five years' worth of tax revenues were appropriated to the work. Avignonet, Fanjeaux, Castelnaudary, Montgiscard, Alzonne, Limoux and Carbonne were among the ruined towns which had to be given extensive exemptions and privileges until their fortunes were restored. These included a moratorium on the enforcement of private debts owed to outsiders and a partial respite from taxation. 'And by God's help, if my lord only had the means, he would expand the limit of the duchy and conquer many places,' concluded Sir John Wingfield, the head of the Prince's household. 'Our enemies,' he added, 'are truly astonished'.[75]

It was the astonishment that was the Prince's real achievement. Although the inhabitants of Languedoc had suffered war taxation and conscription for many years, and occasional military alarms, they were utterly unprepared for destruction on this scale. The ease with which the Prince had penetrated 200 miles into the French King's territory wholly unopposed while a larger French army including a royal Lieutenant and the two senior military officers of the French Crown stood aside, was a shattering blow to French self-confidence. The reverberations in places which he had not touched were even greater than those of Lancaster's invasion of Poitou a decade before. Panic spread through all of southern France. Montpellier demolished its suburbs. The scholars of its famous university fled to Avignon, accompanied by many of the citizens. When they arrived they found workmen reinforcing the gates of the papal palace with iron bracing.[76] A stream of protests was directed at the government in Paris. The King received eye-witness accounts of the destruction from Jacques de Bourbon and Jean de Clermont. But most of the blame was heaped upon them, and on the hapless John of Armagnac. Embarrassed letters of explanation and apology were sent by the King to the principal towns of Languedoc, and promises of energetic steps to defend the province against further incursions. A 'prodigious' army would shortly leave for the south, he said. The Duke of Orléans, John's brother, had already been appointed to command it.[77]

News of the Prince's deeds in Languedoc had reached Paris by the last week of November. But it took another six weeks for reliable information to reach England. When Sir Richard Stafford (the Earl's younger brother) arrived in London with the Prince's despatches in January 1356, he found the country preoccupied with events nearer home: the burning of Picardy, invasion scares on the south coast, the incursions of the Scots and their French allies, the campaign to recapture Berwick-on-Tweed.[78] The King had left Westminster for the north in the second week of December and reached the Tyne on Christmas Eve. Over the new year a great assembly of men gathered in the fortress-town of Newcastle, now already beginning its second career as the coal capital of England. The recruitment of archers and infantry had been in progress in the march of Wales and in every county north of the Trent for a month. Men-at-arms had been retained by the King and his companions all over England. Ten of the King's largest ships had been mobilised and more had been requisitioned in the east coast ports. The great engine of English military administration was slow and noisy. The Scots must have had plenty of warning of what was afoot. But they scarcely knew how to take advantage of it.[79]

The whole mass of men moved north out of Newcastle on 6 January 1356. Walter Mauny went ahead with the advance guard, including 120 miners. When he reached Berwick he took command of the garrison of the castle and began the preparations for the recapture of the town. Tunnels were dug towards the town walls. Plans were made for a simultaneous assault by land and water. The Scots in Berwick did not wait for the signal to be given. Their numbers were small. They were defending a large expanse of wall with a surly and unreliable population at their backs. Their stores were low. Their leaders were quarrelling among themselves. And they no longer had the assistance of Yon de Garencières. He had left Scotland with his men immediately after the capture of the town and was back in France in December as Edward III was beginning his march north. By the time the English King arrived with the bulk of the army, on 13 January 1356, the Scots were ready to surrender. They sent a delegation to the castle gate to parley with him. They offered up with the keys of the town. Edward III took the keys and delivered them to John Coupland as captain of Berwick. The Scots were allowed to withdraw with their lives.[80]

Having accomplished so easily the business for which he had come, Edward III removed his headquarters to Roxburgh, further up the Tweed. Here, the last chapter of the tragedy of Edward Balliol was played out with dramatic symbolism. Balliol, whose title of King of Scotland had been an empty formula for many years, was an old man now and too tired to keep up the pretence any longer. On 20 January 1356, as the English army approached the gates of Roxburgh, he came before Edward III on the road and renounced Scotland in his favour in a bitter speech delivered 'like a roaring lion'. Then he took the crown from his head, scooped a handful of earth and stones from the Scottish ground, and handed them to the King of England. Edward paid off Balliol's debts and saved his dignity with a pension of £2,000 from the English Treasury. Balliol retired to Yorkshire where he lived on in peaceful obscurity until 1364.[81]

Edward rested his army at Roxburgh and prepared to revenge himself on the Scots. They fled from the eastern lowlands in large numbers. They buried their money. They stripped the furniture from their houses. They drove their cattle north before them. They hid in caves and woods. The lord of Douglas sent his agents to meet Edward III on the road with 'sotiles paroles et decevantes' and agreed a ten-day truce with the English King in the great tracts of the region which he controlled. The ostensible reason for the truce was to discover whether the nobility of Scotland could be persuaded to submit to English sovereignty. But in fact Douglas needed more time to complete the evacuation of his own lands. On 26 January 1356, the English army struck east from Roxburgh and marched up the coast through the territory of Patrick Earl of March and Dunbar, the other Scottish lord who had been responsible for the capture of Berwick. Patrick's lands were not covered by the truce. The English spread themselves out in three columns, burning everything across a twenty-mile front. It was the most destructive English expedition in Scotland since the 1330s.

By the time Edward reached Edinburgh, at the beginning of February 1356, he realised that the Scots had no intention of submitting to him. So he burnt the lower town of Edinburgh, which had been abandoned. Then he moved east and set up his headquarters in the small town of Haddington near the Firth of Forth. When he left, a little later, the town was in ruins and the famous gothic church of the Franciscans, which men called the 'lamp of Lothian', had been reduced to rubble.

By now, the King's army was in serious difficulty. The Scots had removed a large part of their animals and stores to the district north of Stirling. The army's foragers were finding it impossible to get supplies. Fresh water was almost unobtainable. To make matters worse the English victualling fleet, which was heading north to meet the King, failed to arrive. It was delayed by unproductive diversions to pillage coastal villages and churches, and then dispersed by a great storm as it made its way along the south shore of the Firth of Forth. Edward was forced to retreat south without further delay. He burned his way across Douglas territory towards the border, while Douglas himself followed at a safe distance, falling on stragglers and independent groups and harassing the army on its way. In the forest around Melrose, Douglas ambushed Edward's own column and inflicted heavy losses on it. Many Englishmen died of hunger and cold on this retreat. By the end of February 1356, the King reached Carlisle. There he paid off the men of the north, and marched south towards Westminster.[82]

English public opinion was very dismissive about the King's campaign. In the northern counties, where the border was always a more anxious concern than France, it was regarded as a waste of time and effort. It was true that Edward had recaptured Berwick and re-established the English positions along the Tweed. But he had also demonstrated the pointlessness of trying to control even the lowlands, let alone the regions beyond the Forth. The very shapelessness of the Scottish government put a permanent settlement out of reach. As soon as the English army had withdrawn across the border, Douglas gathered his men and launched a tremendous onslaught on Edward's few remaining allies in the south-west of the kingdom. The great castles of Caerlaverock and Dalswinton in Nithsdale were stormed and partially demolished. Penetrating west into the Gaelic-speaking regions of the Solway Firth and the Firth of Clyde, the Scots swiftly overran Galloway and Kyle. If Balliol still enjoyed some residual loyalty here, where his family had been great men for more than a century, he completely failed to transmit it to Edward III. The chief power in Galloway, Duncan

MacDowell, had broken with the English in 1353 and maintained a sullen neutrality ever since. He met Douglas at Cumnok Church to surrender the region into the hands of the Scottish Guardian. Only in Annandale, where an English garrison clung on to the great fortress of Lochmaben, did Edward's officers preserve a semblance of control.[83] In April 1356, some two months after the English King had left Scotland, his Lieutenant there, the Earl of Northampton, agreed a truce with the lord of Douglas. It was the end of the attempt to subdue the northern kingdom which had begun at Dupplin Moor and Halidon Hill more than twenty years before. The English did not enter Scotland again in force until 1385. As for Douglas, his own war against the English continued elsewhere. Within a few weeks of the truce on the Scottish march he had taken ship for France with a company of about 200 men-at-arms, including some of the great names among the rising generation of Scottish chivalry.[84]

On 2 December 1355 the Prince of Wales assembled the leaders of his army in the fortress of la Réole overlooking the Garonne. A few prominent Gascons were there, including Jean de Grailly Captal de Buch, Auger de Montaut, lord of Mussidan, and Élie de Pommiers, who were by now virtually full-time soldiers. But most of the Gascons had returned to their homes for the winter. It was an overwhelmingly English gathering. The available troops, some 2,200 Englishmen and a few hundred Gascons, were shared out among the commanders and given winter stations along the northern march. Warwick remained at la Réole. Salisbury was sent to Sainte-Foy on the Dordogne. Suffolk was based at Saint-Emilion. The Prince set up his own military headquarters at Libourne with Audley and Chandos. From these places it was planned to send raiding forces across the march to push out the frontiers of the duchy. The men were allowed three weeks to rest after their exertions in Languedoc.[85]

The fighting began shortly after Christmas. Montravel, the heavily garrisoned French fortress on the Dordogne near Castillon, a thorn in the side of the Seneschals since it had been captured in 1351, was retaken. Two columns of troops then advanced east into the Agenais. The Earl of Warwick invaded the valley of the Lot, capturing Tonneins, one of the few remaining French towns of any importance in the region, and the fortified monastery and bridge at Clairac. Another detachment, about 750 strong, marched up the Garonne under Chandos and Audley. They captured Port-Sainte-Marie in early January 1356. This important

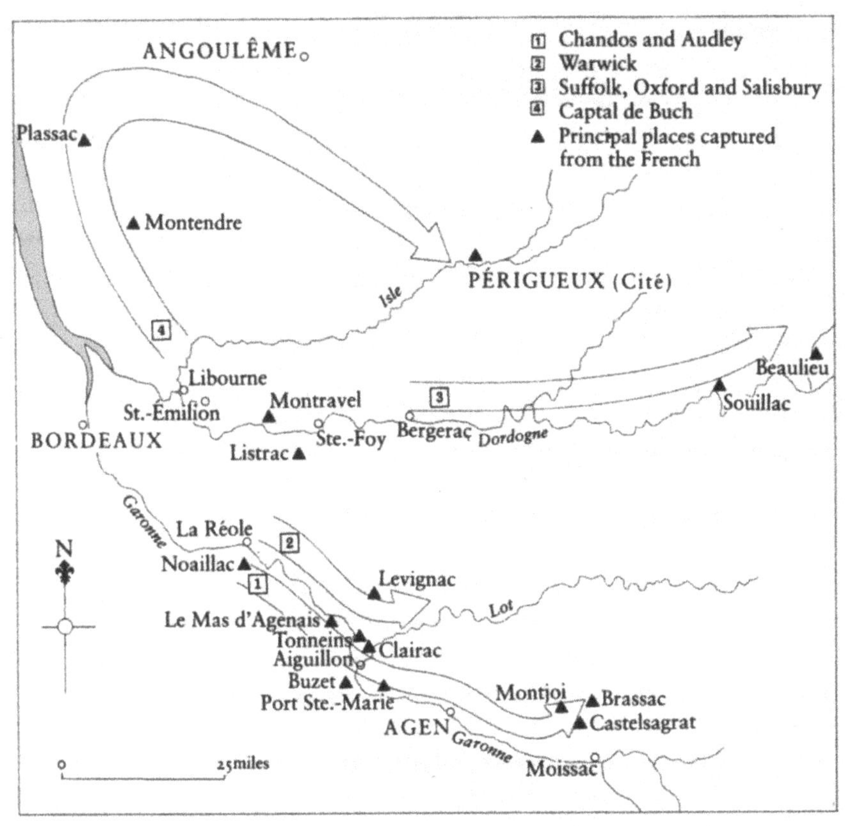

12 English conquests in south-western France, December 1355–February 1356

river port had a garrison of 300 men, the largest in the region after Agen itself. But its commander surrendered without a fight and delivered up all the subsidiary forts around. An outraged French government immediately accused him of treason, perhaps rightly. The English put a large permanent garrison into Port-Sainte-Marie. Then they burned up to the walls of Agen, destroying all the windmills around the town and burning the bridge over the Garonne. The town of Castelsagrat was stormed. The castle of Brassac fell immediately afterwards.

A third force, larger than the others, was commanded by the Earls of Suffolk, Oxford and Salisbury and the lords of Pommiers and Mussidan. They marched up the valley of the Dordogne and invaded the lordship of Turenne, a great barony extending over much of southern Limousin and northern Quercy on either side of the Dordogne. With 1,000 men and the advantage of surprise, they caused mayhem in this rich and vulnerable region. They occupied Souillac. They captured Beaulieu-sur-Dordogne after a short siege, and fortified its famous abbey. These places became nests of bandits whose garrisons established clones in villages and castles across the region, terrorising the viscounty of Turenne and launching raids deep into the surrounding provinces until they were eventually bought out in the autumn of 1357. Further south the men of Quercy, hardened by more than five years of raiding and large-scale banditry, were able to hold their walls. But success brought them no security. At Martel the consuls ordered special processions and intercessions, and had an oath of loyalty administered to every adult inhabitant.[86]

The most spectacular coup was achieved by the Captal de Buch. He collected together a mixed band of Gascons and Englishmen and recaptured a large number of castles on the eastern march of Saintonge. At the end of January 1356, he reinforced his company by drawing on the garrisons of the province and invaded Poitou with about 600 men. But instead of advancing on Poitiers or Angoulême, as had perhaps been expected, he suddenly turned south towards Périgueux. The low-lying and poorly walled *cité* was captured by escalade at night and handed over to the lord of Mussidan. This man, Edward III's principal captain in the region, had passed more than ten years in harassing the men of Périgueux. He installed a large garrison of his own men in the *cité*. The *bourg*, clustered within its own walls around the monastery of St. Front, was assaulted several times during the next few days. The defenders held out, and were eventually reinforced by the Count of Périgord and the Count of Lisle with a large royal garrison. But they could not have suffered more if the *bourg* had fallen. The inhabitants, after enduring a ten-year battle against the Anglo-Gascon garrisons around them, now found themselves caught in the continual cross-fire of rival garrisons occupying different parts of their own town.[87]

The French commanders in the south-west did nothing. The Seneschal of the Agenais shut himself in Agen 'not daring to put his head over the parapet', wrote Wingfield. There was nothing else to be done. The 'prodigious' army which John II had promised to send to Languedoc would take at least two months to recruit and supply. But work did not even begin until the new year. The army which had been recruited locally to confront the Prince of Wales in Languedoc had been disbanded and there was neither time nor money to raise another. The Count of Armagnac was away at Béziers conferring with the ambassadors of the King of Aragon, and then in Avignon for discussions with the Pope. In his absence, the senior French commander in the region was Jean de Boucicaut, whose headquarters were at Moissac. He was an able man, and certainly did not lack boldness. But he had just 600 men under his command.[88]

The damage done to John II's interest in the south in the first six weeks of 1356 proved to be even graver than his humiliation in Languedoc in the previous autumn. It is true that the Prince's territorial gains had been modest: five walled towns and seventeen castles by the third week of January, perhaps half a dozen more including Périgueux by the end of February. But they were concentrated in the strategically important districts of the north-western march, where there were important allies to be found if only they could be convinced that the English presence was permanent. In the spring of 1356 some significant turncoats were convinced. Jean de Galard lord of Limeuil transferred his allegiance to the Prince at the beginning of the year, the fifth time that he had changed sides in ten years. Gaillard de Durfort, who had done homage to Edward III's representatives after the victories of Henry of Lancaster in 1345 and then defected to the French in 1352, returned to the fold. His vast clan controlled no less than thirty walled towns and castles in the Agenais and southern Périgord. Guilhem-Raymond lord of Caumont, who had repudiated the English allegiance in 1342 after a quarrel with the lord of Albret, did homage at about the same time. He brought six walled towns with him, most of them in the crucial region around the confluence of the Lot and the Garonne which controlled the eastern approaches to Bordeaux. Many of these men had ancient disputes with those who were already among the pillars of the English cause, particularly the ubiquitous and quarrelsome Albrets. Accommodating the conflicting ambitions of these touchy and violent men was an exacting test of the Prince's patience and diplomatic skills as well as a drain on his resources. But the Prince's advisers knew that the price was worth paying. Astute men like Gaillard de Durfort were not only men of influence and power. They were the weather-vanes of the south-west. The clans which defected in 1356 were to remain loyal to Edward III and his son for more than a decade, years of victory and riches.[89]

At Westminster, the English King and his ministers were making plans to build on the Prince's work and exploit the increasingly noticeable internal difficulties of John II's government. The old strategic dream of a combined invasion of France from north and south was revived. The Duke of Lancaster's expedition to Brittany, which had been cancelled in the autumn when Edward needed his troops in Picardy, was refixed for

April 1356. The men were summoned to muster with their horses and equipment at Southampton. At about the same time a second fleet was due to sail to Gascony from Plymouth with supplies and reinforcements for the Prince of Wales. [90]

CHAPTER V

Poitiers
1356

On 25 September 1355, John II suspended payment of all royal debts until the following Easter, the second time that this had happened since his accession. He gave as his reason the 'great charges and expenses sustained on account of our wars, particularly in the present year, and the fresh burdens which we shall have to support in future.'[1] The strain had been intensifying since the beginning of the year 1355 as the King had had to deal first with the threat from Charles of Navarre in Normandy, then with Edward III in Picardy, and finally with the Prince of Wales in Gascony and Languedoc. In Languedoc tax collection had virtually ceased since the Prince's raid. Elsewhere, the machinery of collection remained in existence, but functioned badly. Southern Normandy, traditionally one of the most productive regions of France, had been virtually removed from the French government's tax base since the King had fallen out with Charles of Navarre, a state of affairs which was more or less legitimised by the treaty of Valognes. The capacity of medieval communities to produce surpluses for tax collectors was always marginal. The political and administrative difficulties of the French government coincided with a period of sharply rising wages and falling prices, and a severe agricultural depression which wiped out the margin even in regions which were not suffering from direct war damage.[2]

John II had no source of windfall revenues other than coinage operations, the traditional stand-by in financial emergencies. During the year 1355 there had been no less than eight devaluations of the silver coinage. The *monnayage* was generally above 30 per cent and at one point exceeded 45 per cent. These measures had yielded good profits for the Crown. But it was politically impossible to go on in this way for much longer. It was in 1355 that Nicholas of Oresme, Master of the College of Navarre in Paris, had produced his famous treatise on money, one of the most influential works on the subject ever written. Nicholas challenged the whole juridical basis on which the Crown controlled the coinage, asserting that it was the common property of the people and not of their ruler. But Nicholas no populist. He was a skilful pamphleteer writing in the interest of the Church and the landed aristocracy. As he pointed out, the debasement of the coinage could be positively beneficial to peasants and urban wage-earners, who rarely used coin as a store of value and did not depend on revenues fixed in nominal money. The victims were the 'best classes of the community', in particular the landed community which lived on agricultural rents and supplied most of the taxpayers and warriors on which the state depended in its wars. The King's bankruptcy provoked a severe crisis in his relations with the 'best classes of the community'.[3]

Early in October 1355, at his wits' end for money, John II summoned the Estates-General of Languedoil. On 28 November 1355, shortly before it opened, the King was forced to make a major concession in order to prevent the proceedings from being taken over by the victims of his coinage policies. He issued a contrite proclamation that he would never again alter the value of the coinage and would make his sons swear to do likewise.[4] The opening ceremonies took place in the Great Chamber of the Parlement of Paris on 2 December 1355. The Chamber was a large barrel-roofed hall at the north end of the palace on the *Cité*, dominated by a wall painting of the Crucifixion. Raised on a platform at the far corner of the hall was the great canopied divan on which the King sat, propped up on rich cushions embroidered with gold *fleurs de lys*. The principal prelates of the realm sat along the wall at the King's left, the peers and barons on his right. At the back of the hall, on a lower level than the rest, sat the representatives of the towns, perhaps 500 strong. The proceedings began with a report on the state of the King's wars. It must have been a sombre record. The Chancellor, Pierre de la Forêt, admitted that the practice of financing the fighting from the profits of the mints was unpopular and damaging, and reminded them of the King's intention to abolish it. But the war had to be financed somehow. Without the mints, other sources of funds would have to be found. In the stage-managed fashion of such occasions, the spokesman of each estate delivered a loyal address in reply. They promised, in the time-honoured phrase, that they were 'ready to live and die with the King' and that they would deliberate together about supplying his needs.

When the delegates came back to report on their deliberations, they were less accommodating. They told the King that they were as anxious as anyone for the proper defence of the realm. They said that it was his duty to prosecute the war 'on land and sea as vigorously as he might.' They believed that this would require a standing army of 30,000 men each year at a cost which they estimated at 5,000,000 *livres*. The delegates therefore authorised a sales tax of eight pennies in the pound (3.33 per cent) on all commodities and proposed to revive the *gabelle* or salt duty. By historic standards these were generous grants. The yield which the deputies anticipated was twice the amount which the assemblies of 1347–8 had proposed to raise from a larger population. Moreover, unlike previous assemblies the Estates-General of 1355 purported to bind their constituents at once, without the endless succession of local bargains and compromises which had addled previous tax collection campaigns. But this was not all that the delegates had to say. They wanted the collection of the tax taken out of the hands of the King's officials. They proposed to set up a special commission in each province composed of 'good and honest men of means, loyal and above suspicion.' These men would be responsible for appointing local receivers and for supervising their activities in accordance with standard instructions to be prepared for them in due course. Overseeing the work of the provincial commissions there was to be a national commission of nine *généraulx et surintendenz*, three from each Estate. They were to be assisted by two receivers-general, who would disburse the sums collected directly to the paymasters of the army, bypassing the royal treasury. Paymasters were, of course, royal officials. But they were to be made to swear oaths that they would use the money for war purposes and nothing else. Previous schemes of this kind had been largely circumvented by the King's servants, as the estates knew well. They were a temporary body, which was convened at the King's command and then dispersed, whereas the civil service was retentive, experienced and permanent. In the attempt to avoid this difficulty and ensure that their decrees were effective, the Estates-General of 1355 were driven to yet more radical lengths. They proposed to reconvene in Paris on 1 March 1356 to receive the accounts of the collection and expenditure of the tax and to consider whether further grants would be required; and again on 30 November 1356, the anniversary of their first assembly, to review the progress of the war and the means of paying for it in the following year. In the meantime, the King would be left to control his own foreign policy and to conduct military operations as he thought fit, save on one point: he was to make no truce with the enemy unless the representatives of the Estates-General consented.[5]

The ordinances of December 1355 reflected the persistent prejudice of the French political community that the government's difficulties were the result of corruption and fecklessness rather than the scale of its war expenditure and the paucity of its permanent resources. There are grounds for believing that they were driven by the representatives of Paris. The city was the traditional home of political radicalism. The Parisian delegation had for many years taken the leading role in the deliberations of the Third Estate at such meetings. Its citizens had been energetic supporters of the war effort from the outset and generous providers of troops and money. Its mobs were a perennial reminder of the closeness of popular fury and vengeance. The spokesman of the third estate, Étienne Marcel, was the Provost of the Merchants of Paris. All three of the Third Estate's representatives on the supervisory commission were Parisians.[6] We cannot know John's inner thoughts about the proceedings of the Estates-General. But he was very much beholden to the Parisians and had always been inclined to co-operate with national and provincial assemblies in the hope of securing a reliable source of tax revenues such as Edward III enjoyed in England. Like Edward, he was probably prepared to make substantial political concessions in order to get it. There is certainly no evidence that he resisted the ordinances of December 1355. At the same time it is clear that the guiding sentiment among the delegates was distrust of John's government. His conduct was regarded as inglorious in the north and scandalous in the south. Doubts about his ability to govern were now no longer confined to a limited circle of politicians and initiates or directed at all-powerful ministers acting in his name. 'By the blood of Christ,' the Count of Harcourt was heard to say, 'this King is a worthless man and a bad ruler.'

In the background, the magnetic personality and self-serving designs of Charles of Navarre were a perennial source of tension. Charles was ostensibly at peace with the King. But few men doubted that he would offer an alternative government when the opportunity arose. Robert le Coq, the most virulent of John's critics within the administration, was already putting it indiscreetly about that the King should be replaced by the Dauphin under the tutelage of the King of Navarre, or perhaps even by the King of Navarre himself. John, he said, was not equal to the pressures of government. The kingdom was being 'lost and ruined' by his efforts. It is not clear how many agreed with these opinions. They undoubtedly had a great deal of support among the discontented nobility of the realm. They also had friends and advocates among the urban oligarchies of the north and the Île de France, men radicalised by the continually increasing burden of taxation, who had seen the secular decline of their industries accelerated by economic boycott and war-damage. Perhaps most unexpected of all, they had the support of an influential minority of the higher clergy, the legal profession and the resident masters of the University of Paris, who gradually jettisoned the royalist traditions of their caste and threw in their lot with the opponents of the Crown. For all these men, who desired many different and incompatible things, the King of Navarre was an ideal figurehead. He never overtly presented himself as the champion of political reform. So far as could be known, he had no programme but the advancement of his power and the enlargement of his domains. He stood for nothing except opposition. His importance lay in the fact that he was a great prince in an age which respected the claims of birth, yet at the same time an outsider, untainted by the failures of his family.[7]

In December 1355, while the sessions of the Estates-General were still in progress, there occurred what seems to have been a botched attempt at a coup d'état. The facts were not made public at the time and are still obscure. The plot centred on the person of the Dauphin. He was persuaded to meet Charles of Navarre's agents at the bridge of Saint-Cloud outside Paris, on the night of 7 December 1355. From there he would be taken to the King of Navarre's castle at Mantes and sent with an escort of twenty or thirty men-at-arms to take refuge at the court of the German Emperor, his uncle. The principal plotters apart from Charles of Navarre himself were the Count of Foix, Jean de Boulogne Count of Montfort (the Cardinal's brother), the Count of Harcourt, a bastard of the house of Bourbon, an assorted group of lesser noblemen, mainly from Normandy, and some highly placed civil servants including Robert de Lorris. It is probable that once the Dauphin was out of the way it was intended to raise a rebellion in Normandy and perhaps in Paris. Some months later, a series of confessions extracted under torture from one of Charles of Navarre's lieutenants revealed that the ultimate object was to seize the King and kill him. What is far from clear is to what extent the Dauphin himself was privy to the plan. It is unlikely that he knew of any plan to kill his father. But there is a good deal of circumstantial evidence that he was willing to deprive him of his power. The Dauphin was vain, impressionable and debt-ridden. He had already fallen under the spell of the King of Navarre during the few days which they had passed together at Vaudreuil after the treaty of Valognes. Charles of Navarre and Robert le Coq appear to have persuaded him that his father had no intention of allowing him to exercise any real power while he remained alive, and even that his life was in danger at John's court.

At the last moment the plot was revealed. John took it extremely seriously. He immediately had his son detained in Paris and reached a private settlement with him. On 7 December 1355, the day on which Dauphin should have met Charles' agents at Saint-Cloud, he was made Duke of Normandy and granted the duchy as an appanage. In this way John answered the main argument by which the plotters had won over the Dauphin. Moreover, in spite of the difficulty of the government's financial situation, 26,000 *l.p.* was found to pay off the Dauphin's debts and 400 marks of silver was presented to him to make plate for his household. John was wary enough to avoid a major dispute with the King of Navarre's supporters at a time when they were ready and he was not. So he professed to make light of the incident and to accept their apologies and explanations. He pardoned all of them. Never, he declared, would he bear any grudge against his son-in-law.[8]

John's latest reconciliation with the King of Navarre was even shallower than their previous declarations of friendship. His settlement with the Dauphin, although it parried the immediate threat, brought its own dangers as John must have known. The grant of the government of Normandy, however necessary, placed a great deal of power in his unstable hands and brought him into regular contact with the most resentful and disaffected noble community in France. When, on 10 January 1356, the Dauphin received the homage of the Norman nobility in the great hall of Rouen Castle, Godfrey of Harcourt came before him holding the original of the charter extracted by the Normans from Louis X in 1315, which had been taken from the cathedral. He called on the Dauphin to swear before the whole assembled company to observe it, and when the Dauphin temporised, he left without doing homage.[9] During the first weeks of the new year, it became clear to the young prince that he could not effectively govern Normandy unless he distanced himself from the government of his father. Charles of Navarre, who was the chief power in the province after the Dauphin himself, remained close at hand, befriending and impressing him. Robert le Coq filled their ears with poison, 'bad and dangerous words'. Simon Bucy had 'no other object,' Robert said, than 'squandering French blood.' The King was only buying time until he could rob the Dauphin of his power and perhaps even of his life. Was he not secretly plotting his revenge for the incident of December? Such rumours were widely disseminated, and credible enough for John to order public denials to be issued by his officials.[10]

The reorganisation of the government of Normandy was an unwelcome and expensive distraction from the business of preparing the great campaigns which the Estates-General had appointed for the year 1356. The sea was the first line of defence. Yet the government was desperately short of ships to obstruct the major seaborne expedition which was being prepared across the Channel. Several sailing ships were bought in Flanders during the winter, which were manned and victualled in the Seine ports. But it was clear that the main burden of holding the sea would have to fall upon foreign mercenaries, as it had done in the 1330s and 1340s. The Count of Armagnac met the principal ministers of the King of Aragon in January 1356 in a small village near Béziers. Aragon was now the principal source of contract warships in the western Mediterranean. Armagnac obtained for the French government an option to charter up to fifteen galleys, each with a full crew of oarsmen and 25 soldiers for service in the coming campaign. For land operations, the French needed to raise two large armies. One, in the north, was required to resist the army of the Duke of Lancaster, whose plans to invade Brittany had been known in Paris for some time. In the south, the Prince of Wales was thought to be planning another heavy raid into Languedoc. In February 1356 it was announced that the command of the southern sector would be conferred on the Dauphin. By the end of February 1356 the King's ministers had already committed themselves to war expenditure on a large scale.[11]

It was already becoming clear that funds to meet this expenditure were not coming in. When the Estates-General had authorised unusually heavy taxes without referring back to their constituents, they had gone a long way beyond what public opinion in the provinces was willing to accept. There were several unpalatable features of the new taxes in the eyes of the communities which had to pay them. Not only were the rates historically very high, but the whole burden was loaded onto indirect taxes, which significantly increased the cost of living. To make matters worse, the first attempt at collection coincided with the steep revaluation of the coinage required by the Estates-General, a popular policy in principle, but in practice disruptive and disorienting. The result was that the Estates-General's commissioners and receivers were resisted with the same obstinacy and resentment as the King's had been before. Opposition came from two main sources:

the provincial nobility, attached to local privileges and disturbed by the idea of a grant made on their behalf by a distant gathering in Paris; and the urban commons, too poor to be represented at the Estates-General, who resented the high rates at which essential commodities were being taxed. In Beaujolais furious mobs attacked the *bailli* and his men when they tried to collect the tax. The dame de Beaujeu was the principal power in this region. She openly supported the resistance and may even have instigated it. In the neighbouring province of Burgundy, where John II governed as regent of the young Duke, no one would accept the decisions of the Estates-General as sufficient authority for the collection of the tax. The Estates of the duchy, meeting at Chatillon in January 1356, evaded the issue. Another meeting, at Dijon a month later, refused point blank to pay. The King summoned representatives of the Burgundians before him in Paris. He dismissed the governor of the province and appointed another who was thought to be more persuasive. It was all to no avail. A succession of local assemblies meeting in the spring and summer of 1356 resolutely refused to approve the tax and it was never collected. The results were not much better in Normandy. The Dauphin paid the tax on his own domains and Charles of Navarre did likewise on his. But elsewhere, there was general and persistent opposition. In the middle of February 1356, the Dauphin confronted an angry assembly of the nobility of the province at the castle of Vaudreuil. The opposition was led by the Count of Harcourt. He made a bitter speech, full of 'proud and offensive words' against the King. The opposition in this assembly may have been overcome, for the commissioners and receivers of the Estates-General were active in Normandy by the end of the month. But they raised virtually no money. In the villages and towns passive resistance made the task of these functionaries all but impossible.[12]

When the Estates-General of Languedoil reconvened in Paris on 1 March 1356, attendance was poor. Very few prelates were present. Most of the towns of Normandy and the whole nobility of the province declined to attend. So did the towns of Picardy, where the *gabelle* had been particularly ill-received. Other provinces such as Auvergne, which did send delegates to the new assembly, sent them with obstructive messages or no powers. The authority of the Estates was correspondingly diminished. On 5 March 1356, while they were still in session, they were abruptly reminded of the strength of popular feeling by a violent rising in the northern city of Arras. As in other parts of France, the men of Arras divided on class lines, the oligarchy and the rich supporting the new taxes which, they said, were essential for the defence of the realm (and to which in any case they contributed little). But the mass of the population refused to pay. They declared that they would destroy the town and the whole region around it before they surrendered. There was a succession of acrimonious public meetings. When, at length, steps were taken to enforce the taxes, mobs rampaged through the streets. The leaders of the municipality fled to a safe house belonging to one of their number. But the mob stormed it and lynched seventeen of them, casting the bodies out of the windows into the river below. The rebellion was eventually suppressed with much violence by the Marshal Arnoul d'Audrehem, and most of the ringleaders were executed. But by this time the main grievance of the rebels had been removed. The Estates-General ordained another radical change of fiscal policy. They abolished the *gabelle* and decreed that the collection of the sales tax should cease at the end of March. These impositions were replaced by an income tax. There were to be no exemptions except for children, beggars, monks and nuns. Even the spiritual revenues of the Church, which had previously been taxed only by special arrangement with the Pope, were to be assessed for tax on the same basis as the incomes of the laity. The rates were steeply regressive: five per cent was levied on the first ten *livres* and each successive band thereafter was taxed at a diminishing rate. Income in excess of 5,000 *livres* for nobles and 1,000 *livres* for non-nobles was not to be taxed at all. Everyone, however poor, was to pay at least ten *sous*. These arrangements bore all the marks of a painful compromise between the divergent interests represented in Paris and they were no doubt necessary in order to persuade the first two Estates to agree to anything at all. In spite of the regressive rates, the main burden of the new taxes fell on the landed fortunes of the Church and the nobility. The towns and the poor escaped relatively lightly. As a result, the popular clamour died away. Before they dispersed, the Estates-General agreed to reassemble again on 9 May 1356 to receive a report on the working of the new taxes.[13]

All this bustling was wasted. The changes had come too late. An income tax (unlike a sales tax) required a time-consuming process of assessment before a single penny could be collected. The government seems to have anticipated that revenue would begin to flow in during April, as soon as the sales tax ceased. This was completely unrealistic. As winter opened into spring, the symptoms of political disintegration in the north became alarming. The tax strike was still continuing in Picardy. The administration of the new income tax was proceeding with unbearable slowness elsewhere. The Dauphin appears to have been encountering some difficulty in recruiting troops for his great army of the south. Money must have been root of these difficulties.[14]

The Estates of Languedoc met separately in Toulouse to consider the King's financial difficulties for themselves. On 26 March 1356 the proceedings opened in the hall of the Chateau Narbonnais, a massive old fort, the architectural patchwork of ten centuries, which served as the southern citadel of the town. The delegates represented the towns of Languedoc and of the neighbouring provinces of the south, Rouergue, Quercy and Périgord. But some of them, including the representatives of the rich cities of Montpellier and the Rhone valley, had come without authority to agree anything. The nobility were not represented at all. They were expected to make their own grant in separate assemblies, province by province, over the following weeks. The assembly could therefore never have been more than the beginning of an arduous process of negotiation between the government and different bodies of taxpayers. Bertrand de Pibrac, now Bishop of Nevers, was the senior of the King's commissioners at the opening. He addressed the assembled representatives about the misfortunes of the province in the past six months, the imminence of the Dauphin's arrival in the province, the size of the army which he would have under his command and the tremendous efforts which the King was making for the defence of the region. A loyal address was delivered from the hall by one of the *capitouls* of Toulouse. Others, filled with generous sentiments, followed. But, as in Paris, the private deliberations of the delegates were more acerbic than these planted speeches. They continued for more than a week before any conclusion was reached. When they reported, on 4 April 1356, the delegates said that they were willing on certain conditions to grant a sales tax of six *deniers* per *livre* (2.4 per cent). But the conditions were extremely restrictive. These men knew that in spite of all his protestations the King's first priority was the defence of the north. They too were determined that their tax revenues should remain under their own control, and not go to pay the wages of a northern army. They decreed that the subsidy was to be spent exclusively on the prosecution of the war in the south-west. Collection was not even to begin until the Dauphin had appeared there. And it was to cease at once if he withdrew to the north or if the theatre of war shifted elsewhere. Like the provinces of Languedoil the men of Languedoc made it a condition of their grant that the King should renounce the manipulation of the coinage as well as a variety of other irksome money-raising expedients to which the Crown had resorted in past crises. Everything therefore depended on the success of the new tax.[15]

Paris was alive with rumours of rebellion and treason. There were reports of plots against the King and the Dauphin, and of conspiracies between the Dauphin and Charles of Navarre. Persistent gossip circulated about the King of Navarre's dealings with the English. At some point John II was said to have received a cache of documents whose authenticity was hotly disputed but which appeared to disclose a scheme for murdering him and his son and delivering up Normandy to Edward III. Towards the end of March 1356, the King was about to attend a baptism at the Cistercian abbey of Beaupré near Beauvais. As he set out, he received information which suggested that the King of Navarre had devised a plan with the leading malcontents among the Norman nobility to kidnap him there and put him to death. It is difficult to know how much truth there was in this story. But undoubtedly something was afoot. The King reinforced his bodyguard and continued on his way. In the event the plotters realised that they had been discovered and nothing happened. But this latest incident festered in John's mind, and coalesced with the accumulated grievances of the past three years. Out of his capital and away from calmer counsels, he decided to have done once and for all with Charles of Navarre and his Norman allies.[16]

John collected 100 men-at-arms from his household troops and a handful of his closest relations and friends. He sent to Paris for another 500 men-at-arms to join him on the road. Then, without waiting for them to arrive, he led his men to Maineville, a little village at the end of the forest of Lyons, some thirty miles east of Rouen. On 5 April 1356 they rose before dawn and rode through the vast forests of the Seine valley towards the Norman capital. The Dauphin was presiding over a council of the leading men of Normandy in Rouen Castle. It had been called to make arrangements for the defence of the province during the his absence in Languedoc. Charles of Navarre and the Count of Harcourt were there. So were most of the more prominent noblemen of the province and the mayor and leading citizens of Rouen. At midday, when the meeting had ended, the Dauphin entertained about thirty of them at a banquet in the main hall of the castle.

In the middle of the meal, a door was opened in a corner of the hall. The King entered unannounced, wearing a battle-helmet and full armour under his clothes. He was followed by his brother the Duke of

Orléans, his son the Count of Anjou, the Marshal Arnoul d'Audrehem and a large body of armed men. They had entered by a stair tower at the foot of which a small wicket gate leading into the meadows outside had been left open for them. Moving into the middle of the hall, the Marshal drew his sword from under his cloak and shouted: 'Anyone who moves shall die.' The King approached the high table where the Dauphin was sitting with the guests of honour. He grasped Charles of Navarre by the throat and pulled him bodily back from the table. 'Foul traitor!,' he said; 'you deserve to die.' Charles' squire Colin Doublet (who had undertaken the delicate mission to England for him in the previous summer) was serving as his carver. He drew a dagger from his clothes. He was immediately disarmed by soldiers. 'My Lord,' the Dauphin protested; 'what are you doing? These men are my guests and they are under my roof.' The King was deaf to his protests. Charles and Doublet were dragged away. The other guests fled for the doors. A handful of them, including Thomas de Ladit, Chancellor of Navarre, escaped from the hall and managed to find their way out of the castle into the streets of Rouen, where excited crowds were beginning to gather. But most of the diners were stopped and held in separate rooms of the castle until the King's wishes were known.

John singled out three men: the Count of Harcourt, the lord of Graville, and Guillaume ('Maubué') de Mainemares. The first two of these men had been prominent in every Navarrese plot since the murder of Charles of Spain more than two years earlier. The third had been involved in the plan to take the Dauphin to Germany in December and probably in the attempt to kidnap the King in March. They were summarily condemned to death. So was Colin Doublet, who had threatened John with his dagger in the hall. Towards the end of the afternoon, the gates of Rouen were closed, a curfew declared, and the streets emptied of their crowds. The four condemned men were put into two carts and taken out of the city to a large open space called the Champ-du-Pardon, where horse fairs were held. There they were beheaded in the presence of the King with the greatest possible butchery by an amateur executioner. He was a forger and murderer awaiting trial in Rouen prison who volunteered for the job to earn his pardon. When the deed was done, John had their bodies suspended from chains and their heads impaled on lances at the great gallows which overlooked the city of Rouen from the heights of Bihorel by the Abbeville road.[17]

In spite of his terrible anger, John retained enough respect for aristocratic convention to spare his son-in-law the same fate. Charles of

Navarre was taken under armed guard to Paris with two of his closest retainers, Friquet de Fricamps and Jean de Bantalu, both of whom had often been employed in confidential missions on his behalf. All three men were interrogated at length in the cells of the Châtelet. Friquet's confession, part of which was extracted under torture, uncovered much of the complex dealings between Charles and the King's enemies over the past few years, the full extent of which had never previously be appreciated by John's ministers. He eventually escaped from the Châtelet with the aid of two of his servants and found his way to England.[18] As for Charles himself, he was moved from prison to prison for greater security. He lodged briefly in the Louvre, the Châtelet, the huge fortress of Chateau-Gaillard at les Andelys on the Seine, and the citadel of Pontoise. When the English invaded Normandy in June he was taken out of the kingdom to the French protectorate of Cambrai. There they shut him in the great keep of Arleux, a remote and austere old fort surrounded by marsh, where he remained in close confinement for more than a year and a half.[19]

The King's revenge at Rouen must have been profoundly satisfying to him. But it was an act of great folly. The summary execution without trial of the head of the leading noble house of Normandy was profoundly offensive to aristocratic sentiment even among those whose every instinct was to support the Crown. It outraged opinion in a province close to Paris which had a strong sense of political identity and whose wealth had contributed mightily to the French war effort for two decades. It threw the House of Évreux, which had hitherto been extremely chary in its dealings with the English, into their hands, provoking a schism within the royal family and a bloody civil war in western France. To the many in Normandy and elsewhere who remembered the sudden execution of the Count of Eu in 1350 and knew nothing of the conspiracies of Avignon, Beaupré or the bridge of Saint-Cloud, it confirmed the widespread impression that the King was irrational, unstable and impulsive, and that his government lived every day from one expedient to the next. A more skilful politician than John II might have turned opinion in his favour. But John took the authority of his office for granted. Shortly after the event he made it known that the Count of Harcourt had been arrested for treasonable dealings with the English and claimed to have documents to prove it. In May, a statement of the case against Harcourt was prepared and distributed in Normandy, which presumably said much the same thing. But the arrest and imprisonment of the King's son-in-law was too shocking to the pieties of fourteenth-century politics, and the reasons too sensitive and humiliating to be discussed in public. John never explained them. 'No one knows what led to his arrest,' the spokesman of the Estates-General complained when, months afterwards, the consequence of the King's anger was plain for all to see.[20]

The French King was well aware when he planned his coup that the strongholds of the House of Évreux and its allies in Normandy would have to be taken by force. On 7 April 1356, two days after the execution of the Count of Harcourt, eighty mounted men commanded by the *bailli* of Rouen seized the castle of Harcourt in the valley of the Risle. During the next two weeks the 500 men-at-arms who had been summoned from Paris before the coup arrived at Pont-de-l'Arche with the Provost of the Merchants of Paris, Étienne Marcel. Others were mustered in small groups across the province.[21] As the King returned to Paris with his prisoners, his officers laid siege to Évreux and the citadel of Pont-Audemer.

Évreux was the seat of Charles of Navarre's administration in France. But it was not particularly strong. The *cité*, which was the kernel of the old town, was defended by low, crumbling walls dating from late Roman times, reinforced by the castle of the Counts at one end and the cathedral of Notre-Dame at the other. The *bourg*, which had grown up north of the town around the market place, had its own more modern walls. The defence of the place depended mainly on an unenthusiastic population of about 3,000 souls and a determined garrison of Navarrese soldiers, urged on by the principal councillors of the King of Navarre. The Dauphin's marshal captured the *bourg* almost immediately. But he was unable to dislodge the garrison from the walls of the *cité*. The Dauphin took command of the operation in person. He had siege engines brought from Rouen. Impatient letters arrived regularly from the King in Paris. Bloody assaults achieved nothing. A month after the siege had begun Évreux still held out. At Pont-Audemer progress was even slower. Robert Houdetot, who after many years spent defending the French King's territory in the Garonne valley had become Master of the Royal Archers, was in command of this operation. As at Évreux, he was able to occupy the town without difficulty. But he made no impression on the keep. He undermined the walls and ordered one assault after another without success. Six weeks later his troops were still encamped in the fields below.[22]

In this extremity the defence of Charles of Navarre's interests fell to his younger brother Philip, who suddenly found himself at the age of twenty-two the principal protagonist in a civil war. The role became him well. He was an abrasive young man, readily drawn to violent solutions. He did not have Charles' cunning, nor his insight into other men's minds. But unlike Charles, he was a natural soldier, bold, energetic and popular with his men, French and Navarrese alike. After the arrest of his brother Philip made a brief, fruitless attempt to negotiate with John II. Then, when John's troops arrived outside Évreux and Pont-Audemer, he withdrew to the Cotentin peninsula. The Cotentin was the remotest part of the King of Navarre's domains, where opposition to the Crown was a long tradition. Philip proclaimed himself his brother's lieutenant in France, set up his headquarters at Cherbourg and set about forming an army from the scattered groups of Navarrese in the region and from sympathizers among the local nobility. With the King's troops pouring into Normandy, and the Navarrese cause apparently doomed, this was not easy. Most of Charles of Navarre's friends waited in frozen immobility until the direction of events became clearer. Two months after Charles' arrest, Philip had found no more than 100 men-at-arms to fight for him and most of these came from the Cotentin itself. Even the Harcourt family was divided. The dead count's uncle, Godfrey, withdrew to the Cotentin with Philip and supported his cause from his great fortress at Saint-Sauveur in the middle of the peninsula. But his brother Louis, although strongly pressed to join them, remained loyal to the King. He would not make war on his natural lord or dishonour his oath, he said.[23]

It was already plain by the end of April 1356 that the cause of Philip of Navarre would founder unless help could be had from outside. His two chief lieutenants, Martin Henriquez and Pedro Remirez, were sent urgently to Navarre to raise troops. Charles's youngest brother Louis, who had efficiently governed Navarre for the past two years, set about raising money from his subjects and finding allies in the other Spanish kingdoms and at the papal court at Avignon.[24] But Philip knew that England was the only place from which help could come quickly. In the Thames and in harbours along the south and east coasts, long-laid plans to transport an army to Brittany under the Duke of Lancaster were already close to fruition. Twenty-seven ships had been mobilised from the King's own fleet, the largest number that Edward III had ever collected from his own resources. The requisitioning of merchantmen had been in progress since March. By early May there was a sizeable fleet lying in Southampton and a large number of troops in the town waiting to embark.[25]

Two emissaries of Philip of Navarre arrived in England at the end of April 1356. Jean de Morbeke was a disaffected knight from Artois. One of his kinsmen was at that moment serving with the Prince of Wales in Gascony. His colleague, Guillaume de Carbonnel, was a minor lord from the Cotentin. They had several interviews with the English King's Council. They explained Philip's plight. They promised to put all the castles of the King of Navarre in Normandy at Edward's disposal if only he would send an expedition force to help them. They declared that they would fight for the English King against John II with every means at their command. But they needed at least 1,000 men immediately, and enough money to pay the wages of the men-at-arms already at Cherbourg. The English ministers were very circumspect. They were imperfectly informed about what was happening in France. They were uncertain what authority Philip could really claim on his brother's behalf. But they recognised a chance when they saw one. By 4 May 1356 it had been decided to divert Lancaster's expedition to Normandy. Orders were given to the Lieutenant in Brittany to send troops at once into the Cotentin to protect Philip's base there. The King's officers in Gascony were told to find shipping for the men recruited by Martin Henriquez in Navarre, and to give them every assistance on their way. When Philip of Navarre's envoys returned to Cherbourg in the third week of May they were able to report that help was on its way. On 28 May, Philip formally renounced his homage to the King of France in a ringing declaration in which he accused John of tyranny and treachery and announced that he would make war on him with all his strength.[26]

John II's ministers were probably ignorant of Jean de Morbeke's mission to England. But they must have anticipated something of the kind. Certainly they were well aware of the invasion fleet which was being made ready in southern England and of the weakness of their own defences. There were virtually no naval forces available to stop an English landing. The Aragonese galley fleet had been mobilised and manned at Barcelona during April and placed under the command of Francisco de Perellós, a Catalan nobleman of strong francophile sympathies who was close to the King of Aragon. But there were only nine vessels, instead of the fifteen for which the French had options. And there were long delays in beginning the voyage which, in spite of their long experience of foreign contract fleets, the French government had failed to anticipate. The ships did not leave the Mediterranean until July. So, John II had to meet the threat of invasion as best he could by disposing his forces on land. The *arrière-ban* was proclaimed on 14 May 1356. The main body of the King's army was summoned to Chartres on the confines of Normandy and the Île de France, which suggests that he knew that the English attack would come from the west through Normandy or Brittany, rather than from Calais. But the response to the summons was very poor. The *arrière-ban* had to be repeated on 27 May and again early in June.[27]

In the ordinary course, the French government would probably have left the south-western provinces to fend for themselves. But John's representatives had promised the Estates at Toulouse that an army would be sent from the north to defend them. The collection of taxes in the region was conditional on its arrival. The new crisis in Normandy made it impossible to send the Dauphin. So the King's third son, John Count of Poitiers, was appointed in his brother's place. This unimpressive fifteen-year-old, without experience of government or command, became the King's Lieutenant in all provinces of the kingdom south of the Loire. He was assigned a formidable body of tutors and ministers to guide him, including the Marshal Jean de Clermont, Jean de Boucicaut, and a mass of noblemen and functionaries of the southern provinces. A second army was summoned to muster at Bourges at the same time as the army of Chartres, in order to accompany the young prince south.[28]

As the summer wore on, the symptoms of civil disintegration multiplied not only in Normandy but across much of southern and central France. In April 1356 a small Anglo-Gascon army commanded by the lord of Mussidan mounted a sudden raid deep into Quercy. They penetrated to within a few miles of the important market town of Figeac on the eastern march of the province. Here, they laid siege to the small fortified village of Fons, which had a royal garrison, and to the imposing seigneurial fortress of Cardaillac a few miles away to the north. Both places were taken by assault in the first half of June. The inhabitants of the region had had no warning of the attack. The French Seneschal tried to raise the siege of Cardaillac shortly after it had begun. He was defeated and driven off. Representatives of the towns and the local nobility gathered at Figeac to decide what to do. In the middle of June they collected a fresh army to fight off the invaders. Most of its troops were raw men conscripted in the towns. They were wiped out by the raiders. Almost all those who were not killed were taken for ransom.

The brief and destructive raid of the lord of Mussidan was the signal for an explosion of brigandage in the surrounding regions. The raiders left a large number of new garrisons to continue their work in Quercy. Two sons of the lord of Albret installed their men at Fons and used it as a base for plundering the trade of the region and raiding into the valleys of the Lot and the Aveyron. Other captains penetrated into the south of Quercy. Cahors, the administrative and commercial capital of the region, was protected by a complete circuit of modern walls, built only a decade earlier. But it was surrounded by enemy forts which paralysed its trade. The neighbouring province of Rouergue dissolved into chaos, as small groups of armed men splintered off from the Anglo-Gascon bands and roamed unmolested across the province. They seized the fortified village of Clairvaux only eight miles from the provincial capital at Rodez. Although they held it for barely a month, the incident terrified the citizens. The consuls strengthened the watches, redoubled their efforts to build their walls, and patrolled the streets at night with torches. They hired a garrison of 200 men-at-arms. Within a fortnight of the capture of Clairvaux, other raiding parties were reported to be prowling around Najac, Millau, Saint-Affrique and Sauveterre. North of the Dordogne, in Turenne and southern Limousin, enemy garrisons sprang up like summer weeds in delapidated castles, abandoned monasteries and semi-fortified villages. Poitou had been granted to the young prince John as his appanage in April, but much of the it was ungovernable. The southern part of the province was largely controlled by Gascon garrisons. The great castle of Lusignan was 'surrounded on all sides by English fortresses' according to reports reaching John's staff in June. At Poitiers itself the citadel had not been repaired since Henry of Lancaster's disastrous raid of 1346. Gaps in the walls were being hastily filled with timber breastwork. In July, the enemy was raiding up to the gates, seizing goods and men, including the mayor of the city who was carried off and ransomed. Every community turned in on itself, looking to its own salvation. The work of the tax-collectors and recruiting officers was paralysed.[29]

When the Estates-General of Languedoil reconvened in Paris on 8 May 1356 it was already becoming obvious that the great fiscal reform set in train in December had failed. Their deliberations have not been recorded. But the terms of the ordinance which followed show that little or nothing had been collected of the subsidy. The delegates tinkered with it. The rates were altered so as to transfer more of the burden to the richer taxpayers from whom it was easier to collect. Payment was ordered to be made in two instalments, in June and August. An attempt was made to cut short the endless round of petitions, complaints and bargaining by which tax levels were traditionally set, by allowing each province some freedom to decide the basis on which its payments would be assessed. The major concession was that the proceeds of the subsidy should be reserved for the defence of the region in which they were collected. The angry and frightened communities of the provinces might well have forced this on the government anyway. But its consequences were very unfortunate. It meant that the paymasters of the armies of Chartres and Bourges in theory received nothing unless it had been raised in the province where the army happened to be.[30]

The result of all this chopping and changing was chaos. Normandy, which had long ago appropriated the right to regulate its own taxes, ignored the decision of the Estates-General. The districts of Lower Normandy resolved upon a sales tax, to be levied at the punitive rate of 5 per cent with effect from June. This seems to have superseded the income tax which they had approved in March. It was superseded in turn about a fortnight later at an assembly representing the whole of the province, which decided that there should be a hearth tax of 10 *sous* from July. This was followed by a maelstrom of protest as attempts were made to collect all three exactions and taxpayers refused to pay any. In other provinces, the paucity of surviving records makes it hard to say what happened but suggests that probably nothing did.[31]

When the King had agreed to the reformed silver coinage demanded by the Estates-General at the end of the previous year, he had almost certainly anticipated a final glut of income from the mints before the new regime of stable currency reduced it to a trickle. Unfortunately events conspired against him. There was a steep rise in the market price of silver in the first half of the year 1356. This made it impossible for the mints to buy bullion and still make a profit by coining it. The traditional solution, which was to pay more for the bullion and reduce the silver content of the coins, had been ruled out by the terms of the King's agreement with the Estates-General. The government devoted increasing attention to the problem as the prospect of collecting the subsidy declined. Nicholas Braque and Jean Poilevillain, the two principal experts on the art of coinage manipulation in the government's employ, were brought back into the Chambre des Comptes to see what could be done without repudiating the ordinances of November and December. But the truth was that nothing could be done. Two of the largest provincial mints, at Poitiers and Saint-Pourçain, ran out of metal in May. The mint at Troyes ran out in July. Others, like those of Toulouse and Rouen, continued to make coin but surreptitiously reduced the bullion content. As the troops began to arrive at Chartres and Bourges, the government was at its wits' end to find money for their wages.[32]

The last great royal army to be raised in France for nearly three decades was recruited very much as the first had been at the outset of the war. The privatisation of warfare had passed France by, even though the financial and political pressures which had forced it on the King of England existed in an acute form in France. Contract captains tended to be men who, like the Count of Savoy or the Count of Foix, were beyond the reach of compulsion. Conscription was still very much the rule for everyone else. The innate conservatism of an ancient military nation was one reason for this although not the only one. The limited prospects of gain for French armies, who were fighting a defensive war on their own territory; poor morale; the diminished reputation of the Crown: these were all important contributory factors. Money was certainly another. The chronicler Jean le Bel believed that the Kings of France were ill-served because they were tight-fisted. He contrasted their policy unfavourably with the generosity of Edward III to his soldiers. This appears to have been the received opinion. The truth was more complicated. French armies, like English ones, had been paid wages since the early thirteenth century, whether conscripted or not. Moreover, rates of pay in the two armies were roughly comparable and long delays in paying them were common to both. The main difference lay in the more generous advances paid to English soldiers, and in the fact that ordinary soldiers generally received their wages from the man who had retained them. Their final accounts were promptly settled by the great noblemen who recruited and led the principal retinues. These then presented their accounts at the Exchequer and waited to be paid. In effect they bank-rolled much of Edward III's army, enabling him to spread heavy expenditure over a number of years. They were willing to do this because agricultural revenues were high and war profitable, because they were personally close to the monarch and because supporting the King's wars was an incident of their status. None of these conditions except the last existed in France. French men-at-arms received relatively mean advances, and had to claim their final accounts directly from the war treasurers. They would then, as the Estates-General complained in 1356, be strung along for years by 'long delais et. . . mensonges'. Many gave up before they were paid, and even those who persevered had to accept payment in instalments in devalued coin.[33]

At the outset of every campaign the King or his lieutenant summoned all those holding noble fiefs, on pain of losing them, to join the army with a retinue and equipment appropriate to their status. There was a similar system, the exact legal basis of which is unclear, for summoning selected towns to supply infantry and crossbowmen. These arrangements were successful in the sense that they produced the men. But they were highly unsatisfactory from every other point of view. The main problem was an operational one. The French government's method of recruiting troops made it difficult to form cohesive military units. French armies of the 1350s came into existence for particular campaigns. There was no training, except on the march. The troops did not know each other and were not used to fighting together. This difficulty had been resolved, perhaps more by accident than design, by the system of contract retinues which prevailed in England, but no satisfactory solution had yet been found in France. The nearest equivalent to the great contract retinues of English captains were supplied by the holders of princely appanages and a handful of other prominent noblemen, who would appear with large bodies of men at their back, which they had recruited themselves by a mixture of contract and compulsion. Bannerets often did the same thing on a smaller scale. They were rich and prominent knights willing to make a career of warfare, who commanded sections of cavalry in battle and flew a 'banner', a rectangular flag bearing their arms, as opposed to the triangular pennon of a knight bachelor. They too had often recruited their own companies, and some did so among their dependents and neighbours very much as their equivalents did in England. But these were the exceptions. The great bulk of a French army's strength was supplied by hundreds or thousands of individual noblemen and gentlemen, each accompanied by a tiny retinue, often no more than a squire and a page. When they arrived, one of the military officers of the Crown, or a deputy, would receive their muster. They would line up wearing their armour and weapons and holding their horses. The men were counted. The equipment was inspected. The archers were made to demonstrate that their bows worked and that they knew how to use them. Horses were valued and branded as a precaution against fraud. Inadequates were sent away. The new arrivals were then assigned more or less arbitrarily to a battalion commanded by some famous nobleman. In the course of a long campaign, a measure of cohesion must have developed, but long campaigns were not particularly common.[34]

The King's ministers were well aware of this weakness, and within the limits of their difficult situation tried to do something about it. In April 1351 John II had issued an ordinance which required men-at-arms summoned by the Crown to present themselves for service in companies not less than twenty-five or more than eighty strong, under captains who would answer for them. Infantry were to be organised in *connestablies* between twenty-five and thirty strong. However, since there was no peacetime basis for these units and no reason for a captain to assume onerous responsibilities for his fellows, the response was inevitably patchy. In about 1355 the practice was adopted of paying an *état*, or supplementary wage, to captains who presented themselves in units of the correct size. This payment served a function which was in some ways similar to that of the *regard* in English military practice. It produced for a brief period identifiable companies not unlike those which served in English armies, except that they served under compulsion and must have lacked the same comradeship and stability of membership. But for the catastrophic reverses of 1356 the system might have developed into something better.[35]

It is an interesting question why Frenchmen of the 1350s responded to compulsion in the numbers they did, given the political weakness of the government which was applying it. The answer must inevitably be rather speculative. Just as money and spoil were not the only motives of English soldiers, so the lack of it did not stop Frenchmen from fighting for their King whatever they thought of him. In a world where loyalties were owed to much smaller and more local units than the nation, patriotism was not as powerful a factor as it later became. But status and the obligations associated with it counted for a great deal. The Knight of la Tour Landry told his daughters that the ideal knight might hope for 'fat rewards and profits' but should expect to get them from the largesse of his lord. At a more exalted level the Marshal Jean de Boucicaut, who passed his whole adult life in the service of the Crown, used to boast of having added nothing to his inheritance. 'If my children are wise and valiant, they will have enough to get by,' said he.[36]

Sentiments like these continued to be expressed until the end of the middle ages and indeed beyond, but the mid-fourteenth century was the last period in which they were the ordinary currency of the military class. Knighthood, still the universal mark of military status, retained its hold on contemporary minds. The romances of the period celebrated knighthood more than war. Famous knights were recognised everywhere by their banners and pennons. Orders of chivalry were instituted in both England and France, membership of which was much coveted.

The classic image of the soldier hero was still that of Froissart and the artist of the Luttrell Psalter: a belted knight seated on a caparisoned charger, 'lance at his arm and buckler at his neck'. On the eve of great battles young men seduced by this image queued up in hundreds to be dubbed on an occasion that would do them honour if they survived, and celebrated their new-found status by challenging their adversaries to murderous staged fights between the lines. Geoffrey de Charny, himself a famous authority on points of chivalry, found that men wanted to be knights even if they did not want to be career soldiers: to win respect from their peers or to end their days covered with honour. He was well aware that the ideals of knighthood were rarely reflected in the brutal practice of war, but still regarded it as the finest service of God after the Church. There is much evidence that contemporaries who execrated war and its practitioners agreed with him. As long as these ambiguous sentiments retained their force, the pressures of public opinion pushed men to war and sometimes to feats of insane courage, where self-interest would not have been enough. The Thirty who fought their contrived battle in Brittany in 1351 were certainly not the only heroes to be celebrated in verse, just as Jean de Galard, the French captain who lost Bergerac to the English in 1345, cannot have been the only man who found itinerant minstrels singing ballads about his cowardice. Even those too unimportant to be celebrated as heroes or cowards went to war, enduring pain, disease, extremes of heat and cold, and the ever-present risk of death because the conventional views of their peers and neighbours expected nothing less of them. They did it, as the Knight of la Tour Landry said, 'for their honour and reputation'.[37]

The changes were already coming which in the next generation would deprive knighthood of much of its significance. As the war continued, a class of career soldier came into existence which transcended social status. The great armies continued to be commanded by dukes, earls and counts, if not by Kings, a reflexion not just of their rank and of public expectations, but of the sheer military competence of most of them. Yet a squire could command knights, as Robert Knolles did for fifteen years before he was dubbed (by one of his subordinates) in 1359. A knight could command counts and barons, as Bertrand du Guesclin did in the 1360s and 1370s. Equally, a man who was not a knight and had no aspirations to become one could fight with the cavalry. When, in May 1358, the French government ordered suitably trained and equipped townsmen to be received and paid as cavalrymen at musters, they were simply regularising a practice that had been common for years.[38] All these soldiers were simply 'men-at-arms', a generic term comprising anyone who had the right equipment and could handle a lance from the saddle, regardless of his social position.

By the middle of the fourteenth century, there was no longer even a specifically knightly mode of combat. As tactical ideas developed and commanders came to value mobility over numbers, the horse, once the mark of a knight or squire, lost its significance. In English armies and increasingly in French ones, cavalrymen dismounted to fight. Everyone travelled on horseback, including archers and the ballast of every medieval army which went indiscriminately by the name of 'sergeants'. It is true that some horses were finer than others. The leaders of the army rode on *destriers*, large, strong and highly trained creatures like the one on which Sir John Hawkwood is seated in the painting by Uccello in Florence cathedral. Most men-at-arms rode on *coursiers*, light, fast horses which although cheaper than *destriers* were still extremely costly. The records of compensation paid to French soldiers who had lost their horses on campaign suggest that the average banneret rode a horse worth 270 *l.t.* (£54), and that the corresponding figures for knights and squires were 103 *l.t.* (£21) and 40 *l.t.* (£8). Knights were obliged to have two such horses, and expected to have three. At the opposite extreme mounted archers and infantrymen rode on unimpressive beasts known as 'rounceys' which would rarely be worth more than 10 *l.t.* (£2). Yet the quality and value of horses used on campaign inevitably tended to decline as the mass cavalry charge, which was the main justification for their existence, became obsolete. In English armies, which had been the first (after the Scots) to abandon traditional cavalry warfare, the general standard of horseflesh always was lower.[39]

Other military equipment was gradually democratised, very much as horses were. Swords and axes were the common weapons of every rank. The lance, which was the traditional cavalry weapon, became progressively less useful as the frontal cavalry charge became rarer. It was now sometimes used as an infantry weapon, wielded on foot by groups of three ordinary soldiers, two of whom held the end in a belt, the third guiding the tip. Froissart says that at one battle (in 1359) the cavalry were ordered to cut their lances down to five-foot lengths in order to use them in the mêlée. Armour remained a more visible source of social distinctions. The spectacular suits of plate armour which can be seen on funeral sculpture and memorial brasses were the ultimate in protective clothing. They were also impressive to look at, a consideration not lost on those who wore them. The habit of older knights of wearing a flowing robe over their armour disappeared with the arrival of steel breastplates and back-pieces, and pages were kept busy at night keeping them polished and gleaming. But plate was within the means of only the richest or most persistent soldiers. Among the general body of the army, armour was becoming largely standardised. The traditional iron pot-helmet which had been the standard equipment of thirteenth-century knights had almost disappeared except in tournaments, and been replaced by a lighter, rounded piece known as a bacinet, which protected the top and back of the head, and was usually fitted with a throat piece and a movable, conical vizor in front. The bacinet was worn by almost everyone, including ordinary infantrymen and garrison troops. The common *habergeon*, a sleeveless jacket of chain mail, became the most widely used form of body armour. It was heavy and hot, but serviceable. It could be put on quickly, without the assistance of a page. It allowed relatively unrestricted movement. It gave good protection against the cutting edge of a sword, although not against the points of swords, or crossbow bolts. It was comparatively cheap. Squires and even infantrymen commonly wore *habergeons* in the 1350s, while some knights did without metal armour altogether, preferring the lighter padded jacket of boiled leather which had traditionally been the clothing of common infantrymen. In 1356 it would not always have been possible to recognise a knight or a sergeant by his appearance. King John when he was captured in battle would have to ask his captor whether he was a knight. Fifty years earlier, the question would not have been necessary.[40]

On 1 June 1356 the advance guard of the English expeditionary force sailed from Southampton: forty-eight ships carrying 340 soldiers. They entered the great bay of La Hogue in the Cotentin on the following day. On 18 June the ships returned to La Hogue with the Duke of Lancaster and the rest of the army. The Duke set up his headquarters near Valognes, in the Benedictine abbey of Montebourg. Here he passed four days in organising his army. The total number brought from England was 1,300 men. They were joined by Robert Knolles, with 800 more drawn from the garrisons of Brittany, making a total, with Philip of Navarre's retainers, of 2,400 men. It was a small army by comparison with the force at the disposal of the King of France even in his present parlous position. But the men were all mounted, and about two thirds of them were longbowmen. Their arrival, on schedule, in Normandy

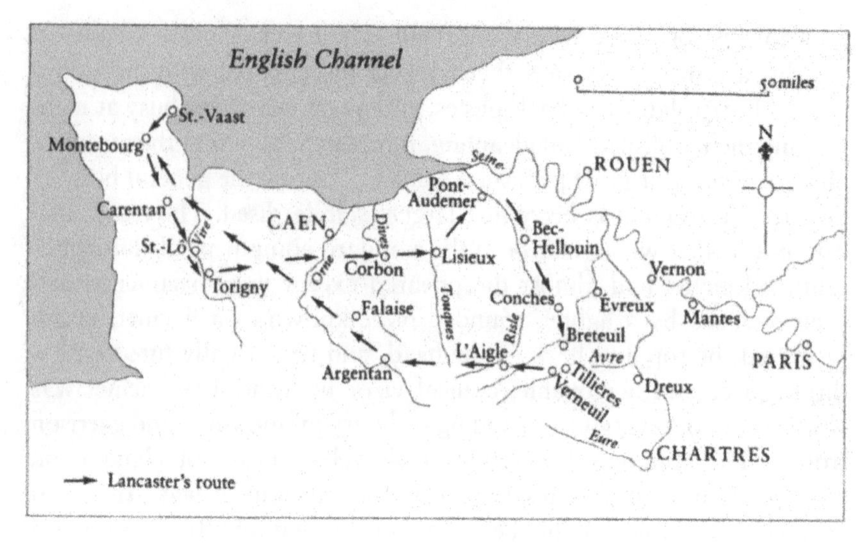

13 Henry of Lancaster in Normandy, June–July 1356

within six weeks of the decision to send them there was a tribute to the growing skill of the English in concentrating their scattered forces in western France and improvising ambitious plans at short notice. On 22 June 1356 the whole force rode south from Montebourg on the road to Caen and Rouen.[41]

Lancaster was too late to save Évreux. The Dauphin's troops had stormed the walls of the *cité* at the beginning of June, at about the time that the first English landings were occurring at la Hogue. They had burst into the town, plundering houses and churches alike. The Navarrese completed the destruction, torching the crowded wooden buildings as they retreated through the streets towards the castle of the Counts. When they were securely barricaded in there, they began to bargain from the walls. They were allowed to withdraw under safe-conduct to join the Navarrese garrison of Breteuil twenty miles away.[42]

At Pont-Audemer, another Navarrese garrison was still holding out against the army of Robert Houdetot. Houdetot redoubled his efforts against the citadel as the English approached. Baudrain de la Heuse, the commander of the Dauphin's troops at Évreux, marched west as fast as he could to reinforce him. But Lancaster made faster progress than either of them. On 29 June, Houdetot learned that he had passed the great fortified passage of the river Dives at Corbon. He abandoned the siege so quickly that most of his equipment, including the siege engines, was left behind for the enemy to take. When Baudrain's reinforcements arrived on the scene they found the French camp empty and Lancaster's standard flying from the walls. Lancaster had Houdetot's mines filled in. He stocked the store rooms of the castle with enough victuals to last a year, and he replaced the Navarrese garrison with 100 English troops under a German mercenary captain from Brabant. The Anglo-Navarrese army stayed for three days at Pont-Audemer. Then, on 2 July 1356, they rode up the broad valley of the Risle towards the forest of Breteuil where at least three Navarrese garrisons were still clinging to their walls.[43]

The King of France had passed the first half of June in the Beauce, contemplating an empty treasury and the disappointing results of three successive proclamations of the *arrière-ban*. When he heard the news of Lancaster's advance into Normandy his first reaction was to refight the campaign of 1346. He moved his army north of the Seine so as to block the way to Paris and the escape to Calais. He had ships sunk in the shallows of the river to obstruct the passage of carts and horses. At the beginning of July he abruptly ordered the Count of Poitiers to put off his march to Languedoc and transferred most of the army of Bourges to his own command. The men marched north through the night from the Cher to the Seine. By the first week of July the French King had gathered round him the Dauphin, the Duke of Orléans and many of the most prominent noblemen of his realm. English scouts reckoned his strength at about 8,000 cavalry, which was probably an over-estimate. In addition he had a large but unwieldy and slow-moving mass of infantrymen from Paris and the northern towns. As Lancaster moved up the Risle Valley, the French army moved south to meet him.[44]

Lancaster's army moved fast. Covering between twenty and thirty miles a day, they reached Conches-en-Ouche on 3 July only to find that the place had just been captured by the French. They recaptured the outer ward of the castle by storm. But they failed to penetrate the keep. At Breteuil, eight miles south of Conches, a small French army encamped around the walls was driven off. The French seem to have been completely surprised by the sudden arrival of the Anglo-Navarrese army. At Verneuil, an important walled town south of Breteuil, the inhabitants only just had time to abandon their walls and carry their valuables into the citadel. After three days of repeated assaults the garrison of the citadel surrendered and abandoned the treasures of the inhabitants to the invaders. The capture of this place, which cost Lancaster's army many lives, was probably no more than a grand plundering venture. The troops were allowed to rampage through the town emptying out the abandoned churches and houses, while the Duke's engineers demolished the citadel. Early on 8 July 1356, Lancaster left Verneuil heading back west towards his base in the Cotentin.

When the English withdrew from Verneuil, the main body of the French army was only a few hours' march away. The French King tried to cut the enemy off, leading his men on a long forced march by the valley of the river Iton. By sundown on 8 July, Lancaster was at l'Aigle, the scene of Charles of Spain's murder two years before. John had reached the small village of Tuboeuf less than three miles away. From here he sent two heralds to Lancaster's lodgings. They brought a challenge of the kind he had often heard before. Since the Duke had ridden so hard from his base, the herald said, the King could only imagine that he had come to fight him in battle. Lancaster replied that he had invaded the region to carry out limited objectives and that having now achieved them he was returning to transact other business elsewhere. If John chose to block his path, then he should have his battle. West of l'Aigle lay the great expanse of the forest of Saint-Evroult where pitched battle would be impossible and the English would be able to melt into the trees at the first sign of danger. John could not block his path, as the Duke knew perfectly well.

Had Lancaster really achieved the 'limited objectives' for which he had come? He had not relieved Évreux or Conches. He had not been able to reach the other Navarrese garrison of the region, at Tillières, which was captured by assault a few days after his withdrawal. But he had planted two important garrisons in parts of southern Normandy which were otherwise controlled by the Crown. And he had left French strategy in complete disarray. There was now no prospect of sending an army to the south for at least another month. As for Lancaster's troops, they certainly achieved the objectives for which they had come. 'Each of the towns where my lord stayed was fine and prosperous,' one of his companions wrote home; 'every day the men captured castles and seized hordes of prisoners and piles of booty; and on their return they brought with them 2,000 horses taken from the enemy.' Lancaster left l'Aigle early on the following morning. By 13 July 1356, he was back in the abbey of Montebourg.[45]

The presence of English armies on both the southern and western fronts was a problem for John II. The English King was determined to take full advantage of it. He intended to throw everything he could into what might at last be the decisive campaign which had eluded him for twenty years. During the spring Edward conceived a plan to land a third army in France to reinforce the Duke of Lancaster. The combined army, under his own command, would then attack the French King from the west while the Prince of Wales marched up from Gascony to the Loire to threaten his rear. All this called for good timing and coordination, better perhaps than was possible with the poor communications and limited intelligence available to medieval commanders. Nevertheless, preparations were put in hand at once. The King began to retain men for the new army in the early summer. In the second week of June Richard Stafford sailed from Plymouth with a small fleet laden with fresh drafts and supplies for the Prince. Stafford reached Bordeaux on about 19 June 1356. It is very likely that he brought the King's plans with him. By the beginning of July the Prince had already begun to act on them.[46]

The French commanders had known for some time that the Prince was gathering his forces in the south-west. But there was much uncertainty about the direction in which the blow would fall. Like John II, the Count of Armagnac was planning to refight past campaigns. He was convinced that the Prince would try to repeat his triumphs of the previous autumn by making another descent on Languedoc, perhaps this time penetrating into the rich unpillaged valley of the Rhone. Armagnac's sombre warnings were read out at gatherings of prominent citizens across the province during the spring and summer. A great assembly of representatives of the towns of Languedoc was held at Béziers to coordinate the defence. On 6 July, the 'season of ripening grain and fat campaigning', the Prince left Bordeaux and marched to la Réole on the River Garonne, where he had arranged to meet the Gascon contingents of his army. By the middle of the month there were between 8,000 and 10,000 men gathered there under his command. The word spread across the region that he would be at the gates of Toulouse within days. Panic. John II belatedly detached his son's troops from his own and sent the young Count of Poitiers back to Bourges to reassemble the army of the south. The Count ordered Armagnac to proclaim the *arrière-ban*. All men of military age were summoned to appear by 1 August. Across Languedoc, the inhabitants were ordered to bring everything that they could carry into the nearest walled town.[47]

John II's own army was still well below strength. Pockets of men were arriving at halting intervals to swell its numbers during June and July. On about 12 July 1356 the King laid siege to the castle of Breteuil, the second time within three months that the place had been besieged by a French army. Breteuil was the only Navarrese stronghold left in eastern

Normandy. But it was by no means an important place. It was an ancient fortress constructed by William the Conqueror in the middle of the eleventh century to defend the march of Normandy against the King of France. It had not been in the front line since the wars of King John and Philip Augustus a century and a half before. Yet it was against this place that the King of France turned all the available resources of his kingdom. Froissart, with unconscious irony, said that it was 'the finest siege with the greatest press of knights, squires and noblemen that had been seen before such a place since the siege of Aiguillon.' It was a pointless endeavour. The castle was defended by a courageous and determined garrison of Navarrese troops. Their stores were full. There was no shortage of water. The besiegers gradually filled the ditches. They brought in teams of miners and carpenters to undermine the walls. Norman castles with their high towers and square plan were always vulnerable to mining. But they failed. In August the French mounted a great assault from a specially constructed mobile scaffolding of huge size, which was filled with men and pushed against the walls. But the garrison destroyed it with burning arrows. The French suffered terrible casualties from burns and missiles.[48]

In the middle of the month of July, the Prince of Wales suddenly moved his headquarters north from la Réole to Bergerac on the Dordogne. He was reported there by the 22nd. It now seemed likely that Languedoc was not the target after all, but that the Prince would strike north towards the Loire or east into the *massif central*. The news caused consternation in the north when it arrived there a few days later. On 26 July the French King's councillors gathered in emergency session in his tents at Breteuil. Although observers vied with each other in finding superlatives to describe the splendour of the royal army encamped around them, and there were indeed many magnificent noblemen among its ranks, John's servants knew that the result of several months' continuous recruitment had been exceptionally disappointing. Moreover, the cost of keeping even a disappointing army in the field for the past eight weeks, before the decisive stage of the campaign had begun, had outstripped the government's resources. The Treasury was almost empty. The yield of the taxes voted by the Estates-General had been negligible. The Council resolved to order the immediate devaluation the coinage. In the ordinance announcing this decision to his subjects John admitted that it was a breach of the undertakings which he had given in Paris the previous winter and contrary to the ordinances of the Estates-General. But 'the subsidies are not and never will be equal to our needs.' The huge cost of sustaining his honour and defending his subjects against the enemy could not be met in time by any other means.[49]

The coinage ordinance of 26 July was never put into effect, for within a few days it became apparent that it was not enough. At Westminster Edward III had presided over a formal session of his own Council a few days earlier. All the principal lay and ecclesiastical magnates of the realm had been summoned. The King had laid before them his plans to send another army to France and obtained their approval. The orders had gone out on 20 July 1356. Shipping was being requisitioned. Archers were being arrayed throughout Wales and central and southern England. The men-at-arms who had been retained during the summer were being told to be ready to move at short notice. Edward intended that all the preparations should be complete by the middle of August. He appointed Southampton as the port of embarkation. News escaped quickly from the palace of Westminster into the gossiping streets of London. The information that a fresh expeditionary force was being recruited in England reached the French King's ministers in less than a fortnight. On 3 August the coinage ordinance was recalled and replaced by another which ordered a yet more drastic devaluation. The price paid for silver at the mints was increased by more than a third and the silver value of the coinage reduced by half. The *monnayage* (or difference between the two) rose to the unprecedented level of 54 per cent. 'And hurry on the business,' the King added; 'for we must have the revenues as fast as you can bring them in.'[50]

On the following day, 4 August 1356, the Prince of Wales divided his forces at Bergerac. One army, which cannot have been more than 2,000 or 3,000 strong, was placed under the command of the Seneschal and one of the sons of the lord of Albret. They were given the task of defending the march of Gascony against the Count of Armagnac. The rest, between 6,000 and 7,000 mounted men including archers, moved north with the Prince. The plan was to cross the hills of the western Limousin and reach the Loire Valley at Orléans through Berry and the Sologne. On 6 August the Prince arrived in the *cité* of Périgueux. He passed two days here as the citizens watched warily from the heights of the *bourg* Saint-Front and the Bishop fulminated excommunications against looters from the pulpit of his cathedral. On 14 August, six days after leaving Périgueux, the Prince crossed the river Vienne near the abbey of la Peruse, some thirty-five miles west of Limoges. Here he unfurled his banner.[51]

The army began to burn. Within hours of the crossing they attacked the abbey of Lesterps, whose great grey granite tower of the twelfth century was held against them for more than a day. For the next four days the army made its way across the county of la Marche, territory dominated by the Bourbon family and, by an odd twist of fate, by the dowager Countess of Pembroke, an adoptive Englishwoman. The Countess's domains were spared by express order of the King of England. But the English seized le Dorat, which was sacked as Jacques de Bourbon's wife and garrison looked on impotently from the castle. Advancing north they burned Lussac-les-Églises on the 19th and sacked Saint-Benoit-du-Sault on the 20th, rifling 14,000 *écus* from the abbey treasury. On 21 August the Prince crossed the River Creuse at Argenton, less than sixty miles from Bourges. The crossing had been undefended. On the 23rd he was at Chateauroux; on the 25th at Issoudun. The garrison of Issoudun watched from the great keep of Philip Augustus as the Prince's troops wrecked the town so thoroughly that parts of it remained uninhabitable for years.[52]

While the Prince marched through central France Edward III's efforts to send a third army across the Channel were obstructed by predictable and unpredictable obstacles. In the first week of August the Aragonese galley fleet finally reached the mouth of the Seine. By 10 August they had been sighted off the coast of Kent. The preparations of the English were still far from complete, and the news had an immediate and disruptive effect on them. Ships waiting to proceed to Southampton were ordered to take refuge in the nearest safe harbour. By 26 August the government in great alarm was ordering men to be arrayed for coastguard duty along the whole coast from the Wash to the Solent.[53] Edward III would plainly not be able to meet his son on the Loire. So it was decided that the Duke of Lancaster would meet him instead. Lancaster was in Brittany by now. He had rather more than 2,000 men distributed among the garrisons of the peninsula. In about the third week of August, Lancaster sent a messenger to the Prince to tell him that he would join forces with him in Touraine at the beginning of September.[54]

From the time that the Anglo-Gascon army left Périgueux their movements were observed day and night by mounted scouting parties of French soldiers. Their reports were sent back to the Count of Poitiers. He had by now set up his headquarters for the second time at Bourges. There, he had gathered about him a small army recruited in the nearby provinces of Berry, Bourbonnais and Auvergne. They were no match for the much stronger force which the Prince commanded. By 18 August, as the prince advanced across the Limousin, the Count of Poitiers abandoned Bourges altogether and withdrew behind the Loire at Nevers. A few days later he established his headquarters a short distance upstream in the fortress-town of Decise.[55]

The French King was 200 miles away at Breteuil immobilised by the increasingly pointless siege of the Navarrese garrison there. John had committed too much of his personal authority to reducing this place to contemplate abandoning the attempt now. Although the news of the Prince of Wales' advance must have reached him very soon after it had begun, he was still insisting publicly that it was at Breteuil that he would find his worst enemies. When it became clear that the fortress could not be taken by force, even John's capacity for self-deception failed him. On about 20 August he paid the Navarrese an enormous sum of money to surrender the castle and allowed them a free passage to rejoin Philip of Navarre in the Cotentin. They were allowed to take with them all the goods that they could carry.[56]

The French plan of campaign did not begin to take shape until after the King had extricated himself from Breteuil, by which time the Prince was almost at the River Creuse. The first decision was to postpone yet again the expedition of the Count of Poitiers to Languedoc, this time indefinitely. It was politically unfortunate, but the Count's troops could not be spared. Instead, he was ordered to hold the line of Loire until the King and the Dauphin could reach him in early September. The two armies were then to join up to confront the Prince of Wales in Touraine. In the meantime the Marshal Jean de Clermont was sent ahead to organise the defence of Touraine. Two large reconnaissance forces were sent south of the Loire to obstruct the Prince's movements and gain time for John's larger plans: one under Philippe de Chambly (known as 'Grismouton') and another, rather larger, under Jean de Boucicaut and Amaury de Craon.[57]

Shortly after these decisions had been made the King moved his headquarters back to Chartres, where he set about reorganising his army. Virtually all the infantry contingents of the towns who had been with him at Breteuil were now paid off. This decision was condemned, even at the time, as an act of folly and variously blamed on the snobbery or insecurity of the noblemen about the King. But it was unavoidable. John had to conserve his resources and to match the mobility of the Prince of Wales, whose army was entirely mounted. The urban infantry were ill-trained, expensive and slow. 'Don't burden yourself with scum, take only picked men,' was the poet Guillaume de Machaut's advice. John's problem was that by comparison with the great hordes of 1340 and 1346, his army was desperately short of picked men. There were still very few men-at-arms. It was probably at Chartres that he was joined by the lord of Douglas and his fine company from Scotland. But the response of John's own subjects was unimpressive. The King renewed his appeals to the nobility of France. It was not until the following month that they began to arrive, and then irregularly.[58]

On 26 August 1356 the Prince's troops reached the River Cher. A large Gascon reconnaissance force commanded by the Captal de Buch crossed the river near Vierzon. The men sacked the town, which had been abandoned by its population, and wasted the whole region for twenty miles around leaving hardly a building upright. Another detachment under Chandos and Audley made a dash for the Loire in the hope of seizing a crossing. They reached Aubigny on 28 August. North of Aubigny they ran into a troop of eighty French men-at-arms, part of Grismouton's force. There was a sharp encounter in the fields. The Frenchmen, greatly outnumbered, were driven off with heavy losses including eighteen of their men who were captured. Beyond the waterlogged flats of the Sologne, with their copses of willow and alder and islands of cultivation among the reeds, the Loire made a meandering course through the shifting channels of its vast sandy bed. For more than two centuries the inhabitants had fought with dykes and earthworks against a river which could capriciously change its course or swell in a few hours to cover vineyards and ploughed fields for miles around. The river was now to be their principal defender. The summer of 1356 had been very wet. The Loire was too deep and fast to be crossed and too broad to be bridged. The English failed to find a crossing.[59]

The main body of the English army followed some way behind the flying columns. On 28 August the Prince occupied the ruins of Vierzon. On the following day the Gascons captured a French scouting party belonging to the company of Amaury de Craon. The prisoners revealed that Craon and Boucicaut were at Romorantin. They also disclosed that the French King intended to concentrate his forces at Orléans. According to them the plan was to confront the Prince on the road to Tours. In fact, John had been seriously delayed. He was still at Chartres struggling with the problems of recruitment and finance. Boucicaut and Craon decided to hold up the Prince's advance on the line of the river Sauldre at Romorantin. Their strength was small, about sixty men-at-

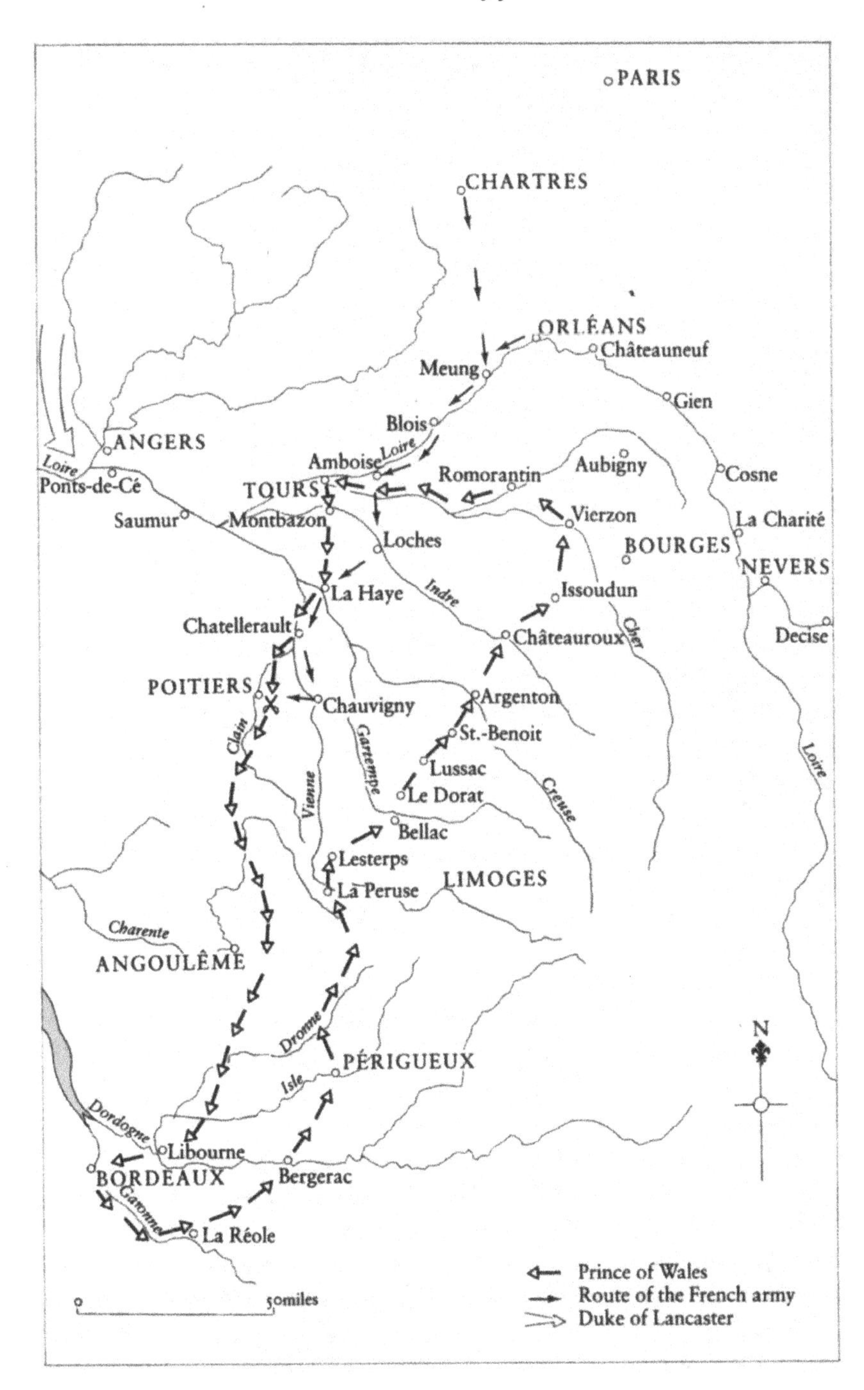

14 The Prince of Wales' march through France, July–September 1356

arms and a few hundred infantry. But they calculated, correctly as it turned out, that the Prince would not want to risk leaving them behind him when he might have to confront a far larger force further west.

Romorantin was a walled town dominated by a large stone keep dating from the eleventh or twelfth century. The region had not seen a major military campaign since the early thirteenth century and it is unlikely that the defences of the town were in good condition. There had been no time to lay in stores of victuals. There was no convenient source of drinking water. The defence of the town had still not been properly organised when the first units of the Prince's army arrived outside it on 31 August 1356 and carried the outer walls by assault. The defenders fled to the citadel and then, when the outer bailey fell, to the keep. Here, they held out for three more days. The English undermined the walls. They built three mobile assault towers. They launched repeated assaults against the keep from several directions at once. On 2 September, one of the assault parties succeeded in setting fire to it. The fire spread upwards through the building and into the roof timbers. On the following day, as the fire was still raging, the garrison surrendered. It was the third time in five years that Jean de Boucicaut had been a prisoner of the English. The Prince left Romorantin on 5 September 1356 and marched along the old Roman road which followed the north bank of the river Cher. On 7 September he arrived outside Tours.

Here he now found himself for the first time in serious difficulty. The French had broken every bridge over the Loire between Tours and Blois. John II had finally left Chartres and begun his march south. He arrived at Meung-sur-Loire on 8 September. Reports had reached the Prince from Brittany that the Duke of Lancaster was on his way. But Tours blocked his route to the west.[60]

Tours was a medium size provincial town of about 12,000 inhabitants. Its main importance for the Prince was that it guarded the great bridge which carried the Roman road from Bourges west towards Anjou and Maine. The town was spread out along a narrow spur of ground which extended for a mile along the south bank of the Loire. At one end stood the ancient episcopal *cité* clustered around the unfinished cathedral, the royal castle and the bridgehead; at the other, the *bourg* of Chateauneuf which had grown up rather later around the famous abbey and shrine of St. Martin. *Cité* and *bourg* were both defended by ancient and dilapidated walls. A third wall, which was destined to enclose both communities as well as the rich and populous suburbs of the valley in between, had been begun two years before. But it had made little progress. The inhabitants of the valley gathered up their valuables, abandoned their homes and took refuge in the episcopal city. The defence of Tours depended on Jean de Clermont and the seventeen-year-old Count of Anjou, the King's second son, who had recently arrived in the town with reinforcements. They had ditches and makeshift defences constructed at weak points. They organised the inhabitants. The Prince established his headquarters on the banks of the Loire in the suburban village of Montlouis. An assault force of 1,500 men was formed. Bartholomew Burghersh was put in command of it. But Burghersh was driven off by determined resistance and torrential rain, which turned the low lying ground south of the town into an impassable swamp. He failed even to penetrate the unwalled suburb.[61]

On about 10 September 1356 John II joined forces with the Count of Poitiers. The combined armies crossed the Loire at Blois and marched downstream to Amboise, within ten miles of the Prince's tents. The Prince learned this early on the following day, 11 September. Faced with the threat of being caught between Clermont and the King he resolved to retreat rapidly south. There was no other option. The army withdrew across the Cher and the Indre on the same day. That evening, they occupied Montbazon on the south bank of the Indre. There, on the following morning, in the great stone fortress overlooking the town and the river crossing, the Prince received the Cardinal of Périgord and a magnificent suite of lay and ecclesiastical dignitaries. They had come with messages of peace.[62]

Élie Talleyrand de Périgord and his colleague Niccolo Capocci were the latest of the long line of papal conciliators sent to plead for peace at critical moments of the war. Talleyrand was a princely personage, 'proud and arrogant' according to the Italian chronicler Matteo Villani, very conscious of his splendid lineage and red hat. Born the son of a Count of Périgord, he had been tonsured at the age of seven, a bishop at twenty, and a cardinal at twenty-seven. By 1356 (when he was in his fifties) he was a rich man, the employer of a vast household of clerks and servants and the patron of a growing band of protégés. His charmed progress through the hierarchy of the Church had in some ways resembled the career of Guy of Boulogne, that other great aristocratic placeman of the papal court. But for all his influence at Avignon, and perhaps in Paris, Talleyrand was a surprising choice for an embassy to the King of England, and his appointment demonstrated more than anything how little Innocent VI understood about English politics. For the cardinal was one of the great ecclesiastical pluralists of his day, and many of the livings by which he endeavoured to support his splendid style of life were in England. This was an extremely sensitive subject at Westminster. In 1343, when the Commons had delivered a fierce complaint about the Pope's provision of foreigners to English livings, they had identified Talleyrand as one of the two principal offenders. He was, they said, the King's 'greatest enemy in the papal curia and the one who does more than any man there to obstruct his enterprises'. Capocci was in some ways an even odder choice. He was a Roman, a member of the Colonna family, a man of austere virtue who was known for his plain speaking in consistory and for having a mind of his own at a court with its due share of time-servers. But he was no diplomat and he quickly fell out with his grander colleague. It hardly mattered, for the two peacemakers encountered obstacles that would have frustrated the subtlest ambassadors. Although they had been appointed in early April 1356, their mission had been delayed by the political tumults which followed the arrest of Charles of Navarre at Rouen. They had not left Avignon until 21 June. By this time the Duke of Lancaster was already in Normandy and Richard Stafford had arrived in Bordeaux with Edward III's orders for the Prince of Wales. By the time they reached the King of France, he was preoccupied with the siege of Breteuil. The cardinals were 'benignly' received at the French court. The problem lay in England, where the news of their mission was received with a glacial respect for forms but no enthusiasm at all. Malicious persons, Innocent had been informed, had persuaded Edward III and the leading men of his realm that the Holy See was not mediating but simply making trouble in the interests of France. Thomas Ringstead, an English Dominican in the Cardinals' suite, was sent across the Channel to soften their hearts. But his visit served only to confirm that Innocent's information was correct. When Ringstead appeared before the King at Westminster he received a venomous lecture about the abortive treaty of Guines, the outcome of the Pope's last attempt at mediation. The most that Edward would do was to issue documents empowering the Prince of Wales to deal with these matters in the field. Perhaps it was convenient for the Prince that he had not received them when the Cardinal of Périgord came before him at Montbazon. It was a bad moment for negotiation. Talleyrand spoke 'at length' of truces and treaties. But the Prince told him that there could be no peace. Not only was he without instructions, but the King of France was already on his way to fight him.[63]

The Dauphin entered Tours on the same day. He brought with him

1,000 men-at-arms from Normandy. John II with the combined armies of Chartres and Bourges was making rapid progress along the royal road from Amboise to Poitiers, a route which would take him round the Prince's army by the east. The Prince was desperately trying to find the Duke of Lancaster, whose army was believed to be somewhere to the west of his own. The English reached la Haye (modern Descartes) on the River Creuse on the evening of 13 September 1356. On the same evening, John II arrived at the immense fortress of Henry Plantagenet at Loches, twenty miles away. John reached la Haye on the following day a few hours after the Prince had left it. On the 14th, the Prince arrived at the bridge-town of Chatellerault on the east bank of the Vienne. Here he paused for three days, almost certainly in the hope of making contact with the Duke of Lancaster. Lancaster, however, was meeting unexpected difficulties of his own. When he reached the Loire he found that all the bridges over the river were either broken or heavily defended. He tried to force the crossing of the river at Ponts-de-Cé, just south of Angers. But he was stopped by the great island fortress which guarded the northern channel. There was no other bridge between Nantes and Saumur, both of which were guarded by great walls and large garrisons. While the Prince waited vainly for news at Chatellerault, the King of France passed round him by the south. On the evening of 15 September 1356 John entered Chauvigny.[64]

According to his own report, written some weeks later, the Prince decided on the evening of 16 September that he would offer battle to the French King. This is certainly consistent with his movements during the next two days. It may be that since John's army was now in a position to cut off his line of retreat to Bordeaux, there was little alternative. The Prince's staff assumed that John would march west from Chauvigny along the road to Poitiers. Their plan was to attack the French army on this road, just west of the bridge at Chauvigny. Medieval armies, encumbered with horses, weapons and baggage carts, took a long time to cross river bridges. The Prince must have hoped to surprise the French while part of their force was still on the east side of the Vienne. So, early on the morning of 17 September, the English left Chatellerault by the Vienne bridge and turned south. They forded the River Clain, then marched south through the dense forest between the valleys of the Clain and the Vienne. The Prince quickened his march as reports began to reach him that the French army was already crossing the Vienne and moving towards Poitiers.

When the Prince's scouts reached the road from Chauvigny to Poitiers

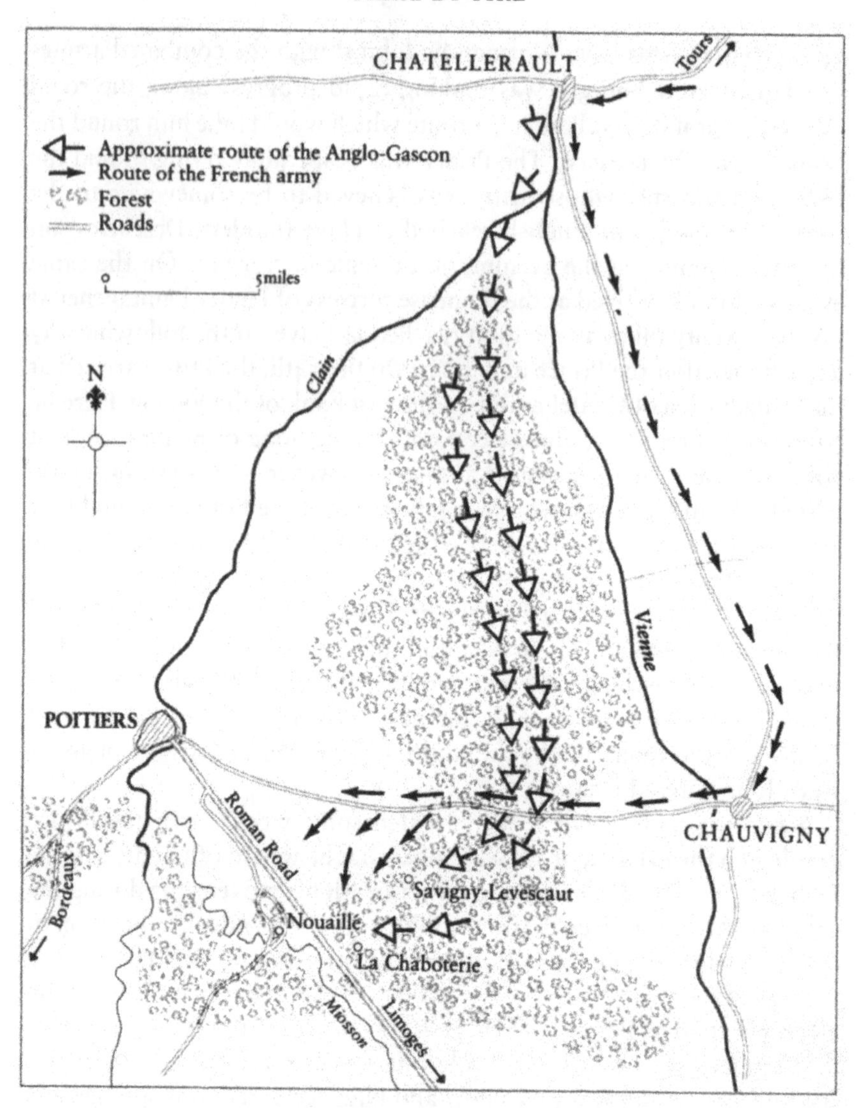

15 The march to Poitiers, 17 September 1356

they found that the French army had already passed by. The English commanders decided to follow them but, instead of taking the road, they resolved to pass south of it and move cross-country through the forest. The route was punishing for the Prince's carts as well as for his men, who had already covered more than twenty miles that day, much of it on rough forest tracks. But it kept his movements concealed from the enemy. Towards the end of the afternoon, a column of Gascons emerging from the forest stumbled upon part of the French rearguard at the manor of la Chaboterie, seven miles south-east of Poitiers by the Roman road to Limoges. There were about 700 French men-at-arms there, most of them belonging to companies from Burgundy and Champagne. The Gascons immediately attacked. Their enemies had no time to organise themselves. They were routed with heavy losses. Some 240 Frenchmen were killed or captured. The prisoners included the Counts of Auxerre and Joigny and Jean de Châtillon, all of them prominent men at the court of France who earned large ransoms for their captors. Some of their men were pursued for several miles back along the Roman road. The fight broke up the marching order of the Prince's army and the pursuit scattered it over a considerable area. Before a counter-attack could materialise, the English and Gascons vanished into the forest, where they rested and regrouped, searched vainly for water, and finally encamped for the night.[65]

The following day, 18 September, was a Sunday. The English army emerged from the forest before sunrise. Unnoticed by the enemy, they moved west along the valley of the River Miosson past the high tower and closed walls of the Benedictine abbey of Nouaillé as if making for Poitiers. The Prince's scouts located the French army soon after dawn. They were drawn up in battle order in the plain north of them, between the city of Poitiers and the village of Savigny-Levescaut, where the Bishops of Poitiers had their country residence. South of their lines the Roman road passed through an undulating landscape of woodland and pasturage and scattered vineyards belonging to the churches and richer citizens of Poitiers. The scouts counted eighty-seven banners in the enemy ranks. But the exact strength of John II's army was rather smaller than this great array of flags suggested. Figures obtained after the battle was over suggested that John had about 8,000 men-at-arms under his command and about 3,000 infantry. This was a larger army than the Prince's. But it bore no comparison with the great hosts of 1340, 1346 and 1347.[66]

The English took possession of a hilltop north of the village of Nouaillé. The French lines were about a mile beyond, just out of sight behind the brow of a hill. Here, the Prince drew up his battle lines. The Earls of Warwick and Oxford were put in command of the first division, which was stationed on the left, where the ground fell away towards the River Miosson. The Earl of Salisbury commanded the right wing. The Prince himself took command of the centre. A small reserve, including 400 archers, was kept at the rear. Their total strength was about 6,000 men, comprising some 2,000 English and Welsh archers, 1,000 Gascon infantry and 3,000 men-at-arms. They occupied a particularly strong defensive position. Immediately behind them was the forest of Nouaillé. Their front was protected by a thick hawthorn hedge which ran across the hillside, and by scattered copses of bush and scrub and rows of vines. The archers took up their traditional place at the two wings of the army. On the right, deep trenches were dug for them. On the left they were protected by the marshes of the River Miosson. But in spite of these careful dispositions, the English and Gascons were afraid. They were hungry and thirsty. There were murmurs in their ranks about the disparity of numbers. It had been a mistake, some of them complained, to leave so many good men behind in Gascony.[67]

The Cardinal of Périgord followed, wringing his hands, in the track of the French army. Shortly after the Prince had completed the disposition of his troops, the Cardinal rode across the open ground between the two armies in a final attempt to stop the battle. He came before the Prince, stretching out his arms and choking back his tears. He begged the Prince to listen. 'Say it quickly then,' the Prince replied; 'this is no time for a sermon.' The Cardinal of Périgord launched into a long and emotional speech. He dwelt upon the waste of human life which would inevitably follow if battle were joined. He implied that the bulk of the casualties would be on the Prince's side. The Prince and his army were in grave peril where they were, he said. Let them not tempt God from pride and over-confidence. He implored the Prince by the honour of the crucified Christ and the Blessed Virgin to grant a short truce so that negotiations could be held. He promised his own good offices to find an honourable way out. The Prince was eventually persuaded to agree to a short conference in the no man's land which separated the two hosts. The delegates of each side met in the open fields. Their deliberations dragged on all day and well into the night. The Prince appointed no deadline, and in spite of his brusque answer to the Cardinal, there is a good deal of evidence that he was anxious to avoid a battle and willing to make significant concessions. The most reliable account is that of the Florentine chronicler Matteo Villani, which was derived from the Italian community at the papal court in Avignon. According to him the Cardinal of Périgord produced a proposal. The English were to surrender all their conquests in France during the past three years; they were to pay a cash indemnity of 200,000 nobles (£66,666) to make good the damage which the Prince's raids has caused in France. Charles of Navarre would be released from prison. The Prince himself would be betrothed to a daughter of the King of France who would bring the whole county of Angoulême as her dowry. Whatever the Prince thought of this hotchpot of ideas, he certainly did not reject it out of hand. But the French did. When John II laid the Cardinal's plan before his Council, an uncompromising speech was made by Renaud Chauvel. Chauvel was the Bishop of Chalons. He had been one of the principal officers of the Chambre des Comptes for many years, a protégé of Charles of Spain who shared his old master's view that the English could be tamed by force alone. He was also a bitter enemy of the King of Navarre, and was bound to oppose anything that might bring about his release. Chauvel's theme was simple. The English had destroyed large tracts of France. The Prince of Wales was trapped in his present position and had no way of escape. His men were outnumbered, exhausted by their march and short of supplies. Any agreement which they might make with him would be ineffective. It would have to be confirmed by Edward III in England, and in the meantime the Prince's men would join forces with the Duke of Lancaster and return to their depredations. When Chauvel had finished, the whole Council was with him.[68]

It was late when the conference dispersed, but Talleyrand did not give up hope. He asked the Prince for authority to agree an indefinite truce. But the Prince was becoming suspicious of the Cardinal's good faith. He believed that Talleyrand's real purpose was to delay the onset of the fighting for long enough to exhaust his remaining supplies and enable reinforcements to reach his enemies. So he refused the request. Just after dawn broke on the following morning, 19 September, the Cardinal rode back across the fields to the Prince's tents with yet another proposal for a more limited truce, this time for a period of one year. The Prince, according to one report, was willing to contemplate a truce until the following spring but no longer. The King of France, however, had already decided on his course. He would have no truce at all. A conference of his chief councillors and captains was already making their final dispositions for the battle. As for Talleyrand, he withdrew empty-handed. Some of his entourage slipped off to fight with the French, thus confirming what Englishmen had always suspected about papal peacemakers.[69]

John II's army was drawn up in three lines one behind the other. Each line consisted of a central mass of men and two smaller wings. The front line was commanded by the Dauphin and the lord of Douglas. The King's brother, the Duke of Orléans, took command of the second line. The King himself was in the rear, together with Geoffrey de Charny carrying the *Oriflamme* and about 2,000 select men-at-arms.[70] The great tactical difficulty of the French commanders was that the English showed no signs of attacking first. Past experience suggested that they would simply stand at their stations for long enough to retreat with honour, and then disappear. Yet if the French attacked first they would lose the advantage of numbers. The Anglo-Gascon army was dug into a powerful position where it was impossible to surround or outflank them. Even a direct assault could be mounted only on a narrow front where gaps in the hedges and vines permitted. So the French decided, for the first time in a major engagement, to abandon the mass cavalry charge which had been the main feature of their battle tactics for more than two centuries. They formed a small corps of about 500 men-at-arms mounted on armoured horses whose task would be to charge the English archers at the outset of the battle and break up their formations. They were placed under the command of the two Marshals, Clermont and Audrehem. The rest of the army dismounted and sent their horses to the rear. They were to follow up the hillside on foot, taking advantage of the carnage which the cavalry hoped to cause among the archers. According to reports which reached the English after the battle Douglas was the man who proposed this plan. He pointed out that ever since the battle of Bannockburn in 1314 the English had fought their battles on foot, a lesson which they had learned from the Scots and might yet teach to the French. But the decisive argument was given by Eustache de Ribbemont, one of the heroes of the battle at the gate of Calais five years earlier. He had been given the task of reconnoitring the enemy's position. He reported that there was no other way of reaching the Prince's lines. The only alternative was not to attack at all, but to wait until hunger and thirst had forced the Prince to abandon his prepared positions and try his chances elsewhere. One of the Marshals, Jean de Clermont, was for this course. But his colleagues taunted him with cowardice and dismissed his advice. 'You will be lucky if you can put the muzzle of your horse to the rump of mine,' Clermont replied to Arnoul d'Audrehem, who had been foremost amongst the scoffers.[71]

In fact the Prince was closer to being starved out than even Clermont realised. His men had been arrayed in battle order for more than twenty-four hours and had slept all night at their stations. They had no water and virtually no victuals, while their adversaries were well supplied with both. The last preliminaries of battle were being completed. Mass had been said. Knighthoods had been conferred. The Prince had harangued his men from his horse. The ordinances of war had been read out to the men. They were commanded to keep strict discipline in the lines and on no account to waste time and effort securing prisoners in the mêlée. But the truth was that the Prince and his commanders had already decided to retreat. They planned to slip away south across the Miosson while keeping the whole army in battle order in case the French tried to attack them on the move. It was an exceptionally dangerous manoeuvre. The Earl of Warwick's division, which was closest to the river, made the first move, picking their way across marsh at the valley bottom.[72]

On the other side of the hill, between the two hosts, the self-appointed champions of each side rode up and down the line challenging all comers to single combat, an exhibition of bravado which traditionally occupied the tense moments before a great battle. The French Marshals were watching from the front of their lines, surrounded by the select cavalrymen destined for the initial attack. Suddenly, they noticed the movement among the enemy's banners, the tips of which could just be seen over the brow of the hill. There was a brief argument about what it meant. Audrehem immediately concluded that the English were retreating. Without further discussion he couched his lance and led half the cavalry force pell-mell across the fields towards the Earl of Warwick's banners on the English left. Clermont did not agree, but was not to be outdone. He drew up the rest of the cavalry and led them in a parallel charge towards the Earl of Salisbury's positions on the opposite wing.

Warwick's men had already reached the lower slopes of the hill when Audrehem's cavalry came into sight, and some of the leading columns had penetrated some distance across the marshes of the Miosson. The archers were still in their original positions by the slimy banks of the river, well beyond the reach of cavalry. But their arrows glanced off the steel plates and leather fringes of the horses' armour. While the rear units of Warwick's division bore the brunt of the French attack, the Earl of Oxford ran along the river bank with the archers until they were able to fire at the flanks and rumps of the French horses. The animals were not as well protected there. The arrows inflicted terrible carnage among them. They fell over and crushed their riders or reared up and threw them helpless to the ground. Some of them turned back in terror towards the French lines, trampling prostrate knights underfoot as they went. Audrehem himself was captured and many of his men lost their lives. Douglas, who had ridden beside him, was severely wounded. He survived only because his companions dragged him from the field.[73]

Clermont's men fared worse. They followed the Marshal over the

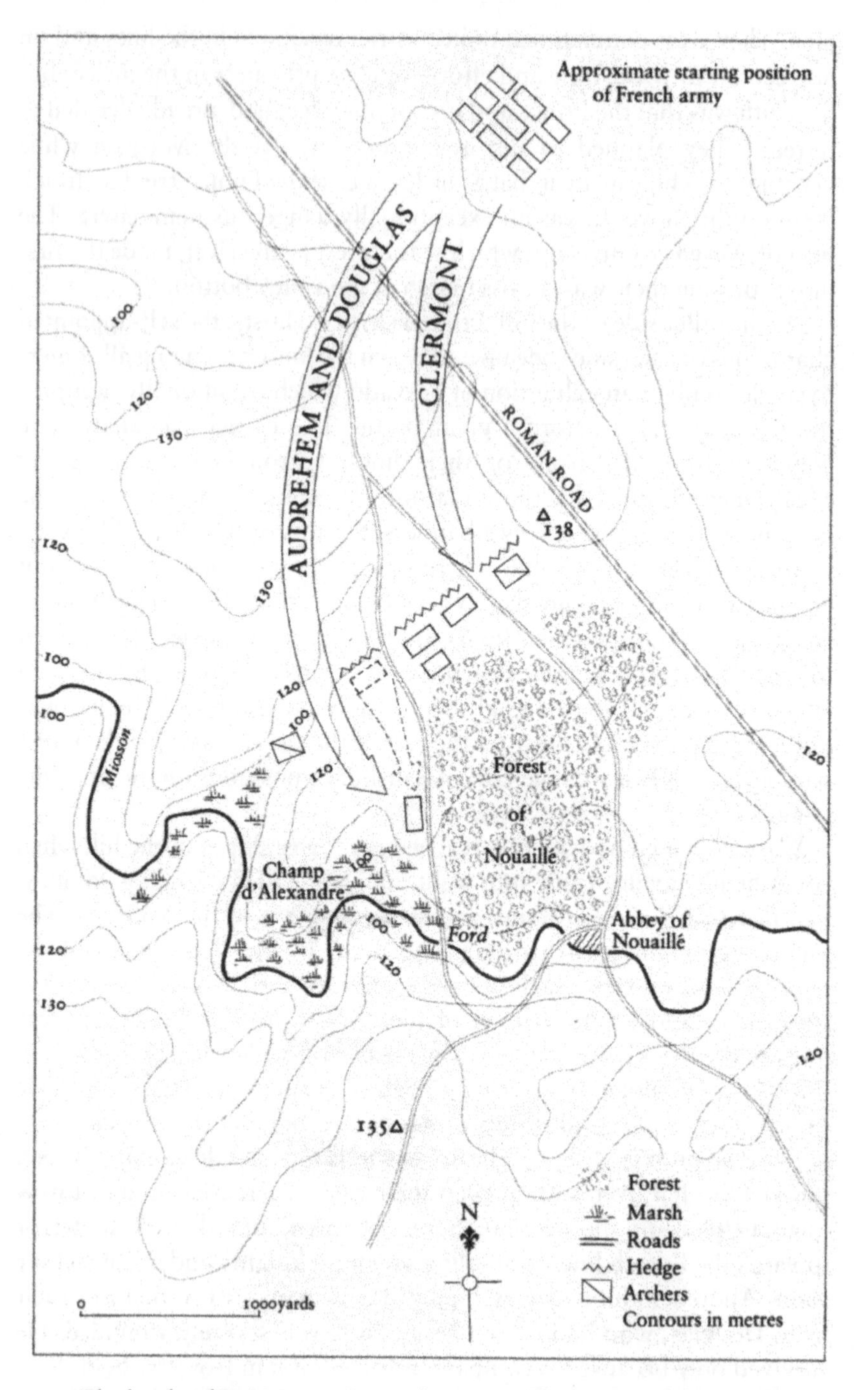

16 The battle of Poitiers, 19 September 1356. The charge of the Marshals

ridge and charged up the slope on which the Prince's army was positioned. Ahead of them was the hawthorn hedge which protected the Earl of Salisbury's lines. There was a gap in it scarcely wide enough for five men to pass through abreast. The horsemen made for this gap. As they approached, they encountered murderous flights of arrows from the trenches in which Salisbury's archers were concealed. As the French horsemen reached the gap the infantry moved forward from Salisbury's lines to block it. There was a bloody mêlée of men fighting with lances, swords and axes, and all the deafening noise of battle: shouted orders, trumpet blasts and cries of 'St. Denis' and 'St. George', screams from wounded men and horses. Salisbury 'glowed in the warm blood which covered his sword.' The Earl of Suffolk in spite of his age (he was nearly sixty) rode up and down the lines bellowing encouragement, redisposing the archers to best advantage and calling up reinforcements. The French horsemen held their own with superb strength and courage, suffering heavy losses before they were finally driven back by sheer force of numbers. The English Marshals and their deputies knew that they had fought only a small detachment of the French army and that the rest were waiting for the order to attack. They passed through the lines of unmounted men stopping enthusiasts from breaking ranks to take prisoners or strip bodies on the hillside below.[74]

The first of the three lines of the French army had already begun to advance before they knew the fate of the cavalry. They moved towards the English lines in good order along a broad front, on foot, led by the eighteen-year-old Dauphin. When they reached the hedge they crammed themselves through the gaps to get to the English troops behind. Many of them were killed or wounded by arrow fire as they came through the hedge. The rest fell on the English and Gascons standing in their lines a short distance behind. The hand-to-hand fighting lasted for some two hours before the Dauphin's officers, finding that they were making no progress, decided to sound the retreat. Once again the English had to be held back. Only Maurice Berkeley followed the retreating French troops. He found himself engulfed in the mass of the enemy, surrounded and forced to surrender. As soon as the Dauphin had withdrawn a safe distance from the English lines he was hurried from the field by his companions. This may have been done by the King's order, for the Dauphin was too important a prize to risk in the rout of defeat. But the King cannot have anticipated what the consequence would be. The Duke of Orléans, seeing the Dauphin leaving, followed him from the field taking with him the young Counts of Anjou and Poitiers and the whole of the second line. After the battle, when reputations were at stake, it was put about that this too had happened by John II's order. But no one believed it. 'Wretches and cowards' Villani called them, echoing the outrage of most Frenchmen. The King was left alone on the field with the third line.[75]

When John was informed of the repulse of the Dauphin and the flight of the Duke of Orléans, he resolved to try to save the battle with his own division. He ordered them to advance. A cacophony of trumpets sounded across the shallow valley which separated the two armies. The crossbowmen went first, the pavisers holding their great shields before them. The men-at-arms advanced steadily on foot behind. As they came up the hill, the archers on the right of the English line loosed volleys of arrows at them. But they were running out of arrows by now, and John's division penetrated almost unscathed to the English positions. The King's troops included many of the most famous knights of his army. They were also fresh men, whereas the English had been fighting with only brief intermissions for some three hours. But the morale of the English was high after the repulse of the first two attacks, and although many of their men were wounded and out of action, they outnumbered what was left of their enemy by a considerable margin. When the English archers had emptied their quivers they left their positions and fell on the French with knives and swords, followed by the men-at-arms.

At the high point of the fighting, the Captal de Buch took sixty men-at-arms and 100 mounted archers from the English reserve and led them in a broad sweep round the side of the battlefield by the north until he reached the rising ground behind the French army where they had encamped for the night. Then, raising the standard of St. George to show which side he was on, he charged down on the French rear. When the Prince saw the Captal begin his charge, he had the horses brought forward from the rear. Every man-at-arms who could be taken out of the line was remounted and sent forward under the command one of the most impetuous commanders on the English side, Sir James Audley. It was one of the rare occasions on which cavalry decided a great battle. John II's troops were unmounted on open ground, and quite unprepared to be attacked by horsemen from two sides at once. Many of them were scattered by the first impact. The rest were driven down the slope towards a field by the river known as the Champ d'Alexandre. Here they were met by a hail of arrows from the archers of the Earl of Warwick's division, who were still holding the marshes of the river. The arrows

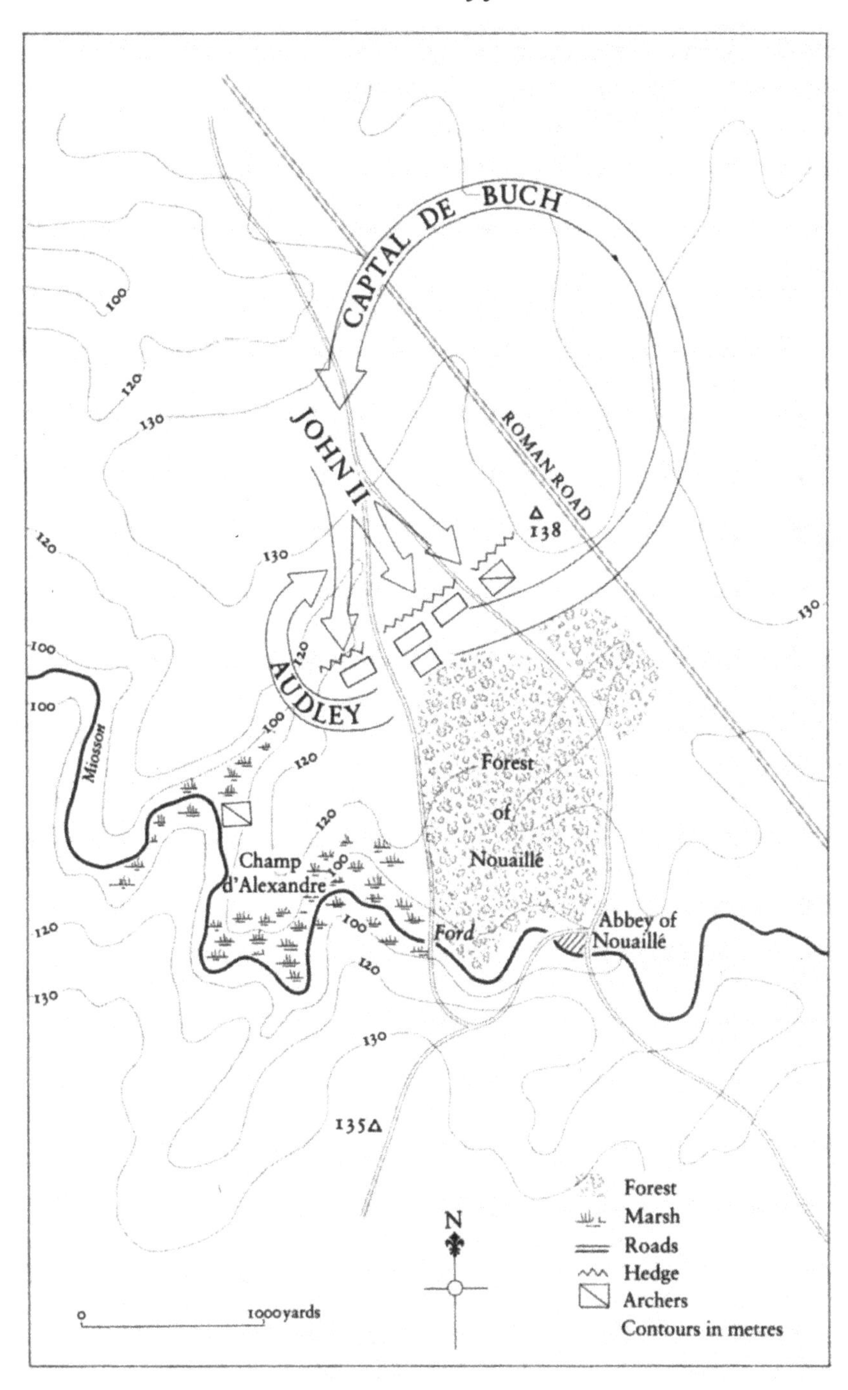

17 The battle of Poitiers, 19 September 1356
The charge of Audley and the Captal de Buch

broke up what remained of the French formations and split them into small groups fighting on every side at once.

> Men trod in their own guts and spat out their teeth; many were cloven to the ground or lost their limbs while on their feet. Dying men fell in the blood of their companions and groaned under the weight of corpses until they gave out their last breath. The blood of serfs and princes flowed in one stream into the river.

The French royal standard was seen to waver in the middle of the mass of men, then fall away. At the edge of the fighting, the survivors of the French army realised that all was lost. They slipped away and fled toward Poitiers. The English cavalry pursued them to the gates of the city and cut them down along the road or at the gates. A handful managed to surrender in time to save their lives. The terrified citizens of Poitiers watched the last moments of the massacre from their walls. But they kept the gates firmly closed.[76]

On the Champ d'Alexandre the fighting slowly dissipated into a disjointed succession of skirmishes. Many of the richest noblemen in France were stumbling towards the road or lying wounded on the field or helpless under the weight of their armour. The English and Gascon soldiers scattered across the field in a frenzied competition for ransoms. They grabbed bits of plate armour, clothing or equipment from their prisoners as tokens of possession, and then rushed off to find others. Years later the Count of Dammartin, who had fought in the King's division, remembered how he had been captured by a Gascon squire in the closing moments of the battle:

> He called on me to surrender, and I did so at once. I gave him my word so that he should protect me. He said that I should be quite safe and need have no fear. Then he tried to take off my bacinet. When I begged him to leave it, he answered that he could not properly protect me unless he took it off. So he took it off, and my gauntlets as well. As he did so, another man came up and cut the strap of my sword so that it fell to the ground. I told the squire to take the sword, for I should prefer him to have it than anyone else. . . Then he made me mount his horse and handed me over to the keeping of a man of his, and thus he left me. But as soon as he had gone, this man abandoned me and made off. Then another Gascon came up and demanded my pledge. I answered that I was already a prisoner, but all the same I gave him my word, simply in order that he would protect me. He took an escutcheon from my coat armour and then abandoned me like the last man. I shouted after him that since he was deserting me I would pledge myself to anyone else who might come up and be willing to protect me. 'Protect yourself, if you can,' he shouted back. Another man, who

belonged to Sir John Blaunkminster then appeared and demanded my pledge. I answered that I had already been captured by two people, but I gave him my word so that he would protect me. This man stayed with me, guarded me, and eventually brought me to the Earl of Salisbury.[77]

The King of France fought on with his youngest son Philip and a dwindling band of bodyguards and friends until he was overwhelmed by the mass of men shouting at him to surrender and grabbing at his clothing. Eventually Denis de Morbeke, a knight of Artois serving in the Prince's retinue and by birth John's subject, forced his way to the front and called upon the French King to submit. John would not surrender until he was assured that his captor was a knight. Then he gave him his word and delivered up one of his gauntlets. Almost immediately, the King was grabbed by several other men and dragged back into the crowd where he was claimed by a group of Gascons led by a squire called Bernard de Troys. 'He's mine! Mine!,' the voices shouted at once. John, who was becoming alarmed for his safety, protested. 'I am a great enough lord to make all of you rich,' he said according to Froissart. Then, from the edge of the crowd, the Earl of Warwick and Reginald Cobham forced their way through on horseback. They commanded every man to stand back on pain of death. Dismounting from their horses, they bowed low before the French King and led him away.[78]

Matteo Villani called it the 'incredible victory', and it suited the English to say the same. 'God is great and wonderful,' Edward III later declared; 'he disposes of all things according to his inscrutable design.'[79] Yet the outcome of the battle of Poitiers was not in military terms extraordinary. The longbow, which was the key to most English victories of the fourteenth century, played a comparatively minor part. The Prince's archers were highly effective against the opening charge of the French cavalry and again in the final stage of the battle when the French were being driven down the hill by Audley and the Captal de Buch. But they proved a great deal less effective against men on foot than they were against horses. Moreover, the battle lasted longer than any other major engagement of the period, with the result that they ran out of arrows well before the end. The traditional thing in this situation was to run forward and pull arrows from the wounded and dead. But the lie of the land and the strict line discipline of the Prince's army had made that difficult to do. As a result, the battle was really a prolonged test of endurance and physical strength fought out between men grappling with each other on foot and wielding lances, swords and axes, followed by a tremendous cavalry charge when it became clear that the last division at John II's disposal had failed to penetrate the English lines. Why were the French defeated? The main reason was that they were attacking a strong defensive position without any local superiority of numbers. Their army was larger than the Prince's, but no more than about a third of it was ever engaged at any one time. But it was also true that in spite of the outstanding courage and discipline of the French soldiers, they were outfought by a more skilful and experienced enemy. To some extent this was because French men-at-arms were not used to fighting on foot. The English, by comparison, had been doing it for four decades as the lord of Douglas had pointed out. However, the most striking contrast between the two armies was at the level of command. Manoeuvring large bodies of men-at-arms who had never trained together was one of the perennial problems of medieval battlefields. Orders were generally transmitted to section commanders by trumpet, occasionally by messenger, and thence by shouting. Signals could be complex, and hard to hear inside a visored helmet. Yet the Prince and his adjutants had shown a remarkable ability to control the movements of their men in the midst of the fighting, far superior to anything that the King of France's staff had been able to achieve. The French divisional commanders had been given their orders before the battle, and they carried them out with grim persistence regardless of what was happening elsewhere. By comparison, the Prince had been able to improvise plans in the heat of the action and to communicate them quickly to those who had to act on them in the line.

When it was all over the trumpets sounded to recall the dispersed English soldiers to their standards. Men turned to dressing their wounds, to finding food and drink and to securing their prisoners. A roll call was taken. Search parties were sent out across the fields to find those who were missing. About forty men-at-arms of the Prince's army were found dead, and an undisclosed number of infantry and archers. Wounded friends were pulled out from beneath the crush of corpses. Sir James Audley, who had led the final charge, was found lying half dead on the ground covered in blood. The Prince was dining with the King of France when Audley was brought into the camp stretched out upon a shield. He left the meal and went at once to comfort his friend, kissing his bloodstained lips and looking about for some soft bedding. John asked what arms Sir James bore upon his shield and, when he was told, remarked that he had seen their owner stand out for his strength and endurance even among so many courageous men. Then he turned to the fate of his own men. Although they had been defeated John knew that they had preserved their honour. 'At least we were not taken like criminals or runaways hiding in corners,' he said, 'but like proud soldiers fighting in a just cause, captured on the field by the judgment of Mars, when rich men were buying their lives, cowards fleeing untimely away and the bravest of soldiers heroically laying down their lives.' The King of France might perhaps have avoided battle altogether, as his father had done three times and Clermont had urged him to do on this occasion. But Clermont's advice was politically quite unrealistic as the King's other councillors had recognised. If John regretted anything, he did not admit it: 'Although the outcome of battles is ever uncertain,' he wrote three months afterwards, 'yet I have done nothing which I would not as gladly do again in the same situation.'[80]

The French had suffered terrible casualties, as the defeated always did in medieval battles. Among the dead lying on the field 2,500 men-at-arms were counted. Many had already been stripped of their armour by scavengers and could no longer be identified. Among the rest the heralds found the Dauphin's father-in-law the Duke of Bourbon; the Constable Walter of Brienne; Geoffrey de Charny, who had been killed defending the royal standard in the last moments of the fighting; Jean de Clermont who had vainly urged the King to postpone the battle; and Renaud Chauvel, who had been foremost among those who were for fighting it. Seventy corpses of the great and famous were collected from the fields by the clergy of Poitiers and buried in the Dominican church. Another 101 were laid to rest in the Franciscan cemetery nearby. But the great mass of unidentified corpses was left to rot until the following February, when they were loaded onto carts and hurled into huge pits beside the Franciscan church.[81]

The very large number of prisoners attracted unfavourable comment in France when it became known. There were about 2,000 of them, nearly a fifth of the army. They included fourteen counts, twenty-one barons and bannerets, and about 1,400 belted knights. In addition to the King, the young Prince Philip and the Marshal Arnoul d'Audrehem was taken; so were Jacques de Bourbon, brother of the Duke; Jean d'Artois, Count of Eu; Guillaume de Melun, Archbishop of Sens; Bernard, Count of Ventadour, a rising star at John's court; and many others who had been closest to the King's counsels during the past two years. The more important prisoners were all taken into the Prince's custody and most of them were later bought by the Prince or his father. But the lesser men and the Count of Eu (who was badly wounded) were allowed to be released on parole if their captors were willing. The captors were usually willing. The only alternative was for them to bring the prisoner back to Bordeaux and keep him at the their own expense for what might be a long period until the ransom could be agreed and paid. And so, much of the night was passed in bluff and haggling as the English and Gascons tried to discover what their prisoners were worth and French noblemen who were used to exhibiting their wealth boasted of their losses, their declining revenues and their accumulated debts. It is impossible to calculate even approximately the total value of the prisoners of Poitiers, and some allowance must be made for those who defaulted. But the more distinguished captives earned very large sums for their captors. The Captal de Buch and five of his companions sold Jacques de Bourbon for 25,000 old *écus* (about £4,700). Élie de Pommiers got 30,000 old *écus* (about £5,650) for the enormously rich Count of Eu. Arnaud d'Audrehem, who was an important man but not a rich one, fetched 12,000 old *écus* (about £2,250). All of these prisoners were sold to the Prince of Wales, and were ultimately acquired by his father. Leaving aside the French King himself, the top seventeen captives alone earned about £65,000 sterling for their captors, which was about two thirds of what Edward III had spent on prosecuting the war for the past year. More than nine tenths of this sum was actually paid. To this was added the great haul of clothing, armour and horses. The Burgundian nobleman Mile de Noyers lost a jewelled belt and a scarlet robe worth 250 *livres* (£62), and he was by no means the most expensively dressed cavalryman in the army. The spoil of the French camp was prodigious. In the King's pavilion the looters found a crown, the jewelled insignia of the Order of the Star and a silver model of a ship which served as the centrepiece of his table. All of these ended up in the possession of the Prince of Wales. John II's illuminated Bible was bought by the Earl of Salisbury for the enormous sum of 100 marks (£67). The whole army, said Froissart, had become 'rich in honour and lucre.'[82]

On the day after the battle the Anglo-Gascon army moved to a new position three miles south of Poitiers to rest their limbs. On 21 September they set out along the road south, followed by carts piled high with booty and lines of demoralised prisoners. On 2 October 1356, the Prince paused at Libourne while the city of Bordeaux was made ready for his triumphal entry.[83] At about the same time the first news of the victory reached England. The messenger was one John le Cok of Cherbourg, who had probably been sent by the Duke of Lancaster. A few days later, the Prince's servant Geoffrey Hamelyn arrived with confirmation and trophies: John II's bacinet and his tunic decorated with the arms of France. Edward III received these reports with almost total impassivity. But he gave Cok twenty-five marks, and he had the news carried to the bishops and announced from pulpits across England. 'We take no pleasure in the slaughter of men,' Edward intoned; '. . . but we rejoice in God's bounty and we look forward to a just and early peace.'[84] On the face of it the King's optimism was justified. He had his enemy in his hands, and within a short time he was to see the kingdom of France sink into anarchy and revolution. Yet it took him four years to achieve the peace which the Prince's victory had earned him, only to find it turn to dust in his hands.

CHAPTER VI

The Estates-General 1356–1357

The battle of Poitiers removed in the space of a few hours the whole higher direction of the French government. The King had last been seen beset by enemies on the Champ d'Alexandre, and his fate remained unknown for several days. Most of his Council had been killed or captured. They included the Constable and both Marshals, the head of the financial administration and all the leading noblemen of the court. The only surviving ministers of any importance were the aged but still vigorous Simon Bucy and the Chancellor, Pierre de la Forêt, who were both in Paris. They had an immediate military crisis on their hands. There was no French army in the field. There were English troops in Brittany, Normandy and Calais. The Île de France was defenceless against attack from any direction. A scratch army was hurriedly put together at Chartres in the last week of September to protect the capital. Within the city, the leading citizens took control of the defence. Chains were piled up at street corners to seal off each quarter. Ditches were dug on the west and south. Weapons were stored by the gates and bastions. A start was made on the demolition of the mass of buildings which had spread out beyond the ancient walls of Philip Augustus.[1]

The English did not attack Paris. But they did not waste their opportunities. In Brittany, the Duke of Lancaster invaded the north-east of the duchy in September in the name of the young John de Montfort, the puppet duke brought up at the English court whom Lancaster had brought to France in his baggage train. He overran most of the remaining strongholds of Charles of Blois virtually without opposition. Lancaster led the attack in person at la Roche-Derrien and Lannion in the Tréguier peninsula. Shortly afterwards another company, commanded by Roger David, entered Charles' favourite residence at Guingamp. Charles of Blois himself had been released from captivity in the Tower of London just a month before, on his undertaking to find a ransom of 350,000 *écus* (£58,333). He was in Brittany throughout the English campaign. But there was nothing that he could do to save his subjects. The terms of the ransom treaty forbade him to enter any place in the English King's obedience, and as a paroled prisoner he was unable to take up arms against the enemy. He had to suffer the indignity of moving from pillar to post as his possessions were eaten up. On 3 October 1356 the Duke of Lancaster arrived with John de Montfort at Rennes, the principal city of Brittany after Nantes, and laid siege to it.[2]

In the midst of the panic, Simon Bucy and Pierre de la Forêt set about filling the void of authority in Paris and replenishing the empty treasury. After hurried consultations with the Dauphin, who was on the road from Poitiers, they summoned the Estates-General of the whole kingdom to meet in Paris on 1 November 1356. This was almost immediately superseded by another even more urgent summons which brought forward the date to 15 October and limited it to the provinces of Languedoil, the only ones which could be expected to send their representatives in time. On 29 September 1356 the eighteen-year-old Dauphin entered Paris. He did not go to the rambling palace on the Île de la Cité. He installed himself in the Louvre, the great round bastion of Philip Augustus at the western edge of the city, guarded by ditches and curtain walls from his father's subjects.[3] Here he began to gather round himself the germ of a new government. Apart from permanent officials of his father like Bucy and la Forêt, there were the two royal princes, the Duke of Orléans and the Count of Alençon; his kinsman Jean de Châtillon, Count of Saint-Pol; and Moreau de Fiennes, an old soldier who was appointed as Constable. Early in October, they were joined by Charles of Blois, fleeing from the disasters of Brittany. He was a more experienced politician than any of them, but possessed by the desire to save Rennes and what remained of his Breton duchy, at whatever cost.

The soul-searching and suppressed anger of the French was even more intense than it had been after the defeat at Crécy, ten years before. Treachery seemed to be the only possible explanation of the defeat of so great an army. There was much rumination about the flight of the second division and the departure of the royal princes from the battle, the news of which had preceded the Dauphin's arrival. Their behaviour was pointedly compared with the heroism of the King and his youngest son Philip. In the course of the autumn, public contempt for the government and the leaders of the army spread to embrace the whole nobility. One man, the author of some bitter verses written in the aftermath of the disaster, accused them of deliberately losing the battle in connivance with the enemy, so as to prolong the war for their mutual benefit. They were too greedy, he said, to kill the invader when they could take ransoms from him instead, and so obsessed with the conventions of aristocratic warfare that they had more natural sympathy for their equals on the other side than for their fellow countrymen. Men remembered the dismissal of the urban infantry after the siege of Breteuil, which they put down to snobbery and arrogance. They remembered the peacock costumes which had been so fashionable among the nobility in the early 1350s:

Bombans et vaine gloire, vesture dishoneste,
Les ceintures dorées, la plume sur la teste.

The evidence is anecdotal but, such as it is, suggests that these feelings were widely shared. According to a more restrained pamphleteer, crowds gathered in the street to hurl abuse at noblemen as they passed by: 'fleeing hares, bloated chest-beaters, craven deserters' every one of them. In one village in eastern Normandy, the inhabitants gathered together to attack a knight travelling unarmed on the road with his squire and servant. 'There go the traitors who fled from the battle', they cried.[4]

In Paris, feelings ran higher than anywhere. The city was a unique force in French politics. For size and population, it dwarfed every other city of Europe. It was a great administrative capital, the artistic and intellectual metropolis of the realm, the dominant market of a vast region, and the centre of a network of roads and rivers extending throughout northern France. Unusually, for so great a city, Paris had no communal government. It was administered in uneasy rivalry by two authorities. The Provost, a royal official with his seat in the Châtelet, held the main civil and criminal courts of the capital, and maintained a small permanent police force. The Provost of the Merchants presided, together with four *échevins*, over a loose association of traders belonging to the corporation (or *hanse*) of the *marchands d'eau*. In theory this body was simply a guild of merchants which had assumed the responsibility for regulating the commerce of the Seine and the wholesale trades within the city. But in practice it had come to exercise many of the administrative and police functions of a municipal corporation. In spite of the absence of any formal political organisation and in spite of strong contrasts of wealth and status, the population of Paris was remarkably cohesive. It was, as it has always been, a city of small workshops without any dominant trade, and without the great unskilled proletariats of Ghent or Florence. It had not suffered the social upheavals which had become endemic in other large European cities since the twelfth century. Its population was bound together by a dense network of guilds and confraternities, and by the pervasive links of neighbourhood, clientage and interest. Within the walls a mass of servants, apprentices and journeymen lived cheek by jowl with the aristocracy of merchants and bankers and with the volatile crowds of immigrants, beggars and criminals, all densely packed into narrow streets where fear and anger spread rapidly and mobs appeared from nowhere in seconds.

For two centuries, successive Kings of France had enjoyed a close alliance with this huge, rich and intensely political community. The city drew a large part of its prestige from the presence the monarchy, visible in the rambling buildings and gardens of the royal palace which filled the western part of the Île de la Cité. Much of its prosperity depended on the business of the King and on the growing population of courtiers, petitioners and administrators who surrounded him. The city was conscious of its debt. The Provost of the Merchants traditionally delivered the loyal speech on behalf of the towns at the opening of meetings of the Estates-General. At moments of crisis, it was usually the first to offer money for the King's coffers and troops for his armies. Paris was a community of resonant patriotism at a time when patriotism was still, for most Frenchmen, a juridical abstraction. Yet this impressive solidarity was dangerous as well as valuable. In 1356 the French cause, which the Parisians had fiercely supported, had collapsed in bankruptcy and defeat. The frustrated enthusiasm of the Parisians quickly turned to anger and violence.

The man who articulated the anger and eventually led the violence was Étienne Marcel, the Provost of the Merchants. Marcel belonged to a prominent family of Parisian drapers and money-changers. He had not originally been a rich man or even a particularly successful one, and his commercial activities seem to have been on a modest scale. The foundation of his fortune was his marriage, in about 1345, to an heiress, Marguerite des Essarts. Her father, until he was disgraced and imprisoned in the purges which followed the battle of Crécy, had been the greatest native banker in France. Marcel's marriage brought him a dowry of 3,000 *écus* and an introduction to the extensive network of lawyers and financiers at the heart of the royal administration. To these he added the traditional alliances of a wealthy and ambitious Parisian. It was presumably by these means that he became Provost of the Merchants in about 1354. But the manner of his rise is obscure and even the date is uncertain. As Provost of the Merchants, he was naturally drawn into the events of the time. He spoke for the Third Estate at the Estates-General of December 1355, as his predecessors had done. He recruited and led the small army which Paris sent to the aid of John II after the arrest of the King of Navarre at Rouen. He organised the defence of Paris during the panic which followed the battle of Poitiers. He became the dominant figure in the Parisian revolution of 1358. In some ways his career, like his ultimate fate, resembles that of Jacob van Artevelde, that other great urban dictator of the mid-fourteenth century. Marcel certainly shared the ruthlessness and brutality of the great captain of Ghent. But in other ways he was a very different kind of man. He was no orator, and although he was a skilful organiser, he seems never to have acquired a mass following of his own. He was also guileless, impulsive and lacking in political judgment.[5]

The proceedings of the Estates-General began conventionally enough on 17 October 1356 in the Great Hall of the Parlement. It was one of the largest assemblies of its kind in recent times. Some 800 delegates were present as the Chancellor, Pierre de la Forêt, went through the now familiar catalogue of calamities which had caused them to be summoned. He spoke of the valour of the King, of the tragedy of his capture, and of the sacrifice which every Frenchmen would now be called upon to make to ransom him. After the Chancellor had finished, the Dauphin added a few 'wise and gracious' words of his own. But although the customary loyal addresses were delivered from the hall, the government's proposals were coldly received. The kingdom was exhausted and much of it was being overrun by armed bands of English, Gascon and Navarrese adventurers. John's courage on the battlefield was genuinely admired, but few men regarded the payment of his ransom of the first call on their resources. Whatever might be said about his military leadership, John's management of his finances had been deplorable and his ministers, several of whom could be seen among the courtiers around the Dauphin, were cordially loathed and despised.

The delegates withdrew from the palace to consider what to do. They repaired to the convent of the Franciscan friars in the university quarter, a rambling group of buildings by the south wall of the city where the École de Médecine stands today. Several members of the Dauphin's Council went with them to guide their deliberations. But they did not stay long. The meetings were almost immediately taken over by dissidents and protestors. After a brief and unruly discussion in each of the Estates, the delegates resolved to elect a joint committee of eighty members, which would be able to act with greater resolution than the unwieldy gatherings from which they were drawn. These men were charged with drawing up a list of demands to be presented to the Dauphin. They swore a great oath that they would all assume collective responsibility of their decisions. None of their discussions would be disclosed. The Dauphin's councillors were summarily expelled.[6]

According to the version of events which was later circulated by the Dauphin's ministers, the Council of Eighty was dominated from the outset by inveterate enemies of the King and his son. They identified thirty-four of its members as overt partisans of the imprisoned King of Navarre. The truth was more complicated. There certainly were supporters of Charles of Navarre on the Council of Eighty. These included some of its most vocal and influential members, such as the Bishop of Laon Robert le Coq and the disaffected Picard nobleman Jean de Picquigny. But many of the government's opponents on the Council of Eighty were never partisans of the House of Navarre, and others only became so later. The dominant groups were drawn from the representatives of the industrial cities of the north and from a band of reform-minded noblemen, ecclesiastics, and academic theologians. Paris was particularly well represented. Étienne Marcel and his cousin Gilles sat among the Eighty. So did the money-changer Charles Toussac, one of the four *échevins* who assisted Marcel in the government of the *hanse*. In addition there were a number of men who represented the towns from which they originated but who lived in Paris and were for all practical purposes Parisians. But it was the role of the disgruntled nobility which was paramount. Their loyalty to the Crown was in most cases beyond question. But they were dismayed by the mismanagement and the corruption which they saw everywhere in the government. So far as any man stood out as typical of the government's opponents, it was probably not the Provost of the Merchants of Paris or even the fiery pro-Navarrese Bishop of Laon but the Archbishop of Reims, Jean de Craon, who spoke for the Church: a well-connected nobleman who came from one of the great families of western France and whose brother had been captured fighting with the King at Poitiers.[7]

After a week of deliberation, the Eighty submitted their report to the three Estates. It consisted of a long and miscellaneous catalogue of grievances, the collective complaints of a large number of different interest groups. But the main theme was common ground between all of them. The King, they said, had surrounded himself with sycophants, parasites and profiteers who had mismanaged his wars, his finances, his mints, and his courts. The Eighty protested against the arbitrary and violent methods used to raise revenues and against the squandering of the proceeds. They declared themselves oppressed by the continuous manipulation of the coinage. They painted a vivid picture of the economic ills of the nobility, which they attributed to tax exhaustion, coinage operations, war damage, and the non-payment of their war wages, to the breakdown of civil justice and to the failure of the King to respond to their petitions for grants and favours. For this reason, the Eighty declared, 'towns, castles, cities and fortresses had fallen, whole regions had been wasted and destroyed, and many good men killed, while others had deserted to the enemy taking their strongholds and domains with them.' The Estates-General unanimously adopted this bleak and superficial diagnosis of France's ills. There was not a single dissenting voice.

On 26 October 1356 the Council of Eighty summoned the Dauphin to appear before them to receive in private the advice which the Estates intended to give him. The Dauphin came, attended by a small group of noblemen. Nothing can have prepared him for the message which followed. The spokesman of the Eighty was the Archbishop of Reims. He had three demands to make. First, certain of the King's officials who were 'manifestly useless' were to be summarily dismissed, deprived of all their property, and put on trial for their crimes. He named the Chancellor, Pierre de la Forêt; Simon Bucy, the First President of the Parlement; the Chamberlain, Robert de Lorris; and the four chief financial officers of the Crown, Nicholas Braque the former Treasurer, his successor Enguerrand du Petit-Celier, Jean Poilevilain, master of the mints, and Jean Chauvel the senior war treasurer. The Archbishop added the names of some other, comparatively minor officials. Apart from Pierre de la Forêt, all of these men were either closely associated with the King's financial administration or else, like Simon Bucy and Robert de Lorris, had done too well out of a government which had served no one else's interest. Neither of these accusations could be made against Pierre de la Forêt. But he was too prominent a minister to be left out of the purge. The Archbishop's second demand was that the Dauphin was to govern in future on the advice of a permanent commission to be appointed by the Estates-General. This, he said, would comprise four prelates, twelve knights and twelve representatives of the towns. They were to exercise viceregal powers in all matters of state. For all practical purposes they would displace him as John's Lieutenant. Thirdly, the Archbishop observed that nothing good had befallen the realm since the arrest of the King of Navarre six months before. The Estates therefore insisted upon his release. The Dauphin listened in silence. He said that he would take advice. But he would like to know before he did so what financial assistance the Estates-General were proposing to give him in return for meeting these demands. The Archbishop replied that the clergy and the nobility would pay 15 per cent of their revenues for a year, subject in the case of the clergy to the consent of the Pope; and that the towns would pay the cost of one soldier for each hundred households. The Eighty regarded these offers as outstandingly generous and said so. They believed that the taxes, if properly administered, would raise enough to pay for an army of 30,000 men. They had been advised by the military men among them that this was 6,000 more than the number required to clear the enemy from France and to garrison the main cities and fortresses. The Dauphin replied that he would give his answer on the following day. Then he left.[8]

The Dauphin did not give his answer on the following day. He repeatedly put it off while the implications were discussed among the small group of noblemen and lawyers around him. Their first instinct was to negotiate. Delegations passed between the Louvre and the Franciscan convent as the councillors tried to soften the demands of the Eighty. But they were intransigent. The Council's next instinct was to capitulate. Without funds, as they pointed out, the government was defenceless in the face of the English. Charles of Blois had an eye to the fate of Rennes, which might depend on the Estates-General's subsidies. He appears to have been one of the foremost advocates of capitulation. He told the representatives of the Eighty that the Dauphin had been advised by all his councillors (except one) that their demands were 'good, just, loyal and reasonable'. This may have been true. But if so they changed their minds within twenty-four hours. The Dauphin convened a new meeting of his Council. He questioned whether it was right to make such weighty concessions without consulting his father in captivity. For their part, the officers of the Chambre des Comptes had been working on the Estates' proposals for taxation. Their calculations showed that the yield of the taxes on offer was likely to be much smaller than the Eighty had claimed. Taking account of the difficulties of assessment and collection, they were able to demonstrate that far from supporting an army of 30,000 men, the taxes were unlikely to support more than 8,000 or 9,000. This concluded the argument even in the eyes of the natural compromisers. It was decided that the demands of the Estates would be rejected.[9]

The grievances of the Estates-General and their proposals for reform were due to be announced at a public session in the Great Hall of the Parlement. After several postponements the date had been fixed for 31 October 1356. An inflammatory sermon was being prepared for the occasion by Robert le Coq. Crowds had already begun to gather in the hall several hours beforehand. The Dauphin did not dare to announce his decision in this highly charged atmosphere. Instead he summoned a deputation of the three Estates before him in the privacy of the Salle de la Pointe, a little lodge at the western extremity of the island, by the landing stage. He told them that he was expecting to hear shortly from his father. He said that he wished to wait for the advice of the German Emperor and the Count of Savoy, to whom he had written. He asked them to put off the closing session of the Estates for a few days, until 3 November. Then, on the 2nd, the eve of the adjourned session, the Dauphin addressed the same delegates again, this time behind the walls of the Louvre. On this occasion, his message was very different. He told them that the Estates-General was to be suspended indefinitely. Its members were to disperse to their homes. In due course, he added rather disingenuously, he would recall them to complete their work. Early on the morning of 3 November, the Dauphin rode out of Paris with his entourage, leaving behind him instructions that his officers were to prevent the Estates-General from reassembling. Then he rode twelve miles down the Orléans road and shut himself in the massive keep of Montlhéry.[10]

As the delegates of the Estates-General began to leave the city for their homes, the leaders of the Council of Eighty who had been present at the Louvre gathered their colleagues together at the Franciscans. They decided that all the delegates who could still be found in the capital should be assembled to hear how the Dauphin had frustrated their demands. A manifesto was to be prepared to justify what they had done, which each of them could carry home to his constituents. In defiance of the Dauphin's orders, several hundred men crammed into the chapter house of the Franciscan convent. There they were treated to a tremendous oration by Robert le Coq. Robert went through the demands of the Council of Eighty and the tortuous history of its dealings with the Dauphin and his councillors. He did not mince his words. He dismissed the young men about the King and the Dauphin as 'slanderers, flatterers and boot-lickers'. He denounced the central administration as a snakepit of envy and ambition, filled with men who never gave advice without an eye to their own fortunes. He railed at the incompetence and greed of the provincial officials of the Crown. He denounced the institutionalised embezzlement to which he attributed the reverses in the war. Every time the King had raised significant sums in tax revenues, Robert asserted, he had patched up some shabby truce with the enemy and diverted the proceeds into private pockets instead of laying it aside in preparation for the next round of fighting. Then, when the truces failed, he would turn in desperation to coinage manipulation and fines for exemption from the *arrière-ban*. In the main, this analysis of the government's financial problems was a travesty of the truth. But the symptoms which Robert described were real enough, and few members of his audience can have been in the mood for questioning the diagnosis. The remedy, he concluded, was the wholesale replacement of the King's advisers with experienced men who would speak for the great interests of the realm. Robert proposed the appointment of two standing commissions of the Estates-General. One of them would meet daily to consider the great affairs of the realm and to set the Dauphin's government on the path of virtue. Another, composed of experienced military men, would sit in permanent session in Paris to guide the military officers of the Crown and the captains of the principal garrisons. Robert le Coq proposed a thorough purge of the royal administration, and especially of its financial departments. The leading ministers whose dismissal had been demanded on 26 October ought to have been summarily imprisoned and all their assets confiscated. Their guilt was too obvious to call for any kind of trial. But, he said, it was surely unreasonable to single out just seven or eight men when the incompetence and corruption of the King's administration was so widespread. Groups of *réformateurs* should be sent to tour the provinces, chastising oppressive or corrupt officials who were less easily identified and punished than their superiors in Paris. There ought to be a general confiscation of all Crown lands which had been granted out to the King's friends since the beginning of the reign. Robert le Coq spoke out, as the Eighty had done, for the King of Navarre:

> He is of the blood royal of France on his father's and mother's side. He is married to the sister of my Lord the Duke [of Normandy, the Dauphin]. Yet, because of his arrest, the province of Normandy has been shattered; the dioceses of the Coutances, Avranches, Bayeux, Lisieux, Sées, Évreux, Rouen, Chartres and le Mans have been wasted: others have suffered grave damage. Unless he is released from prison yet greater evils may befall us. The Navarrese soldiers who are still in occupation of his castles may totally destroy Normandy or, even worse, let in the English.

Finally, Robert turned to the Estates-General itself. The Dauphin, although he was wise for his years, was still very young, he said. He needed sound advice and guidance. The men who were now offering him these prescriptions for the conduct of his government had invested their honour and their fortunes in the survival of the French nation: 'men of conscience, men of high rank and dignity, men of wisdom and loyalty from every part of the realm who have seen for themselves the ills of the nation about their own homes.' As Robert warmed to his theme, he began to refer darkly to the possibility of more abrasive measures. He suggested that if necessary the Estates-General could depose a monarch who refused to heed their advice. There were, he suggested, historical precedents. At this point, Robert's colleagues began to feel uncomfortable. One of them stepped sharply on the orator's foot. Robert hastily corrected himself. It was the Pope, he said, who had deposed past tyrants, at the invitation of the Estates-General. Winding up his speech, Robert called on every delegate present to collect a written summary which had been prepared of the advice which the Dauphin had spurned, and to carry it home to his own community. With the Bishop's words ringing in their ears and the document stuffed into their satchels, the delegates dispersed across the provinces of France.[11]

The suspension of the Estates-General temporarily relieved the Dauphin's political difficulties. But it did nothing to improve his financial situation, which was becoming desperate. The taxes voted before the battle of Poitiers had been remitted in October on the assumption that fresh ones would be granted by the Estates-General. There was now nothing left in the treasury, and nothing coming in. The Dauphin passed most of November in Paris trying to raise money. He despatched *réformateurs* to levy fines and compositions for the innumerable infractions of the coinage ordinances and other lucrative peccadilloes of his subjects.[12] He attempted to raise taxes by private treaty, approaching the municipality of Paris and other traditional supporters of the Crown. Étienne Marcel, who was still not wholly won over to the radical opposition, seems to have seriously contemplated making a local grant. But he was abused and threatened by Robert le Coq, and eventually refused to help unless the Dauphin would agree to recall the Estates-General.[13]

In the provinces the government fared rather better. The Estates of Languedoc, which had not been represented in Paris, met in October in Toulouse under the presidency of that experienced political manager the

Count of Armagnac. There was no radical agitation there. The men of Languedoc were a great deal more generous than the Estates-General in Paris, and their offers were not accompanied by unwelcome proposals for political reform. They voted a *capage* (or poll tax) of three pennies per head per week, payable by all persons over the age of twelve, and a small tax on movable and immovable property. The delegates at Toulouse expected that the yield of these taxes would be enough to finance an army of 5,000 men at arms and 5,000 mounted infantry for a year. But their generosity brought little relief to the Dauphin, because they stuck to their traditional practice of reserving the proceeds for the defence of their own region. Two standing commissions of the Estates of Languedoc and a hierarchy of local treasurers and receivers were nominated to supervise the collection and expenditure of the money. The King's officers were largely excluded from the process. Other parts of France reacted in much the same way. The Dauphin sent agents out to several of the *baillages* which had been represented in Paris in the hope of negotiating grants of taxation directly with the local communities. Some of them unquestionably did make grants. The provincial estates of Auvergne, for example, granted a hearth tax in the towns and an income tax on the revenues of the nobility. But they reserved the proceeds for local defence just as the Estates of Languedoc had done. None of it reached the Dauphin's treasury.[14]

For all this, the decisions of the local politicians in Toulouse and Clermont were welcome evidence of support for the Crown, and symptomatic of a widening gulf between Paris and the provinces. There was little sign outside the capital of the anti-government feeling which had animated the debates in the Franciscan convent. In Languedoc this was no doubt due, at least in part, to the strong royalist tradition of the region and the presence of an English army on its borders. But there is some evidence, even in the provinces of the north, that men had no time for the radicalism of the Council of Eighty. When the delegates of the town of Soissons returned home, they were beaten up by a mob. Their assailants were outraged by the offensive speeches which they were reported to have made against the King's ministers. This was not an isolated incident. In the following year, when the delegates returned to Paris, they complained that many of them had been attacked by friends of the King's officers and demanded the right to go about with up to six bodyguards.[15] In Paris, these men had found themselves caught up in the collective emotions of the crowded capital and of angry meetings dominated by skilful and manipulative politicians. But the communities which they represented were increasingly preoccupied with organising and financing their own defence and with the task of surviving in the face of the bands of English, Gascons and Navarrese operating in their midst. The fate of the Dauphin, the terms of peace, the release of John II, the reform of the constitution, all these were increasingly distant distractions as the King's administration fell apart and his realm disintegrated into a loose federation of self governing-regions.

John II followed the events of the north as best he could from his prison. At Bordeaux, he was accommodated in a securely guarded apartment in the palace of the archbishops, a vast and dilapidated Roman mansion wedged between the nave of the new cathedral and the ancient city walls, where the Prince of Wales had established his court. Here he was honourably treated as befitted his status. The Count of Armagnac sent him furniture for his rooms, silver plate for his table and provisions to eat from it. The King was not kept in solitary confinement. He was attended by his personal servants and surrounded by many of his former ministers, advisers and companions in arms who had been captured with him at Poitiers. Around the figure of the captive King arose a shadow court, injecting fresh uncertainties into an already difficult political situation. Its leading personalities and the strongest influences on the King were the Archbishop of Sens, Guillaume de Melun, and the Limousin nobleman Bernard de Ventadour. Guillaume de Melun was a masterful ecclesiastical politician, shrewd, determined and calculating, who had fought in person in the battle with his own company of two dozen men-at-arms. Bernard de Ventadour was a practised and well connected courtier and who had become very close to the King during the crises of the past year. But John II's court in Bordeaux was isolated. Its members were obliged to ruminate impotently over events which they could no longer influence and about which they were only indistinctly informed. News arrived from Paris at uncertain intervals, mainly through fellow prisoners who had returned to Bordeaux after a period on parole. Much of it was garbled or out of date. Even so, it cannot have taken these men long to perceive the growing chasm which was opening up between the King and his subjects.[16]

John's consuming desire was to be released, and to this end he was prepared to sacrifice almost anything. His subjects saw things in a different light. The captivity of the King was a complication and an embarrassment, an occasion for brooding on the malice of fortune and the source of a constitutional void that seemed likely to be filled by violence. But his release was far from being their main priority. The Dauphin had asked the Estates-General in Paris for subsidies to pay for his father's ransom, but they had only been interested in taxes for the more effective prosecution of the war. The Count of Armagnac had made the same demand in Toulouse and received the same answer. The representatives of Languedoc ordered public mourning for a year to mark the King's capture. But they would contribute nothing for his release. By the end of the year 1356 it had dawned on the group of men around John II in Bordeaux that there was no prospect that he would ever be ransomed, except as part of a general peace. As a result, they became increasingly opposed to the prosecution of the war, and were more and more inclined to see in the radical patriotism of the Estates-General the main obstacle to his release. 'You must realise', John wrote to Étienne Marcel in December, 'that you will never get me back by making war: negotiation is the only way.'[17]

John's first instinct was to negotiate with his English captors in Bordeaux. They at least were close at hand. But they would do nothing without instructions from Westminster, which were slow in coming.[18] The next approach was made through the two papal peacemakers. Unfortunately the senior of them, Talleyrand de Périgord, was largely discredited in the eyes of the English by the enthusiasm with which certain members of his entourage had thrown themselves into the battle of Poitiers on the French side. His colleague, Niccolo Capocci, maintained his impartiality. But he quarrelled violently with Talleyrand and withdrew to Paris, where he tried to carry on his own private peace-making mission without regard to the parallel efforts of Talleyrand and the Pope, and to the mounting fury of both. He conducted an inconclusive correspondence with the English government for several weeks during October and November 1356, using as a go-between an Anglicised Italian called Hugh Pelerin who had served for some years as the collector of papal revenues in England. But Edward had no proposals to make to him. As he pointed out, he could hardly be expected to negotiate with the French when it was impossible to know who represented them.[19]

The French King was already trying another approach, this time through the good offices of the German Emperor Charles IV. Charles was the son of John of Luxembourg, King of Bohemia, a life-long francophile who had died a famous death in the ranks of the French army at Crécy. The Emperor had been brought up at the French court. His sister had been John II's first wife. All his personal sympathies must have been with the King of France. The problem was that he had virtually no influence over the English King. Some months before the battle of Poitiers, when John was becoming alarmed by the scale of Edward III's military preparations, he had planned to send the Dauphin to attend the Imperial Diet, which was due to meet at Metz in May. The ostensible purpose of this visit was to present the Emperor with a gift of two thorns from the crown of thorns preserved in the Sainte Chapelle in Paris. But its real object was to enlist the Emperor's help in setting up an international peace conference to find an accommodation with England. Unfortunately, the Diet was postponed and the plan came to nothing. Conditions were even more unpromising when the scheme was revived in October after the battle of Poitiers had been fought and lost. The idea of using the Emperor's good offices came this time from Pope Innocent VI. But it was enthusiastically taken up by the captive King. Towards the end of October the Archbishop of Sens was released on parole and allowed to travel to Paris. He arrived there at the beginning of the following month in the last days of the Estates-General. He seems to have brought with him a plan for the Dauphin to attend the Imperial Diet, which was now due to open at Metz in December. There could hardly have been a worse time for the Dauphin to leave France or a more hopeless diplomatic enterprise to undertake. Edward III had no intention of engaging in premature negotiations in Germany. When early in November 1356 the Emperor's messengers arrived at the court of Edward III to invite him to participate in a conference at Metz, he did not in terms refuse. But his answer was a masterpiece of benevolent and wordy emptiness.[20]

Edward saw as clearly as John II did that it was in his interest to hold onto his prisoner until he could be bargained away as part of a general peace. He was in no hurry. His situation, as he saw it, could only improve as political disorder spread in France and his own strategic plans matured. Neil Loring, the knight whom the Prince of Wales had sent to England to discover the King's intentions, was detained at court for several weeks and did not return to Gascony until the end of December 1356. The secret instructions which he brought back with him would have dismayed the French King if he had known them. Edward authorised his son to go through the motions of diplomacy. A conference with representatives of the King and of the government in Paris was due to open on 6 January 1357. The Prince of Wales was to use the occasion to test how much the French might be induced to concede, but to agree nothing for his own part save possibly a truce for a limited period. Even that must exclude Normandy and Brittany. Edward planned to reopen the war on a large scale in the summer. In his view the Prince had served his purpose in Gascony. His instructions were to allow a decent period to elapse after the conference had ended and then to return to England, bringing the King of France with him.[21]

As these instructions were being prepared, the Dauphin was already on his way to Metz, as his father had commanded. He had left Paris on 5 December 1356 and was making stately progress across north-eastern France, accompanied by a bodyguard of liveried archers and an entourage of 2,000 men. The splendour of his passage exhausted the revenues of the treasury and excited unfavourable comment in Paris. With the Dauphin travelled several of the paroled prisoners of Bordeaux, the Archbishop of Sens, the Count of Tancarville and Jean de Boucicaut, as well as the two ministers of the government in Paris who were closest to John II: Pierre de la Forêt and Simon Bucy. They were joined in Metz by the Cardinal of Périgord. The French contingent attended the tremendous ceremonies which accompanied the proceedings of the Imperial Diet. They dispensed largesse on a handsome scale. They ate at banquets of legendary opulence. They achieved almost nothing. The Emperor renewed the old treaty of amity between France and Germany, which had been largely discarded since it was first made in 1347. He lent his nephew 30,000 *livres* towards his expenses. Nothing could be done about the French King's captivity. Edward III ignored the affair and sent no one to represent him.[22]

In the Dauphin's absence Paris exploded. The occasion was a recurrence of the perennial affliction of French public finance, the manipulation of the coinage. The government's timing could not have been worse. But they had little choice. Virtually no tax revenue had been received since the summer and coinage operations were the only resource to which they could turn. John II had devalued the coinage twice during the Prince of Wales' march through France, once at the beginning of August and again a week before the battle of Poitiers. After the battle, the Dauphin's officers continued the process, stretching his treasure by surreptitiously reducing the bullion content of the coinage still further. The process accelerated during the autumn as the Dauphin broke with the Estates-General and as the military situation deteriorated in Normandy. The masters of the mints were ordered to increase their rate of production, without regard to the consistency of the coin. Defective coin which had been kept back was put into circulation with the rest. Then, when these stocks were exhausted, the government published an ordinance which made the coins legal tender for reduced amounts. The silver penny, for example, which was probably the most widely used silver coin, became worth only three *deniers tournois* in money of account, instead of eight. This decree was notified to the Parisian money changers on 7 December 1356. Just three days later, on the 10th, a fresh ordinance was proclaimed in the streets of Paris. This instrument, which had been prepared in secret at the end of November but held back until the mints could exhaust their supplies of the old coin, announced the withdrawal of the whole of the existing coinage (apart from the gold *écu*) and its replacement by a new coinage with a slightly increased bullion content. The *monnayage* would run at nearly 40 per cent. These measures were cynically conceived to boost the revenues of the Crown and to protect the interests of the traditional enemies of coinage devaluation: the Church and the great aristocratic landowners drawing fixed money rents from their tenants. But they were too much for the merchant communities of the great cities and the mass of urban wage earners, and they were anathema to the radicals of the Council of Eighty. In Paris, this was a powerful combination. Étienne Marcel and his allies on the Council of the Hanse des Marchands ordered a boycott of the new coinage. On 12 December he appeared at Louvre with a delegation of prominent citizens of Paris to confront the representatives of the government. They demanded the complete withdrawal of the ordinance.[23]

The chief representative of the government was the Dauphin's younger brother Louis, Count of Anjou. He was a quick witted young man, but he was only seventeen years old and even less experienced than the Dauphin. All the more practised ministers of the Dauphin were on the road to Metz. Louis temporised. He put off his answer for a day, then for another. On the third day Marcel returned to the Louvre, this time at the head of an intimidating mob. Louis could prevaricate no more. So he agreed to send an urgent message to the Dauphin to obtain his decision. In the meantime the ordinance would be suspended. The new coinage went into production at some provincial mints and must have generated a certain amount of revenue. But it was not recognised in Paris, where the old coins continued to circulate at the old rate. Parisian resentment of the coinage ordinance was no doubt perfectly genuine. But their leaders had larger ends in view. They were concerned that a successful reissue of the coinage might enable the Dauphin to do without taxation. Without the revenues of the mints the Dauphin in his penury would be forced to recall the Estates-General and to submit to its demands. As the military situation deteriorated, the pressure on him could only increase.[24]

During the winter of 1356–7 the English and their Navarrese allies mounted an offensive in western France which severely tested this dangerous calculation. The numbers involved were small. The Duke of Lancaster had about 2,000 English troops in Brittany. Most of them were encamped around Rennes. Some were serving in the garrisons of the peninsula. Another 100 men were holding thc citadel of Pont-Audemer in Normandy. Philip of Navarre's troops were by now working in close concert with the English. He had some Norman retainers at his disposal and rather more than 2,000 Navarrese soldiers spread among the garrisons of the Cotentin and the English-occupied parts of Brittany. In the course of the autumn, several shiploads of fresh men arrived from Navarre via Bordeaux to reinforce them. Between them Lancaster and Philip of Navarre must have had between 5,000 and 6,000 mounted men at their disposal.[25]

In the Cotentin the followers of Philip of Navarre had almost entirely driven out the garrisons of the King of France by the end of 1356. Avranches, an important cathedral city on the Breton march, was occupied by a Navarrese garrison at about the beginning of December 1356. Coutances, which was then partly unwalled, was virtually abandoned. The *bailli* of Coutances, who was the principal French officer in the region, was obliged to withdraw with his men to the nearby fortress of Saint-James de Beuvron, which Philip VI had rebuilt in the 1340s to serve as the southern bastion of Normandy. Here, he endeavoured as best he could to obstruct communications between Brittany and the Cotentin and engaged in a continuous guerrilla war with the Navarrese intruders. By the end of 1356 Saint-Lô, in the centre of the Cotentin peninsula, was the only significant surviving garrison holding out for the Dauphin. From their strongholds in the Cotentin, the Navarrese joined with the English in pillaging the adjoining provinces of France. Along the south shore of the Seine estuary, they raided over the Bessin with a few hundred men at a time, smashing and grabbing across the fertile land south of the cathedral city of Bayeux. Messengers from Paris or Rouen reported that the roads were impassable west of Caen.[26]

The main English operation of the autumn was the siege of Rennes. Rennes should not have been difficult to take. The walls were old. Their circuit was small, about three quarters of a mile. The population had long ago spilt out into straggling, undefended suburbs which were now much more extensive than the city itself. Help was far away. Although the city stood at the hub of the roads leading to Dinan, Caen and Nantes, they were obstructed on every side by the garrisons of Knolles and Calveley. Yet Lancaster failed to take Rennes. He tried to carry the walls by assault, then to undermine them, then to batter them with stone-throwers. Within a short time of its arrival, the English army was digging in for a long blockade through one of the harshest winters for many years.[27]

The English were destined to pass more than nine months glaring at the walls and gates of Rennes. But they were not idle. The Duke of Lancaster formed mounted raiding parties out of the besieging army and sent them to range across eastern Brittany and the neighbouring provinces of Anjou, Maine and Lower Normandy. Between October 1356 and the following March these beautiful regions, much of which had never previously been invaded, were looted and burned, then divided into ransom districts as Brittany had been years before. Their populations were cowed into submission. Their principal inhabitants were carried off for ransom. The *baillis* and their lieutenants retreated behind the walls of the cathedral cities, followed by crowds of refugees encumbered with carts, sacks and animals. Traditional bonds of loyalty dissolved as the English overran the undefended open country. The mass of the population readily paid their *patis* to the invaders to secure their lives and what remained of their possessions.[28]

Some impoverished local noblemen cast off their allegiance to the King of France and joined in the plundering. One of them, a local knight called Philippe de la Chèze, caused even greater havoc than the English. This man recruited a band of some 200 men, including minor noblemen of the region, Breton soldiers of fortune, petty criminals and displaced clerics, with which he seized the castle of Fresnay-le-Vicomte in Maine and harassed the country around just as the English were doing a few miles away. When after a few weeks his garrison mutinied and took over Fresnay for themselves, Philippe made common cause with the bands of English raiders. Together they seized the castle of Sillé-le-Guillaume, west of le Mans, by escalade at night, and began the daily round of destruction afresh. The owner of the castle, who was partly paralysed from wounds received at Poitiers, was seized in his bed and bundled off to the headquarters of Robert Knolles at Gravelle in eastern Brittany. Why did men like Philippe de la Chèze act as they did? Local politics and ancient vendettas usually had a part in it. Philippe had a long-standing quarrel with the vicomtesse of Beaumont, who was the owner of Fresnay and the territorial lord of Sillé. But self-preservation counted for at least as much. The war had ruined men of Philippe's class. Their fortunes lost to looters, they turned to looting themselves. And to whom should their loyalty have been due? To the King, a prisoner of the enemy? To the Dauphin, who was impotent to defend them? Like Edward III, they asked themselves who represented France. The career of Philippe de la Chèze was brought to a sudden end in the following summer when he was captured by the Dauphin's officers near Tours and hanged. His band dispersed.[29] But there were plenty of others like him to abet the English in their advance. Within a few months of the invasion a broad belt of territory extending from Angers to Caen was pock-marked with English, Breton and Navarrese garrisons. The easy fortunes made by their captors became well known in England, and during the winter hordes of fresh adventurers left for western France to find their share of the pickings while there were still some to be had. They milled about in disorderly groups in the streets of Southampton and other ports of southern England waiting for ships to carry them to the promised land. Edward III encouraged them on their way. He made them grants to buy equipment and to pay advances to their men. He had ships requisitioned to carry them to Barfleur, Cherbourg, Brest or Vannes. Then he left them to make their profits and pay their expenses as they might.[30]

The Dauphin and his ministers were impotent spectators of these events. All their efforts were concentrated on keeping the English and their allies away from the Seine valley and the road to Paris. The garrison of Pont-Audemer, which was the only significant enemy force east of Caen, was hemmed in by French troops and bought out at the beginning of December 1356. Successive royal Lieutenants at Caen made it their task to hold the line of the river Orne against invaders from the west. But they were hampered at every turn by want of money, and rapidly outflanked by the enemy's advance into Anjou and Maine. So far as can be discovered, they had to rely entirely on local sources of revenue to fund their operations. This meant, in the main, the proceeds of taxes voted by the Estates of Normandy during the summer, before the disaster at Poitiers. In current conditions, these taxes were extremely difficult to collect. Even when they were successfully collected, they had to be prised out of the hands of local communities who resented their expenditure in a neighbouring town let alone another province. In order to extract money from the *vicomte* of Falaise the Lieutenant, then

Amaury de Meulan, had to summon him to Caen and hold him there while a troop of soldiers went to Falaise to rifle through his coffers. As a result of problems such as this the Dauphin's representatives in Lower Normandy never disposed of any very substantial forces. At best they were able to find between 600 and 800 men for occasional field operations.

This was far less than they needed to defend their huge territory. It was just about enough for hit-and-run raids against enemy-occupied towns in the Cotentin. The broad sandy estuary of the Douve and the Vire east of Carentan, which marked the boundary between the Cotentin and the Bessin, was stained with blood and littered with corpses abandoned after each raid and counter-raid. The only notable result was the death, towards the end of November 1356, of Godfrey of Harcourt. The old conspirator, who had dabbled on and off with Edward III since 1342 and had become the most stalwart supporter of the House of Navarre in Normandy, was worsted in a fight as he tried to ambush a French raiding party at night. Cornered by eight men-at-arms and a crowd of archers, Godfrey contemptuously rejected their challenge to surrender. 'By my mother's soul, the Duke shall not have me alive,' he is said to have shouted as they cut him in pieces.[31]

In the course of the autumn, the Dauphin's ministers devised a doomed plan to confront the army of the Duke of Lancaster outside Rennes. If this had succeeded, it would no doubt have drawn off the English troops in Anjou, Maine and Lower Normandy. But it was never likely to succeed without much larger forces than the Dauphin could find. He had laid his plans in mid-October 1356, when the Estates-General was about to open and there were still hopes of raising large sums from taxation. Charles of Blois was the obvious leader of such a campaign and must have been the prime mover. But as his ransom was unpaid, he could not take part. The command was given instead to Thibault, lord of Rochefort, a prominent partisan of Blois with estates around Nantes and Fougères in eastern Brittany. Thibault was an experienced soldier who had fought at Ploermel and Mauron. But he was allowed only a limited budget, reckoned to be enough to pay 1,000 men-at-arms and 500 mounted archers for two months. Charles of Blois added a contribution from his own pocket, which he took out of the money raised from his subjects to pay his ransom. Another, smaller force was recruited in Maine and the provinces of Loire. These men were commanded by Guillaume de Craon, whose family had been powerful men in the region for several generations. Neither army achieved anything. The cost of Thibault's campaign turned out to have been grossly under-estimated. It took him two months and all his funds to raise an army much smaller than he planned. Lacking the strength to confront the Duke of Lancaster directly, he conducted operations from the distant safety of Vitré and Dinan. If any damage was inflicted on the English army it has not been recorded. The southern army fared even worse. For some reason Guillaume de Craon was replaced at a late stage by Fulk de Laval, the flamboyant captain who had led the highly successful French invasion of Bas-Poitou in 1349. Fulk began operating in Maine at the beginning of the December. But shortly afterwards his army encountered a large English raiding force and was wiped out. Four hundred of his men were killed or captured. Fulk himself was among the prisoners.[32]

In the absence of effective reinforcements, the defence of Rennes fell mainly to its citizens and garrison, and to a hero of the future, the young Bertrand du Guesclin. This obscure Breton squire from the district of Dinan had passed several years leading bands of irregulars and drop-outs in the woods and marshes of eastern Brittany, a life like that of so many English commanders, halfway between warfare and banditry. Du Guesclin hung about the siege lines at Lancaster's rear, attacking his supply trains, destroying his equipment, ambushing and killing isolated groups of his men. The Dauphin contributed nothing to his efforts. But Bertrand received 200 *livres* per year when Rennes had been saved, and his deeds passed into legend, celebrated in the mediocre verses of the last *chanson de geste*.[33]

In the new year, when the English and Navarrese began to push beyond the borders of Normandy into the Île de France, the French commanders in the region could do nothing to stop them. Philip of Navarre rode east out of the Cotentin at the head of a mounted force of about 800 men. Most of them were his own Navarrese soldiers and Norman retainers of his family. But there were also 100 English and German men-at-arms and about the same number of archers who been recruited for Philip in England. Their commander, Richard Totesham, was an experienced knight of Edward III's household, with years of service in Brittany and the march of Calais. The small army took the road through the Bessin. They occupied a string of castles east of Bayeux without encountering any serious opposition. Then, avoiding Caen, they lunged directly towards Paris. On 11 January 1357 they were reported at l'Aigle, apparently heading for Dreux. Gossip magnified their strength several times over. Panic spread through the

Île de France. Dreux appealed for help to Paris. Paris appealed to all the major towns of the north. They were begged to proclaim the news in the streets and call for volunteers. 'You know that the King and most of his captains are in the hands of the English,' the Parisians said; 'they can do nothing for us now.' In about the third week of January 1357, the Anglo-Navarrese army passed Chartres. Riding through the flat plains of the Beauce, they came to within eight miles of the capital. Then they turned away and returned home.[34]

Had Philip and Totesham achieved anything other than terror? The English had once hoped, and perhaps even expected, to achieve their political objectives in France by spectacular raids such as this, destruction on a large scale combined with diplomatic pressure and the occasional engagement of great armies. They had adopted this method of making war for financial, not military reasons. It made few demands on the King's purse or on his administrative resources. But its limitations were obvious. The immediate political impact of the English raids was very great, but unless they could hold on to the territory which they traversed, it was necessarily short-lived. The Duke of Lancaster, who had been largely instrumental in perfecting the great *chevauché*, was among the first to recognise this. The very fact that he was prepared to undertake a long siege in order to capture Rennes, a town of considerable administrative and economic importance but little military value, was symptomatic of a renewed interest among the English leaders in the permanent occupation of territory.

The turning point had come a little earlier in Brittany with the lieutenancy of Sir Thomas Holland in 1354 and 1355. Holland devised, or at least put into effect, the first financially sustainable system of occupation which the English were able to achieve outside Aquitaine. Although the fact is nowhere documented, it is reasonably clear that within a short time of his arrival in the province, he reached a settlement with the independent captains who controlled the garrisons of the interior who had made life so difficult for his predecessor. All the principal fortresses of Brittany controlled by the captains were taken into the English King's hands. If, like Robert Knolles and Roger David, they had obtained royal charters recognising their claims, these were rescinded. The castles were then regranted to the same men at the King's pleasure and on terms which required them to pay a farm (or rent) for the privilege of exacting *patis* from the surrounding districts. Fresh conquests were dealt with in the same way. They were either granted out to the conqueror for a limited period, or taken in hand at once and let out to him at a fixed rent. None of the indentures have survived. But they are likely to have involved the same kind of obligations on the part of the captains as Edward III expected in other parts of France, including service in the Lieutenant's armies when it was required. The end result was that the King's officers maintained garrisons at his wages in Vannes, Brest and Bécherel and, from time to time, in Ploermel, while some two dozen other places were garrisoned in his name by men who were bound to him by contract and in some cases, such as Knolles', by a broader understanding which extended beyond contract and indeed beyond Brittany.[35]

The relatively high degree of administrative control which the King's Lieutenants were now able to exercise in Brittany was reflected in their revenues. In their own castles they appointed castellans who instituted the systematic collection of *patis*, much as the independent captains had been doing for years, but on a larger scale and in the more formal and methodical tradition of the English civil service. A staff of clerks was installed in the larger places. Assessors prepared quotas for every parish, payable twice a year in cash or kind or in labour services according to a rough assessment of its ability to pay. Local collectors were appointed to do the rounds of the villages. Arrears were meticulously recorded. Applications for reassessment on the grounds of penury, or for remittance on the grounds of war damage were methodically considered. For all practical purposes it was a system of general taxation. At the end of the 1350s, the royal castellan of Bécherel was claiming *patis* from more than 160 parishes of north-eastern Brittany. These extended from Mont-Saint-Michel in the east to the Tréguier peninsula in the west, and south almost as far as Ploermel. The *patis* of Bécherel had a theoretical yield of £7,400 a year, nearly two thirds of which was actually collected. The Treasurer of Brittany in Vannes received revenues amounting in total to £11,500 from the combined *patis* of Bécherel, Ploermel and Vannes and from miscellaneous fees and dues. The captain of Brest and the contract captains of the interior accounted directly to the Exchequer at Westminster and their records have not survived. But the total revenues of the Crown in Brittany must now have been large enough to meet most, if not all, of the ordinary costs of occupation. Indeed, the English King's decision in 1358 to take over the cost of the defence and appropriate the revenues to himself suggests that by this time there was a surplus.[36]

These were very satisfactory results which the English endeavoured with varying success to reproduce elsewhere. During the winter of 1356–7 the Duke of Lancaster set about transforming the disorderly looting of Anjou, Maine and Lower Normandy into a permanent occupation based on small garrisons in well-sited castles, and on the systematic collection of *patis* from the local population. The Duke of Lancaster's principal garrison in the region was based in the massive twelfth-century *donjon* of Henry I at Domfront above the gorges of the river Varenne. This place had originally been captured by the Navarrese. But Lancaster took it over from them and installed two of his own retainers, Sir Thomas Uvedale and Sir Thomas Fogg. The two men were also made responsible for subsidiary garrisons at Villiers and Bois-du-Maine in the valley of the Mayenne, and further north at Messei and Condé-sur-Noireau and the fortified abbey of Le Val in the valley of the Orne. These six fortresses, together with the places in the Bessin which were captured during Philip of Navarre's *chevauché*, gave Lancaster control of a line of garrisons extending from the Loire valley to the estuary of the Seine. Uvedale was one of Lancaster's closest adjutants, a full-time soldier who had fought with him since his first campaign in Gascony. Fogg was a rather different sort of man, an ambitious adventurer who operated very much as he pleased and was to make a considerable fortune for himself in western France during the next five years. The extremely incomplete record of his stewardship shows that he made at least £2,400 over this period and probably more than twice that much. This was a considerable sum. Fogg's own share was two thirds even on the assumption that he accounted honestly with his master.[37]

The acid test of Edward III's determination to occupy these regions came when it brought him into conflict, as it inevitably did, with his allies of the House of Navarre. Philip of Navarre passed most of the second half of 1356 with his Chancellor Thomas de Ladit in England, settling the terms of his alliance with Edward III and planning fresh wars of conquest. He did homage to the English King as King of France and Duke of Normandy. He promised to serve him against every man alive, his brother alone excepted. At the end of August, Edward and the Navarrese leaders had left London for Clarendon in Wiltshire, where the English King had recently renovated the famous hunting lodge of Henry II. There, they reached a formal agreement on the division of the spoils. Philip was to be placed in possession of anything which had belonged to him or his brother. He was to be allowed to keep all his conquests up to the value of 60,000 *écus* per year, an enormous sum.

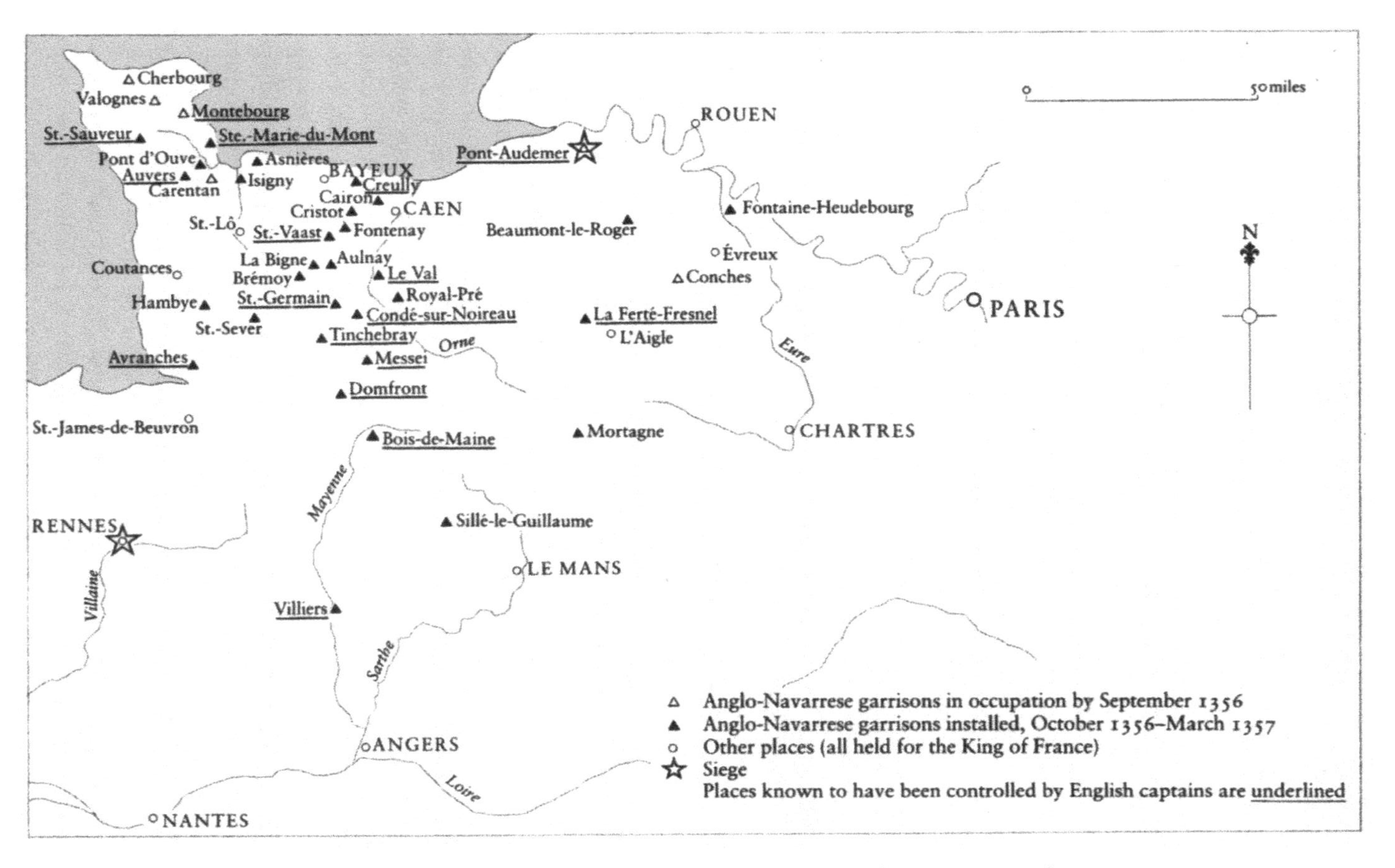

18 Anglo-Navarrese operations in western France, October 1356–March 1357

But Edward was to have the whole of the demesne lands of the dukes of Normandy and everything else that Philip might conquer. And he was to be entitled to require Philip to surrender to him (in return for compensation) any place of special military or political value. Philip returned satisfied from England at the beginning of December 1357 with the treaty in his satchels and letters patent appointing him as the English King's Lieutenant throughout Normandy.[38]

Philip probably assumed that his lieutenancy would involve a purely nominal subordination to the King of England. If so, he was quickly disabused. All the more substantial places occupied on Philip of Navarre's *chevauché* through Lower Normandy in January were garrisoned by Englishmen, although the English had contributed only a small part of his strength. Richard Totesham, who was no doubt there to serve Edward III's interests, saw to that. At about the same time, Avranches was officiously taken out of the hands of its Navarrese garrison by the Duke of Lancaster just as Domfront had been. He appointed an English captain, Richard Scholl, and a clergyman called William Tutbury to serve as receiver of revenues. Philip of Navarre was outraged. On his return from the Île de France, he rode into Lancaster's camp at Rennes to protest. 'Grosses paroles' were exchanged between the two men. Eventually Lancaster agreed to reinstate the Navarrese garrison. But Scholl and Tutbury remained in possession, and they presumably accounted for the revenues to him.[39] Edward III was even less accommodating. At about the time that Philip of Navarre was quarrelling with the Duke of Lancaster over Avranches, he became embroiled in a far more serious dispute with the King of England about the castle and barony of Saint-Sauveur-le-Vicomte. The immense thirteenth-century fortress, which guarded the Cherbourg road ten miles south of Valognes, was one of the strongest of the region and the centre of a valuable barony. It had belonged to Godfrey of Harcourt, who had recently given it to the King of England, apparently reserving the usufruct for himself during his lifetime. It was Godfrey's revenge against his family, all of whom had supported the King after the judicial murder of the head of the house of Harcourt at Rouen. When Godfrey died in battle Philip of Navarre claimed it on behalf of his brother. But Edward III sent an officer out from England with a company of soldiers to take possession for himself. Philip's Chancellor went to Westminster to complain, but his protests were ignored. Edward made his position very clear. The claims of the House of Navarre, he said, had been most carefully considered by his Council. However, 'since Philip has done homage to the King as his sovereign lord, King of France and Duke of Normandy, it must follow by all law and reason that the King may exercise his sovereignty by taking actual possession of his domains.' The King appointed one of the Duke of Lancaster's lieutenants in Normandy as the permanent captain of Saint-Sauveur and ordered him to put his own garrison into the place at once. In spite of the warmth of their dealings in England, there can be little doubt that Edward distrusted Philip of Navarre, and his brother even more. He had had enough of trying to control France through fickle allies and malcontents.[40]

The Dauphin returned to Paris from Germany on 14 January 1357 to find his capital in a state of incipient revolution. He had nothing to show for the conference at Metz. Civil order had collapsed in much of the west and centre of the kingdom. Étienne Marcel had taken control of the capital with his friends. Philip of Navarre was less than forty miles away. There was no army in the field and no money in the treasury. For a few days the Dauphin endeavoured to face out his adversaries and to avert the humiliation of having to recall the Estates-General. It was a hopeless endeavour. The crisis came on 19 January 1357. A delegation of some of the chief members of the Council, led by the Archbishop of Sens, had arranged a meeting with the leaders of the Parisians at the church of St. Germain l'Auxerrois, a short distance from the Louvre. The object was to discuss the new coinage. But they had evidently under-estimated the strength of feeling among their opponents. Marcel arrived at the meeting at the head of an armed mob. When the Archbishop demanded that they put an end to their boycott of the coinage, there was a spontaneous outburst of anger. Marcel refused point blank. As the news spread, workmen went on strike throughout the city. The streets filled up with angry crowds. Marcel called every citizen to arms. Ministers and officials began to fear for their lives. Some of them packed up what they could carry and fled. Inside the Louvre, the Dauphin himself was locked in discussion with his principal advisers. They decided to capitulate.

The Dauphin announced his surrender in person. On the following morning, 20 January 1357, he addressed the representatives of the Parisians in the Great Hall of the Parlement. He agreed to withdraw the new coinage. He recalled the Estates-General. He announced that he would invite them to reform the coinage in a manner 'pleasing and profitable to the people.' As for the seven ministers who had been condemned by the Estates-General in October, the Dauphin agreed as an earnest of his good faith to dismiss them all, and imprison them 'if they could be found'. Marcel's response was that he wanted to see it in writing. A notary was called as men began to search for the proscribed ministers. They found Jean Poilevillain, the master of the mints. But the others had gone. Simon Bucy and Pierre de la Forêt had left to join the diplomatic conference which had just opened in Saintonge. They had taken the King's great seal with them. Robert de Lorris fled after them. The rest were nowhere to be found. In their absence, soldiers were sent to occupy their mansions in Paris, and clerks to list and confiscate their property.[41]

On 5 February 1357 the Estates-General reassembled in the Franciscan convent, the scene of Robert le Coq's venomous tirade three months before. Attendance was patchier now. Since there had been barely a fortnight's notice of their recall, the representatives of the towns must have been drawn mainly from Paris and the Île de France. The great fiefs, Flanders, Artois, Burgundy and Alençon, stayed away. Among the clergy and the nobility, attendance was adequate but no more. But the opposition was there in force. Years later, in calmer times, the Dauphin said that the delegates were for the most part gullible men, fools rather than rebels. They had allowed themselves be swayed by an organised group of malcontents, by men who hid their private rancours and jealousies behind a façade of patriotism. That is what successful counter-revolutionaries commonly say. It may be true nonetheless. When, after a month of deliberations, the delegates reassembled in the Great Hall of the Parlement for their concluding session, the spokesman of the clergy was none other than Robert le Coq. The Bishop of Laon spoke in more measured language than he had used on the last occasion. But his message was equally uncompromising. The kingdom, he said, had been ill-governed for many years. The coinage had been debased. Property had been arbitrarily requisitioned. Tax revenues had been squandered on grants to greedy courtiers. All this, Robert declared, had been done by the advice of guilty men. He named the seven dismissed ministers, and another fifteen lesser functionaries, making a total of twenty-two. The list included six of the principal officers of the Treasury and the Chambre des Comptes, five judges and officers of the Parlement, four officers of the royal household and three members of the Dauphin's personal household. All were to be summarily dismissed. Not content with these proscriptions, the Bishop declared that every principal officer of the Crown throughout the land would be suspended from his duties while a commission of *réformateurs-généraux* investigated their past conduct and considered whether they were fit to be reinstated. When Robert le Coq had finished, his demands were endorsed on behalf of the nobility by Jean de Picquigny and by a radical lawyer from Abbeville on behalf of the towns. Étienne Marcel wound up with his own endorsement on behalf of the city of Paris. It was as if the capital had become a fourth estate. In return for the satisfaction of these demands, the Estates-General was prepared to offer the same taxes which they had proposed in the previous autumn. In spite of the doubts which had been expressed then, they still professed to believe that with honest and efficient administration this would be enough to raise an army of 30,000 men. They must also have believed that its collection would be well under way within six weeks, for they proposed to reassemble of their own accord on 17 April 1357 to examine the accounts of the collectors.[42]

The demands of the Estates-General, great and small alike, were embodied in an enormous ordinance which was solemnly read out to the assembled crowd. The greater part of this remarkable document was directed to the reform of the central and local administration and to the elimination of the idleness and corruption which they conceived to be endemic in the government of the realm. The Chancellor was stripped of most of his political power and reduced to the status of chief secretary, presiding over the preparation and issue of letters under the great seal. Elaborate provision was made for the conditions of service of the King's judges and administrators. The work of the Great Council was minutely regulated. Its members were to be at work by sunrise, failing which they would lose a day's wages and regular offenders would be removed. They were to work through the day's business strictly in order of importance. The pay, fees and perquisites, recruitment and hours of work of civil servants were specified in exacting detail. Extensive regulations were ordained for the administration of justice. Judicial office was no longer to be sold. Provision was made for dealing with the perennial and, in truth, insoluble problem of competing jurisdictions. There were ruthless measures to accelerate the processes of civil justice. The civil chamber of Parlement were henceforth to sit in three divisions working through the lists in order until the whole backlog had been cleared. A root and branch attack was made on the system of grants ('excessive and useless gifts to unworthy persons'). All grants out of the royal domain since 1314 were to be cancelled and the property recovered, except for grants to the Church and the royal princes and those made for genuine services. The Chancellor was not to seal any document in future which alienated part of the King's domain without referring it to the Council, notifying them of its exact value. Ministers were to swear an oath not to seek grants for themselves unless it be overtly at meetings of the Council, and not to form secret alliances to support to each other's claims. Strict rules were to be observed limiting the powers of the King's military officers and regulating their exercise. The *arrière-ban* was never again to be proclaimed save on the advice of the Estates-General or in cases of 'evident necessity'. The requisitioning of supplies was abolished and the owners of goods authorised to resist requisitioning officers by force. There was to be no billeting of soldiers for more than one day at a time. The ordinance committed the government absolutely to the continued prosecution of the war. Tax revenues were to be collected and spent under the supervision of commissioners appointed by the Estates-General and used exclusively for military purposes. No truce was to be made without the consent of the Estates-General.[43]

The work of purging the administration began at once. The commission of *réformateurs* comprised a mixture of experienced officials and ardent malcontents. More than half of them had been members of the Council of Eighty. Within days the royal administration was reduced to chaos. In accordance with the ordinance all principal departmental officers vacated their offices while their position was considered. Some were quickly reconfirmed. Most were not. The Parlement, that great reservoir of authoritarianism, found the number of its judges reduced from sixty to sixteen. The administration of justice had to be suspended in Paris for several days as the commission deliberated on whether to confirm or replace the royal Provost. The fifteen masters of Chambre des Comptes, who had been particularly severely criticised by the Estates-General for the idleness and the irregularity of their ways, were all dismissed and replaced by four inexperienced laymen. They gave up after a day and begged the Council to reinstate some of the former officials so as to show them what to do. In the provinces, the ranks of the royal officials were decimated as local men seized the opportunity to complain of maladministration, real or imagined.[44]

The great reform ordinance of March 1357 marked a brief moment of solidarity between the disparate enemies of the government before they fell out in a welter of mutual antagonism. The deliberations of the Estates-General have not been recorded. But there is a good deal of evidence that they were dominated by the nobility and by the powerful and well-connected caucus of aristocratic bishops. They may have been no more coherent a political party than any other class of French society, but many of them, and particularly those with interests in western France, had become increasingly frustrated by the financial impotence and military paralysis of the royal government. Charles of Blois was an extreme example of a political conversion which other noblemen had made less conspicuously. The failure of the Estates-General in October 1356 had been a very personal misfortune for him, since it had led directly to the Dauphin's inability to raise money for the relief of Rennes. By the following January this fundamentally loyal prince who had depended for fifteen years on the military and political support of the Crown, had become wholly converted to the cause of administrative reform. Robert le Coq and Étienne Marcel had become his friends and colleagues, allies in a common cause. The decisions of the Estates-General embodied many of the superficial remedies which such men proposed for curing the ills of the French state. It was almost entirely directed against the class of professional administrators which had been growing larger and more prosperous for more than half a century. There were no significant measures of constitutional reform in the great ordinance, no demands for a permanent council of the Estates-General to oversee the workings of government. Instead, its sixty-one clauses were largely concerned with comparatively trivial administrative regulation. When the Dauphin's Council was reconstituted in the immediate aftermath of the Estates-General, its membership exactly reflected the coalition of interests behind the ordinance. There were a few radical opposition politicians such as Robert le Coq, and a handful of representatives of the northern towns. But its membership was largely drawn from the princes of the blood and the military nobility. The jurists and permanent officials who had dominated the Council for so long were conspicuously excluded.

What destroyed the efforts of the Estates-General of February 1357 was not the conflict of classes or ideologies. That came later. It was the schism between the King in Bordeaux and the reformed government in Paris.[45]

The castle of Mirambeau, above the road from Saintes to Bordeaux, was among the last remaining fortresses in Saintonge still in French hands. Here, in the second half of January 1357, as the Dauphin surrendered to the Parisians, Pierre de la Forêt and Simon Bucy and a small body of French diplomats gathered to negotiate a peace with the Prince of Wales. The conditions were not favourable. The Prince's representatives were twenty miles away at Blaye. Messages passed laboriously between the two. Neither side was empowered to agree very much. In the last week of January, the news arrived that the two leaders of the French delegation had been dismissed from their offices and that Bucy's commission from the Dauphin had been cancelled. The conference then broke up. The two displaced ministers remained behind and joined the court of John II at Bordeaux. The rest returned empty-handed to Paris in time to witness the Dauphin's humiliation at the hands of the Estates-General.[46]

The French King, isolated in the *archevéché* of Bordeaux, surrounded by frustrated fellow prisoners and political refugees, received the news of the tumults in Paris with mounting fear and resentment. The ordinances of the Estates-General had made no provision at all for his ransom. On the contrary, the tax revenues voted by the assembly were strictly reserved for a fresh military offensive. The possibility of a negotiated peace with England was not even contemplated. It is not clear when John II decided to repudiate the government of his son and the work of the Estates-General and to take the conduct of affairs into his own hands, but his preparations must have been well advanced by the time that the Estates-General closed at the beginning of March. At about that time the Cardinal of Périgord and his colleague arrived in Bordeaux to give fresh impetus to the peace process. They found the French King more than willing. When, early in March 1357, a fresh conference opened in the Gascon capital, the French King nominated a team of eleven ambassadors of his own. No less than eight of these were drawn from the prisoners who were with him in Bordeaux. The other three (Simon Bucy, Pierre de la Forêt and Robert de Lorris) were all ministers in exile who had been proscribed by the Estates-General. On 18 March 1357, after only a few days of negotiation, they agreed the terms of a treaty of peace. Since the Prince of Wales had only very limited authority from his father, the treaty was subject to Edward's approval. Its terms were kept secret and no copy of the text has survived. But if it was acceptable to the Prince's ambassadors, the likelihood is that it included very considerable cessions of territory. There were no doubt sound reasons for ensuring that the hotheads in Paris did not learn how much had been conceded until the final act had been performed. In order to preserve the status quo in the meantime it was agreed to proclaim a truce in all parts of France for two years, until Easter 1359.[47]

The truce was sealed in Bordeaux on 23 March 1357. Immediately afterwards, three of John's ambassadors, the Archbishop of Sens, his brother the Count of Tancarville, and Jean d'Artois Count of Eu, were released on parole and sent to Paris with letters patent to be read out by the criers in the markets and street corners. In these letters John announced the truce to his subjects and commanded them all to observe it. He ordered every Frenchman to refuse to pay the new war subsidies voted by the Estates-General. The adjourned session of the Estates-General, which was due to open in the capital on 17 April, was to be cancelled. In other letters, addressed to the principal cities of the realm, John directly instructed them not to attend. The assembly, he said, 'could bring no benefit to the King or the realm.' The King was satisfied that his son was no longer a free agent but the prisoner of political partisans. Neither the ordinances of the Estates-General nor the acts of the Dauphin giving effect to them were to obeyed.[48]

The news of the King's letters caused uproar in the streets of Paris. Mobs began to gather within minutes of the first announcement. The whole city was put in a state of readiness, for fear of a coup by supporters of the King. All the gates on the south side were closed. The guards were reinforced. Trenches were dug outside, and heavy chains stretched once more across street corners. The three emissaries from Bordeaux were covered in abuse. They fled for their lives. The Dauphin, who was now virtually a prisoner in the Louvre, was brought under irresistible pressure by Robert le Coq and Étienne Marcel as well as by the standing committee of the Estates-General which was responsible for overseeing the collection of the subsidy. On 10 April 1357, he was forced to issue a personal proclamation countermanding his father's orders. Criers went through the streets once more, announcing that the taxes ordered in March would be collected in spite of the King's orders and that the Estates-General would reconvene after all. To allow time to resolve the confusion, the meeting was put back to the end of April.[49] The news of this act of defiance never reached the French King. On 11 April 1357, the day after the Dauphin's proclamation, John boarded the *Sainte Marie* in Bordeaux, accompanied by most of the more important prisoners of state. The *Sainte Marie* sailed out of the Gironde with the rest of the Prince's fleet and arrived in Plymouth on 5 May 1357.[50]

When the Estates-General reassembled on 30 April, several days were passed in deliberating on the King's act of sabotage. There was nothing they could do about it, except to reconfirm the taxes and ease the burden slightly by providing for payment in instalments every two months over a period of a year. But Frenchmen were notoriously unwilling to pay taxes in time of truce, even when their sovereign had not ordered them to keep their money. The assessment and collection of the new tax was controlled by a commission of *députés-généraux* in Paris, which was drawn from all three estates, and by local commissions of *élus*. It depended very much on the co-operation of the taxpayers of the Church and the nobility (who were paying the lion's share) and of the leading inhabitants of the towns. In Normandy, which was the principal war zone of the north, the towns continued to pay. But the clergy and the nobility refused absolutely. Elsewhere, the King's orders not to pay were gratefully obeyed and attempts to collect the tax were met with violence. When the *élus* arrived in the County of Forez, they were met by officers of the Count, who informed them that neither he nor his subjects had consented to this tax and that it would not therefore be paid. The *élus* returned after a few days with a troop of soldiers and set up a collection office at Montbrison. They fined the Count's officers and arrested his receiver. But before they could begin to collect the money, a large mob gathered round the building, summoned by bells and trumpets and led by the wife of the receiver. They broke down the doors with axes, and drove the *élus* out of the town. Forez was far away in eastern France, where English armies and fighting bands had not yet penetrated. But the attitude of the Foréziens was very common, even in places where the danger was immediate and the case for war taxation obvious. In Languedoc the Lieutenant, John of Armagnac, summoned representatives of the nobility and the towns to Toulouse at the beginning of May 1357. Languedoc was not affected by the decisions of the Estates-General in Paris or by the King's annulment of them. It had granted its own tax. But since the grant had been conditional on there being no truce, Armagnac needed their consent to its continued collection. The delegates allowed him to collect half of it. Even that was too much for some of their constituents. As soon as the decision had been made, crowds began to gather outside the Lieutenant's headquarters in the Chateau Narbonnais. On 9 May 1357 they attacked the building with siege engines, shouting 'Death to the traitors!', and set fire to it with burning arrows. Armagnac was forced to suspend the collection of the tax and flee covertly by night. The mob celebrated their victory by pillaging the building and rampaging through the streets looting the houses of royal officials and destroying the archives of the collectors. They remained in control of Toulouse for several weeks. What violence did in these places was achieved in other parts of France by the sheer weight of passive obstruction. On 10 May 1357 the Dauphin announced another moratorium on the payment of royal debts. A little money trickled in from the collectors in the towns of Languedoil during the summer. Less than a fifth of the theoretical yield of the tax was brought in. The government was bankrupt and impotent.[51]

The truce of Bordeaux expressly contemplated its own failure. The perennial problem of irresponsible subordinate commanders, which had destroyed every previous truce, was dealt with by providing that neither party should be held to have broken the truce if such men continued to fight, provided that the principals did not support them. Special provision had to be made for the Duke of Lancaster, who was on any view one of the principals. He had committed his honour to the capture of Rennes and was still, after more than six months, engaged in besieging it. Lancaster was to be notified of the truce and ordered by the Prince of Wales to abandon the siege. But if he declined to do so, then he was to be allowed to take nominal possession of the city with up to twenty of his men and to hold it until he received the personal command of the King of England to withdraw. If he declined to comply even then, the truce would remain in force, but Lancaster would be regarded as fighting a private war of his own against the partisans of the house of Blois, in which neither the King of England nor the French government might interfere.[52]

The Duke of Lancaster was as obstinate in the defence of his honour as everyone had expected. His response to the proclamation of the truce was that since he was fighting not only for Edward III but also for the young John de Montfort, he was not bound to withdraw and could not properly do so. He refused to leave Rennes either in response to the Prince's command or in response to the King's when in due course he received it. Nor would he agree to content himself with a nominal and temporary occupation. It was not until July, when Charles of Blois was raising a new army of Bretons to relieve the city and the English King was coming under strong diplomatic pressure from the two cardinals in London, that Lancaster at last received a command couched in language which showed that he was really expected to comply. Edward sent Richard Totesham, to reinforce the message by word of mouth. By the time Totesham reached Rennes, however, Lancaster had already made his own deal with the representatives of the Dauphin. He was paid 100,000 *écus* for his 'expenses' in addition to the 40,000 *écus* or so which he had made from the ransoms of prisoners captured during the siege. An elaborate charade was devised to save his face. The Duke was formally presented with the keys of Rennes and allowed to send a small troop into the city to plant his banner on the wall. Then he solemnly restored the keys to the French captain of the town on his undertaking to deliver the place up in accordance with whatever terms might be included in the treaty of peace to be made between the two Kings. No one was deceived. It was the first major defeat suffered by a man who for fifteen years had been Edward III's most persistently successful commander.[53]

When Lancaster left Brittany he appointed Robert Knolles and James Pipe, two of the chief English captains of western France, to look after his interests in Normandy. Such men had neither the strength nor the inclination to control the excesses of their fellow countrymen, and during the following weeks a spring tide of adventurers spread over Lower Normandy and Maine. Prominent Gascon captains appeared in the region. The Bascon de Mareuil, who had been lost from sight since his participation in the murder of Charles of Spain, suddenly reappeared in Normandy at the head of several companies of Navarrese and joined the garrison of Avranches. Fresh drafts of violent young men from England crossed the Channel. They went out as foot soldiers and pages and came back as belted knights with fortunes, wrote the chronicler Knighton. 'A horde of yobs,' the conservative Sir Thomas Gray called them; unknowns, some of them mere archers, who quickly took to this war of fortlets and hedgerows without the long training in arms that he and his kind had had. The rush of volunteers whetted the ambitions of the English captains in western France and enormously extended the range and scale of their operations. Thomas Fogg, Lancaster's captain at Domfront, launched a succession of ambitious military enterprises for his own account, seizing castles from the French and even buying out other garrisons of the Duke of Lancaster and placing them under his personal command. Lesser bands spread out in groups of a dozen or two from the major fortresses into the interstices of the country around, making their bases in manor houses, church towers and abbey buildings. An indefensible farmhouse like the manor of Vaudry, just outside Vire, which had been occupied by two old ladies, could be seized by two or three men and transformed in a few weeks into a powerful fort capable of withstanding a sustained assault by an army of several hundred. Vire was surrounded on every side by improvised forts like this. So were many other major towns. An important road, like the main road from Bayeux to Caen, could be cut at will by the diminutive garrisons of two converted monastic churches. Even minor roads became impassable without safe-conducts from two, three or more garrison commanders of the district. Most places survived only by accepting the protection of the nearest garrison irrespective of its nationality and by paying *patis* and safe-conduct fees to its collectors. But there were areas of Lower Normandy where villages and hamlets and roadside farms were entirely abandoned as their inhabitants took refuge in walled towns or in caves, marshlands and forests. The principal walled cities, Bayeux, Caen and Rouen were overwhelmed by the tide of refugees. 'And all Normandy was at war from Mont-Saint-Michel to Eu,' a contemporary wrote.[54]

The Anglo-Navarrese garrisons of Lower Normandy were competitors, but common bonds of politics or nationality joined them together in a loose alliance. On the whole, they respected each other's territory. And from time to time the dispersed bands came together for mutual assistance against the local population or the armies of the Dauphin's lieutenants or to launch a major raid or establish a fresh centre of operations. In about July 1357, some 600 of them, English, Navarrese and Gascon, joined together to capture Honfleur, a small harbour-town on the south shore of the Seine estuary, which belonged to the lords of Briquebec. The population panicked when they realised that the enemy were within. They fled into the fields around or made for their boats and put to sea. The invaders took possession without opposition. The capture of Honfleur was a catastrophe for the inhabitants of the lower Seine, for it immediately became the advance headquarters of some of the chief English captains of western France. They found it an ideal base. It could be supplied and reinforced by sea from other ports of Normandy or Brittany, or from England. Its possession enabled the companies to extend their range much further east, preying on the shipping of the estuary and mounting raids deep into the Seine valley towards Rouen and the Île de France.[55]

Robert of Clermont, who was then in command of the government's troops in Lower Normandy, was overwhelmed by the scale and range of the companies' operations. He spent most of the summer of 1357 trying to clear the roads around the towns of Caen and Vire, attacking one improvised fort after another. For every manor which he demolished another church tower or millhouse was occupied by another enemy. The fall of Honfleur, which lay well to the east of the line of the Orne, was the last straw. A determined effort was made to expel the English from the town. In August Robert of Clermont and Louis of Harcourt managed to raise for a brief period an army several thousand strong in the regions threatened by intruders. Rouen alone contributed 200 men-at-arms and a large force of crossbowmen. Yet the enterprise was a valiant failure. The plan was to attack the harbour from the sea at the top of the tide, while the rest of the army assaulted the walls on the landward side. Unfortunately for the French the defence was ready and skilfully led by the Duke of Lancaster's Lieutenant in western France, Robert Knolles. The two attacks were poorly co-ordinated. A large number of French troops was landed from merchant ships on the beaches in front of the town. But the garrison fought them off until the tide fell and the ships were stranded. The assailants eventually made off along the shore. By the time that the overland attack began, the defenders had been able to regroup and concentrate their strength on the walls. The French assault ended in a humiliating rout when Knolles led a sortie party out of the town and attacked the French army in the rear. The triumphant defenders burst out of the gates, burning the ships abandoned on the beach and destroying the tents in the French camp. That military operations on this scale, conducted by the principal lieutenants of the two governments, could occur in a time of truce showed what kind of truce it was.[56]

The exertions of the Dauphin's commanders in Lower Normandy may not have achieved much, but they exhausted his strength and his treasury. The rest of France was left to defend itself as best it could with the aid of local officers of the Crown and whatever funds they could scratch together in their own districts. Even in the heart of France the government was powerless to defend its subjects. A bandit leader called Ruffin who, so far as can be discovered, acknowledged no allegiance to either side, burned a trail of destruction from the Loire to the Seine, looting and burning open villages and monasteries, and the deserted suburbs of a dozen walled towns. All the roads south of Paris were cut. Ruffin's army came within fifteen miles of the walls of the capital before turning south and dispersing. No one knew how many men Ruffin had under his command, but he cannot have had more than a few hundred. According to Jean le Bel, they operated in semi-autonomous units of only thirty to fifty men. Outside the walls of the main towns and fortresses, a band of thirty to fifty men could sweep all before it.[57]

On 24 May 1357, three weeks after his arrival in England, the Prince of Wales made his triumphal entry into London, accompanied by the King of France, the King's son Philip and the chief prisoners of Poitiers. The mayor, Henry Picard, met them with the leading citizens of London on the road from Kennington. At the northern end of London Bridge the

French King entered the capital of his enemy, a city about half the size of Paris, with perhaps a quarter of its population. The events of the past twenty years had had a special resonance here. The city had seen the parting of armies and the sailing of fleets. It had witnessed the dramatic return of Edward III from the disaster at Tournai in 1340. It had organised processions to celebrate the victories of Caen and Crécy, and watched as the King of Scotland was paraded through the streets to captivity in the Tower. London like Paris had been among the most consistent and vociferous supporters of the King's wars. A month before the entry of the Prince and his prisoners, the Corporation had had occasion to remind Edward III how much that support had cost them. Over the years, they said, they had sent men-at-arms, archers and ships to Scotland, Gascony, Flanders, Brabant, Calais, Brittany and Normandy. They had borne the burdens of war taxation. They had suffered prolonged disruption of their trade. They had lent the King nearly £140,000, including £60,000 for the campaigns in the Low Countries between 1338 and 1340, and £40,000 for the year-long siege of Calais. Much of this had never been repaid.

In spite of this catalogue of burdens and misfortunes, Londoners had done well out of the war. The royal courts and the great departments of state had returned to Westminster from the north. The civil service had progressively expanded to cope with the administrative burdens of the war. Chancery clerks were spilling out of their accommodation off Fleet Street into the neighbouring houses. New buildings were being added to the Palace of Westminster. The royal court had become more showy and expensive, a buoyant market for purveyors of luxuries. London's war contractors flourished mightily, and particularly the armourers and victuallers, whose prices rose steeply with the news of every fresh expedition. It is true that there had been some spectacular bankruptcies. But most of London's war financiers had done well enough. Henry Picard was not the only man who had taken good security for his loans and made fat profits out of less cautious men by speculating in royal debts and licences to export wool. When, in the mid-1340s, the war had turned in England's favour, London had received much of the spoil of France. Londoners had been foremost among the new colonists of Calais. Henry of Lancaster built a palace and Walter Mauny a chantry on the profits of war. Now, in 1357, the English capital was enjoying peace and security, historically low taxation, and the fourth year of a commercial boom. The richer men among them were laying out their profits in buying estates in Surrey, Kent and East Anglia, just as the commercial oligarchies of French cities were abandoning the suburbs and the countryside to find security behind their walls.[58]

No pains were spared in the effort to impress the Prince's prisoners. Bows and armour hung from every window on his route. Gold and silver leaf was showered on him from above. An escort of 1,000 mounted men was provided by the London guilds to escort them through streets that would hardly take three men abreast. Guilds and companies drew up their members in livery at the roadside. Curiosity and pride brought many thousands out to see the King of France go by. The Bishop of London met the procession at St. Pauls churchyard, with the entire clergy of the city. Crowds crammed every building and alleyway. The press was so great that it took three hours for the Prince and his prisoner to cross the city from Bridge Street to the Savoy Palace. 'And then there was dancing, hunting and hawking,' sang Sir John Chandos' Herald, 'and great jousts and banquets, as at the court of King Arthur.'[59]

In the sumptuous residence which Henry of Lancaster had built from the ransoms of French prisoners, the King of France set up his household in exile. He was provided with 5,000 florins 'discreetly and cautiously' by the papal collector in England. Although he was watched continuously, John was treated with every outward mark of respect and allowed a good deal of personal freedom. He hunted at will in the forests around the capital. He surrounded himself with his own servants, brought from France. He had his own secretarial and accounting staff. He was allowed to send messengers freely back and forth across the Channel.[60]

The diplomats gathered in London for what was expected to be the final act of the treaty of peace. On 24 June 1357 the cardinals Talleyrand and Capocci arrived at Dover. They came with a magnificent train of clerks, servants, messengers and guards and 200 outriders. Talleyrand was accommodated in the rambling London mansion of the Bishop of Lincoln at the corner of Chancery Lane and Holborn, and Capocci in the neighbouring mansion of the Bishop of Chichester. They and their households were destined to spend more than a year in England, supplied with regular doles from the revenues of the English Church, and groceries requisitioned from five counties. The cardinals were followed by the principal ministers and advisers of the French King. Gilles Aycelin, whom John had now appointed as his Chancellor, had accompanied him to England. His predecessor as Chancellor, Pierre de la Forêt, had recently been raised to the cardinalate. But he was still about, playing an ambiguous role as a prince of the Church and the confidant of the King. Guillaume de Melun, Archbishop of Sens, arrived at the same time. Nothing happened. The cardinals and the King exchanged compliments and banquets. Much time was passed in quarrelling about the agenda for the conference, which made no reference to Edward III's claim to the Crown of France. The opening was put off until the end of August. More lawyers and politicians were announced from France, including members of the Paris municipality and the agents of Philip of Navarre from Cherbourg. The King of England bided his time, waiting for the situation in France to deteriorate.[61]

While the King of France and his friends and advisers kicked their heels in the Savoy Palace, his allies in Scotland finally bowed out of the war. There was no help to be expected now from France. They had made contact with the councillors of Edward III within a few weeks of arrival of the news of the battle of Poitiers. But negotiation with the demoralised and divided factions in Scotland had proved a long-drawn business. Although the diplomats had reached agreement at Westminster by early May, the terms were not finally approved until 26 September 1357, when a great conference gathered for the purpose at Edinburgh, attended by most of the leading lay and ecclesiastical magnates of Scotland. The terms were mild by comparison with what Edward III might have demanded years before, when he had been more interested in Scotland and more willing to invest resources in its occupation. The Scots undertook to pay a ransom of 100,000 marks in instalments over a period of ten years, a modest sum in the budget of the King of England but a crushing burden for a small and impoverished kingdom suffering from economic recession, war damage and a severe shortage of coin. Pending payment, the Scottish King would be released on parole in exchange for an impressive list of hostages: three of the leading lay magnates of the land, the heirs of Robert Stewart and of nineteen other prominent Scottish noblemen. No attempt was made to resolve the underlying differences between the two kingdoms and perhaps, in the absence of the King, it would have been unrealistic to try. The treaty was therefore nothing more than a ransom agreement. But the Scots understood the implications perfectly. It meant an indefinite truce while France remained at war, a departure from the main axiom of Scottish foreign policy for the past six decades. The Scots bound themselves not to take up arms against the King of England until the last instalment of the ransom had been paid. David Bruce was brought to Berwick to put his seal to the agreement. On 7 October 1357 he was released.[62]

The whole affair had lessons for both sides in the larger drama being played out at Westminster between the representatives of England and France. The possession of a King was not the unanswerable argument which Edward III had perhaps assumed. It had taken him eleven years of military and diplomatic effort to get much less than he had hoped out of the capture of David Bruce. To achieve even that he had had to negotiate with the Scots and not simply with their captured King. David's stature in Scotland had visibly shrunk with each year of his captivity, just as John II's was now beginning to do in France. In the last resort it was clear that the Scots had been willing to do without their King if the alternative was an unacceptable peace and an unaffordable ransom. There were always ambitious politicians, such as the Stewart in Scotland and the King of Navarre in France for whom the absence of the King was an opportunity to be seized, not a misfortune to be lamented.

In Paris, the Dauphin lurched from one extreme to another in the effort to escape the grip of rival groups of French politicians. The Estates-General of Languedoil reassembled on 22 July 1357 to consider the accounts of the tax commissioners whom they had appointed in March.[63] The new assembly had little to do but recognise its own impotence. The tax ordinances had been ignored by the nobility and the Church and by many of the towns. The main consequence of its deliberations was to persuade the Dauphin that there was nothing to be gained by co-operating within a body which was filled with radical troublemakers and had proved incapable of solving his financial difficulties. Within a few days of the dispersal of the delegates the Dauphin returned to the confrontational manner of the previous autumn. At the end of July he left Paris and installed himself in the abbey of Notre-Dame at Maubuisson outside Pontoise. Here he dispensed with the Council which had been imposed on him by the Estates-General. He appointed his own Chancellor. He banished Robert le Coq to his diocese. Charles did not dare to restore the twenty-two officers who had been proscribed by the Estates. But he did reinstate many of the lesser officers who had been dismissed in the spring purges, and he suspended the work of the commissions of *réformateurs* who were busy investigating the failings of others. In the middle of August 1357, Étienne Marcel and his henchmen Charles Toussac and Jean de Lisle were summoned to Maubuisson to be told that the Dauphin proposed to dispense with the tutors which the Parisians and their allies had given him. He instructed them to keep their noses out of the government of the realm in future.[64]

This brief mood of defiance lasted less than two months. For if the Estates-General could not raise money from taxpayers, neither, it was clear, could the Dauphin alone. At the end of August, the young prince visited Rouen to plead for money with representatives of the Church and nobility of Normandy. They were willing to concede a hearth tax in their domains, which proved impossible to collect. A number of towns were also approached for contributions but appear to have refused absolutely. At Maubuisson, the Dauphin's councillors tried some other expedients: devaluation, farming out domain revenues for instant cash, the creation of new offices, almost certainly for sale. At the beginning of October 1357, the Dauphin gave up the unequal struggle and surrendered to the Parisians.[65]

He made a bargain with Étienne Marcel and his Parisian allies. They agreed not to renew the attack on the Dauphin's officers. They said that they would stop demanding the release of the King of Navarre from prison. The Dauphin for his part agreed to summon an assembly of some kind, even if it was not the Estates-General. It was an awkward compromise and a humiliating failure. The Dauphin called together the representatives of seventy selected towns of Languedoil. The object seems to have been to devise an assembly in which the radical allies of Paris would be diluted by others from regions traditionally loyal to the Crown. But when the delegates of the towns eventually appeared in Paris, around the middle of the month, they refused to agree to anything without the recall of the full Estates-General. The Dauphin had been baulked. On 15 October 1357 he reluctantly called a fresh meeting of the Estates-General. Étienne Marcel's reputation now far surpassed the Dauphin's. He marked his new-found authority by joining his own letters to the official summonses. On 7 November 1357, only three weeks after their despatch, those delegates who were able to reach the capital in time gathered once more to witness the formal opening of the proceedings. The opening address must have been a sombre oration. We do not know what he said. It very quickly became irrelevant. On 9 November 1357, the third day of the assembly, the news arrived that Charles of Navarre had escaped from his prison.[66]

CHAPTER VII

Revolution in Paris 1357–1358

Charles of Navarre's escape from Arleux and his re-emergence as a force in French politics were due mainly to the citizens of Amiens. Amiens had been hit hard by the economic misfortunes of the mid-fourteenth century. Once among the most populous cities of northern France, a great centre of cloth making, dye manufacture and metal-work, its industries had suffered from the secular decline of the cloth industries of northern Europe. The war had accelerated the process. The city's commercial links with England had been cut and those with Flanders severely strained. Its population, which had expanded during the thirteenth century into spacious suburbs beyond the walls, had lived under the shadow of fire and pillage ever since Edward III had first invaded France in 1339. Then came the extension of the city's walls, decided on the morrow of the battle of Crécy, which had involved the construction of four miles of wall, fifteen towers and three gates on the south side of the city, a crushing financial burden, coming on top of heavy war taxation imposed by the central government. Two years after Crécy the strain of reduced incomes and increased expenditure had been aggravated by the sudden disaster of the Black Death. The plague took a particularly heavy toll in the cramped industrial quarters within the old walls, and inaugurated a long period of social tension as labour became scarce and the upward pressure on wages cut further into the profits of Amiens' manufacturers. In the face of these hardships, the city had become by the middle of 1350s a centre of political radicalism second only to Paris. It had had no less than three representatives on the Council of Eighty in addition to Jean de Picquigny, the hereditary *vidâme* of Amiens, who had been one of the spokesmen of the nobility. These men had been prominent among the delegates clamouring for the release of Charles of Navarre in October 1356, and among those who had refused to disband when the Dauphin dismissed them.[1]

Jean de Picquigny had been a consistent and dedicated partisan of the House of Navarre from the outset. Even at the lowest point of Charles's fortunes, Jean believed that only the King of Navarre could lift France from the depths to which it had sunk under the Valois. When, early in November 1357, he resolved to spring him from his prison, his declared motive was to save the honour of France and to bring about the defeat and expulsion of her enemies. Jean recruited a band of about thirty men in Amiens. Before dawn on 9 November 1357, they scaled the walls of Arleux with ladders and grappling irons. After eighteen uneventful months, the small garrison had grown careless and the watches were poorly kept. Within a few minutes, Charles was dressed and on his way to Amiens, 'without even taking leave of my host' as he later boasted. The city received him like a returning hero. He was cheered through the streets and laden with gifts. He was heard with respect as he delivered a wordy and passionate oration full of 'sweet words' about the injustice of his arrest and the sufferings of his captivity. The municipality made him an honorary citizen. They swore to support him in his struggle. From his quarters in the city (the residence of one of the cathedral canons) Charles of Navarre began to recruit an army and to plan his march on Paris. He had all the prisoners released from the city's prisons. He hired men on promises among the citizens. He recruited the retainers and friends of Jean de Picquigny. He wrote to neighbouring cities and old allies. He intended no ill to the good people of France, he said, but only to win their friendship and support and to vindicate his honour and his rights.[2]

The reappearance of Charles of Navarre transformed the balance of power in Paris. Charles's chief confederate in the government was Robert le Coq, who had rejoined the Council in October. He immediately assumed control over the administration. The Dauphin was forced to issue a safe-conduct permitting the King of Navarre to enter the capital with as many followers as he wished, armed or disarmed. The Dauphin's hopes of escaping the tutelage of the politicians with the aid of the Estates-General were dashed. As attention shifted to the plans of the King of Navarre, the assembly gradually broke up in confusion. Many of the delegates, including all those of Burgundy and Champagne, believed that they were being used to put a veil of legitimacy over a coup d'état. They took no further part in the proceedings. The nobility who remained behind quarrelled with the delegates of the Third Estate. Then they too began to withdraw. Most of the others drifted away to their homes. Shortly, only a rump of ecclesiastics and delegates of the towns remained behind in the Franciscan convent.[3]

On 29 November 1357 the King of Navarre and a host of friends and allies from Picardy and Normandy entered Paris by the Porte Saint-Denis. He was escorted through the streets by an imposing company. The Bishop of Paris came to meet him at the city gate with the Provost of the Merchants and a press of prominent citizens of the capital. More than 500 armed attendants rode with him down the rue Saint-Denis, the triumphal way of generations of French Kings, where Charles was received like a newly crowned monarch and cheered across the city to his lodgings in the abbey of St. Germain. That evening the criers went through the streets announcing that Charles would address the citizens of Paris in the Pré-aux-Clercs on the following morning.

The Pré-aux-Clercs was a vast meadow on the left bank of the Seine, beyond the walled enclosure of the abbey of St. Germain, covering much of what is now the seventh *arrondissement* of Paris. It was the place where gangs of university students fought each other, where duellists settled their quarrels, where the lists were laid out for the great state and civic tournaments. Against the walls of the abbey there was a large wooden grandstand. At about 9 o'clock on 30 November the King of Navarre began to address the crowd from the top of this structure. About 10,000 Parisians were gathered in the meadow to hear him. It was a very long speech, so long that the rest of Paris had eaten its midday meal before he had finished. He inveighed against those who had imprisoned him without cause for a year and a half, just as he had done at Amiens. He described his sufferings in language so affecting that the crowd began to weep. He lambasted the ministers and servants of the Crown. He declared that he felt nothing but loyalty for the kingdom of France. Indeed, if he were ever to claim the Crown, he would be found to have a better claim than either John II or the King of England. It was a 'fine and wise' speech, according to Jean le Bel; 'elegant and prolix' said another.[4]

The speech had its effect. The Dauphin's capacity to resist, already weakened by the events of the past two months, collapsed entirely. On the following morning, 1 December, Étienne Marcel appeared before him in the palace on the island at the head of an intimidating delegation of citizens of Paris and representatives of the Third Estate. They had come, they said, to demand justice for the King of Navarre. Without pausing to consult the Dauphin, Robert le Coq rose from his seat to announce that the King of Navarre would have 'not only justice but all the favour and courtesies that should exist between brothers.' None of the other councillors dared to say a word. The 'brothers', who had not seen each other since the day of Charles's arrest at Rouen, met on the following afternoon in the enormous Parisian mansion of the Counts of Évreux by the south gate of the abbey of St. Germain. For the Dauphin, it was a humiliating occasion. The King of Navarre arrived after him, accompanied by an escort of armed men who promptly seized and expelled all his attendants. The two young men exchanged frigid courtesies in the presence of the dowager Queen Joan, and then departed.

On 3 December there was a tumultuous meeting of the Council in the presence of the Dauphin. The numbers were swollen by many new councillors co-opted by Robert le Coq and his allies. The demands of the King of Navarre were read out to the assembled company. Charles required the immediate restoration of all the castles and domains which the Crown had seized from him since his arrest. He wanted an indemnity against all the damage done to them during his imprisonment. This Charles reckoned at 40,000 *écus*. Then there was to be a free pardon for all his crimes and those of his supporters, including the four men executed by John II at Rouen. Their skeletons, which were still hanging from chains at the gibbet of Bihorel, were to be taken down and honourably buried. As the Council began to deliberate, there was a great commotion in the next door room. Étienne Marcel burst in, followed by the leaders of the Third Estate and a mob of hangers-on from the assembly at the Franciscans. They remained in the council chamber while each councillor in turn was asked his advice on the demands of the King of Navarre. Every one of them sat terrified and gave it as his opinion that they should be conceded. The Dauphin submitted. A former royal Lieutenant in Lower Normandy, Amaury de Meulan, who had thrown in his lot with the King of Navarre, was to be given documents sealed by the Dauphin which required all royal captains holding castles of the House of Navarre in Normandy to deliver them up immediately to Charles's representatives.

This was only a beginning. There were also Charles's long-standing claims to be granted an endowment equal to his status. His demands were exorbitant. They included the Dauphin's own duchy of Normandy and to the whole county of Champagne. Possession of these provinces would have given him a large part of the royal domain and made him for all practical purposes the ruler of northern France. It would be necessary, the Dauphin was informed, to discuss these matters with Charles in person. During the next few days the Dauphin had a series of disagreeable interviews with the King of Navarre. They took place in the unfriendly atmosphere of the Hotel de Navarre in the Bourg Saint-Germain and Robert le Coq's mansion in the rue Pavée (now rue Séguier). Charles pressed his claims. The Dauphin temporised as best he could. The negotiations were still in progress when the news reached Paris that John II had reached agreement with Edward III in England.[5]

The diplomatic conference in London had opened at the beginning of September and had quickly got bogged down in irreconcilable differences.[6] Events in France had an electrifying effect on the proceedings. For John II, the implications of the escape of Charles of Navarre were obvious. It threatened to propel his realm further into chaos before he could return to it. It revived old fears that the King of Navarre might make common cause with Edward III to dispossess him. Ironically, the English government was equally dismayed. They had always been equivocal about Charles of Navarre. They had achieved a reasonable working relationship with his brother Philip, a much more straightforward personality, but experience had taught them to distrust Charles. And, although they were Charles's declared allies in the fight against the French Crown, they were well aware that the alliance was founded on his continued imprisonment. Once he was released, anything might happen. When Philip had tried to persuade the King of England to make the release of his brother a condition of the truce with France, he had been brushed off with declarations of goodwill and courteous evasions. Louis, the other cadet of the House of Navarre, had made the same application to the Prince of Wales and received the same response. Edward III was quite content that Charles should languish at Arleux indefinitely.[7]

Within a month of his escape, the councillors of the two Kings at Westminster had reached provisional agreement. In the rush to devise something which could be announced in France, the terms were agreed in outline only. Many points of detail remained to be negotiated. But even the outline was humiliating enough for the King of France, and certain to be disagreeable to his subjects. The ransom of the King was fixed at 4,000,000 *écus* (£667,000). Of this immense sum 600,000 *écus* (£100,000) was to be paid before John left English territory and the rest by instalments over a number of years thereafter. The terms provided for the surrender to Edward III in full sovereignty of about a quarter of the territory of France. In the south-west, Edward III was to have, in addition to the Bordelais, Saintonge, Poitou, Angoumois, Périgord, Agenais, Limousin, Quercy and the Pyrenean territories of Bigorre and Gaure. In the north, Edward was allowed to retain Calais and the pale of land around it; the county of Ponthieu and the town of Montreuil in Picardy, which he had held until 1337; and the lands which Godfrey of Harcourt had given him in the Cotentin peninsula. Philip of Navarre was to be restored to everything that he had held in France before the current civil war. Elaborate provision was to be made for resolving the disputed succession to the duchy of Brittany. Performance of all these undertakings was to be secured by the delivery of a great number of hostages. The list annexed to the draft included almost all the principal noblemen of France and two prominent citizens each from twenty of the largest walled cities. From the French point of view, the most that could be said for these terms was that they were better than those on which Edward III had been insisting until recently. The English King dropped his claim on Normandy, which he had been demanding since the early 1350s; and to the provinces of the western Loire, which had actually been granted to him by the draft treaty of Guines in 1354.[8]

During the conferences, John II's prison had been transferred from the Savoy Palace to Windsor Castle. From here, he wrote at the beginning of December announcing the agreement to his subjects. But he said nothing about the terms. He knew very well how unwelcome they would be. Public opinion would have to be carefully prepared. The King of England did his best to help. Four prominent prisoners in England were released on parole at the end of December 1357 to explain the draft treaty to the Dauphin and the various factions in Paris. John selected the Archbishop of Sens, the Counts of Vendôme and Tancarville and the Lord of Derval, all of them men who were close to his counsels but not too distasteful to the radicals in Paris. At the same time, John planned a direct appeal to the southern provinces which had virtually detached themselves from the rest of the kingdom. The Dauphin had recently reappointed his younger brother John, Count of Poitiers, as his Lieutenant in Languedoc in place of the Count of Armagnac, who had resigned. The King appointed him in his own name, with extended powers. His main function was to be to raise the first instalment of the ransom in the only part of France on whose loyalty the King could now count.[9]

The work of the two Kings was almost immediately swept away in a great tide of fresh violence in western France. During the autumn of 1357 Martin Henriquez arrived at Cherbourg from Navarre with nearly 1,400 reinforcements.[10] Allowing for casualties and desertions, this must have brought the total number of Navarrese troops in western

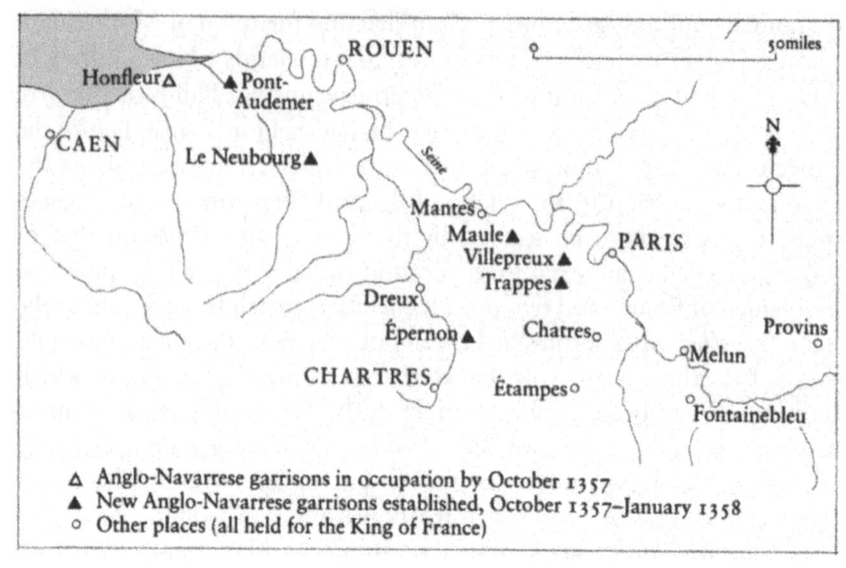

19 Anglo-Navarrese offensive, October 1357–January 1358

France to well over 3,000 men. In addition English, Gascon and German soldiers of fortune had been pouring into the region all year. Towards the end of the year the principal English and Navarrese captains in Lower Normandy launched a coordinated offensive from Honfleur into the Seine Valley and the Île de France.

The leading light was an Englishman called James Pipe. Pipe was a Staffordshire knight who had begun his career as a protégé of the Earl of Stafford. He had served with Stafford in Scotland in the 1340s and had briefly held the office of keeper of Berwick-on-Tweed. He had fought with him at the siege of Calais. And, when the Earl went to Gascony as royal Lieutenant in 1352, Pipe went with him. He became the first English captain of Blaye after the recapture of the place from the French and, after Stafford's return to England in October, served as acting Seneschal of the duchy. Unfortunately for ambitious retainers like Pipe, the Earl of Stafford played little part in the military campaigns of the mid-1350s, which was no doubt why Pipe transferred his allegiance to the Duke of Lancaster. He joined Lancaster's expedition to Normandy in 1356, and served with him at Rennes. When the Duke left France in July 1357, Pipe remained behind as one of the two lieutenants charged with protecting his interests in the west. But it was never entirely clear in what capacity he was acting. Like so many English soldiers of his time, he occupied an ambiguous position, never wholly amenable to the orders of the English King's ministers, but not quite an independent freebooter either.[11]

The first important step came with the capture of le Neubourg, a market town with an ancient castle, where the roads from Rouen, Tours and Paris met. The English had established a garrison here by the early autumn of 1357, from which they were able to obstruct much of the road system of southern Normandy and to range freely over the whole of the fertile territory between the Seine and the Risle. Then, on 9 November 1357, in the middle of the night, a troop of Englishmen and Germans from Honfleur fell on the town of Pont-Audemer. Pont-Audemer had a large royal garrison. But fifty of its number were German mercenaries. They were suborned by the Germans fighting with the English and let them into the town. The rest of the defenders fought a courageous rearguard action in the streets until they were cornered and forced to surrender. The citadel, which had a separate garrison, held out. But there was nothing that they could do. They watched impotently from their walls as the invaders pillaged and burnt the town below them.[12]

From Pont-Audemer, the English and Navarrese burned a trail up the left bank of the Seine. By mid-December they had invaded the Île de France and penetrated within a few miles of Paris. Villepreux and Trappes, two small seigneurial castles on the road from Paris to Chartres, were occupied by English garrisons. A few days later another English company occupied the small town of Maule, south of Mantes. Penetrating east across the forest of Fontainebleu, the English appeared around Montereau, one of nodal points of the lacework of navigable rivers east of Paris. By the end of the year 1357 the first English garrisons had penetrated into Champagne, where several fortified manors around Provins were reported to have fallen into their hands. From each of these centres, small groups spread out seizing merchandise on the roads, burning villages, taking travellers for ransom and butchering those who were not worth the trouble. The numbers involved were still small. Estimates varied between 800 and 1,200 for the whole Paris region, and these were probably too high. But there was no one to resist them. Most of the population were frozen in panic. West of Paris the villages were deserted as their inhabitants crammed through the gates of the capital, laden with their possessions. The nuns of Poissy, Longchamp and Melun abandoned their buildings, closed their doors and joined the mass of people clogging the roads to the city.[13]

*

The agreement of John II with the King of England was a serious threat to Charles of Navarre. Like many other Frenchmen, he probably underestimated the remaining diplomatic obstacles and assumed that the King's release from captivity was imminent. The end of the war or the premature return of the King of France to his country could only reinforce the position of the Crown and undermine his own. So, when the first news of the agreement reached Paris, on about 9 December 1357, Charles embarked on what can only be regarded as a deliberate attempt to hasten the disintegration of the French state and satisfy his demands before the first instalment of the ransom could be found and paid to Edward III. He had all the prisons of Paris opened, like those of Amiens a month before. Their occupants were released in a brawling mass onto the streets of the city. The Dauphin, now little more than a cipher in the hands of Charles' friends, meekly sealed the necessary orders. The Estates-General, or the rump of it which was still in Paris, was formally adjourned to the middle of January. As for the King of Navarre's negotiations with the Dauphin, they were brought to an abrupt and inconclusive end. Charles' territorial claims were referred to the adjudication of a commission comprising the dowager Queens and two nominees of the Dauphin, assisted by the three Estates when eventually they reconvened. On 13 December 1357 the King of Navarre left Paris to build up his strength in Normandy, his great cavalcade forcing its way along roads packed with refugees pressing in the other direction.[14]

In Charles' absence, the Dauphin struggled to free himself from the politicians. Robert le Coq exercised an iron grip on the government. He dominated the Council. He controlled all the principal administrative departments. He had the support of the leaders of Paris. He was virtually the agent of the King of Navarre. He luxuriated in his new found status, issuing statements and orders without reference to the Dauphin or the rest of the Council. At the beginning of the New Year, when he was at the height of his power, he had letters drawn up in the Dauphin's name calling on the Pope to make him a cardinal. But the ambitious prelate readily made enemies even among those who shared his principles. There was a sizeable group of noblemen who found Robert's overbearing manner intolerable. Some of them regarded the King of Navarre as a dangerous schemer whose actions could only help the English. In the course of December 1357 three men emerged as the leading members of this group. Jean de Conflans, the honorary Marshal of the county of Champagne, and Gerard de Thurey, who held the same office in the duchy of Burgundy, were prominent and well-connected noblemen on the Dauphin's Council. They came from profoundly conservative regions of eastern France, hitherto untouched by the fighting, which regarded the radicalism of Paris with indifference or outright hostility. Robert of Clermont, the Marshal of Normandy and the Dauphin's Lieutenant at Caen, came from a completely different background. He was the man responsible for the conduct of the war in its main theatre, but found himself spending an increasing amount of his time in Paris, endeavouring to shore up the Dauphin's failing political strength. These men had limited influence on the decisions of the Council. But there was one area where they represented a considerable threat to the Bishop of Laon and his allies, and that was the control of military operations. Because the Dauphin's troops in the field were largely paid from local receipts collected by the commanders on the spot, they were in the last resort in a position to make up their own minds about whom they would regard as representing the Crown. The three provincial marshals on the Council could count on the support of most of the officers who were struggling to maintain the French positions in Lower Normandy and on the Breton march. In practice they disposed of such reserves of manpower as the French government still had.[15]

At about Christmas time orders were issued on the Dauphin's behalf summoning large numbers of soldiers to be in Paris by 14 January 1358. There is every reason to believe that the three marshals were responsible for this momentous step. 14 January was the date when the Estates-General was due to reopen and the King of Navarre was expected to return to Paris. The ostensible reason for the summons was to protect the capital against the Anglo-Navarrese companies in the Île de France. But there can be little doubt that the real object was to enable the Dauphin to hold his own against the partisans of Navarre and the mobs of Étienne Marcel. Most of the men were recruited in eastern France and the francophone territories beyond the Rhone, where the Dauphin and his friends still had strong personal connections to call on. Burgundy and the Dauphiné supplied the largest contingents. During the month of January about 2,000 of them responded to the Dauphin's summons and arrived outside the gates of Paris. Meanwhile, Amaury de Meulan, who was in Normandy trying to recover the confiscated castles of the House of Navarre, found himself baulked at every point. The royal captains in command of these places refused to surrender them even when they were presented with the Dauphin's personal command. At Breteuil, Évreux, Pont-Audemer and Pacy the garrison commanders all returned the same answer. They had been appointed, they said, by John II and would answer to no one but him. There is no evidence that the Dauphin or his friends were behind this, but it is likely.[16]

The King of Navarre responded in kind. He regarded the Dauphin's summons as a provocation. He accused the young prince of secretly encouraging the defiance of the royal castellans in Lower Normandy. He declared that the Dauphin had repudiated his engagements, and summoned his allies and their retainers to support him by force of arms. It was a declaration of war. On Christmas Day 1357, the French prisoners in England attended the splendid celebrations of Edward III at Marlborough in a mood of fresh optimism. At Mantes Charles of Navarre sat down to dinner in the great castle overlooking the Seine with the captains of the principal English and Navarrese companies and took them into his service for the coming civil war.[17] Then, at the beginning of January 1358, Charles travelled to Rouen to exact revenge on the King of France in the most public way he could devise. He had agreed with the Dauphin to take down the skeletons of Bihorel 'without ceremony'. But on 10 January he had them carried on biers in the failing light of the afternoon to the site of their execution, where a requiem mass was sung by the light of a hundred torches. The bodies were then carried back along the route of the tumbrils to Rouen cathedral, where they lay in state all night as the crowds filed past to pay their respects. On the following morning, Charles made an impassioned speech to the inhabitants of Rouen from an upper storey, full of pity for his own sufferings and recrimination against his enemies, in which he referred to the executed men as 'martyrs'.[18]

In the first few weeks of the New Year the English and Navarrese companies passed through the Beauce south-west of Paris, destroying everything before them. The Seine valley became impassable. The main roads to Chartres and Orléans were blocked. On 16 January 1358 an English company sacked Étampes, just thirty miles from the capital, taking many prisoners. Another destroyed the village of Saint-Cloud. The flames must have been visible from the gates of Paris. A few days after this, James Pipe established his headquarters in the castle of Épernon, a great square keep of the eleventh century belonging to the Counts of Montfort l'Amaury, which stood by the main road from Paris to Chartres at the edge of the forest of Rambouillet. Pipe installed a garrison of about 120 men here and turned it into a centre for the systematic devastation of the western and southern Île de France. Other

Englishmen, and some Navarrese, followed in his path. Most of them claimed to be operating under the authority of the King of Navarre. Pipe called himself Charles' Lieutenant.[19]

The Dauphin could do nothing. His garrisons were thinly spread and unpaid. His treasury was empty. At one point he was reduced to authorising his garrisons to plunder his own subjects in lieu of wages. The result was to reduce to chaos the few areas which were still loyal and reasonably secure. For most of the population there was now little to distinguish the troops of the government from those of the English and Navarrese. At Étampes the garrison of the Dauphin based in the church of Notre-Dame and the garrison of the Count of Étampes based in the keep of la Guinodie were engaged in a full-scale war with each other and with the inhabitants of the town and surrounding region. It is not surprising that when the English arrived they were able to destroy the town without effective interference from either garrison.[20]

In desperation, the Dauphin appealed to Edward III to control his subjects. He sent the Seneschal of Anjou to England with a catalogue of complaints about the conduct of the English in France. Edward was genuinely concerned. He could see his hard-won agreement with John II failing before it was even sealed. Too late, he ordered his bailiffs and constables in the harbours of southern England to stop the flow of soldiers and weapons across the Channel. He sent two of his most reliable officers to France to command obedience from his subjects there. The officers, Richard Totesham and Stephen Cusington, arrived in late January 1358 in the Île de France. But they could do no more than the Dauphin could. They toured the war zone under heavy guard, accompanied by the Seneschal of Anjou. Most of the English captains refused to acknowledge their authority. They claimed to be fighting for the King of Navarre. A few declared themselves for some other French politician who, they said, would recognise them sooner or later as his own. None of them was willing to surrender his gains or to abandon the looting of one of the richest regions of Europe.[21]

Tensions mounted in the streets of Paris as the delegates began to arrive for the reopening of the Estates-General. The capital was crowded with refugees. The English were within a day's march of the walls and had cut most of the routes to the south and west. The schism between the military men on the Dauphin's Council and the majority of radicals and pro-Navarrese in control of the administration made it difficult to know who was to defend Paris and who was to attack it. Étienne Marcel and his friends began to adopt an independent and increasingly militant role. They took into their service a Norman knight, Pierre de Villiers, an experienced soldier who had served for several years in Brittany and Scotland. They put him in command of a ramshackle army consisting mainly of soldiers of the city watch and recruits from the streets and suburbs of Paris, which failed to clear the enemy from the main routes around the capital.[22] The city put its own guards on the gates of Paris. The Dauphin's troops, arriving in answer to his summons, were turned away at the gates as they tried to enter. They had to lodge themselves instead in great encampments in the suburbs and across the plain of Saint-Denis where, bored and angry, they began to steal and burn like the enemy. Within the walls Marcel called on all his supporters to declare themselves by sporting hoods of crimson and blue (the colours of the city). Some embroidered theirs with the words 'À bonne fin', which Marcel had adopted as the motto of his revolution.[23]

The Dauphin, who could see himself becoming the prisoner of the Parisians, made a bold attempt to appeal for their support over the heads of his keepers. Early on 11 January 1358, he had criers sent through the streets to announce that he would address the people in person. Étienne Marcel and Robert le Coq were taken by surprise. They did their best to dissuade him. They said that his life would be in danger. He brushed their protests aside. In the middle of the morning the Dauphin appeared at the market at les Halles with just six or eight attendants and addressed the crowd from a high platform. Although he did not name them his speech was obviously aimed at Robert le Coq and Étienne Marcel. He denied that the troops encamped beyond the walls had been hired to intimidate or attack the Parisians, and denounced the men who had said so. He denied responsibility for the failure to confront the companies in the Île de France. This, he said, was due entirely to 'those who had taken over the government'. He himself had not received a single penny of the taxes voted by the Estates-General. Turning the accusations of waste and corruption against his adversaries, he invited those who were in control of his financial affairs to render an account of what they had collected. Henceforth, he said, he intended to govern in person and to carry the fight to the enemy. He would 'live and die', he said, with the people of Paris. The Dauphin had learned a great deal from the demagoguery of his cousin of Navarre. His words made a considerable impression on men who were used to hearing public pronouncements of the Crown filtered through the marmoreal orations of a spokesman, as the King sat impassively by.

On the following day Marcel responded with a great demonstration of his own at the church of St.-Jacques-de-Compostelle, a pilgrims' hospice by the Porte Saint-Denis. For Marcel this was home territory. The church was the seat of a powerful confraternity to which Marcel and many of his friends belonged. The quarter was heavily populated with his supporters. But before the meeting could begin the Dauphin unexpectedly arrived. He was accompanied by Robert le Coq and by the Chancellor of Normandy, Jean de Dormans. It must have been an uncomfortable occasion for the Bishop of Laon. The Dauphin took over the proceedings. Jean de Dormans delivered a speech in his defence along much the same lines as his own address at les Halles. By the time he had finished, much of the audience was evidently with him. Marcel was speechless. His chief henchman Charles Toussac tried to say something, but no one would listen. It was not until the Dauphin and his company had departed that he was able to make himself heard by the remnant of the audience. Toussac was followed by a lawyer who had been one of the commissioners of the Estates-General for the assessment and collection of the new taxes. The tax receipts, said the lawyer, had not been embezzled by the commissioners. He claimed that some 40,000 or 50,000 *moutons* had been disbursed on the Dauphin's personal instructions. He even named the captains to whom it had been paid. Toussac wound up with a eulogy of Étienne Marcel, a man, he said, whose every decision had been guided by the welfare of the people and who would not hesitate to withdraw from public life entirely if he ever lost their support. Marcel's friends in the crowd bellowed out their support. But not everyone was convinced. When the Dauphin received a deputation from the city guilds on the following day their enthusiasm for his cause was evident. Taking up his own phrase at les Halles, they declared themselves willing to 'live and die' with him. It was not a moment too soon, they said, to take over the government in person. The Dauphin gained vastly in confidence during December and January, but if he believed that sentiment was shifting decisively in his favour, he was deceiving himself. The anxieties of the city and the menace from outside polarised opinions, intensifying extremes. For every group which could find a delegation to promise their loyal support to the government, another watched the Dauphin's acts with growing jealousy and suspicion.[24]

On 14 January 1358 the Estates-General reopened. The towns were well represented. But there were few representatives of the Church present and hardly any of the nobility. The King of Navarre remained at

Mantes. Little is known about the debates except that they were disorganised, acrimonious and inconclusive. As always, the main bone of contention was finance. After ten days of deliberation the delegates resolved to authorise a devaluation of the coinage: a return to the old expedients of the Crown and a recognition perhaps of their own impotence. Four fifths of the profits, they decreed, were to be reserved for the war effort, the remaining fifth for the expenses of the Dauphin's household. But the delegates were unable to agree upon any measure of general taxation. On about 23 January 1358 they adjourned for three weeks to consult their constituents. In their absence the capital moved closer to the edge of violence. A minor incident on the evening of 24 January 1358 brought it close to civil war. The Dauphin's Treasurer was attacked and killed in the street by an unpaid creditor of the household. The murderer fled to sanctuary in the nearby church of St. Merri in the rue Saint-Denis. But a group of courtiers, led by Robert of Clermont, arrived with a troop of soldiers and took him out by force. According to a report which was widely believed in Paris, Robert declared as the man was hanged at Montfaucon that he would do the same to the richest and greatest citizens of Paris. The Dauphin attended the funeral of his Treasurer in person, while a few hundred yards away his murderer was magnificently interred in the presence of Étienne Marcel and a crowd of angry Parisian supporters.[25]

It was in this atmosphere that the representatives of John II arrived in the city at the end of January 1358 with the details of the proposed treaty. Gilles Aycelin, John's Chancellor and chief negotiator, was the leader of the group. With him came Jean de Champeaux and Regnaut d'Acy, his two principal assistants at the Westminster conferences, and the group of aristocratic prisoners whom Edward III had released on parole specially for the purpose. The Dauphin's councillors are said to have found the document wholly satisfactory. The important point was that it provided for the release of the King and offered some prospect of peace and stability in his realm. The enormous financial and territorial concessions were passed over in silence. But public opinion in the capital was less easily satisfied. The terms were kept secret from the populace in the hope of forestalling opposition. It was not a wise decision. In the absence of firm information the supporters of peace were silent, while its opponents assumed the worst. With so many Navarrese sympathizers in the administration, it is unlikely that the terms remained secret from the King of Navarre.[26]

At the beginning of February 1358 Charles of Navarre sent Jean de

Picquigny to Paris to present his terms for co-operating with the Dauphin. A brief, arid conference was held in the presence of the two dowager Queens. Jean de Picquigny demanded the immediate surrender of the fortresses of Normandy, which were still excluding Charles' officers, and the payment of the indemnity of 40,000 *écus* which he had been promised in December. The Dauphin replied that Jean was not a man to whom he owed any answers. If such a man were to appear, he added, his answer would be that the King of Navarre had got everything to which he was properly entitled. The interview then ended. Charles moved at once to extremes. He sent a messenger to the King of England to say that his ambassadors would shortly arrive at Westminster to discuss matters of common interest. In the streets of Paris his allies mobilised their support. Charles' words in the Pré-aux-Clercs were still ringing in the ears of the mob. They did not criticise him for the collapse of civil order in the Île de France and the Beauce. What prodigies might he not have achieved for their defence, they asked, if the Dauphin had not broken his agreements? Others from whom the Dauphin might have hoped for better, agreed. When a delegation from the university came before him to report the views of the masters of the faculties, they were escorted by Étienne Marcel and many prominent citizens of his party. They thought that the Dauphin should surrender the disputed castles and pay the indemnity at once. They demanded that he start negotiating with the King of Navarre about his territorial claims. They threatened to preach against him from their pulpits.[27]

At Westminster, the drafting of the finer points of the treaty continued in an atmosphere almost completely insulated from the currents of opinion in either country. When the English Parliament assembled at Westminster on 5 February 1358 to approve the terms, Edward III was taken aback by the depth of their indifference. In the counties and towns men were satisfied that the French no longer represented a threat to the coasts of England or the livelihood of its inhabitants. They knew that the alliance of France and Scotland was moribund, and that the ransom treaty with David II had more or less secured the northern border. There was not much left to raise enthusiasm outside the ranks of the military aristocracy, the civil service and the war contractors. The Commons decided to use the treaty as an occasion for satisfying their ancient and unconnected grievances about papal taxation of the clergy and appointments to English benefices. They required a 'solemn' embassy to be sent to Avignon to resolve these matters before they would approve the treaty. That meant a bishop or an earl, an imposing retinue, a slow progress through France with escorts and safe-conducts, great expense and long delays. The Commons did not mind. The Pope, they believed, wanted a peace treaty badly enough to make some major concessions. Edward's ministers were gravely embarrassed. They told the cardinals that the King would not comply with the Commons' conditions. There would have to be an embassy. But a knight and a clerk would do.[28]

John II was full of optimism. He wrote to his officials in Paris telling them to prepare for his return. He asked them to send him notaries to draw up the treaty in due form, and knights and prelates to dignify his diminutive court in its last days at Windsor. He began to wind up his affairs in England, which consisted mostly of unpaid debts to tradesmen and sympathizers. John can have had little idea of the true condition of his realm.[29]

In Paris opinion was moving decisively against the treaty. The masters of the university pronounced against it. The municipality and the clergy of the city declared themselves opposed.[30] On 11 February 1358, six days after the opening of the English Parliament at Westminster, the Estates-General reassembled at the Franciscan convent. They showed even less interest in the draft treaty than the English assembly had done. The proceedings were once again dominated by the representatives of the towns. The nobility was once again almost entirely absent. The delegates were filled with the obsessions of the past eighteen months. They insisted on the dismissal of the officers proscribed the year before, several of whom had found their way back into the Dauphin's service or were sheltering at the court in exile at Windsor. They demanded the resumption of the purge of royal officials in the provinces, which the Dauphin had interrupted during his brief show of independence the previous August. They set about breathing fresh life into the flagging French war effort. A survey was ordered to be made of all recently constructed castles and defensive works. A campaign of tax raising was ordained. Arrears from the previous year were to be enforced. Fresh impositions were authorised. Heavy discounts were provided for towns and regions overrun by the companies, 'le fort portant le faible'. The Dauphin was permitted to take just one twentieth of the yield for the expenses of his household. The whole of the rest was reserved for the war. Moreover, its collection was placed in the hands of avowed partisans of the King of Navarre and of Parisian supporters of Étienne Marcel who could be relied upon to enforce these stipulations to the letter. The ransom of the King and the draft treaty with England must have been discussed. But in the ordinances which closed the sessions they were passed over in complete silence.

Having ignored the King's wishes, the Estates-General resolved that John's ability to intervene in the affairs of the realm from his prison should be brought to an end. The lord of Aubigny, one of the prisoners who had come from England to prepare public opinion for the treaty, was summarily removed from the office of Admiral to which the Dauphin had appointed him. In current conditions, the Estates declared, a fighting man was wanted in that office, not a prisoner bound by his parole. Another of the messengers from England, John's Chancellor Gilles Aycelin, found himself frustrated at every turn in Paris, forced to abandon his office and retire to his native Auvergne. There was nothing that the Estates-General could do about the regular flow of missives from Windsor addressed to the King's servants in Paris and the provinces. The King had been careful to keep his seal with him in England when his Chancellor left for France. But the delegates insisted that the Dauphin should assume the title of Regent instead of being a mere lieutenant of his father. They wanted to see him clothed with an authority of his own which would displace the King's, for if they could not control the father at least they had the son in their power. To maintain their grip on affairs, the delegates resolved that they would reconvene themselves in May. To prevent the Dauphin from outflanking them by direct appeals to the provinces, as he had done before, they decreed that there were to be no more assemblies of provincial Estates. The only permitted assemblies were to be those of all Languedoil, and they were to meet nowhere but in Paris, the 'finest, most imposing city of the realm' where they could count on the protection of Marcel's mobs.[31]

The Dauphin put his seal to the ordinance of the Estates-General on about 21 February 1358. But he was already planning to throw off his shackles. As the delegates of the Estates-General began to disperse to their homes, the Dauphin's officers ordered the soldiers whom they had summoned to the capital to advance on the city from their encampments in the plain of Saint-Denis. The city authorities had been holding the gates against them for several weeks. But the Dauphin's men controlled access by the Louvre. Realising what was up, the leaders of Paris, Étienne Marcel, Charles Toussac, and a rich wholesale grocer called Pierre Gilles, resolved to pre-empt the Dauphin with a counter-stroke of their own. On the evening of 21 February 1358 they summoned the city guilds to bring their men fully armed to the church of St. Eloy on the following morning.[32]

The Benedictine priory of St. Eloy was one of the oldest churches of the Île de la Cité. It occupied a rambling enclosure opposite the royal palace, all yards and gardens, outbuildings and tenements, penetrated by an irregular lacework of narrow lanes. The whole quarter was flattened in the nineteenth century and replaced by the frigid blocks of the Prefecture de Police and the Tribunal de Commerce which stand there now. At sunrise on the morning of 22 February 1358 a huge armed mob gathered here in answer to Marcel's summons. They passed through the lanes into the rue de la Barillerie, which ran past the Treasury building and the east wall of the palace enclosure. About 3,000 of them forced their way through the gates into the great court of the palace. Most of them had probably never seen it before. In front of them stood the Sainte-Chapelle. On the north side was the Great Hall of the Parlement. Joining these two buildings was the Galerie des Merciers, an arcaded edifice on three storeys where the royal apartments were situated. The Galerie was approached by an imposing marble stairway from which royal summonses and proclamations were traditionally announced. Marcel entered the building with a handful of colleagues and an escort of armed men, wearing the crimson and blue hoods of their party.

The Dauphin was in his private rooms on the second floor. He had his closest advisers around him, including two of the marshals, Jean de Conflans and Robert of Clermont. Étienne Marcel burst in, the mob at his back. 'We have business to do here,' he announced. Then, turning to his men: 'My good friends, do what you have come to do and do it quickly.' A group of men threw themselves on Jean de Conflans and hacked him to death with their swords as he clung for protection to a corner of the Dauphin's couch. Robert of Clermont fled into an adjoining room. But they followed him there and butchered him like his colleague. The terrified Dauphin appealed to Marcel for protection. Marcel handed him his hood of crimson and blue to draw over his head. He stood beside the prince as men dragged the corpses of the marshals through the building to the top of the marble staircase. From here they were hurled into the courtyard below in front of the yelling crowd.[33]

The clerks and officers working in the palace had seen the crowd break in. They were fleeing from every available exit. One of them, Regnaut d'Acy, had the ill-fortune to be passing through the street outside the palace enclosure just as the mob was streaming from the gate. Regnaut stood for most of the things which they hated. He was a lawyer and a *parlementaire*, a man whose family had been influential about the Crown for at least two generations and had earned golden rewards too quickly. He had been one of the twenty-two officials proscribed by name by the Estates-General the year before. He was also one of the agents of the King who had negotiated the draft treaty with Edward III in England. Regnaut was recognised at once. He fled down a side-street. But they caught him in a baker's shop, and battered him to death.[34]

Later in the morning Étienne Marcel addressed his followers in the Place de Grève. The great open space sloped gently down to the Seine, where the grain barges were beached along the strand. The *Hanse des Marchands* had recently bought as their headquarters the Maison aux Piliers, an imposing mansion overlooking it on the east side, on a site which has been occupied by the municipality of Paris ever since. Marcel knew the enormity of what he had done and the danger in which he had placed himself. He wanted to wrap himself in the approval of the mob. Speaking from an upper window he told them that they had acted for the good of the realm. Their victims had been 'false, evil, treasonable' men who had deserved to die. He called on them to support him. 'With one voice' the thousands cried out that they took the deed as their own and would live and die with Étienne Marcel. Marcel then led them back across the bridge to the palace. The crowd was now so large that it filled the whole of the courtyard in front of the Galerie des Merciers as Marcel and his companions mounted the great stairway for the second time. The Dauphin was still in his apartments where they had left him. The bodies of the marshals could be seen through the windows, spreadeagled on the marble paving below. Marcel told the Dauphin that he had no reason to fear for his own safety. What had been done had been done by the will of the people and to avoid yet worse misfortunes. He called on the Dauphin to show that he was at one with his subjects. He must ratify the murder of the marshals. He must issue whatever letters of remission were required of him. The young prince was beyond resistance. He replied that he would do all that Marcel asked and 'prayed that the Parisians might be his good friends as he would be theirs.' That evening the Parisians had bales of crimson and blue cloth delivered to the palace so that the Dauphin, the royal princes and the officers of the administration could robe themselves in the colours of the revolution which they had now adopted. Later that afternoon, as it was growing dark, the bodies of the two marshals were picked up off the ground and taken away in a cart to be buried covertly in the church of St. Catherine by the eastern wall of the city. The clergy was so cowed by the events of the day that they would not inter the bodies without first enquiring of the Provost of the Merchants whether he had any objection.[35]

Marcel and his companions closed their grip on what remained of the French state. The delegates of the Estates-General who were still in Paris were called together in the Augustinian convent on the left bank of the Seine, where they were harangued in the presence of a crowd of armed citizens by Robert of Corbie, the radical delegate of Amiens. With evident misgivings they were persuaded to declare that the marshals had been murdered for good and proper reasons. They solemnly ratified the act. Letters were addressed by Marcel to the principal walled cities and towns of northern France, calling on them to approve what the Parisians had done and inviting them to show their solidarity by wearing the crimson and blue. On 24 February 1358 the Dauphin's Council was reorganised at a public session in the Great Hall of the Parlement. Many of its old members had by now fled the capital. The survivors were purged of those who were overtly hostile to the revolution, and over the next three weeks several prominent Parisians including Marcel, Toussac and Robert of Corbie were added to their ranks. Early in March the Dauphin began to call himself Regent and to deliver acts under his own seal from which the King's name was entirely omitted. But although the seal was his, the decisions were those of Robert le Coq and his supporters.[36]

Some months after the murder of the marshals, when the surviving participants were interrogated by their judges they declared that the King of Navarre had been behind it. One of them even said that the real object was to kill the Dauphin and to put Charles in power. There is, however, no reason to believe the confessions of these tortured wretches. The coup of February 1358 was a purely Parisian affair. Among the leaders, it was a calculated response to what they regarded as an attempt by the Dauphin's officers to reverse the work of the Estates-General by force; among the crowds of panic-stricken citizens, an over-reaction to the news that the Dauphin seemed to be about to move his undisciplined troops into the capital where they would have their lives and property at their mercy. But although the King of Navarre was not the instigator of the violence of 22 February, he was certainly its main beneficiary. Marcel knew very well that for all the promises of immunity that he had extracted from the Dauphin, he had made an everlasting enemy of him. He may even have had some inkling of the impact which the murder of the marshals would have in the provinces, where the news produced a surge of support for the Dauphin as soon as it began to spread. Marcel needed every ally that he could find. So, on the evening of the murder, the Provost of the Merchants rode to the Hotel de Navarre and obtained an audience of Joan of Navarre. According to reports, he asked her to arrange for Charles of Navarre to come urgently to Paris.[37]

At all events Charles came. On 26 February 1358 he entered Paris with a large armed escort and installed himself in the Hotel de Nesle, on the left bank of the Seine opposite the royal palace. Over the following fortnight Robert le Coq, Étienne Marcel and the two dowager Queens negotiated in the utmost secrecy an agreement by which in return for the King of Navarre's support and protection of the revolution, the Dauphin would be made to grant many of Charles' more exorbitant demands. It is true that they did not surrender Champagne or Normandy. But they agreed to make over a large swathe of territory in the Pyrenees, including the county of Bigorre, the whole of the county of Mâcon in eastern France, and yet further territory worth at least 10,000 *livres* per year to be identified in due course. Moreover, the Dauphin was to be made to finance from his non-existent resources a standing army for the King of Navarre numbering 1,000 men-at-arms, for use in whatever fashion Charles thought fit. On 13 March 1358 the King of Navarre left Paris. He had had his way in large measure, without any effort of his own at all.[38]

Outside the walls of Paris, the enemies of the city were gathering round. James Pipe had agreed to observe a brief truce, presumably for money, which had been extended into March while the King of Navarre haggled in the Hotel de Nesle. When it expired in the second week of March, Pipe began a fresh offensive. From their headquarters at Épernon, his men launched a succession of devastating raids along the Orléans road south of Paris. On 12 March 1358 they sacked Arpajon and Montlhéry in one day. Resistance was sporadic and disorganised. Small unpaid garrisons fled at the first appearance of the enemy or looked down impassively from their citadels at the mayhem below. Robert le Coq and his colleagues on the Dauphin's Council alternated between resistance and appeasement. On 15 March 1358 they ordered Pierre de Villiers, the commander of the troops in the capital, to clear the roads to Chartres and Orléans. On the following day an emissary was sent out to Épernon to try to buy another truce from Pipe. Both strategies failed.

To the depredations of the English and Navarrese was added the increasingly violent reaction of the aristocracy of the Île de France against the Parisian revolution. A minor nobleman called le Bègue de Villaines, who had been a friend of Robert of Clermont, declared a private war on the city of Paris in March. He gathered a large band of like-minded men and began to raid the road and river routes around the forest of Fontainebleu, south-east of the city. He posed an even greater threat to the Parisians than Pipe did. For two days in March he succeeded in occupying Corbeil, a major river port on the Seine where the produce of Brie and the Gâtinais was loaded on barges for the markets of Paris. This event caused consternation in the city, since it temporarily cut off the population from its main surviving source of grain. A scratch force of citizens and soldiers had to be found by the Provost of the Merchants to deliver Corbeil from the enemy. But although le Bègue de Villaines was quickly expelled from Corbeil and the Seine reopened to traffic, it was impossible to stop the progressive occupation of the smaller castles and country villages. By the end of March 1358 much of the Île de France south of the Seine was controlled by enemies of one sort or another, and the ring of fire had come within ten miles of the walls of Paris.[39]

Within the city the threat from outside intensified the political passions of the moment. The rhythms of life were marked now by an unending succession of demonstrations and public meetings. Citizens went about armed in the streets in readiness for some unknown danger. For the Dauphin, Paris had become a prison where his movements were continually watched and his decisions made by others. Among his small household of servants and friends there must have been many who overtly sympathized with le Bègue de Villaines. There were continual rumours of plots to seize the Dauphin and take him out of the clutches of Marcel's followers. Some of the rumours were true. When in the middle of March the Dauphin visited the suburban manor of Saint-Ouen, a group of sympathizers tried to kidnap him. One of those responsible was arrested and executed with much publicity in the market of les Halles.[40]

In the event the Dauphin escaped from his tutors without violence or subterfuge. The Parisians and the partisans of Navarre began to realise that if they were to govern France through the Dauphin they could not keep him permanently immured in his capital. The immediate problem was that the nobility, which accounted for a large part of the taxable capacity of the realm, had refused to take any part in the meetings of the

Estates-General in February and were insisting on a separate assembly of their own. After the murder of the marshals they were not willing to hold it in Paris. Accordingly, on 12 March 1358 the Dauphin's Council summoned the nobility of Picardy, Artois, Beauvaisis and Upper Normandy to meet on 25 March in the cathedral city of Senlis some thirty miles north of Paris. Champagne had also boycotted the Estates-General. Another assembly, representing all three estates of the county, was therefore summoned to the town of Provins on 9 April. The Dauphin's presence would be required on both occasions. Arrangements were made for him to be escorted by Charles of Navarre. But at the last moment the plans went awry. Charles was laid low at Mantes by abscesses in his groin and was unable to move. Shortly before 25 March 1358 the Dauphin left Paris. He was accompanied by his uncle the Duke of Orléans and by his cousin the Count of Étampes, by selected councillors and a small military escort. After the gathering at Senlis, which was ill-attended and uneventful, the Dauphin and his companions proceeded to Compiègne to celebrate Easter and freedom. In this small walled town on the Oise which was firmly under the control of his officers, the Dauphin was able to draw on the rising tide of anger among the nobility against the excesses of the Parisian revolution, and to plan a counter-revolution of his own. He closeted himself with two agents of his father who had arrived from England: John's confessor the Dominican Guillaume de Rancé, and his private secretary Yves Derrien. Their discussions were shrouded in secrecy. It was probably at Compiègne that the decision was made to break with the King of Navarre and force the Parisians into submission.[41]

The Estates of Champagne opened at Provins on 9 April 1358. The scene was probably the hall of the palace of the old Counts of Champagne at the summit of the town. The men present came from a vast region which had been barely touched by the fighting south and west of the capital. They viewed the violence in Paris with anger and the Dauphin's apparent adoption of it with incomprehension. The Dauphin addressed them at the opening. He told them that their country was in great peril. He made an emotional appeal to them to remain united in the face of recent disasters. Terrible things had happened in Paris, he said, things which would perhaps be better understood when they had heard them explained by the men responsible. With heavy irony, the Dauphin turned towards the representatives who had been sent by the city of Paris to observe the proceedings. 'Here we have Master Robert of Corbie and the Archdeacon of Paris,' he said; 'they will surely have something to say to you on behalf of the good citizens of Paris.' The two Parisians were evidently taken by surprise. They had no explanation to give. Robert of Corbie declared that the citizens of Paris held the men of Champagne in high regard and earnestly hoped for their support. As for the recent tumults in the city, they would hear the reasons one day from those who had made the decisions. He was sure that they would be satisfied.

The delegates withdrew into the palace garden to talk among themselves. After a short delay the Dauphin and his attendants were invited to join them there. The spokesman of the Estates was Simon de Roucy, Count of Braisne. He declared all those present to be 'good and loyal subjects' who were more than willing to commit their support to the Dauphin. It would be necessary, however, to adjourn the final decision until the end of the month so that certain important absentees could attend. The men of Champagne would attend no more assemblies in Paris. Their next meeting would be held in the small town of Vertus, just south of Épernay. Robert of Corbie's intervention was passed over with contempt. The Estates, said the spokesman, did not see fit to answer him. However, since Jean de Conflans had been the Marshal of Champagne and a great figure in these parts, they would like to know whether the Dauphin himself knew of anything against him which could justify his murder. The Dauphin replied that the Marshal had 'served and counselled him loyally and well'. The spokesman thanked him. The men of Champagne, he said, expected those responsible for his death to be brought to justice.[42]

Early on the following day, 11 April 1358, the Dauphin sent the Count of Joigny north from Provins with a company of sixty men to take possession of the Marché de Meaux, the great island fortress on the Marne east of Paris. The Dauphin himself rode twenty-five miles to Montereau at the confluence of the Seine and the Yonne, upstream of the capital. The castle and fortified bridge at Montereau belonged to the dowager Queen Blanche, Charles of Navarre's sister. Together they formed one of the principal fortresses of the Île de France, commanding the road and river approaches to the Paris from the south-east. The captain of the place appeared above the main gate in full armour and *bacinet*. He refused to open without the personal order of the dowager Queen or the King of Navarre. But on the third summons his nerve failed him. He surrendered possession.[43]

The Dauphin placed garrisons in both Meaux and Montereau and called for artillery to be brought from the stores in the Louvre to strengthen them. A few days later he set up his headquarters at Meaux and issued a series of proclamations addressed to the provinces of the north. One of them declared that the meeting of the Estates-General of Languedoil, which was due to take place in Paris on 1 May 1358, was cancelled. The delegates were to present themselves three days later, on the 4th, at Compiègne. Another proclamation called on all loyal noblemen to join his army on the Marne. The Dauphin had no money to offer them. But they were drawn by anger and enthusiasm, and it was noised about that they would have the plunder of Paris. They came in great numbers, from Champagne, from the Dauphin's own duchy of Normandy, and from the miscellaneous bands of men already recruited by royalist *routiers* such as le Bègue de Villaines and the flamboyant Breton captain, Fulk de Laval. The prospect of recovering Paris did much to boost the morale of the Dauphin's supporters. The proscribed ministers of March 1357 began to come out of hiding. Some of them appeared in the Dauphin's suite, including that great enemy of the Parisian radicals, Simon Bucy.[44]

Even in prosperity great medieval cities lived on the edge of famine. They depended on an elaborate network of road and river routes carrying supplies from great distances and were always vulnerable to natural and human disasters. Paris lay at the centre of a vast shallow basin whose fertile ground and dense population was largely devoted to producing for city's mouths. After two centuries of clearances and intense cultivation, the landscape already looked very much as it did in the age of Corot. To the north, the horizons were limited by a range of gentle hills extending from the Marne at Meaux to the Oise at Chantilly, crowned by dense forest in which generations of French Kings amused themselves in hunting and building. East and south of the capital an intricate pattern of rivers ran through the heavy marshy ground of Brie towards the valleys of the Auxerrois and northern Burgundy. To the south, beyond the broad fringe of forest which extended from Fontainebleu to Rambouillet, the flat featureless plateau of the Beauce Chartrain, then as now one of the richest cereal-growing regions of Europe, extended as far as the eye could see. Paris had grown fat on 200 years of political stability and royal favour. Its citizens had been able to exert absolute economic control over much of this region and, beyond it, over the valleys of the Seine and its major tributaries as well. A ring of rich commercial cities served as economic satellites of the capital, accommodating wholesale markets where grain and wine were incessantly shipped onto barges to meet the demands of the city. Even after the Black Death a population of at least 100,000 depended on the continuance of this commercial miracle. The number must have been swollen in 1358 by the great tide of migrants and refugees fleeing from the English and Navarrese companies.

From Montereau and Meaux, the Dauphin was able to block the whole of the traffic reaching the city from Champagne and Burgundy. These regions had so far seen almost nothing of the war: 'pays de paix et sans guerre' as Étienne Marcel put it in the letter of protest which he addressed to the Dauphin. Although James Pipe and his friends were nominally allies of the King of Navarre their operations perfectly complimented the Dauphin's own, severing Paris from its hinterland to the south and west as completely as the Dauphin was doing from the east. Pipe's garrison at Épernon extended their range east into the forest of Fontainebleu, almost as far as Montereau. The smaller English and Navarrese companies followed his lead. On 19 April 1358 they sacked the walled town of Chateau-Landon and crossed the river Loing, penetrating to within a few miles of Sens and collecting 50,000 *moutons* in ransoms. A few days after the attack on Chateau-Landon another even more destructive raid was mounted in the Gâtinais. The town of Nemours was reduced to ashes. The road to Orléans and the Loire was cut at several points. The region around was stripped bare, although much of it was dower land of Blanche of Navarre and the chief victims were Charles of Navarre's Parisian allies. By the end of April 1358 the city was almost encircled. The only direction from which supplies were still flowing freely was the north. For the moment the valley of the Oise and the great north road to Flanders were at peace. But it was a fragile peace. In the second half of April the Dauphin travelled across the Beauvaisis and into Picardy, building up his support among the nobility of the region. The owners of all defensible castles there were ordered to equip and man them for war. They were encouraged to stop all supplies bound for Paris.[45]

Within the city the Dauphin's operations were regarded as a declaration of war. When the news arrived of the capture of Meaux and Montereau, Étienne Marcel immediately occupied the Louvre, expelling the Dauphin's garrison and replacing them with his own men. The Dauphin's artillery train, which was being loaded onto barges for Meaux, was seized and hauled to the Place de Grève. Marcel did what he could to placate the Dauphin, but it was not much. He addressed a letter of protest to the young prince, defending his actions in language so arrogant and inept that the document was rejected as an impertinence: 'crude, ugly and ungracious'.[46] He begged the King of Navarre to go before the Dauphin and intercede for the city. Charles of Navarre was hardly an appealing ambassador and he had no concessions to offer. But the meeting did take place at the beginning of May, in the open country south of Clermont-en-Beauvaisis where neither prince could ambush the other. The Dauphin arrived with a large body of men-at-arms at his back. The King of Navarre was accompanied by an enormous military retinue in which prominent English and Navarrese captains could be recognised. It must have been a cold occasion and it was certainly an unproductive one. The Dauphin declared that he had nothing but love for the city of Paris and was well aware that there were good men there. But there were others who had treated him with violence and contempt, killing his officers in his presence and seizing his artillery. He did not intend to return to the city until these matters were addressed. The conference continued into a second day. But the Dauphin was immovable. On 4 May 1358 Charles of Navarre returned to Paris to a hero's welcome but with nothing to show for his efforts.[47]

The Dauphin's strength increased from day to day. He had already received a generous grant of taxation from the Estates of Champagne who had reassembled at Vertus, as they had promised, at the end of April. On the day Charles of Navarre returned to Paris the Dauphin entered Compiègne to preside over the Estates-General of Languedoil. The meeting was poorly attended. This was due in part to the sudden change of venue, and in part to the decision of some of the Dauphin's enemies to boycott it. The Parisians appear to have been unrepresented and the same was probably true of their allies among the northern towns. But the nobility and the supporters of the Dauphin were there in force. They included many friends of the murdered marshals and other victims of Étienne Marcel, as well as men who without being touched personally by the events in Paris had been profoundly shocked by them. The delegates were not wholly supine before the Dauphin. They did not abandon the cause of administrative reform, so dear to previous assemblies. They adopted a modified and much reduced version of the great reform ordinances of March 1357 and February 1358. Nor would they have any truck with proscribed ministers such as Simon Bucy, who disappeared at once from the Dauphin's entourage. However, they faithfully reflected the tide of opinion in the provinces, and unequivocally supported the Dauphin against the capital. They replaced all the commissioners appointed by their predecessors for the collection of the taxes, who were close associates of Étienne Marcel working in Paris. They granted a fresh tax to finance the Dauphin's household and his army. Unlike the Parisian assemblies of the past eighteen months, they made some attempt to deal with the problem of the captive King. Although no provision was made for his ransom, a substantial grant was made towards the expenses of his household in exile. The Dauphin appealed directly to the delegates to help him against Étienne Marcel and the murderers of the marshals. 'With one heart and mind' they urged him to take Paris by force and to put the guilty men to death. Robert le Coq, who was present among the representatives of the Church, found himself abused and threatened by members of the Dauphin's entourage. Voices were raised against him in the assembly. They accused him of 'evil' and 'treachery' and called for his dismissal from the Dauphin's Council. Before the proceedings had ended Robert had fled back to Paris in fear of his life.[48]

The decisions of the Estates-General at Compiègne caused great despondency in Paris when they were reported there. The leaders of the city made a final attempt at conciliating the Dauphin before the fighting began. A delegation of masters of the University of Paris came before him to plead for peace. But the Dauphin told them that he wanted the ringleaders of 22 February delivered up to him. He promised that they would not be executed, but that was all. The Parisians ignored him. Their city was already becoming an autonomous republic. The tightening circle of fire beyond the walls and the universal fear of siege and sack generated a brief but intense solidarity among the inhabitants. Marcel and his friends were able to assume dictatorial powers without resistance and virtually without opposition. Their first preoccupation was money. The treasury of Notre-Dame was raided, and coin and plate removed to the coffers of the municipality. Guillaume Marcel, a money-changer distantly related to the Provost of the Merchants, was in charge of this. The Paris mint was taken over and a new municipal coinage issued. At first the metal content was the same as that of the King's coinage. But as metal became scarcer and the municipality's needs more pressing there were frequent and severe devaluations. All around, the city was preparing itself for a siege. Timber breastworks were constructed over the walls and men set to guard them day and night. Ditches were cleared and deepened outside. A whole new wall was constructed on the east side of the city, by the suburb of Saint-Antoine (the modern Bastille quarter). On the south side three of the six gates were closed and ditches and dykes constructed in front of them. The warren of lanes which had been pierced in the walls over the years was blocked. Acres of buildings were razed around the Porte Saint-Jacques, the Porte Saint-Germain and the Louvre. Marcel had plenty of manpower at his disposal. But there was a distinct shortage of experienced soldiers and weapons, which was never overcome. The Provost of the Merchants tried to buy weapons and hire mercenaries at Avignon, then one of the centres of the Mediterranean arms trade. But contact with the world outside was becoming increasingly difficult. Marcel's agent was arrested on the road by officers of the Count of Poitiers.[49]

In the streets the first signs of mass fanaticism had already appeared, bringing to the city something of the atmosphere of 1792 and 1870. Crimson and blue parti-coloured hoods were seen everywhere. Demonstrations filled the markets and public places. Leagues and brotherhoods sprang up to organise processions and to bind their members by great oaths to defend the city against its enemies. A concerted campaign of persecution was mounted against the few noblemen remaining within the walls, who were assumed to be in league with their fellows outside. Many of them were arrested. Some were beaten up. A few were killed. In May, the *maitre du pont* of Paris and the carpenter of the royal household were arrested on charges of plotting with the Dauphin's agents to admit his troops into the city. They were beheaded before an enormous crowd in the Place de Grève. Those who had successfully escaped from the city had their property confiscated behind them. Some of them had their houses pulled down. Agents of the municipality forced their way into the house of the Dauphin's secretary after his departure in order to seize his furniture, disfiguring the royal coat of arms on the wall and abusing his servants as they did so. When Jean de Chambly was found to have joined the Dauphin's army at Meaux his Parisian banker was visited by Guillaume Marcel with twelve armed men at his back. They went through his deposit books and relieved him of 1,100 *écus* which he was found to be holding for the knight. The Provost of the Merchants was 'all powerful', the bankers' relatives protested when the crisis was over and Jean called for his money. Nobody had dared to resist him.[50]

In most of the larger provincial cities of the north there were ardent partisans of the Parisian revolution, men like the mayor of Meaux, who told the Dauphin's officers to their faces that he would have held the town against them if he had had the chance. His feelings were widely shared in the river ports of the Île de France, which were bound to Paris by long tradition and economic interest. In most other places the issue was decided only after bitter divisions among the citizens and some violent incidents. The King's officers, without money or troops, were impotent spectators of this process. When at the end of April 1358 the Dauphin did a brief tour of Picardy, there were plenty of people in Amiens who would willingly have acknowledged his authority. They may even have been the majority. But the mayor, supported by a self-appointed 'captain' of the town and most of the magistracy, were for Charles of Navarre. These were the men who had welcomed Charles on his release from prison and had given him the freedom of their city. They repeatedly called the citizens to arms, organising military exercises and generating an atmosphere of insecurity and fear in which few men were willing to challenge their decisions. When the Dauphin and his escort were at Corbeil, ten miles from the city, the 'captain' summoned the populace to the market square and told them that the Dauphin's men would rape their wives and daughters and reduce their houses to ashes. Not everyone was convinced. A royal sergeant tried to rally the Dauphin's supporters in the crowd. He called on them to divide, the 'French' on one side of the square and the 'Navarrese' on the other. Then they would see which was the stronger. But he was knocked down by one of the leaders of the mob and half strangled by another until, dazed and bleeding from the mouth, he was rescued by his supporters. The outcome was a resolution, ratified by the crowd, to defy the Dauphin and exclude him from the city unless he was prepared to come virtually unescorted. In the following weeks the crimson and blue hoods of Paris appeared in the streets of Amiens. Demagogues at the crossings and markets poured out abuse against the Dauphin, calling him a 'scoundrel', a 'turd' and a 'son of a whore'. Most of the larger cities of the north went the way of Amiens and fell under the control of partisans of Paris and Navarre. In Laon, which had no municipal institutions, the revolution was organised by a miscellaneous group of clerics and lawyers. Their leader was a man who had represented the city at the Estates-General of October 1356 and had sat on the Council of Eighty. The pattern was much the same as it had been at Amiens: demonstrations and mass meetings, speeches against the Dauphin and the nobility, hoods of crimson and blue.[51] By midsummer Étienne Marcel had forged alliances with Rouen, Beauvais, Amiens, Noyon, Soissons, Laon, Reims and Châlons-Sur-Marne, all of whose leaders had sworn to defend the 'holy ordinances of the Estates-General'. Marcel's agents and associates claimed to exercise authority in no less than sixty towns of Languedoil.[52]

Amiens and Laon were certainly not the only places to be drawn into the revolution by radical ideologues. But the great majority were probably drawn to it by fear. The occupation by *routiers* of the *plat pays* around their walls was a disaster for the northern towns, cutting off their food supply, throttling their markets and devastating the suburban gardens and estates of their inhabitants. The class hatreds which were beginning to surface in Paris and in cities like Amiens and Laon struck a sympathetic chord in places which were suffering from the flowing tide of military banditry. Noblemen had failed France at Poitiers and yielded her up to looters. Noblemen had filled the ranks of the companies. Noblemen owned the private fortresses which speckled the landscape around the towns, turning them into centres of organised pillage or failing to stop the likes of James Pipe from doing so. Noblemen were even now flocking to the Dauphin's standard to fight a civil war against Parisian patriots while the English and Navarrese overran the rest of the Île de France.

Rouen was a particularly revealing case. Its mayor may have taken dinner with the King of Navarre during Charles' dramatic visit to the city in January, but he was no Navarrese client. His city had a strong royalist tradition. It was the capital of the Dauphin's duchy of Normandy. It was no friend of Paris, for the two cities had competed for more than a century to control the navigation of the Seine. Yet Rouen defied the Dauphin's representatives and aligned itself with Étienne Marcel, because its citizens were terrified of falling to the bands of *routiers* roaming outside the walls. They did not trust the garrison, which was commanded by noblemen, to defend them. The mayor and leading citizens demanded to be allowed to place their own troops in the citadel. When this was refused they attacked it from the town side for three days until it surrendered. As they explained to the Dauphin months later, they did this 'not as enemies but to defend themselves against the perils about them.' The incident provoked a savage class war between the inhabitants of Rouen and the nobility of the surrounding district. For several weeks the men of the city launched raids against the manors and castles of the nobility in the *plat pays*. They burnt down the buildings. They demolished the walls. They destroyed the stores. The noblemen, led by the royal captain of the *baillage*, responded with a series of equally destructive attacks on the suburbs of Rouen. The revolt of Rouen was more violent and more prolonged than that of most other northern cities. But its root causes were very typical. It was quite commonly believed that city garrisons had more in common with their friends and kinsmen among the *routiers* of the district than with the people whom they were supposed to be defending. The city of Reims joined the revolt for much the same reasons as Rouen did. The Archbishop had refused to block up a gate which allowed direct access between the citadel and the fields outside. The inhabitants believed that the garrison would plunder them or let in the enemy. These fears were not fanciful. The city of Évreux was sacked by the royal garrison in the citadel at the very time when the Parisians were reaching out for allies in other towns. For most townsmen there was now little to choose between the brigandage of angry French noblemen like Fulk de Laval or le Bègue de Villaines and that of an English captain such as James Pipe or the Navarrese subordinates of Martin Henriquez.[53]

On St. George's Day, 23 April 1358, Edward III held a particularly splendid Garter feast: a 'pompous, pointless extravaganza', the Florentine Matteo Villani called it. The celebrations were held at Windsor, where the King had recently begun at prodigious cost the sumptuous restoration of the royal lodgings in the upper ward. Spectators reported tremendous parades of knights carried on magnificent war horses and wearing dazzling plate armour decorated with their arms; ladies clothed in bright colours, jewelled garlands, belts and buckles. On a painted dais draped with gold cloth the King and Queen sat with the King of France and the other guests of honour to watch some hundreds of knights competing in the lists. They included all five of Edward's sons, the Duke of Lancaster and specially invited champions from all over England, Germany and the Low Countries. At the banquet which followed, Edward III and his councillors discussed the draft treaty with John II. They were becoming as concerned as John was by the turn of events in France and by the accelerating dissolution of civil order. They had decided to dispense with the embassy to Avignon which the House of Commons had insisted upon in February. They wanted to complete the draft treaty as soon as possible.[54]

After two weeks of intense negotiation at Westminster the councillors of the two Kings reached agreement. The agreement did not cover all of the points of contention which had been left over in December. But it covered enough to enable John to present the treaty as a *fait accompli* in France before men entirely lost interest in it. The remaining issues were referred to a fresh conference which was to be conducted under the auspices of the cardinals during the summer. On 8 May 1358, in the presence of the Chancellor of England and all the chief councillors of

Edward III, the two Kings appeared in public in the hall of Windsor Castle. The terms were read out. Refinements apart, they appear to have been along the lines of the earlier draft agreed in December. The main advance was the inclusion of a timetable for the payment of John's ransom. The first instalment was now agreed to be payable in November 1358. The French King would then be released on parole. The Kings kissed each other on the lips several times. They exchanged signet rings. Then they took supper together 'moult amicablement'.[55] When the news of these events reached Paris on 15 May it was received with weariness and cynicism. Men did not believe that the English were serious. Some of them, a contemporary said, did not want to believe it. Others had heard it too often before. It was in any event too late to forestall a civil war.[56]

Within a fortnight of the arrival of John's messengers in the capital, the Île de France and the surrounding provinces of the north were consumed by an unparalleled explosion of civil violence and class hatred. The Jacquerie began in the valley of the Oise, north of Paris, in the last days of May 1358. The first recorded incident occurred at Saint-Leu d'Esserent, a large village lying in the shadow of a Cluniac priory on the right bank of the river, which had recently been occupied by a band of armed men. They included two nephews of Robert de Clermont, the murdered Marshal of Normandy. They were almost certainly in the service of the Dauphin. On 28 May a mob of peasants drawn from places up to ten miles away invaded Saint-Leu and fell on them, killing nine and driving the rest to flight. This event was the signal for a spontaneous uprising in the royal castellanies of Senlis and Creil and the neighbouring lordship of Clermont-en-Beauvaisis, which belonged to the Duke of Bourbon. Within a few hours much of the eastern Beauvaisis was in arms.[57]

The origins of the Jacquerie are exceptionally obscure, and not always illuminated by social theorists of the fourteenth or twentieth centuries. Most of the obvious explanations are inconsistent with the facts. The poorest parts of the Île de France, south-west of the capital, and the regions such as the Beauce Chartrain which had suffered the worst war damage, were largely unaffected by it. By comparison the Beauvaisis where the Jacquerie began, like most of the regions to which it spread, was rich agricultural land which had so far suffered very little from the incursions of armed bands. It was a region of free peasants, most of whom worked as tenants on large agricultural estates in return for a variety of customary services. It had suffered like most of northern France from continual war taxation, from the secular decline of agricultural prices and from the progressive attempt of debt-laden landowners to reassert ancient claims to services. It was also exceptionally densely populated even after the Black Death. But these were ancient problems suffered by most of the peasant communities of northern France.

The main causes of the great revolt of 1358 were political. The Dauphin was trying to close the route to Paris by the valley of the Oise, the only one by which supplies could still reach the capital. His partisans had introduced a large number of garrisons into the seigneurial castles of the region. Heavy *corvées* were being imposed on the local communities in order to carry out essential repairs. These developments were scarcely a month old. But they intensified the chronic insecurity of communities which knew all about the devastation of Normandy and the charred villages of the Beauce. In the kaleidoscopic pattern of the war there was no longer any distinction between friend and foe. The men-at-arms of the Dauphin or the King of Navarre, the bands of English and Navarrese freebooters, the garrisons of local towns and castles, no longer had any allegiance which could be counted on. As the inhabitants of the villages and towns of the Oise faced the prospect of being engulfed by the same disasters as the rest, the only recognisable enemy was a nobleman. 'These men are good for nothing but pillaging the common man,' a demagogue shouted. 'Hear! Hear!' the mob answered. Huge crowds of leaderless men spread through the region attacking the manors and castles of the nobility, lynching the occupants, smashing the furniture and burning down the buildings. The Duchess of Orléans was lucky to escape to Paris as the rebels began to destroy her castle at Beaumont-sur-Oise and to murder her retainers. Some sixty noble residences were destroyed in the diocese of Beauvais alone. Stories spread of appalling atrocities: whole households burnt alive, gang-rapes of women, men tortured to death in front of their families. Some of these reports were true.[58]

In the ordinary course the undirected fury of these lynch mobs would quickly have dissipated. But the Jacques, like the Parisians in February, were too frightened of what they had done to disperse meekly to their homes. They needed to stay together to defend themselves against the inevitable reaction. Within a few days of the first outbreak they found a leader, a man called Guillaume Cale. Cale was a rich peasant from the village of Mello, south of Clermont, a 'shrewd well-spoken man with a fine presence', according to a sympathetic contemporary. At the outset of the revolt he proclaimed himself 'Captain of the men of Beauvaisis'. He was assisted by a number of local lieutenants, who probably appointed themselves. Together, this small group of men formed an army of about 5,000 men. They were recruited by a mixture of enthusiasm and force. Cale organised them in units, with banners. He had arms distributed to them. They began within a few days to look like a formidable force. They achieved a brief dominance in the region where the rebellion had begun, which they extended down the valley of the Oise beyond Beaumont and east across the plain of the Beauvaisis.[59]

Guillaume Cale could not have achieved this degree of organisation if he had had only peasants to call on. It is clear that his army included a number of educated men with military experience, and some noblemen. Most of these were very minor figures, village *hobereaux* little better off than their tenants. But others were men of some consequence on a local scale. Jean Bernier, a minor nobleman from Montataire, had been charged by the Dauphin with the defence of the royal castellanies of Senlis and Creil. Colart le Maunier was the Duke of Bourbon's captain at Conti. Germain de Reveillon, who served as one of Cale's deputies, was a retainer of the Counts of Montfort. Lambert d'Autrefontaine was the brother of one of the presiding judges of the Parlement de Paris. The great majority of these men later claimed to have been forced to join the Jacques, and some of them undoubtedly had been. But this was by no means generally true. Contemporaries who witnessed their meetings noticed a significant minority of 'rich men and townsmen' among them, and when the rebellion had ended there were several hundred who had the resources and connections to obtain letters of pardon from the royal chancery. Their motives are unknown. A taste for violence? Greed for booty? An old vendetta? Frustration and fear, born of the progressive collapse of civil authority?[60]

The main source of support which the peasants found from outside their own ranks came from the towns. The townsmen, with their habitual fear of pillage, closed their gates and guarded their walls against the Jacques. But they laid out tables in the suburbs to feed them as they passed by, and some made common cause with them against the nobility. In a number of places townsmen took advantage of the situation to lead the Jacques against local castles which were thought to represent a threat to their security. The men of Senlis recruited companies in the streets to assist the Jacques. Together they sacked and ruined most of the major castles of the Senlisis: Chantilly, Courteuil,

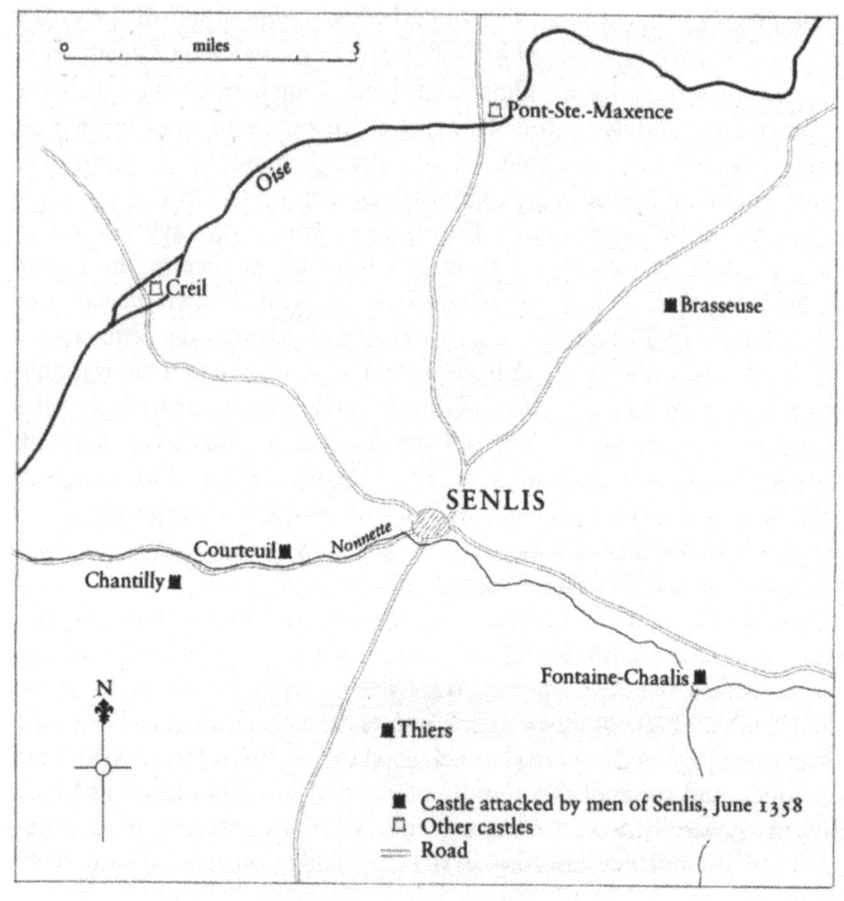

20 The Jacquerie at Senlis, June 1358

Thiers, Fontaine-Chaalis, Brasseuse. Their reasons are obvious when one looks at a map. These places were disposed in a ring around Senlis. In the wrong hands, they were in a position to block every road leading to the city.[61]

By the beginning of June 1358 the rebellion was only a week old, but the Jacquerie had already spread beyond the Beauvaisis into the neighbouring provinces. From the walls of Paris flames could be seen lighting up the ring of hills around the horizon. The castle of Montmorency, seat of one of the great lordships of the Île de France, was captured and burnt. The peasants of the district gathered round the ruins and elected a captain who led them on a ferocious rampage through the lordship, murdering noblemen with their entire families and households, and leaving their corpses to be cremated in the ruins of their homes. East of the capital, the movement spread through the valley of the Marne into the heart of Champagne. Eighty castles and manors were reckoned to have been destroyed between Paris and Soissons.[62] Further north, an army of about 4,000 Jacques including many of Cale's followers from the Beauvaisis, rampaged through Picardy and the provinces of the Somme basin. They laid siege to four of the principal castles of the region, where much of the local nobility had taken refuge. It was the great walled towns which took the initiative in organising the peasants, supplying food, direction and reinforcement just as the men of Senlis had done. The radical mayor of Amiens sent 100 men to reinforce the Jacques attacking castles around the city, only to find himself overruled by the city magistrates and forced to recall them. But the nearby town of Montdidier was more confident of its role. The citizens, led by their mayor, took advantage of the crisis to destroy most of the significant fortresses within five miles of their gates.[63]

The rising of the peasants took the politicians by surprise. Some time passed while they calculated how it might best serve their interests. As soon as he had taken command of the Jacques in Beauvaisis, Guillaume Cale sent a delegation to the leaders of Paris. Étienne Marcel and his friends received them with overt sympathy. They saw in the rebellion an opportunity to clear all fortified structures from the approaches to the city, to settle scores with enemies new and old, and to break the Dauphin's encirclement. They sent back messages of support urging the Jacques to complete the destruction of noble castles and residences around the capital. After the Jacques had captured Montmorency, their captain received a letter from the Provost of the Merchants inviting him to level every castle from the Oise to the Marne: 'They must never rise again,' Marcel wrote.[64] Meanwhile the Parisians set out about fomenting a second Jacquerie south of the Seine, a region hitherto unaffected by the rebellion. Marcel's commissioners organised attacks on the castles of the county of Étampes. They provoked a co-ordinated series of risings in the territory between the Orléans road and the Seine west of the capital. Within the walls a citizen army was being raised. The kernel of this body was found among the *chevaliers du guet*, the nearest thing to a police force which existed in medieval Paris. Marcel used this force to attack castles and noble residences beyond the city walls. They destroyed the keep of Trappes by the road to Dreux, which was occupied by the Dauphin's men. They seized the keep of Palaiseau on the road to Chartres, drinking the cellars dry. Most of the Parisian raids, however, had no discernible strategic purpose. They were simply acts of vengeance against enemies of Étienne Marcel and his allies. The first of their victims was Simon Bucy himself. The great wealth accumulated over his long career in royal service was publicly flaunted in Bucy's three fine suburban mansions at Vaugirard, Issy and Viroflay. All three were wrecked. Two other influential and authoritarian government lawyers, Pierre d'Orgemont and Jacques de la Vache, were despoiled in the same way. When d'Orgemont's manor at Gonesse proved too solid to burn, they pressed the local roofers and carpenters into service to break the roof timbers by hand. But the most spectacular feats of destruction were reserved for the magnificent estate of Robert de Lorris at Ermenonville, the fruits of a decade of corrupt accumulation and sinuous political manoeuvre. The old trimmer was in residence when the Parisians arrived with a mob of Jacques led by Guillaume Cale in person. Robert saved his life by renouncing his knighthood and declaring before the assembled multitude that he was as much a partisan of Paris and an enemy of nobility as any of them. But he could not save his property. The house was stripped bare before his eyes and methodically destroyed. Robert later assessed his losses at 60,000 *livres*.[65]

The Dauphin was still at Meaux. He was preoccupied with his preparations for the siege of Paris, and hardly stirred in defence of the nobility of Picardy or the Beauvaisis, even when the violence began to spread into the regions of Brie and western Champagne around his headquarters. Casting around for some champion who would lead them against the peasantry, a large part of the nobility of the north turned to Charles of Navarre. 'My Lord,' they said to him according to one account; 'you come from the noblest stock in the world; surely you will not stand aside while the whole noble order is obliterated.' Charles assessed the position perfectly. The Parisians were his allies. But he could see that the Jacques would do nothing for his cause and that Marcel's folly in throwing in his lot with them would undo him. The opportunity to present himself as the leader of the united nobility of France was not to be missed. At the beginning of June 1358 Charles put himself at the head of the counter-Jacquerie. He assembled a small but select army, some 400 men drawn from his supporters in Normandy and Picardy, and a contingent of English mercenaries commanded by an adventurer called Robert Scot. They were joined within a few days by about 1,000 noblemen from the Île de France and the Beauvaisis.[66]

The crisis of the peasant rebellion came in the second week of June 1358. The great horde assembled by Cale at the beginning of the month was beginning to disperse into small undisciplined groups wandering about in search of loot. There were two peasant armies still in being. One of them, about 500 strong, was encamped at Silly-le-Long, north-east of Paris, gorged with the loot of Ermenonville. They were commanded by a renegade official of the royal mints called Jean Vaillant.[67] Another much larger force was still assembled south of Clermont-en-Beauvaisis where the revolution had first begun. They were encamped in a strong defensive position on the plateau of Mello.

On 7 June 1358 the King of Navarre reached Mello with his army. He drew up his men in front of the peasants' positions. Cale was away conferring with his captains at Silly. He rushed back early on 8 June to make his preparations for battle. He drew up his men quite skilfully in two lines. He placed the archers in front and protected his flanks with carts and trenches. A small force of cavalrymen, poorly armed and mounted, were kept together in reserve. But Cale did not lead them in the fight. On the morning of 10 June 1358 he was tricked into crossing the lines into the King of Navarre's camp to parley under the protection of a truce. But a King owed no obligations to a peasant, regardless of his word. As soon as he arrived Cale was seized and taken to the rear. Charles gave the signal, and the mass of heavily armed cavalrymen in his lines charged down on the confused and leaderless mass of peasants. The Jacques suffered appalling casualties. Their lines broke up. The rest of Charles' army, led by the King in person, then followed on foot, killing everyone in front of them. The survivors of Cale's army fled north in terror and dispersed. Most of them were caught by horsemen as they ran and butchered on the ground. Cale himself was taken into Clermont and beheaded. The greater part of Charles' army then drifted spontaneously off towards Senlis, where they made a brief and unsuccessful attempt on the town before dispersing.[68]

Meanwhile, Jean Vaillant's army had moved south from Silly. They joined forces with about 300 men sent from Paris under the command of one of Marcel's closest associates, Pierre Gilles. On 9 June 1358 they appeared outside the gates of Meaux where the Dauphin's headquarters were. The Dauphin himself was away, recruiting troops in Burgundy. Most of his army was with him. When the Jacques and the Parisians arrived the mayor of Meaux, who had never made any secret of his hostility to the Dauphin, threw open the gates of the city and laid out food and drink for them on tables in the street. The people of the town overwhelmingly supported him.

Meaux was a small cathedral city on the north bank of the Marne.

On the opposite bank, joined to it by a stone bridge, stood the huge stone fortress known as the Marché, whose walls were reinforced by towers and bastions and surrounded by water on all sides. The Marché was occupied by the Dauphin's wife and baby daughter, a group of ladies of the court, and a bodyguard commanded by the lord of Hangest and le Bègue de Villaines. By chance, they also had with them a small troop of crusaders who were on their way back from fighting with the Teutonic Knights on the march of Prussia. They included that famous antagonist of the Valois, Gaston Phoebus Count of Foix, and one of the heroes of the Anglo-Gascon army at Poitiers, Jean de Grailly, Captal de Buch. Rarely had political divisions been so completely closed by the common interest of caste.

When they had eaten their fill, the Jacques, the Parisians and a crowd of men of Meaux formed themselves up in units on the north side of Marne bridge opposite the fortress, and prepared to storm it. The sequel demonstrated the impotence of even quite large bands of armed men without training or prepared positions in the face of experienced cavalrymen. The men-at-arms in the Marché, only about two dozen strong, emerged mounted from the bridge gate, led by the lord of Hangest. They charged over the bridge into the ranks of the Parisians of Pierre Gilles. They dispersed them with the loss of only one of their own number. The rest of the peasants and townsmen panicked and fled, pursued through the streets by the lord of Hangest's men. The cavalrymen cut down everyone on their path, trapping the fleeing men in the narrow, twisting lanes. Some pursued their prey through the gates into the meadows beyond the walls and cut them down as they fled. The ringleaders were seized whenever they could be found and sent back to the Marché. Then the men-at-arms lit fires in the empty houses at regular intervals across the town. A huge conflagration was started which reduced much of the city to ashes. The ruins were still smouldering two weeks later. When they had finished with the city, the noblemen rode out of the gates to join forces with their fellows in the *plat pays* around. Together, they invaded the villages around Meaux. They killed every peasant that they encountered.[69]

The Jacquerie was over. The only red embers remaining were in Picardy, where several large and organised bands of Jacques were still at large. Some of them had not yet heard about the fate of their fellows at Mello and Meaux. Around the middle of June 1358, the nobility of the Beauvaisis assembled in the village of Gerberoy, north-west of Beauvais, where they were joined by fresh companies drawn from all the provinces of the north. Some even came from regions such as Normandy, Flanders and Hainault, where there had been no Jacquerie. Together, they marched north towards the Somme. An army of peasants was besieging the castle of Plessis-de-Roye, south-east of Montdidier, when the noblemen arrived. Their lines were broken up by a cavalry charge. Most of them were killed. About 300 who took refuge in a nearby monastery were burned alive in it. Another group of Jacques, about 1,300 strong, was surprised at an encampment at Poix. They were wiped out to the last man. Isolated groups of peasants engaged in plundering missions of their own were rounded up and killed. Those who had sloped back to their villages were identified and summarily executed. The atrocities attributed to some of the noblemen engaged in these operations were as bad as anything for which the Jacques had been responsible in the first flush of brutality. Jean de Clermont, a nephew of the murdered marshal of Normandy, personally severed the hamstrings of two men, father and son, who had burned down his manor-house near Montdidier.[70]

The sudden collapse of the Jacquerie was followed by an orgy of vengeance on the part of the nobility. Immediately after his victory over the ragged army of peasants, Charles of Navarre issued instructions for the methodical repression of the rebellion. In every village which had taken part in the 'excesses' four ringleaders were to be selected for execution. The whole of the *plat pays* of the Beauvaisis and the Vexin français was to be laid under a special levy to compensate noblemen for the loss of their houses and crops. Whether this tidy scheme was ever implemented is far from clear. Most of Charles' followers had already embarked on their own campaigns of retribution. The nobility of the Beauvaisis organised themselves in armed bands which rode through the villages of the province burning down houses and destroying property. Large tracts of the northern Île de France were laid waste as if they were enemy territory. In Champagne the counter-Jacquerie was conducted with particular ferocity although the region had been by no means the worst affected by the Jacques. Self-appointed justiciars gathered in armed companies to exact terrible revenge on real or imagined fomenters of rebellion. The lord of Coucy collected his neighbours to kill and burn around his castle. The lord of Saint-Dizier, who believed that he had personally been the target of the Jacques around Vitry-le-François, led a *chevauché* of several hundred noblemen through the villages of the district, identifying supposed ringleaders to be summarily beheaded or hanged from trees. In a few places the cavalrymen indiscriminately murdered all the inhabitants that they could find.[71]

The Jacquerie was triumph for the King of Navarre but a disaster for his cause. Although the Dauphin had contributed nothing to the suppression of the rebellion, the violence of the Jacques provoked a surge of loyalty to the Crown among the nobility of France. His efforts to recruit an army to recapture Paris from Étienne Marcel became increasingly fruitful. On the day when the Parisians led the Jacques against the Marché de Meaux the Dauphin was received as a hero at Sens in northern Burgundy. From here he made a triumphal progress through the towns of western Champagne. In these regions, isolated outbreaks of rebellion among the peasantry were just beginning to coalesce into a great uprising when the whole movement collapsed. The nobility had received a severe shock. They turned in venomous resentment against the Parisians who had encouraged and assisted the peasants. They flocked to the Dauphin's standard. Too late, Étienne Marcel ordered the city's troops and the confederate towns of the Île de France to restrain the indiscriminate violence of the Jacques. Too late, he offered shelter within the walls for more than 1,000 noble refugees from the surrounding regions. These gestures counted for very little beside the widely publicised sack of Gonesse and Ermenonville and the incident at Meaux. Charles of Navarre's carefully constructed scheme of political alliances depended on the strength of feeling against the royal government among the nobility of northern and western France, and on the support of the belligerent population of Paris, two elements which in the aftermath of the class war found themselves separated by a gulf of mutual incomprehension and hatred. He had led the nobility against the Jacques of the Beauvaisis, but he could hardly lead them against Paris.[72]

Charles did not spend long contemplating his dilemma. Shortly after the battle of Mello, as his army was marching on Senlis, he rode south with his retinue to the manor of the kings of France at Saint-Ouen, by the Seine north of Paris, to confer with Étienne Marcel. Then, on 14 June 1358, he entered the capital. He was welcomed by cheering crowds, as dense as those who had greeted him after his escape from prison. On the following morning Charles addressed them in the Place de Grève, from a window of the town hall. His brief but powerful oration was an open bid for power. He spoke of his great love of his country, and of the support which he had received from Paris and the other great cities of the realm. He reminded his audience that he was born of the *fleur de lys* on both sides. If his mother had been a man, would she not have been King of France? Marcel's chief lieutenant and public orator, Charles Toussac followed with a bitter lament about the sad condition of the realm and the misconduct of its government. The hour had come, he said, to elect a 'Captain' who would govern it better. Could there be a better candidate than the King of Navarre himself? Some shouts of 'Navarre! Navarre!' went up from men planted in the audience. Charles was declared elected by acclamation. He swore a solemn oath to defend the city against every assailant 'without exception'. The realm, he declared, was 'profoundly sick'. Its ills were too deeply rooted to admit of any fast cure. 'Do not lose patience with me if I cannot do all that is required at once.' It is far from clear how much support there was in Paris for this radical departure, which had obviously been prepared in private between Marcel and Charles of Navarre at Saint-Ouen. Among the partisans of the revolution, the pure were troubled by the King of Navarre's recent campaign against Jacques on behalf of the nobility of France. Others were disturbed by the spectacle of a man 'of the *fleur de lys* on both sides' surrounded by English and Navarrese men-at-arms. Even the most ardent partisans of the king of Navarre were reluctant to let these men into the capital. Yet what use were they outside it? For the moment men suppressed their misgivings in the face of the common danger. It was the beginning of Marcel's fall from power.[73]

Charles of Navarre's emergence as Captain of Paris cost him a great deal of support among the nobility, as he must have known it would. Although his friends in Normandy and Picardy stood by him, others took their leave to join the growing army of the Dauphin around Meaux. The Burgundians in his retinue told him as they left that they would never fight against the Regent or undermine the cause of the nobility. Undeterred, Charles and Marcel set about organising the defence of Paris. Charles summoned his troops from the garrisons of Lower Normandy and the Beauce. He took into his service all the mercenaries that he could recruit. Inevitably, most of those who answered his summons were Englishmen. They included many of the most notorious brigands then operating in France: James Pipe, who came with troops from the garrison of Épernon; John Standon, a murderer who had fled to Brittany years before to escape trial in England, and made his career in the retinue of Roger David before ending up as a garrison commander in Normandy; John Jewel, another captain of growing notoriety who had made his name in the sack of Pont-Audemer and was destined to achieve greater fame than any of them. An English garrison occupied the fortified bridge over the Seine at Saint-Cloud at the end of June. Companies of English and Navarrese garrisoned Poissy on the Seine. Marcel for his part sent out commissioners to recruit men in the villages beyond the city wall. He wrote a circular letter to the cities of the north urging them to make common cause with Paris. He called on them to elect the King of Navarre as their captain. He begged them to send contingents to help defend the capital against the Dauphin. The results were very meagre. On 22 June 1358 the King of Navarre reviewed his forces in the village of Gonesse north of Paris by the shattered remains of Pierre d'Orgemont's mansion. Some 600 men drawn partly from his own English and Navarrese retainers, partly from the soldiers of the Paris watch and partly from volunteers raised in the streets, joined forces with a few hundred more from the dependent towns of the Paris region. Charles told them that he intended to lead them to Compiègne, where the Dauphin then was. But they got no further than Senlis. Some of them turned aside to make a pointless and unsuccessful attack on Senlis, which was ostensibly an allied town. Then the news arrived that the Dauphin had begun his march on Paris.[74]

The Dauphin moved slowly down the valley of the Marne during the last week of June 1358, followed by an enormous cavalry army. According to contemporary estimates he had about 12,000 men with him, and the true number may well have been about that. On 29 June he set up his headquarters at les Carrières, a small lodge belonging to the Kings of France by the banks of the Seine at the edge of the Bois de Vincennes. His army spread itself out across the eastern approaches to the capital, engaging in running fights with the defenders of the Porte Saint-Antoine and looting villages and hamlets for twenty miles around. The King of Navarre scurried back from Senlis with his miscellaneous army and established himself on the opposite side of the city in the abbey of Saint-Denis, where he could receive reinforcements and supplies brought up by river from the west. Between the two armies, the frightened and suspicious citizens of Paris guarded their walls. They were no more willing to admit Charles' English and Navarrese mercenaries within their walls than the Dauphin's Burgundians and Champagnards.[75]

The King of Navarre did not take long to perceive that the cause was lost. Few of the Parisians had much military experience. Charles himself had no more than about 800 professional soldiers, including some 200 or 300 English archers.[76] They were plainly not enough to confront the Dauphin's army in pitched battle. Yet without being admitted into the city they could not fight from the walls and gates either. The obvious course was to negotiate with the Dauphin while there was still something to bargain with. The problem was the Parisians. They still entertained an altogether unrealistic view of their chances. Moreover, their leaders had no appetite for compromise since they were almost certain to be executed if the Dauphin ever laid hands on them. At an early stage, discreet contact was made between Charles of Navarre and the Dauphin. The dowager Queen Jeanne acted as broker, as she had done in all previous dealings between the two enemies. She was assisted by a commission of mediators who had been appointed for the purpose by the Pope: the Bishop of Paris, the Prior of St. Martin des Champs and the Archbishop of Lyon. At least two of these men had known sympathies for the House of Navarre. On 8 July 1358, when the siege had been progress for about ten days, the Dauphin and the King of Navarre met at a tense conference. It was held in a pavilion erected on open ground outside the Porte Saint-Antoine. The Dauphin made his proposals. He was willing to buy Charles off with landed domains worth 10,000 *livres* a year and a cash sum of 400,000 *écus*, payable in instalments. It was less than he had been demanding during the winter. But it was a substantial offer. As for the Parisians, they were to be required to pay by way of indemnity the whole of the first instalment of the ransom of John II. In return the Dauphin would remit all criminal penalties for their many acts of rebellion. According to those in Dauphin's camp, Charles agreed to be bound by these terms for his own part and to do his best to obtain the agreement of the Parisians. But Charles was uncharacteristically hesitant throughout these negotiations, and evidently uncertain where his best interest lay. At the last moment he got cold feet about abandoning the Parisians before they had the opportunity to consider the terms for themselves. What guarantee would he have, without their support, that the Dauphin's promises would ever be observed? The two men were invited to swear on the body of Christ to observe the agreement. But as the Bishop of Lisieux tendered the divided communion host which would have completed their oath, Charles suddenly excused himself. He had not fasted, he said. It was necessary for him to return to Saint-Denis.[77]

When the leaders of the Parisians were told the terms, they rejected them out of hand. They were suspicious of Charles himself, 'because he was a nobleman.' They were suspicious of the Dauphin, who was

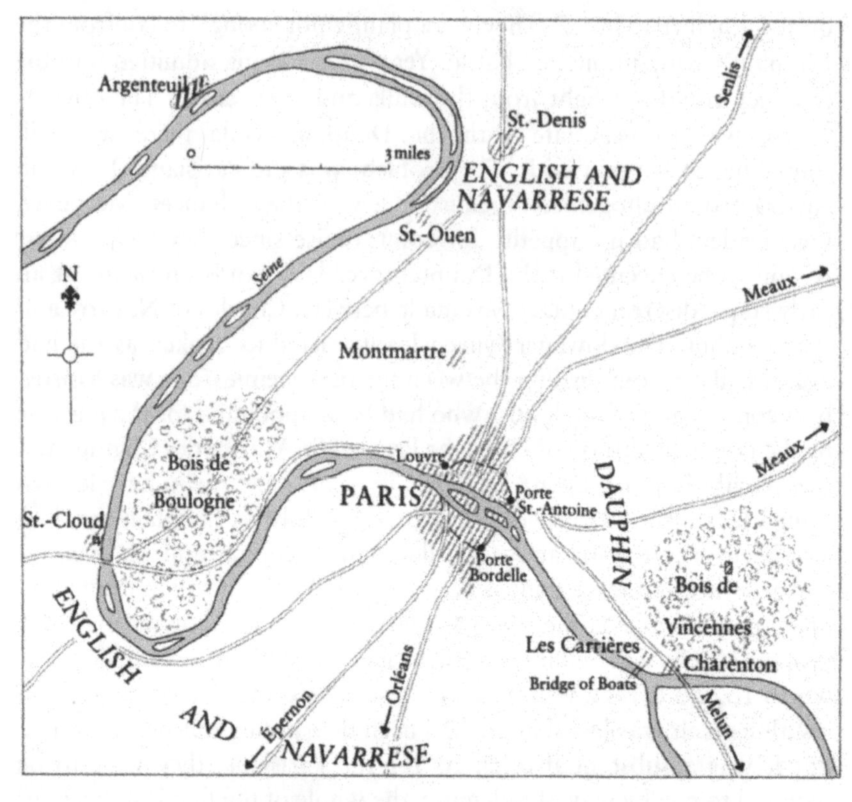

21 The siege of Paris, 29 June–31 July 1358

reported to have sworn to see them dragged on hurdles to their deaths. They were suspicious of the proposed treaty itself, which manifestly served Charles' interests better than their own and might contain further, undisclosed clauses. They declared that if necessary they would fight the Dauphin's army on their own. So the agreement was abandoned. The King of Navarre promised to fight on with the Parisians. But he insisted that it would be on his own terms. The Parisians would have to allow his troops to come within the city walls, and to pay their wages as well. Marcel and his colleagues were obliged to agree. Early on 11 July 1358 some of the English and Navarrese companies and assorted Norman and Picard henchmen of the King of Navarre entered the capital and installed themselves in the royal palace on the Île de la Cité. On the same day Étienne Marcel made his last and most emotional appeal for support to the cities of the north. It included a comprehensive defence of everything that the Parisians had done, from the reforms of the Estates-General to the murder of the marshals of Normandy and Champagne, and a bitter denunciation of the Dauphin who preferred to raise armies for use against his own subjects than to defend the realm against the enemy. Parisians, Marcel said, were free men; they would 'rather die than be reduced to servitude.'[78]

Behind the bravado there were already serious misgivings among some of Marcel's followers. The irony of condemning the Dauphin for failing to defend the realm while challenging him by force with a corps of English mercenaries must have struck many of them. The arrival of the English and Navarrese within the walls turned out to be serious mistake, intensifying the insecurity of the Parisians and the terror of sack and pillage which they had in common with most medieval town-dwellers. For although the men quartered in the palace behaved well enough, the ones in the suburban garrisons continued to kill, burn and steal right up to the walls, notwithstanding that they were now taking regular wages from municipal funds and that their compatriots were defending the city from within.[79]

While the Anglo-Navarrese companies blocked the routes to the capital from the west and north, the Dauphin's men closed it off from the east. On 12 July 1358 they completed the construction of a bridge of boats across the Seine at les Carrières, which enabled them to pass round by the south side of Paris as well. The encirclement of Paris was now almost complete. The critical point of the siege came on 14 July 1358, when the defenders made a determined attempt to destroy the bridge. They planned a triple sortie. One force would emerge from the Porte Bordelle in the university quarter, south of the Seine, while another would issue from the Porte Saint-Antoine north of it. Both would consist mainly of English troops, supported by armed citizens. A third force was to come out of the city by river on fortified barges. The three attacks were badly coordinated. The southern sortie and the barge party reached the Dauphin's bridge first. But the alarm was sounded before they could take possession of it. Although they inflicted heavy casualties on the Dauphin's troops and took some valuable prisoners, including his marshal, they were driven off. The northern sortie started late and was repulsed with heavy loss of life, especially among the supporting citizenry. For the first time Marcel's partisans came to terms with the difficulties of their military situation. Some of them began to demand a resumption of negotiations with the Dauphin. They found enough support among the leaders of the city to force their point.[80]

During the next few days the Parisians made contact with the

Dauphin through Jeanne de Navarre. Another conference was arranged. It was held on 19 July 1358 in the middle of the bridge of boats at les Carrières. The dowager Queen presided, together with the three papal commissioners. The King of Navarre was there. The Dauphin came with a small group of unarmed advisers and no escort. The representatives of Paris came with a large and intimidating company of archers and men-at-arms. But none of the leaders of the revolution was among them. Their principal spokesman turned out to be Jean Belot. He was one of the four *échevins* of the *hanse*. But he had played little or no part in Marcel's revolution and was regarded by the Dauphin's advisers as a loyal servant of the Crown. He and his colleagues were prepared to accept the terms which the Dauphin had offered on 8 July, and eventually a modified version of them was agreed by all parties. The only significant change was that instead of offering a general amnesty the Dauphin required the Parisians to throw themselves on his mercy. However, he promised to take no steps against any of them except by the unanimous advice of four named individuals. Since they included the dowager Queen and the King of Navarre himself, this was a sufficient guarantee for the leaders of the revolution if the Dauphin's word could be trusted. The weakness of the agreement was that, as everyone appreciated, the Parisians who were present only represented a party within the city. A period of persuasion would be necessary before their fellow-citizens could be brought to agree. The whole arrangement therefore had to be made subject to confirmation five days later on 24 July 1358.[81]

When the conference on the bridge was over, the Dauphin decided to take a momentous risk. The main obstacle to the confirmation of the treaty by the Parisians was the presence of a large army at its gates, filled with men whose attitude to the city was a mixture of loathing, fear and lust for plunder. Once the city was open, the assembled nobility in the Bois de Vincennes would be beyond control. The Parisians knew this, and so did the Dauphin. So he decided to disarm himself. Criers passed through the ranks of the army announcing the agreement. The greater part of its strength was dispersed. The Dauphin himself withdrew to Meaux with a small military retinue to wait upon the decision of the Parisians. It was an act of folly, or perhaps of great statesmanship.[82]

Inside the capital the announcement of the treaty was followed by violent recrimination between rival groups of citizens. Charles of Navarre may never have intended to observe the agreement and certainly did not propose to do so if the Parisians were willing to carry on the fight. Étienne Marcel and his friends rejected it outright. They installed themselves in the monastery of St. Eloy on the Île de la Cité under the protection of the garrison in the palace, and began to make plans to hold out. The die-hards were still a sizeable part of the population and they included many of those who were in control of the walls and gates. Bands of them gathered in the streets to attack houses belonging to the Dauphin's officers and friends. The Dauphin's treasurer, who was found within the walls, was threatened with death and finally expelled. But there were other mobs on the streets, whose leaders were losing confidence in Marcel and were outraged by the presence in the city of his praetorian guard of English and Navarrese soldiers. There had already been a number of serious incidents involving the Anglo-Navarrese garrisons of Saint-Cloud and Saint-Denis. Anti-English feeling was rising. On the afternoon of 21 July 1358 the anti-Navarrese party came onto the streets in force and took over much of the city. Thirty-four Englishmen were lynched in the streets or at their billets. The crowd invaded Charles of Navarre's headquarters in the Hotel de Nesle. They seized another forty-seven English officers who had just finished dining with him. More than 400 others were rounded up in their lodgings in the course of the evening. Marcel did his best to keep control. He persuaded the mob to surrender the English prisoners on the pretext that they would be exchanged for French prisoners of war in England. Then he took them under his own protection, behind the walls of the Louvre.[83]

Charles of Navarre was alarmed. He called for reinforcements from his allies and retainers in the west. The Captal de Buch joined him, fresh from his fight against the Jacques at the Marché de Meaux. Philip of Navarre scoured the garrisons of Brittany and Normandy for men. He assembled a considerable force. Like Charles' army around Paris, it consisted mainly of English troops. But they were no longer simply English mercenaries hiring out their arms. Several of the principal English commanders on the Breton march now joined Philip's force with their men, including Robert Knolles, Hugh Calveley, and a Northamptonshire man called John Fotheringhay, who served as Philip's marshal. There cannot have been time to consult Edward III's ministers at Westminster. But his representatives on the spot were certainly implicated. The new army was accompanied by two men very close to the King of England's thoughts, Gilbert Chastelleyn and Stephen Cusington. Chastelleyn, a knight of the royal household for many years, had been one of Edward's ambassadors at the conference which produced the truce of Bordeaux. In 1358 he was one of the King's two personal representatives in Normandy. Cusington, who was the other one, was also the captain of Edward III's garrison at Saint-Sauveur-le-Vicomte. He had been the Prince of Wales' aide-de-camp at the battle of Poitiers and was frequently employed by the King in difficult and confidential missions. Since he had been with Edward at Westminster as recently as June, he knew the King's mind if anyone did.[84]

On the morning after the anti-English riots, there was a tense meeting in the town hall, attended by all the leaders of the Parisian revolution. Charles of Navarre, Étienne Marcel and Robert le Coq were all there. The building was full of armed guards. Outside, in the Place de Grève, a huge and threatening mob gathered, shouting anti-English slogans. Charles tried to address them. He spoke to them in 'belles parolles et douces', He said that the English troops were his retainers, and that they were working for the defence of the city. They had saved it from being pillaged by the Dauphin's army. It was wrong to attack them. But the oratory had lost its spell. He was shouted down. The mob wanted the English prisoners in the Louvre put to death. They demanded that the King of Navarre and the Provost of the Merchants should lead them at once against the garrisons of Saint-Cloud and Saint-Denis. The two men were in no position with their small forces of bodyguards to defy the furious crowd. They were forced to put themselves at the head of a disorderly armed mob and to march against their own mercenaries. In the early evening, between 2,000 and 3,000 Parisians poured out of the gates in the north wall of the city. The King of Navarre and the Provost of the Merchants played for time. They hoped that the anger at their backs would dissipate with time and darkness. They called a halt just beyond the northern suburbs, at the foot of the hill of Montmartre. They formed up their men into three battalions. Then, after a certain amount of delay, they continued north before ordering an about-turn towards the bridge of Saint-Cloud. The Parisians' route passed through a dense wood just east of the bridge. Here, they marched straight into an ambush laid for them by the English garrison. About 600 Parisians were killed. Many of those who escaped were drowned in the bends of the Seine. The King of Navarre looked on impassively from the rear, without intervening. The Parisians believed that he had deliberately betrayed them. They were probably right. Immediately after the disaster, Charles rode as fast as he could to Saint-Denis and shut himself behind the walls of the abbey.[85]

Étienne Marcel returned to Paris to try to appease his people. But he had completely failed to take the measure of their fury. His following drained away before his eyes. Men hurled abuse at him in the streets. They began to gather round the Louvre, baying for the blood of the English whom he was protecting there. A faction of prominent citizens decided to put an end to the Provost's tottering regime.[86] Their leader was a man called Jean Maillard, a rich draper who had once been among Marcel's closest confederates. He gathered around him in secret a group of prominent citizens, including several of Marcel's former allies and at least three of Marcel's kinsmen. Their motives were straightforward. Paris was out of control. The city was now effectively under siege by both the Dauphin and the King of Navarre. Supplies of food had stopped and stocks were low. The city was even cut off from the suburban windmills which ground its grain. The conspirators knew that Philip of Navarre was on his way with fresh troops and might arrive at any time. They believed that unless Paris made peace with the Dauphin, it would shortly be sacked by the soldiers of the King of Navarre. They sent a message into the Dauphin's camp, inviting him to enter the city to restore order. They offered to open the gates to his men.[87]

Marcel was well aware of these covert contacts. At least one letter between the Dauphin and the plotters was intercepted and laid before him. In desperation he decided to take control of the city with the aid of army of the King of Navarre before the Dauphin was admitted to the capital. On 27 July 1358, in defiance of the mob leaders, Marcel released the English prisoners from the Louvre to rejoin their fellows at Saint-Denis. They were escorted past the sullen crowd by an enormous guard of men-at-arms and crossbowmen with drawn bows. Then he arranged with the King of Navarre that he and his friends would take over the guard of one of the gates and admit the Anglo-Navarrese army by night. The chains would be removed from the street corners to allow them to pass rapidly through the city. Lists would be prepared of prominent enemies to be murdered in the first hours. According to Jean de Venette the plan was to proclaim Charles of Navarre King of France. In the last few days of July troops poured into Saint-Denis and the encampments around it. James Pipe brought up the rest of his men from Épernon. The English soldiers at Saint-Cloud joined them. The first companies of Philip of Navarre's approaching army arrived. The coup was fixed for the night of Tuesday 31 July 1358.[88]

On the Tuesday morning Paris was alive with rumour. During the night the houses of men listed for assassination had been marked out with paint. The guards had been changed on some of the city gates and

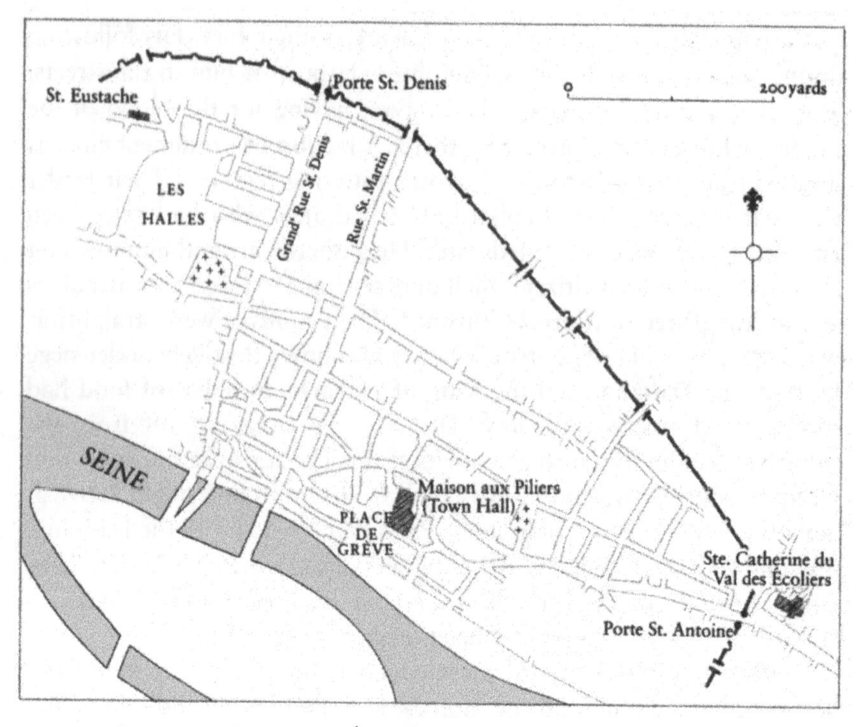

22 The fall of Étienne Marcel, 31 July 1358

the keys removed. A huge demonstration was organised by the anti-Marcel factions. The crowds crammed into the market of les Halles. They turned quickly to violence. They began to attack known supporters of the King of Navarre. Led by two confederates of Maillard's, lynch mobs invaded the mansion of Josseran de Maçon, the King of Navarre's treasurer, which was by the church of St. Eustache. Josseran had fled. He was closeted with the Provost of the Merchants and a handful of his closest associates. It began to look as if Marcel and his friends had been baulked. They believed that without swift action, their enemies would open the gates to the Dauphin before they could let in the English and Navarrese.

Towards the middle of the morning the mob at les Halles, deprived of their prey, began to drift across the rue Saint-Denis towards the Place de Grève. Marcel made for the northern gates of the city. He was accompanied by Josseran de Maçon, a few close colleagues and about fifty armed horsemen, some of them in full armour with helmets. Without warning they appeared at the Porte Saint-Denis. This was in the sector commanded by Jean Maillard, and Maillard's men were still in control of it. Marcel confronted the gatekeepers. The garrison of the bastion, he said, was too large. It ought to be reduced. He ordered them to deliver up the keys to Josseran de Maçon. The gatekeepers refused. In the midst of the altercation, Maillard himself arrived. He told Marcel that the keys would not be surrendered. Then, cutting short the dispute, Marcel and his companions remounted and escaped as fast as they could towards the Porte Saint-Antoine in the east of the city. Maillard rode back down the rue Saint-Denis to find help. As he went, he shouted out the war cries of the kings of France: 'Montjoie! Saint-Denis!'. The cry passed through the spreading crowd as it was taken up by one group after another. The head of the mob had by now reached the Place de Grève. In the town hall, they found a banner of the Dauphin's arms. Then, with the banner held aloft before them, they pressed through the narrow lanes of the Grève quarter to cut off the Provost of the Merchants.

The Porte Saint-Antoine was a large fortified gate on the east side of the city which opened onto the old Roman road to Melun. It stood just west of what is now the church of St. Paul-St. Louis in the rue Saint-Antoine. In the mid-fourteenth century, when the Bastille was yet unbuilt and most of the Marais was still a marsh, it was one of the principal entrances to Paris. The gateway had been put in the hands of partisans of the King of Navarre. But they were no more willing to surrender possession to Marcel than Maillard's men had been at the Porte Saint-Denis. They were indistinctly informed about what was happening and suspected a counterplot. Marcel pretended that the guard needed to be changed. They demanded to know why. He told them that he had letters of authority from the King of Navarre. They asked to see them. Voices were raised. The mob was already appearing through the streets behind them. Marcel and his companions tried to break out of their corner. But they were hopelessly outnumbered. The first bands of men fell on the Provost's escort and butchered them. Someone raised a sword high above the crowd and brought it crashing down on Marcel's head. Outside the Porte Saint-Antoine stood the church of Ste. Catherine du Val des Écoliers, which belonged to the Augustinian friars. It was the place to which the bodies of the marshals had been taken in February, which was now destined to receive the bodies of their murderers. The remains of Marcel and one of his companions were retrieved from the carnage, stripped naked and spread out on the steps in front of the church, where they were left unburied in the summer heat for several days.[89]

As the news of Étienne Marcel's death spread, there was a spontaneous uprising all over the city. All the fury which had once been directed at the friends and servants of the Dauphin was turned against the associates of Marcel and Charles of Navarre. Men stuffed their parti-coloured hoods into hidden corners of their homes, said Jean de Venette, and went out on the streets to cheer and shout out the Dauphin's name. Gilles Marcel, the Provost's cousin, and Jean de Lisle, one of the captains of his militia, were found hiding near the Place de Grève in the mansion of the Abbot of Ourscamp. They were summarily put to death. Another of the Provost's associates was found at the Porte Saint-Martin, trying to get out of the city. He met the same fate. All three corpses were dragged to St. Catherine's Church to be exhibited on the steps beside Marcel's. On the following morning the lynchings were stopped, and replaced by more methodical procedures. A systematic search was organised and most of the leaders of Marcel's government, together with a large number of sympathisers, were rounded up. Thomas de Ladit, Charles of Navarre's tireless chancellor and ambassador over more than five years, was found disguised as a monk. Charles Toussac and Josseran de Maçon were arrested and escorted through the screaming crowd to the Châtelet to await the Dauphin's pleasure with the rest.[90]

In the abbey of Saint-Denis the King of Navarre proceeded immediately to extremes. He resolved to embark upon a full scale civil war against the Dauphin and the Parisians, in alliance with the King of England. A commission of six of his closest councillors sat down with Gilbert Chastelleyn, Stephen Cusington and John Fotheringhay to work out what terms would be acceptable to Edward III. They drew up an agreed memorandum to be presented to the two principals. It envisaged nothing less than the partition of France between Charles of Navarre and the King of England. Charles was to have Champagne and Brie. Subject to further negotiation, he was also to have Picardy, the county of Chartres and the whole duchy of Normandy. He would have become the dominant power in northern France. Edward III would become King of France with the rest of the royal domain and his own conquests and inheritances in the south-west. This remarkable document was sealed on 1 August 1358, on the day after Marcel's violent end.[91] On the following day Charles of Navarre and his brother Philip began to test the defences of the capital. They led their army round the north side of the walls. They occupied the abbey and suburb of Saint-Laurent on the Senlis road. It looked as if they were preparing for an assault on the city.

But they were too late. On the evening of 2 August, the Dauphin entered Paris by the Porte Saint-Antoine. His cavalcade rode past the battered corpses of his enemies, still exhibited on the steps of St. Catherine's church. From Saint-Laurent, the King of Navarre could see the great cloud of dust thrown up by their horses as they came up the Roman road. He retreated with his men to Saint-Denis. There, he plundered the abbey and marched away to Mantes, to prepare larger schemes of revenge.[92]

The purge of the Dauphin's enemies continued for several days. A commission of ten men, most of them professional judges, was set up to find and punish supporters of the defeated revolution. Charles Toussac and Josseran de Maçon were dragged on hurdles from the Châtelet to the Place de Grève a few hours before the Dauphin's entry into the city, and beheaded in front of the town hall. Pierre Gilles, who had led the Parisian army at Gonesse and Meaux, was beheaded at les Halles two days later. Gilles Caillard, a renegade knight who had held the Louvre for Étienne Marcel, died with him. A succession of minor figures followed to their deaths during the next few days. Others died more obscurely, the victims of public or private vendettas. We do not know what crimes caused the Dauphin to have Jean Beauvoisin immured in an oubliette until he died. Michel de Saint-Germain, a long standing enemy of the brothers Braque, the Dauphin's coinage specialists, was taken to the Châtelet and drowned without trial, record or confessor. For every man who died there were scores more who were denounced by neighbours or enemies for real or imagined connections with the revolution. They fled, or passed uncomfortable weeks in prison, or had to plead for pardons to save themselves. 'Les choses sont trop nouvelles et trop chaudes', a cowed sympathizer said, turning away the messenger who brought him a letter from the King of Navarre at the height of the proscriptions. This man, a canon of the Sainte-Chapelle, had already been arrested once and had had his silver taken from him. Robert of Corbie, the radical representative of Amiens at the Estates-General, was found hiding in the house of the parish priest of St. Genevieve and taken to the Châtelet. Jean Marcel, who had played a very minor role in his brother's revolution, was kept in prison for some time before he was eventually pardoned and released. Many others had their possessions confiscated and distributed to friends and ministers of the Dauphin and to the rapidly growing band of time-servers and sycophants who were congregating around them. They included some very insignificant revolutionaries: a sergeant of the watch, a valuer who had appraised the confiscated goods of Marcel's victims, a man who had been seen wearing a parti-coloured hood, assorted loudmouths who had been heard to utter imprecations against the Dauphin.[93]

On 10 August 1358 a general amnesty was announced. It extended to the city of Paris, to its officers and to all its inhabitants, except only those who had been in the 'secret councils' of Étienne Marcel. By then, almost all those who had been in Marcel's 'secret councils' were dead. Of the great figures of the revolution only Robert le Coq had succeeded in escaping from the city. The last victim of the purge was Thomas de Ladit. Being an ordained priest, he could not be condemned to death. But he was kept in custody and interrogated at length about the whole of Charles' conduct from the time of his escape from Arleux. He was made to produce an extravagant confession, part of which he had to recite in public before the Dauphin and a large audience of invited guests. Then, on 12 September, he was taken from the royal palace to be transferred to the Bishop's prison. As he emerged with his guards into the rue de la Barillerie, he was attacked by a band of assassins lying in wait for him and battered to death. His death was undoubtedly convenient, and probably officially arranged. His body lay exposed for several hours in the street under the torrential rain until, as evening drew in, men came to drag it to the strand and cast it into the Seine.[94]

CHAPTER VIII

The Companies 1357–1359

Encouraged by the complaisance of the King of England and the disintegration of the French government, successive hordes of soldiers spread through the provinces of France, occupying castles, manors and church towers from which they subjected the districts around to a brutal military occupation before passing on to find fresh prey. Contemporaries looked upon these incursions as random catastrophes, visitations of a capricious God. Yet the movements of the companies followed a logical and more or less consistent geographical pattern. They spread outwards from two sources: from the marches of Brittany and Normandy the companies moved across the plains of the north; from Gascony they penetrated up the great river valleys into the *massif central* and from there to the provinces of the Rhone and the Sâone. It was not until 1358 that the two streams mingled in the valley of the Loire. There was a pattern too in the regions which they left alone. Provinces such as Poitou and Saintonge, which had been exhausted in the wars of the 1340s, escaped relatively lightly in the 1350s. Others, such as the principal seneschalsies of Languedoc and the duchy of Burgundy, which had strong local institutions and well developed systems of defence, succeeded in fighting off the invaders until the 1360s.

Gascony, the territory of the victorious power and the home of most of the companies, enjoyed a brief and golden peace. There were no major French operations there after the Count of Armagnac's raids in 1355. The last significant French garrison on the lower Garonne, at Marmande, was captured at the end of 1359. The finances of the duchy steadily improved as the profits of the mints and custom-houses rose from the disastrous levels of the 1340s and expenditure on war wages and garrisons fell. In the heartlands of the English duchy, around Bordeaux and Bayonne, the government slowly re-established its prestige and its authority.[1]

Edward III's officers attempted with some success to spread this *pax anglicana* beyond the traditional heartlands of the duchy into the disputed provinces of the march. In the valley of Dordogne around Souillac, where the provinces of Périgord, Limousin and Quercy met and the Bordeaux government was at the limits of its reach, the King of England's representative, Élie de Pommiers, established his own authority over much of the region and eased out the larger companies within a year of the battle of Poitiers. Most of them were led by young men from prominent Gascon families whose worth was concentrated in the Bordelais and the Landes and whose fathers and uncles were closely associated with the government of the duchy. They were vulnerable to official pressure. The eldest son of the lord of Albret was bought out of Fons and its satellite garrisons in eastern Quercy by the local communities. Pierre de Montferrand, whose garrison at Bétaille in the viscountcy of Turenne was one of the most dangerous in the region, sold out to the viscount in August 1357 after only five months of occupation. The price was just 2,500 florins at a time when a well defended castle in virgin territory could command more than 20,000. None of these places was reoccupied so far as is known, and some may have been demolished. Other captains were more obstinate. The captain of Nadaillac, who preyed on the roads around the hill town of Gourdon, refused to go notwithstanding direct commands from Bordeaux and Westminster. In January 1358 the Seneschal of Gascony, Sir John Cheverston, came up the Dordogne valley with 2,000 men-at-arms, a train of canon and a safe-conduct from the French conservators of the truce to deal with men like him. In this corner of south-western France it is possible to follow events in detail from the accounts, minutes and newsletters in which the towns recorded their tribulations.[2] But it is very likely that a similar process was in train in Périgord and the Agenais as well. The sparseness of the evidence is itself suggestive. War is better recorded than peace. The French retained important garrisons in both provinces, including those at Agen and the *bourg* of Saint-Front at Périgueux. But the lesser towns and the *plat pays* were so far under English control that they had to be omitted from the summons of the Estates of Languedoc.[3]

Languedoc, which bounded the English duchy on the south-eastern side, was the paradigm example of a successful locally organised defence. The province comprised a tight political union of the three southern seneschalsies of Toulouse, Carcassonne and Beaucaire, which were loosely associated with the outlying dioceses of Rodez, Cahors, Albi and le Puy on their northern flank. In the middle of the 1340s Henry of Lancaster's campaigns in the south-west had made it necessary to put the defence of Languedoc on a more or less permanent war footing at a time when the government in Paris was preoccupied with events in the north. Philip VI stopped trying to organise the defence of Languedoc from Paris, and under the pressure of war the region gradually grew apart from the rest of France.

The critical development was the emergence of efficient local assemblies with extensive tax-raising powers. Some of these represented a single seneschalsy. Some represented quite small districts. But the most important were the assemblies of the whole province, which met at frequent intervals under the auspices of the Lieutenant or his deputies. The history of the Estates of Languedoc really begins with the great assembly in Toulouse in February 1346 which was presided over by John II when he was Duke of Normandy and royal Lieutenant in the south-west. From this time until the end of the wars, in the second half of the fifteenth century, they met separately from those of the rest of France, and developed on lines which were in some respects peculiar to themselves. In the first place, they generally represented only the towns. The towns formed a political community of their own, disposing of much of the taxable wealth of the province, linked by the habit of consultation, by firm local alliances and by common fear for the security of their walls and trade. They were the financial strength and organising spirit of the defence. The nobility and the Church by comparison played a more subdued role, generally confined to granting approval for the collection in the *plat pays* of the taxes ordained by the towns. The Estates of Languedoc voted regular taxes for the defence of the region throughout the 1350s, which were collected and spent under the control of its own officers. They established a system of assessment by which the towns made themselves responsible for raising lump sums based on a conventional figure for the number of hearths or, occasionally, heads. It was a great deal more productive than anything so far achieved in the more fragmented provinces of the north.

The dominant political figure in Languedoc remained John, Count of Armagnac, a man profoundly sympathetic to these developments. Even after January 1358, when he was replaced as Lieutenant by the ineffectual Count of Poitiers, he retained most of his influence over the affairs of the province. Armagnac deliberately encouraged the autonomy of the Estates in order to free himself from the financial and auditing departments of the government in Paris, which had crabbed and confined his predecessors. It was Armagnac's decision, when John II was captured at the battle of Poitiers, to countermand the Dauphin's orders summoning representatives to attend the Estates-General in Paris and to convene them at Toulouse instead. In the next four years Languedoc conducted its affairs almost entirely independent of the Dauphin's government, organising and financing its own defence, formulating its own foreign policy and dealing directly with the captive King without reference to the views of his ministers in Paris. The province called itself a *patria*, the natural instinct of men who spoke in another idiom, observed another law and referred in their letters to 'Paris en France'.[4]

In May 1358 the Estates of Languedoc meeting at Toulouse were persuaded to swallow their traditional distaste for taxation in time of truce and to finance an army of 2,000 men for two months. A scheme of defence was devised, directed by local captains appointed for each seneschalsy. Fortified places were to be inspected to ensure that they were either properly defended or demolished. There was of course a world of difference between ordaining these matters and carrying them out. But some of them undoubtedly were carried out. There are signs of work on the urban fortifications of Languedoc in the spring and summer of 1358 and some evidence that cavalry forces were being raised at short notice to reinforce vulnerable points on the march as danger threatened them.[5] Although official missives continued to lament the weak defences and anarchic condition of Languedoc, the truth was that the region was well off by comparison with almost every other part of France. The outlying dioceses, particularly those of Rodez and Cahors, suffered from continual incursions by the Gascon companies. However, the three principal seneschalsies were virtually untouched. Both the major threats to their security in this period, from the Archpriest's horde in 1357 and from Robert Knolles in 1359, were beaten off with ease.

The main consequence of the growing authority of Bordeaux and the remarkable resilience of Languedoc was to drive the Gascon companies north and east towards Auvergne and the mountains of the *massif central*. By 1357 these had become the principal field of the Gascons' operations. Auvergne was a large province comprising several geographically distinct regions. Haute Auvergne, corresponding to the diocese of Saint-Flour and the royal *baillage* of the Mountains, was a thinly populated area of lava hills, dense forest and high grassland used by shepherds as summer pasturage. To the north, beyond the Monts Dore, the landscape opened out into the broad valley of the Allier, a rich and populous land, 'bon pays et fertil de blez, de vins, de bestail',[6] which contained the chief cities of Auvergne: the ecclesiastical city of Clermont, its twin town of Montferrand, and Riom which was the administrative capital. West of the Monts Dore, extending towards the high Limousin plateau, lay the scattered territories of the county of la Marche, poor land shared between rye, meagre pasturage and dense forest, which had for many years been dominated by the princes of the house of Bourbon. Auvergne had none of the advantages of Languedoc in the fight against the companies. The region had lost its autonomy when it was absorbed into the royal domain at the beginning of the thirteenth century. It had no tradition of political organisation. The provincial Estates, which had come into existence in the last decade in response to the Crown's demands for war finance, met regularly enough during the crises of the following decade. But their authority was not always accepted by taxpayers and they proved to be a very ineffectual forum for organised resistance. The defence of the province depended mainly on the two royal *baillis* and on the Dukes of Bourbon. None of them was in a strong position. The authority of the *baillis* had suffered grievously from the collapse of the government in Paris and from want of funds. As for the Bourbons, they had recently experienced some serious reverses. The previous Duke had died at Poitiers, leaving his domain crippled by debt. His younger brother Jacques, Count of la Marche, the ablest soldier of his family, had been captured and taken off to England. The fortunes of the house were left in the inexperienced hands of the late Duke's widow and his nine-year-old son.

The first Gascon bands had entered Auvergne from the west in 1355. At the outset their operations were confined to the district of Aurillac and the foothills of the Cantal. But in the last few months of 1355 they became bolder. An attempt on Saint-Flour was beaten off. Then, in March 1356, they found a foothold in the county of la Marche, where they seized the walled town of Felletin and made it into a base for raiding across the mountains and into the valley of Allier. They attacked the suburbs of Clermont. Their spies were found reconnoitring the defences of Issoire. At Saint-Pourçain, the mint had to be temporarily closed and moved within the castle walls. These events caused much alarm in the region. The Estates of Auvergne met in emergency session. The *bailli* organised a siege of Felletin which continued fitfully from April to August without effect.[7]

Arnaud d'Albret of Cubzac, the captor of Felletin, belonged to a family which had been intimately concerned in the looting of Périgord and Quercy. The rape of Auvergne during the next decade was to be very largely a cooperative venture of his famous and prolific clan. Arnaud was bought out of Felletin by the Duke of Bourbon in the autumn of 1356 for 21,000 *écus*, then one of the largest ransoms ever paid for the delivery of a single castle. He must have promised to withdraw from the province, but he certainly did not withdraw very far. Instead he joined forces with his cousin, Arnaud-Amanieu d'Albret and together they occupied the castle of la Chapelle-Taillefer just across the border in the diocese of Limoges. The two men set up a new centre of operations there and at another fortress further south in the fortified manor of Beaumont near Tulle. From these places they recruited fresh bands of adventurers from every part of the south-west. Early in 1357 the Gascons re-invaded Auvergne. They briefly occupied Volvic on the eastern face of the Monts Dôme and the great keep of Sermur, only fifteen miles from Arnaud's former headquarters at Felletin. Other Gascon bands pushed up the valley of the Allier and established themselves in the Bourbonnais.[8]

The defence failed throughout the region. Jean de Boulogne, the King's brother-in-law served briefly as royal Lieutenant during the wretched winter of 1356–7 without achieving anything. The nobility of Auvergne was paralysed by its own quarrels and divisions. Some of them tried to ride out the tempest by making tactical alliances with the *routiers*. The provincial Estates met in January 1357 and voted fresh subsidies. More was voted later. But although the first fruits of these taxes were relatively abundant, as the disorder spread collection became increasingly difficult. As the companies extended their operations the tax base was gradually destroyed and with it the last prospect of expelling them without outside assistance: a vicious circle which much of France would soon experience.[9]

The truce of Bordeaux made no difference at all to the fate of Auvergne. In the first place its enforcement was entrusted largely to the bandits themselves. The four conservators nominated by the Prince of Wales included Arnaud d'Albret himself, together with his brother and another of his cousins, all of them active protagonists in the guerrilla war. Some six months into the truce Arnaud took into his service his bastard cousin Bertucat, who was probably the ablest and certainly the most brutal of his ambitious tribe. Bertucat d'Albret, like many of his kinsmen, had begun his career in Quercy. He had probably served under his half-brother at Fons. In the early autumn of 1357, after Fons had been bought out, he suddenly appeared in Auvergne at the head of Arnaud's company and reoccupied Sermur. Here he established a permanent base and resumed the spoliation of Auvergne as if nothing had happened. The Dauphin's Council was helpless. They were prevailed upon to appoint a captain for each of the two *baillages*, but neither of these men made the least impression on the companies. The nobility of Auvergne raised another local army. They called it the army of the 'Sermur front'. It could not even contain Bertucat's men within the walls.[10]

Episodes like these were followed with intense interest among the nobility of Gascony and reports of the fortunes to be made in central France drew crowds of ambitious and violent young men up the river valleys to the mountains of Auvergne. In January 1358 fresh bands were reported to have arrived at Sermur and more were gathering at Beaumont on the march of Limousin to 'waste, smash and loot' in Auvergne. Bertucat's garrison held out at Sermur until May 1358 when they were bought out by the Estates of Auvergne for 3,000 *écus*. The price, which was low, suggests that the Auvergnats had finally had the better of the fighting. But even as they were leaving Sermur fresh men were gathering in force in the valley of Dordogne to join them. Within weeks Bertucat's bands and their emulators were once more roaming freely over the hills. At the southern extremity of the province, one of his subordinates, a Castilian by the name of Sandoz, occupied the small castle of Montbrun on a spur of rock 10 miles south of Saint-Flour and used it to wage a long guerrilla war against the inhabitants of the town. Years later, after the garrison had gone, the men of Saint-Flour counted the cost: 1,000 local men killed; a parish church destroyed; more than 400,000 florins worth of damage to property; suburbs burnt to the ground; the town penetrated several times by armed bands and whole quarters devastated before they could be expelled. The implications for the surrounding regions were graver still. Auvergne, together with the adjoining parts of Limousin and la Marche, became the reservoir where the companies collected their strength and from which they spilled out into the valleys of the Loire, the Saône and the Rhone.[11]

Rivers are rarely natural frontiers. The great corridor of the Rhone and Saône marked the frontier of the French kingdom, dividing it from the principalities of the east which were loosely associated with France but belonged politically to the German empire. But the regions on either bank had economic and political links of great antiquity. As late as 1365 a German emperor would have himself crowned by the archbishop of Arles in the church of St. Trophime as sovereign of the Kingdom of Arles and Vienne, a ramshackle structure which nominally comprised most of the territories of the east bank. However, for more than a century before this event the kingdom of Arles and Vienne had been little more than a prestigious abstraction. Its component parts were deeply penetrated by the language and culture of France and by the pervasive influence of French wealth and power. The last of the independent imperial Counts of Burgundy had abandoned the county to Philip the Fair of France at the end of the thirteenth century. Lyon, the great city at the confluence of the two rivers, was annexed by France at the beginning of the fourteenth. Savoy, a huge ungainly territory straddling the Alps from the Rhone to the plains of northern Italy, was ruled by princes who were usually dependable allies of France. The Dauphiné, an immense mountainous principality wedged between the Rhone on the west and north and the Drome on the south, was acquired for cash at one of the lowest points of France's fortunes in July 1349. The territory and title of the Dauphins passed to the eldest son of the King of France.

Of all the francophone lands beyond the Rhone the must vulnerable was Provence. Fourteenth-century Provence was a loose association of territories belonging to a Mediterranean culture which extended from Barcelona to Genoa. There was the county of Provence proper, which stretched from the river Durance to the sea; the dependent county of Forcalquier north of the Durance; a medley of scattered, semi-independent lordships at the margins; and the Comtat Venaissin, north of Avignon, which had been severed from Provence at the beginning of the thirteenth century and ceded to the papacy. The whole region had been a dependency of France since 1246, when the heiress of the last independent count had married Charles of Anjou, the ablest and most ambitious of Louis IX's brothers. As a result of Charles of Anjou's conquests in Italy Provence had become an outlying possession of the Angevin kingdom of Naples, thoroughly taxed but rarely visited by its rulers. It was a political backwater. Ambitious Provençal noblemen, lawyers and churchmen made their way to the court of Naples, where some of them achieved high office and great wealth. They left behind them a territory governed by an uneasy coalition of competing local interests. In the coastal regions the government depended mainly on the city of Marseille, whose trade had prospered mightily by the Mediterranean empire of the Angevins; and on the more capricious affections of the lords of Les Baux, the main power in the plains and marshes of the lower Rhone, whose leaders had traditionally been powerful figures at the court of Naples. In the interior Naples seemed infinitely more distant, and the government's position was more difficult. Authority was contested between the Seneschal, who was the count's representative; the Estates of Provence, meeting regularly at Aix; and a small group of powerful barons from the north. The natural tensions of this troubled region were aggravated by economic misfortune. The Rhone valley had suffered like the rest of eastern France from the shift of Europe's trade routes as well as from the disruption of the western Mediterranean in the successive naval wars of Genoa, Naples and Aragon. To these problems were added the natural disasters of the 1340s: torrential rain, floods, crop failure and famine. The Black Death had a particularly severe impact in Provence.

Provence had belonged since 1343 to Charles of Anjou's great-great-granddaughter Jeanne d'Anjou, Queen of Naples, a dissolute and conspiratorial young woman who passed her long reign in violence and intrigue in Italy until she was finally murdered in 1382. In the latter part of the 1340s there had been a grave crisis in the affairs of the kingdom of Naples. Jeanne's husband Andrew of Hungary had been strangled outside her bedroom door in September 1345. Two years later, she had married her cousin Louis of Taranto, an ambitious and unscrupulous politician who was probably responsible for the murder. He filled the administration with his clients and friends and antagonised powerful interests in Naples. They included the house of Les Baux, two of whose most prominent members were killed resisting his ambitions. The disorders of the kingdom of Naples inevitably spilled over into the politics of Provence where so many of the principal actors originated. Jeanne's enemies multiplied as her new husband attempted to impose a succession of unpopular Italian seneschals on the resentful lawyers and noblemen of Aix. In the spring of 1357 Raymond des Baux and his cousin Amiel, together with a large coalition of local malcontents, planned a rebellion against the authority of the Count in Provence. They proposed to raise an army locally from their own resources and another in France from the mass of unemployed soldiers thrown onto the market there by the truce of Bordeaux. To do this they turned to a famous captain, Arnaud de Cervole, who was universally known in his lifetime as the 'Archpriest'.[12]

Arnaud de Cervole was the cadet of a minor noble family of the Castillonais on the Gascon march. At an early stage he entered the

Church and became the archpriest of Vélines in the diocese of Périgueux, from which he derived his famous soubriquet. Long before Arnaud was deprived of his benefices by the archbishop of Bordeaux he had become a man of war mixing (according to a disciplinary report) with 'brigands and men of base extraction'. In the early 1350s he appears in the pay rolls of the French army in the south-west with his own company of eighty men. There is some evidence that he was already well known for his skill in taking walled towns and castles by escalade which was to become the trade mark of his later years. For these services and perhaps because he was too dangerous an enemy, he received the grant of Chateauneuf-sur-Charente, a substantial fortress on the western march of Angoumois. But like so many of his kind on both sides of the war the Archpriest repeatedly crossed the blurred line between military service and banditry. When Charles of Spain was assassinated in 1354 he seized three of the chief castles of the county of Angoulême as security for the arrears of his wages. During the French siege of Breteuil, when he was serving in the army of John II, he suddenly seized a castle in Normandy. 'Simple theft', was the verdict of the royal officer sent to investigate. By this time Arnaud had abandoned his native province and transferred his operations to the north. Here he began a determined social ascent. He fought in the battalion of the Count of Alençon at Poitiers, where he was wounded and captured. He married a rich widow who controlled several important lordships in Berry. In March 1357 he was named in the truce of Bordeaux as one of the four French conservators for Berry. He became a man of substance.[13]

It was Arnaud de Cervole who first perceived the larger opportunities for independent freebooters which were opened up by the paralysis of the French government. The traditional Gascon companies, such as those of the Albrets, had been small groups of men, a hundred or two strong at the most, recruited mainly from clients and kinsmen of their leader, who had spread themselves thinly across large expanses of territory looking for the line of least resistance. Arnaud created what contemporaries called the 'Great Company'. It was not in fact a single company but a succession of large temporary armies, which was formed and re-formed by combining the forces of many different companies, each under its own leader, but acknowledging the overall leadership and strategic direction of one captain or sometimes a small group of captains. The core of the Great Company was always Gascon. But there was added an unstable ballast recruited from every province of France and every rank of society except the highest: unemployed foot soldiers and archers; professional criminals from the towns; penniless gentry; a handful of knights. Initially, Arnaud de Cervole found his recruits among the Gascon companies of Auvergne and Limousin. Then, in about May 1357 he transferred his operations to the Dauphiné. By midsummer, he had more than 2,000 men assembled on the border of Provence on the right bank of the Rhone. All of this happened under the noses of the Dauphin's officers and almost certainly with the connivance of his councillors. In spite of Arnaud's chequered past they still regarded him as a loyal and useful soldier whose acts of indiscipline would have to be tolerated, rather as Edward III's ministers must have regarded Robert Knolles. Besides, they had their own quarrels with the Queen of Naples and were no friends of the house of Taranto.[14]

Provence was extremely attractive to the sort of man who followed the Archpriest. The law of diminishing returns which constricted their activities elsewhere as portable wealth was exhausted and the defence became more alert, had hardly begun to operate here. The past riches of the region were still to be seen in the fine buildings and golden treasuries of the great pilgrimage churches at Saint-Gilles and Saint-Maximin, and in the rich suburbs built by the merchants of Marseille and Arles and the lawyers of Aix. The principal cities were protected only by their Roman walls, which were low and unrepaired. For all the economic difficulties of the region, the traffic of the Rhone valley was still busy. Marseille remained a major centre of the seaborne trade of the Mediterranean. However, the main magnet for looters was the tremendous wealth generated by papal court at Avignon. Clement V had established the papacy at Avignon five decades before, in 1309, initially as a temporary refuge from the disorders of Rome and the wars of central Italy. Over the years the city had gradually become a permanent capital. Benedict XII and Clement VI had built the great palace on the Rocher des Doms to replace the temporary accommodation which had done for their predecessors. The huge financial and legal departments of the papal administration and the expanding offices of the papal household had moved into it. Some two dozen cardinals maintained establishments of their own which they installed in luxurious palaces in the city or at Villeneuve on the other side of the river. A horde of courtiers, petitioners, messengers, soldiers, bankers, furnishers and suppliers followed, with numberless crowds of hangers-on behind them. Avignon became a boom town. The demands of this great official and spiritual community drew a continuous flow of luxury goods along the unprotected roads of Provence: wine from Burgundy, jewellery from Paris, fabrics from

Champagne and paintings from Italy, and above all money. The papacy consumed only a modest proportion of its revenues in Avignon itself, yet during the reign of Innocent VI (1354–62) the Apostolic Chamber handled an average of 253,000 florins of Florence (about £36,000) in cash and bullion every year.[15] Almost all of this had been brought into city on boats or pack animals.

On 13 July 1357 the Archpriest's army crossed the Rhone north of Valence. The invaders marched down the east bank of the river, then burned and smashed their way across the Comtat Venaissin. By 24 July 1357 they had crossed the Durance, joined forces with Amiel des Baux and occupied the great castle of the Bishop of Marseille at Saint-Cannat north-west of Aix. From here they spread out over the whole of Provence. The Archpriest and his army occupied much of the Comtat Venaissin and the county of Forcalquier north of the Durance. East of Aix, local bands loyal to Raymond des Baux seized Brignoles and burnt Draguignan. In the great plain west of Aix, a huge undisciplined mob overran the open country under the leadership of a priest of Salon, breaking open granaries and stores and cutting off the cities of Aix and Marseille from their hinterland. The pickings were easy. The chief cities, Aix, Arles, Marseille and Toulon were the only significant centres of resistance. Crowds of refugees abandoned the open country and took refuge within their walls.[16]

Struck by the boldness of the Archpriest's enterprise and the ease of his conquests, other captains of the south-west began to cast envious eyes on the territories beyond the Rhone. According to reports reaching the papal court, the Captal de Buch, the lord of Mussidan and the Count of Armagnac were all arming to join in the rape of Provence. This may or may not have been true of the first two, but it was certainly true of the last. Armagnac had large territorial claims of his own in Provence, which he had unsuccessfully pressed on the Queen of Naples for several years. In about May 1357 when the preparations of the Archpriest became public knowledge, he began to raise his own army, the kernel of which consisted, like the Archpriest's own, of disbanded Gascon soldiers. It was probably the advance guard of this army which was reported to be gathering on the west bank of the Rhone during August 1357. In the middle of the month, as the Archpriest's men were filling the valley of the Durance, those of the Count of Armagnac crossed the Rhone south of Saint-Gilles.[17]

The chief representatives of Jeanne's government in Provence were her brother-in-law, Philip of Taranto, and the Seneschal, Fulk d'Agout.

Both of them were quite unequal to the challenge. Philip had collected a small force of cavalry on the Archpriest's approach with which he had failed to hold the line of the Durance. He had then fled to Avignon where he was swiftly joined by Fulk.[18] The papal city was in a state of panic. The ancient walls had been partly demolished at the time of the Albigensian wars in the early thirteenth century and never rebuilt. The Pope ordered hurried works to be carried out in the gaps and hired several hundred extra garrison troops. Urgent appeals for help were addressed to the Emperor, the imprisoned King of France, the Count of Savoy and other potentates. Some of them promised to help. None did so.[19]

At the beginning of September 1357 the frightened politicians in Avignon decided to play off one group of *routiers* against the other. They sent that practised compromiser the cardinal of Boulogne to treat with the Count of Armagnac. On 13 September 1357 Armagnac was bought out. He agreed to enter the service of the Queen of Naples for two and a half months with an army of 1,000 calvary and 1,500 mounted infantry. For their part the Queen's officers undertook to raise another 8,000 men to fight under his command. Together they would confront the horde of the Archpriest. For these services, Armagnac was to have all his territorial claims in Provence satisfied promptly and in full, and to receive in addition a large cash fee: 65,000 gold florins. It was probably worth paying this to get rid of him. But it made very little difference to the fight against the Archpriest. At the beginning of October 1357 the Count of Armagnac's army set up its headquarters at Tarascon on the east bank of the Rhone. In November they marched east towards Aix and joined forces with the Seneschal. Here they attacked two castles north of Aix in which the rebels had established themselves. But they made no impression on one and, having failed to capture the other, eventually bought out the garrison for 4,000 florins. The great army which the Seneschal had promised to raise in Provence never materialised. In the new year Armagnac fell out with his employers and returned abruptly to Languedoc, whence he carried on an acrimonious correspondence with the Seneschal about the arrears of his pay. The Seneschal, who was struggling to raise money in Avignon, suffered the indignity of being arrested as a common debtor.[20]

As soon as the Count of Armagnac had departed, the Provençal rebels launched a fresh offensive, the ultimate object of which was the capture of Marseille. The troops were mostly mercenaries from south-western France commanded by Raymond des Baux: 'Gascons, but worse than barbarians or Sarracens', as the terrified inhabitants of one village reported. Operations began in the middle of January 1358 in the coastal region east of the city. The Archpriest's army advanced simultaneously from the north. They poured across the Durance from Forcalquier to Manosque in bands of a few hundred at a time and converged on the agreed meeting point. This was the pilgrimage town of Sainte-Maximin-la-Sainte-Baume. Sainte-Maximin had had many warnings of their coming. The relics of Saint Mary Magdelen had already been carried off to the hills. But the inhabitants were taken by surprise. The Great Company approached with banners bearing the arms of the Queen of Naples and the city of Marseille. They remained undetected until they were almost at the walls. Men working in suburban vineyards fled for their lives. On 21 February 1358 the town was carried by assault and subjected to a brutal sack. The remnant of the Count of Armagnac's army, some companies of which had stayed behind after the count's precipitate withdrawal, melted away. At the beginning of March 1358 the Archpriest established his headquarters at Pélissanne, east of Salon, and began to make the final preparations for the assault on Marseille. By his own reckoning he had about 2,700 men with him, not including the inevitable tail of camp followers and thieves.[21]

Marseille saved Provence. Its citizens cut fresh ditches around their walls. They demolished the bridges leading to the gates. They expelled every inhabitant born on the domains of Raymond des Baux. They were ready for the assault. But it never came. The Archpriest assembled a good deal of intelligence about the layout of the defences and drew the obvious conclusions. The city was too large and too populous to be taken by storm. It could not be blockaded without a fleet. The rebels and their auxiliaries were in much greater danger of starvation than the inhabitants. The failure of the harvest, the looting of the granaries and the scorched earth policy organised by the officers of the Queen had brought the *plat pays* north of Marseille to the edge of famine, leaving her enemies with no means of feeding themselves. There was little booty left to be taken. Reports from the Île de France, where the Anglo-Navarrese companies were closing in on Paris, suggested that the prospect of loot was better in the north. In the course of March 1358 the troops of Raymond des Baux and the Archpriest began to drift away.[22]

The Archpriest himself turned north in April. He left some of his lieutenants behind to extract protection money from the communities of

Provence. But as their numbers declined, so did their bargaining power. In September 1358 Arnaud returned to make a deal with the representatives of the Pope. He agreed to withdraw his companies from Provence and to restore all the castles which they had occupied in the papal territories of the Comtat Venaissin and the neighbouring parts of the county of Forcalquier. In return, he received the comparatively modest sum of 20,000 gold florins, which was to be levied on the communities of Provence. Innocent himself advanced the first instalment. In October the Archpriest led the last remnants of the Great Company back up to the Rhone valley.[23] Deprived of the support of the Gascons, the rebellion in Provence swiftly fell apart. The rebels strangling Aix, Marseille and Toulon were picked off one by one by troops sent out by the cities. Raymond des Baux went on fighting until the end of 1359. But his cause was ruined and his career ended in disgrace and imprisonment.[24] How much the soldiers of the Great Company had got out of the whole enterprise is hard to say. The sack of Sainte-Maximin and the ransoming of the Durance valley must have been very profitable. But the Great Company had failed to take a single large city or to establish themselves on the Rhone. Most of them must have been disappointed by their receipts and glad enough to head north.

Charles of Navarre renounced his homage to the Crown on 3 August 1358, the day after the Dauphin's triumphal return to the capital. On the 4th, a fresh chapter opened in the story of the companies' operations in the north. Three hundred Navarrese and English soldiers arrived at Melun by boat. Melun was an ancient town of the royal demesne, built on an island in the Seine some forty miles upstream of Paris. The old town stood under the shadow of the collegiate Church of Notre-Dame at one end of the island and the castle at the other. On either bank, large walled *bourgs*, or suburbs, separated it from the plains of the Gâtinais and Brie. The place had been assigned as part of the dower lands of Joan of Navarre, widow of Charles IV. She was the King of Navarre's aunt and his most persistent ally within the royal family. Joan had been forewarned. When the Anglo-Navarrese company arrived, she admitted them into the island citadel. When the inhabitants of Melun took to arms and began to put up barricades, she sent messengers to calm them with lies. The soldiers, she said, were loyal men who had only come for rest and a meal, and would quickly be gone. On the following morning her Chancellor appeared on one of the bridges leading to the west bank with 200 men at his back. They threw down the barrier at the gate, swept aside the guards, took the keys out of the hands of the keepers and occupied the whole of the western *bourg*. The Dauphin did his best to root out the invaders before they were firmly established. He sent every soldier to Melun that he could pay, and many that he could not. But the King of Navarre moved faster. At the beginning of September 1358 Charles arrived with several hundred English and Navarrese troops, and installed his principal commander, Martin Henriquez, as captain of the town.[25]

At almost exactly the same time, another group of Charles of Navarre's partisans took over Creil, which occupied an equivalent position on the northern side of Paris. Creil was a large thirteenth-century fortress on the Oise belonging to Beatrice de Bourbon, the widow of John of Bohemia, hero of Crécy. Like Melun, it was sited on an island in the river, linked by bridges to both sides. The occupation of this place was the work of Jean and Robert de Picquigny, the King of Navarre's principal lieutenants in Picardy. But the custody of the place was conferred on Philip of Navarre's English marshal, John Fotheringhay. He brought in an enormous garrison of English and Navarrese soldiers from Normandy. At the height of the war there were reckoned to be 500 men-at-arms at Creil which suggests a total garrison strength of at least 1,000 when archers, foot soldiers and auxiliaries are counted.[26]

The King of Navarre already controlled the three principal bridge towns of the Seine downstream of Paris at Mantes, Meulan and Poissy. From these places and the island fortresses at Melun and Creil his followers set about occupying the whole of the Île de France, Beauvaisis and Picardy. The pattern of events was broadly consistent everywhere. The great walled towns, with their developed suspicion of all soldiers, turned against the King of Navarre as soon as he had become the overt patron of the companies. Densely populated and highly organised, these places were rarely captured. But in the *plat pays* around, it was a different story. Resistance was fitful and disorganised and failed almost everywhere at the first appearance of the enemy.[27]

In Picardy, for example, Jean de Picquigny failed to capture Amiens at the beginning of September 1358 in spite of the presence within the city of a powerful group of pro-Navarrese citizens, some of whom opened the gates of the outer walls for him at night. The town bells sounded the alarm and crowds of armed citizens drove out the Navarrese before they could reach the inner wall. The Dauphin's Lieutenant in the region arrived in time to complete the rout. After this incident, five of Charles

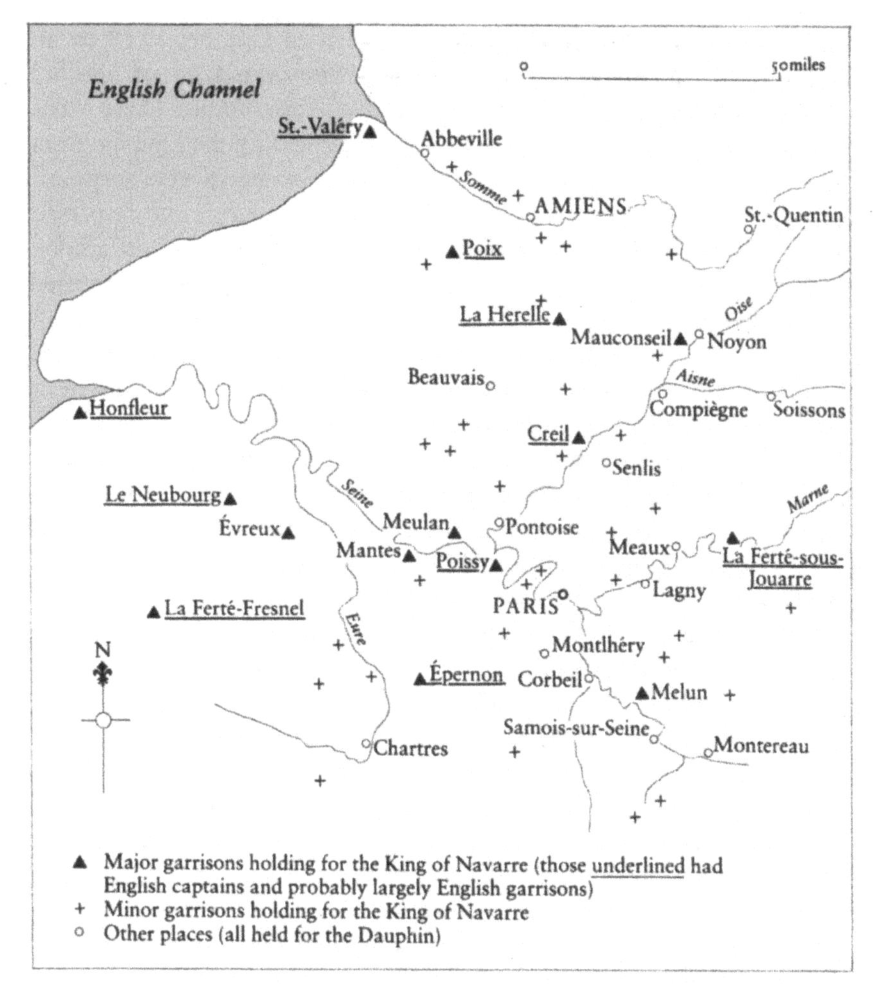

23 Principal Navarrese garrisons, 1358–1359

of Navarre's most prominent supporters in the town, including the mayor and the captain, were beheaded in the market. Not long afterwards a rather similar attempt was planned against Abbeville. This time the plot was betrayed to the town authorities and suppressed almost as soon as it had been conceived. By comparison most of rural Picardy was swiftly brought under control from a handful of garrisoned castles: Creil itself; Mauconseil near Noyon, which was captured by Jean de Picquigny at about the same time; Poix, south of Amiens, which was occupied on his behalf by Englishmen from the garrison of le Neubourg in Normandy; and the small port of Saint-Valéry at the mouth of the Somme, which was seized early in October 1358 by an Anglo-Navarrese troop and placed under the command of another English adventurer from Normandy called William Bulmer. There was a brief attempt at resistance. An army was collected by the Lieutenant in Normandy. It laid siege to Mauconseil. But the besiegers were surprised before daybreak by a force of cavalry sent out from Creil, and dispersed with heavy casualties. The Bishop of Noyon, who was found among them, was sent off a prisoner to England. After this, all organised defence in Picardy collapsed.[28]

The Île de France lacked even the limited capacity for concerted resistance shown by the men of Picardy. The region was the garden of the Kings of France, and its government had always been peculiarly dependent on the monarchy. There was virtually no provincial organisation. The Jacquerie had destroyed the social cohesion of the Beauvaisis and the Senlisis and left many rural castles and fortified houses ruinous or abandoned. Nowhere else in France was the vacuum of power at the centre so keenly felt. More than sixty places were effortlessly occupied by the Anglo-Navarrese companies in the course of August and September 1358.

The inhabitants of these regions were assigned to ransom districts and systematically mulcted. They were in no position to refuse. Martin Henriquez threatened the villages around Melun with 'death, pillage and arson' unless they made ransom agreements with his officers. They succumbed. The people of Ableiges and Santeuil just outside Pontoise, who tried for a time to resist, had their barns emptied and their vines uprooted just before the vintage. They too succumbed. The enemy 'rode from one castle to the next, smashing or taking whatever they felt like, carrying off the inhabitants for ransom, burning down houses and barns, pillaging their contents,' they explained to the Dauphin's officials; 'several of the inhabitants had already been killed or executed.' Most places bought protection. The cost was high. Antony was a large and once prosperous village beyond the southern suburbs of Paris, which belonged to the abbey of St. Germain-des-Près. Even with the aid of the monks it must have been hard for them to find the twenty gold florins, eight barrels of flour, eight barrels of wine, two bushels of salt and fifty pounds of candle wax demanded by the Navarrese garrison of Amblainvilliers. Larger garrisons could exact much more from comparable places. The village of la Ferté-Alais, at the edge of the forest of Fontainebleu, was attacked at the end of September 1358 by several hundred soldiers from Melun. They killed the inhabitants who had not managed to flee in time, raped the women and looted and burned a large number of houses. The community had to find 500 gold deniers, 50 barrels of wine and 50 of flour or grain in order to prevent a repetition. Many were quite unable to pay their ransoms or lived in villages which could not afford the *patis* demanded of them. Those who were not beaten up or simply murdered, were led off tied to the horses of their captors to be locked in prison, or were made to serve the garrison in lieu of payment. Some of these may have been perfectly content with the relative security of garrison life and the liberation from the burden of ransoms and *patis* and served their new masters with enthusiasm. But others were virtually slaves. The clerk who wrote out the safe-conducts at Creil was a prisoner, like many of those who filled his office in Anglo-Navarrese castles. So was the miller who ground the garrison's grain, the farrier who shod their horses, and the surgeon who tended their wounds.[29]

The worst affected region lay north of Paris within marching distance of Creil. John Fotheringhay may have been 'possessed by cruelty and tyranny' in the conventional phrase of the Dauphin's chancery clerks. But the driving force behind his activity was not sadism but simple financial calculation. He had to maintain one of the largest garrisons in France and make a profit for himself, all from the traffic of the Oise valley and the *patis* of villages lying within range of his walls. During the period of two years when he commanded at Creil, Fotheringhay was reputed to have taken 100,000 francs in safe-conduct fees alone. It is perfectly possible. His revenue from *patis* cannot even be guessed, but must have been considerable. Simply in order to keep itself supplied and fed, the garrison of Creil had to levy ransoms at a heavy rate, which rapidly exhausted the villages within their power and obliged them to extend their range over ever greater distances. They came down the Senlis road as far as Gonesse, within ten miles of Paris, burning recalcitrant villages and kidnapping those found on the roads without safe-conducts. They burnt Montmorency, the second time in the space of a year when the fires of this place had been seen from the walls of Paris. They captured Argenteuil by storm and planted a subsidiary garrison in the fortified priory there. To the north they reached up the valley of the Oise as far as Noyon. At its greatest extent the effective operating range of the garrison of Creil was about thirty miles.[30]

Resistance was as disorganised and ineffective as anywhere. A few communities fortified their parish churches. One or two prepared retreats on islands in the Oise, to which they fled when danger threatened, carrying what their arms would hold. The peasants of Longueil near Compiègne barricaded themselves into a fortified farm house belonging to the Benedictines of Saint-Corneille and fought off Fotheringhay's troops with such savagery and courage that the story was retold, with embellishments, across northern France and even in England. However, the great majority of village communities paid up until the burden became unbearable. Then they fled, abandoning their possessions in their homes and their stores piled up in their barns. Ecclesiastical landowners, who usually had important investments in buildings and livestock, faced a more difficult dilemma. Several of the greater houses, such as the Cluniac priory of Saint-Leu-d'Esserent and the great royal foundation of Royaumont paid *patis* to the companies over a considerable period. But without men to bring in the harvests, no monastic community could support itself for long. Sooner or later most of them fled to the safety of the towns leaving one or two monks behind them to look after the conventual buildings and negotiate with the soldiers. The brother left in charge of the empty buildings of Saint-Eloi-aux-Fontaines confessed to being terrified. He lived alone in the priory, finding his food in the surrounding fields and running into the woods at the least alarm. He survived. But he lost five horses and the only cart to casual raiders. The vestments in the sacristy were saved only by being concealed in some nearby lime-kilns. Less personal, but equally evocative, was the testimony of the account books: deserted farms, abandoned harvests, ruined buildings, stolen livestock and equipment, no income. Before the war Beauvais cathedral had been one of the richest in France. But when the Dauphin's Chancellor Jean de Dormans was elected to the see in July 1359 he found the revenues reduced to a trickle and entirely consumed by the cost of repairing and manning the castles and manor houses of the domain. In Paris, the chronicler Jean de Venette saw plenty of once rich ecclesiastics who were worse off than Jean de Dormans. Abbots and abbesses who had once administered huge estates and travelled with clattering escorts of body servants, attendants and men-at-arms, now struggled on foot through the gates of the capital with one servant and a monk for companions, elbowing their way through the jostling crowds of fellow refugees.[31]

How much Fotheringhay gained personally from the operations of his garrison is hard to say. He certainly lived well. He indulged the taste for swagger which was so common to men of his kind, helping himself to padded saddles, beaver hats, ostrich feathers and other plunder of the road. And he accumulated money for himself. When in 1360 his activities became embarrassing to Edward III and his assets were seized, they included in Brittany alone a stable of war horses, 500 gold *moutons*, 1,000 old *écus*, eighty English nobles and a variety of gold and silver objects in safe-keeping at Vannes, Hennebont and Quimperlé, not to speak of what he must have amassed in England and at Creil itself. This was not fabulous wealth by any means, but it would have bought gentility and a substantial manor in England for a man who had hardly been heard of before the mid-1350s.[32]

By the end of August 1358 the Navarrese garrisons of the Île de France had put the capital in a collar almost as tight as the one which had enclosed it back in June. The roads north and west were blocked. The Seine and the Oise were closed to navigation except by leave of the King of Navarre's captain. For a few weeks after the Dauphin's entry into Paris it was still possible to reach the city more or less unimpeded from the east by the valley of the Marne. But towards the end of October 1358 the Navarrese and their allies put to an end to that. Moving east from Creil they took possession of a group of castles by the main road from Paris to Soissons, which they filled with Breton troops drawn from the English garrisons of the west. Shortly after this a major garrison consisting mainly of Englishmen was established in another island fortress at la Ferté-sous-Jouarre on the Marne. This place, which belonged to the lords of Coucy, closed the river a few miles upstream from Meaux. It is true that even after these conquests the blockade of Paris was never entirely complete. Garrison commanders needed to sell safe-conducts to make money, and there were always men willing to run the gauntlet without one. A system of escorted convoys was organised on the Seine between Corbeil and Samois-sur-Seine which enabled some supplies to be got past Melun. Paris never starved. But the trade of its inhabitants was depressed and their life was wretched. Grain became scarce. Wine, most of which came from Burgundy, was almost possible to find. Some supplies, such as salt, could not be had at all. Prices too rose to astronomical levels. Within the walls tension ran as high as at the most dangerous moments of Etienne Marcel's revolution. Citizens worked shifts at the walls and gates. Apart from the clock tower of Notre-Dame the bells were silenced to avoid false alarms. Rumours flew about of plots and traitors.[33]

'I have not the strength to fight the English,' the Dauphin protested to his relatives.[34] It was true. The Dauphin and his ministers had no authority except in Paris and in parts of Normandy. In both regions he moved quickly to take what advantage he could from the brief enthusiasm which followed his victory over Etienne Marcel. But it was not much. The Parisians submitted to a heavy sales tax, a *gabelle* on salt and an income tax on rents, none of which can have been very productive while the blockade continued. The canons of Notre-Dame sold their plate, and other churches no doubt did the same if they still had any. In Normandy a group of the Dauphin's councillors passed from town to town addressing local assemblies and appealing for funds. Much help was promised. Hardly any was received. Normandy was exhausted. In the whole viscounty of Falaise only Falaise itself and the small town of Saint-Pierre-sur-Dive paid anything. Caen, one of the richest towns of Normandy, had exhausted its resources fighting the enemy garrisons around it and contributed nothing.[35]

Behind the walls of the Louvre, the Dauphin turned to the traditional expedients. The silver coinage, which had been revalued in August 1358 in accordance with the demands of the Estates-General of Compiègne, was devalued again at an accelerating rate as the crisis deepened. In September, when the Lieutenant of Normandy ran out of money to pay his troops, the mint at Rouen was ordered to reduce the silver content of the coinage by 60 per cent for two weeks to stretch out its stocks of bullion. Shortly after this brief and fraudulent device had been tried, the Dauphin took back into his service his father's old master of the mints, the notorious Jean Poilevilain. Poilevilain, bruised by the dismissals and confiscations which he had suffered in the past for his unpopular craft, agreed in return for the strictest immunities to milk the coinage for all he could. He undertook, after an initial period of reorganisation, to produce 32,000 gold royals each month from the mints until July 1359 and 40,000 thereafter. At the end of October 1358 the Dauphin issued an apologetic ordinance declaring that in spite of his promises to the Estates-General the threat to the realm and the absence of other revenue left him with no alternative but to order a general devaluation. Another followed just two weeks later. It cost him a great deal of political goodwill for a very limited return. The profits of Poilevilain's coinage operations fell far below what he had promised. But they were virtually the only regular source of revenue available to the government.[36]

The Dauphin had no troops at his disposal apart from his personal entourage and the garrison of a few royal castles outside Paris: the Louvre, Saint-Denis, Montlhéry, Corbeil and Lagny-sur-Marne. In the winter they were reinforced by some crossbowmen hired in Italy. These tiny forces had not been paid for months. They could not even be counted on to defend themselves. In January 1359 the English garrison of la Ferté-sous-Jouarre succeeded in penetrating the walls of Lagny in spite of the presence of a large garrison in the town, many of whom were carried off to be ransomed.[37] Further from Paris the few castles which still acknowledged the Dauphin's authority were garrisoned by demoralised soldiers, unpaid, unfed and without orders. For them the only alternative to desertion was to support themselves in the same way as the enemy. The Dauphin's captain at Lagny led his men on plundering raids through the valley of the Marne. The royal captain at Autrèches rode through the Soissonais pressing labourers and seizing wine for his men. The royal garrison at Gandelù requisitioned victuals and supplies without payment, burnt down houses and trafficked with the English of la Ferté.[38]

These problems, originating in the penury of the government, were aggravated by well meaning but ill-judged attempts to prevent the payment of *patis* and safe-conduct fees to the enemy. Villagers who had been forced to pay money to the English or Navarrese found themselves accused of treason and pillaged by the troops in the service of the Dauphin as if they had been accomplices. Travellers found with safe-conducts issued in the name of the King of Navarre were arrested and ransomed by officers of the Dauphin. The unfortunate Robin Louvrier of Neuville-en-Hez in the Beauvaisis fled when the town was occupied by the enemy, but ran into a troop of soldiers from the French garrison of Mouy on the opposite side of the valley, who attacked and injured him. Robin was forced to return to Neuville, only to be charged with treason two years later when the place was recovered and he was found working there. Incidents like these added to the impression of random violence, a war without logic and increasingly without sides. How was a Frenchman or Breton in the garrison at Creil to be distinguished from his compatriot in the service of the Dauphin? How was the looting of a Navarrese garrison commander different from the requisitioning of a French one? There must have been many who, like the inhabitants of the small walled town of Crevant, 'did not know who to trust, who to deal with, who to treat as loyal Frenchmen.' So they closed their gates against everyone and attacked mounted men on sight, whether they were bandits, *routiers*, honest travellers or royal officers.[39]

It was some time before the King of England recognised that events in France had destroyed his treaty with John II. The main problem was the ransom, the first instalment of which, 600,000 *écus*, had to be found by 1 November 1358. It was a sisyphian task in a country torn apart by civil war and ruined by brigandage. Languedoc was probably the only region where any substantial sum could be raised and most of the King's efforts were directed there. Gilles Aycelin, John's Chancellor, achieved heroic feats. In spite of his years, he travelled indefatigably from town to town, addressing groups of local politicians. In July 1358 there was an assembly at Montpellier, attended by representatives of the seneschalsies of Beaucaire and Toulouse and the province of Rouergue. They voted a generous subsidy for the release of the King, on top of the considerable sums required for the defence of their own province. The seneschalsy of Carcassonne met separately and made its own grant. Quercy, which was torn apart by war and partly occupied by Gascon garrisons, offered nothing. The nominal worth of these grants was 216,000 *moutons*. However, although Languedoc was second to none in its loyalty to the Crown, the amounts actually collected were disappointing. The reasons are unclear, but lack of time was certainly one of them. Towards the end of the summer the King's tireless private secretary Yves Derrien arrived in the south to urge on the laggards. By September a note of desperation entered the King's correspondence as he tried to anticipate the unbearably slow processes of collection by bargaining for advances. He was wasting his time. Even if the whole amount had been produced, the balance would have had to come from the provinces of the north and centre. There was not a hope of collecting any substantial amount there. John's agents hardly tried. They must have counted on persuading Edward III to accept less than was due.[40]

The two papal legates in London were not so sanguine. They had already concluded by the middle of August 1358 that the treaty was doomed. They applied for their passports. At Avignon Innocent VI reached the same conclusion. He ordered his legates to proceed at once to France to reconcile the warring contestants. Perhaps, he wrote, their remarkable diplomatic skills, which had brought about the treaty in the first place, could now be directed to making it work.[41]

In November 1358, Yves Derrien returned to London bringing with him the tale of the difficulties and delays which had frustrated his efforts. The French representatives came before Edward III and told him what had been evident for several weeks, that the financial provisions of the treaty could not be performed. The English King, who always seems to have felt that he could have got more out of the treaty, was in no mood for compromise. 'If you default in a single point,' he had told John when the treaty was completed at Windsor, 'I shall be as free as I was before.' There is some evidence that he would have been willing to release John II without having received the whole of the first instalment of the ransom if the security had been good enough. But the French could not provide that either. The treaty called for the surrender as hostages of forty of the principal noblemen of France and the leading citizens of twenty walled cities. None of them was ready. John's representatives seem to have hoped for further time. They protested that performance of the treaty was impossible in the current state of France. They complained that this was mainly due to breaches of the truce by Edward III's own subjects. Edward replied with passion. These men, he said, referring to the English companies in the service of Charles of Navarre, were outlaws, criminals, murderers, thieves. He denied all responsibility for their acts. On 20 November 1358 he returned his formal answer to the Dauphin. He would no longer be bound by the treaty of Windsor. When the truce expired, the following Easter, he would assert his claims by force.[42]

In the last ten days of November 1358 Edward III's Council decided to mount a fresh invasion of France through Calais in the spring. A general requisition of shipping was announced on 6 December. During the next six weeks the tremendous bureaucratic preliminaries to the gathering of a great army were put in motion for the first time in more than three years. Clerks toured the ports arresting merchant ships on behalf of the admirals. Commissioners of array were appointed to recruit archers in every county of southern and central England and throughout Wales. Purveyors cleared the stocks of fletchers and bowmakers to fill the stores of the Tower of London. Carts and packhorses were taken from monasteries. The timetable envisaged that the fleet would be ready in the Downs by the middle of April 1359. On 13 December 1358, a week after these decisions had been made, the cardinal of Périgord and his colleague entered Paris. They had taken ten weeks to cross the savage wastes of northern France, only to find that the treaty which they had come to save had been renounced by both sides.[43]

It is tempting to see in these events the triumph of Navarrese intrigue. There was certainly no shortage of observers to draw that conclusion at the time, including John II's principal counsellors in England, who firmly expected that Edward III would now throw in his lot with the King of Navarre. They offered new and extravagant terms of peace in the hope of pre-empting this outcome. They planted hints among Edward's ministers that Charles could not be trusted, indeed was already negotiating with the Dauphin. They need not have troubled themselves.

Edward and his ministers had not forgotten that the King of Navarre had double-crossed them twice. And the truth was that Edward's interests were fundamentally incompatible with Charles's. The King of Navarre desired at all costs to prevent a treaty of peace between England and France while his own exorbitant claims against John II remained unresolved. The King of England on the other hand badly needed a treaty with France on the right terms. Without it, his possession of the French King, which had once seemed such an overpowering diplomatic ace, could bring him no advantage. If the treaty could not be the one made at Windsor in May 1358, then sooner or later it would have to be another. Yet it was becoming increasingly clear that whatever terms the English might impose on the King of France would mean very little until his authority was restored in his realm, and that Charles of Navarre was the main obstacle in the way. Men like James Pipe and John Fotheringhay may have been Edward III's subjects, but they were helping the King of Navarre to destroy the fruits of two years' careful diplomacy and well timed compromise in London and Windsor. Edward's venomous outburst against them in the presence of the French representatives at Westminster had been perfectly sincere.

So, far from throwing in his lot with Charles of Navarre Edward kept his distance as his military preparations took shape. The draft treaty drawn up at Saint-Denis on 1 August 1358, on the morrow of Etienne Marcel's death, had been brought back to England at the end of September by the King of Navarre's new Chancellor, Robert de la Porte, and by Stephen Cusington, the chief English signatory. Edward had received Cusington at the royal manor at Woodstock, north of Oxford, on 21 September 1358. A week later, on 29 September, the Council had gathered there to hear his report. Their discussions are not recorded, and may have been inconclusive. What is clear is that the draft treaty was never ratified. On 12 December 1358, after the English government had decided to re-invade France, Edward sent a remarkably cagey letter to Charles of Navarre. He informed him of his plan. But he had no terms to propose. He simply assured Charles that he would make no treaty with the French King until he had reliable news of the Navarrese King's intentions. In the meantime Edward did his best to deprive Charles of the services of English mercenaries. On 20 December 1358 Stephen Cusington returned to France with Richard Totesham. Their instructions were to control the 'disturbers of the peace' there, most of whom were fighting for the King of Navarre.[44]

*

In the brief interval since Cusington had last been in France, the operations of the 'disturbers of the peace' had become even more extensive and their grip on the provinces of France tighter than ever. The river Loire, with its broad, treacherous channels, unpredictable floods and heavily defended bridges had stopped two English armies in 1356 and was still a formidable strategic obstacle even for irregular soldiers. For many years it had separated the Gascon operations in the south and centre of the kingdom from those of the English, Bretons and Navarrese in the north. It was only in the course of the year 1358 that the valley became a highway rather than a barrier, as the companies penetrated from the east and west at once, then mingled and spread through the adjacent regions on either bank. The invasion had begun on a small scale at the end of the previous year, when bands of Gascons had started to feel their way north from the high Limousin plateau into Berry and up the valley of the Allier into the Nivernais. Their attacks were scattered and difficult to contain. The defence was a disaster.

The main power in the Nivernais was Louis de Mâle, Count of Flanders, who held the county of Nevers from the Crown, but left the government of its affairs in the hands of his mother, Margaret of Flanders. She was another of the politically inept dowagers who found themselves in possession of strategically important places in France at the crisis of its affairs. Her response to the Gascon invasion of her domain was to appoint the Archpriest, Arnaud de Cervole, as her captain and to pay him a large sum of money to garrison her chief fortresses against the companies. This unfortunate decision was made in about April 1358. The Dauphin aggravated the mistake by confirming the Archpriest's appointment in his own name and extending his authority to the neighbouring province of Berry, which depended directly on the Crown. The Archpriest was admittedly a man with important domains of his own in the region and every interest in defending them. But he was also fickle, greedy and unprincipled, and his followers were worse. Moreover, for the first six months of his appointment he was preoccupied with the affairs of Provence and only intermittently present in the territory which he was charged to defend. He installed garrisons in Nevers and in several of the principal fortresses of Berry and Nivernais, and appointed deputies to command them. Most of these men were drawn from the Great Company. They included Spaniards, Gascons and even some Englishmen. They treated the *plat pays* around them as if they had conquered it, looting villages for supplies, levying *patis* for their upkeep and provoking riots among the

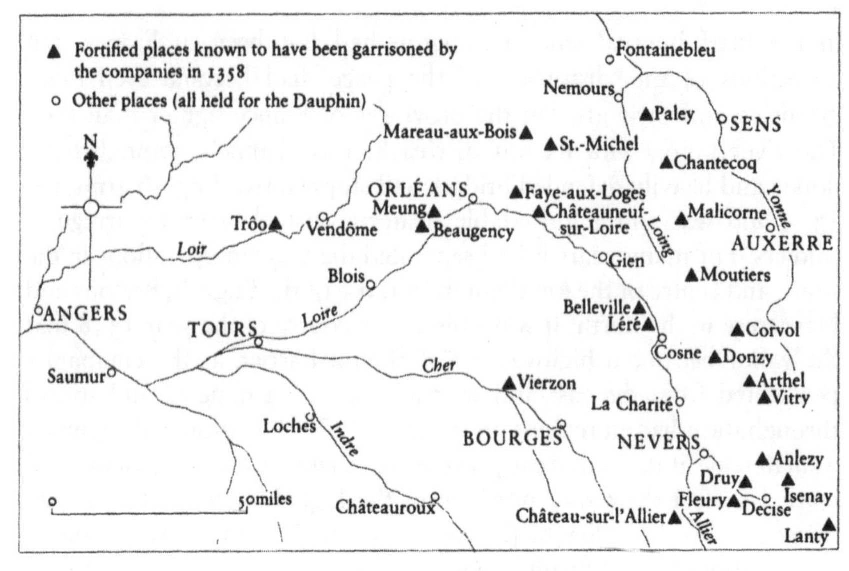

24 The Loire valley, 1358

inhabitants of Nevers. If they did anything to halt the seeping invasion from the south, it has not been recorded. The result was that the Gascons advanced virtually unopposed through much of the southern part of the region. The castellan of Decize, who controlled one of the three bridge-towns over the Loire in the Nivernais, reported that the enemy held 'more than a hundred' fortified places around his walls. Thirty years after these events, when the chronicler Froissart passed through Béarn, he met a man at an inn in Orthez who had participated in his youth in the occupation of Berry and the Nivernais. Warming himself by the fire as he waited for his dinner, this man reminisced happily about the easy times of the autumn of 1358. 'There was not a knight or squire or well heeled fellow who dared to put his nose outside his door unless he had a ransom treaty with us,' said he.[45]

Larger and better organised bands were already making their way along the Loire from the west. Most of these were Bretons and Englishmen from the garrisons of lower Normandy and the Breton march, part of the great eastward migration occasioned by the progressive exhaustion of these regions. In the spring of 1358 a group of companies, mainly Bretons, had appeared without warning at Trôo, a market town set into the side of the cliffs above the banks of the River Loir. From here, the *routiers* launched a succession of raids into the Orléanais.[46] The Orléanais was as unprepared as the other Loire provinces. It was the appanage of John II's younger brother, Philip Duke of Orléans. He was preoccupied with events in Paris. The defence was therefore entrusted to the Seneschal of Poitou and Limousin, Regnault de Gouillons, an experienced but overburdened officer who was thus obliged to add a new and populous territory to the enormous region for which he was already responsible. In about May 1358 the companies captured Meung, a small town downstream of Orléans which had a stone bridge over the Loire. This enabled them to operate simultaneously on both banks and to stop the traffic of the river. On midsummer day, 24 June 1358, they were let into the nearby walled town of Beaugency under the nose of Regnault de Gouillons, who had established his headquarters in the citadel. The inhabitants who were responsible for this treachery preferred to pay *patis* than to run the risk of a sack. It was a reasonable calculation.[47]

During the autumn of 1358 a great army of English and Breton *routiers* invaded the Loire provinces under the command of the famous English captain Robert Knolles. Knolles' army was formed after the model of the Great Company of Arnaud de Cervole. It was a federation of smaller companies who accepted the leader's broad strategic direction, but fought under their own captains and were always liable to detach themselves in search of their own prey when the opportunity arose. For this reason the estimates which contemporaries made of its strength are more than usually unreliable. There were probably between 2,000 and 3,000 effective troops in addition to hangers on.[48] It was widely assumed in France that Edward III was behind Knolles' operations, but there is no reason to suppose that he was and some evidence that he was not. Knolles fought under the banner of the King of Navarre. But according to Froissart he proclaimed wherever he went that he fought 'simply for himself'. This was closer to the truth, whether he really said it or not.[49]

Knolles moved fast. By early October 1358 he had reached Orléans, where he passed three days in pillaging and burning the suburbs. A few days later he captured Châteauneuf-sur-Loire, with its important bridge over the river. Here he installed a permanent garrison and set up an advanced base for further operations during the winter. Scattered companies from his army split off from the rest and fanned out across the forest of Orléans and into the Gâtinais, establishing subsidiary garrisons and marking ransom districts for themselves.[50]

In the year of Our Lord 1358 the English came to Chantecoq, and on the evening of 31 October they took possession of the castle and burned almost all of the town. Then they brought the whole of the region around under their control, ordering every village great or small to ransom itself and buy back the bodies, goods and stores of every inhabitant, or see them burned, as they had been in so many other places. The people appeared before the Englishmen, confused and terrified. They agreed to pay in coin, flour, grain, or other victuals in return for a temporary respite from persecution. Those who stood in their way the English killed, or locked away in dark cells, threatening them daily with death, beating and maiming them, and leaving them hungry and destitute.

Thus begins the story of his tribulations, written by Hugh de Montgeron, the superior of the small priory of Saint-Thibault, eight miles from Chantecoq at the edge of marshes of the Gâtinais. When the invaders approached, Hugh hid the treasures of the priory and fled into the forest with the peasants. The English broke into the abandoned buildings. They drank the wine. They carried off the grain. They stole the horses and the vestments. In the forest, Hugh and the other refugees built themselves huts to live in. They 'ate their daily bread together in fear, sorrow and anguish.' They took turns to keep watch, catching occasional glimpses of the enemy attacking hamlets and isolated houses and listening to the distant sounds of fire and violence. But they did not remain undisturbed. The English wanted the fruits of the land. They were not prepared to allow the fields lie unsown and the wealth of the district to be strangled by weeds. They searched the forest, pulling out everyone they found there. They killed some of them, and ransomed others. A few remained hidden or escaped. One winter night, the soldiers evaded the forest sentries and found Hugh's hut. The noise of their approach woke him up before they reached the door, and he escaped naked into freezing swamp, clutching his habit in his hand. He eventually found his way to the walled city of Sens, ten miles away, where he was put up for a while by a relative. The captain of Chantecoq did not give up. He sent messages after him at Sens. He sent him a safe-conduct to return to Saint-Thibault. He threatened to burn down his priory unless he came. In February 1359 Hugh finally returned to Saint-Thibault and submitted. He bought protection for the priory and its domain until midsummer. It did him no good. Not long afterwards, the captain of Chantecoq was captured by the French, and the garrison was taken over by another adventurer who declined to recognise his predecessor's agreements. The newcomer seized Hugh on the road and robbed him. The priory was invaded again. The church plate was taken, then restored and taken again. The pigeons were eaten. Hugh sowed his harvest and paid more ransom money to protect it from destruction.

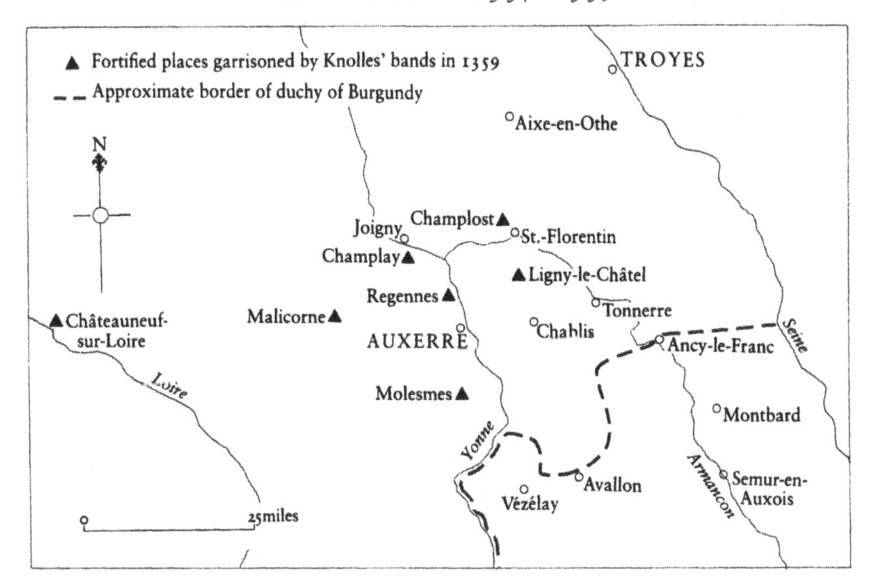

25 The Auxerrois, 1358–1359

Then he built himself a hiding place at the back of his barn for the day when the soldiers would return. In the following July, he sat down there and wrote down what had happened to him on the inside cover of a manuscript book, which still survives in a Paris library. 'What can you have experienced of sufferings like mine,' he wrote, 'all you people who live in walled cities and castles?'[51]

In the last few days of October 1358 Robert Knolles left Châteauneuf and advanced east into the Nivernais. At about the end of the month they occupied Malicorne, a great castle belonging to Margaret de Courtenay, situated in isolated, densely wooded country about twenty miles west of Auxerre. Here they established a fresh centre for exacting *patis* and long-distance raiding. When the Archpriest returned from Provence early in November 1358 he found the region which he had been charged to defend prostrate before the invader. Urged on by the Dauphin, Arnaud tried to organise a counter-attack. The result was a humiliating fiasco. The Archpriest led his own company and a miscellaneous force of local men east in Knolles' tracks, until they came to Malicorne. After a brief and ineffective siege of the place, he withdrew in circumstances which are obscure but were evidently regarded at the Dauphin's court as discreditable. There was worse to come. On his retreat the Archpriest laid siege to the castle of Corvol l'Orgeuilleux in the eastern Nivernais. Corvol was occupied by a splinter group from Knolles' host, commanded by an adventurer from Cheshire called John Waldboef. There he was captured by a sortie party and forced to sign a ransom contract for an enormous sum. His troops dispersed without achieving anything.[52]

At the beginning of December 1358 Robert Knolles' bands reached the River Yonne north of Auxerre. The departure of some of his companies on their own adventures and the need to leave garrisons in Châteauneuf and Malicorne had by now rather depleted his numbers, and it is unlikely that he had more than about 1,400 men with him. On 8 December they captured Regennes, a large fortified manor on the left bank of the river which belonged to the bishops of Auxerre. This place became the headquarters of Knolles himself and the shared base of at least three English companies: those of David (or Dakyn) Heton, John Dalton and Nicholas Tamworth. Heton was already well known as a garrison commander in Lower Normandy. Dalton was a retainer of the Duke of Lancaster whose background was rather similar. Tamworth was probably one of Knolles' lieutenants on the Breton march. All of them were to become notorious in the Auxerrois and northern Burgundy during the following months. Another Englishman called William Starkey, a criminal of ill repute from Chester, installed himself on the opposite side of the Yonne in the castle of the Counts of Tonerre at Ligny-le-Châtel.[53]

The Auxerrois proved to be the natural limit of Knolles' range. East and south of him lay the duchy of Burgundy, an ancient territory with a cohesive nobility and large cities, which conserved something of its ability to recruit troops and raise taxes. The Duke of Burgundy, Philip de Rouvre, was a minor, and the direction of affairs was in the hands of the Queen of France, who had been appointed as his guardian. She was a woman of limited political skills and perennially short of funds. But her council included some able soldiers and administrators. They had been able to build up the garrisons along the north-east march of the duchy, at Semur, Avallon, Montréal and Montbard, and to assemble more than 2,000 men along the border as Knolles approached. Further assistance had been summoned from the Count of Savoy.[54] As a result the English companies made no serious attempt on the duchy of Burgundy. Some of them turned north instead, and tried to penetrate into Champagne and the upper valley of the Seine. Moving up the Roman road they established a forward base at Aixe-en-Othe, a small village clustered by a fortified manor house. About 400 men gathered here in the new year. The great cathedral city of Troyes stood twenty miles away to the east, an inviting target. Troyes was a major centre of cloth manufacture, filled with rich churches and mansions, the monuments of an even richer past. Its defences were weak. There were ill-kempt ditches and a circuit of low earth works. Two wooden forts stood in front of the principal entrances. Otherwise there was nothing. The urgent need to do something about this had been pointed out by the royal *baillis* as long ago as 1346, but the project had been lost in indolence and disputation. Nonetheless, the place was energetically defended in 1359. The leading spirits were the Bishop, Henry of Poitiers, a resolute and worldly military clergyman, and the Count of Vaudémont, one of the Dauphin's Lieutenants in Champagne. On 12 January 1359 the English appeared before the walls. Vaudémont and the Bishop led their men through the gates, followed by a horde of armed citizens. The English were unused to being challenged in open country. They were caught unprepared and routed. They left 120 dead on the field and lost about the same number of prisoners, in all about two thirds of their strength. The survivors returned to their forts around Aixe and set fire to them. Then they retreated back into the Auxerrois.[55]

Knolles' army remained in the Auxerrois for nearly five months, an altogether exceptional period for a body of men of that size to stay in one place. A rough territorial division was worked out between the garrisons of Regennes and Ligny. This left Starkey with the territory east of the Yonne, while the garrisons of Regennes despoiled the west bank. Starkey was particularly active. He extended his ransom districts east across the county of Tonerre and south to the border of the duchy of Burgundy. The inhabitants of the villages around Auxerre joined in the pillage, as the only way of feeding themselves.[56] The situation of Auxerre itself was appalling. The city had once been one of the great river ports of eastern France. Surrounded by the famous vineyards of the Auxerrois and by those of the neighbouring districts of Tonerre and Chablis which produced the most expensive white wines in Europe, the citizens lived on the wine trade and on the traffic of the Seine. The city must have suffered grievously from the partial closure of the Seine at Melun just before the vintage of 1358. The destruction of the vineyards by the English completed the disaster.

The walls of Auxerre dated from the 1160s. They were not easy to defend, partly because of the steeply sloping hillside on which the city was built; partly because of their irregularity, the legacy of the clutter, demolitions and repairs of the years; and partly because of their great length, nearly 2 miles for a city whose male population of military age was probably much less than the official reckoning of 2,000. The townsmen had expelled their garrison a year before, at a time when many cities of France had come to distrust professional soldiers of whatever allegiance, and resolved to defend themselves. Yet they had neither the skills nor the experience to do so. There were no obvious leaders. The lord of the city, Jean III de Chalon, was a prisoner in England. His son was living in the citadel, but had no troops. On 10 January 1359 the Bishop of Auxerre lay dying in his palace attended by the clergy of his cathedral, swords in hand, as the bells rang out the alarm and the English launched the first of a succession of assaults against the walls. Two months later, on 10 March 1359, catastrophe befell Auxerre. About 1,000 men drawn from Regennes and the surrounding garrisons of the region approached the Porte d'Égleny. The watchmen were not at their posts. No one raised the alarm as the English scaled the wall, opened the gate to their companions waiting outside, and spread through the streets. Before the sun had risen the whole city including the citadel was in their hands. When it was all over Knolles, who still ranked no higher than a squire, received his knighthood at the hands of two of his subordinates.[57]

It was the first time that a city of comparable importance had been captured since the fall of Poitiers to Henry of Lancaster in 1346. But there was no repetition of the frenzied sack of Poitiers. This was to be a careful appropriation of the city's wealth by disciplined professional thieves whose procedures were calculated to maximise their profits. Hardly anyone was killed. Soldiers posted at the gates stopped the inhabitants from leaving so that they could be assessed for ransom. The floors were dug up and secret caches hacked out of the walls in which they had been hidden. In the cathedral the great silver lamps which hung before the high altar were taken down and the treasury was emptied. The portable booty of a city of more than twenty churches must have been prodigious. Some English reckonings gave the total value of the spoil at 500,000 *moutons*. No one tried to count the value of the personal ransoms. When the English had taken everything that could be found and carried away, they set about extracting the value of the rest. Knolles gathered together the leading citizens of Auxerre and stated his terms for refraining from the physical destruction of their city. After prolonged negotiation the inhabitants agreed to ransom their buildings for 50,000 *moutons* payable within three months, with an extra 50,000 payable in default. The citizens had the utmost difficulty in finding the money to redeem these pledges. The monks of the great abbey of St. Germain dug out the treasures which they had managed to conceal, including the jewelled reliquary of the saint, and pledged them to the conqueror. A deputation was sent to Paris to borrow from moneylenders on the security of other choice items from the treasury of St. Germain. But some of them refused to return, and the rest were robbed on the road home and lost everything that they had collected. The citizens managed to placate the English with a payment on account of sixty pearls, said to be worth 10,000 *moutons*, in exchange for which they received back the front plate of the reliquary. Later in the year, they were able to borrow another 32,000 florins by mortgaging future vintages to a syndicate of Parisian vintners. Further sums were raised by levying tolls on goods passing the city wall. But Knolles was never entirely paid off. Part of the debt remained outstanding until, many years later, he resolved to make his peace with God and was obliged by the Pope to make reparation for his sins. 'Moved by pity and remorse for the suffering of the city, and by love of God and reverence for the Holy Father', Knolles remitted what remained and surrendered the reliquary of St. Germain.[58]

A few days after the sack of Auxerre the cardinals of Périgord and Urgel passed through the region on their way back to Avignon, after the complete failure of the longest papal peacemaking mission of the fourteenth century. Their train made an imposing sight as it moved down the Dijon road. Passing Gyé-sur-Seine it was attacked by an armed band. The cardinals and their attendants were robbed of everything they had.[59]

The nakedness of the French countryside had rarely been more obvious. The ubiquitous lawyers who had served as *baillis* and seneschals before the war had long ago given way to professional soldiers. Royal captains had been charged with co-ordinating the defence of whole regions, and had rushed with clattering escorts from place to place. Yet these representatives of the central government had proved incapable of dealing with the dispersed menace of the companies. By the end of the 1350s the mass of the population had to put their faith in walls and ditches. The rash of minor fortifications which appeared across the French provinces, most of them designed to defend tiny areas, reflected a major shift of sentiment: the fragmentation of provincial communities, paralysis in the face of violence, the urge to hide away from danger, and underlying all these things a lack of confidence not only in the King's government but in all institutions of collective defence except for the most local.

France had always been densely scattered with castles and fortified houses. On the eve of the war, there was an average of one every 5 miles in the Agenais. The tax records of the *prévôté* of Montferrand, which comprised the most prosperous parts of Auvergne, point to a very similar density there. These figures are probably typical of fertile districts with fragmented landholdings and a tradition of political instability, in fact of much of eastern and southern France. During the war few new castles were added to their number. But a very large number of improvised forts was created out of of other buildings. The chronicler Jean de Venette, who lived in Paris throughout the tumults of the 1350s, describes how the villagers of the Île de France fortified their parish churches as the King of Navarre's partisans overran the region. Everywhere, he said, men were building timber platforms around the tops of their bell towers, digging ditches at the base, collecting stocks of food and piling up great stones to throw down on their assailants. Some churches were permanently converted into fortresses with reinforced walls, arrow slits and projecting stone galleries. If the parish church was unsuitable, the villagers turned to fortifying other massively constructed buildings: stone barns, large farm houses, local manors, water-mills. The royal commissioners who were appointed to inspect the defences of the *baillage* of Caen in 1371 found no less than 111 fortified places, including walled towns, fortified abbeys and churches, 'forts' and village citadels. A similar inspection in the western Gâtinais a few years earlier had disclosed in this small region alone six castles, twelve forts, five towers, five fortified houses, twenty-eight fortified churches and a fortified bridge, an average of one fortified building every three miles not including walled towns and villages. Most of these buildings and virtually all of the churches are likely to have been fortified since 1356. The great majority were militarily useless. When the English entered the Île de France in March 1360 they captured them all. Even the most elaborate, like the village church at Orly, with its fixed crossbows, garrison of 200 and victuals laid in for weeks, fell to them within a day or two. Some of these places became death traps when the enemy lit fires at the foot of the tower and watched as the defenders at the top were burnt alive or smothered by smoke.[60]

Castles were the prime centres of local defence, but they were of very variable strength. At one extreme there were the great fortresses of the King and the principal feudatories of the realm. These places were defended by experienced captains with large professional garrisons. They were usually in adequate repair, and many had been improved by

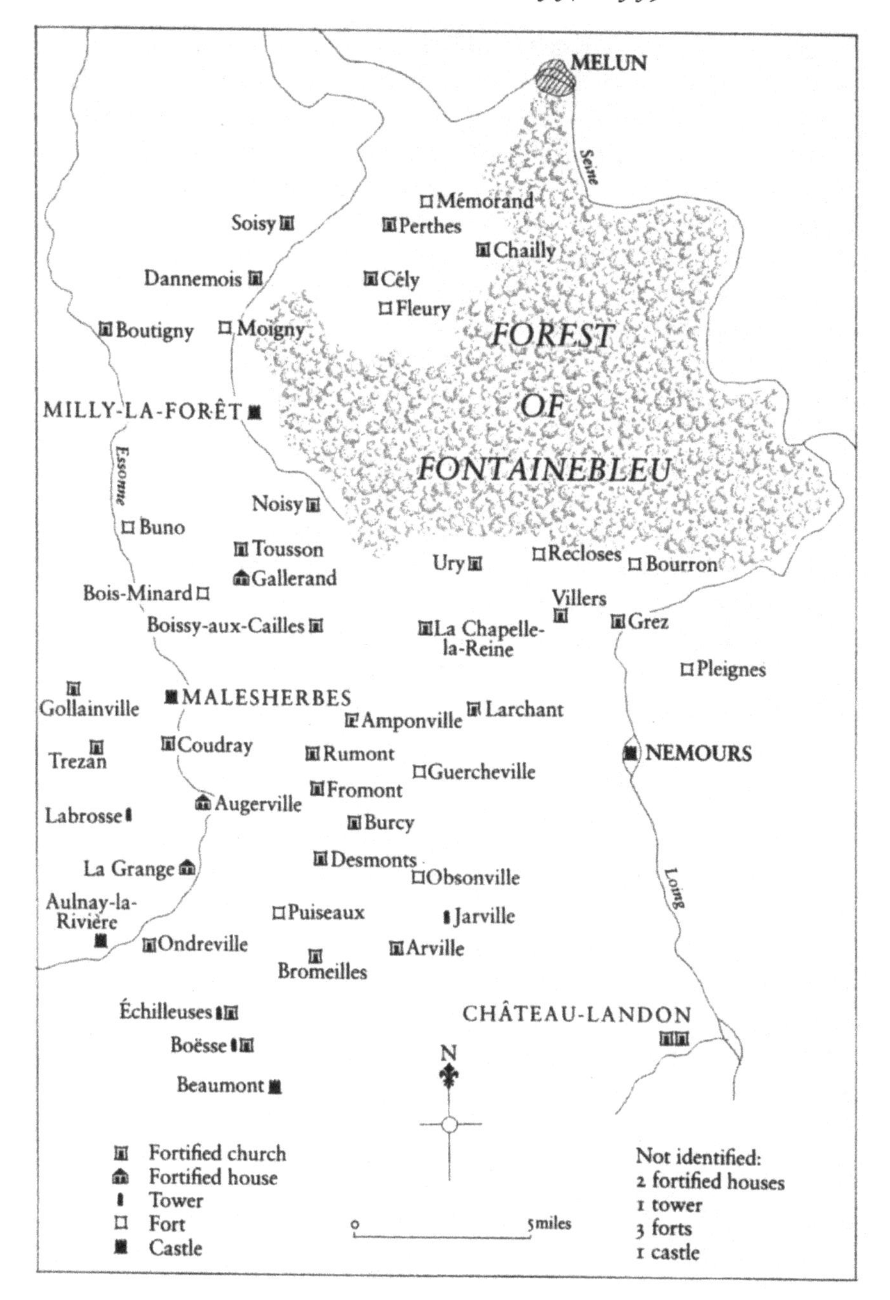

26 Fortifications of the Gâtinais, 1367

the techniques of an age which had learned a great deal about how fortresses fell. Curtain walls were raised to the level of the towers, defeating scaling ladders and making possible a continuous circuit around the walls. Great machicolated galleries of stone appeared around the crown of the walls and towers. Gateways were shouldered between enormous flanking towers. Crossed arrow slits, designed for crossbowmen, became virtually universal. Some of these places were also extremely well equipped. Bioule near Montauban, which was for practical purposes a royal castle since its owner was the royal captain in Quercy, had at least twenty-one pieces of gunpowder artillery mounted on the walls and towers, as well as the traditional stone throwers and fixed crossbows.[61]

Such places, however, were hardly typical. Much more familiar to most countrymen was the aged seigneurial castle or small fortified manor: a solitary tower surrounded by farm buildings and shallow ditches; or a farmhouse with thick walls and bricked-up windows. These small rural strongholds were often well-sited and massively built, but they were poorly repaired and guarded by a garrison comprising the owner's retainers and family and pressed men from the surrounding district. The rich surviving documentation of the imperial county of Burgundy suggests that such places rarely had garrisons more than twenty-five strong, and ten or twelve was commoner. They could be extremely cramped when filled with refugees with their carts, animals and household goods. Not all of them had proper working wells or baking ovens. Moreover, they were heavily dependent for their defence on the arrangements which the owner was able to make with the nearby communities. The law, building on ancient and largely forgotten custom, entitled the owner of any defensible castle to call for assistance from communities who lived near enough to take refuge there. They could be required to serve watches on the walls or to labour on the ditches. They could be mulcted for contributions to the cost of maintaining and supplying the place. During the first quarter century of the war, the King's courts developed a large if rather miscellaneous body of jurisprudence on the subject. But duty was one thing, performance another. In practice the defence of places like these varied with the resources and negotiating skills of the owner. The fortified farm Longeil, defended by peasants, resisted John Fotheringhay's companies for the best part of eighteen months, but the renown which these peasants earned by their achievement is perhaps the best evidence of how unusual it was. In the county of Burgundy, a hundred men were reckoned to be quite enough to capture the average fortified manor.[62]

Where castles were not available, the most satisfactory alternatives were generally monasteries. They generally stood behind walled enclosures, and their spacious, massively constructed buildings were readily converted into fortresses. By the end of the 1350s the great majority of rural monasteries which had not been abandoned or demolished, had been fortified to serve as refuges for the inhabitants of the surrounding country. The collegiate church of St. Aignan outside Orléans, which was fortified in about 1356, is described as having a captain, a new well, a mill and a baking oven, store-rooms filled with victuals and a permanent garrison of thirty men. Many of these conversions were the result of elaborate bargains between the monks and the inhabitants, by which the latter undertook to contribute to the cost and to do guard duty on the walls. The church of the famous Benedictine abbey of Bec had only recently been completed when, in the autumn of 1356, the royal Lieutenant in Lower Normandy offered the monks the alternatives of demolishing or fortifying it. According to the domestic chronicle of the house, they conferred with the nobility of the region and with representatives of the outlying villages and eventually chose a combination of both options. They demolished three walks of their cloister, the whole of the dormitory and most of their outbuildings. With the stone obtained from the demolitions, they constructed masonry walls across the chapels of the apse and battlements around the roofs of the church, belfry and chapter-house. They surrounded them all with ditches. They bought a great quantity of equipment and hired a large professional garrison, which consumed all their revenues and stores and left them hardly any space in which to conduct their services.[63]

The rapid proliferation of fortified places was regarded by the population of the provinces as a source of strength. It was in fact a serious weakness. It meant that resources were too thinly spread to provide effective defence. The King's captains in the provinces were forever trying to encourage the use of a much smaller number of forts, which could be better built, better supplied and better defended, albeit that countrymen might have a longer trek to reach them. But the results of their efforts were very meagre. The problem was well described by the Bishop of Albi, who complained in 1359 about the construction by a local nobleman of a new keep at Carmaux in the northern Albigeois. Hitherto, the Bishop said, the inhabitants of the Cérou valley had always taken refuge with their stores and possessions in his own castle at Monastiès five miles downstream. They had served watches there day and night and manned the walls against passing bands of *routiers*. Now, those who lived in the eastern part of the valley went to Carmaux instead because it was nearer. As a result, neither place was properly guarded. The Lieutenant of Languedoc ordered the partial demolition of Carmaux. But the decline of royal authority in the regions made it easy to ignore such orders. The keep of Carmaux was still in use a year later. The citizens of Maçon had a very similar problem. The town was desperately short of manpower to defend its enormous circuit of walls. But villagers living within walking distance of the town of Maçon were prevented by their lords from doing watch duty there because they were wanted for the defence of innumerable seigneurial fortlets in the valleys around. Not only were most of these places incapable of protecting the men of their district and liable to undermine the defence of stronger places nearby, but they frequently provided ready-made keeps for *routiers* who knew much better than their owners or the local villagers how to defend them. Raymond de Mareuil, whose company operated in Périgord in the early 1350s, had garrisons in no less than eleven fortified churches, most of which had probably been fortified against him.[64]

The only solution to these problems was the wholesale demolition of minor rural fortifications, a difficult and ultimately perhaps an impossible task. The Crown had always asserted the right to make the owners of ill-defended or indefensible forts improve or demolish them. 'To us alone belongs the duty of protecting our realm and its inhabitants, of directing its defence and of ordaining its wars,' the advocates of John II declared in his name, 'and to us alone therefore belongs the right to build and defend the fortresses of the land.'[65] But few people accepted this proposition, even in theory. Although the power to order demolitions was occasionally exercised, the King's officers were inevitably resisted by the minor nobility who owned most of these places and often by their subjects, who preferred a weak refuge nearby to a strong one far away. The main supporters of the policy of demolition were the larger towns. They needed the manpower and stores of the agricultural population for their own defence. They also objected to minor forts on the roads around them which if they fell into the hands of the companies could be used to choke off their trade. When the castle of Faye in Poitou was demolished in 1357 the initiative came from the citizens of the nearby town of Saint-Maixent. They met in the chapter-house of the Franciscan convent and, seeing that Faye was an 'isolated place where enemies prowl about day and night', resolved to petition the royal captain and the provincial estates for its destruction. Other towns simply took matters into their own hands. The radical cabals which took over the government of many northern towns in the late 1350s embarked on ferocious campaigns of demolition against the seigneurial castles of their regions. The Parisian mobs of Etienne Marcel attacked dozens of manors of the Île de France. Abbeville demolished five seigneurial castles in its district in 1358 and took over a sixth. Orléans demolished a large number of fortified houses and monasteries on the approach of Robert Knolles' bands later that year. Tours slighted five castles of Touraine in 1359.

It was the urban radicals of the Estates-General in Paris who drew up in February 1358 the first comprehensive programme of demolition. All the 'petites forteresses' which had been put up in recent times were ordered to be destroyed, and all other fortifications to be placed in the hands of people who could be relied upon to defend them. Class hatred was at least part of the motive for this legislation. But a slightly less ambitious version of this decree was included the great ordinance of May 1358 which followed the Dauphin's Estates-General at Compiègne. This ordained that commissioners should be appointed in every region to inspect fortifications, ensure that those which were defensible were properly manned and supplied, and demolish the rest. A similar ordinance was issued by the Estates-General of Languedoc. In spite of the extremely difficult conditions of the time, it is clear that a great deal of survey work was done. Sporadic evidence survives of the commissioners' activities in the Paris area, the Orléanais, the Beauvaisis, Champagne and Picardy, and what survives is probably fairly typical of their unrecorded activities elsewhere. The problem was that their orders were not always obeyed once they had passed on to the next district. The commissioners for the Beauvaisis ordered the destruction of two castles there in early 1358 which were still standing when the Jacques destroyed them several months later. Even those demolitions which occurred were not always skilfully done. The castle of Verdey in Champagne, which was partially dismantled in 1359, was almost immediately occupied and refortified by the bands of Eustache d'Aubricourt. The citizens of Tours blew up the curtain walls of Azay with gunpowder in the same year, but it was still being used by the companies in the 1360s. The commissioners' task was so immense that it would have been hard for them to make much impression on it even in ideal conditions, and the conditions of the late 1350s were very far from ideal.[66]

By the end of the decade the organised defence of the countryside had been virtually abandoned, and all efforts were being concentrated on holding the principal walled towns. The defence of these places owed little to the efforts of the Crown or its servants, but it was much the most significant achievement of the defenders of France in the first quarter-century of the war. The record speaks for itself. Poitiers was taken by assault in 1346 at a time when few French towns had even begun to think seriously about organising their defence. Calais fell to the largest English army seen in France until the Napoleonic wars, after an eleven-month siege by land and sea which bankrupted Edward III. Auxerre was captured by escalade in 1359 as a result of the negligence of the watch, and le Puy followed later in the same year, certainly by the same method and probably by the same cause. Every other attempt to capture a major walled town in this period failed. In particular, no large town (except Calais) was successfully besieged. The great sieges of Bordeaux (1339), Tournai (1340), Rennes (1356–7), Melun (1358–9), Reims (1359–60) and Paris (1360) all had to be abandoned. In every case except the last at least one assault *en masse* against the walls had been attempted. All had been repulsed. The failure of the ten-month siege of Rennes is particularly eloquent, for Rennes was neither well situated nor well walled. Its only resource was the determination of its inhabitants. Yet they successfully resisted a large English army led by one of Edward III's most talented generals.

The main reason for the relative invulnerability of the larger towns was their sheer size. A small town or castle could be surrounded by ditches and temporary forts (or *bastides*) and completely blockaded. This was impractical for a great city. It was usually necessary to distribute the besiegers on either side of a river and, in the case of cities on a confluence, on three sides. The divided sectors of the besieging army generally found it difficult to communicate with each other. They were always exposed to the risk of being attacked in detail by a garrison operating on internal lines with the advantage of surprise. Cutting off the city's river communications was particularly problematical. A shallow river could be blocked by sinking barges in the navigable channels, as the Charente was during the siege of Tonnay in 1349–50. But it took 300 carpenters several weeks to build a boom across the Garonne at Aiguillon in 1346. The Dauphin built a boom upstream of Paris in 1358 but never succeeded in cutting the city off. The forces required for these spectacular sieges were huge and tended to outrun their supplies of food long before the defenders of the city did. Jean de Marigny withdrew from Bordeaux in 1339 because his army was starving whereas the city was plentifully supplied by river and had not even begun to feel the pinch.[67]

The mid-fourteenth century was the last age in which properly constructed and defended walls were more or less invulnerable to attack. There was no artillery available in the 1350s capable of doing serious damage to them. The traditional wooden stone-throwing engines, operating by torsion and counterweights, were still built according to a design which had barely changed for 150 years. They were inaccurate and unwieldy and had to be erected on site, a process which could take a considerable time. Their high trajectory made them extremely effective for breaking roofs and crushing heads, or generating panic in crowded streets, but that is all. In this period, gunpowder artillery was a weapon of defence, mounted on the terraces of walls and towers for use against men. Cannon, with their more level trajectory, would eventually provide besieging armies with a formidable weapon against masonry walls, but not until the last years of the fourteenth century. Mining was occasionally tried, and specialist sappers accompanied most large armies. The citadel of la Réole on the Garonne was forced to surrender in 1345 after the Earl of Lancaster's mines had made the place untenable. The citadel of Cormicy in Champagne was actually brought down by mines in 1359. Froissart has a memorable description of the props in the gallery taking fire and the great square tower slowly splitting open from the top as the masonry collapsed into two great mounds on either side. But this dramatic moment was rarely seen. Mining could only be attempted in suitable ground conditions, and even then was usually prevented by deep ditches and moats. Modern walls were built to withstand mines, and garrisons were wary of them. They listened to the ground, or took bowls of water to the summits of the towers to watch for vibrations rippling the surface. They then dug countermines. The commonest method of attacking a town or castle was still the traditional assault *en masse* over the walls, which depended on sheer force of numbers to overcome the defence. Various devices, such as assault towers and mobile shelters known as 'cats' were constructed to enable men to reach a wall under the merciless rain of missiles but they rarely remained intact for long. Scaling ladders remained the main means of attack. Geoffrey de Charny gives a graphic account of this appallingly dangerous operation of war: the ladders swinging overhead against the wall, the terrified mass of men at the base running up encumbered by their armour into a thicket of lances and swords, thrown back by huge boulders and the falling bodies of their companions on the rungs above. The attempt almost always failed, with heavy casualties.[68]

From the mid-1340s onward almost all French cities sought to improve their natural advantages by great programmes of wall-building. At the beginning of the war French city walls had been in a lamentable state. Most of them dated from the last great age of medieval wall-building in the eleventh and twelfth centuries and some, particularly in the south, from Gallo-Roman times. Fat suburbs had long ago spread beyond them. There was a particular problem at cities like Tours, Limoges, Périgueux, Rodez and several dozen others, which had grown up around two centres, a 'city' and a 'bourg', with separate circuits of walls that did not intercommunicate, and unprotected suburbs in between. Few city walls had been properly maintained in the long years of peace. They generally comprised an irregular mixture of stone gates and towers with walls of mud, rubble or timber. Gaps had often been left by the builders or pierced by the inhabitants for access. Houses had been built through the whole thickness of rampart, with stone pillaged from it. The cleared path behind the walls, which was conventionally supposed to be at least twelve palms (eight feet) wide, was commonly blocked up with hovels and variegated junk, leaving parts of the circuit of the walls inaccessible to the defenders.[69]

Complete circuits of stone walls were prodigiously expensive to build. The walls of Cahors were completely rebuilt in twenty months in the late 1340s at a cost of 67,000 *l.t.* the whole of which was advanced by the Crown. The walls of Avignon, which were in the main built between 1359 and 1373, cost the Papal Chamber well over 120,000 florins. But expenditure on this scale was possible only for governments, and not always for them. Most French cities received very modest grants from the Crown towards their walls and were authorised to levy tolls and duties for their wall-funds, but were otherwise left to find the money as best they could. A good deal of ingenuity was applied to the business of raising money by mortgaging tax revenues and selling annuities (in effect, the earliest municipal bonds). Even so, most major programmes of wall building had to be spread over many years, and often over generations. The most remarkable example was probably Reims, whose walls were completed in 1359. These vast walls, extending over four miles, with six gates, two fortified bridges and fifty-two towers represented one of the most impressive municipal investments of the period. But they had taken 150 years to build, years punctuated by ferocious internal quarrels about their precise course, the requisitioning of land and materials and above all about the payment of murage taxes. Even under the pressure of war Dijon took twenty-five years, from 1355 to 1380, to rebuild its twelfth-century walls. Dijon was rich, and supported by the even richer Dukes of Burgundy. Others ruined themselves in the process of building walls against the enemy. The great southern city of Montpellier borrowed 15,000 florins for immediate repairs after the Prince of Wales' raid of 1355, and further large sums at intervals over the next few years, as well as levying heavy internal taxes and diverting huge sums from various urban charities. Montpellier became one of the most secure cities in France, but by 1362 it was bankrupt. The consuls' houses were being taken in execution for taxes which the city owed to the King. The Pope was threatening to enforce the debts owed to him by excommunication. Ultimately Montpellier was to decline from the first commercial city of Languedoc to a modest country town by the beginning of the fifteenth century. The financial burdens of defence were a major cause of its misfortunes.[70]

The main burden of defending towns invariably fell on their inhabitants. Permanent garrisons were unpopular. They cost money, and tended to steal and riot. Royal garrisons, which the town had to pay but did not control, were particularly unwelcome. In 1351 the citizens of Saint-Maixent in Poitou arrested the entire garrison of their town and locked them in a tower after a series of disorders for which they were held responsible. Violent incidents like this were surprisingly common and became even more so after 1356 when the pay of royal garrisons fell into arrears and discipline largely broke down. As a result of these animosities, town garrisons were few and small, except in frontier areas. Where they existed, their main function was not to defend the walls but to guard the citadel, which commonly belonged to the King or to the lord of the town and whose defence was organised independently. Some towns employed their own garrison troops on the walls. Paris maintained a permanent body of 200 professional crossbowmen at the end of the 1350s in addition to the full-time knights and sergeants of the watch. Similar corps of municipal crossbowmen are known to have been employed at Rouen, Caen, Arras, Amiens and Saint-Omer. Poitiers had some professional soldiers permanently in its pay. Rodez hired mercenaries for short periods in emergencies. Two hundred of them served the city during the campaigns of 1356. All the walled towns of Picardy are said to have hired professional troops to stiffen the defence during the English invasion at the end of 1359. Many towns hired professional captains to train and inspect the citizens of the watch and command the defence of the walls during an attack.[71]

Yet professionals never displaced the inhabitants of the town, even in a rich and highly organised community like Paris whose fate was intimately bound up with the Crown's. Compulsory military service was an almost universal feature of urban life. The regulations made for the city of Poitiers in 1347, after its sack by Henry of Lancaster, were fairly typical of arrangements which prevailed almost everywhere. Every adult male living within the walls or in the immediate suburbs was liable for military service, and expected to serve with equipment suitable to his wealth and status: the rich with the full range of personal armour and weaponry, the middling sort with a lance, buckler and padded jacket, the poor with a sword or spear or any other implement which they could lay hands on. The men were usually organised in units, conventionally ten or fifty strong, which were assigned a specific function in the event of attack. Nîmes may have been a more bureaucratically governed city than most, but the arrangements which it made in 1358 for the organisation of its defence were typical of those made less formally elsewhere. The citizenry was divided into fourteen units of fifty householders, each under a *cinquantenier* with five *dixeniers* under him. Every *cinquante* was charged with the defence of a particular sector of the walls. Precise ordinances were distributed in which every man was assigned his place and the weapons that he should be carrying. In times of 'great necessity' the householders belonging to these units were expected to bring out all the able bodied men of their household to help repel an attack.

In principle two kinds of duty were expected of citizens in addition to the *levée en masse* which occurred when an assault was imminent. The richer ones, who could afford good armour and weapons, were posted in shifts at the gates during daylight hours. This was undoubtedly the more congenial form of service. At Poitiers, the regulations of 1347 required that each gate should be permanently manned when open by ten 'personnes notables et convenables', whose main function was to fight off any attempt to rush the entrance for long enough to close the gates and sound the alarm. The second duty was the watch on the walls, mainly at night, which was the lot of the ordinary citizen and could be extremely onerous. The accounts of Rodez for a slightly later period suggest that in this medium-sized provincial city a single shift of the watch involved about fifty men. These figures imply about one man for every fifty yards of wall and at least one duty a week for able-bodied males. But this was light by comparison with other cities. Lyon was protected on three sides by the Rhone, and walled only on the fourth, but it organised the watch in shifts of 200, all drawn from the 'common people', in addition to the thirty-two 'tradesmen' who did duty on the towers and forty 'notables' who served in mounted patrols. Parisian tradesmen were being required to do three shifts a week during the troubles of 1358. The job was extremely dull and usually had to be combined with a full day at work before and after. Many places fell because the guards were asleep or absent when the enemy came over the walls.

At night a curfew was imposed. The town councillors took possession of the keys and patrolled the streets on horseback for signs of trouble. The gates were opened for no one. There are few images more evocative than Froissart's account of the attempt of the Constable of France and the Count of Saint-Pol to enter Saint-Quentin with a company of men-at-arms at five o'clock one morning in 1359, in order to cross the Somme bridge. 'We are friends. . .', they cried from the clearing beyond the gate; 'we command you to open at once in the King's name.' The guards had to wake the consuls to ask for the keys. A hurried meeting of the town council was convened. Then a head appeared at a window above the gate to offer the town's apologies to the assembled men-at-arms below, and its refusal to let them in on any account. 'Gross and base words' were exchanged, but the gates remained firmly closed.[72]

The funding of wall-building and the organisation of the watch were the main preoccupations of almost every French municipality, and the fears and pressures of urban life turned many of them into tiny republics governed on increasingly authoritarian lines. In October 1352, during the English invasion of Quercy, Martel, a small town of about 2,500 souls, placed itself under the command of a committee of eight, presided over by a 'governor'. The committee raised taxes greatly exceeding the King's. They compulsorily recruited citizens to work on the ditches. They ordered the inhabitants of the suburbs within the walls. They demolished buildings which interfered with the defence and seized private stocks of building material. They administered oaths of loyalty to the inhabitants. They arrested and tortured suspicious strangers and occasionally executed them. These local committees of public safety became very common. At Tours, a city riven by internal strife for centuries, John II instituted in March 1356 an elected commission of five men armed with despotic powers to organise the defence of the city without regard to private interests. Most cities did not wait for royal authority before organising themselves on similar lines. When the Breton companies began to raid around Orléans in 1358 the inhabitants, frustrated by what they saw as the supine inactivity of the Duke of Orléans, elected commissioners for their defence who taxed them, directed work on the walls and carried out large scale demolitions inside and outside the town. In the following year Reims was to become the model of these miniature despotisms created to withstand a sudden military threat from outside.[73]

The larger towns extended their power beyond their walls, assuming control of the rural districts around them, very much as the cities of northern Italy had long ago taken control of their *contade* to fill the vacuum left by the disappearance of a powerful central authority. In this they were encouraged by the King's officials and judges, who saw in these arrangements the only effective defence of the peasantry of the *plat pays* against the companies. Walled towns, like castles, were entitled to claim services and money from the inhabitants of all places from which men were wont to come and find refuge in times of danger. The conventional size of this *ressort* was two French leagues (about five miles) from the walls. But it could be greater if there was no other suitable refuge in the vicinity. The *ressort* of Chateaudun in the Beauce included villages as far as eleven miles from the walls. Fifty-five villages around Châlons-sur-Marne were obliged to contribute to the cost of its defence, each of which was responsible for a short section of the walls. Forty villages within ten miles supported the defence of Troyes. And where law stopped, force began. In the mid-1350s contributions to the fortification of Saint-Lô in the Cotentin were being exacted by gangs of thugs sent out from the town to terrorise villages across the whole of the dioceses of Avranches and Coutances. The town sergeants of Auxerre seized men by main force in the villages of Auxerrois to guard their walls and dig their ditches, fighting off wives and mothers as they did so. This was fair enough, or so the townsmen told themselves. The towns needed the manpower, stores and above all the money of the surrounding peasantry, and the obligations which they assumed in return could be extremely burdensome. Space had to be found for refugees. At Martel a municipal officer was charged with requisitioning rooms and assessing rents for them. Rouen put up hundreds of them in the ruined buildings of the Hotel-Dieu de la Madeleine. Other cities organised great shanty-towns in clearings within their walls. Refugees disrupted the economic life of the city, introducing traders and artisans who competed with their hosts and could not be accommodated within the monopolistic structures of the urban guilds. Some of these wretches became semi-permanent additions to the population as the villages from which they had come were burnt out and the countryside outside became an uncultivable wilderness.[74]

Cities had traditionally lived among countrymen, but the experience of war increasingly insulated them from their surroundings, creating fortified islands of security in the midst of the desolation around. The almost complete disappearance of suburbs was the most visible symptom of the divergent fortunes of town and country. Suburbs, which had once had sprawled formlessly outward from the gates to merge with the landscape of vegetable gardens and vineyards, had been the chief legacy of the great urban boom of the previous century. Here were the residences of the richest citizens and the sites of the churches of the Dominican and Franciscan friars, who were forbidden without papal licence to establish themselves within the walls. Much of the vitality of pre-war French towns had been concentrated in their suburbs. But they tempted enemies by their wealth and gave them cover behind their buildings. By the end of the 1350s most towns which could not wall their suburbs had cleared them. The citizens of Orléans, who before 1358 had been surrounded by rich, unwalled districts with fine churches and monasteries, now looked on a desert of ruins. In 1359, when the *bailli* of Sens was preparing to defend his town, he ordered the demolition of two monasteries, two suburban churches, a Franciscan convent, a hospital, a pilgrims' hospice, two groups of water mills and a number of fortified houses, not to speak of humbler dwellings whose owners could not afford to complain and whose fate therefore went unrecorded. City walls now rose sheer from newly cut ditches and the charred masonry of their former suburbs and, as these were gradually covered by vegetation, from a sea of green like the idealised townscapes of the miniatures of the Duke of Berry's *Très Riches Heures*.[75]

Other changes, less visible perhaps to outsiders, must have been equally obvious to those who had grown up in pre-war towns. Most of the gates through which townsmen had once looked out into the open country beyond were now permanently closed for reasons of security. At Nîmes, only two of the seven gates were in use in 1359, and those only on alternate days. The others were walled up. At Poitiers, three of the six gates were permanently shut. At Montauban, and no doubt in other carefully defended towns, even the main gates were not opened until patrols had searched the woods nearby for armed men, and asked after enemies at local fords and cross-roads. Vineyards and vegetable gardens by which urban families once supplied their needs were abandoned. Essential services were brought within the walls. Markets were crammed into narrow streets instead of extending over suburban meadows. Grain mills, traditionally located in the suburbs, were dismantled and brought into the city, like the suburban water mills of

Bourges which were re-erected inside the river gates in 1359. The butchers of Martel, who had always been required to carry out their filthy trade outside the walls, were relocated in the city. The streets stank as people living away from the open gates could no longer take their rubbish outside. The inhabitants crowded into ever more densely populated tenements as the suburbs and countryside emptied out. These changes brought significant transformation in the mentality of the inhabitants. Cities protected. Cities enclosed. Cities repelled. The watchman in the bell-tower looking out over a hostile world, the petulant guards at the gates who recognised every citizen who belonged, and inspected strangers who did not, searching their luggage and reading their letters, were the paradigm figures of the self-contained, perennially suspicious world of late medieval towns.[76]

During the winter of 1358–9, as the progressive deterioration of the situation in France became known in England, the prisoners and counsellors around John II grew desperate. To these men, who were by now willing to concede almost anything to be free, the real enemy was no longer the King of England but Charles of Navarre. The solution seemed obvious: a further substantial cession of territory to the English, in exchange for their armed assistance in putting down Charles' rebellion. John himself seems to have become a passive spectator of events. He passed the winter at the Savoy palace, waiting to be removed to Somerton, an austere moated castle in Lincolnshire to which the King of England had banished him when the treaty of Windsor failed. At the beginning of February 1359, just as his baggage was being loaded into barges in the Thames, the move was cancelled and John was told to stay in London until further notice. By the end of the month letters from the French exiles in London were reporting fresh negotiations, a new peace and a joint plan to wage 'bonne guerre et forte' against the King of Navarre. The Chancellor of Navarre, Robert de la Porte, and Charles's old confidant Friquet de Fricamps, were sent in great haste to England without notice or safe-conduct to protect his interests. Whatever arguments they employed fell on deaf ears. The treaty was complete by the middle of March. On the 24th it was sealed by the two Kings in London. The treaty of Windsor had required nearly a year of painstaking haggling. But the essential terms of the treaty of London which replaced it were agreed in less than a month.[77] It was an almost complete capitulation.

The provisions for the French King's ransom were much the same as those of the earlier treaty. But the transfers of territory were far more extensive. Edward III was now to have, in addition to the provinces ceded by the treaty of Windsor, the whole of Brittany, Normandy, Maine, Anjou and Touraine in full sovereignty. The surrender of these provinces would have reconstituted the Angevin empire as it had been at the high point of the reign of Henry II in the twelfth century. Moreover, the English enclave around Calais and Guines, which Henry II had never owned, was to be extended southward to include the Boulonnais. Edward III would have obtained just under half the territory of France, including all the Atlantic provinces other than Flanders and Picardy. These terms were certain to be unacceptable to the King of Navarre. Not only did they provide for the release of John II, which it was Charles' main purpose to prevent. They also ceded to the English King virtually all of Charles' domains in France, which were concentrated in Normandy. A joint embassy was to be sent to call on him to submit and to accept suitable but ill-defined compensation elsewhere. If he failed to do so by 24 June 1359, then the Kings of England and France proposed jointly to make war on him.

The Florentine chronicler Villani called it the 'phoney peace'. He thought that Edward III had simply imposed it on his hapless prisoner in order to justify invading France when it proved impossible to enforce. But there is no doubt that both signatories took it entirely seriously. The English King postponed his expedition until June 1359. John II for his part set about meeting the extremely tight timetable for the remaining formalities. He was given two and a half months in which to consult his subjects and confirm that the treaty could be performed. This process was to be completed by 9 June 1359. Some minor bones of contention were to be sorted out between the councillors of the two Kings by 24 June 1359, when it was evidently intended that the treaty would be ratified. Assuming that all these matters were satisfactorily dealt with, the first 600,000 *écus* (£100,000) of the ransom had to be found by 1 August 1359. On the same day, ten prominent French noblemen and twenty castles and walled towns were to be delivered up as security for the rest of John's obligations. He would then be released. John busied himself with the task of persuading his subjects of the excellence of the bargain. The Marshal, Arnoul d'Audrehem, was released on parole to carry the news to Paris. He was followed by the Archbishop of Sens and the Counts of Tancarville and Dammartin bringing the full text and a clutch of instructions addressed to the Dauphin and to various functionaries in the principal government departments.[78]

When, however, these emissaries arrived in France with the terms it became apparent that John had seriously miscalculated the balance of opinion there. The treaty undoubtedly had some support. But its terms offended a large number of disparate interests which were united in opposition to it. The provinces of Normandy and the lower Loire were close to the political heart of France in a way that Périgord or Angoumois or even Poitou never had been. They contained some of its chief ecclesiastical and industrial cities, and some of the principal political families of the realm, all of whom would become subjects of Edward III if the treaty were confirmed. Even those parts of France which were not directly affected by the cession of the western provinces were gravely affected indirectly. The loss of every major river estuary of the Atlantic coast except for the Somme had grave implications for some of the larger inland cities, which would lose their access to the sea. The prospect that Paris, for example, would be dependent on Rouen in the same way as the cities of the south-west had for decades been dependent on Bordeaux must have been extremely unattractive to the Parisians. Moreover, the truncated remnant of France would now have to meet the financial burden of the ransom and of the future defence of the realm without the contributions of some of its richest regions. The Dauphin's own sentiments are not recorded, but must have been highly equivocal. For all his public professions of loyalty to his father he cannot have welcomed a peace which deprived him of the duchy of Normandy and partitioned the kingdom that would one day be his.

Frustrated by the interminable deliberations at Westminster and the continual advances of the English bands in northern France, the Dauphin had been looking for some months at more aggressive solutions to the stalemate. Some idea of how desperate he had become can be had from the fantastic scheme which was occupying his mind at the very time when his father was agreeing to the bleak terms offered by the English. This involved a projected landing on the east coast of Scotland by 12,000 mercenaries hired in Germany and Denmark, who were supposed to join forces with the Scots and descend on England to ravage the country and rescue John II by force from his prison. The author of this plan was Waldemar III, King of Denmark. He had not the slightest personal or political interest in the French war and had simply put the package together as a commercial deal. A fee had been agreed of 600,000 florins, payable as soon as the troops were mustered and the fleet ready. How serious Waldemar was is difficult to say. But he sent the most optimistic reports to the Dauphin of the state his preparations. He had already (he said) made contact with the Scots and with native leaders in Wales who were willing to raise a rebellion there. His fleet was almost ready. The French were invited to send representatives to Denmark to see with their own eyes.[79]

On 19 May 1359 the Estates-General met in the royal Palace in Paris to consider the terms of the treaty of London. It was a poorly attended assembly. There had been no time for the representatives to arrive from the more distant places, and even those close at hand were deterred by reports of brigandage on the roads around the capital. The dominant group is likely to have comprised the officials and councillors of the Dauphin, who made no secret of their objections; and the delegates of the municipality of Paris, which had always been foremost among those who wanted to resist the English. The merits of the treaty were vigorously debated, but in the end most of the delegates were agreed on their response. 'Unacceptable, impossible', they called it. They urged the Dauphin to repudiate it and wage 'bonne guerre' against the enemy. Only two months after it had been sealed, the 'phoney peace' was dead.[80]

The delegates struggled with the consequences of their decision until well into June. The Dauphin's treasury was certainly not equal to the strain of a fresh campaign without a large inflow of tax revenue. The representatives of the towns were eventually persuaded, subject to the approval of their constituents, to finance an army of 12,000 men for the defence of France. They were also willing, they said, to contribute 200,000 florins to the cost of Waldemar III's invasion of England. The other two estates fell in behind the towns. The nobility agreed in addition to serve in the Dauphin's armies without pay for a month. Much of this was fanciful. There was no prospect of raising these sums in the current condition of France, even had the delegates' constituents been willing, which they were not. Only the Parisians responded with any enthusiasm. Most of the provincial towns replied that they had suffered too much war damage and were too burdened by the cost of their own defence. Some returned no answer at all. The Dauphin's views of the taxable capacity of the realm were entirely unrealistic. He was advised, for example, that the towns of Auvergne could afford to contribute the cost of 500 soldiers at a time when they were struggling for survival against a great influx of Gascon companies and at their wits' end to find money for their own safety. They contributed nothing.[81]

The extraordinary Danish project limped on for a few weeks longer. Early in June the Dauphin's emissaries left for Toulouse to try to raise the rest of Waldemar's fee from the communities of Languedoc. The southerners were not enthusiastic. When their representatives met at Béziers in August 1359 some of them were apparently prepared to join in a grant of about half the sum required, on condition that the rest did the same. A few even made arrangements to send their agents to inspect the preparations said to be on foot in Denmark. In the event, nothing was granted by the men of Languedoc and the 200,000 florins promised by Languedoil were never collected. As for the Scots, they were sufficiently interested to send two ambassadors to discuss the project in Paris in June: Robert Erskine, Chamberlain of Scotland and principal director of Scottish foreign policy for many years, and an Aberdeenshire knight, Norman Leslie. These two haggled with the Dauphin's councillors in the Salle Neuve of the Palace, and eventually agreed to renew the old alliance in return for a subsidy of 50,000 marks. The whole negotiation was unreal. The Scots could not make war on the English without first paying the 90,000 marks outstanding from David II's ransom, while the French could not even afford the 50,000 marks that they had promised. Neither the Danes nor the Scots received their subsidies, and neither stirred in the Dauphin's interest. Erskine and Leslie left Paris for Avignon in June. Erskine eventually returned to Scotland in the autumn. Leslie, who was a seasoned adventurer, stayed behind in France, taking service with the Queen in Burgundy. There he was almost immediately captured by *routiers* from the English garrison of Regennes.[82]

At Westminster Edward III's Council was occupied with more practical plans. When Arnoul d'Audrehem returned from Paris at the end of May 1359 with the verdict of the Estates-General on the treaty, the English King's reaction was immediate. He reissued the recruitment orders which had been revoked or scaled down when the treaty had first been made, and announced his attention of invading France in the following weeks. In the course of June Edward prepared his plan of campaign with his advisers. They resolved to launch a large-scale raid from Calais into northern France with the principal object of capturing the city of Reims. Reims cathedral was the traditional place of coronation of the Kings of France. Edward almost certainly intended to have himself crowned there.[83]

CHAPTER IX

Edward III's Last Campaign The Treaties of Brétigny and Calais 1359–1360

The vast plain of Champagne, devoid of natural frontiers, crossed by three great river valleys with their fine highways and navigable waters, was as open as any in Europe; and rich, filled with ecclesiastical cities and market towns still gorged with the wealth of its golden age in the twelfth and thirteenth centuries. Yet Champagne was one of the last regions to be invaded by the companies and one of the first from which they were successfully expelled. It was in about November 1358 that the Navarrese garrisons of Picardy and the Beauvaisis first began to spread into the Laonnais and the Soissonais towards the metropolitan city of Reims. The pioneers were two men of very similar backgrounds. One was an English squire known to the French as Rabigot Dury, whose identity is lost in the distortion of language. Dury had been in the service of the King of Navarre for at least five years. He was one of the men who had sunk his sword into the body of Charles of Spain at l'Aigle in 1354. More recently he had served in the Navarrese garrison at Mauconseil. His colleague, Robert Scot, was another English adventurer in Navarrese service. He had commanded Charles of Navarre's English mercenaries against the Jacques, and then become the captain of the Navarrese garrison of la Herelle in Picardy. These two men had entered into a partnership agreement by which they undertook to share the costs and profits of war.[1] At some stage they joined up with a third captain, a German called Frank Hennequin who was believed to hail from Cologne, but was in fact probably a Hainaulter like so many of the despoilers of Champagne. In the autumn of 1358 they collected a band of several hundred others, mainly Englishmen, Picards and Hainaulters, and invaded the Aisne valley.

The early pickings were easy. Dury and Scot made themselves a base in the castle of Vailly, a few miles upstream of Soissons. Within a few weeks they had captured at least five more castles in the district. At about Christmas time they capped these feats by entering the castle of Roucy by escalade. The Count of Roucy, one of the principal barons of

Champagne, was in the castle with his wife and daughter. His chamberlain had been bribed to leave the walls unwatched. This famous coup brought them 12,000 florins in ransom money and a great fortress on the Aisne within fifteen miles of Reims, as well as putting them in an excellent position to expand their empire even further in the spring. At Easter there was another great push. A fresh garrison, under Hennequin's command, was planted at Sisonne. These three places, Vailly, Roucy and Sisonne, served as the bases for a dense colonisation of the castles and manors around Laon and Soissons, and for occasional hit and run raids against the cities themselves.[2]

At almost exactly the same time a more miscellaneous group of adventurers was entering Champagne by the south. The leading light here was another Hainaulter, Eustache d'Aubricourt. Eustache's family had been closely connected with England for many years. His elder brother had participated in the siege of Calais and become one of the founding members of the Order of the Garter. He himself had served with the Prince of Wales in Gascony and fought at Poitiers. Aubricourt was new to Champagne, but he joined forces with two partners, the Englishmen Peter Audley and a German called Albrecht, both of whom had been in the region for some time. Albrecht was probably the same person as Albert Sterz, a brutal professional commander who later became famous as a soldier of fortune in Italy and died on the scaffold in Perugia in 1366. At this time he was the captain of Blanche of Navarre's castle at Gyé-sur-Seine, some miles upstream of Troyes. Peter Audley was probably the younger brother of the great Sir James, who had fought with the Prince at Poitiers. According to Froissart he was the captain of the occupied fortress of Beaufort at Montmorency on the eastern march of Champagne. These three men combined their forces early in 1359 to produce an army of about 1,000 men.[3]

In about February or March 1359 they occupied Pont-sur-Seine, a small market town on the south bank of the Seine dominated by the twelfth-century castle of the Counts of Champagne. Shortly afterwards they seized the much larger bridge-town of Nogent, a short distance upstream, where they established their headquarters. From here they began to extend their territory north towards the Marne in the spring. Vertus and Épernay were sacked, both substantial towns with important royal castles. The inhabitants of Vertus had time to reach the citadel, 'noble habitacion et puissant', and to watch the destruction of their homes from its walls. But the men of Épernay were caught unawares and killed or captured in large numbers. At Rosnay, the seat

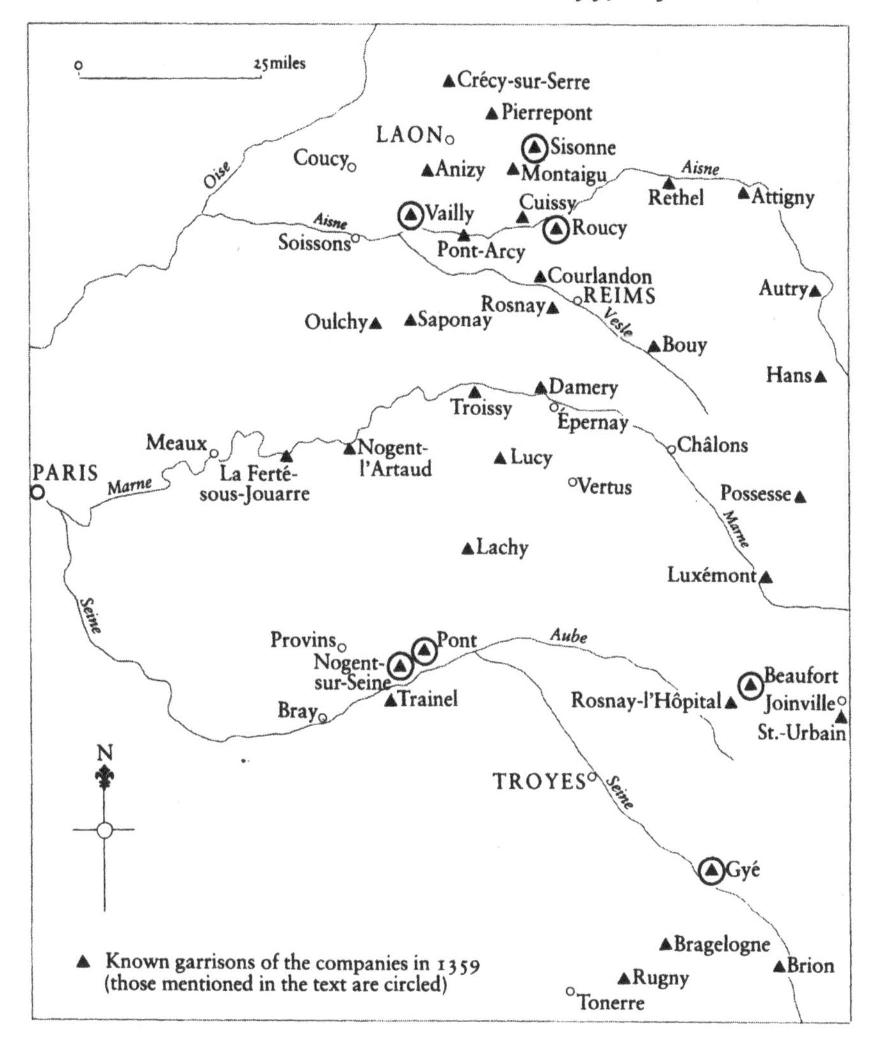

27 Champagne, 1358–60

of another royal castellany, the soldiers burst into the church as the inhabitants were at mass, snatching the chalice from the priest's hands and leading him by the ear into captivity. By the end of April 1359 Aubricourt and his partners were occupying a chain of castles and manors south and east of Reims and joining hands with the garrisons of Dury, Scot and Hennequin on the west. As in other parts of France the successes of these famous and well organised exploits attracted hordes of imitators. Very few were Englishmen. Some were French. The great majority came from Brabant, Hainault and Lorraine and from the principalities of the German Rhineland. Jean le Bel, writing the final pages of his chronicle in 1359, recorded that the whole county of Champagne from Rethel in the north to Bar-sur-Aube in the south was in the hands of the bandits.[4]

The invasion of Champagne offered a number of lessons for both the *routiers* and their enemies. The most notable feature of the companies' operations in Champagne was their tendency to form themselves into coalitions disposing of relatively large forces of men capable not just of holing themselves up behind the walls of captured castles but of fighting pitched battles against an organised enemy. When the young lord of Coucy led his retainers and a hired company of German mercenaries against the garrison of Vailly, the *routiers* challenged them on open ground. The Germans went over to the enemy and the rest fled for their lives. The Counts of Roucy and Porcien fared even worse when they tried to evict Frank Hennequin from Sisonne with troops recruited for the most part in the streets of Laon. Most of their army fled and both leaders were captured, in Roucy's case for the second time in half a year.[5] But the size of these companies was not always an advantage. A few hundred men besieged in a narrow castle were liable to exhaust its stores very quickly, without being strong enough to confront an enemy force of any strength in the open. The optimum size of *routier* armies was either very small, like the Gascon bands which flourished in the south-west and in Auvergne, or enormous, like those of the Archpriest or Robert Knolles or the great bandit hosts of the 1360s. Most companies responded to this dilemma by occupying three or four castles within easy marching distance of each other, and combining their garrisons when they needed to raise a siege or meet an enemy in battle. At any one time Dury, Scot and Hennequin occupied at least three major fortresses and several minor ones, and moved their troops from one to the other as the prospect of booty and the danger of annihilation suggested. This technique worked well enough where the defence was weak and localised. But where it was able to call on troops recruited over a larger geographical area the companies were rapidly outclassed, too large to sustain themselves for long in a blockaded fortress and too small to fight their enemies outside. This is what happened in Champagne in 1359.

The royal Lieutenants in the province were both outsiders. Jean de Chalon, lord of Arlay, was one of the principal barons of the imperial county of Burgundy. His colleague, the Lorrainer Henry, Count of Vaudémont, was an experienced soldier who had taken the leading role in the successful defence of Troyes against the bands of Robert Knolles earlier in the year. They could call on large forces of infantry of rather variable quality from the towns, and smaller forces of cavalry supplied by the nobility. In addition, they struck a deal with an officer of the Duke of Lorraine called Brocard de Fénétrange, who undertook to produce a contract army of 500 men-at-arms in return for a lump sum of 100,000 *écus*, the payment of which was secured on three castles belonging to the Count of Vaudémont. Another smaller company was hired from the Count of Bar. The whole force gathered in the Seine valley, east of Troyes, during June 1359. They were supported by a large body of infantry and some men-at-arms from the city of Troyes, led by their martial Bishop. Their total strength seems to have been between 2,000 and 3,000 men.[6]

The first target was Eustache d'Aubricourt's headquarters at Nogent-sur-Seine. Aubricourt was not willing to run the risk of being starved in Nogent. So he called together his men from the outlying garrisons, some 600 or 700 in all, and leaving Nogent in the charge of one of his Lieutenants retreated down the Seine. On 23 June 1359 he found a good defensive position near Bray-sur-Seine, some fifteen miles downstream from his headquarters. Here he drew up his men on foot, in the English fashion, on rising ground in a vineyard where the rows of vines would break the momentum of the enemy's cavalry. Although Aubricourt was considerably outnumbered, he was confident of victory. But he was not victorious. The Lieutenants made good use of their superior numbers. They divided their army into three battalions. They attacked Aubricourt's men from several quarters at once and overwhelmed them. Large numbers of the *routiers* were killed. Those who were worth a ransom were captured. They included Aubricourt himself.[7]

After the battle, the men of Troyes returned to their homes. Vaudémont himself marched north with the men-at-arms and joined up with a fresh army which had been assembled by the Archbishop and the captain of Reims. Just as they had done in the Seine valley, they made directly for the largest garrison in the region, which would be easiest to starve out: Frank Hennequin's garrison at Sisonne. Dury and Scot tried hard to relieve their colleague. But they did not have the numbers, and were forced to withdraw. Hennequin eventually surrendered on terms after a siege of about a month. Dury capitulated at Roucy three weeks after that. Vailly was abandoned a few days later. Under the terms of the capitulations the garrisons and their captains were to be permitted to leave under safe conduct. But the common people would have none of that. They fell on the *routiers* as they left and killed as many as they could. Hennequin, who had aroused particular hatred, was led off to be executed in the market at Reims. He was only with the utmost difficulty extricated by the nobleman who had promised him his life.[8]

This short, highly effective campaign cleared all the larger enemy garrisons from the valleys of the Aisne and the Marne. Aubricourt was taken to Troyes where, like Hennequin, he narrowly escape being lynched. He was held a prisoner for several weeks while he found his ransom. Scot returned to Picardy whence he had come. Dury left the region, no doubt also to Picardy. Albrecht returned to Gyé. Hennequin is never heard of again in Champagne although he reappeared some years later in Brittany. Peter Audley had withdrawn from his partnership with Aubricourt shortly before the battle of Bray, taking 60,000 *moutons* as his share of profits. He tried to continue on his own. Some weeks afterwards he and his band scaled the walls of Châlons-sur-Marne by night and briefly occupied part of the town before being expelled by the garrison, a famous but wholly unprofitable adventure and the last notable exploit of his career. Audley banked his takings with the merchants of Mechelen and Sluys, and died in his bed at Beaufort early in 1360. The garrison of Pont-sur-Seine survived for a few months longer until, in the spring of 1360, its captain Jean de Ségur went to Troyes to negotiate the surrender of the place. The Bishop of Troyes gave him a safe-conduct, but as soon as the news of his presence spread, a furious mob gathered outside the Bishop's palace baying for his blood. 'Kill him! Kill him!', they shouted. Eventually, they forced their way in and dragged him away to be butchered in the street. The only notable survivor of the campaign was Brocard de Fénétrange, who quarrelled with his employers as so many of his kind did, and for much the same reasons. The Lieutenants were unable to raise the money to pay his fee. As a result he occupied several castles and embarked on his own campaign of plundering which lasted until his accounts were finally settled at the beginning of the following year.[9]

The companies which invaded Champagne were large and well organised, and their leaders included some of the most experienced professional soldiers operating in France. It is an interesting question why they were so swiftly and completely defeated when in other regions bands with fewer advantages had swept all before them. To some extent the credit belonged to individuals: the two Lieutenants, the Bishop of Troyes, the Archbishop and captain of Reims. But their energy might have been wasted elsewhere. The main explanation is that the resilience of France's historic provinces in the face of these incursions depended very much on their political traditions: on their social solidarity, on the willingness of their inhabitants to come to the aid of another district before they had themselves been attacked, and on their ability to organise and pay for the operation. The critical time was the immediate aftermath of the invasion. Once the companies had achieved a significant degree of penetration, the sheer scale of the devastation was usually enough to prevent any co-ordinated response. The tax base was destroyed. No one dared to leave his own district. The institutions of the province rapidly ceased to function. The virtual extinction of the central government at the end of the 1350s revealed where the real strengths of French society lay. The ancient *pays* which had conserved something of their autonomy and institutions in the face of a century and a half of expansive royal government succeeded much better than those which had been thoroughly subordinated to the King's judges and officials. In a region as weak and diverse as Auvergne the attempt to organise the defence on a provincial scale had collapsed within a few weeks. In the Limousin, it had failed almost at once. The Île de France with its long tradition of subordination to the crown scarcely stirred in its own defence. Champagne by comparison was, like Languedoc, a province of populous cities, linked by a dense network of local alliances. It had enjoyed a considerable measure of political autonomy as recently as the mid-thirteenth century. And, although it had become since then a possession of the Kings of France, it had retained many of its institutions as well as a strong political identity, which had been demonstrated in the rebellions of 1314 and 1315 and more recently at the meetings of the provincial estates during the crisis of 1358.

Robert Knolles withdrew from the Auxerrois at the end of April 1359 and returned to his base at Châteauneuf-sur-Loire, followed by a train of wagons piled high with booty and by long lines of prisoners, including many women and children. His next great enterprise had been planned since the beginning of the year. As early as February 1359 the companies operating in Berry and the Nivernais had begun to gather around Châteauneuf for the feast. Their leaders were John Waldboef and Jack Wyn. Waldboef was a Cheshire man (like Knolles) who had previously commanded the garrison of Corvol l'Orgeuilleux in the Nivernais. He was already famous as the man who had captured the Archpriest in the previous autumn. Wyn, a colourful Welshman who called himself the 'Poursuivant d'Amours', had recently been bought out of his holdings in the Nivernais and was looking for fresh opportunities elsewhere. They were joined in the following weeks by several English captains from other parts of France. One of these was Hugh Calveley, Knolles' kinsman and comrade-in-arms in Brittany, who had passed the last year in the service of Philip of Navarre.[10] In the second half of May 1359 all these companies joined up with Knolles' own men and began to march south. It was a largely English and Breton army. Their ultimate objective, like the Archpriest's two years before, was the Rhone valley.

Their route was determined by the strength of the defence in the various provinces in their path. The roads up the Loire valley towards Forez and the Lyonnais were blocked by an army of men from Beaujolais and Bresse. Knolles therefore made his way up the valley of the Allier, across the Bourbonnais, towards Auvergne. At the end of May, they reached Saint-Pourçain, a prosperous walled town situated in an enclave of the county of Auvergne in the southern Bourbonnais which contained the principal royal mint of central France. Reports reaching the Count of Poitiers put their combined strength at this stage at about 4,000 effective men.[11]

The defence of Auvergne was ultimately the responsibility of the Count of Poitiers, but he was far away in the south. The conduct of affairs was in the hands of his deputy, the young Duke of Bourbon, and a royal captain, Hughes de la Roche. Neither of them played any significant part in the crisis. They were paralysed by the breakdown of the machinery of tax collection and the perennial jealousies of the local baronage and had neither troops nor money at their disposal. It could hardly have been more different from the situation in Champagne. The initiative fell instead to an unconventional military contractor, Thomas de la Marche. Thomas was the offspring of an adulterous union, some forty years before, of the estranged wife of Charles IV of France, one of the most embarrassing scandals in the history of the royal house. Shunned by his family until quite recently, he had passed his youth as an errant adventurer fighting in the service of other princes in Cyprus and the Levant and in Italy. Although he had no previous connection with Auvergne, the Dauphin had granted him in the previous year the important lordship of Nonette, south of Issoire. At the end of April 1359 he became the Duke of Bourbon's deputy. Thomas de la Marche received almost no co-operation from the local nobility, who regarded him as an ambitious outsider, and very little from the towns, who were

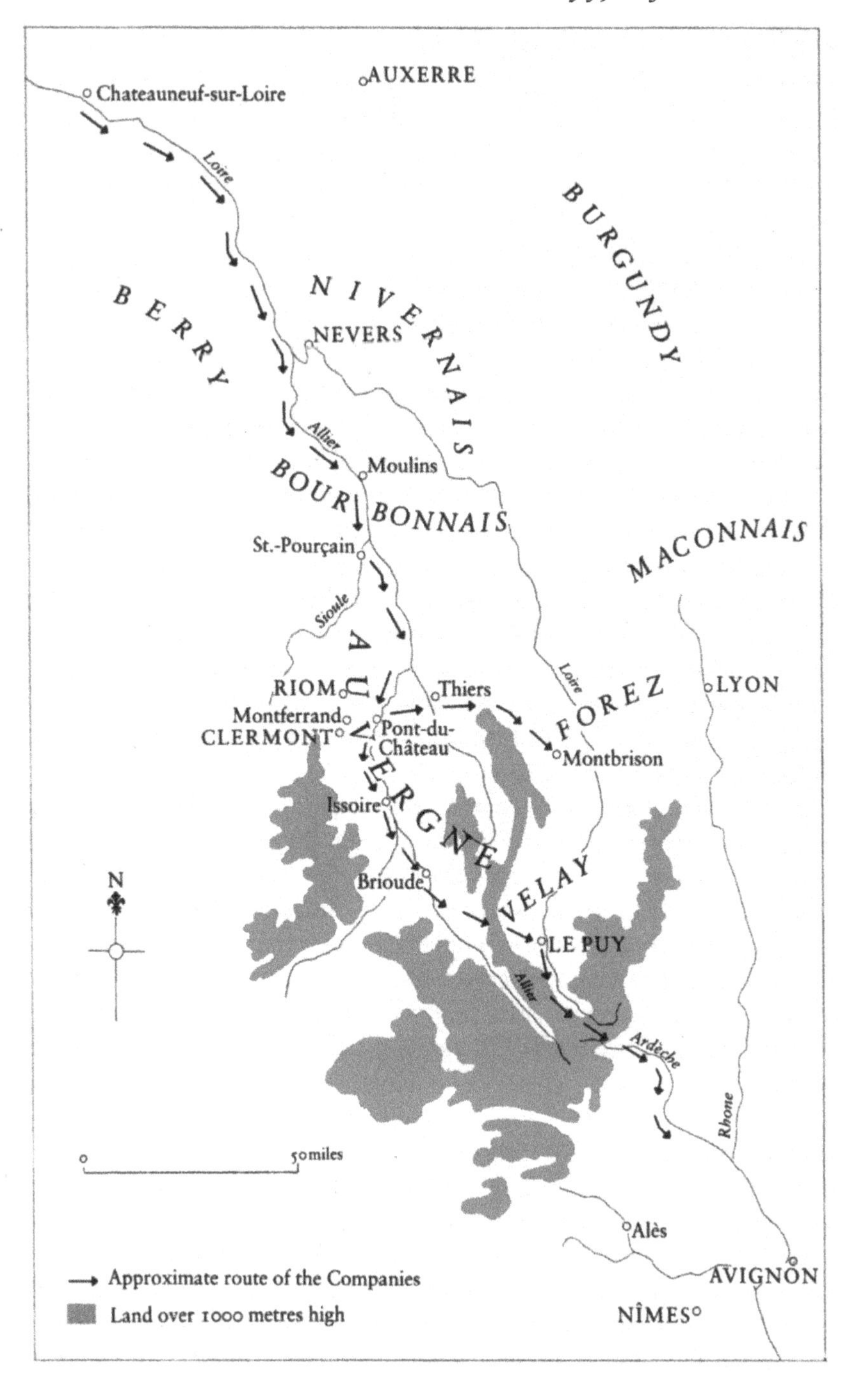

28 Robert Knolles in Auvergne and the Velay, 1359

more interested in defending their walls than the distant frontiers of the province. On 24 May 1359 the Estates of Auvergne, meeting at Clermont, were induced to provide him with a small force of men-at-arms and archers. That was all. With these men at his back Thomas marched north and established his headquarters at Saint-Pourçain, three days before the arrival of Knolles' companies.[12]

The English had no intention of being drawn into a long siege. They burnt the suburbs of Saint-Pourçain and withdrew south towards the plain of the Limagne and the great cities of Riom, Clermont and Montferrand. West of Clermont they established a new headquarters in the cliff-top fortress of Pont-du-Château, which stood over the main road from Lyon and controlled the only bridge over the river Allier between Moulins and Brioude. Here Knolles joined forces with the Gascon bands of Bertucat d'Albret already operating in the region. They prowled around the three cities waiting for the moment to strike. Riom appealed to the royal captain for help but he could do nothing. 'Point de gens d'armes, ne de finance,' was his answer. Thomas de la Marche sent what he could spare. But he was finding it impossible to recruit men-at-arms in Auvergne itself even for good money. As a result, he was obliged to leave his subordinates to make what progress they could in the province while he himself left to recruit troops elsewhere, in Burgundy, Bresse and the Maçonnais.[13]

By mid-June 1359 Knolles' companies began to split up. Frustration at the lack of booty was probably the main factor. Knolles' captains were not interested in the kind of warfare which the Albrets and their Gascon bands had successfully practised in Auvergne since 1356. They had neither the time nor the inclination to drain the province gradually of its resources by occupying scattered castles with small garrisons and taxing the population year after year. Knolles' targets were not roads or villages, but the great walled towns and cathedral cities which alone could produce the spoil to satisfy his horde quickly. But the townsmen of Auvergne were hardened by two years' experience of guerrilla warfare and they were extremely vigilant. Hugh Calveley was the first of Knolles' confederates to break away on his own. His band moved south with about 1,000 mounted men. On 17 June 1359 the cavalcade passed Issoire. At Toulouse the Count of Poitiers anxiously studied reports while his officers speculated on the *routiers'* ultimate destination. It was thought possible that they might be heading south-west towards the Rouergue, or east into the Rhone valley. In the event Calveley's army turned south-east, traversing more than 60 miles of difficult terrain, and appeared without warning in the Velay. On 20 June 1359 they were reported within twelve miles of le Puy.[14]

The invasion of the Velay was a serious threat to the security of the lower Rhone. On the east bank of the river, in the papal states and Provence, the authorities were gripped by panic.[15] Languedoc, however, was well prepared. An unusually full assembly representing the three Estates of all seven seneschalsies had met at Montpellier as soon as the first reports arrived of Knolles' plans at the end of March 1359. They were frightened into agreeing to a number of emergency measures, including the temporary reintroduction of the hated *gabelle* or salt duty. The machinery of tax collection and military recruitment in Languedoc was far from perfect, but it operated more efficiently than in any other part of France. During the spring and summer of 1359 large loans against the proceeds of the *gabelle* were raised in all the principal towns, and many troops were recruited.[16]

The Seneschal of Beaucaire was Jean Bernier, an energetic officer of the royal household who had been sent from Paris in the previous autumn to take charge of the defence. As soon as the news of Calveley's invasion reached him he marched north with the troops of his seneschalsy to relieve le Puy. By the beginning of July 1359 Bernier had already set up an advance base at Alès near the northern limits of his seneschalsy, where the baked scrub of the Garrigues gave way to the granite foothills of the Cevennes. He was joined there by the Viscount of Narbonne with the levies of the seneschalsy of Carcassonne, and by John, son of the Count of Armagnac. Meanwhile, Thomas de la Marche had returned to the north of Auvergne with a hired company of 700 men-at-arms and 2,000 infantry recruited in the neighbouring provinces. It was a remarkable achievement for a man with no funds at his disposal. The men had been recruited entirely on promises. At the beginning of July 1359 Thomas was at Saint-Pourçain appealing to the communities of Auvergne for another 400 men-at-arms.[17]

The subsequent course of events has to be pieced together from incoherent fragments of evidence. The return of Thomas de la Marche with a substantial army behind him put the remaining companies in Auvergne at a considerable disadvantage. Knolles' companies appear to have responded by abandoning their positions around Riom and Clermont, and splitting into at least two groups. Waldboef and Wyn headed east along the Lyon road into Forez, fertile unpillaged territory which was virtually undefended. It was their companies which captured Montbrison, the provincial capital, a few days later. The place was unwalled and must have been indefensible. But even if its capture was no great feat of arms, it gave the companies their first notable prize.[18] Knolles himself went south, following in the tracks of Calveley. In about the middle of July 1359 the two joined up in the Velay. The loose siege of le Puy, which had been in progress for about three weeks, was now brought to a swift and bloody end. The *routiers* scaled the walls at night and captured a gateway. There was a terrible massacre in the streets. Some of the inhabitants tried to fight the invaders. They were cut down mercilessly by the professional roughs pitted against them. Some of them were killed as they fled. Some broke their necks or drowned trying to escape over the walls.[19]

The English had little leisure to enjoy their conquest. They were in danger of being caught between two enemy armies. Thomas de la Marche began to move south from Saint-Pourçain in the last ten days of July. His army crossed the length of Auvergne at high speed and entered the Velay behind the invaders. As they approached, the Anglo-Gascon horde withdrew south before them. Their route is uncertain, but the probability is that they were making for the Rhone by the valley of the Ardèche. On 29 July 1359 they were reported, apparently heading for Avignon, about thirty-five miles from the city. Here they found their way barred by the army of Languedoc. Their nerve failed them. They dispersed and turned back. Knolles made his way across the Limousin with about half the army. The companies of Calveley and Albret, about 900 men in all, moved north with the army of Languedoc in hot pursuit.[20]

Early in August 1359 the men of Languedoc effected a junction with Thomas de la Marche, who took command of the combined force. Somewhere close to le Puy Calveley found himself cornered by a vastly superior French army. He drew up his men after the fashion of the Prince at Poitiers and Eustache d'Aubricourt at Bray, on a hillside planted with vines. A full day passed as each side waited for the other to break ranks and attack first. On the next day the French advanced to within a stone's throw of the English line. There was a brief, inconclusive skirmish between a few men on either side. As evening drew in the Viscount of Narbonne was for attacking. But John of Armagnac shared his father's famous distrust of the chances of battle. He was for waiting until the following day. During the night Calveley's men folded their tents and stole away.[21]

Knolles' Great Company had failed on the march of Languedoc for much the same reasons as the invaders of Champagne had failed. They were too numerous to hide behind the walls of captured castles, yet not strong enough to fight battles in open country against an army drawn from the vast area of Languedoc and the provinces of the Saône. By the autumn of 1359 virtually all of the bands which had invaded Auvergne and Languedoc in the summer had vanished. Knolles was back in Brittany. Calveley had reappeared in western Berry, where he was planting garrisons in the valley of the Indre. Jack Wyn returned to the Yonne to rejoin his friends in the rape of the Auxerrois. Waldboef is never heard of again. Only the Gascons and the companies of Thomas de la Marche remained behind. They returned to Auvergne, the first to resume their guerrilla war in the hills, the second to present their accounts. The Estates of Auvergne were no more able to settle them than the Lieutenants in Champagne had been able to pay Brocard de Fénétrange. They dutifully assembled in July to vote a hearth tax for the purpose at the swingeing rate of one *écu* per hearth. It could not be collected. It was not so much a question of resistance as exhaustion. The commissioners appointed to levy the money gave the same explanations to the officers of the Estates: war damage, desertion, plague, administrative collapse. In December 1359 Thomas's men were still cantoned in the province waiting for their wages and threatening mutiny.[22]

Knolles' second great *chevauché* no doubt made him some money, but it was much less profitable than the first. Most of the humbler troopers in his following must have been disappointed with their winnings. A lucky man like the eighteen-year-old Jacques Dupré might make sixty florins in a few months, mainly in pillaging around the greater monastic *bourgs* of Auvergne. This was equivalent to the earnings of a building craftsman over two years. Others, who took no rich prisoners or found themselves in the wrong place at critical moments, made next to nothing. Geoffroy Sabatier, a cobbler's apprentice from Aubigny-sur-Nère in Berry, was kidnapped by a Gascon captain at the age of sixteen and served in his band for more than a year. He was fed, clothed and mounted, but had nothing to show for his service when he deserted except for two low-grade horses worth five francs between them, plus one *écu* of Philip VI and a florin of Florence. His fortune was probably more typical than Dupré's. According to the English chronicler Knighton the loot of le Puy was enough to enrich the lowest man in the army. But he was probably exaggerating. The most valuable prizes escaped them. The cathedral, one of the greatest Marian sanctuaries in France, filled with the treasures of four centuries of piety, was situated on a hill protected by its own independent line of walls, which the raiders never penetrated.[23]

*

In the spring of 1359 Charles of Navarre's positions started to collapse in northern France. The process began in Picardy, the home of his strongest supporters and largest garrisons. Jean de Picquigny, Charles's chief partisan there, died at Évreux in the spring. It was said that in his final weeks he had gone raging mad, gnawing at his hands and strangling his own chamberlain. As he raged, the Picards and Normans joined forces to drive out his garrisons. Saint-Valéry at the mouth of the Somme surrendered on about 21 April 1359. The garrison, a mixed company of English and Navarrese, withstood a siege of nearly a month and then bargained for their lives before their water finally ran out. In spite of the orders of their commanders, angry mobs of foot soldiers separated themselves from the French army and fell on the English and Navarrese as they were being ferried across the Somme. More than a hundred of them were lynched. In May, a few days after the fall of Saint-Valéry, Jean de Picquigny's garrison at Mauconseil on the Oise was bought out by the local communities. The citizens of Noyon pulled down the walls with their own hands. This left Poix, west of Amiens, and la Herelle near Montdidier as the only significant garrisons in Picardy still holding out for the King of Navarre.[24]

Philip of Navarre did his best to keep his brother's flag flying. He came up from Mantes with an army composed mainly of Englishmen just too late to save Saint-Valéry. He conducted a noisy military demonstration along the valley of the Somme and into western Champagne over the next six weeks, pouncing on unwary garrisons, skilfully evading the counter-attacks of the enemy. Philip certainly succeeded in making fools of the Constable and the Admiral of France, who commanded the defence. They were more afraid of the urban roughs among their own infantry than of the English and Navarrese on the other side. But Philip had little to show for his pains when he returned to Normandy at the beginning of June 1359.[25] As the King of Navarre's support ebbed away, the Dauphin acquired a new confidence. The old anti-Navarrese officers of his father began to reappear in the ranks of his councillors: the authoritarian Simon Bucy, the coinage experts Jean Poilevillain and Nicholas Braque, and other vilified figures from the corrupt beginnings of John II's reign. The great alliance of radical reformers, rich cities and Navarrese clients had fallen apart. During the sessions of the Estates-General in May 1359 the Dauphin reinstated all the ministers who had been prosecuted by the assembly of 1357. No one turned a hair.[26]

As soon as the Estates-General had dispersed, the Dauphin laid siege to Melun. How he found his army or paid it is far from clear. It seems to have consisted mainly of men-at-arms withdrawn from the garrisons of Normandy and the Île de France, noblemen serving out the free month which their representatives had promised at the close of the Estates-General, and Italian crossbowmen hired by the city of Paris. The Dauphin established his headquarters in the wrecked Cistercian convent of le Lys, a mile and a half west of the walls. He built a great fortified barbican across the main road from Paris. He brought up a barge load of artillery from the arsenal in the Louvre, including two large gunpowder cannons. His men repeatedly stormed the island citadel, achieving great feats of personal heroism. But they made no impression at all on the garrison. A month after the siege had begun, the Dauphin's army had hemmed in the island fortress from both sides of the Seine, but they were no nearer to conquering it.[27]

Both sides in this increasingly pointless civil war were now looking over their shoulders at events elsewhere. Edward III's long-promised invasion of France was expected to begin in August. Walter Mauny was noisily retaining men-at-arms on the northern borders of the kingdom, in Hainault and the neighbouring provinces of Germany and the Low Countries. There were agents of Edward's government on the quayside at Sluys and Bruges, ordering English ships to return at once for war service, and others buying vast quantities of stores in the market places of Flanders. Within their own island the English ministers made determined attempts to hide their preparations from the great community of French prisoners, officials and diplomats now almost permanently resident in London. On 5 July 1359 all Frenchmen (other than prisoners) were ordered out of the kingdom. The prisoners themselves were removed from the capital and dispersed among a large number of fortresses in the midlands and western counties. King John, whose household was more than seventy strong and French down to the laundrywoman, was obliged to send almost half of them home. At the end of the month he was taken to the austere security of Somerton castle, where his correspondence was controlled, his guard doubled and armed men were posted at every entrance. It was useless. French spies were reported to be at large in London and the south-east. Some of them appear to have been Englishmen naturalised in France who were virtually undetectable. Wartime tensions no doubt amplified their reports, but someone 'exceptionally reliable and well placed to know' had undoubtedly disclosed all of Edward III's plans to the Dauphin by early July and supplied him with an accurate list of the towns to be attacked.[28]

The King of Navarre was determined to reach an accommodation with the Dauphin while the continuing resistance of Melun gave him something to bargain with. On 26 July 1359 he gathered an 'enormous company' at Mantes on the Seine, nominally to relieve Melun, in fact to maintain his unsteady position at the negotiating table.[29] His representatives were already haggling with the Dauphin's councillors. They had provisionally agreed by the end of July 1359 that Charles would do homage to the Dauphin and that in return he would receive everything that he had held at the outbreak of hostilities, plus 600,000 *écus* payable in instalments over twelve years and a grant of land worth 12,000 *livres* a year. These terms were acceptable in principle to the Dauphin and his Council. They were also acceptable, after a certain amount of persuasion, to the perennially suspicious Parisians who were by now the main pillar of the Dauphin's government. The difficulty which remained to be resolved was the precise location of the land which Charles was to receive, a question of exceptional sensitivity to a man who cared much more for status than revenue. Charles of Navarre wanted the whole of the viscounties of Falaise, Bayeux, Auge and Vire. This would have given him a concentrated domain comprising most of Lower Normandy. The Dauphin's men would not agree.

On the afternoon of 19 August 1359 the brothers-in-law met for the first time in a year and a half. The scene was the treeless plain west of the royal fortress of Pontoise, where ambush was impossible and forty men-at-arms was a sufficient bodyguard. Large numbers of troops stood back at a discreet distance on both sides. Hostages were exchanged. The two princes rode back together into Pontoise. But in spite of a whole day of disputation their councillors were quite unable to agree on the vital question. The Dauphin sent the Count of Étampes to Charles's apartments to tell him that his demands could not be met. If he persisted, he would be escorted out of Pontoise and there would be no peace. Everyone believed that the negotiations had failed. In the course of his impulsive career the King of Navarre had often surprised his contemporaries, but few things surprised them more than the manner of his reconciliation with the Dauphin. On the following morning, the King of Navarre called the Dauphin's councillors to his private room. The kingdom, he told them, was on the verge of destruction. Surely two princes who were so intimately related on both sides of their families should not stand idly by as it was torn apart. He did not want any money. He did not want any land but what he had before. He wanted nothing more than to do his duty to his country. No doubt if he did it well he would be suitably rewarded. All this, he told them, he would willingly repeat in public.

The Dauphin's advisers could hardly believe their ears. They sent out into the streets of Pontoise for witnesses. Later in the day the citizens crammed into the great hall of the castle to hear the King of Navarre repeat his declaration before the world. He told them that he would order his garrisons to abandon the castles which they had occupied since the civil war had begun. He received the Dauphin's peace offering of wine and spices. There was naturally a good deal of speculation about the King of Navarre's motives. Some of his hearers thought that he had been touched by the Holy Spirit. Some took his declaration at face value. Some suspected a trick. At Avignon the theory was put about that the King of England was behind it all, believing that Charles would do more damage to the government of France from within. The truth was probably quite simple. Once the King of Navarre perceived that the Dauphin would not give him the four viscounties of Lower Normandy, he preferred to postpone a territorial settlement altogether until he should be in a better position to force one that was to his taste. Like almost everyone else in France Charles of Navarre believed that Edward III's strength was greater than it really was. He had nothing to gain by the extinction of the Valois dynasty to which he belonged, or its replacement by an outsider who owed him no favours. So, on 1 September 1359 the Dauphin and the King of Navarre rode through the streets of Paris side by side and feasted together at the Louvre.[30]

The King of Navarre's surrender at Pontoise made no difference to the operations of the companies and it was ignored by many of his own partisans. In Lower Normandy the English were temporarily deprived of the use of Cherbourg, which was firmly under Charles's control. But they lost no time in making alternative arrangements to secure their sea communications with England. Sir Thomas Holland, Edward III's captain at Saint-Sauveur-le-Vicomte, occupied the fine harbour at Barfleur in the north-east of the Cotentin peninsula, transforming the parish church into a fortress. Other officers of the English King took control of the port of Honfleur from the international brigade which had occupied it in his name since 1357. But these precautions proved largely unnecessary. Even in the heart of Charles's domain in the Cotentin, his Navarrese soldiers maintained their tactical alliance with the English and served their own interests as they had always done. Charles's brother Philip, who was their natural commander, declined to follow him into the

Dauphin's peace and remained in the service of the King of England.[31]

In Picardy, the Pays de Caux and the Île de France Charles instructed all garrisons holding towns and castles in his name to surrender them to the Dauphin. A few of them complied. They were generally the smaller and more isolated ones. One or two others were taken by force. Poix in Picardy, which was already under siege, was bought out. James Pipe's garrison at Épernon was recovered at the end of the year. His watchmen had grown slothful with prosperity. The enemy entered the place with ladders through a window and seized the famous captain in his bed. But these places were the exception. All the greater garrisons ignored the King of Navarre's orders and held on to their strongholds like winkles on rocks. Those which had large English contingents simply declared themselves to be holding them for the King of England, now that his truce with France had expired. They included la Ferté-sous-Jouarre on the Marne and the fortress of la Herelle, the last of the Jean de Picquigny's garrisons in Picardy. Charles of Navarre could not even procure the surrender of Melun. His captain there, Martin Henriquez, refused his orders to his face. A compromise was eventually agreed by which he was allowed to remain in the citadel and to levy tolls on the traffic of the Seine for long enough to satisfy the garrison's arrears of pay. In the event his men remained there for more than a year.[32]

As might have been expected there were particular difficulties at Creil. John Fotheringhay contemptuously refused the 6,000 royals that the city of Paris raised to buy him out. His garrison, which had always been one of the largest in France, had recently been swollen by soldiers evicted from the Anglo-Navarrese garrisons of Picardy and the Beauvaisis. He had also been joined by a number of adventurers in the service of the King of Navarre such as the Captal de Buch, who now had to look elsewhere for excitement and profit. In November 1359 it was necessary to pay Fotheringhay and his friends 24,000 royals to go away, plus 2,000 royals to each of his two principal lieutenants. The garrison broke up into a number of smaller groups each under its chosen captain. They did not go very far. Fotheringhay himself was let into the castle of Pont-Sainte-Maxence just eight miles upstream of Creil by a group of English prisoners of war who were incarcerated there. The Gascon contingent from Creil followed the Captal de Buch. They seized the great castle of Clermont-en-Beauvaisis, 10 miles west of Creil on the night of 18 November 1359 and used it as a base for fresh looting. 'Across the Amienois and the Beauvaisis we took towns and castles one after another,' an ageing retainer of the Captal told Froissart many years later; 'truly, we were lords of the fields and rivers and amassed marvellous fortunes.'[33]

Further south, in regions where the King of Navarre had never claimed partisans, his reconciliation with the Dauphin made no difference at all. In the provinces of the middle Loire the jurisdiction of the Dauphin's officers was reduced to the walled towns and their immediate suburbs. In the Orléanais the Breton companies succeeded in ransoming much of the open country. The inhabitants of the larger towns watched impotently from their walls, while those of smaller places were reduced to hiring their own companies of Bretons to defend them. Touraine, which had more or less held its own during the invasions of 1358, was engulfed by a fresh wave of Gascon brigands who penetrated into the region by the south from Poitou. The first and chief of them was the large and highly organised company of the Gascon captain Pierre Descalat. Descalat, who called himself the 'Basquin de Poncet', had arrived in the region in March 1359, when his company suddenly fell on the town of Cormery on the Indre, south-east of Tours. They occupied the Benedictine abbey, demolished its outbuildings and used the stone to transform the church and enclosure into a formidable fortress. From here they established another garrison on the Cher at Veretz. Descalat's conquests drew fresh hordes of Gascons into the region to swell his numbers or set up in competition. Tours, the principal city of the middle Loire and the hub of its road system, was the great magnet. In the autumn of 1359 a minor Gascon captain called Jean Gros occupied the huge tenth-century keep of the Counts of Anjou at Langeais. Another garrison occupied Montbazon and raided up to the walls of Tours. All the efforts of the towns and the local officers of the French Crown failed to dislodge them.[34]

Like the Île de France, the Loire provinces had few regional institutions and their administration had always depended on the Crown. They suffered very much from the government's demise, and proved unable to raise funds or recruit troops even on the limited scale which had been found possible further north. The defence depended on a handful of royal garrisons who behaved very much as the Gascons did. The French captain of Loches, a minor nobleman from Montreuil called Enguerrand d'Eudin, was accused some years afterwards of a formidable catalogue of crimes and abuses, all recorded by his enemies in a 'certain roll of paper'. He stuffed the garrison of Loches with friends and retainers from Picardy. He ransomed local villages. He supplied his garrison by large-scale theft. He rounded up animals in the fields and sold them to the highest bidder. He forcibly collected the taxes voted by the Estates-General even after the King had remitted them. Yet for all this he achieved nothing against the Gascon companies of the region, apart from strengthening the aged defences of Loches. It cannot have been easy to disengage truth from malice in documents such as this. But similar crimes were undoubtedly being committed by other French garrison commanders and they were probably committed by Enguerrand d'Eudin. The crippling want of money experienced by frontier captains like him left them little choice.[35]

If Enguerrand d'Eudin with all his unscrupulous energy and an armed retinue of loyal outsiders could not raise enough money to defend the small district of Loches, it is hardly surprising that the Dauphin could not do so on a national scale. The tax collection programme announced in June 1359 failed throughout northern France. The towns were unable to make any workable proposals for raising the taxes promised by their representatives. Eventually the Dauphin and his Council lost patience and imposed a *gabelle* on their own authority. The Estates of Normandy granted a separate subsidy in September, to be raised from a sales tax. In the current condition of the realm, however, all this effort was doomed to failure.[36] The autumn of 1359 and the following winter was a wretched time in northern France, even by the standard of recent years. It rained continuously from the beginning of September. The grain rotted in the fields. The vintage failed in Burgundy. Prices soared. These misfortunes were accompanied by a steep decline in the value of the silver coinage. In October 1359 Nicholas Braque reported that the coinage had never been worth less. It had fallen from sixty to 150 florins to the mark of silver in less than half a year. It was to reach 500 before the crisis was out. The result was that when Edward III's invasion finally came there was no French army to confront it, the first time in the prolonged agony of the French Crown that such a thing had happened. In October 1359 the Dauphin returned from haggling with his subjects at Rouen and withdrew within the walls of Paris until the end of the campaign.[37]

The English army which invaded France in 1359 was the largest which Edward III had raised since the *annus mirabilis* of 1347, and probably the most impressive that had ever left England's shores. About 10,000 English and Welsh troops took part. A high proportion of the men, about half, were mounted archers. The whole force, including the archers, had been raised from volunteers and contract companies. It represented an unusual concentration of experience and talent which the county arrayers of earlier campaigns could never have matched. All the leading captains of the past generation, the Prince of Wales, Lancaster, Northampton, Stafford, Warwick and Mauny, were there. Much attention had been given to the logistics of the campaign. In view of the season, the condition of the French countryside and the scorched earth tactics of the defence, the army would have to bring with it a large part of its stores. The English organised a supply train and ancillary services on a scale which astonished contemporaries. Two hundred sappers, carpenters, fletchers, farriers and other 'artificers' accompanied the army on its march, as well as 300 clerks. Thousands of spare bows and bow staves were packed up in chests and barrels and sent to Sandwich, together with strings, arrow heads and crossbow winches. A mass of equipment was collected: mobile forges, portable corn-mills and ovens, leather-skinned boats for crossing rivers and fishing in lakes, a ton of iron for horse-shoes, vast quantities of building lime, nails and rope, as well as the staple provisions of English armies in the fourteenth century: wine, oil, grain, dried vegetables, salted meat and fish. The transport of all this material required a wagon-train comprising about 1,000 carts and teams requisitioned in southern England or bought in the Low Countries. A fleet of 1,100 ships was assembled in the Downs to ferry men, animal and stores across the Channel.[38] Edward told his troops, to the audible dismay of some of them, that he intended to remain in France until he had achieved his war aims or died in the attempt. This, then, was to be a long campaign, not a brief hit-and-run raid like Edward's invasion of Picardy in 1355, which he had been forced to abandon after nine days for want of equipment and stores.[39]

The cost of all this was enormous, £130,000 on war wages alone, not to speak of the expenses of shipping, equipment and supplies. Yet the expedition of 1359 was not a great national enterprise as the siege of Calais had been, but a peculiarly personal venture of Edward's own. Not only was the army was raised without conscription; it was financed without direct taxation, the only major campaign of the Hundred Years War of which this was true apart from Henry V's expedition of 1421. Edward found part of the money from customs revenues and part of it from opportune windfalls such as the instalments of the ransom of David II of Scotland and booty collected on the campaign itself; but the greater part of the cost was financed by credit supplied by the leading captains who fought in it, most of whom accepted Exchequer tallies and allowed their debts to be deferred until well into the following decade.

The King's reluctance to approach his subjects was wise, and revealing. The emotions of 1347 and 1356 had subsided as the internal collapse of France made men feel more secure. The threat from the sea and from Scotland, which had largely created the mood of national solidarity fifteen years earlier, had vanished by 1359. The English were not much interested in Edward's personal ambitions.[40]

The departure of the invasion force had originally been fixed for 8 September 1359.[41] But it was repeatedly held up by the bureaucratic difficulties associated with the assembly of men, shipping and stores on such a scale. As the delays continued things began to go wrong in Calais. In addition to the invasion force which was to come from England, Walter Mauny had been recruiting men-at-arms in Hainault, Brabant and other principalities of Germany during the summer. About 1,000 of them had been retained for the campaign. They began to arrive in late August. Many had come without money, expecting to fill their pockets at once from the spoil of France. There were no lodgings for them in the town. They could not pay the high prices which local shopkeepers were demanding for basic provisions. Some of them rioted and caused much damage. At the beginning of October 1359 an advance guard of 2,300 men had to be sent hurriedly across the Channel from England under the command of the Duke of Lancaster to restore order. Lancaster busied the Germans by leading them on an extended raid into Picardy. He penetrated east as far as Péronne, and then south to Amiens, before doubling back to Calais. The main lesson of this improvised campaign was that even Edward III's great supply train was unlikely to be enough for his needs. Lancaster's men found nothing to plunder or even to eat in the regions through which they marched. Some of them had to do without bread and wine for days at a time. The Duke also found that although there was no French army to resist him in the field, the walled towns were defended by large and determined garrisons. Whenever his men tried to assault the walls they were invariably repelled with heavy casualties. It was not a good augury for the larger enterprise to come.[42]

Edward III landed at Calais on 28 October 1359. On 4 November the English army marched out of the town in three columns towards Champagne. The King with the main body of the army took the northerly route through Artois and the Cambrésis. The Prince of Wales followed on a parallel course by the valley of the Somme. The Duke of Lancaster took the middle route. The course of the campaign was determined from the outset by the problems of supply. Not even

Edward's great wagon-train could supply the army's needs for more than a week or two. At best it could even out the alternating periods of feast and famine. The Dauphin's strategy was simple, cheap and effective. The countryside was abandoned to the enemy. Its inhabitants were ordered into the walled towns, taking with them all the stores that they could carry and burning whatever had to be left behind. English foraging parties were persistently attacked by mounted troops sent out from the garrisoned towns and castles. But otherwise no attempt was made to hinder the King of England on his march. The French stood behind their walls as the enemy marched by. Or, where their walls could not be counted on, they abandoned them. On the English side, there was only one casualty of the march. He was injured by a 'gun', one of the earliest recorded victims of this new weapon.

In spite of the low casualties the army began to suffer severe hardship within a few days of leaving Calais. The winter was one of the worst for many years. The rain poured down throughout November, drenching the men and turning the roads into marshes. The rivers were black with mud and debris and the water undrinkable. Fodder was unobtainable. The three English columns lost contact with each other for much of the time. Progress was exceptionally slow, 10 miles a day at best. The German mercenaries had come, like their compatriots a generation earlier in 1339, without supplies and in some cases without even proper mounts or equipment. Edward III dismissed the company of Henry of Flanders before he had even left Calais, and another 450 Germans on the second day of the march. He had enough mouths of his own to feed, he said. Between 28 and 30 November the three English columns came together, 30 miles west of Reims. The men rested while their leaders considered the next move. On about 4 December 1359 they arrived outside the walls of Reims.[43]

Reims was a divided community. For many years its government had been contested between the Archbishops, who were the lords of the town, and an increasingly organised and assertive citizenry. As in so many other episcopal cities of France, the inhabitants' efforts to organise a coherent scheme of defence had been obstructed by successive Archbishops and other ecclesiastical proprietors, who jealously guarded their urban estates and political prerogatives, and were notoriously reluctant to contribute to common taxes. Only by dint of periodic compromises and occasional riots had it been possible, in September 1358, to complete the circuit of walls after many years of intermittent work. Even then a vital section was defended only by the so-called

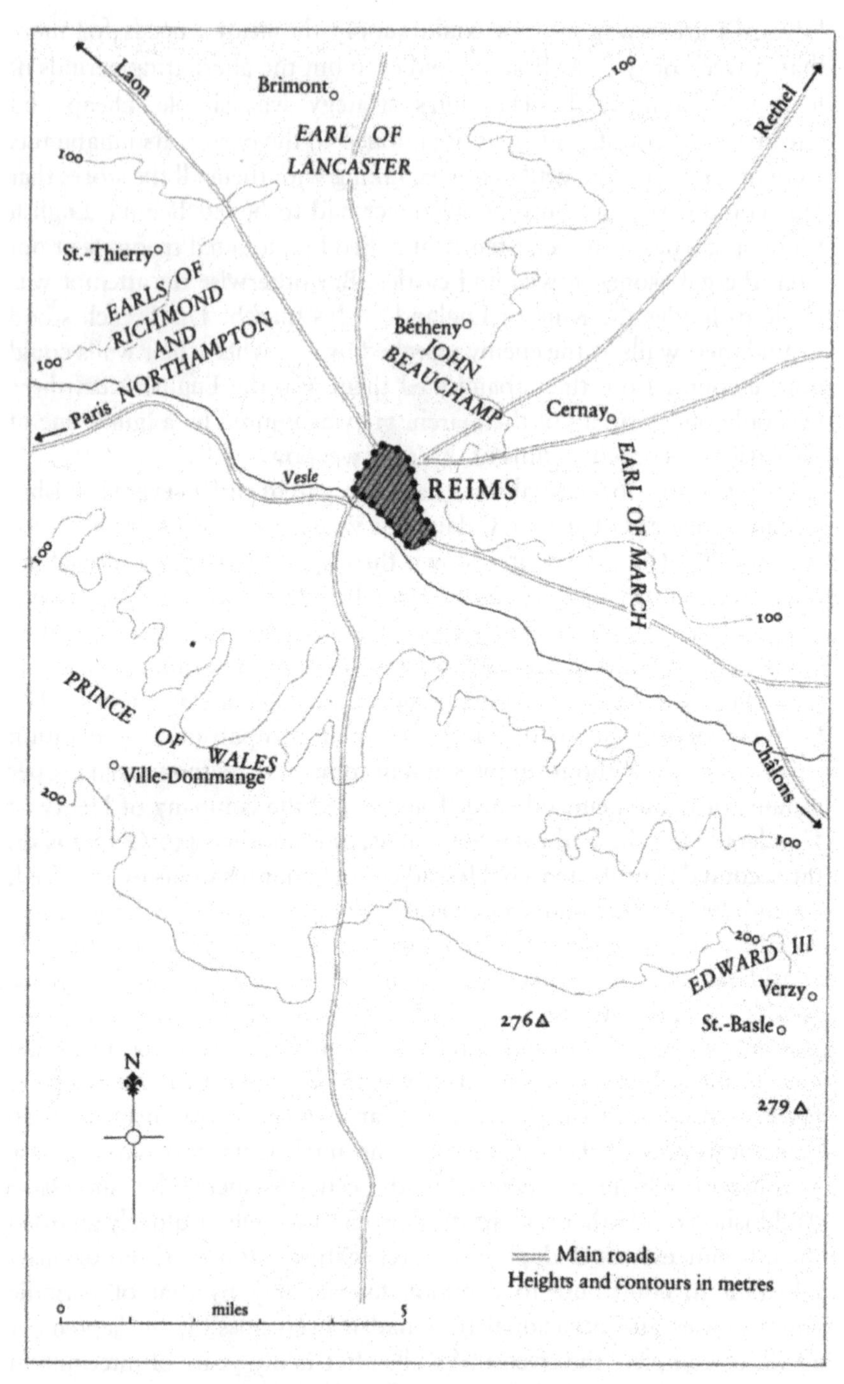

29 Siege of Reims: December 1359–January 1360

chateau de Porte-Mars, a fortified triumphal arch dating from the third century, surrounded by a low dilapidated wall, where the Archbishops had laid out a garden and which they resolutely refused to demolish or improve. The current tenant of the cathedral, the aristocratic Jean de Craon, had had a particularly abrasive relationship with the town. The citizens quarrelled with him about guard duty and money. They resented his relationship with the nobility of the outlying district, whom they regarded as plunderers little better than the English. They were irritated by the way his officers boasted of his kinship with the King of England. Some of them believed that he was in league with the enemy.[44]

If Reims was equal to the English challenge at the end of 1359, this was due mainly to one man, Gaucher de Châtillon. He was a member of one of the most prominent noble houses of Champagne, whom the Archbishop and the townsmen had agreed in a rare moment of concord to appoint as captain of the city. Jean de Craon came to regret his part in the nomination of this ruthless and energetic man, who put himself at once at the head of the citizenry and briefly became dictator of Reims. Gaucher built a huge wall with high towers between the cathedral and the chateau de Porte-Mars. He raised large sums of money by taxing the habitants of the town and its suburbs, as well as the great number of refugees who had brought their households and possessions into the city. Three of the eight gates were walled up and their drawbridges dismantled. An additional circuit of ditches was dug. Everything close to the walls that might give cover to an enemy was razed regardless of who owned it. An entire forest belonging to the cathedral chapter was felled for building materials. Carts and beasts of burden were requisitioned, including the horses in the Archbishop's personal stable. Supplies were confiscated in the surrounding villages to fill the garrison's stores. Great quantities of artillery were brought into the city. Chains were piled up at street corners to block the progress of the enemy should they penetrate the walls. The citizens were organised in units of ten and fifty and rostered for guard duty day and night. The tower of the church of St. Symphorien was taken over and its bell used to call them to arms, in spite of the Archbishop's protest that the town was his and had no right to 'corps ne commune, arche ou cloche'. Even the ageing poet Guillaume de Machaut, a canon of the cathedral, was made to put on a coat of mail and stand grumbling at the gates. Gaucher de Châtillon saved Reims, and perhaps France.[45]

The King of England established his headquarters at Saint-Basle, a Benedictine monastery at the highest point of the Montagne de Reims.

From this place – General Gouraud was to direct the east wing of the French armies from it in the summer of 1918 – Edward could look across the vineyards of the River Vesle to the city, ten miles away on the far bank. Beyond it the encampments of the Duke of Lancaster and the Earls of Northampton, Warwick and March were spread out in an arc from the heights of Saint-Thierry to the meadows of the Vesle. A series of conferences was arranged with the leaders of the city. A temporary truce was called and the army ordered to abstain from plundering while attempts were made to persuade them to surrender. But the citizens were uncompromising. They replied that they would resist 'as long as there was breath in their bodies.' Shortly after this, probably on 18 December 1359, the English came down from the hills around the city and began a close blockade of the place. Prisoners captured by the defenders all told the same story. Edward was planning a long siege.[46]

The Dauphin was prince of Paris, but nothing more. Outside the capital, his government scarcely existed. Even provinces closely connected with the royal house increasingly acted like independent states. In Poitiers the royal Lieutenant Jean de Boucicaut, desperate to find coin to pay his troops, took over the local mint and began to set the value of coin and the price of bullion on the advice of a local monetary committee of his own without reference to the rest of the kingdom. The Normans virtually declared independence. They appropriated the local receipts of the taxes voted in the previous autumn. They organised their own defence in alliance with the communities of Picardy. In the following year, they would elect their own Lieutenant in place of the Dauphin's nominee, who had been captured in battle. Indeed their first instinct was to offer the job to the King of Navarre. He refused it only because he did not wish to be 'misinterpreted'.[47]

The only troops at the Dauphin's disposal, apart from the garrison of the capital, was a small cavalry force commanded by the Constable. When the King of England left Calais, he was at Auxerre, rebuilding the walls and gates thrown down by Robert Knolles and trying to expel the English garrisons of Ligny and Regennes. As Edward approached Reims the Constable patched up a rapid treaty with the English captains of these places, by which they agreed to vacate the two fortresses and return to Normandy in return for a promise of the enormous sum of 26,000 *écus*. It was a face-saving formula, but worthless as both parties appreciated. For it was subject to the approval of the King of England and expressly reserved the brigands' right to carry on the fight under Edward's commanders if they were ordered to. Having achieved this much, the Constable marched north to Troyes, pillaged the churches of the city for plate to pay his men, and judging the position around Reims to be hopeless, returned to Paris for consultations with the Dauphin. Shortly before Christmas a messenger from the town managed to penetrate through the siege lines to carry to Paris a full report of the situation of Reims and an appeal for help. The Dauphin and his Council could do nothing.[48]

The only notable French military project of the winter was a much diminished version of the grandiose plan which had foundered in October to invade England with aid of the Danes and the Scots. The new version relied simply of the exiguous resources of France. The idea was to collect a fleet together in the ports of Normandy and Picardy and land it on the coast of England to rescue the King of France from his prison. The men behind this unrealistic scheme were Louis of Harcourt, the royal Lieutenant in Normandy, and a Picard nobleman called Jean de Neuville, who was the nephew of the Marshal Arnoul d'Audrehem and was deputising for him during his captivity in England. The Dauphin made a small financial contribution, and sent the Constable to Picardy to help. Otherwise he had very little to do with it.[49]

Shortly after the investment of Reims, the English tried to capture the city by storm. Three divisions attacked the walls simultaneously. One assaulted the south-west corner, close to the fortified bridge over the River Vesle. The other two approached by the east near the great monastery of St. Remi. The English archers brought a deluge of arrows down on the walls, forcing the defenders to keep their heads down while great quantities of trees and building timber were thrown into the ditches below and two wooden towers were rolled forward towards the wall. The defenders fought back with ferocity. They showered the assailants with stones shot from machines within the city. They sent out sortie parties, who fought their way into the ditches and set fire to the timber fillings under a hail of arrows from the banks. After a whole day's fighting, the Prince of Wales' division succeeded in creating a causeway some thirty feet wide across the ditch on the western side. But he failed to reach the walls. The others, on the eastern side, did not even achieve this much. The attack was called off at dusk. No attempt was made to repeat it.[50]

The defenders of Reims were better placed to withstand a long siege than the English were. Their stores were still crammed with provisions. The besiegers, by comparison, sat encamped in the freezing rain on the fringe of cleared land around the city walls and ate through the last of the supplies which they had brought with them from Calais. Edward's army was the equivalent of the population of a large provincial town. It rapidly exhausted the resources within foraging distance. The King of England celebrated Christmas in the village of Verzy, close to his headquarters, with most of his army around him. After the festivities had ended the pattern of operations changed. Lust for spoil and an increasingly urgent need to find forage and victuals were almost certainly the reasons. A curtain of troops was left around the city, while the rest of the army formed itself into a number of separate bands under the principal commanders and dispersed across northern Champagne. In the nearby town of Cernay the Duke of Lancaster's troops fought their way across a line of ditches and captured the place from scaling ladders. At Cormicy on the other side of Reims Bartholomew Burghersh entered the town by escalade at night, undermined the citadel and took it by storm. Several *routier* captains followed on the English army's coat-tails, thus re-establishing themselves in a region from which they had been expelled by the Lieutenants in the previous summer. The most famous was Eustache d'Aubricourt, who bought his way out of prison, reconstituted his company, and fell on the town of Attigny, thirty-five miles north of Reims on the River Aisne. Here, he and his men drank the cellars dry and set up a base from which they plundered the county of Rethel and raided down into the plain of Reims. At the beginning of January 1360 Aubricourt joined up with the Duke of Lancaster. Together they launched an exceptionally destructive raid east towards the forest of Argonne. These operations briefly relieved the pressure on the English army's supplies. But within two weeks of the new year they had exhausted all the resources within reach of Reims. There was no alternative but to leave. On 11 January 1360 Edward III swallowed his pride and abandoned the siege. His men sloped away in the middle of the night. The morning watch found them gone.[51]

For some time after he had left Reims the English King's strategy was determined mainly by the need to feed his army. The plan was to march in a great circle round the east and south of Paris, keeping his army on the move until a fresh supply train could be organised. The new supply train was to come from Lower Normandy. This ambitious project involved reinforcing the garrison of Honfleur at the mouth of the Seine and creating a great depot there. Some of the stores would be found by large-scale foraging raids from Honfleur into the region around. Some would come by sea from England. Preparations were already under way in January 1360.[52]

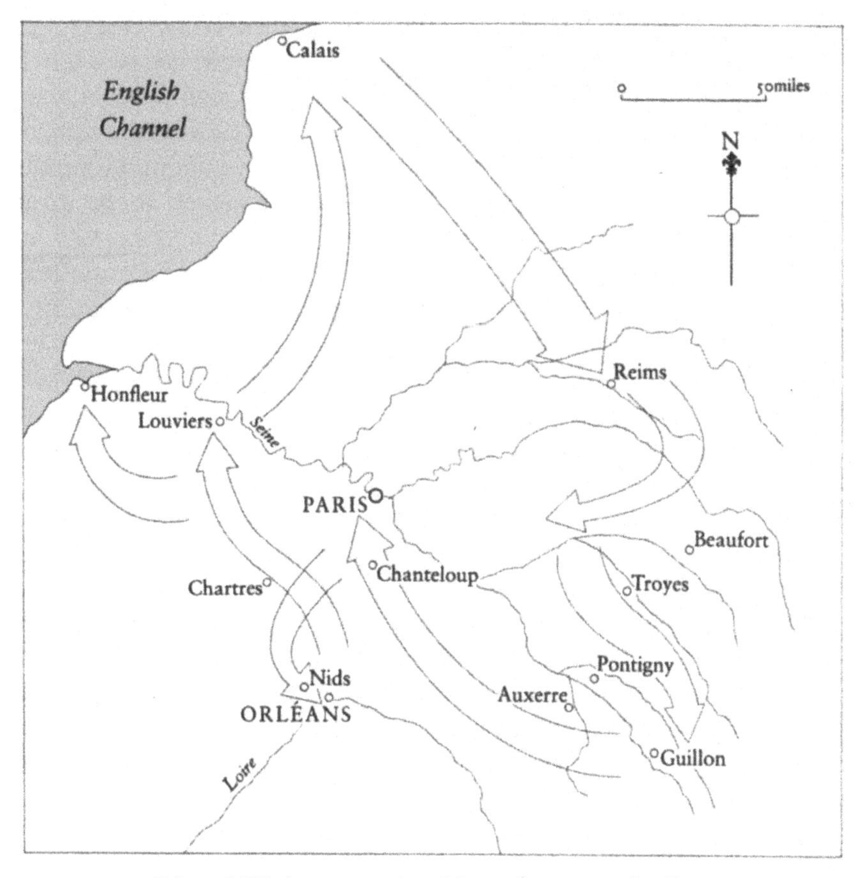

30 Edward III's last campaign, November 1359–April 1360

From Reims, the English marched south through a green desert. All stores had been removed to the walled towns and garrisoned castles. The inhabitants fled before them. There was no organised resistance, only the constant harassment of small guerrilla groups. Englishmen who slept in unguarded quarters were knifed in their beds. Those who ventured too far from their companions in search of food were ambushed and killed or, like the poet Chaucer, taken for ransom. The army advanced in three columns spread across a broad front some fifteen miles wide, doing damage which for its scale and organisation far exceeded the worst ravages of the independent companies. When they had passed by, mobs of French looters followed in their wake, breaking into abandoned houses and churches, clearing out whatever the English had left behind. The Italian poet Petrarch, who travelled through the region a few months after the passage of the English army, wrote to his friends that he could hardly recognise it. 'Everywhere was grief, destruction and desolation, uncultivated fields filled with weeds, ruined and abandoned houses. . . In short wherever I looked were the scars of defeat. The ruins go right up to the gates of Paris.' In about the middle of February 1360 the English columns came together at the great Cistercian Abbey of Pontigny, north of Auxerre, a place rich in historical associations with England, where one Archbishop of Canterbury had passed his exile and another had died in the odour of sanctity. From here they advanced on Burgundy, a 'land lush with riches' said Jean le Bel, where the English would be able to fill their bellies and their pockets. In the middle of February, Edward called a halt at Guillon, a small village east of Avallon. Here he opened negotiations with the Queen and the Council of the duchy of Burgundy.[53]

The men of Burgundy had defended themselves with skill and vigour against the companies of Robert Knolles, but they were in no position to resist the host of Edward III. A thin fringe of Burgundian garrisons defended the northern march of the duchy. The English companies in the Auxerrois had already torn up their treaty with the Constable and penetrated the duchy's defences in several places. By the time that Edward III reached Guillon, Nicholas Tamworth and the companies from Regennes were firmly ensconced in the castle of Courcelles and the abbey of Flavigny on the eastern side of Semur-en-Auxois. At Dijon, which was barely a day's march from Tamworth's new headquarters, the Estates of Burgundy gathered in the great convent of St. Benigne to approve the terms of surrender. They agreed to pay a ransom on behalf of the whole duchy of 200,000 *moutons*, payable in instalments over the next fifteen months. This was a large sum, roughly equivalent to an English parliamentary subsidy. In return Edward III granted the Burgundians a truce of three years. He promised to take the town of Flavigny out of the violent hands of Nicholas Tamworth and restore it to the Queen's officers. Tamworth, who had to be given some reward for his travails, was allowed to keep Courcelles but made a separate agreement of his own by which the Burgundians were granted an option to buy him out when they could raise the money. This treaty was sealed at Guillon on 10 March 1360. There was a curious proviso about Edward III's claim to the French Crown. If Edward III succeeded in having himself crowned King of France with the assent of a majority of the peers of the realm, and if the Duke of Burgundy was in the minority, then Edward should be entitled to take armed measures against him notwithstanding the truce. Perhaps the Queen and her advisers regarded this contingency as too remote to be taken seriously. In Paris, however, the terms of the treaty of Guillon provoked much indignation. If the Burgundians had truly done this thing, men said, they would be despised forever. In fact, it was difficult to blame them. They had been left to defend themselves with forces far inferior to the enemy's. The Constable had left the region and was now in Picardy, engrossed in the preparations to rescue John II in England. The terms which the Burgundians negotiated were very favourable considering the wealth of the duchy. They paid no more for their immunity than the smaller and poorer county of Bar had promised the English King in January. It was certainly much cheaper than allowing Edward to continue his advance to the south, instead of turning west.[54] In the middle of March 1360 the English army crossed the Yonne south of Auxerre and entered the Nivernais. Then, turning north through the Gâtinais, they quickened their pace and advanced on Paris.[55]

Jean de Neuville's preparations to invade England were soon discovered by Edward III's ministers at Westminster. There had been rumours for some months of a French counter-stroke, possibly in conjunction with the Scots, and contingency plans for dealing with it had been on hand since the previous autumn.[56] As always, bureaucratic reactions were slow, ready money was scarce and precise intelligence was late and incomplete. From the beginning of the year 1360 the Council had ships sent out to reconnoitre off the Channel ports of France. It was presumably in this way that at the beginning of February 1360 they received reports that a fleet was gathering in the great open harbour of le Crotoy at the mouth of the Somme.

The government of England was in the hands of the Chancellor, William Edington, and the Treasurer, the learned John Sheppey, Bishop of Rochester. It is not clear how seriously they really took the threat, for they had every interest in exaggerating it. They were keen to assist Edward III's campaign in France, which was beginning to lose momentum. But they were short of cash, and a direct threat to the realm was much the best way of getting some. So they immediately ordered the requisitioning of ships along the south and east coasts of England. All men of an age to bear arms were summoned to defend their counties. And a number of regional councils was hurriedly summoned to meet at Westminster and at various of provincial towns. These were not Parliaments, but gatherings of the county courts of each region, which technically could grant no taxes. But they were bound to pay for the cost of defending their counties against an enemy. The King's ministers persuaded them to raise this money by levying funds according to the assessments used for parliamentary taxation. Half the amount was to be collected at once, but held in sealed chests in cathedrals and abbeys across England. When the enemy invaded, the first half would be released and spent under the direction of the King's officers, and the collection of the second half would begin. There was very little to distinguish these levies from a Parliamentary subsidy.[57]

These arrangements were made at great speed and were still far from complete when Jean de Neuville's fleet sailed from le Crotoy at the end of February 1360, declaring to the assembled well-wishers, gossips and spies that they would return with their King. The commanders of the French expedition must have known that John II was at Somerton. But their knowledge of the geography of England was very uncertain, and they initially made for Sandwich, apparently believing that Somerton was close by. Within a day or two of their departure the Council at Westminster was precisely informed of their intentions. The fleets of the south and east coast ports were concentrated in the mouth of the Thames. Troops were arrayed along the Kent coast. The Council ordered the King to be removed from Somerton and taken under escort to the enormous twelfth-century fortress of Berkhamstead in Hertfordshire, which was stronger and further from the sea.[58]

In the event the French did not land at Sandwich. For more than a week, they were pinned against their own coast by strong headwinds, and when they did find a landing place it was at Rye Bay in Sussex. On 15 March 1360, after their ships had been at sea for more than a fortnight, they anchored and disembarked without opposition on the marshes of the Rother. Contemporary estimates of their strength varied between 1,500 and 2,000 men, in addition to the crews of the ships. Very few of them were men-at-arms. Most were bowmen and foot soldiers from the towns of Normandy and Picardy or volunteers from Flanders. They formed up on the beach in three battalions, and marched along the shore until they came to Winchelsea.

The sea has retreated a long way from Winchelsea in six centuries. In the fourteenth century the town stood on a cliff overlooking the bay. It was a poor prize: a new town never completely colonised and already in decay only seventy years after its foundation by Edward I. It was still largely unwalled. The invaders encountered little resistance. They swiftly occupied the place, killing the inhabitants who had not had time to flee, clearing out the warehouses of wool, tin and wine, and sending raiding parties into the villages and hamlets around. There was then a pause for reflection, and for quarrels about the distribution of spoil. While this continued about 300 horsemen of the Sussex county levies gathered at the approaches to the town. The invaders learned from their prisoners that more troops, raised in other parts of southern England, were on their way, which was true, and that the King of France had been removed to Wales, which was not (he was still at Somerton). When they had digested this information, the French captains decided that there was nothing more to be done. They waited until the following day. Then they set fire to Winchelsea and withdrew towards their ships.

It was a difficult and bloody withdrawal. By now the county levies were present in force around the town. They moved into the streets as the French left, cutting down some 160 of them who were still engaged in looting it. The rest of the French army made its way in formation along the beach, followed at a short distance by the English cavalry. When at length the French reached the ships, they were obliged to break ranks in order to wade into the sea and climb aboard. At this point the English charged down on them across the sloping sand. A large number of the invaders were killed in the mêlée and many more were drowned. The French lost about 300 of their men and two ships which they had beached and were unable to refloat. The rest escaped across the Channel.[59]

For the ministers at Westminster, the incident was an unmitigated boon. Although the danger had passed almost as soon as it had appeared, the money which the counties had resolved to collect for their defence was now at the government's disposal. Edington intended to spend it. The Council described its plans as purely defensive. But what they in fact had in mind was a large-scale raid along the French Channel coast, followed by a landing in support of Edward III's operations around Paris. The preparations were conceived on an ambitious scale. The fleets of both admiralties, which had been assembled for the defence of the coast, were ordered to wait in the Thames. Men recruited for the defence of England were directed to embarkation points at London, Sandwich and Pevensey. All men-at-arms waiting for passages to Normandy or Brittany were ordered to join them. John Wesenham, the famous grocer and war financier of Lynn, advanced £4,500 for this project against assignments from the county taxes. Henry Picard, vintner and former mayor of London, who was the richest merchant in

England, is likely to have subscribed a substantial part of this. He took command.[60]

In March 1360 the sleet and driving rain which had made life a misery for the English in France suddenly gave way to warm clear skies. Entering the Beauce south of Paris, they found themselves in a land in the first budding of recovery. It was one of the few regions in the north where the King of Navarre's surrender had been followed by real peace. The granges were filled with the previous year's harvest. At the end of the month the King of England installed himself in the manor of the Dukes of Burgundy at Chanteloup by the Orléans road, some 20 miles south of Paris, while the rest of the army encamped along the left bank of the Seine from Corbeil to Longjumeau. From their encampments by the river, they spread out for many miles around, breaking into deserted churches and houses, emptying the storehouses, smashing and burning what they did not need or could not carry.[61]

Edward III had virtually no chance of capturing Paris. It is unlikely that he expected to. Even 10,000 men were not enough to invest three and a half miles of wall or fight through narrow streets inhabited by 100,000 determined citizens and perhaps as many refugees. Edward's purpose was to force a treaty on the government of the Dauphin while he still had an army in the field and while there were still supplies in the region to feed it. Terrorism on a great scale was Edward's only means of doing this. The French knew this as well as he did. For at least a month both protagonists had been setting the scene for the negotiated settlement which both desperately needed. The key was the captive king at Somerton. John II was past caring what it cost to regain his liberty. He had been outraged by the way in which the Estates-General had rejected the treaty of London the year before and, no doubt, by his son's overt connivance in it. One of his first acts after receiving the news had been to strengthen his own grip on the government in Paris. Three of John's councillors and fellow prisoners had been released on parole to represent the King's interest at the Estates-General: the Archbishop of Sens, his brother the Count of Tancarville, and Charles de Trie, Count of Dammartin. They did not return to captivity after the treaty had failed. Instead, some arrangement was cobbled together with their captors to pay off at least part of their ransoms and allow them to remain in Paris. John II personally borrowed heavily in England to raise part of the Archbishop's ransom. The three prisoners, together with John's old councillor Simon Bucy, now became the dominant figures in the Dauphin's Council. They worked assiduously to make peace with the King of England.[62]

As at previous crises of their affairs, it was to the papacy that the French government looked to bring them together with their enemies. Pope Innocent VI had had two agents following the progress of the English campaign ever since it had begun. One of them was Simon of Langres, the general of the Dominican Order, an intelligent and independent-minded Parisian theologian who had acted as the spokesman of the University of Paris during the revolution of February 1358. The other was William Lynn, who had once been employed by Edward III as a diplomatic draftsman and was now working in the papal judicial service at Avignon. Simon and presumably his colleague had spent the first weeks of 1360 passing between the Dauphin's court and the English King's field headquarters. They presumably reported some willingness to compromise. At the beginning of March 1360 the Pope was persuaded to appoint a full legation to preside over a new diplomatic conference.

Innocent's choice of principal was not entirely satisfactory. Androin de la Roche, abbot of Cluny, had frequently been entrusted by the Pope with difficult diplomatic missions, including a legation in England in 1355. Innocent had great confidence in him, but it is far from clear why. The abbot was an upright man and a graceful speaker. But he was unworldly and incapable. That shrewd Florentine, Matteo Villani, who had witnessed his conduct as papal legate in Italy, dismissed him as 'uomo molle e poco pratico' ('soft and inexperienced'). His colleagues were more impressive. One was Simon of Langres himself. The other was Hugh of Geneva, lord of Anthon, a long-standing anglophile, now at least sixty years old, who had fought with Edward III in the Low Countries in 1339 and served as his Lieutenant in Gascony for two years in the early 1340s. Simon of Langres was already in Paris. Androin and Hugh received their instructions at Avignon on 4 March 1360 and left for the north in the next day or two.[63]

Edward III learned of the Pope's initiative while he was still at Guillon on the march of Burgundy. On 14 March 1360 he sent William Burton, a knight of his household, to discuss the issues with Innocent in person.[64] A more significant pointer to the English King's intentions was a sudden change in the arrangements for the custody of John II in England. The Council's instructions to send John to Berkhamstead were cancelled. Instead the French King was to be brought to London, where he would be in closer touch with Edward's ministers and with events in France. On the 21st he was removed from Somerton and taken under heavy guard down the Great North Road. On the 29th he was lodged in the Tower. Three days after his arrival, John executed a power of attorney empowering the Dauphin to represent him at the 'forthcoming negotiations for peace'. But the Dauphin never exercised this power in person. It was exercised on his behalf by John's ministers in Paris. The Dauphin was nowhere to be seen. He was living in the Hotel de Sens, the private mansion of the Archbishop of Sens by the suburb of Saint-Antoine, where he could be kept under more exacting supervision.[65]

On 31 March 1360, the day of Edward III's arrival at Chanteloup, Simon of Langres came before him to propose a preliminary conference. It was held three days later on Good Friday, in the buildings of a leper hospital at Longjumeau, a short distance from Edward's headquarters. The debates of the ambassadors are not recorded, but it seems that the demands of the English were exorbitant. The conference broke up on the same day without achieving anything.[66] Edward began to increase the pressure. The village of Orly was attacked only 5 miles away from the conference while it was still in progress. Half the population of the village was massacred in the parish church, where they had gathered for protection. On 4 April the English burned Longjumeau and a large number of villages around it. The town of Montlhéry was gutted under the eyes of the Dauphin's garrison in the castle. One of the worst incidents occurred at Arpajon, within sight of Edward's headquarters. The Benedictine priory there had been turned into an improvised fortress guarded by a small garrison of soldiers. A great number of refugees from the town and surrounding country had taken refuge in it with their goods and furniture. After being battered for several days by English artillery posted on the hill above them, the garrison withdrew to a gatehouse. When the occupants of the church found themselves abandoned by their defenders, they decided to surrender. The garrison then turned on them. They set fire to the church. About 900 people perished in the flames. Some 300 survivors tried to make their way out of the enclosure, letting themselves down from the walls with ropes. As they reached the ground the English killed them.[67]

On 7 April 1360, after a brief pause to celebrate Easter, the King of England and the greater part of his army moved up the Orléans road towards the walls of Paris. As the army cut off the city from the south, the English garrisons operating on the other side of the Seine closed in from the north. One of them, at la Ferté-sous-Jouarre on the Marne, was taken over by one of Edward's captains, James Audley. Robert Scot brought his bands down from Picardy and briefly occupied the island-fortress of l'Isle

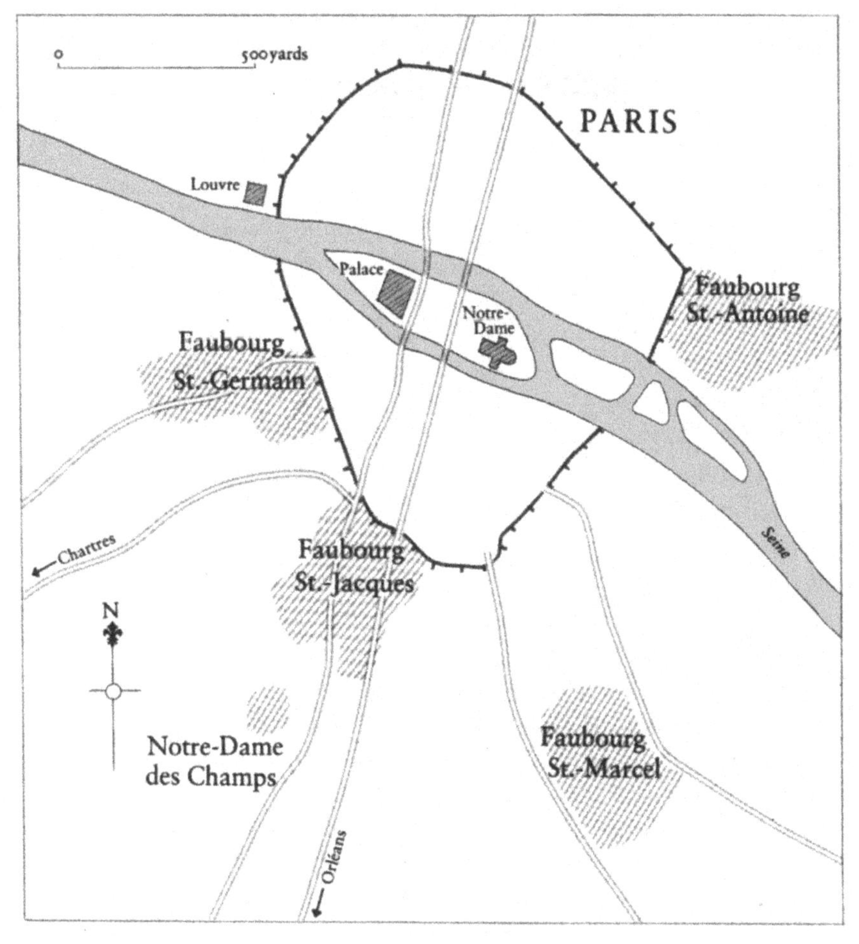

31 Paris, 7–12 April 1360

Adam on the Oise. Inside the capital, morale was high, but conditions were difficult. Severe shortages and the continuing devaluation of the coinage drove up prices in the city's markets to unheard-of levels. The price of grain more than doubled. Wine cost so much that men would not share it with their closest friends. Fish almost disappeared from the shops. What food there was had to serve for a vastly increased population. The first great tide of refugees had arrived in the southern suburbs as the Beauce and the Île de France emptied out before the advancing English army. On Easter Sunday the inhabitants of ten country parishes shared the Carmelite church of Notre-Dame des Champs outside the gates, each parish taking a side chapel in which to receive the sacrament from their own priest. On the following day, as smoke and flames covered the horizon, the Parisians began to destroy their southern suburbs to deprive the enemy of cover. Their inhabitants took up their possessions and crammed into the narrow streets of the city.[68]

The English army occupied the plateau of Chatillon, overlooking the city from the south-west: gently sloping ground, densely planted with vines and scattered with the suburban villas of rich Parisians and the farmhouses of the great monasteries of the capital. Edward III drew up his men in battle order in three lines just below the burnt out village of Notre-Dame des Champs. A cacophony of bugles and trumpets was directed at the closed gates of the city, just 600 yards away across the charred ruins of the *faubourg* Saint-Jacques. For the next few days the English marched back and forth through the southern suburbs wrecking whatever the Parisians themselves had left standing, in the hope of provoking a pitched battle with the Dauphin's troops. But the defenders had received strict instructions to stay at their posts. A single troop of sixty men-at-arms emerged to fight a staged battle *à outrance* beneath the walls. Otherwise no one came out to take up the challenge.[69]

In the midst of these events the abbot of Cluny and Hugh of Geneva arrived in Paris to settle the preliminaries of peace. The English King assured the Dauphin's emissaries that he would consider 'any reasonable proposals'. But his views about what was reasonable were still a long way from theirs. On 10 April 1360, the representatives of the two sides met at la Banlieu by the Orléans road, another of the suburban leper houses of Paris. The proceedings were brief. As soon as they opened, the English disclosed that their minimum demands still included the whole of the territory ceded to Edward III by the abortive treaty of London which the Estates-General had already rejected. The French delegation replied that they would not dare even to report such a demand to the Dauphin. They tendered their own proposal, which has not survived but was rejected as inadequate. The conference then broke up without agreement.[70]

The French could afford to wait. As in most major sieges of the fourteenth century, the situation of the besieging army soon became far more parlous than that of the defenders within. The immediate vicinity of Paris had been efficiently stripped of its stores before the English had arrived. The grain which the English had plundered in the Beauce had been eaten. Edward III's ambitious attempts to create a new line of supply from Honfleur were not working according to plan. Large quantities of salted fish, vegetables, grain and wine had been requisitioned in the English counties or bought from wholesalers in London. But not all of it had been shipped, and not all that had been shipped had arrived. One vessel, which put into Winchelsea on the way, had been captured in the French raid. Another had been wrecked on a sandbank in the Thames estuary. Some of the vegetables went bad before they reached their destination. As for the foraging raids of the garrison of Honfleur, they encountered unexpectedly stiff resistance and disintegrated into cock-fighting in the Seine valley. A very small quantity of victuals reached Edward III from Honfleur in early April 1360. It can hardly had been enough to feed his personal staff. By the second week of the siege the army had almost run out of food. Fodder for horses was in particularly short supply. The leaders of the French were well aware of these facts, for Edward's soldiers complained often and loudly. An Englishman called John Cope, who had lived for many years in Paris, slipped out to mingle with his fellow countrymen in their encampments. He delivered a full report to the Dauphin's Council.[71] Early on 12 April 1360 the King of England, the Prince of Wales and the Duke of Lancaster drew up the bulk of their forces on the plain before the suburb of Saint-Marcel. The defenders massed on the walls opposite. It was only a diversion. Behind the English lines the retreat had already begun. The great wagon-train had been moving slowly west along the Chartres road since before dawn. At about 10 o'clock in the morning, Edward's battalions beneath the walls of Paris turned round and marched after them.[72]

On Monday 13 April 1360 disaster struck the English army. After six weeks of unseasonal warmth the weather turned again. As the army was passing the town of Galardon the towers of Chartres Cathedral came into view across the flat plain. A great thunderstorm broke above. There was no cover in the open prairie. The long columns trudged on into fierce winds and driving rain. The baggage wagons sunk deep into lakes of mud. Most of them had to be abandoned. Equipment, stores and booty were all lost. The temperature fell and the rain turned to sleet and hail. Then it froze hard. No one could remember such conditions. Men and horses, many of whom were sick and underfed, died of exposure. Others were killed or wounded by enormous hail stones. Their corpses were left by the roadside. The survivors had no transport, tentage, saddlery or cooking utensils. 'Wherefore,' an Englishman wrote many years later, 'unto this day it is called Black Monday and will be long time hereafter.'[73]

Close to Chartres Edward III received another delivery of victuals from Honfleur, this time several cart loads, which were distributed among the principal retinues. It was a minor miracle of logistical organisation. But it cannot have made much impression on the needs of such a large army, and it was the last delivery which they received. The bedraggled and much reduced horde turned south across the Beauce Chartrain. Everywhere the French withdrew before them, carrying their foodstuffs into fortified places. The French garrisons of the region harassed the English supply operations with great skill. Their scouts watched the progress of the army. Mounted parties fell on any groups who got separated from the main force. English foragers had to operate over great distances and under heavy guard. South of Bonneval the army spread out in order to ease their supply problems. One part headed south into the Vendômois, another east into the Orléanais. On about 18 April 1360 Edward III established his headquarters at the Priory of Nids, ten miles north-west of Orléans. Here, he paused to reflect upon the next move.[74]

The storm and the supply crisis finally forced the English King to abandon the uncompromising line which he had maintained at Longjumeau and la Banlieu. According to Froissart, it was the Duke of Lancaster who made the decisive point:

> Sir [he is supposed to have said], you are waging a tremendous war in France and fortune has so far favoured you. But while your subjects are making money out of it, you are just marking time. You now have a choice. You can press on with your struggle and pass the rest of your life fighting; or you can make terms with your enemy while you can still come out of it with honour. My advice is to accept the offers which have already been made to you. You know perfectly well that in one day we could lose all that we have gained in twenty years.

Whether Lancaster in fact gave this advice we cannot know, but it would be surprising if someone had not done so. Edward's army may have been impressively large and superbly equipped, but the Dauphin's policy of refusing battle and defending the walled towns had left them with no way of coming to grips with the enemy before they starved. So Edward authorised a message to be sent to the abbot of Cluny. He told him that he was willing to treat with the Dauphin. In the last week of April 1360 it was agreed to call a new diplomatic conference near Chartres. The Dauphin's ambassadors left Paris on 26 April 1360 and arrived at Chartres on the following day. The King of England came north from Nids. On about 30 April 1360 he established himself 6 miles from Chartres in the house of the Hospitallers of Sours.[75]

*

At the end of April 1360, the fleet which William Edington had gathered in England for the defence of the coast appeared off Picardy. After cruising south from port to port, about 160 English ships entered the great natural harbour at Leure on the north side of the Seine estuary and landed a large number of seamen and soldiers. The strength of this fresh invasion force was probably somewhere between 3,000 and 5,000 men. They occupied the harbour. They forced the surrender of the old royal fort by the beach. Then they advanced on Harfleur, an important walled town three miles inland. It was the mirror image of the French raid on Winchelsea in March, and proved to be equally fruitless for much the same reasons: the follow-up was too slow and too little thought out. The news of the landings shocked the region into a spasm of activity. The English made no impression on the defences of Harfleur, and within a few days the royal Lieutenant in Normandy, Louis of Harcourt, had arrived on the scene with substantial forces raised in Rouen and the Pays de Caux. With these, he hemmed in the English against the coast, blocking the routes inland and making it all but impossible for the invaders to find food.[76]

The diplomatic conference opened under the shadow of these events on 1 May 1360 at Brétigny, a tiny hamlet in the flat plain between Sours and Chartres. Into this insignificant place were crammed sixteen French ambassadors, twenty-two English ones, three papal legates and an observer sent by the King of Navarre, all with their bodyguards of soldiers and their staffs of clerks, servants and messengers. The chief negotiators were all veterans of past occasions of this sort. The Dauphin was represented by his Chancellor Jean de Dormans, Jean de Boucicaut, Simon Bucy and the Count of Tancarville; the King of England by the Duke of Lancaster, the Earls of Northampton, Warwick and Suffolk, Reynold Cobham, Bartholomew Burghersh and Walter Mauny. Once the English had made it known that they were no longer maintaining the territorial demands which had brought the earlier conferences to an end, negotiations rapidly reached a conclusion. The ground had been worked over so many times before, usually between the same people. The essential terms were already agreed by 3 May 1360, the third day of the conference.[77]

They were substantially the terms of the treaty of Windsor which Edward had repudiated eighteen months before. The English King abandoned his demands for the cession of the huge additional territories which had been included in the abortive treaty of London. But he was to hold all the provinces of the south-west which had once belonged to the

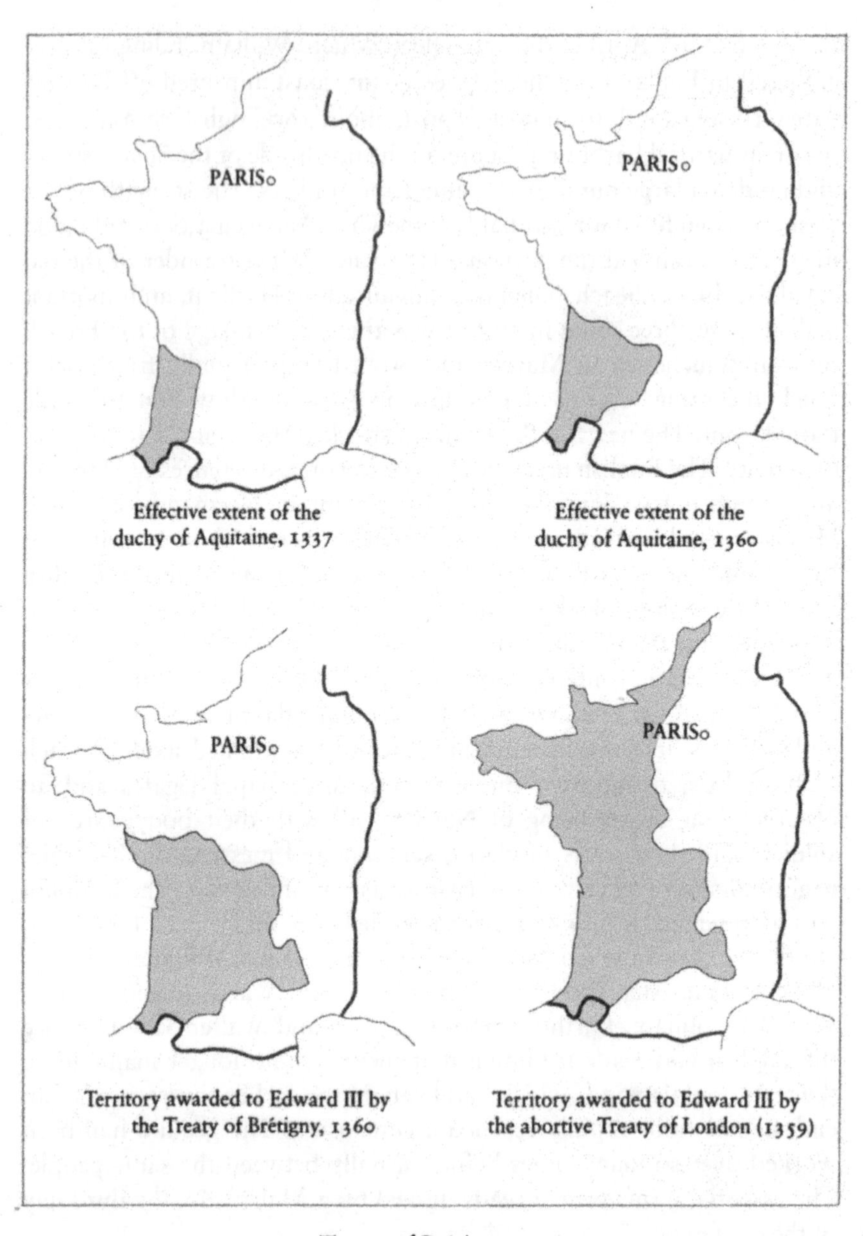

32 Treaty of Brétigny, 1360

Angevins in free sovereignty 'in the same manner as the King of France and his ancestors held them'. In addition to Gascony, this meant Poitou, Saintonge, Angoumois, Périgord, Limousin, Quercy and Rouergue, together with certain territories bordering on Gascony in the western Pyrenees. In the north Edward III was to be restored to the county of Ponthieu and the town of Montreuil in Picardy and he was to retain Calais and its dependencies. The King of France was to renounce all of these territories by 29 September 1360. In exchange for this renunciation, the King of England was to renounce all his claims to the throne of France which he had first asserted twenty years before in the market-place at Ghent. As for John II himself, he was to pay a ransom of 3,000,000 gold *écus* in instalments over a period of six years. This represented a large reduction from previous figures. It was 1,000,000 *écus* less than the sum required by the treaties of Windsor and London. Moreover it was to include the ransoms of sixteen of the most famous prisoners of the battle of Poitiers who were still in captivity in England. They would have been worth at least 500,000 *écus*.

The most elaborate arrangements were prescribed for the French King's release. John was to be brought to Calais by the middle of July 1360. There, some outstanding questions concerning the cession of territory and the renunciation of Edward's claims were to be resolved and the essential preliminaries to the performance of the treaty to be carried out. The two Kings would then formally ratify it. A small number of strategically vital fortresses in the ceded territories would be surrendered to the English at once: the French fortifications around Guines east of Calais, and the walled town and port of la Rochelle in western Poitou. The first 600,000 *écus* of the ransom would be paid. Twenty-five hostages selected from a list of the most prominent noblemen of the realm would be delivered up to the English King to secure the payment of the rest and the cession of the remaining territories. All this was to be accomplished within four months of John II's arrival in Calais. As additional security, Edward III stipulated that he was to keep in his power all sixteen of the prisoners of Poitiers whose ransoms had been remitted, and to receive a large number of further hostages selected from the leading citizens of twenty French towns.

Several days were passed in drafting and tidying up the details before the formalities at Brétigny were completed. On 7 May 1360 a truce was agreed to 29 September, to enable the provisions of the treaty to be carried out. On the following day, 8 May, the ambassadors applied their seals to the main instrument. As the heralds passed through the

English encampments proclaiming that peace had been made, the English soldiers processed barefoot into Chartres to give thanks to the Blessed Virgin in the cathedral dedicated to her.[78]

The Dauphin did not care for the treaty of Brétigny. He is reported to have believed that the English would soon have been forced to leave France anyway by shortage of supplies. This was probably true. But the Dauphin's views were by now irrelevant. The terms agreed at Brétigny were largely the work of the King's chief confidant in Paris, the Archbishop of Sens. The Dauphin may not even have been consulted. He certainly played no public part in the peace conference. He was suffering from an ulcer, it was explained. The final act, however, occurred in his presence. On Sunday morning, 10 May 1360, the Dauphin, surrounded by his councillors and by the leading citizens of Paris, received six knights of the King of England in the hall of the Hôtel de Sens. The treaty was read out to him and he confirmed that he was content. The Archbishop said mass. As the celebrant came to the *Agnus Dei*, the Dauphin approached the altar and swore on the consecrated host that he would perform the treaty in all respects that lay within his power. A sergeant-at-arms opened a window overlooking the courtyard to proclaim the peace to the crowd waiting below, and all the bells of Paris rang out. Whatever the Dauphin's private misgivings there was no doubt about the spontaneous joy of the French. Some, it is true, regretted the vast territorial concessions made to the English, and others feared the heavy fiscal burden which the ransom clauses implied. But in the northern towns which had borne the brunt of the war over the past three years everyone was relieved that the nightmare had apparently ended, except (says Jean de Venette) traitors, freebooters and arms manufacturers.[79]

The English could hardly wait to leave France. They burnt all their cumbersome equipment and marched north as soon as they heard the news of the Dauphin's assent. The Prince of Wales led his own division to Louviers on the Seine. Here, in the cavernous austerity of the church of Notre-Dame he ratified the treaty for his own part in a ceremony which was deliberately modelled on the Dauphin's ratification in Paris a week before. Edward III deferred his own ratification until it could be exchanged for John II's in England. On 19 May 1360 he and his sons embarked for England at Honfleur on the fleet which had attacked Leure. The rest of the army marched across Picardy to take ship at Calais.[80]

*

News of the treaty reached London before them. John II received an official report from the Count of Tancarville and another from Queen Philippa. The Queen's messenger received the enormous tip of 100 nobles for his pains. John was overjoyed. The conditions of his captivity were eased at once. The Chancery record office in the Tower was emptied out to make more spacious accommodation for him. He dined out with the Queen, with Henry Picard, with the countess of Pembroke. He visited St. Paul's Cathedral, the shrine of the Three Kings at Bermondsey, and the great monastic churches of London. He went boating on the Thames and inspected the lions in Edward III's private zoo. On 14 June 1360 John solemnly ratified the treaty of Brétigny at a banquet in the Tower which was attended by the King of England, the Prince of Wales and their courtiers, and by most of the French prisoners in England. The two kings, as John's agent told the King of Aragon, agreed that they and their children would be brothers together and would live in perfect love and perpetual peace. On the last day of June 1360 John II began his journey back to France, travelling slowly down the Old Kent Road to Dover. On 8 July 1360 he was delivered to Edward's officers in Calais.[81]

The main concern of the King of France was now to find the first instalment of his ransom. One of his last acts before leaving England had been to write from Canterbury to the officers of the Chambre des Comptes urging them to redouble their efforts to raise the 600,000 *écus* required. Another letter, repeating the same message in even more urgent terms, was sent as soon as the King reached Calais. In fact the Chambre des Comptes had been bending itself to the task for the past two months. There was no question of seeking formal consent for the necessary taxes. The ransom of a lord was one of the few occasions on which the custom of France recognised that taxation could be imposed as of right. The problem was not the principle but the endless haggling over assessments and the long delays before any money actually arrived in the King's coffers. It was therefore decided in the first instance to raise a large forced loan. Commissioners were despatched on 22 May 1360 to every part of France to extract money from rich individuals and walled towns. Everyone who was thought to have money was called before them to make his offering. Their instructions declared that they were not to take no for an answer. Those who were reluctant to lend were to be threatened with ostracism, and if necessary with force. There were to be no exceptions, even for the clergy. The King wrote to many of the greater towns himself, adding his personal entreaties. But it was one thing to insist, and another to collect. Paris agreed to lend 100,000 royals. Rouen, which after Paris was more closely associated with the fortunes of the Crown than any other French city, borrowed 200,000 *moutons* from the Count of Namur. Other towns did the same on a smaller scale. But many of the most important places had suffered too much from war damage to make any serious contribution at all. At Saint-Quentin the government's commissioners raised less than tenth of their target. Reims, which had been ruined by the expense of building its walls and fighting off the English army, took six months to raise just 2,600 *écus* in spite of three personal letters from the King, a peremptory order from the Chambre des Comptes, and a visit from one of the Marshals. The province of Normandy raised almost nothing until the end of the year.[82]

A special treasury was set up at the abbey of St. Bertin at Saint-Omer, to which all receipts were to be sent. But when the Dauphin arrived at Saint-Omer in the middle of June 1360, the chests were still almost empty.[83] By October 1360, when the money was required, only two thirds of it was there. Even that had been raised with the utmost difficulty. The surviving documents (which are far from complete) suggest that about 300,000 *écus* had come from the Paris area and the provinces of the north. The rest was in due course received from the highly unconventional sale of John II's eleven-year-old daughter Isabella to the Duke of Milan. Galeazzo Visconti, the rich and ambitious dictator of Milan and the principal Ghibelline prince of northern Italy, was keen to make a dazzling marriage for his eight-year-old heir. He was, it is true, a parvenu and an enemy of the papacy with which the French Kings had traditionally aligned themselves. But he was prepared to pay a high price in cash down. The Dauphin's agents had been despatched to Milan within a week of the execution of the treaty of Brétigny. They negotiated at great speed a marriage agreement by which the French obtained almost nothing but cash. Agreement was reached by July. The young princess was on her way to Italy by August. In return for Isabella and an extremely modest dowry, John's ambassadors received from Visconti a sum reported to be 600,000 *écus*, equal to the whole of the first instalment of the ransom. Of this sum 100,000 *écus* appears to have reached the Abbey of St. Bertin shortly after the agreement was signed in July. The Guelph chronicler Matteo Villani was profoundly shocked. Here, he said, was the ultimate abasement of France at the hands of the 'little King of England'.[84]

For six weeks after John II's arrival at Calais nothing happened, partly because neither the hostages nor the 600,000 *écus* were ready, partly because the Pope wanted his legates who had broked the treaty of Brétigny to be on hand for the final act. They did not arrive until late August. As for Edward III, he left the Prince of Wales to sort out with John II the matters which had been left unresolved at Brétigny. He transported his household to the Isle of Sheppey at the beginning of September 1360, where a flotilla of ships waited to carry him across the Channel as soon as the signal came from Calais that the stage was set. He evidently regarded the outstanding negotiations as formalities.[85]

In fact they proved unexpectedly difficult. The main issue concerned the precise timetable for the mutual renunciation of claims by the Kings of England and France. Edward III was pathologically suspicious of the French. He was afraid that John might not honour the terms once he had regained his liberty and Edward's claim to the throne had been abandoned, these being in his view by far his best bargaining counters. He therefore refused to renounce his own claims until the ceded territories had actually been given up. The French for their part appear to have insisted that if Edward's renunciation of his claim was postponed, their own renunciations of sovereignty in the ceded provinces would have to be postponed as well, since the terms agreed at Brétigny required them to be made simultaneously. In addition, they were becoming anxious about the activities of the English, Gascon and Navarrese companies. It had hitherto been assumed that they would lay down their arms when the war between the Kings came to an end. But this assumption was beginning to seem rather unrealistic. Edward had to wait at Sheppey for more than a month while the diplomats argued about these matters in vain. In the event the dispute had to be resolved by the Kings in person.

The King of England arrived in Calais on 9 October 1360. During the next few days there was a great gathering at Calais of the principal actors of the war. The Count of Flanders arrived on 12 October, making a flamboyant entry into the great hall of the castle in the midst of the banquet given by John II for his captors. The Dauphin came on the following day. They were followed by the Bishop of Avranches, Chancellor of Navarre. Charles of Blois appeared to plead his own cause. So did seven representatives of John de Montfort. An elaborate series of side agreements was then negotiated which resolved all major outstanding points.[86]

The solution to the problem of the renunciations was particularly complex. Edward III promised to procure the surrender of all the fortresses occupied by his subjects in the provinces which were to remain part of the French kingdom. An incomplete list of more than eighty occupied places was drawn up, for whose garrisons Edward was prepared to accept responsibility. Their removal was to be completed by the beginning of February 1361. John II was to be allowed to retain for a short time some of the lesser territories which he had promised to cede, as security for the performance of this ambitious undertaking. The county of Ponthieu, which was a minor territory but symbolically important to the Kings of England, was to be retained by the French to secure clearance of the enemy garrisons from the provinces of the north and east side of Paris and in the middle Loire. The county of Montfort-l'Amaury (which was to be delivered under the treaty to Edward III's protégé John de Montfort) was to be retained pending the clearance of the provinces south-west of the capital. Saintonge was to be held against the clearance of Normandy, and the Angoumois against the clearance of Touraine and the upper Loire. These concessions cost Edward very little, for come what may the territories in question had to be delivered up to him by the beginning of March 1361, failing which a large number of prominent members of the local nobility and each of the provinces in question would have to be sent to Calais as hostages for their eventual surrender.

The rest of the ceded territories were dealt with by a separate document containing the agreement which later became notorious as the 'clause *c'estassavoir*', so called after the word which introduced its operative provisions ('that is to say'). The clause *c'estassavoir* laid down that the remaining transfers of territory agreed at Brétigny would be completed by 24 June 1361. Once this had been done, the two Kings would send their representatives to exchange their renunciations in the convent of the Augustinians at Bruges on 15 August 1361, or failing that by 30 November 1361 at the latest. In the meantime John II would continue to enjoy nominal sovereignty in the ceded provinces, but he undertook not to exercise it. For his part Edward would retain in theory his claim to the throne of France until he came to renounce it, but undertook not to assert it. The matter of sovereignty having been dealt with by this side agreement, the main treaty was amended to delete all references to the mutual renunciation of claims. A separate agreement was made about the release of hostages, which was to occur in stages as the treaty was performed. John's sons, the Counts of Anjou and Poitiers, his brother the Duke of Orléans and two other royal princes would be released as soon as the second instalment of the ransom had been paid, the main territories of the south-west transferred and the renunciations duly made at Bruges. A fifth of the remaining hostages would be released as soon as the rest of the ceded territories had been transferred, and another fifth each year as the instalments of the ransom were paid. Edward III was destined to pay a high price for his caution, and for the complexity which was thus introduced into what had once been a reasonably straightforward agreement. For in the event the renunciations were never made, a fact which gave the French the pretext on which years later they were to repudiate the treaty altogether.[87]

Even now John's trials were not over. The citizens of la Rochelle, which was one of the strategic places to be handed over forthwith, were uncooperative. Like many other communities threatened with transfer to the King of England, they were concerned not so much about the territorial integrity of France as about the numerous civic privileges which they had received over the years from successive Kings of France, which would not necessarily be honoured by another sovereign. It was necessary for John II to send the Marshal Arnoul d'Audrehem to the town to reason with them. Then there was the problem of Charles of Navarre, whose co-operation was indispensable in view of the number of companies who acknowledged his authority, at least in point of form. A separate treaty was made between the King of France and his estranged son-in-law, under the auspices of the Duke of Lancaster and Walter Mauny, who acted as mediators. Charles was forgiven his many crimes against the Crown and restored to all his rights and properties. He was also allowed to nominate up to 300 of his followers for a royal pardon. In return he promised to renew the act of homage which he had renounced in 1356 and to co-operate in clearing hostile companies from the provinces of France. The next problem was to induce the noble hostages named in the treaty to present themselves. They were naturally unenthusiastic. They lay low, or inordinately prolonged their preparations. The King's second son, the Count of Anjou, who had just married, had to be compelled to go. His third son, the Count of Poitiers, did not appear until he had been summoned 'moult asprement'.[88] Finally, when everything else was ready, only two thirds of the first instalment of the ransom could be produced. Most of Galeazzo Visconti's money was still awaited. Edward had to put up with this difficulty. He agreed to accept 400,000 *écus* down and the rest later. This sum was brought to Calais from Saint-Omer, counted out across a table and assayed in the presence of the English King's commissioners.[89]

The final ceremony was held on the evening of 24 October 1360. The two Kings and their families and principal councillors swore to observe the treaty and its ancillary documents. They exchanged the kiss of peace. John was loaded with jewellery and precious gifts by his enemy. Then he was formally released from his obligations as a prisoner. A few days after his departure from Calais an English clerk took possession of the French fortifications at Guines, the only constructions still standing in the bleak waste around the castle. It was the first French territory to be ceded to England under the treaty.[90]

CHAPTER X

Unfinished Business
1360–1364

John II must have been shocked by the first sight of his kingdom. In Picardy, which had been wasted for two years by the garrisons of Jean de Picquigny, the country was a desert and the towns surrounded by the charred ruins of their suburbs. At Amiens, where part of the town itself had been burnt, the King's distress was visible to everyone.[1] Conditions in the Beauvaisis and the Île de France, which had suffered the worst of the Jacquerie and the raids of John Fotheringhay, were bleaker still. Between Saint-Denis and Paris there can hardly have been a single significant building standing. Like most of those who had made the treaties of Brétigny and Calais, John had high expectations of what the peace would do for regions like these. They proved to be quite unrealistic.

The available documents record more than 120 castles in the provinces retained by John II which were garrisoned in the name of Edward III. Even this figure is a considerable underestimate. It does not include the thirty or so substantial fortresses occupied by the English in Brittany, nor the hundreds of occupied farm-houses, mills and church towers too obscure to be counted. The main concentrations were in Lower Normandy, in the provinces of the Loire from Anjou to Auvergne, and in the broad wedge of territory east of Paris between the Marne and the Yonne. But there were hardly any parts of France which were free of enemy garrisons except for the three principal seneschalsies of Languedoc and the heartlands of the duchy of Aquitaine. Edward III had undertaken at Calais to procure the *videment* (or emptying) of all of these places and to control the further operations of his supporters in France by whatever means should prove necessary. These were bold promises, which the King was soon to regret.[2]

After the conclusion of the treaty of Brétigny, Edward III left the Earl of Warwick in France to see to its observance. Warwick was the first of many Englishmen to learn how difficult it was to enforce the King's will on his subjects in France. In May 1360 he negotiated the voluntary departure of the ten major garrisons of the Île de France and Beauvaisis in return for the global sum of 24,000 florins. A substantial part of this was paid. But only the four smallest garrisons left on time. John Fotheringhay refused to abandon Pont-Sainte-Maxence on the Oise in spite of the confiscation of his assets in England and Brittany. The officers of the Captal de Buch declined to leave Clermont-en-Beauvaisis, although he was to have half the promised 24,000 florins. At la Ferté-sous-Jouarre on the Marne, James Audley's captain, an English squire called Thomas Bagworth, refused to recognise Warwick's authority. He embarked on a series of fresh destructions around Meaux, until the communities of the region agreed to buy him off for more. The garrisons of these places, and three other fortresses of the Beauvaisis, clubbed together to extract an extra 17,000 old *écus* from the French government before they would go away.[3]

The *videment* of the Île de France, Beauvaisis and Picardy was expensive and slow, but it was at least complete and durable. The clearance of the remaining provinces did not begin until early 1361 and by comparison its results were patchy and impermanent. Normandy was the next to be systematically cleared. The operation was begun in February 1361 by Sir John Chandos and the French King's Lieutenant in the province, Louis of Harcourt. In some ways, it ought to have been a straightforward task. Most of the garrison commanders here were English and many were retainers of the King or the Duke of Lancaster. They were much more amenable to pressure than the Gascons, Bretons and Navarrese who controlled most of the garrisons of the centre and south of the kingdom. And Chandos himself counted for something among these men: friend and companion of the Prince of Wales and founder member of the Order of the Garter, he was a considerable figure in English chivalry. He was also accompanied by a small army: 160 men-at-arms plus at least that number in the entourage of Louis d'Harcourt. Yet even in Normandy the garrisons were able to exact large sums of money as the price of their departure. In the year after the treaty of Calais the Estates of Normandy bought out sixteen large English-controlled garrisons at a total cost of 84,000 *écus* in cash and promises. Even money was not always enough. The garrison of Honfleur did not agree to go until Louis d'Harcourt came before the walls with a large armed force. Even then they demanded and received nearly 20,000 *écus* in ransom money and miscellaneous charges and remained in occupation until it was paid.[4] When the King of France protested, Edward III's answer was that arrears of *patis* which had accrued before the treaty had to be paid. A captain was entitled to be compensated for forgoing them, he said. The consensus of the fighting classes on both sides of the Channel supported Edward's view rather than John's. So did the lawyers. They held it to be self evident that conquests of war belonged to the conqueror. Perhaps the most remarkable illustration of this frame of mind concerned the five great fortresses of Maine and Lower Normandy which had been occupied since 1356 by officers of the Duke of Lancaster. Lancaster was as closely associated with the treaty as any man and had sworn an oath at Calais to observe it. Yet he sold these castles to the communities of Normandy for 20,000 *écus*. When only a third of this sum was paid, his executors sued for the rest in the courts of the King of France. The arguments in this long-running litigation are interesting. The defence was that the contract was void for duress and its enforcement contrary to the treaty. But the executors answered that this was irrelevant. The sale was a private transaction. It could not be affected by an act of state between two sovereigns. The Parlement of Paris agreed, and gave judgment in their favour.[5]

It was only the richer and better organised provinces which were able to rid themselves of enemy garrisons. The relatively well organised political community of Champagne, for example, had more or less cleared the remaining garrisons from their province by the spring of 1361. This was largely due to the energy of the Count of Vaudémont and the wealth of the cities of Reims and Troyes. In Touraine another energetic local magnate, the Marshal Jean de Boucicaut, expelled all the larger garrisons in the first half of 1361. The main financier here was the city of Tours. But at the opposite extreme, in the Bourbonnais and northern Auvergne, regions racked by war damage where political organisation had collapsed and the principal territorial magnate was a prisoner in England, the clearance commissioners achieved next to nothing. Edward III's choice of commissioners cannot have helped. Arnaud and Bérard d'Albret belonged to the family which had been among the chief plunderers of the region and still controlled the most dangerous companies operating there. Shortly after the treaty of Brétigny, probably in July 1360, the Albrets sold at least five major fortresses of the Bourbonnais to the duchess of Bourbon. But their garrisons continued in occupation pending payment of the price. Some places remained in their hands for several years while the duchess struggled to raise the money from the ruined communities of her son's domain. Those captains who were not confederates of the Albrets simply ignored the commissioners. The Navarrese *routier* le Bourc

Camus, for example, who was probably the worst of them, continued undisturbed about his pillaging, kidnapping and torturing for eight years after the treaty.[6]

The main problem of the clearance commissioners in rich and poor provinces alike was that the most that they could hope to do was to shift the problem elsewhere. Two decades of war had created a large class of semi-professional soldiers who knew no trade but fighting. It was all very well to buy up occupied castles and turn out their garrisons, but where were they to go? Most of the English must have returned to England. A few settled permanently in France. It would be interesting to know more about John Bell, who stayed behind in 1361 to marry a rich Norman widow; or William Welles, an English squire serving in the French royal household in 1364; or the former university student known only as 'Lucas' who commanded his own company in Lower Normandy until he was captured and took service with the French government; or the various English men-at-arms who served in the household of Philip Duke of Burgundy in the 1360s, such as the squire John 'Poupon', who was at one stage engaged to be married to a formidable aristocratic widow; or the man (also a squire) who appears in the duchy accounts under the unrecognisable name of 'Hoschequin Warin' as Philip Duke of Burgundy's English interpreter. At a more exalted level, Robert Marshall, who had been one of the Duke of Lancaster's captains in Normandy in the 1350s and ended the war with three garrisons of his own in Normandy and the Beauce, sold out for a fortune and was employed by John II to defend the Vendômois against his fellow countrymen. The Welshman Jack Wyn, who had arrived in Burgundy with the companies in 1359, settled there after the treaty and became a substantial local potentate, participating in the close politics of the region and by and large observing his obligations to its duke. When the war broke out again in 1369, Wyn threw in his lot with the French and served Charles V and his successor for rest of his life. These are, however, interesting exceptions to a more humdrum rule. Most of the English *routiers* who stayed in France were outcasts or criminals with no talent to sell. They were incapable of settling down in either country.[7]

Brittany was the destination of most such men. The duchy remained for several years an open sore from which the neighbouring parts of France were repeatedly re-infected. Because the dispute between the houses of Montfort and Blois about the succession was still unresolved, it had been more or less excepted from the treaties. The two Kings had merely agreed to try to broke a settlement, and if that failed to let the protagonists fight it out with which such allies as they could find. When the attempt at mediation predictably failed, Brittany was left in an anomalous position: legally a fief of the King of France, in fact governed by the King of England in the name of his young ward John de Montfort. In June 1362, when John came of age, Edward surrendered the duchy to him. But in practice it remained an English protectorate for several years longer. John had been brought up among the English, and anyway had too many enemies to be able to do without them. He was to spend a great deal of time in the next two years in Aquitaine in the company of the Prince of Wales, who became his close friend and mentor. Towards the end of the year 1365 John entered into a military alliance with the Prince, and married his step-daughter Joan Holland. The English were everywhere found in positions of influence and power. The rapacious William Latimer, Edward III's former Lieutenant, emerged as one of the Duke's principal lieutenants. Edward himself kept Bécherel and Trogoff, the two principal English-occupied fortresses in the north of the duchy, as security for the debts which John had accumulated in his minority, and stuffed them with English soldiers. Other important castles continued to be held in John's name but by English captains with largely English companies. They lived off the profits of war for several years after the peace. Walter Hewitt, the captain of Collet castle in the bay of Bourgneuf, continued to exact *patis* within the duchy and, when that became impossible, across the border in Anjou. He was still doing it five years after the treaty. Hewitt was probably one of the more aggressive English captains in the region, but he was by no means untypical.[8]

Froissart thought that the build-up of unemployed English soldiers in Brittany was deliberately encouraged by Edward III so that they could continue their violent careers on the other side of the Channel instead of coming home to wreak havoc in England. Certainly it is what happened. Soldiers of the Calais garrison were reported to be deserting their posts in order to find excitement and profit in Brittany. Robert Scot, scourge of Picardy and Champagne, re-emerged as the captain of Hennebont on the Breton coast. He was succeeded by Thomas Fogg, formerly one of Henry of Lancaster's captains in Normandy. The Lancashire brigand Hannequin Tyldesley, after plying his trade for two years in Perche, took service in the garrison of Bécherel. The march of Brittany became an armed camp from which raids could be launched into the neighbouring provinces of France. Robert Knolles, for example, who still controlled the great fortresses of Fougeray, Chateaublanc and Gravelle in eastern Brittany, re-invaded Maine in the summer of 1360. Hugh Calveley, one of the most active English captains in Brittany in the year before the treaty, raided around Alençon and le Mans for several months after the treaty of Calais had been sealed. At the end of 1360 he fought a pitched battle against the forces of the French Lieutenant in Lower Normandy in which he captured Bertrand du Guesclin, the celebrated French captain of Pontorson. Yet, by the standards of freebooters, Knolles and Calveley were relatively sensitive to the wishes of the King of England. Both of them called a halt to their activities early in 1361, probably at his request. Knolles even sought absolution from both Pope and King for his past misdeeds. He had made his fortune and could perhaps afford to repent. His example was not widely followed. The veteran Sir Matthew Gournay was a more characteristic figure. He had been a soldier for at least twenty years. He had fought, like Chaucer's knight, against the Moors at Algeciras, and against the French at Sluys, Crécy and Poitiers, before becoming captain of Edward III's garrison at Brest in 1357. Gournay had no intention of retiring to his house at Stoke-under-Hamden in Somerset when the treaties were sealed. He became an independent military contractor and at the age of fifty or so entered upon the most profitable time of his life. He hung on to his lucrative position at Brest for at least two years. He hired out his company. He raided into Normandy. He bought and sold castles. Gournay was briefly imprisoned in the Tower of London for his insensitivity to Edward's diplomatic interests, but the discomfort was no doubt worth it. He invested some of his profits in buying the right to sell Breton *brefs de la mer* at Bordeaux and la Rochelle. He had substantial sums on deposit with bankers. The commissioners charged with the confiscation of Gournay's assets in England reported that in 1361 a Somerset merchant was holding for him no less than £1,000 worth of gold plate and a quantity of gold *moutons,* all of which must have represented the loot of France.[9]

The operations of the English companies in France were a serious diplomatic embarrassment. However, the English were not the main problem. Their strength tended to decline over the years. The Breton march was the only region where they were ever present in force. Far more damage was done over a wider area by men of other nations: Bretons, Béarnais, Navarrese, Germans and above all Gascons. They began to form large and cohesive companies of men of their own language, who wandered through the provinces of France killing in the open villages, exacting protection money from the towns. The larger political and strategic objectives of the Anglo-French war had never meant much to them, and when it ended they continued to fight as if nothing had changed.

Indeed nothing much had. For although the agents of violence were often outsiders, the root cause of their success lay in the fragmentation of French society during the war years. Vast transfers of land had occurred in the 1350s as a direct or indirect consequence of the war. Ancient allegiances had been renounced. Confiscations had been ordered on a large scale. Houses, farms and castles had been occupied by force and then abandoned to others. Major landowners had been ruined and forced to sell onto a buyer's market. Whole districts had been deserted as the fighting made the land uncultivable and the roads impassable. These problems were aggravated by the severe economic difficulties of France in the aftermath of the war with England. War damage was extensive, especially in the open country, and was not easily repaired. Burnt out barns and broken equipment represented years of investment written off. Seed had gone. Mature vines would take many years to replace. The loss of cattle ruined upland regions. In grain-growing areas, the theft or killing of beasts of burden reduced the productivity of the land for years. To these were added the instability occasioned by the return of bubonic plague to western Europe in the winter of 1360, which persisted on and off for the next five years. It was not easy in these conditions to turn swords into ploughshares. All this left a venomous legacy among Frenchmen when the peace was made, which the diminished institutions of the Valois monarchy could not contain. It not only undermined any collective resistance to brigandage, but provoked frequent private wars in which the protagonists indiscriminately hired French, English, Gascon, Breton or Navarrese men-at-arms to man their garrisons and fight against other Frenchmen. The result was always to concentrate large numbers of footloose soldiers in one area for brief spasms of intense military effort before releasing them to survive in strange regions by whatever means they could. In parts of France private war was as endemic in the 1360s as public war had been in the decade before. When the citizens of Péronne, on the northern march of the kingdom, rebelled against their royal captain in May 1360, he treated them like an enemy city, laying siege to the walls with a mixed army of French and English troops. The many enemies of the Bishop of Albi hired multinational armed bands who turned much of the Albigeois into a desert in the early 1360s. The Bishop replied in kind.

One of the principal magnates of Berry, Hutin de Vermelles, fell out with a stepson about a family settlement, and pressed his arguments with the aid of English, Gascon, Breton and German soldiers. For every example which is recorded, there must have been a dozen more which were not.[10]

The career of Charles of Artois, son of the old traitor Robert, was perhaps the classic case. Charles had been reconciled to the house of Valois after his father's death. He had made a rich marriage, and had acquired valuable domains in Lower Normandy, to which the King added the great county of Longueville, part of the confiscated estates of the King of Navarre. But Charles was captured at Poitiers in 1356 and ransomed. His Norman lands were occupied in his absence by the King's cousin Pierre, Count of Alençon. The county of Longueville was lost when the King of Navarre made peace with John II in 1360 and recovered his old estates and titles. Charles of Artois returned to France a much diminished man. In 1361 and 1362, he embarked on a series of violent attacks on Alençon's lands in Lower Normandy and Touraine, indiscriminately hiring English, Gascon and Breton *routiers*. Alençon retaliated by much the same methods. John II did nothing to stop them. Charles of Artois later claimed that the King had encouraged him. Neither protagonist gained much. The main beneficiary was the Englishman James Pipe, former captain of Épernon, and his confederate Robert Marshall. They fought first for Alençon and then for Artois, always in reality for themselves. Pipe launched a devastating series of raids in Normandy and Maine in the autumn of 1361. He was bought out of his principal conquests in February 1362 and pardoned by both kings. But within six weeks he had returned to the task and occupied the fortified Benedictine monastery of Cormeilles near Lisieux. From here he was able to ransom the whole of the region from Lisieux to Pont-Audemer until he was eventually bought out again. James Pipe had plenty of emulators. Most of them were either bought out or forcibly ejected by the local forces of the French Crown. But the process was costly and time-consuming, and quickly undone by fresh incursions. In large parts of the region the new war of raid, ambush, escalade and siege was indistinguishable from the old war of the 1350s.[11]

Most of the soldiers who decided to continue practising their trade in France ended up serving with one or other of the free companies. These brigand armies varied in size from ten or twenty to several hundred men. Most of them had a strong national or regional identity. The Navarrese, most of whom had been brought to France by Charles of

Navarre in the mid-1350s, were concentrated in Lower Normandy. The Germans were for the most part migrants from Brabant, Hainault and the Rhineland who had been bought out of garrisons in north-eastern France or had been paid off from the mercenary army of Brocard de Fénétrange. They operated almost exclusively in Champagne and northern Burgundy. Their acknowledged leader was Albrecht, the former captain of Gyé-sur-Seine, who had recently established his headquarters in the great castle of the Joinvilles on the west bank of the Marne. Then there were the Breton companies, a growing force among the *routier* bands. At the time of the treaties they were occupying a large number of places in the middle and lower valley of the Loire which had been seized at about the time of Robert Knolles' great *chevauchée* through the region in 1358. Over the next few years they spread through much of eastern and central France in search of employment. The largest concentration of them belonged to the loose association of Breton companies formed by Maurice Trésiguidi, a squire who had fought for many years as a partisan of the House of Blois. Trésiguidi led his bands into Auvergne at the end of 1360 and hired them out to Thomas de la Marche to fight in the ferocious series of private wars which he had undertaken against his many enemies. By the autumn of 1361, when the main protagonists in these wars were exhausted or dead, his companies had begun to spread into the Limousin.[12]

By far the most significant regional group comprised the companies of Gascons and Basques. Not only were their numbers much greater but, unlike the German, Navarrese and Breton companies, who tended to waste away over the years, they enjoyed a constant flow of recruits from south-western France. They were also less exclusive, more readily making up numbers by recruiting Frenchmen and Englishmen when they needed to. As a result their companies enjoyed a longer and more continuous existence than any of the others. By 1360 there were Gascon companies operating in most parts of France. But the nodal point of their operations was always the *massif* of Auvergne. The flotsam of unemployed soldiers and hopeful adventurers made their way there up the valleys of the Lot and the Dordogne from Aquitaine. From the mountains of Auvergne they descended by the valleys of the Loire and the Allier into Berry and the Nivernais; through Rouergue and across the Great Causses to Languedoc; or down to the plain of Forez and the great highways of the Rhone and the Saône. And it was to Auvergne that they retreated when conditions became difficult in the lowland areas. The larger companies never could stay together for more than a short time without running out of food, and they could not split up to forage without being picked off by the local population and the troops of the King's *baillis* and captains. They therefore moved constantly between the plains and the hills to keep themselves supplied, to get rid of bulky spoil, to dispose of prisoners and to regroup and recruit.

During the summer of 1360 a large number of companies came together in eastern France to form a 'Great Company'. Bands of unemployed soldiers drifted east towards the borders of the kingdom away from the desolation of more traditional war zones towards the unpillaged riches of the Saône valley: Burgundy, Maçonnais, Beaujolais and Lyonnais. Here, they gradually coalesced into vast unstable mobs of armed men, the largest of which was said to number 4,000 or more. The Bascot de Mauléon, who entertained Froissart with his stories twenty-five years later, remembered this period well. 'The kings have made peace, but we must make our living,' the captains told their men. In the autumn of 1360 they were joined by some important Gascon companies and by large contingents of Germans from Champagne. These included the celebrated Albrecht, who had by now sold out of Joinville. There was also a small but prominent group of Englishmen: William Starkey, who brought his English company south from the Auxerrois; Sir John Hawkwood, later to become famous as a soldier of fortune in Italy; John Verney, banished from England for his crimes, now self-styled lieutenant of the curious Sienese adventurer Giovanni Guccio who claimed to be John I King of France. The first recorded leader of the Great Company was a Scottish knight known as Walter. This man cannot be identified with certainty, but he was probably Sir Walter Leslie, adventurer and professed crusader, who had arrived in France on a diplomatic mission in 1359 and stayed behind to fight.[13]

The name of the 'Great Company' had originally been used to describe the large self-governing armies of Werner von Urslingen and Fra Moriale which grew up in northern Italy in the 1340s and 1350s. It had also been applied in 1357 to the rather similar coalition of companies which Arnaud de Cervole had formed to invade Provence. The French Great Companies of the 1360s were very similar organisations. A fluctuating body of the principal captains formed a council to liaise among themselves and to co-ordinate the movements of the larger mass. There was a hierarchy of command. There was an administrative service, generally staffed by clerics and directed, in at least one case, by a 'chancellor'. Their style of operations was quite different from that of the smaller Gascon companies of the 1350s from which they grew.

These had concentrated on holding strategically situated castles with the minimum forces required for the purpose, and on levying tolls and taxes in the districts around them. The Great Companies, with their superior strength and organisation, made war in much the same way as the expeditionary armies of the King of England and the Prince of Wales, in which many of their captains had learned their trade. They moved through open country exacting protection money from whole provinces one after the other. They rarely occupied any place for very long, generally looting it, selling the ruins back to the inhabitants and moving on.[14]

Froissart's informant, the Bascot de Mauléon, reckoned that the total strength of the Great Company of 1360 was about 12,000 men at the end of the year. It was certainly much larger a year later. About a third or a quarter of these men, he thought, were experienced professional soldiers. The rest were untrained and undisciplined thugs. Their stories, when they were caught, were a complete cross-section of the ills and grievances of French society. In addition to the riff-raff of the military underworld, there were large numbers of criminals and fugitives from justice; displaced monks whose communities had been broken by the war, or clerks in minor orders who had no living; prisoners who were not worth a ransom but could be persuaded to serve instead. Many more were unremarkable men who volunteered when the companies passed through their villages offering adventure and an escape from the destitution of the countryside.

> Received: thirty florins from the sale of all the goods of Belier le Gustet of Villaines, whom the English and other enemies of the Great Company took with them when they left Villaines at Christmas 1360. He has not since returned and no one knows what has become of him, but the common rumour at Villaines is that he has died in the service of the said Company.

The judicial records of the 1360s are full of functional biographies like this.[15]

At about the beginning of December 1360 the leaders of the Great Company resolved to invade Provence. How they came to this decision has not been recorded, but their reasons are obvious enough. Provence lay outside the legal frontiers of France, still an important consideration at a time when men over-estimated the capacity of the two governments to maintain order and enforce the treaties. And the riches of Avignon and Villeneuve were still as enticing as they had been when Arnaud de Cervole had operated there. At about Christmas time, the first units penetrated into the seneschalsy of Beaucaire on the French side of the Rhone, looking for a crossing of the river.

At that time, a large consignment of coin, representing part of the contribution of Languedoc to the ransom of the King, was being moved up the Rhone valley. It was believed to have reached Pont-Saint-Esprit, a walled town about 20 miles north of Avignon which stood at the western end of a famous stone bridge over the Rhone. On the night of 28 and 29 December 1360 the *routiers* came silently over the walls. The Seneschal of Beaucaire, who was in the town, attempted to fight them back through the streets. But he fell from a wall and was mortally injured at the critical moment of the fight. His followers were overwhelmed, and the invaders occupied the whole of the town. When the companies came to inspect their capture, they found to their dismay that the consignment of coin was not there. It had been delayed in Avignon and ultimately reached Paris by another route. But Pont-Saint-Esprit itself proved to be as great a prize. The *routiers* were now in a position to stop the whole traffic of the lower Rhone and to launch raids across the bridge into Provence and the papal states. The small force of papal troops guarding the east end of the bridge was swept aside. Bands of men raided up to the walls of Avignon and beyond. Others passed down the west bank and penetrated deep into the seneschalsies of Beaucaire and Carcassonne. The news of the Great Company's first triumph drew to the south hordes of fortune-seekers who had previously held back. In the first three months of 1361 there was a vast migration of companies towards Pont-Saint-Esprit down the corridor of the Rhone and the Saône and across the hills of Auvergne. By the spring of 1361 the town had become the headquarters of a very large army of brigands.[16]

The resistance (such as it was) was organised by the Pope. In Avignon, the papal palace was a scene of hysterical activity. Men were set to work on the walls and ditches, which were still incomplete and in bad condition. The city's food supply, which came mainly from the river, was interrupted and its dense population threatened with starvation.[17] The captain of the Comtat Venaissin, an Aragonese nobleman, was summoned urgently back from his native country. Soldiers were hired in France and neighbouring countries. Appeals for help were despatched to the kings of France and Aragon, the Duke of Burgundy, the Count of Savoy and seventy-two cities of western Europe. At the end of January 1361 the Pope publicly excommunicated the soldiers of the Great Company and proclaimed a crusade against them. It was a complete failure. The cardinal appointed to organise it set up his headquarters at Bagnols and waited for men to come to his colours. A few turned up under the impression that they would be paid, most of whom withdrew when they discovered that only indulgences were on offer.[18]

The appeals to neighbouring princes proved more effective. The King of Aragon promised 1,800 men, several hundred of whom actually appeared. John II sent the Constable of France, Robert Fiennes and the Marshal Arnoul d'Audrehem to the Lower Rhone in February 1361. Between them, they briefly checked the operations of the invaders. The Great Company was becoming too large and too concentrated to feed itself. Faced with an increasingly organised defence they sued for peace. In March 1361 they made a treaty with the representatives of the Pope and another with the Constable of France. They were offered comprehensive indemnities. In return they promised to go away. But where were they to go? Everyone appreciated that they would have to be found employment killing people somewhere else. So, in the course of the next few weeks, a series of rather complicated arrangements were made to use some of them in Italy and others in Spain.[19]

Fourteenth-century Italy was an inviting country for professional mercenaries. The cities were richer than those of France and their trade more extensive and vulnerable. There was no dominant power. The perennial wars of the northern cities, the territorial ambitions of the Visconti rulers of Milan and the unending struggle of successive papal vicars to control the papal state in central Italy, had created anarchic conditions very similar to those in which the companies had flourished in France. For many years the wars of the Italian peninsula had been fought by armies of soldiers of fortune recruited by contract captains ('*condottiere*'). Many of these were foreigners, mainly Germans and Hungarians. Most were in the service of the Pope's enemies. They included the most powerful of them all, the Great Company of the German captain Conrad of Landau, who served the Visconti. Italy had hitherto been untouched by the wars of England and France except during the brief period when the Genoese had supplied contract fleets to Philip VI. It was now to become, like Scotland, the Low Countries, Provence and, later, Spain, one of the countries on the periphery of the Anglo-French wars which experienced the reflected violence of the main protagonists.

It was Pope Innocent VI who arranged the departure of part of the

Great Company of Pont-Saint-Esprit across the Alps. He saw in them a weapon to be used against the Visconti and their German auxiliaries in Piedmont and Lombardy. He struck a deal with the marquis of Montferrat, a prominent Piedmontese nobleman and, like Innocent himself, an enemy of the Visconti. Montferrat agreed to lead the *routiers* into Piedmont. Once there, they would be hired for an initial period of two months by the Pope's formidable Vicar-General in Italy, the Castilian cardinal Gil Albornoz. A large subsidy, said to have been 100,000 florins, was paid to the marquis for this service. Another 30,000 florins was paid to the companies themselves. The cost of the whole venture was shared between the papal chamber and the city of Genoa, then the leading Guelph power of northern Italy. A large number of the captains at Pont-Saint-Esprit signed up to this scheme. They formed themselves into a new company which became known as the 'White Company', whose combined strength was reported to be about 6,000 men. They included all the Germans and most of the English companies who had been operating in eastern France. Their leader was an English-speaking German called Albert Sterz, who was probably the same person as 'Albrecht', the notorious captain of Gyé-sur-Seine. After much delay, occasioned by the difficulty of collecting the money for their fees and wages, the White Company eventually left Provence at the end of May 1361. In June they appeared in Italy.[20]

The surviving accounts of the operations of the companies in France were written by men to whom such sights were by now too familiar for detailed notice. They are spare by comparison with Italian sources of the 1360s, which have all the freshness and detail of surprise. They referred to the invaders indiscriminately as 'English' and, although only a minority of them were in fact native Englishmen, it was these who made the greatest impact. 'They were all young men,' Filippo Villani wrote; 'bred in the long wars of England and France, fierce, enthusiastic, quite used to the routine of killing and looting.' The White Company, like the Great Company in France, was a coalition of different units under their own captains, employing the methods and organisation which English armies had perfected in France. It was governed by a captain-general, a council representing the main contingents, and a hierarchy of constables, marshals, sub-marshals and corporals. The single-mindedness and discipline of these men astonished the Italians. They were indifferent to their own comfort. They marched through the night. They fought in winter and summer alike in a country where warfare had traditionally been a seasonal activity.

Their equipment was quite unlike that of existing armies in Italy. They wore light armour, often no more than a leather doublet or metal breastplate, with a thigh-piece, leg-armour and unvisored bacinet. Their cavalry dismounted to fight on foot. They formed themselves up in units (or 'lances') of three, which advanced on the enemy on foot, holding their lance between them. Their archers used huge bows of yew, 'which they hold from their head to the ground and from which they shoot long arrows.' They used specially constructed scaling ladders which were assembled in sections, each one fitting into the top of the one below. But what was most shocking about the White Company, even to communities which had grown used to the German companies of the 1340s and 1350s, was its brutality. They set new standards of savagery in war. They wreaked appalling and systematic destruction in the countryside of Piedmont and Lombardy. They burnt to the ground open villages and captured towns. They tortured prisoners who would not make ransom agreements and murdered those who could not.[21]

The White Company remained for two years in the service of the Church in Italy. During this period they briefly transformed the balance of power in Lombardy, inflicted terrible damage on the territory of Milan and virtually destroyed the Great Company of Conrad of Landau. But, like other associations of its kind, the White Company was inherently unstable. It was divided by the ambitions and rivalries of its captains, and by the language and habits of the two main national groups of which it was composed. Its losses were severe. Men died in battle or were culled by disease. Bubonic plague, which was endemic in the towns of northern Italy, claimed many lives. These losses were difficult to replace. The Germans could recruit from their fellow countrymen already in Italy, but the English had only a trickle of new arrivals from Gascony and England to maintain their numbers. They remained the most disciplined and effective part of the White Company. But three years after their arrival in Italy there were only about 800 of them left, perhaps a fifth of the company's total strength.[22]

In the summer of 1363 the White Company split into two. Most of the companies belonging to it passed into the service of the city of Pisa, which employed them to prosecute its 'tedious war' (Villani's phrase) against Florence. Sterz remained in command of the company.[23] But although most of the troops were Sterz's fellow Germans, he was gradually supplanted by English officers. In October 1363 Pisa appointed one of these officers over Sterz's head as captain of the city and commander of its forces. This man, the 'astute and vulpine' John Hawkwood, became one of the most successful and adaptable English adventurers of the period. Hawkwood was a man of lowly origins. He had been born in about 1320, the son of a tanner in Essex. According to Villani he learned his fighting skills from an uncle who had served in France. In 1360 when the armies were being paid off in France, Hawkwood had formed his own company and led it to join the Great Company in Burgundy. He took part in the capture of Pont-Saint-Esprit and joined the first wave of military migrants to Italy. There he acquired a reputation as a skilful commander and strategist and a military contractor who kept his bargains, which was rare among professional mercenaries.[24]

Hawkwood survived longer in Italy than the companies which had arrived with him. The original White Company finally broke up in 1364, three years after its formation.[25] Most of the English corps and some companies of Hungarians and Gascons formed themselves into a new White Company. Their leaders were two English adventurers in the classic mould, scions of famous but diminished noble families who needed to live by war. Hugh Mortimer de la Zouche, a young man in his mid-twenties, was the grandson of Queen Isabella's 'gentle Mortimer', who had been executed and dispossessed in 1330. He became Captain-General of the new White Company. His marshal and second-in-command was Andrew Beaumont, an older man, probably the illegitimate son of the adventurer who had invaded Scotland in 1332 in the name of Edward Balliol. The history of their enterprise was very brief. They took service with Cardinal Albornoz, who employed them against the rebel city of Perugia. At the end of July 1364, they suffered a catastrophic defeat at the hands of the Germans of Sterz, who had been hired by the Perugians. Both of the English commanders were captured and remained in prison in Perugia for several years. Most of their followers were killed. The remnant who survived drifted from side to side and gradually merged with the indistinct mass of foreign men-at-arms in Italy. As for Sterz, he was shortly afterwards detected in treasonable correspondence with Albornoz and ended his life on the scaffold in Perugia. Of the leaders of the great invasion of 1361 only Hawkwood survived with a dwindling handful of English officers commanding a largely Italian company and selling his services as a general to whoever would pay him. He eventually married a daughter of the Visconti, and when he died in 1394 he received a state funeral in Florence Cathedral. His tomb and the famous equestrian portrait by Uccello can still be seen there. Few English generals enjoyed such an apotheosis even in their own country.[26]

*

Not all of the Great Company of 1360 went to Italy. A large part, which included almost all the Gascons, remained in the Rhone valley. The leadership of these men passed to another famous soldier of fortune, Séguin de Badefol. Séguin was the son of the lord of Badefol, a castle on the south bank of Dordogne not far from Cadouin, territory which had been disputed between the English and the French for decades and produced many of the leading captains of the age. Séguin's experience as a *routier* had probably been gained in Auvergne in one of the Albret companies. But by 1360 he was already a man of some notoriety in his own right. His company, which was known as le Margot, was one of the largest of the Great Company. In addition to his own men, he had been able to draw to himself a great number of satellite companies of Gascons, Basques and 'false French'. He was probably no more than about twenty-five years old when Pont-Saint-Esprit was taken.[27]

When the companies at Pont-Saint-Esprit made their agreements with the Pope and the Constable of France, the intention was that those which did not go to Italy should go to Aragon, there to dissipate their strength beyond the Pyrenees in the long-running wars between Aragon and Castile. The Gascons tried to perform their covenant. The disorderly mass of men began their march south in March 1361, confronted everywhere by manned walls and closed gates and watched at a respectful distance by the troops of the Constable of France. But their plans were frustrated by events elsewhere. On 13 May 1361 Aragon and Castile had concluded the treaty of Terrer, bringing an end to their five-year war. When the brigands passed south of Perpignan to cross over the Pyrenees they found the Aragonese border closed against them.[28]

Trapped in France, without employment or supplies, Séguin de Badefol's Great Company became progressively more dangerous. Most of them kept together and struck north into the Albigeois and Rouergue to regroup.[29] Then, in August 1361, they moved down from the hills, re-invaded Languedoc and swarmed across the Narbonnais. Every day their numbers were swollen by fresh arrivals. As the commissioners of the two kings emptied out the castles of the Loire and began to pacify the provinces of the *massif central*, a tidal wave of military migrants passed through Burgundy, Beaujolais and Lyonnais and down the Rhone valley to join them. The largest of the new bands were those of the Albrets. Bérard d'Albret, the younger brother of the lord of Albret, was a young man in his early twenties who had previously been active in the Bourbonnais. Bertucat, his illegitimate cousin, had passed several

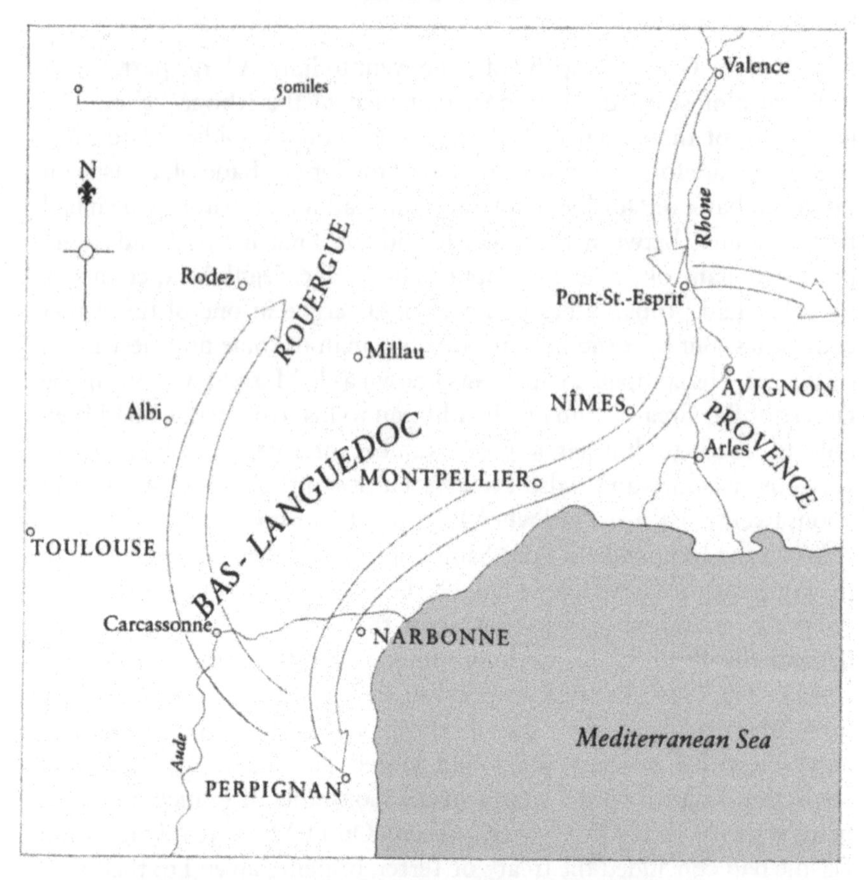

33 The Great Company of 1360, November 1360–November 1361

years in wasting Auvergne. These two men arrived in Bas-Languedoc with their companies at the beginning of August 1361 and joined forces with Séguin de Badefol outside Narbonne. From the Narbonnais, their combined companies first headed south, invading Roussillon. Then, finding nothing there, they turned west in the middle of August 1361. Riding secretly by night 40 miles up the Aude valley, they appeared suddenly in the Carcassès and the Toulousain before the news of their approach. This enabled them to capture three market towns and to provision themselves, their only notable success since the capture of Pont-Saint-Esprit. From here they retreated back into Rouergue and began to look for the best price for departing. At the beginning of November they accepted the paltry sum of 5,200 florins from the Seneschal and Estates of Rouergue to go away. Another 3,000 florins was extracted from the Bishop of Albi to withdraw from his diocese. Three weeks later, on 23 November 1361, the Great Company made a similar deal with the three seneschalsies of Toulouse, Carcassonne and Beaucaire. Séguin de Badefol kept to his bargain. He abandoned his companies and returned to Périgord. From the companies' point of view, the invasion of Languedoc had not been a success. They seem to have been unprepared for the high degree of organisation of the defence, which was a great deal more effective than anything that they had encountered in the central provinces.[30]

On 11 August 1361 Sir John Chandos appeared before John II and his Council at the royal manor of Vincennes to claim the territories ceded to the English King at Brétigny and Calais. Thus began the most significant change in the political geography of France since the same territories had been conquered by the French Crown in the first half of the thirteenth century. The proceedings began in Poitou at the end of September and continued at an efficient pace. Chandos 'had no intention of tolerating any more delays or being taken out of his course by verbiage', he told Marshal Boucicaut, the chief French commissioner for the transfer, who was languishing on his sick bed unable to move. They passed through all the principal towns of Poitou, Saintonge, Angoumois, Périgord and Limousin. Early in the new year they moved into the march provinces of Quercy and Rouergue. The transfer was largely completed by the end of February 1362. The course of events was more or less the same everywhere. The commissioners of the two kings arrived outside the closed gates, watched by the magistrates of the town from the wall. The senior French commissioner read out John II's letters commanding his subjects to transfer their allegiance to the King of England. The gate was opened and the keys delivered up, and the Englishmen entered the town. They proceeded to some public place, a market square, a clearing or a cloister, to receive the oaths of the chief citizens. They promised that the existing privileges of the town would be honoured. A seneschal was appointed in the provincial capitals. Garrisons and captains were installed in walled places. Subordinate officials were reappointed. The arms of Edward III were painted above the main gates. Then the crowd of functionaries, clerks and soldiers moved on to the next town.[31]

How did Frenchmen receive this change of allegiance? It is a difficult and controversial subject, clouded by the patriotic prejudices of other ages. There was certainly no resistance and very little overt reluctance. The nobility generally accepted the transfer without demur. Guichard d'Angle, for example, who was one of the French King's commissioners, had passed fifteen years fighting against the English and Gascons on the marches of Saintonge, and had twice been captured by them. Yet he changed his allegiance readily enough, eventually becoming Marshal of Aquitaine under the Prince of Wales. So did Louis of Harcourt, the long-standing Lieutenant of the French Crown in Lower Normandy, who was lord of Chatellerault in northern Poitou. He had remained loyal to John II even after the execution of the head of the House of Harcourt in 1356. After fighting most of his adult life against the English King, Louis became his loyal subject, serving against the French in Spain and eventually in France. Among the great men of the ceded provinces only a handful objected, and they had special reasons of their own.[32]

Among the towns, which were perhaps more sensitive barometers of opinion, there was a sharp divide between the maritime regions of the west and the provinces of the south-eastern march. In Poitou, Saintonge, Angoumois and Périgord, the main concern of the towns was to have the privileges granted over the centuries by the Kings of France confirmed by their new sovereign. Once this was agreed, as it always was, they submitted readily enough and remained conspicuously loyal to the new order for many years. Further east, men had suffered more heavily and more recently at the hands of the companies and had learned to treat the English and Gascons as natural enemies. There was reluctance and unease, and sometimes open protest. Limousin was the first case of overt opposition commissioners encountered. The region's experience of organised brigandage went back to 1348, as long as any province of France, and the Breton companies were still active there in 1361. In addition, part of the province belonged to Charles of Blois, pretender of Brittany, who was not party to the treaties and whose captains refused to co-operate. Boucicaut had to explain to the citizens of Limoges, who wanted to check his instructions with the government in Paris before complying with them, that the King had ordered them to submit 'not because he hated them, but for the sake of peace and to free himself and his son from captivity.'[33] Further south, the local communities pressed matters rather further. In Rouergue the Estates of the province were summoned to Rodez to consider the intended transfer. They were addressed by the Count of Armagnac, who urged them (in vain) to insist on at least maintaining a right of ultimate appeal to the King of France against the acts of English monarch. They submitted, some of them with visible unease. The city of Rodez declined to paint the arms of their new sovereign above their gates until 1365. Quercy, which had probably suffered more by the war than any other province of the south-west, openly declared its objections. Gourdon, which Chandos reached only in July 1362, barred its gates until he undertook to restrain the Gascon garrisons of the district. Cahors refused to surrender until it had consulted other towns around, and then accompanied the act with a remarkable display of emotion. The consuls wept and groaned. They declared that it was not by their will that they renounced the sovereign whom they loved above all others and to whom they had sworn oaths of perpetual loyalty. Their protest was ignored by Boucicaut, who released them from their oaths; and by Chandos, whose clerks did not even record it in their minutes. These protests were not simply the prelude to a haggle about privilege. They evidently reflected a genuine attachment to France and the French monarchy. Cahors was among the first places to renounce English rule when the opportunity presented itself seven years later, whereas by and large the provinces of the west fought for their new master until his cause collapsed. The Count of Armagnac was yet to lead a French army against an English one, whereas Guichard d'Angle would end his days as Earl of Huntingdon, an exile in England.[34]

Because the English and Gascon companies by and large respected the territory of their own sovereign, the sudden enlargement of that territory in the winter of 1361–2 had an immediate impact on the geography of the companies' operations. Terrorism more or less ceased in the ceded provinces, except for Limousin and Rouergue, both of which were rather special cases. In Limousin the main companies were Breton, not Gascon or English. They had no reason to change their ways because they were now in the dominions of Edward III. Sir John Chandos raised 1,000 men to confront them at the end of 1361. The command of these troops was given to the newly appointed Seneschal in the region, William Felton. He inflicted a severe defeat on the Bretons at le Garet early in the following year. It was the first serious campaign against the companies in Limousin for many years. The pattern was much the same in Rouergue. When Chandos arrived there he found the province threatened by several *routier* garrisons, including the large Anglo-Breton company of John Amory and John Cresswell, which was based at the bridge-town of Espalion on the Lot. Chandos expelled Amory and Cresswell from Espalion and established garrisons of his own at more than a dozen places. Rouergue's position as the main transit route between Auvergne and Languedoc meant that it was never wholly free of armed bands. But the level of activity was much reduced and the larger companies were prevented from operating there altogether.[35]

These developments coincided with a determined push by the French commanders in Languedoc against the companies operating on its northern march. In January 1362 the Lieutenant in Languedoc, Arnoul d'Audrehem, marched up the Tarn and cleared the main companies from the Gevaudan. In February he was in the Velay. Over the following weeks, Arnoul was reinforced by fresh troops raised at the expense of the Estates of Languedoc, bringing his strength to about 4,500 men. In March he led them against the fortress of Saugues, which was occupied by the company of Perrin Bouvetault (or 'Boias'). Saugues was by now the last major centre of *routier* operations on the northern march of Languedoc.[36]

The result of the simultaneous operations of Chandos and Felton on one side and Arnoul d'Audrehem on the other was to drive the companies north and east. As winter softened into spring, the companies flowed from their redoubts in Auvergne into Forez and the Lyonnais. In the absence of Séguin de Badefol, the leading part in this new migration was taken by a gangster by the name of Hélie (or 'Petit') Meschin. This man was a Gascon, like most of his followers. He had begun his career as a squire of the lord of Fronsac, one of the few magnates of the French obedience in the Bordelais. In 1360 he had been among the mercenaries hired by Arnoul d'Audrehem to fight against the Great Company at Pont-Saint-Esprit and Montpellier. After the treaties with Séguin de Badefol in November 1361, he was paid off by the French, and turned to banditry for his own account. 'Uomo. . . di niente, . . . maestro e pratico di arme', Villani called him, with the alternating awe and contempt of so many of his contemporaries: a 'worthless man, but a great master of war'. In January 1362 Petit Meschin and his band led the tide north. He occupied the priory of Étivareilles at the edge of Forez and turned it into a base for heavy raids towards the valley of the Saône. Within a few weeks he had occupied several places in the Lyonnais and was beginning to penetrate into the Maçonnais and southern Burgundy.[37]

The duchy of Burgundy, in spite of being one of the richest agricultural provinces of France, had hitherto suffered very little by the war. The Jacquerie had hardly touched it. The English had not penetrated there until the raids of Nicholas Tamworth at the beginning of 1360. The community had bought off the army of Edward III for

200,000 *moutons* in March 1360, something which no other province of France except Languedoc would have had the resources or organisation to do. Yet political conditions there were changing. In the winter of 1361–2 there was a major crisis in the internal affairs of Burgundy. The Queen, Jeanne de Boulogne, who had governed the duchy in the name of the fifteen-year-old Duke, Philip de Rouvre, died of the plague in September 1361. Two months later, on 21 November, Philip himself died of injuries sustained in a riding accident. Philip had neither children nor siblings. There was no obvious heir. It was in some ways a repetition of the crisis of Brittany in 1341, which had been followed by twenty years of civil war. The councillors of the late queen tried to keep the news secret as long as they could. 'The companies are everywhere about us . . .,' they said; 'every nobleman has withdrawn to his castle. No one knows to whom he is answerable or who is the lord of the land.' There were two main claimants. One was the King who, although only distantly related to the dead child, was his closest kinsman in the male line. The other was Charles of Navarre, who could claim an equally distant kinship in the female line. It might have been a difficult legal question. But the succession was decided as it had been in Brittany, by politics not law. John II declared the duchy to be annexed to the Crown. At the end of November 1361 he sent his Chamberlain, Jean de Tancarville, to take possession of it. Two days before Christmas, the King made his *joyeuse entrée* into Dijon in an atmosphere of dense gloom. The region was racked by plague. The nobility was resentful of the threat to its ancient independence. The troops of the Great Company were making their way north from Languedoc and had already penetrated the duchy's southern borders in several places.[38]

The threat to Burgundy provoked the government of John II to the most disastrous of its confrontations with the Great Companies. On 20 January 1362 John II issued orders at Dijon requiring the inhabitants of the open country to take their goods within the walls of the nearest strongholds, always the first signal of emergency. The five eastern provinces of Champagne, Burgundy, Maçonnais, Lyonnais and Forez were united shortly afterwards in a single military command. Jean de Tancarville, a competent but pedestrian general, was appointed royal Lieutenant in the whole region and entrusted with its defence against the advancing companies. He pursued his task with energy. In February and March 1362 men-at-arms were summoned from every part of Burgundy and Champagne. The various sections of the army came together at Autun in about the middle of March. As they began their march south, they were joined by troops from neighbouring regions. Arnaud de Cervole came with the men of the Nivernais and a band of Bretons whom he had recruited into his private company. Another soldier of fortune of the 1350s, Brocard de Fénétrange, appeared with an army of Lorrainers. Jacques de Bourbon came with the men of Lyonnais, Bourbonnais, Auvergne and la Marche, and Louis Count of Forez with the recruits of his county. Other contingents were contributed by the Count of Savoy. The whole army was reckoned at about 4,000 men. It never occurred to the commanders that such a force might not be enough, still less that it could be defeated in the field.[39]

In the third week of March, the army arrived at the small castle of Brignais, about 8 miles south-west of Lyon, which was occupied by a detachment of Petit Meschin's company. In itself, the place was not worth much to either side. But the leaders of the Great Company could not ignore the challenge. They were in danger of being caught between the army of Jean de Tancarville advancing from the north and that of Arnoul d'Audrehem coming up with the army of Languedoc from the south. The captains of the Great Company responded to this challenge with a remarkable display of discipline and organisation. In the course of March 1362, Petit Meschin brought together most of the major independent companies operating in central and eastern France. His own company, fractions of which were spread across a wide area from the Rhone at Lyon to the borders of Auvergne, was now concentrated in Forez. A number of bands had been operating in the valley of the Saône under Arnaud de Tallebard (known as 'Tallebardon'). They gathered north of Lyon. The various groups which had previously acknowledged the authority of Séguin de Badefol were collected together by his erstwhile deputy Garciot du Châtel. The Anglo-Breton company of Amory and Cresswell came from Rouergue. Perrin Boais and his men, who had finally been expelled from Saugues by Arnoul d'Audrehem at the end of March, joined the others in early April. The combined strength of the *routier* army was about 5,000 men, rather more than the army of the French government.

The army encamped around Brignais was entirely unprepared for a counter-attack on this scale. Froissart's account of this campaign is as unreliable as anything he wrote, but he may well have been right in saying that the government's forces suffered from defective reconnaissance. Tancarville and Bourbon, who were in command, had no respect for the fighting capacity of the companies. They had taken few steps to protect their encampment from attack from behind. When, on the early morning of 6 April 1362, the companies attacked them without warning, the fight was no more than a disorganised mêlée. Many of Tancarville's men were not yet armed. Most of them were unsure what was happening. About 1,000 of them were captured. The rest were killed or put to flight. Tancarville and Arnaud de Cervole were among the prisoners. The Count of Joigny, who commanded the contingents of Champagne, was killed. So was the Count of Forez. Jacques de Bourbon survived, but died later of his wounds.[40]

The battle of Brignais was a spectacular feat of arms and a terrible shock to the government of John II. It created a brief but intense panic throughout eastern France. But it was almost entirely devoid of political consequences. The companies themselves could hardly believe what they had done, and their brief unity of purpose evaporated with victory. The usual logistical problems would have prevented them from following it up even if they had had the will. Their great numbers created intolerable pressure on supplies and severe competition for spoil. They could not act together for long periods unless they kept moving. Yet neither could they separate into their component units without exposing themselves to attack. Arnoul d'Audrehem's army was still in being in the northern Velay. The remnant of Tancarville's defeated force had reassembled at Lyon. So, instead of trying to crush the remaining forces of the government, as they had been expected to do, the captains of the Great Company released Tancarville on parole, and agreed a short truce until 26 May 1362 for negotiations.[41] Then, when this period was about to expire without agreement, the bandit army broke up. In the summer of 1362 the victors of Brignais were operating in two main groups. The larger of them had retreated into Auvergne. A significant minority drifted north into Burgundy, where they spread across the province, seizing vulnerable castles and living off the land. The damage was completed by the mercenaries of Arnaud de Cervole, who had fought with Tancarville at Brignais but joined their former enemies in the looting as soon as they found themselves unemployed.[42]

Tancarville had not given up hope of making an agreement which would finally dispose of the companies. In the weeks after Brignais, the old project of expelling them to Spain was revived. The peace between Aragon and Castile, which had frustrated the last attempt, was failing, and Peter IV of Aragon was once more interested in the services of the companies. In June 1362 he arrived in Perpignan to discuss the project with John II's representatives in Languedoc.[43] The real author of the new scheme, however, was neither Peter nor Tancarville. It was one of the more remarkable adventurers of the late fourteenth century, Henry of Trastámara.

For thirty years to come the ambitions of this young Castilian prince would be mainly responsible for drawing the Spanish kingdoms into the secular conflicts of England and France. Henry of Trastámara was the illegitimate son of Alfonso XI, King of Castile. He was born in about 1333. His mother was the King's mistress, Leonora de Guzman, with whom the King had lived openly in the latter part of his life. She had enjoyed enormous political influence while her husband lived, much of it deployed in the interests of her son. Henry was endowed with vast domains and obviously destined for great power in the state. Unfortunately Alfonso died prematurely in 1350, before his son had been able to consolidate his position in Castile. The Crown passed to his younger (but legitimate) half-brother Pedro I. Leonora was swiftly arrested and then murdered. Henry himself was expelled from all his possessions. From that moment his entire life was devoted to supplanting his half-brother on the throne by whatever means lay to hand.

In the course of his long reign Alfonso XI had imposed order and a large measure of centralisation on the fragmented kingdom of Castile. Many powerful groups, particularly among the Castilian nobility, had been bruised in this process. They had hopes of a more emollient regime under his successor. But they were to be disappointed. Pedro shared all the political purposes of his father and proved to be even more ruthless in carrying them out. He entirely lacked his father's instinct for political possibilities and well timed reconciliation. His temper and brutality when crossed were legendary. The early years of his reign were therefore dominated by a succession of aristocratic rebellions, some of which came close to deposing him. Henry of Trastámara threw himself with energy into these revolts. And when at length they failed, he carried on the fight by joining Castile's external enemies. When war first broke out between Castile and Aragon in 1356 he did homage to the King of Aragon and raised a company of 600 Castilian malcontents and hirelings to fight alongside the Aragonese armies.[44]

Castile had traditionally been a client of France, but in the past fifteen years the two countries had drifted apart. There were a number of reasons for the change of sentiment. The revival of English power in Gascony and the renown of Edward III after the battle of Crécy had brought about a significant reassessment of Castile's interests. For their part the French were drawing closer to the kingdom of Aragon, 'a powerful country with vigorous people who can do much damage to your realm', as John II's ambassadors once advised him. Pedro's father had toyed with the idea of an English alliance at the end of the 1340s, and Pedro himself had briefly been betrothed to an English princess. This might have been an aberration. Certainly Pedro after his accession returned to the diplomatic traditions of his predecessors. He renewed the Franco-Castilian alliance and married a French princess, Blanche de Bourbon. But it proved to be a troubled and short-lived alliance. Pedro quarrelled with John II about Blanche's dowry, which John was unable to pay. As a result Pedro repudiated her almost as soon as they were married and installed his mistress in her place in the most public and insulting fashion. In about July 1361 Blanche died in mysterious circumstances. It was widely believed, probably rightly, that she had been murdered. Relations between France and Castile, which might have subsided into indifference after the treaty of Brétigny, became openly hostile.[45] Pedro's reaction was to draw closer to France's enemies. In June 1362, after more than a year of negotiation, an Anglo-Castilian treaty was concluded in London. Among its clauses was one which obliged Edward III and the Prince of Wales to provide troops at Pedro's expense to serve against his enemies in the peninsula, and particularly against any French auxiliaries which they might employ. A month before, in the Dominican Church at Estella, Pedro's representatives had sealed a treaty of alliance with the agents of that other great adversary of the Valois monarchy, Charles of Navarre. There are good reasons for suspecting that the English suggested this alliance and acted as brokers between the two sides.[46]

Henry of Trastámara exploited this situation with great skill. The peace of Terrer, which had briefly reconciled Aragon and Castile in May 1361, obliged Peter IV of Aragon to expel Pedro's enemies from his realm. As a result Henry had been forced to go north with his younger brother Sancho and a considerable company of Castilian supporters, Navarrese mercenaries and other men-at-arms, intending to enter France. Arnoul d'Audrehem and Robert Fiennes, the two senior military officers of the French Crown in Languedoc, were uncertain what to do. At first they tried to hold the Pyrenean passes against him. Then, at some point in the summer of 1361, they made a deal with him. He was allowed to pass unmolested through Languedoc and ushered out of France across the Rhone, where he might do his worst to the people of Provence. Henry fell in with this arrangement. But he had no desire to live the life of an errant *routier* captain. His ultimate object was to reach an accommodation with the French government which would enable him to continue his vendetta against his half-brother. In January 1362, after wasting much of the dioceses of Arles and Avignon, Henry accepted a large lump sum from the Estates of Provence to leave them alone and agreed to enter the service of John II's representatives in Languedoc. He received a stipend of 10,000 florins a month for himself and his company of about 400 men. Henry did well for his new employers. Arnoul d'Audrehem stationed him on the northern march of Languedoc to guard the approaches from Auvergne and the Rhone valley. In March 1362 he took part in the siege of Saugues. After the battle of Brignais, he pursued the remnants of the routier army across Auvergne. On 3 June 1362 he caught le Bourc de Breteuil, one of the principal captains of the Great Company with several hundred men at Montpensier near Vichy and inflicted a bloody defeat on him. Half the enemy's strength was reported to have been killed and 200 more captured. Henry's standing as a soldier had never been higher.[47]

During June and July 1362, preparations were being made for a simultaneous campaign against the companies from three sides: by Arnoul d'Audrehem and Henry of Trastámara in Auvergne, Jean de Tancarville in the Lyonnais and Robert de Fiennes in Burgundy.[48] The companies might perhaps have attempted another Brignais, but they were not willing to chance their luck. They sued for terms. The negotiations were conducted by Arnoul d'Audrehem and by Séguin de Badefol's former lieutenant Garciot du Châtel. On 23 July 1362 a treaty was made at Clermont between Henry of Trastámara, various royal councillors, and ten captains representing between them all the 'companies from here to Paris'. At about the same time the Constable made a similar agreement with the *routiers* operating in Burgundy and with the Breton mercenaries of Arnaud de Cervole. Under the terms of these instruments, the companies agreed to enter the service of Henry of Trastámara. He undertook to lead them out of France within six weeks. In return, they were to receive at the border a sum of money which was not specified in the text but is known from other sources to have been 53,000 florins (about £7,500) for Henry himself and 100,000 florins (about £14,000) for the captains of the Great Company. Their destination (likewise unspecified) was obviously Aragon. A month before the treaty was made, Pedro I had torn up the treaty of Terrer and invaded Peter IV's kingdom. The hard pressed Peter now needed all the help that he could get.[49]

In due course, the companies made their way south again, towards the Pyrenees. Most of them passed down the Rhone valley, escorted by the army of Arnoul d'Audrehem. The Spaniards migrated through Rouergue into the seneschalsy of Carcassonne watched at a distance by a large armed force raised by Edward III's officers. By 15 September 1362 virtually all the companies had passed through Montpellier. Henry of Trastámara took up the rear, followed by his wife and fifty-four mules laden with her baggage. The whole mass of men encamped around Pamiers and Mazères and waited for their pay.[50]

It was as close to Spain as they got, for the second attempt of the French government to export its problems to Spain failed as completely as the first. There were two main reasons. The first was that the government encountered great difficulty in raising the 153,000 florins which they had promised to pay. The money had been expected to come from the taxpayers of Languedoc, which was the only province which could pay. But the negotiators had not allowed nearly enough time for the lengthy negotiations which were always the prelude to a successful tax-raising campaign in Languedoc. November came and the money was still unpaid. Several captains lost patience and drifted back north. Le Bourc de Breteuil was making his way up the Rhone valley in late October 1362. Perrin Boias, who commanded one of the largest companies and had been among the first captains to march south, was back in his old hunting grounds by the beginning of November. John Amory returned to Rouergue.[51]

The second cause of the failure was more fundamental. The planned exodus of the companies to Spain coincided with a grave crisis in the affairs of the south-west, the war of the Counts of Armagnac and Foix. The ancient rivalry between these two houses had been intensified during the 1350s by the powerful position which the Count of Armagnac occupied, first as the King's Lieutenant in Languedoc and then as adviser to his successor, the Count of Poitiers. He had never hesitated to use his authority to forward his own territorial interests at the expense of his rivals, including the Count of Foix. The resulting tensions had produced brief outbreaks of violence in 1359 and again in the winter of 1360–1. This last incident had been brought to an end by a series of short truces which were bought by promises of very large sums of money from the Estates-General of Languedoc.[52] No one expected them to endure. Both counts spent the best part of 1362 finding allies among the Gascon nobility and the captains of the Great Company in preparation for the coming civil war. When the treaty of Clermont was made, so many of the captains were found to be retainers of Armagnac or Foix or of their allies that a proviso had to be included that if war were to break out between the two counts they would all be free of their obligations. This proviso undid the treaty. It meant that Armagnac and Foix were virtually bound to open hostilities in the autumn before their allies and mercenaries disappeared across the Pyrenees. In early October 1362 Gaston Phoebus received reliable reports that Armagnac was gathering his retainers. He went to Pamiers and Mazères to try to persuade the companies to leave at once for Spain. But he was wasting his breath. The companies double-crossed him, and Arnoul d'Audrehem as well. Arnoul had now finally raised the money for their fees, mainly by taking the funds collected to pay the ransom of the King. A hundred thousand florins was found and carried under armed guard to Pamiers. As soon as it had been paid, most of the captains abandoned Henry of Trastámara and his schemes in order to take sides in the impending civil war in Languedoc. Bérard and Bertucat d'Albret, Garciot du Châtel and several others withdrew to join the Count of Armagnac. A rather smaller number of captains, including Petit Meschin, went to join Gaston Phoebus.[53]

On 5 December 1362 a great battle was fought outside the village of Launac in the plain north-west of Toulouse. The Count of Armagnac had the larger army. But he was completely defeated. The battle was won, like so many unequal contests of the fourteenth century, by the concealed archers of the victor. Armagnac himself and all the leaders of his host were captured and carried off to the keep of Orthez. The prisoners included Garciot du Châtel and no less than five prominent members of the Albret family. The ransoms amounted to more than 600,000 florins. For the remainder of his long reign, Gaston Phoebus was to be one of the richest and most flamboyant princes of the west, the man who could maintain a permanent war treasury and an army of 4,000 or 5,000 men and who 'gave, no man more' to foreigners, knights and squires, heralds and minstrels who passed through his small and ill-endowed territory.[54]

For Languedoc the treaty of Clermont had been a disaster. It had made possible a brief but bloody and destructive civil war. It had cost a fortune in war wages and payments to the companies, all wasted. And it had brought the *routiers* back into the province in force without expelling them at the other end into Spain. Henry of Trastámara abandoned his plans. His Castilian company spread themselves around the seneschalsies of Beaucaire and Carcassonne, alternately serving in Arnoul d'Audrehem's army and exploding in bouts of indiscipline and rioting. They did not leave the region until 1363 when they were eventually paid the 53,000 florins promised to them at Clermont. This too was taken out of the ransom fund.[55]

As for the rest of the Great Company, they were gradually pushed and shoved out of the three seneschalsies in the course of the winter of 1362–3. For another six or eight months after that, they continued to operate in the arc of territory beyond the northern march of Languedoc between the valley of the Tarn and the plateau of Velay. Two places in particular proved to be a continuing menace to the security of Languedoc: Combret in Rouergue and Saint-Chaffre-du-Monastier in Velay. Neither lasted for long. Saint-Chaffre du Monastier was a fortified Benedictine monastery by the main highway south of le Puy, which was occupied in the autumn of 1362 by Perrin Boias. Boias's men raided over a great distances from Saint-Chaffre, mainly southward down the Rhone valley. Their monastery was eventually taken by assault by the levies of the seneschalsy of Beaucaire on 7 March 1363. Combret was a thirteenth-century keep in a remote valley north of Marcillac in Rouergue which was occupied by the Englishman John Amory at the end of October 1362. Detachments of his garrison operated in much the same way, roaming freely through the seneschalsy of Beaucaire, collecting loot and prisoners before scuttling back to base. Amory also sheltered other captains there, including the notorious Provençal brigand Louis Rabaud of Nice. It was from Combret that Rabaud organised his most famous coup, the capture of the entire train of the ambassadors of the King of Castile on their way to Avignon in March 1363. The place was eventually abandoned in the middle of 1362 as a result of persistent pressure from Edward III's Seneschal of Rouergue. These events marked the final extinction of the Great Company of 1360.[56]

They also represented a remarkable success for the defenders of Languedoc from which the northern and central provinces were to learn a great deal in the following years. As in 1361, however, the wider problem remained. The expulsion of the companies from Languedoc simply pushed them further north and east, aggravating the problems of other, less efficiently defended provinces. The cities of the three seneschalsies were willing when they were pressed to spend money on the defence of a region like the Velay which had close administrative links with their own and was the key to the defence of their northern frontier. But they had little interest in the territory beyond. The companies were therefore able to regroup with impunity in Auvergne and find fresh ambitions. The history of the Great Company of 1360 was destined to repeat itself in 1363.

The catalyst was the return of Séguin de Badefol. Séguin had taken no part in the affairs of the companies since his agreement with the Estates of Languedoc and Rouergue in the autumn of 1361. He had honoured his word and withdrawn to his native Périgord. But in the summer of 1363 he reappeared on the march of Languedoc with a huge new company, comprising not only his own men but a large number of other bands which had previously operated together in the Rhone valley and Bas-Languedoc. They included Petit Meschin, who had taken over the leadership of the Great Company of 1360 after his withdrawal at the end of 1361; the redoubtable Louis Rabaud; Arnaud du Solier, otherwise known as 'le Limousin', who appears at about this time as Louis' partner in arms; and the Béarnais *routier* Menaud de Villars, who although hitherto little known was to become notorious under the name of 'Espiote'. Séguin's strength of personality and large strategic views made this new Great Company even more dangerous than its predecessor.

Before they had struck a blow in anger, Séguin de Badefol's confederation succeeded in extracting the enormous sum of 40,000 florins from the city of Toulouse in return for leaving the Toulousain alone. The towns of Bas-Languedoc, however, proved more robust. At Montpellier the consuls summoned an enlarged meeting of the council to decide whether they should follow the example of Toulouse. The assembly, which was joined by representatives of the suburbs and outlying villages, unanimously resolved to fight. The Great Company therefore divided into two wings. Louis Rabaud, accompanied by a native Languedocien bandit by the name of Bertuquin, invaded Bas-Languedoc to take up the challenge. They established their headquarters at the end of July 1363 in the castle of Lignan, just north of Béziers. Béziers was known to be vulnerable. The commissioners who had inspected its defences the year before had found the walls unrepaired, the gates unprotected by barbicans or outworks, and the ditches decayed. The city suffered heavily at the hands of the companies of Lignan. But their operations extended over a much wider area, embracing the whole of the Mediterranean coastal region from the Rhone to the Pyrenees. At one point, they even succeeded in penetrating the walls of Montpellier with eighty men, doing great damage to the town as well as abducting a number of prominent citizens. Yet Languedoc's formidable powers of resistance squeezed them out before

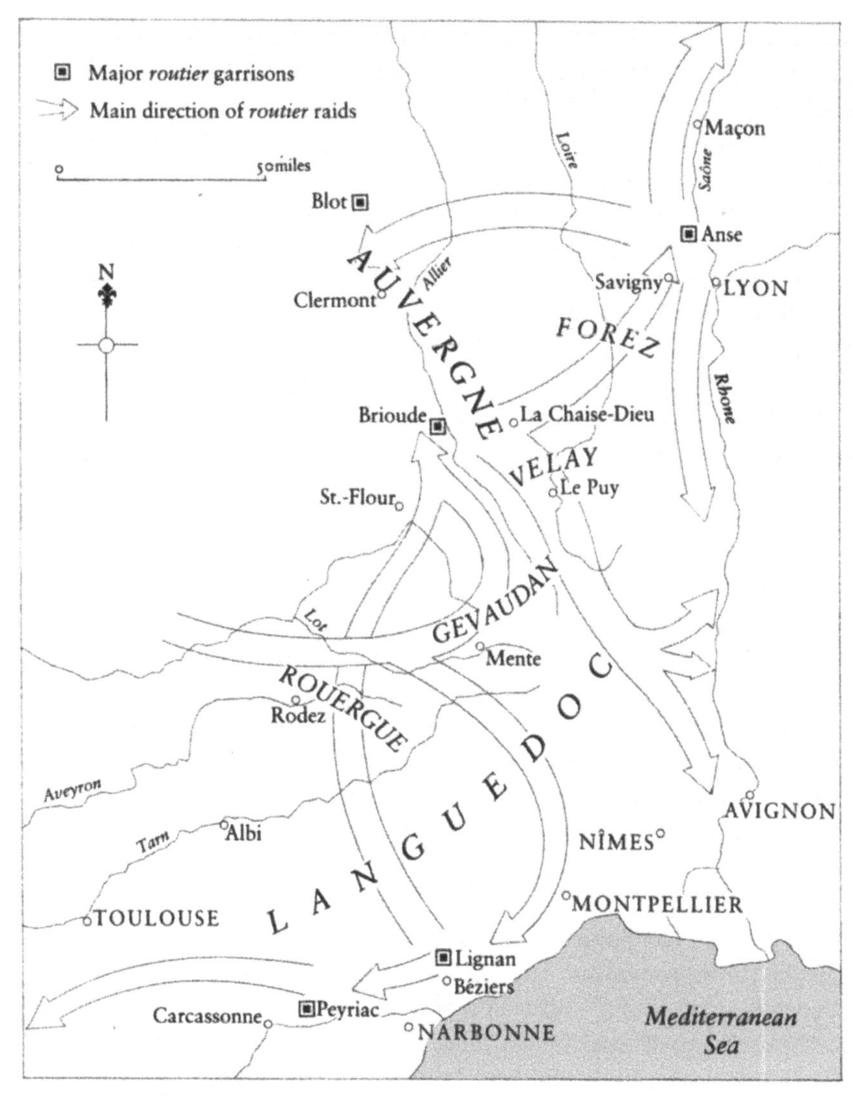

34 The Great Company of 1363, June 1363–September 1365

long. The citizens of Béziers, less strong-willed than those of Montpellier and certainly less strong-walled, bought Rabaud and Bertuquin out of Lignan at the beginning at the beginning of November 1363. Rabaud withdrew to Auvergne to rejoin the rest of the Great Company. Bertuquin's men stayed in Languedoc and within a few days had occupied another fortress at Peyriac on the road from Béziers to Carcassonne, blocking one of the major commercial arteries of the south. It took six months of intermittent siege operations to get him out of this place. He eventually took refuge over the border in the kingdom of Navarre.[57]

At the beginning of September 1363, Séguin de Badefol with the rest of the Great Company entered the Gevaudan and joined forces with Bérard and Bertucat d'Albret. On 13 September, he fell on the walled town of Brioude. This small town on the marches of Auvergne and the Velay belonged to the chapter of St. Julien, one of the richest ecclesiastical foundations in France. Like many ecclesiastical towns it was poorly defended. The invaders got in at night through the deserted houses built against the walls. No one had troubled to demolish them. The town was systematically looted and much of the population ransomed. Then it was converted into a permanent base for wider operations. The governor of Auvergne was exaggerating when he described Brioude as 'the strongest, best and richest town in all Auvergne', but it was certainly an important place and much the largest walled town to be occupied by the companies since the capture of Pont-Saint-Esprit. Its fall was indeed 'une très grand mal aventure'. As the news spread, fresh bands of *routiers* flocked to Brioude from across southern France. Louis Rabaud came up from Lignan. Part of the Castilian company of Henry of Trastámara followed. The French government's officials in Auvergne were well informed about the movements of the principal companies. They expected the combined strength of the army of Brioude to attain 2,000 men-at-arms and 8,000 foot-soldiers and archers. At its height, it was probably not far short of that.[58]

At first the companies at Brioude concentrated their attention on the neighbouring provinces. The Velay, which had owed *patis* to Séguin de Badefol since 1361, received special attention. The province was completely devastated by burning parties sent out from Brioude. To the north, powerful raids were launched against the major towns of Auvergne. The suburbs of le Puy, Saint-Flour, Clermont and la Chaise-Dieu were all wrecked. To the south, raiding parties from Brioude penetrated across the Rouergue into the plain of Bas-Languedoc. To the east they reached the valley of the Rhone and the marches of the papal state.[59] But such a large body of men quickly reached the natural limits of their operations. They exhausted the available spoil around them and required much greater supplies than their foraging organisation could produce. Séguin de Badefol needed to expand his territory. The governor of Auvergne reported rumours from Brioude that Burgundy was the target. 'Unless we can recover this place by negotiation or force,' he told the Council of the Duke of Burgundy, 'every region will be lost.' As if to bear out this warning, Séguin's bands appeared in Forez within a month of the fall of Brioude. In the autumn of 1363 they briefly occupied the great Benedictine abbey of Savigny and extracted a large ransom from the surrounding region before withdrawing. Savigny was only 12 miles from Lyon. In April 1364 the Estates of Auvergne agreed to buy the companies out of Brioude. Séguin promised to surrender his conquests and to release all his prisoners without ransom in return for a royal pardon, a papal absolution and 40,000 florins in cash. It was largest recorded ransom ever exacted for the *videment* of a single place.[60]

John II's ministers in Paris had no time to attend to the problems of the Midi. They were overwhelmed by the tide of violence in the north of the kingdom. The north was different. The main actors were not Gascons, who rarely penetrated north of the Loire. They were Navarrese, English, German and above all Breton. Yet the travails of the north had much the same origin as those of the south: the collapse of royal authority, the destruction of the internal political organisation of the provinces, the growing number of unemployed soldiers and drop-outs.

The creative vice here, as everywhere, was private war. In the autumn of 1362 Henry, Count of Vaudémont, the royal Lieutenant in Champagne, embarked on a vicious war for his own account against a number of German princes beyond France's eastern frontier, principally the Duke of Lorraine and the Count of Bar. The origins of the dispute are obscure and perhaps do not matter. The important feature of the conflict is that unlike earlier wars on the north-eastern frontier, which had been largely local affairs, this one was fought on Vaudémont's side by a large *routier* army recruited in other parts of France. Most belonged to the great diaspora of Breton soldiers of fortune which had been scattered across the basin of the Loire and the provinces of the *massif central* since 1358. But there were also many Navarrese and a few Gascons. The chief war contractor was yet again Arnaud de Cervole, who was hired by Vaudémont to collect this great host.[61] The Archpriest's recruits migrated in unruly mobs through the Loire valley and across the Île de France. They occupied several places south of Paris on their way. They attacked major cities, including Orléans. Great concentrations of them built up in Burgundy, which, precisely because it had been so successful in beating off earlier invasions, still contained great unmined veins of plunder. A rash of castles was seized by Breton companies on the west side of Dijon in January 1363.[62]

Very similar conditions were produced in the west of the kingdom by the continuing civil war in Brittany. When the last of a long succession of truces expired at the end of September 1362, Charles of Blois embarked on a rapid strike across the north of the Breton peninsula with the assistance of the French captain of Pontorson, Bertrand du Guesclin. In the spring of 1363 this campaign reached its climax with a prolonged siege of the fortress of Bécherel. Bécherel was a place of great strategic importance. It blocked the road from Dinan to Rennes and controlled much of the north-east of Brittany, effectively dividing Charles of Blois' territory in two. In order to meet the new threat, John de Montfort turned to the English-led companies based in the duchy. A large relief force (about 2,400 men) was recruited mainly from their ranks. The result was an unstable truce, patched up between the two pretenders in July, as the rival armies confronted each other by the Dinan road.[63] But the effect on the rest of western France continued for long after. There was an effervescence of fighting throughout the march of Brittany and the neighbouring regions of Normandy and Maine, as the soldiers paid off at Bécherel reformed themselves under new captains and looked about them for employment. 'The baillage and district of Caen is destroyed,' the King's officers came to tell him at the beginning of 1363; 'every day and night the garrison of Aulnay penetrates into the suburbs of Caen, and the country around is so racked and wasted that no one ventures outside the walled places.' As the summer began to cool, the French authorities began to take the problem in hand. Bertrand du Guesclin joined forces with Philip of Navarre (the King of Navarre's Lieutenant in the region) and attempted to root out the more important of *routier* garrisons. The chief occupied places around Bayeux and Caen were captured. Some of them were demolished. But the proximity of the Breton march made even these achievements provisional, and fresh places were occupied as soon as the campaign had ended. Unfortunately for the French, they lost one of their most useful allies at the end of August 1363, when Philip of Navarre died of a chill caught in the closing stages of the campaign. He had stood loyally by the peace which he had sworn to preserve and had kept at least some measure of control over the Navarrese troops in the region. His successors had neither the ability nor, in most cases, the will to do so.[64]

Within a few weeks the violence had spread east into the Île de France. In the late summer of 1363, two adventurers, John Jewel and

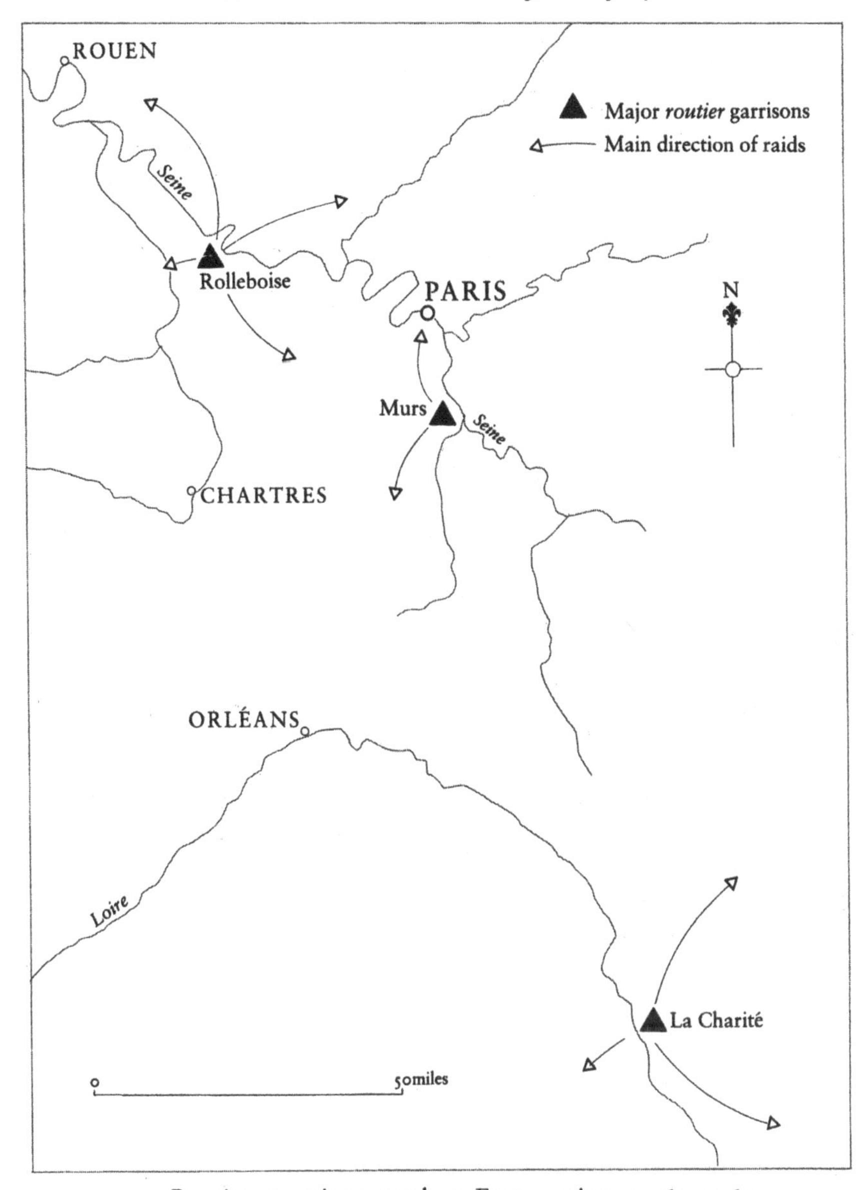

35 *Routier* operations: northern France, winter 1363–1364

Walter Strael, formed a new company to invade the Seine valley. Jewel was an Englishman who had been active in Normandy for some years. One report had it that he was acting on the instructions of the King of England, but there is no reliable evidence of this and it is not particularly likely. As for Strael, he was a professional mercenary from

Brabant, who had previously been employed by Edward III, probably in the garrison of Calais. In September, these two men captured the fort of Auvillers on the march of Normandy and Picardy. Then, moving south, they crossed the Seine and invaded the Chartrain. It was shortly after this, in October 1363, that they seized the famous old keep of Rolleboise, dominating the bend of the Seine below Mantes. From here their company was able to interrupt the traffic of the Seine and to terrorise much of the Vexin français.[65] A few days after the fall of Rolleboise another band captured the fort of Murs outside Corbeil, thereby blocking the Seine on the other side of Paris as well. They entered the castle gates disguised as drovers and blocked the drawbridge for long enough to enable their companions to jump out of their hiding places and rush the entrance: an old trick which some gatekeepers never got wise. The captors of Murs are known to have come from the garrisons of Maine and Lower Normandy. They were probably led by Englishmen. At almost the same moment a mixed group of Gascons and Bretons captured la Charité-sur-Loire at night and established a large permanent garrison there. They were soon joined there by freebooters of every nation. La Charité was a substantial walled town. It provided a secure base for raiding across Berry, Orléanais and the Nivernais. It also commanded the great stone bridge over the Loire which provided the companies with a secure crossing of the river. These three garrisons, appearing almost simultaneously at strategic points of the river network of northern France, represented a major threat to the government's security, the more dangerous for being dispersed.[66] The winter of 1363–4 was one of the coldest in living memory. The Seine froze over, and the companies were able to ride their horses freely across the river to plunder the suburbs of Paris on both sides. By Christmas one French army was besieging Rolleboise and another was encamped outside Murs. The resources of the government, already severely strained, were wholly committed to the defence of the capital.[67]

In Burgundy the King's youngest son Philip of Touraine scratched together packets of troops with which he besieged one small castle after another. Like others before and after, he found himself obliged to recruit companies to confront other companies. Arnaud de Tallebard, who had been plundering the Maçonnais for much of the past two years, entered the service of Philip of Touraine in the autumn of 1363. The Poitevin *routier* Guiot du Pin was hired to recruit a company for the defence of Burgundy, which he employed instead in a campaign of spoliation for his own account. Arnaud de Cervole hired out his Bretons for service against other Bretons in the duchy. Gascons were hired to fight other Gascons. They included Jean d'Armagnac, the son of the former Lieutenant of Languedoc, and Amanieu de Pommiers, one of the Prince of Wales's companions at Poitiers. The policy was a disaster. Few mercenary companies were prepared to fight whole-heartedly against their friends and kinsmen. And their indiscipline was legendary. They stripped bare the places through which they passed. They burned villages and destroyed crops in the search for food, booty and money. They stood at the gates of towns that they were required to guard, manning the barriers as if they had conquered them, and exacted *patis* and safe-conduct fees just like the enemy they were supposed to contain. Most of them ended up by quarrelling about the arrears of their wages and visiting destruction on their hosts until their claims were settled. Many established themselves permanently in Burgundy, joining forces with their fellows, filling the roads with disorderly mobs of armed men.[68]

As much of northern and central France dissolved into chaos, the peace which reigned in the new duchy of Aquitaine, whence the worst of the bandits came, offered an increasingly painful contrast. On 19 July 1362 Aquitaine had been ceded by Edward III to the Prince of Wales, together with all the powers of the Crown there. Almost a year later the Prince arrived in Bordeaux with a great fleet and a magnificent retinue to receive the homage of his new subjects, including many whose kinsmen were waging overt war in the rest of France. 'Since the birth of Christ, such fine state was never kept as this . . .,' wrote the herald of Sir John Chandos; 'and there abode there nobility, joy, largesse, courtesy and honour.'[69]

Under the terms of the treaty of Calais, John II retained a nominal sovereignty over the ceded provinces for a limited period while the transfers of territory were made and the rest of the kingdom was cleared of 'English' garrisons. But it had been envisaged that by November 1361 at the latest John would renounce his sovereignty over the enlarged duchy of Aquitaine and Edward for his part would renounce his claim to the Crown of France. It would not have been surprising if John had looked for some escape from this obligation. He had gained little from the treaty of Brétigny except his liberty, and his subjects nothing at all. But John was an honourable, uncynical man, and he did not. At the end of October 1361, a month before the appointed date, two French ambassadors were sent to Westminster to propose that the renunciations should be made at once.[70] Yet they were not made, a fact pregnant with consequences a few years later when the French throne was occupied by a less malleable monarch.

There is no doubt that it was Edward III who was responsible for the delay. His reasons, however unwise, were at least straightforward. The King of France had undertaken not to exercise his nominal sovereignty, even before it was renounced. No great inconveniences therefore seemed to follow from the delay. Edward had always overrated the bargaining value of his claim to the French throne, and he was unwilling to abandon it until the French King's obligations had been performed to the last letter. His conception of those obligations was exacting. In November 1361, two rather low-grade English agents, Sir Thomas Uvedale and Thomas Dunclent, arrived in Paris to demand John's renunciations forthwith. But they had no authority to make Edward's. Instead, the whole of the three months which they passed in the French capital was devoted to airing their master's complaints about the French fulfilment of the treaties, a task which they seem to have performed without even the minimum of skill or tact. John's councillors responded by complaining with rather better justification about the very large numbers of major fortresses in France which were still, nearly a year and a half after the agreement at Calais, in the hands of Edward III's subjects. The treaty provided for the renunciations of the two Kings to be made simultaneously, and even John was not so supine as to waive this point. 'As soon as our brother is ready to make them,' he told a papal legate, 'we shall do likewise.' Easter passed. Nothing happened.[71]

As the transfers of territory proceeded the English King's complaints became more numerous. Some of them were trivial, like the corner of the county of Ponthieu which was still being held by a recalcitrant French prince. Some were more serious but quickly resolved, like the refusal of the Count of Armagnac to do homage to the King of England or to surrender the county of Gaure in southern Gascony which had been ceded to England by the treaty. This particular problem was diplomatically sorted out by the Prince of Wales after his arrival in the south-west in 1363. Other difficulties were insoluble. There was, for example, nothing that John II could do to make the Count of Foix do homage for Béarn, since the Count claimed that Béarn was an independent state. He had maintained the same pretensions against the Kings of France for years with impunity. But the most intractable and damaging arguments were those which raised highly debatable issues to which the treaty provided no answer. Pre-eminent among these were the long-running disputes about the terre de Belleville and the fortress of la

Roche-sur-Yon. The terre de Belleville in Bas-Poitou had been expressly ceded by the treaty. But what was the terre de Belleville? Was it the relatively small castellany of Belleville which generated some 200 *livres* a year in revenues, or was it the whole of the vast lordship of Belleville, worth an estimated 30,000 livres a year, which had been possessed by Jeanne de Belleville at the time of its confiscation by the Crown in 1343? As for la Roche-sur-Yon, this place was geographically part of Poitou but it had been administered since 1287 as an enclave of the *baillage* of Touraine. The French King's officers therefore continued to occupy it. Such anomalies as these, which depended on the tortuous and fluctuating administrative geography of France, could and did take years to resolve. The process engendered resentment and suspicion between the two parties out of all proportion to their real importance.[72]

The matter was complicated by the considerable difficulty which the French King experienced in collecting the money for his ransom. On 5 December 1360, six weeks after his release, John II issued at Compiègne a great ordinance which determined how the money was to be raised. It introduced in Languedoil a number of new indirect taxes (later known as 'aids') and reintroduced a much hated old one, the *gabelle du sel*. These two corner-stones of the fiscal system of the *ancien régime* were destined to last for more than four centuries. Languedoc, as usual, made its own arrangements. Actual collection, however, was extremely slow throughout France. In Languedoc, which was economically best placed to meet the burden, the demands of the treasurers of the ransom competed with the heavy indemnities payable to the Count of Foix to buy brief respites from his feud with the Count of Armagnac, and with the continuing cost of keeping the peace against the companies. To these problems were added the reappearance of bubonic plague at the end of 1360 which was particularly virulent in the south. Judging by the accounts of the subsidy in the seneschalsy of Toulouse, only about a third or a half of the total assessment was collected. Of that a good deal never reached the ransom treasurers because it was 'borrowed' by the Lieutenant to deal with successive military crises. If Languedoc could not pay its share, the more heavily war damaged regions of the north and centre were still less able to do so. The few surviving fragments of accounts present a picture of economic exhaustion, administrative confusion and waste, and of manipulation by monopolistic syndicates of tax farmers, the abiding vice of French public finance from the fourteenth to the eighteenth centuries. After an encouraging start, receipts fell precipitately. Payment of the ransom began to fall into arrear. Payment of the first instalment was completed more or less on time in course of the winter following the treaties. But none of the 400,000 *écus* due to be paid in the year 1361 had been received by the end of the year.[73]

The delay in performing the territorial and financial provisions of the treaty caused severe friction not only between the two Kings but within the French political community. The treaties provided for forty-one prominent noblemen and forty-two representatives of the leading walled towns of France to be held in England and released in stages as the money came in. Many of these men had been extremely reluctant to go. Some had packed their bags only when they were threatened with the sequestration of their lands and goods.[74] All were anxious to return. Edward III had undertaken that they would be treated not as prisoners but 'decently according to their character and status', and the promise was by and large observed. Places of residence were appointed for them, which they were allowed to leave for up to two days at a time or longer with permission. The noble hostages lived in much the same outward style as they would have done in France. The grandest kept large establishments in England with ample stables. They came with their own servants, secretaries, household officials, chaplains, musicians and retainers. According to Froissart, who spend some time in England in the 1360s and must have met a good many of them, they enjoyed themselves gambling and hunting and travelled about England calling on lords and ladies as they pleased. The Duke of Bourbon played dice with the Queen and passed from one noble household to the next. But this glossy existence must have felt very pointless after the first few months. The poet Guillaume de Machaut went to England, probably in the household of the King's son Jean de Berry (formerly Count of Poitiers). He must have led as full a life as any, but still complained of the 'exile's drudgery', surrounded by foreigners speaking an incomprehensible language. It was, moreover, a cripplingly expensive way of life. Apart from the royal princes and a handful of others who were favoured with allowances from the King, the hostages had to maintain themselves. Some of them raised the money by taxing their tenants and dependents at home. The 100,000 gold francs which the Duke of Bourbon spent during his six years were paid by the inhabitants of his domains in the Bourbonnais and Beauvaisis. Some were helped out by their relations. Some ran through their capital or borrowed from moneylenders. Charles de Montmorency reckoned that his expenses in England exceeded the entire income of his considerable French domain. He had to sell his mansion in Paris to another hostage to pay them.[75]

The hostages of the towns had more modest requirements, which were generally provided for by the communities which sent them. Most towns made elaborate agreements with their hostages, which provided for them to receive a salary and a living allowance and promised to send a substitute after a specified period, generally a year. But these provisions were not always honoured. The allowances were sometimes paid late and in a few cases not at all. This caused great hardship to men residing in a country where they were unable to earn a living. Some towns failed to send substitutes, leaving the original hostage languishing indefinitely in England. But boredom was probably the main peril of their existence. Those who survived had no occupation or entertainment, and they were presumably not received, as their betters were, in the palaces and manors of the great. They also suffered from disease. All the hostages of the towns were assigned to live in London, which was probably the most insalubrious place in England. More than a quarter of them died there in the terrible bubonic plague epidemic of the summer of 1361.[76]

In the course of the year 1362 the hostages became increasingly angry and frustrated at the prospect of indefinite detention in England while the two governments squabbled about parcels of land in France. Most of the noble hostages were men of influence in France. They often had kinsmen and agents in Paris to press their cause and publicise their complaints. The most significant of all were the four royal princes: the King's brother the Duke of Orléans, his two sons Louis of Anjou and Jean de Berry, and the Duke of Bourbon. The treaty provided for them to be released only when the main transfers of territory had occurred, the renunciations had been made and the second instalment of the ransom had been paid.[77] They bore their captivity particularly ill. Lesser hostages were sometimes allowed back to France for limited periods on parole or exchanged for others of equivalent status. But the royal princes were too important to be released on parole and there was no one of equivalent status to substitute for them.

In April 1362, after the mission of Uvedale and Dunclent had ended in failure, John II's government made a determined attempt to get at least some of the royal princes released. Androin de la Roche, now a cardinal, arrived in England to mediate. He was followed by a distinguished French embassy, led by Marshal Boucicaut, 'sage et beau parleur sur tous les chevaliers'. Here was a man who knew better than Dunclent and Uvedale how to make himself agreeable to kings. By now a total of 600,000 *écus* of John's ransom was overdue. Of this sum, the ambassadors brought 108,800 *écus* with them in cash. Another 90,000 was promised by the Pope and treated as paid. It was in practice paid by the English clergy, since the money was transferred by the papal collectors in England from tax receipts in their hands. As for the rest, Boucicaut and his colleagues asked Edward to extend the timetable for payment and to release the royal princes in the meantime. They also pressed him to make the long-delayed renunciation. Edward was uncompromising on both points. He would agree to their requests only if he received yet more territory in France as security. This was to be forfeited to him for ever if the revised terms were not strictly adhered to. Edward also wanted John II's renunciations at once, before he made his own, and a dispensation from having to clear his subjects from the places occupied by them in John's domains. Neither the cardinal nor the ambassadors could move him from this position. When Edward's response was received by the King of France it provoked a bitter protest. John pointed out that he had paid large sums already. He could not pay more owing to the operations of the companies, 'most or all of them English or Gascons of your obedience.'[78]

In the autumn of 1362, another instalment of the ransom fell due and the territorial disputes were no nearer to being resolved. The four 'lords of the *fleur de lys*' in England decided to take the negotiations into their own hands. On 1 November they concluded in London a private treaty with the English King's Council which if it had been performed would have given Edward most of what he wanted. They undertook to procure that Edward would promptly receive another 200,000 *écus* of the ransom money, and that within a year the disputed territories of Belleville and Gaure would be delivered up to him. They also promised that the English King would not be required to do any more than he had already done to rid France of the Anglo-Gascon garrisons and companies, with the single exception of Pierre Descalat's garrison at la Roche-Posay. This was to be rooted out, if necessary by the combined forces of both Kings. Once all this was done, the renunciations would take place mutually and at once. Meanwhile the four princes, together with six other noble hostages, were to be released on parole on providing suitable security. The princes offered by way of security five important castellanies belonging to the Duke of Orléans in territory now ceded to Edward III. The other noblemen promised three major fortresses in the kingdom of France: Dun-le-Roy and Ainay-lès-Dun in Berry and la Roche-sur-Yon in Poitou. John II does not seem to have been consulted at all about these agreements. When the text was brought to him to be confirmed he was away from his capital at Villeneuve-lès-Avignon conferring with the Pope. The French King was evidently dismayed by what he read, and made a brief and unsuccessful attempt to negotiate something better. But on 13 March 1363 he confirmed the treaty as made. In May, after the French King's confirmation had been received in England, the princes were moved to Calais, where they were to be held until the security was delivered.[79]

It is not clear why the treaty of the *fleurs de lys* failed. But it is possible to guess. The most likely explanation is that John II's councillors were appalled by what he had agreed at Villeneuve and made difficulties about the delivery of the security. In mid-July an English officer, Thomas Driffield, left England with sixty men-at-arms to take possession of Dun, Ainay and la Roche-sur-Yon. The story of his mission is unknown. But it is plain that it failed. Then, early in September 1363, the Duke of Anjou, one of the signatories of the treaty, escaped. Anjou, an able and ambitious young man of twenty-four, had married for love (and without his father's consent) a daughter of Charles of Blois shortly before he had surrendered as a hostage two years before. He had borne his captivity particularly ill. Like the other royal princes he was allowed to absent himself from Calais on his parole for up to three days at a time. He made use of the privilege to visit the shrine of Notre-Dame de Boulogne and to see his wife at his father-in-law's castle of Guise. He decided not to return. It was an unusual event among those who were bound by the aristocratic code of honour. John II was furious. He summoned his errant son to a family conference at the town of Saint-Quentin. The prince, afraid that he would be arrested and forcibly returned to England, would only meet them in an open field some four miles from the walls. All their entreaties failed to move him. The treaty of the *fleurs de lys* was dead. Many in France must have been relieved.[80]

At the end of November 1363, the Estates-General of Languedoil met at Amiens. When the sessions ended, the King announced, to the surprise of those present, that he intended to go to England. His reasons were not given, and gave rise to much speculation. Some said that he intended to surrender himself as a hostage in place of his perjured son. Some said that he wanted to interest Edward III in a joint crusade to the Holy Land. Some said that he wanted to have a good time at Edward III's court. The truth was much simpler. John hoped that by dealing personally with the English King he would succeed where his ambassadors had failed and obtain a deferral of the instalments of the ransom and the release of the royal princes. His closest advisers urged him to think again, but he was adamant. So, on 3 January 1364, the King embarked at Boulogne with an escort of 200 mounted men. A few days later he was lodged in his old prison, the Savoy Palace in London. Shortly after his arrival the treasurers of the ransom brought him another 107,000 *écus*, at least part of which had been borrowed from moneylenders at short notice and usurious rates. It was all that they had been able to find to pay the ever mounting arrears of the ransom. It brought total payments to date to about half the sum promised at Brétigny.

Edward III appointed a committee of his Council to conduct the negotiations with the French King. According to one source, some progress was made. Another suggests that agreement was actually reached. John II's superb gesture almost worked. But at the beginning of March 1364, before anything had been signed, John fell ill and the discussions had to be suspended. His health had been giving rise to concern among his familiars for some time. The winter was bitterly cold, and the plague was still rife in London. Edward III visited him several times and provided all the comforts and medical attention that he could. But on the night of 8 April 1364 the King of France died.[81]

The English King had splendidly entertained John II while he was alive, and laid on the most magnificent obsequies for him now that the was dead. The body lay in state in St. Paul's Cathedral. A requiem mass was sung before a great crowd which included the King and Queen, their children and the whole court robed in mourning. The body was carried by night along the Old Kent Road to Dartford by the light of 4,000 torches. On 22 April 1364 the cortege reached Dover, where the body was loaded onto a ship and carried back to France.[82] Edward III's regret at his rival's death was certainly sincere. John had been a generous and attractive man. But Edward may have regretted the politician even more than the man. For John had also been an incompetent soldier and a bad diplomat. He had made great concessions under the pressure of captivity and had he lived might have made more. The abortive negotiations in London in January and February 1364 were the last occasion on which a durable peace might have been made on terms acceptable to the English King. John's successor was a very different and less tractable adversary.

Edward III was to live for another thirteen years, but he was no longer the man he had once been. He was fifty-two years old, an old man by the standards of those around him. He had always been an impulsive ruler, given to headstrong decisions, obdurately maintained.

But he had also listened to advice, and depended on trusted friends to restrain him. There were few of them left to perform this office now. Almost all the companions of his years of triumph were dead. They included all six of the earls created in the first year of the war, who had served as his principal commanders in the 1340s and 1350s. Of the great captains of his own generation only Walter Mauny, a reckless but much revered figure, survived. The Duke of Lancaster, by far the wisest and most influential counsellor of the King as well as his most skilful diplomat and commander, had been the ideal partner of Edward's ventures: judicious, cautious, realistic, always willing to take a longer view of England's interest. He had died in 1361. William Edington, whose stewardship of the government's finances had been the major factor in Edward's recent successes, retired two years later in 1363. These men had no successors, and their disappearance left a large gap in English policy-making. The rising stars at court were the King's second son, John of Gaunt, and his son-in-law, John Hastings Earl of Pembroke, neither of whom had the capacities of the great Duke of Lancaster, or even much experience of public affairs. Within the administration power was increasingly being drawn into the retentive hands of Edward's former private secretary William of Wyckham, who had become keeper of the privy seal in 1363. Wyckham was an ambitious ecclesiastical politician in the mould of John Stratford, who would shortly become the dominant figure in English politics. But although no one doubted his intelligence and energy, he was also unscrupulous and self-interested, lacking in judgment and largely uninterested in foreign affairs.

It is difficult to enter Edward's thoughts at any time of his life, and particularly difficult to do so in the 1360s. One reason for the increasingly erratic quality of his judgments was certainly his obsession with money. By 1364, England had shed many of the major financial burdens of the war years. The cost of maintaining the garrison at Calais had been reduced to about a fifth of its wartime level. The defence of Gascony had been abandoned to the Prince of Wales and that of Brittany to John de Montfort, each of whom was expected to conduct his affairs at his own expense. But the burden of Edward's war expenditure continued to weigh heavily in his accounts. The cost of the campaign of 1359–60, which had been financed very largely from the assignment of future customs revenues, was being paid throughout the following decade. And new burdens were replacing old ones. Edward embarked in the early 1360s on a prolonged and expensive attempt to pacify his long neglected possessions in Ireland. He had to meet most of the heavy initial expenses of the Prince's expedition to Gascony, and the cost of setting up households for his other sons, all of whom were now of age. Moreover, with the coming of peace, Edward had begun to spend more expansively on display. He erected grandiose and prodigiously costly buildings at Windsor. He presided over tremendous festivities there. He invested heavily in land, jewellery and prisoners of war.

The revenue situation was not healthy. There could be no question of parliamentary subsidies in peacetime. The customs grant was renewed in 1362, but at half the previous rate. This, combined with the disruption of the customs administration following on the transfer of the staple to Calais in 1363 and the slump of English wool exports during the 1360s, reduced the yield to about £40,000 a year, about a third of its best levels during the previous decade.[83] These difficulties meant that the collection of overdue ransoms tended to overshadow other issues of greater long-term importance. When John Barnet, Bishop of Worcester, became Treasurer in February 1363, he had a series of budgets and financial statements prepared. They were erratic and inconsistent, but had the common feature of reporting large structural deficits. In January 1365 the Chancellor explained to a group of influential peers that the government's ordinary revenues covered barely half its expenditure. It is fair to say that these statements were prepared at a particularly difficult period in the government's financial history and were not entirely candid about Edward's resources. But even allowing for this they demonstrated how far Edward had come to depend on ransom receipts, mainly from the King of France, but also from the King of Scotland, the duchy of Burgundy, Charles of Blois and a large number of prisoners captured at the battle of Poitiers whom Edward had bought from their captors.[84]

Edward's intransigence about ransoms, however, is only part of the explanation of his inability to make lasting peace with his enemies. The truth was that Edward III, who had never had the Duke of Lancaster's diplomatic imagination or his empathy with France, did not regard the treaty of Brétigny as the final peace which it purported to be. He was jealous about comparatively trivial slights, such as the harmless act of John II in presiding over a judicial duel between two knights of Saintonge.[85] His perennial suspicion of the good faith of the French led him to cling on to his claim to call himself King of France. His continual insecurity led him to look for allies in Castile in 1362 and Flanders in

1364, the first stages in a system of alliances intended to encircle and contain the traditional enemy. Few monuments were more evocative of this mood than the two great towers of the reconstructed fortress at Hadleigh, overlooking Canvey Island from the Essex coast and the huge circular fortress (now demolished) which Edward built on the opposite side of the Thames estuary at Queensborough on the Isle of Sheppey. They were the most costly and elaborate defensive works built in England since the castles of Edward's grandfather in Wales.[86] But what is remarkable about them is not simply their cost, but the fact that they were begun within a year of peace of Brétigny to defend the Thames and the Medway against a French invasion. Edward never really believed that he had won. And perhaps he was right. Perhaps it was simply John II who had lost. Perhaps England had simply exploited the momentary weakness of a richer and more populous nation to extract a peace which was unlikely to survive its inevitable recovery.

CHAPTER XI

Closing the Wounds 1364–1366

While John II feasted and died in a foreign capital, Charles of Navarre embarked upon another bloody bid for power in France, the fourth since he had first commanded the murder of Charles of Spain in 1354. Its failure, which was swift and complete, was followed within a few months by the conclusion of the Breton civil war and, over a period of years, by the gradual readmission of Brittany to the French political community. These two critical events marked the beginnings of France's recovery from the catastrophes of John's reign. Few at Westminster noticed Edward's opportunities passing.

The King of Navarre had returned to his Pyrenean kingdom in November 1361, carrying with him all the resentments accumulated in six years of violence and intrigue, sharpened by failure. Distance had not made him any fonder of his cousins, and political developments in France quickly brought him fresh grievances against them. The abrupt dismissal of his claim to the duchy of Burgundy, although hardly surprising, caused much bitterness in Pamplona. The claim was by no means absurd and would (if it had been accepted) have given Charles the position at the heart of French politics which he had always craved. His chief counsellor and confidant at this time was the famous Gascon paladin, Jean de Greilly, Captal de Buch, who had recently been betrothed to his sister. The Captal was not the man to reconcile Charles to his loss. He had little experience of politics and none of French politics. He had been continuously engaged in war since he had come of age, and peace had not dampened his appetite for fighting. Yet it was he who was sent to stake out his master's claim to Burgundy before the French King's Council at Vincennes and, later, before the Pope at Avignon. He was not listened to in either place. The Pope temporised, and John II was no more inclined to compromise on such a vital territorial issue than Charles was. On 6 September 1362 John secretly made his youngest and best-loved son Philip, Duke of Burgundy, ordering the grant to take effect on his death.[1]

By this time the King of Navarre had already resolved to follow his natural instinct for the violent solution. In May 1362 he was planning a rising of his supporters in Normandy. His agents were hiring mercenaries and buying weapons in Bordeaux under the nose of the Seneschal, Sir John Chandos. When the date came the commander of his troops (the Captal de Buch) was ill, and money had run out before the troops had even gathered. The enterprise failed so completely that the French Government was not even aware of it until several years later.[2] The King of Navarre's next plan was more ambitious, and too noisy to remain hidden. In the autumn of 1363 Charles proposed to form two armies in the following summer. One of them was to go by sea to Normandy. The other, under his brother Louis, was intended to join forces with the Gascons operating with the Great Company in central France and invade the duchy of Burgundy. The idea was to raise the enemies of the Valois in the imperial county of Burgundy east of the Saône and to advance on the duchy from both sides.

Navarre was a landlocked kingdom, and all the practicable routes into France passed through the duchy of Aquitaine. These plans therefore depended critically on the support, or at any rate the acquiescence, of the Prince of Wales. The Prince had no compelling political reasons to help the King of Navarre attack the French Crown. Yet there is a good deal of evidence that he did. In January 1364, in the middle of one of the coldest winters in living memory, Charles travelled over the Pyrenees to meet the Prince at Agen. Their discussions have not been recorded, but it is plain from the sequel that Charles was promised free passage for his men through the duchy as well as the right to hire shipping in its ports and mercenaries among the population. According to the French government's sources, the Prince also did his best to stop Gascons serving in the armies of the King of France. His motives are difficult to divine. Friendships are likely to have played a large part, as they generally did in the Prince's political decisions. The Prince had been a close friend of the Captal de Buch since the Poitiers campaign of 1356, and was reputed to have arranged his betrothal to Charles of Navarre's sister. Sir John Chandos, the Prince's closest adviser, was the lord of Saint-Sauveur in the heart of Charles' Norman domain. Some of his principal household officers, including his marshal Guichard d'Angle and his steward Sir Henry Hay, had been retained by Charles to promote his interests at the Prince's court. In a quarter century of war an instinctive antipathy to the interests of the French Crown had perhaps become habitual. In March 1364 the Captal de Buch marched freely through the duchy with an advance party of troops to secure the main towns and fortresses of Charles' domain in Normandy.[3]

In the absence of the King in London, the government of France was in the hands of the Dauphin. He could hardly fail to be aware of the preparations of the Navarrese. Several French noblemen reported that they had been approached by Charles' agents. Enguerrand d'Eudin had even been buttonholed on his way back through Navarre from a pilgrimage to Santiago. The Captal's men swaggered along the roads of Poitou and Touraine, making no secret of their intentions. Unfortunately for the King of Navarre, the government had about 1,000 men and a train of barges and siege artillery already gathered in Normandy for a renewed attack on the garrison of Rolleboise. They had arrived beneath the walls of the great fortress on the Seine on 25 March 1364, just as the Captal was approaching Tours. The nominal commander of these men was the son of the Count of Auxerre. But, as the crisis broke real authority passed to a much greater soldier, Bertrand du Guesclin, now on the threshold of his years of fame.[4]

There were no precedents for du Guesclin's remarkable career. Born in about 1323, the son of a minor nobleman of north-eastern Brittany, he had first made a name for himself by organising a guerrilla campaign against the English army besieging Rennes in the winter of 1356–7. His subsequent ascent was due mainly to the patronage of two men: Charles of Blois and King John's younger brother Philip, Duke of Orléans. In December 1357 du Guesclin had been appointed captain of the important border fortress of Pontorson. From here he threw himself into the war of raid and counter-raid in Brittany and Lower Normandy. Du Guesclin's unconventional background as a guerrilla fighter and a captain of small companies is the main explanation of his success as the commander of the French King's armies in the next reign. Like many of the great English and Gascon captains he was really an adventurer and a military contractor for whom war was a business venture as well as full time occupation. He was an outstanding strategist with a remarkable ability to execute rapid movements over great distances and to concentrate his forces at the critical point. His ability to maintain control on the field of battle over the amorphous and undisciplined armies of the period was legendary. In these and other respects du Guesclin was the only French captain of his generation equal to the great English generals of the period, Dagworth, Lancaster, Knolles, Chandos and the Prince of Wales. He stood head and shoulders above their mediocre successors in the 1370s.

Early in April 1364 the Dauphin and his advisers decided to use the army gathered outside the walls of Rolleboise to carry out a pre-emptive strike against the King of Navarre. Before dawn on 8 April, 120 men commanded by du Guesclin's cousin Olivier de Mauny disguised themselves as shepherds and seized the main gate of Mantes on the left bank of the Seine. The citadel of this place, which was the seat of the Navarrese administration in Normandy, was taken by assault before the garrison realised what was happening. Another force, eighty strong, seized the Navarrese fortress of Vetheuil, a few miles downstream on the opposite bank of the river. The important town of Meulan, which guarded the main road from Paris to Rouen, had more time to prepare its defences but fared little better. It held out for just three days. The citadel was brought down later with mines. All these places were sacked. The King of Navarre's officers who were found in them were treated as traitors. They were arrested, and some of them sent off for execution in Paris. By the middle of April 1364 the only substantial place still holding out for the King of Navarre in the Seine valley was the bridge-town of Vernon on the left bank of the Seine, which belonged to Charles of Navarre's sister the dowager Queen Blanche. On about 16 April 1364, as troops surrounded the town and sappers began to mine the outer defences, the Dauphin met Blanche at the head of the fortified bridge which joined the town to the right bank of the river. Blanche recognised defeat. She agreed to put royal captains into the main fortified places of her domain and to retire from the fray. The government now controlled all the crossings of the Seine from Paris to the sea and occupied the whole of the Norman domain of the King of Navarre apart from the town of Évreux, the Cotentin peninsula in the far west, and a few isolated castles.[5]

When the Captal de Buch reached the march of Normandy in the last few days of April he was met on the road by Charles of Navarre's Chancellor Robert de la Porte with news of the disaster. He went at once to Évreux and set up his headquarters in the citadel. There he proceeded to assemble an army from whatever elements were available: the garrison of Évreux; soldiers expelled from other Navarrese strongholds of the region, many of whom had drifted into the town; the nobility of the Cotentin; a few remnants of the old Navarrese party from Lower Normandy and Picardy. Much the most important contingents were furnished by the English and Navarrese companies operating in western France. John Jewel brought most of his company over from Rolleboise. The Bascon de Mareuil came with recruits from

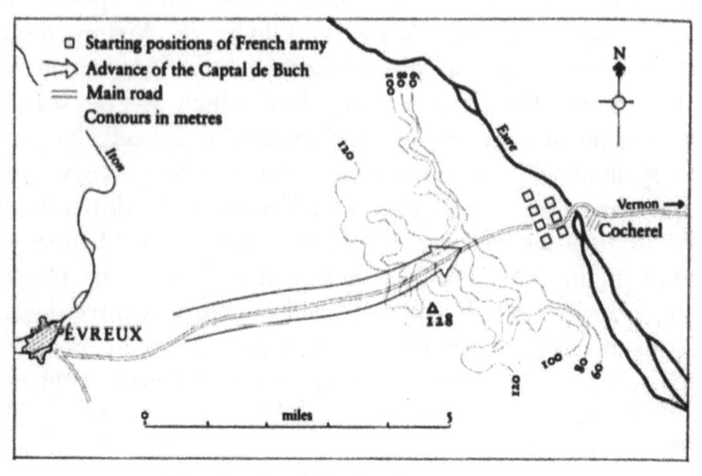

36 The battle of Cocherel, 16 May 1364

the garrisons of Lower Normandy and Maine. Messengers were sent to find help among the English companies in Brittany and the Gascons operating in Berry, Nivernais and Bourbonnais. The whole army was assembled at Évreux by the middle of May. Its numbers are not known, but there were probably between 1,500 and 2,000 men, virtually all cavalrymen. The formation of such an army in so short a time and from such disparate elements was almost as impressive a feat as the gathering of the companies before the battle of Brignais.[6]

The outcome, however, was very different. On 14 May 1364 the Captal de Buch led his army out of Évreux and marched east towards Vernon and Mantes. As they came over the brow of the hill which sloped down to the banks of the River Eure, they saw their path blocked by the government's forces, standing dismounted in prepared positions in the meadows in front of the river. Behind them was a narrow bridge. Close by lay the small hamlet of Cocherel. Du Guesclin had about 1,200 men under his command. In addition to the men who had been operating with him in the Seine valley there were contingents brought over from the service of Philip the Bold in Burgundy, including the Breton companies of the Archpriest; and several Gascon companies retained by the Crown. The Captal de Buch is said to have buried his head in his hands when a herald brought him the news of their presence on the other side: 'By St. Anthony's head, Gascon against Gascon!'

Fourteenth-century chivalry was a small world, in which the same men encountered each other time and again, by chance in the course of operations, by design at tournaments or on social or diplomatic occasions. Obligations accumulated which often crossed the line of battle. The lord of Albret sent his men to join Bertrand du Guesclin but stayed away himself, presumably because the Captal de Buch was his brother-in-law. The Archpriest also left his men to fight for du Guesclin without him. The Captal's host included men whom he had met before on the field of Brignais, and to whom he still owed money for his ransom: 'There are knights over there against whom I may not fight', he said.[7]

The presence of Gascons in both armies raised in an acute form one of the perennial practical problems of medieval armies: distinguishing friend from foe. Uniforms were only beginning to be worn, and were still largely confined to infantrymen. English infantry in the Welsh wars of late thirteenth century had worn white tunics known as 'blaunchecotes' and arm-bands with red cross of St. George. In the Scottish wars of 1330s and the first campaigns in France, uniforms had sometimes been provided for bodies of infantry of common origin, such as the Welsh or Londoners, or specialist corps such as miners or the artificers who constructed siege engines. From these small beginnings, the usage gradually came in of using uniform emblems to identify the members of a whole army. It is not clear when English soldiers began to wear red crosses of St. George on their chests and backs. Shortly after he set out on his raid across Languedoc in 1355, the Prince of Wales had it proclaimed that everyone in the army should wear the sign of St. George. When the Count of Armagnac summoned the men of Languedoc to resist him, he ordered them to wear prominently on their outer clothing the distinctive white cross which was eventually to become the uniform of all French armies. The practice was obviously not new, even then, but complete uniformity was not achieved in either country before the fifteenth century.

It is unlikely that any one in the largely cavalry armies confronting each other at Cocherel wore uniform. They depended on the traditional means by which knights had recognised each other on the battlefield: by the heraldic arms carried on their cloaks, banners and pennons. They were much more widely recognised than one would think. In the famous litigation between Scrope and Grosvenor in 1386 about the right to bear the arms *azur a bend or*, more than a hundred knights gave evidence that they remembered seeing these arms borne by Scropes in fights dating back to the Scottish wars of the 1330s. One of them, Sir Robert Laton, told the court that his father, who had 'long time travailed in foreign wars and in tournaments in time of peace' had been able to recite from memory the arms of all the kings, princes, dukes, earls, barons, knights and squires. When Sir Robert was young (this must have been in the 1350s) his father had made him write them down and learn them by heart. The problem of identifying those who had obscure arms or none at all, was resolved by the primitive but almost universal practice of yelling out war-cries in the mêlée: 'St. George' for England, 'Guienne' for Gascony; 'Montjoie' or 'St. Denis' for France; or, often, the name of the captain in command of the army. The leaders of the French army at Cocherel gave much thought to the war-cry that they would use. At the conference of its leaders which preceded the battle, some were for 'Nostre Dame! Aucoirre!' after the son of the Count of Auxerre, because he was the nominal commander and had 'the greatest income, lands and lineage of all those present'. When he modestly declined, it was agreed 'with one accord' that cry would be 'Nostre Dame! Claiekin', after the real commander, Bertrand du Guesclin. Professional experience was overtly placed before social rank.[8]

For the rest of 14 May and the whole of the following day the two armies stared at each other across the fields. Neither of them was willing to sacrifice the advantages of the defensive. But on the third day du Guesclin's men began to move. They sent their baggage back across the bridge and then retreated towards the river as if withdrawing. The movement was later said to have been a clever feint. But it was probably genuine. There could be no question of du Guesclin's army advancing uphill to attack a superior force. After two days standing in the meadows they were running short of food and were unable to hold their positions for any longer. When the Captal saw the enemy retreating, he resolved to force a battle before they could escape him. A group of cavalrymen was detached from the main army and sent ahead to outflank du Guesclin's army and block their access to the bridge over the Eure. The rest of the Captal's men began to advance slowly down the slope on horseback towards du Guesclin's lines. The two armies crashed into each other amid a cacophony trumpets, war-cries and screams of pain. In spite of the relatively small size of both forces, it was one of the bloodiest fights of the period. Newly made knights threw themselves into suicidal feats of valour. The Captal was seen in the thick of the battle laying about the enemy with an axe. Du Guesclin personally felled the Bascon de Mareuil. John Jewel was mortally wounded with two sword gashes in his side. For most of the time, the Captal's army, which was the larger and more experienced force, seemed to be prevailing. But at the critical moment du Guesclin committed his reserve, a large troop of Bretons standing dismounted at the rear of his line. They advanced around the flank of the Captal's army and turned the fortunes of the day. The Captal's men began to fall back. The retreat quickly became a rout. The Captal himself was left to fight with about fifty companions where his front line had been, until he was wounded and thrown to the ground. A Breton squire took him prisoner. Almost all of his followers were either killed or captured. Among the leaders of the army only Robert Scot escaped. Froissart's informant the Bascot de Mauléon, who fought in the battle, was captured by his own cousin.

News of the victory of Cocherel was brought to the new King on 18 May 1364 outside Reims. On the following day Charles V was anointed as King of France in the Cathedral of Reims with an elaboration of ceremony which masked the diminished stature of his realm. In this moment at least, as the official ordinal put it, the Kings of France 'shone out above all other kingdoms of the world'.[9]

Charles V of France was twenty-six years old at his accession, a handsome man but physically weak. An obscure illness which had struck him about five years before his accession had left him thin, pallid and sickly for the rest of his life, and his poor health necessarily affected his style of kingship. He travelled little, passing almost all his time in Paris and the Île de France. Unable to wield a weapon at thirty or ride a horse at forty, Charles could not cut the classic figure of a king. He made up for his physical disabilities by the strength of his personality, his formidable intelligence and his astute choice of subordinates, none of them strong points in his father or grandfather. Charles had learnt politics in the hard school of the civil war of the 1350s. He did not have his father's openness or chivalrous instincts, nor his respect of agreements which had served their purpose. 'You will find the new King a good friend and brother, a man to nourish your goodwill and stay within your peace,' the Count of Tancarville wrote to Edward III at the beginning of the new reign. But Charles had never been enthusiastic about the treaties with England. He had had almost no part in making them. There is little doubt that he nursed from the outset of his reign an ambition to avenge the defeats of Crécy and Poitiers and reverse the partition of France effected at Brétigny and Calais. Not long after Tancarville wrote his letter, Charles' principal secretary Gontier de Bagneux candidly discussed his master's ambitions in a confidential interview with the Count of Foix. The new King, the secretary said, intended to bring an end on his own terms to the vendetta between the Crown and the King of Navarre and the civil war in Brittany. Then as soon as he had brought the hostages ('or at the least the most important of them') back to France, he would turn on the English in alliance with the Scots to 'recover what had been lost and finally destroy them.' Charles was already considering the possibility of fomenting rebellions against the Prince of Wales' authority in Gascony. These exchanges, which the Count of Foix repeated to the King of Navarre in a Pyrenean garden as an English spy listened from behind a wall, may have gained something in the telling, as most spies' reports do. But as a statement of Charles' long-term plans it is substantially accurate and borne out by everything that he subsequently did.[10]

One of the first and most significant acts of the new reign was the investiture of the King's younger brother Philip with the duchy of Burgundy, in accordance with the dead King's wishes. The immediate effect of this act was to make the breach with the King of Navarre irreparable.[11] In other circumstances it might have been wise to leave the previous, ambiguous situation in being. But Charles V's act only recognised the reality on the ground. During the summer of 1364 there was a general assault on the surviving strongholds of the King of Navarre and on the independent garrisons in western France which were the main source of recruits for his armies. At the beginning of July 1364 Bertrand du Guesclin invaded the Cotentin with an army composed largely of the Bretons who had been with him at Cocherel. Within a few days they had captured the important town of Valognes, the largest of the peninsula and the hub of its road system. Not long afterwards, Barfleur, the main harbour after Cherbourg, fell to them. A second army, commanded by the Marshal of Normandy and the royal *bailli* of the Bessin conducted a successful sweep through Lower Normandy before laying siege to the great fortress of Échauffour, west of Argenton. This place, which was commanded by an English renegade clergyman, was believed to contain the largest Anglo-Navarrese garrison of the region. It eventually surrendered on terms after its walls had been wrecked by persistent mining and some 3,000 rocks had been hurled at them by siege engines. A third force, recruited mainly in Upper Normandy and Picardy, and commanded by two old veterans, Mouton de Blainville and the Admiral of France Baudrain de la Heuse, began to operate simultaneously in the valley of the Eure. On 26 July 1364 these men laid siege to the Navarrese capital at Évreux. Yet another army, probably larger than any of them, was collected at Vernon on the Seine by Jean de Boucicaut and the young Duke of Burgundy. This group, comprising men from the Île de France, Paris and Burgundy, with 200 Gascon retainers of the lords of Albret and Pommiers, carried out a rapid sweep of the *routier* garrisons blocking the roads between Paris and the Loire. These were the largest co-ordinated military operations conducted by the French Crown since 1356.[12]

The key to the government's new self-confidence was money, ironically the last legacy of the feckless old King John. The aids and the *gabelle du sel* had been collected every year throughout the provinces of Languedoil ever since John II had first imposed them by decree in December 1360. Although they were intended to pay the ransom of Brétigny and were only juridically justifiable on that basis, they provided a flow of cash much of which was in practice diverted to war expenditure either at source by the communities which collected them or by the royal treasurers in Paris. An even more important source of revenue became available as a result of the decisions of the Estates-General held at Amiens in November 1363, John II's last important political act before he left for England. The Estates introduced an additional tax which was overtly designed to fund war expenditure. Called, rather misleading, a *fouage*, it was in fact a graduated direct tax designed to yield an average of three francs per hearth per year: 'less than a penny a day' according to the text of ordinance. The tax, which was intended to finance a standing army of 6,000 men, was to run indefinitely for as long as it should be required. Ultimately it became a permanent tax, the precursor of the *tailles* which were to be the mainstay of the Crown's finances until the Revolution. Unlike the aids and other indirect taxes, which were levied on merchandise passing through market towns, the *fouage* was collected in rural and urban parishes alike. No one escaped except for very limited categories of the religious and indigent. Moreover, in another break with tradition, the *fouage* was voted by the Estates-General on their own authority, so as to bind their constituents. It was not, as grants of taxes had traditionally been, merely the prelude to a wearing round of negotiations in which the Crown lost much of what it had been promised.

These measures were accompanied by a radical reorganisation of the machinery of collection. The government adopted the system of local *élus* which had originally been imposed on the Crown by the Estates-General after the great national crises of 1346 and 1356 in order to take control of tax raising out of the hands of royal officials. The *élus* were commissioners elected for each diocese. They supervised the local assessors who fixed the contributions in the parishes and the tax farmers who bid for the right to collect them. They were made answerable to the Treasurers-general in Paris. The quality of the system was variable, but it was a great improvement on anything that had gone before. Much later, Charles V complained that the yield of the *fouage* had been disappointing and sufficed to pay less than a quarter of the proposed standing army. The disappearance of almost all the financial records of the Crown for this period makes it difficult to test this assertion, but it is likely to have been an exaggeration. There is evidence that very large sums were spent on warfare between 1364 and 1369 which were not raised by borrowing or coinage manipulation, the two great fallbacks of previous reigns. Indeed the combined revenues generated by the aids, the *gabelle* and the *fouage* were enough to enable the King to start accumulating a surplus for emergencies.[13]

Undeterred by the loss of most of his Norman domain, the massacre of his allies at Cocherel and the constraints of poverty and distance, Charles of Navarre pressed on with his quixotic projects for re-invading Normandy and conquering Burgundy from the opposite extremity of France. The long-awaited counter-attack began in the west in August 1364. In the first few days of the month a small company of men surprised Moulineaux, the great twelfth-century fortress of Richard Coeur-de-Lion which dominated the left bank of the Seine south of Rouen. The assailants were Gascons in Charles' service, commanded by a Béarnais adventurer called Pierre de Sault. They came over the walls in a thick morning mist while the garrison commander was away at the siege of Évreux. The gates had fallen by the time that the alarm went up. These men must already have been in Normandy. The small expeditionary army with which Charles intended to reinforce its strength there was on its way from Navarre. Some 430 men, mostly Navarrese, had embarked at Bayonne at the end of July, under the command of a Navarrese nobleman, Rodrigo de Uriz, and the Hainaulter Eustache d'Aubricourt, another high-born adventurer in the mould of the Captal du Buch who had found it hard to adapt to the end of the war. Eustache had recently served with English armies in Ireland, and married a niece of the English Queen. They turned a blind eye to what he was doing.[14]

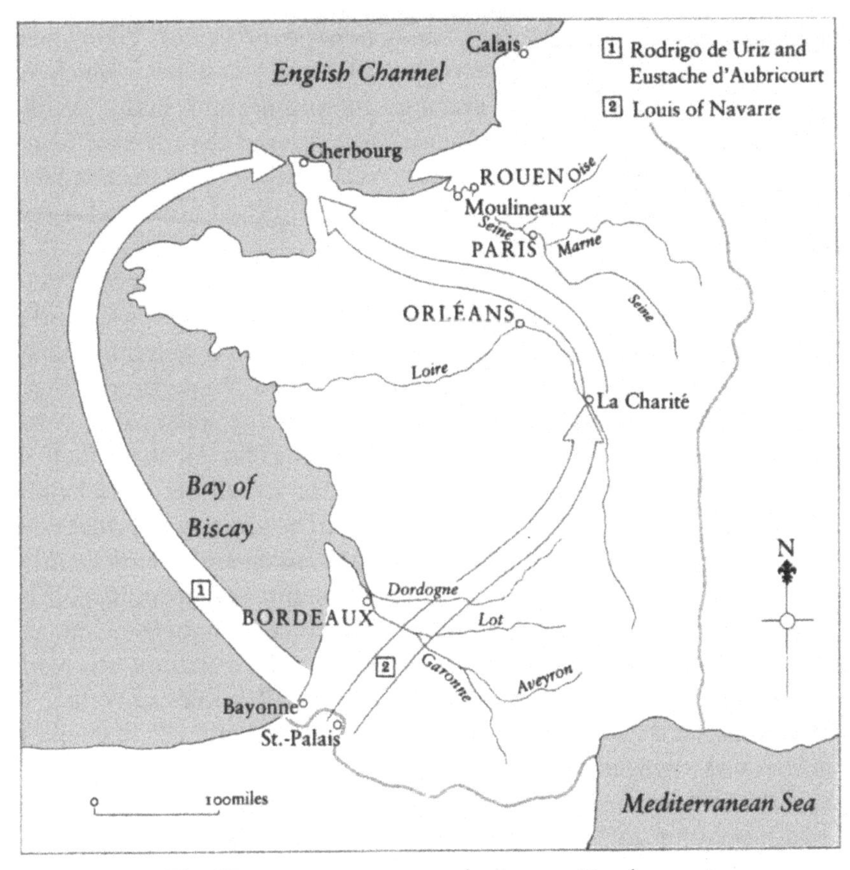

37 The Navarrese counter-attack, August–October 1364

The second arm of the Navarrese pincer was the more lavishly provided expeditionary force of Louis of Navarre. This included several hundred Navarrese. But the bulk of its strength was supplied by the captains of the Great Company. In April 1364, a delegation of four of the principal captains operating in Languedoc and Auvergne had visited the castle of Orthez in the county of Foix to bargain with Charles' representatives under the auspices of Gaston Phoebus. They promised to bring their men to the foothills of the Pyrenees in the summer to join forces with Louis. They received 20,000 florins (about £2,800) in fees and advances. Shortly after this, in May, another deal was made with Séguin de Badefol, who had recently been bought out of Brioude and was looking for fresh employment. His allotted role appears to have been to operate in conjunction with Louis' army once it reached

Burgundy. The King of Navarre had high hopes of Séguin's companies, and made him extravagant promises of money and land which he would later regret. The Navarrese contingent and many of the companies gathered in early August 1364 around the town of Saint-Palais on the march of Béarn. Reports reaching the French commanders in Languedoc put its strength at about 800 men-at-arms and 2,000 infantry.

The French reckoned that Louis of Navarre would try to break out through the valley of the Aveyron. They had concentrated a powerful army there to stop him: 800 cavalry and some 6,000 infantry. But Louis escaped them. He passed swiftly north through the territory of the Prince of Wales, entering France instead through the upper valley of the Dordogne. By 22 August 1364 he was at Aurillac on the march of Auvergne heading north. By early September it had become obvious that he was making for la Charité-sur-Loire. The great stone bridge over the Loire was still under the control of the Gascon and Breton *routiers* who had occupied the town in the previous autumn. From here, if he could reach it, Louis' army would be able to cross unopposed into the Nivernais and the valley of the Yonne. A determined attempt was made to stop him reaching it. There were two small armies operating in Normandy at the beginning of September 1364: Mouton de Blainville's, which was engaged in the siege of Évreux; and a rather larger force commanded by the Duke of Burgundy and Marshal Boucicaut, which had just begun to besiege Moulineaux. On 12 September 1364 both operations were abruptly ended and the two groups joined forces to march to la Charité. But Louis of Navarre got there first. He reached the bridge on 23 September, while Philip of Burgundy was still 18 miles off. The Duke tried to bottle up the Navarrese in la Charité. But it was a hopeless endeavour. His army had outrun its supply train on the march, and the whole region around la Charité had been stripped of supplies by the enemy. Philip lost 1,000 horses to starvation within a few days of his arrival. He was able to invest the town only from the right bank of the river, while the garrison freely drew their supplies across the bridge from the provinces of the left bank. Early in October, Philip abandoned the attempt and withdrew.[15]

While these events unfolded in the valley of the Loire, the plans of all the major protagonists were disturbed by the swift and unexpected conclusion of the twenty-three-year civil war in Brittany. Charles of Blois' attempt to capture the English-controlled fortress of Bécherel had ended in July of the previous year with a tense confrontation and an untidy agreement in the plain north of the walls. The terms have not survived, but it is clear from the subsequent recriminations what they were. The two claimants had agreed to partition the duchy of Brittany between them. It seems that John de Montfort was to have the south and west including the city of Nantes, and Charles of Blois the north-east. As to the title and peerage of Brittany, they agreed to submit their claims to the binding decision of the Kings of England and France. The rivals swore to comply with these terms and exchanged hostages to secure the bargain. It must be doubtful whether the scheme could ever have worked, but in the event it was never tested. Charles of Blois repudiated it almost at once. The circumstances are obscure. There is some evidence that Charles' wife Jeanne de Penthièvre, in whose right he claimed the duchy, refused to ratify it. The whole affair lost him a good deal of support among the Breton nobility, who were weary of war and whose leaders had been among the makers of the treaty and the chief hostages for its performance. They found it hard to sympathise with Charles of Blois' stiff-necked defence of a cause which had little chance of prevailing now that he had been all but abandoned by the Crown while his rival was still supported by several hundred English soldiers and officials. Some of them may have found John de Montfort, an attractive man unburdened by the bitterness of a generation of civil war, the more promising candidate. It was probably these men who pushed Charles into submitting his claim to the Prince of Wales, a most unwelcome arbitrator who was closely connected with Charles' rival. On 24 February 1364, the two claimants appeared before the Prince in the hall of the palace of Poitiers. All the great men of the Prince's court were there, together with the principal officers of the duchy of Aquitaine and the leading English captains of Brittany. The parties and their representatives argued their cases. The Prince reserved his judgment. He had still not pronounced when the truce between the rivals expired in April and both of them threw themselves into a fresh war.[16]

In about July 1364 John de Montfort laid siege to Auray, a small port on the west shore of the Gulf of Morbihan, which was one of the few places held by Charles of Blois on the south coast of the Breton peninsula. Charles resolved to relieve the place. He could probably have done nothing less if his cause were to remain alive. Both sides called on their natural allies engaged in the civil wars of France. Charles summoned help from the Breton companies of Bertrand du Guesclin and Olivier de Mauny, which were still operating against the surviving strongholds of the King of Navarre in the Cotentin. Some of the leading officers in royal service in Normandy came with them. By September 1364 he had raised between 3,000 and 4,000 men. Charles V gave them no encouragement. Indeed he deprived Bertrand du Guesclin of his captaincy in Normandy and the revenues that went with it as soon as he heard of his departure for Brittany. The attitude of the English was much the same: neutrality at the highest level, complicity among the men on the ground. John de Montfort raised about 2,000 men, mainly from the English companies in Brittany, including those of Knolles, Calveley, Hewitt and Latimer. Sir John Chandos came north from Gascony with about 200 English men-at-arms and a force of archers. At the end of 1364 John de Montfort's agents succeeded in making contact with Louis of Navarre on his march through central France. Eustache d'Aubricourt, who had recently landed at Cherbourg, hurried to Auray with a largely Navarrese army drawn from the garrisons of the Cotentin and from the expeditionary force that he had brought with him.[17]

Charles of Blois came within sight of the walls of Auray on 29 September 1364. The decisive battle occurred on the same day. On the Anglo-Breton side Sir John Chandos took the command. He drew up his army in a strong position on rising ground behind a river, a short distance north of the town. He and Sir Matthew Gournay stationed themselves on the right with their men-at-arms and most of the archers. Knolles commanded the left and John de Montfort the centre. There was much ill-feeling within the English camp about the command of the reserve, which Chandos wished to give to Sir Hugh Calveley. Calveley was not at all pleased to be denied a place of honour in the front line, and took up his allotted place with ill grace. Charles of Blois arranged his own men in the same fashion. There were three front-line divisions, commanded by Charles himself, Bertrand du Guesclin and Jean de Chalon, son of the Count of Auxerre, with a reserve behind. Both sides dismounted and sent their horses to the rear. Before battle was joined, there was short interval for negotiations. According to contemporary reports John de Montfort was willing to make large concessions, which the leading Breton noblemen on the other side were inclined to accept. But the English wanted to fight. They threatened at one point to kill Charles of Blois' negotiators if they returned with yet another counter-proposal. There were those on Charles' side, mainly the companions of du Guesclin, who took the same view. 'I will restore the duchy to you, clear of all these wretches,' du Guesclin is said to have told Charles. Almost immediately, a large body of Bretons deserted from his own division and marched away. Minutes later the two armies clashed. The Anglo-Breton army encountered Jean de Chalon's division first. At an early stage Chalon lost an eye and was taken prisoner. His followers were driven into the flank of du Guesclin's division, which was in the process of trying to reform itself. Seeing that things were going ill for them, the Bretons in Charles of Blois' division followed the example of their compatriots and began to desert. Charles and his companions were left isolated and exposed. Chandos and John de Montfort immediately directed the force of the assault against them. They charged them on foot with their men. Charles' standard was seen to waiver above the crowd and fall to the ground. The rest of his army turned and fled. Calveley came in with the reserve in the closing moments of the battle and completed the rout.

The English archers, although present in force, made almost no contribution to the outcome of the battle. Arrow fire had never been quite as effective against men on foot as it was against cavalrymen, whose horses were unarmoured and easily frightened. And the French were becoming more practised at fighting on foot, and better at protecting themselves. Du Guesclin crammed his heavily padded men into tight lines behind a roof of shields held aloft. According to Froissart the archers, having achieved nothing with their bows, threw them away and joined the mêlée. The casualties on the winning side were light, just seven men-at-arms and an uncertain number of archers and sergeants, another tribute to the quality of modern armour. As always, the losers suffered appalling losses, gashed by swords and axes, crushed and suffocated as they lay wounded in the front line by men forcing themselves forward from behind. The greatest slaughter occurred in the rout at the end. Charles of Blois and nearly 800 of his army were left dead on the field. Some 1,500 were captured, including Bertrand du Guesclin, his brother Pierre, and his cousin Olivier de Mauny, as well as many of the leading noblemen of eastern Brittany. Du Guesclin, who was claimed by Sir John Chandos, fetched 100,000 francs (about £20,000) in ransom money. The more mundane prisoners were so numerous that even very minor captains in the victorious army made small fortunes. Froissart's informant, the Bascot de Mauléon, made 2,000 francs from his captives, one of the best paid days he had ever had. In a memorable, perhaps apocryphal passage of his work, a Norman chronicler described how the English and Breton men-at-arms stuck their pennons and lances in a hedge after the battle and took off their armour to cool down, while a trumpeter began to play his instrument and the heralds went through the field identifying the bodies of the dead. When they returned to report that they had found the corpse of Charles of Blois, Chandos left the group to see for himself. He had du Guesclin taken out of the crowd of prisoners and brought before him. Pointing to where Charles' body lay, Chandos told him that it would have been better for him never to have been born than to have been responsible for the death of so many of his own followers. Then, turning to the young John de Montfort, who was standing among the onlookers, Chandos said to du Guesclin: 'Sir! Behold this "wretch" de Montfort. By your act is he today made Duke of Brittany'.[18]

Charles of Blois' cause collapsed as soon as the news of his death was out. His body was carried in state to Guingamp to be buried in the Franciscan convent. His sons were prisoners in England. His widow fled to the protection of her son-in-law the Duke of Anjou at Angers. His partisans submitted to the victor in droves. Apart from the great cities of Nantes and Rennes, with their dense populations and powerful walls, the only supporters of Charles of Blois who put up any serious resistance were the garrison of Quimper in the south-east of the peninsula. This place withstood a siege of several weeks in October and November 1364, until the townsmen refused to carry on the fight any longer and forced the garrison to surrender.[19]

Edward III was visibly delighted when the news of the battle was brought to him. He made John de Montfort's messenger a herald on the spot.[20] But the truth was that having vanquished his rival John would have less need of the English and, over the years to come, Edward's influence in the affairs of Brittany tended to decline. On the morrow of the battle of Auray, John sent two messengers to Charles V to declare his loyalty to the Crown and to offer his homage for the duchy. There were those in the French King's Council who would have rejected him even now. Charles himself was more realistic. He sent a conciliatory message to the victor, and broked a settlement of the war which was very favourable to him. The last act of the Breton civil war occurred on 12 April 1365 in the small collegiate church of St. Aubin at Guérande. There, the representatives of Jeanne de Penthièvre acknowledged John as Duke. In return she was allowed to keep her personal domain in northern Brittany and the viscounty of Limoges. A few days after the treaty of Guérande, John Montfort entered Nantes.[21]

The battle of Auray gave a brief fillip to the cause of the King of Navarre. It deprived Charles V of most of his troops in the Cotentin and

Lower Normandy, as well as of his principal captains, who were either dead or prisoners. It also released the English companies in Brittany to serve Charles' cause elsewhere. Louis of Navarre abandoned his plans to invade Burgundy as soon as he heard the news. Instead, he marched swiftly across the undefended plains of the Gâtinais and the Beauce into Normandy and arrived in the Cotentin in mid-October. Eustache d'Aubricourt came up from the Breton march to join him, bringing his own Navarrese troops and many of the English captains who had fought at Auray. Between them, they reconquered Valognes and Barfleur from the lieutenants of Bertrand du Guesclin and recovered control of the peninsula for the King of Navarre.

In eastern France the cause of Charles of Navarre was left to Séguin de Badefol and the Gascons of the Great Company, hirelings who were much less committed to his cause than the English captains in Brittany. Séguin did no more for Charles of Navarre than he would have done in any event for himself. He joined forces with Louis Rabaud and his partner 'Limousin'. In the earlier hours of 1 November 1364 they captured Anse by escalade. Anse was a small walled town in an important position at the confluence of the Saône and the Azergue, 15 miles north of Lyon, from which it was possible to control the road and river communications of much of the region. Its walls had given concern to local officials for several years. They were cluttered inside and out with extraneous constructions, some of which penetrated their entire thickness. Nothing had been done to avert disaster. Once inside the town, Séguin proclaimed himself captain of the place for the King of Navarre. For the next nine months Anse was an even greater scourge than Brioude had been. It became the centre of a network of some fifty occupied castles in the Maçonnais, Forez, Velay and southern Burgundy, whose garrisons co-ordinated their operations over a vast area of eastern France. Small groups penetrated even further afield. One of them rescued Bertucat d'Albret's castle of Blot in Auvergne, which was under siege by troops of the Duke of Berry. Others raided south as far as the papal state and northern Provence. Lyon was in a state of almost continuous siege. Several hundred villages and small towns were pillaged. The roads of the region became impassable. Its trade dried up. In January 1365 Pope Urban V excommunicated Séguin de Badefol and his accomplices. He commanded them to surrender Anse within two weeks, and offered the indulgences of the crusade to anyone who would turn them out.[22]

The operations of garrisons like Anse and la Charité inevitably brought diminishing returns over time. None of them did any good to the King of Navarre. The companies at la Charité had exhausted the region by March 1365, and accepted 25,000 gold francs for its surrender. In the west, Louis of Navarre achieved nothing of value after the recapture of Valognes and Barfleur, in the end the only trophies of his remarkable enterprise. But his brother was nothing if not persistent. In February 1365 Charles of Navarre appointed a new lieutenant in France, none other than the lord of Albret who had furnished men to fight against him at Cocherel. Albret's motive was straightforward enough. His fortune was burdened by the heavy ransoms which he and his kinsmen and retainers owed to the Count of Foix. The possibilities of profitable war service elsewhere were diminishing. He needed the money. Charles offered him a great deal of money: 60,000 florins (about £8,500), part of it secured by the immediate delivery of a large quantity of jewellery. For this Albret agreed to take over the leadership of the companies in central and eastern France and to carry on the war in his name. A Navarrese clerk in the government offices in Bordeaux sent Charles a list of other Gascon captains who might be for hire at rates like these. But it was already clear that the only realistic option was to negotiate with the King of France. Preliminary soundings had already been made by the Captal de Buch, who had been a prisoner in Meaux and Paris ever since the battle of Cocherel, and by the two dowager queens who had so often performed this office in the past. Early in March 1365 they agreed terms with Charles V's ministers which they were willing to recommend to the distant conspirator. A draft treaty was carried to Pamplona in the spring of 1365 by the Captal himself and Ramiro de Arellano, the commander of the Navarrese troops in France. They were able to give their master a first-hand account of the hopelessness of his position.

After several weeks of uncertainty the King of Navarre submitted at the beginning of May 1365. It cannot have been easy for this proud and obstinate man to accept what amounted to a dignified surrender. There was to be a general amnesty for his supporters in France, with a handful of exceptions such as Robert le Coq, who were beyond forgiveness. The grim remains of Navarrese partisans executed for treason, whose heads still stood on pikes above the gates of various Norman towns, were to be taken down and restored to their families. Prisoners, including the Captal, were to be mutually released without ransom. The territorial provisions were humiliating. Charles V kept all the valuable cities which his troops had taken in April 1364, as well as the county of Longueville, which had been granted to Bertrand du Guesclin. The citadel of Meulan, which commanded the western approach to Paris, was to be razed to the ground. In compensation Charles of Navarre received the valuable but remote city of Montpellier in Bas-Languedoc. As for Charles' claims to Burgundy, they were to be submitted to the binding arbitration of the Pope, together with miscellaneous financial claims which Charles had accumulated over the years. Even these limited concessions were never made in reality. Charles of Navarre never required real control of Montpellier. The Pope never pronounced on his claim to Burgundy. It was the end of his fifteen-year struggle to create a large consolidated appanage for his line in the political heart of France.[23]

With the sudden termination of two French civil wars and the appearance of fresh crowds of displaced soldiers on the roads, the search for some way of disarming the *routiers* assumed fresh urgency. The first efforts in this direction were the work of the Papacy. Urban V, who had been elected to the papal throne in 1362, was the most austere of the Avignon popes after the formidable Benedict XII, and perhaps the most spiritual of all: a man of meticulous intellect and ordered ways who prayed, walked in his garden and did every act of his daily round at set times. Urban, however, was no strategist. And, while he expressed a becoming concern about the activities of the companies everywhere, his vision was limited by the immediate concerns of the papal court at Avignon. His object was to restore peace in the valleys of Rhone and the Saône on which the papal administration depended for its contacts with northern Europe and on which the papal city depended for most of its supplies. Anse mattered much more to him than Rolleboise or Mouli-neaux.

Urban's efforts were uniformly unsuccessful. The first of a succession of projects for exporting the problem elsewhere involved sending the *routiers* overland through Germany and south-eastern Europe to fight for the Byzantine Emperor John V Paleologus against the Turks. The origins of this scheme are exceptionally obscure, but the Pope, the German Emperor and the King of France all appear to have taken it seriously for a time and may even have contributed funds. The task of organising it was confided to the hard-headed Arnaud de Cervole. It is not clear how seriously he took it. But he was busy recruiting crusaders throughout the spring and early summer of 1365.[24] There were many obstacles. The major problem was to persuade the various confederations of *routiers* operating in Auvergne and the Lyonnais to join the crusade, without which the plan was hardly worth the effort. In the middle of July 1365, after several months of negotiation, terms were eventually agreed between a commission of cardinals and Séguin de Badefol, the acknowledged leader of the companies in the Rhone and Saône valleys. The essence of it was that Séguin and his associates would gather their entire strength at Anse. They would then surrender the place and withdraw in a body from France in return for a papal absolution and 40,000 florins. At about the same time a very similar deal was struck with the major Gascon companies still operating in Auvergne under the loose command of Bertucat d'Albret. In August 1365 Bertucat agreed to surrender Blot, his most significant fortress in Auvergne. He then withdrew to join the great gathering of the companies at Anse. Unfortunately, it took much longer than anyone had anticipated to raise the money. The three seneschalsies of Languedoc refused to contribute a penny on the revealing ground that Anse was 'a place in French-speaking country which has nothing to do with Languedoc'. In the end the money had to be found by the city and cathedral chapter of Lyon and by the provinces of the Saône. They borrowed most of it from the Pope and from various magnates and moneylenders. It was not until 11 September 1365 that Anse finally surrendered in the presence of a great army recruited throughout eastern France. Two days later the horde of *routiers* marched away.[25]

By this time, Arnaud de Cervole's crusading venture had collapsed. Most of his followers had probably never intended to go any further than the rich provinces of the imperial border. In the event their crusading zeal was never tested, for all the German cities of the region closed their gates, and the Archpriest's horde was unable to cross the Rhine or the Moselle. When they ran out of booty and food, the project was abandoned. By the early autumn they were streaming back towards their old hunting grounds in Burgundy. The only result of Urban V's well-intentioned efforts had been to create an exceptionally large and dangerous concentration of brigands in the Saône valley. By October 1365 the remnants of the Archpriest's army were spread along the east bank of the river in the county of Burgundy, where they did appalling damage to the domains of Margaret of Artois but were successfully prevented from re-entering France. The companies of Anse and Auvergne were quartered in the Lyonnais on the west bank of the Saône, carefully segregated from them.[26]

To resolve this unstable situation, a new plan was devised which was hardly more realistic than the old. All the companies on both sides of the river were now to be brought together under the command of the Count of Savoy, Amadeus VI. He proposed to lead them across the Alpine passes to Italy, where they would embark for the east on ships provided by the Venetians and the Genoese. The Pope and the French authorities evidently believed that the companies had agreed to this. But it soon became clear that the only person who had agreed was the Archpriest himself. He had the greatest difficulty in persuading the men assembled on the east bank to go with him. As for the companies in the Lyonnais, some stayed where they were, while others resumed their business. Bertucat d'Albret formed a new company of 160 men-at-arms and 200 foot-soldiers from the garrison of Anse and marched off north into Burgundy. There he joined up with some of the Gascon companies which had fought with Louis of Navarre in the previous year, and together they invaded the Chalonnais.[27] Séguin de Badefol, always a scrupulous observer of his contracts, had nothing to do with this enterprise. He withdrew to the Pyrenees to settle his accounts with the King of Navarre. Charles was not pleased to see him. He was truculent and resentful of the high price which he had promised Séguin for services that had brought him in the end very little value. So when the mercenary became too pressing, he received him in his private room in the castle of Falcès and fed him a crystallised pear laced with poison. After six days of agony the terrible man died.[28]

The origins of the next scheme to export the companies from France lay in the conspiratorial politics of the kingdom of Aragon and in the budding ambitions of France in the Iberian peninsula. In July 1364 Bernat de Cabrera, the disgraced chief minister of the Peter IV of Aragon, had been beheaded in the market-place of Sarragossa. The main charges against Cabrera at his brief travesty of a trial had been that he had first provoked and then mishandled the disastrous war with Castile, which had now been in progress almost continuously for eight years. The real reason for his fall was his attempt to bring it to an end. With much of western Aragon occupied and Castilian troops within sight of Valencia, Cabrera had finally realised that the war was unaffordable financially and unwinnable militarily. He sued for peace on the best terms that he could obtain. These terms proved so unpalatable even to the war-weary Aragonese that the minister's many enemies persuaded Peter IV not to ratify them, and seized the opportunity to destroy the man who had proposed them. The leading figure in the cabal which procured Cabrera's downfall was the King's chamberlain Francisco de Perellós, who succeeded him as Peter's chief councillor. Perellós was a native of Roussillon, then a salient of the Catalan kingdom on the French side of the Pyrenees. He was the man who had commanded the galley fleet sent (too late) to the assistance of France in the year of Poitiers. He it was who had provoked the Castilian war by attacking shipping in the Castilian port of Sanlúcar de Barrameda on the way. Perellós was committed, both by his past actions and by the circumstances of his rise to power, to the prosecution of the war.

Perellós was perceptive enough to see that without external assistance the war was likely to end in yet worse humiliations for the Aragonese. Peter IV had paid for it by selling assets of the Crown, by plundering those of the Aragonese Church, and from grudging and irregular grants from the Cortes of the three kingdoms that made up his Crown. These sources had not been enough even while they lasted. His main problem was a dire shortage of heavy cavalry, the arm in which Castile was strongest. In 1364 the utmost that Catalonia, the richest of his domains, could grant him was enough to pay for just 1,500 cavalry. Altogether, it is unlikely that he ever raised a cavalry army of more than 3,000 and then only for a short period. Many of these were not even his own subjects but disaffected Castilians recruited by Henry of Trastámara.[29] Aragon badly needed an ally. For Perellós there could be no question of any ally but France. France had strategic interests which could be harnessed to Aragon's own: in containing the new principality of Aquitaine from the south and in maintaining pressure on the kingdom of Navarre. This suited Perellós' own instincts, which were strongly francophile. He had excellent contacts at Charles V's court. Shortly after Perellós' rise to power the French King appointed him as one of his chamberlains, and thereafter treated him as if he were his own agent in Barcelona rather than Peter IV's in France. This oddly ambivalent status persisted right up to 1368 when Perellós finally left his native country, established his home in Paris and became Admiral of France.[30]

On the French side the momentum behind the government's interventions in Spain came mainly from Charles V's brother Louis, Duke of Anjou, who had been appointed as Charles' Lieutenant in Languedoc in November 1364. Louis of Anjou was a good foil for the sinuous Perellós. Then twenty-five years old, he was a gifted man, an astute politician and the only one of John II's sons to achieve any repute as a soldier. He was also intensely ambitious. He longed to cut a great figure, to rule a kingdom or to play a role of his own in shaping the fortunes of

France, to amass riches beyond anything that his small appanage in the lower Loire could furnish. For this reason he aroused widespread suspicion and distrust, even within his own family. 'His brilliant qualities, which might have won him immortal renown, were tarnished by his unbounded greed', a measured obituarist wrote after his death. Even the usually sycophantic Christine de Pisan thought so. He was always hungry for dominions and money, she wrote. Within the French political community Louis of Anjou was one of the most persistent and resourceful enemies of the settlement of 1360 with England. He had borne with extreme resentment his time as a hostage in England. Edward III never allowed him to forget the circumstances of his escape. 'A shame on his honour and on the reputation of his whole family', was what the English King had said about him in appealing to the peerage of France. Perhaps for this reason there was always an element of personal venom in his dealings with the English which was largely absent from his more calculating brother. Yet Charles V allowed Louis his head. One of the main reasons for sending the Duke of Anjou to Languedoc was to work for the long-term destruction of the principality of Aquitaine. Louis would make a greater figure by doing that, Charles told him, than by persistently nagging the King for largesse. In Languedoc, Louis would enjoy the status of royalty and some of its authority while remaining too far from Paris for his breaches of the treaty to engage the King's responsibility.[31]

In the winter of 1364–5 Francisco de Perellós had a number of informal meetings with Louis of Anjou in southern France. Some of these were attended by Charles V's confidential secretary Gontier de Bagneux. This man was certainly privy to Charles' ambition to expel the English from south-western France. It is hardly conceivable that it was not discussed. What is known is that when Perellós returned to France in February 1365 for further talks at Toulouse, his instructions, which he must have had a large part in drafting, envisaged an alliance of France and Aragon against Castile. The bait was that after defeating Pedro I the two powers would turn together against Navarre and the English principality of Aquitaine. This idea is unlikely to have sprung unprompted into the King of Aragon's thoughts. It has all the marks of Louis of Anjou's mind, sedulously flattered and encouraged by Perellós himself. On this occasion, nothing came of it, probably because the cautious Charles V regarded it as premature. The treaty which was made between Perellós and the Duke of Anjou on 9 March 1365 was directed against Navarre alone. It therefore almost immediately became redundant when Charles V was reconciled with the King of Navarre a few weeks later.[32]

Perellós quickly found another justification for French intervention in Spain. In the spring of 1365 he was at Avignon canvassing a new plan to recruit the companies to a great army which would be sent into Spain, ostensibly to fight a crusade against the shrunken remnant of the Moorish kingdom of Granada in the southern extremity of the peninsula. Some of the promoters of this project may genuinely have intended to fight the Moors, once they had achieved their main purpose.[33] But no one was deceived about what their main purpose was: the conquest of the Christian kingdom of Castile on behalf of the King of Aragon and the Castilian pretender Henry of Trastámara. The pretence was probably essential if the Church was to contribute to the cost, and indeed if recruits were to be found among the subjects of Edward III and the Prince of Wales who were at least nominally allies of Castile. The Pope was wholly won over. His agents were despatched to Bordeaux to interest the Prince of Wales and prominent Gascon noblemen. Louis of Anjou, the Dukes of Berry and Bourbon and several ambassadors of the King of France were all at Avignon in May for the reception of the Emperor. They all fell in with enthusiasm. A total of 300,000 gold florins was to be raised to pay for the expedition, one third each to be provided by the King of Aragon, the King of France and the Pope.[34]

The scale of the funding was the main reason why the Spanish project got so much further than earlier schemes of the kind. In July 1365 Urban V imposed two successive tenths on ecclesiastical incomes throughout the French kingdom, the undeclared object of which was to pay the subsidies which would be required by the companies going to Spain. In the middle of July 1365 Peter IV's Queen, presiding over a secret session of the Cortes of Catalonia at Barcelona, broached the question of the 100,000 florins due from Peter's kingdom. Two months later, in September, as opposition mounted among the Catalans, she informed them that the die was now cast. The companies were coming anyway. If they were not paid they would simply destroy Catalonia and quite possibly put themselves at the disposal of the Castilians as well.[35]

As far as the French government was concerned the object was to remove the companies operating between Paris and the Breton march, and not only those in the Rhone and Saône valleys which interested the Pope. This was probably why, almost from the outset, Bertrand du Guesclin was identified as the man to lead the horde into Spain. Bertrand looked upon the project as a straightforward business proposal. Since the battle of Auray, he had been a prisoner on parole. In order to obtain his services the King of France had to guarantee 40,000 florins (about £5,700) of the enormous ransom which Sir John Chandos was demanding, and to pay 30,000 florins (about £4,250) to Bertrand himself as an advance of his fees and expenses. In addition Bertrand received some kind of financial commitment from the Pope, the precise nature of which was never clear. The core of his army comprised the large English-controlled companies of the Breton march, including most of the captains who had fought against him at Auray: Hugh Calveley and Matthew Gournay, who went into partnership to exploit the risks and profits; Eustache d'Aubricourt; Robert Scot, the former ravager of Champagne; Robert Briquet, an Englishman commanding a Breton company who now becomes prominent for the first time. The process of recruitment was accelerated by buying out any garrisons who showed signs of wishing to stay in the region, and propelling them onto the roads. Rolleboise was bought out in April 1365. Moulineaux surrendered in August, probably for money. Many of the survivors of these garrisons appear to have joined the exodus to Spain. Their numbers were swollen by French noblemen quite unconnected with the companies, who joined for adventure and to repair their damaged fortunes. They included Jean de Bourbon, Count of la Marche, whose father had died fighting the companies at Brignais; le Bègue de Villaines, the captain who had fought a guerrilla war against Paris on the Dauphin's behalf in 1358; and the Marshal Arnoul d'Audrehem, until recently royal Lieutenant in Languedoc. In the autumn of 1365 Bertrand's agents began to recruit among the companies in Burgundy and the Lyonnais who had originally been intended for the crusade against the Turks. He was joined by some remnants of the garrison bought out of la Charité, including the Anglo-Breton company of John Cresswell, and Séguin de Badefol's old deputy at Anse, Arnaud du Solier ('le Limousin'). Loot was the spur for all of these men. 'I will make you all rich', the poet has Bertrand say to the assembled brigands.[36]

The whole mass of men began to move south in September. The English contingents from the west marched down the Atlantic coast into Gascony and then across Rouergue. Bertrand du Guesclin with the French noblemen and the companies of the east passed down the Rhone valley, the countryside emptying out before them as they approached. The two groups joined up somewhere near Avignon in November. Here, there was a long pause while the leaders of the army extracted absolution for their sins and the payment of their fees, and the Pope desperately looked around for the means of paying them. According to the poet Cuvelier, whose account is exaggerated but probably contains grains of truth, Bertrand du Guesclin's men lay about Villeneuve-lès-Avignon threatening to sack the papal city unless their demands were met. Five thousand florins were promised by the Comtat Venaissin; thirty thousand florins by the county of Provence; another ten thousand francs was later extracted from the city of Montpellier. Large sums were paid on account by the papal chamber. In the course of December 1365 the entire horde arrived at Perpignan on the march of Aragon. The best estimates of their numbers suggest that they were between 10,000 and 12,000 strong. At Perpignan they received the first instalment of their wages from the agents of Peter IV and marched out of France on the road to Barcelona.[37]

The departure of the largest of the companies, together with their most resourceful and ambitious captains, proved to be a turning point in the recovery of France from the wars of the past three decades. Many *routier* bands, it is true, remained behind. But they were generally the smaller ones with a limited range of operations, and within a year most of them had vanished. To a large extent this was the achievement of administrators and town governments, not of soldiers. For although the companies were gone for less than two years, the brief respite made it possible to re-establish patterns of authority which had faded since the middle of the 1350s and to complete the restoration of the machinery of tax collection.

As order began to return to the French provinces public opinion became progressively more intolerant of those who supported the companies or bought their pillage from them, the intermediaries in towns and villages without which they could not operate. The French chancery registers of the period contain a large number of pardons recording the hunting down and lynching of men who guided them, traded with them or gave them information. The mood was reflected in the increasing ruthlessness of the King's officers in dealing with notable *routiers* who fell into their hands. The companies had traditionally benefitted from the laws of war which protected prisoners, partly in order to encourage them to surrender and partly for the financial advantage of their captors. Public opinion had always been uncomprehending and intolerant of such compromises. The lynching of Jean de Ségur at Troyes in 1360 in spite of all the efforts of the Bishop to save him was a classic confrontation of opposing attitudes to *routiers*, one of which treated them as criminals and the other as irregular men of war. In the course of the following decade there was a perceptible movement among officials and judges towards the popular view. When the castle of Chamerolles, north-east of Orléans, surrendered to the Duke of Burgundy in August 1365 after a brief and violent siege, the English, Gascons, Navarrese and Germans in the garrison were allowed to ransom themselves; but the subjects of the King of France were summarily put to death. The fate of Louis Rabaud, one of Séguin de Badefol's principal lieutenants at Anse, was symbolic. He was captured in an ambush in May 1365, betrayed (it was said) by his partner-in-arms after a row about a girl. The Duke of Anjou bought the prisoner for 3,000 francs plus an unspecified fee to the man who had betrayed him. Rabaud was then taken to Villeneuve-lès-Avignon so that he could be beheaded with the greatest possible ceremony and his quarters exhibited by the roads of eastern Languedoc.[38]

In western France the clearance of minor companies who stayed behind was swift and virtually complete. A small group of English garrisons around Bayeux commanded by a pair of brigands called Morville and Wilston was rounded up in July 1365. The survivors were taken into Bayeux to be drowned in the river. Saint-Sever, west of Vire, which had been occupied by successive companies since 1356, was evacuated by treaty early in 1366. The local officers of the Crown, remembering what had happened after the last round of *videments*, responded rapidly to attempts to reoccupy such places. In the following May, when a group of English soldiers surprised the castle of le Hommet in the marshes of the Cotentin they were expelled within a month by the royal captain in the Bessin. Orders to raise troops were given on 16 May within a few days of its capture. The place was recaptured on 14 June. The officers of the King of Navarre (in whose domains le Hommet was) had agreed a negotiated surrender. But the royal captain in charge of the operation would have none of that. He ordered his archers to kill the garrison as they came through the gates trying to escape across the flat marshland. 'And if this had been the practice in the past', said the local chronicler who tells us this, 'the wars would not have lasted as long as they did'.[39]

In the east the work of pacification began in the mountains of the *massif central*, for ten years the companies' chief refuge and base and the great crossroads of their operations. After the departure of Bertucat d'Albret's bands to Anse in August 1365, teams of *réformateurs* passed through Auvergne with military escorts, rounding up the remaining *routiers* and sending them off for execution, fining and confiscating the property of those who had dealt with them. In the neighbouring province of Bourbonnais, where the garrisons had never been linked to the Great Companies, the Duke of Bourbon's lieutenant undertook the systematic reduction of most of the surviving garrisons. Once the mountains had been cleared the companies of the plain withered away.[40]

In Burgundy the officers of Philip the Bold had been engaged since 1364 in a vigorous purge, executing *routiers* from the highest to the lowest. The chief agent of this policy was Hughes Aubriot, *bailli* of Dijon, an ambitious, low-born official of great energy destined for a famous and ultimately tragic career in royal service. He entered upon the task with special relish. Great numbers of freebooters were drowned, beheaded or hanged in the public spaces of the principal towns. When the *routiers* fell into the hands of private captors, the Duke's officers were prepared to buy them for large sums in order to make a spectacle of their deaths. Guiot du Pin, the Poitevin captain who had operated in Burgundy for several years, was bought for 200 *livres* and executed in Chalon. His remains were exposed at the pillory for eight months. Gilles Troussevache was purchased and executed at Semur-en-Auxois. The Duke paid 1,000 gold francs for the person of the Breton *routier* John de Cornouailles who was executed at Dijon.[41]

After the departure of Bertrand du Guesclin's army to Spain there remained two substantial concentrations of *routiers* in eastern France: the remnants of the Archpriest's crusaders quartered in the imperial county along the east bank of the Saône; and the companies of Bertucat d'Albret, who had refused to go to either Turkey or Spain, and were being contained on the west bank of the river from Chalon to Lyon. Neither group can have found this twilight phase of their existence very profitable. All the towns and castles of any size were carefully defended. The river crossings were guarded so as to prevent different groups from joining forces. Deprived of most of their leadership and numbers, they could no longer operate the network of alliances which had made them such a formidable enemy only a little while before. They never found a new Brioude or Anse. At the beginning of December 1365 the leading captains encamped east of the Saône in the imperial county were persuaded to enter into a fresh treaty with the Archpriest in the small village of Corcondray near Besançon, by which they undertook to leave the region in return for a modest ransom of 21,000 florins. During the following weeks those of them who were unwilling to join the crusade against the Turks were escorted under armed guard across the river and contained with the rest in the Maçonnais. A few crusaders were found among the companies of Bertucat on the west bank and were ferried across the river in the opposite direction. Several months were passed in trying to arrange the passage of the eastern group to embarkation ports in Italy, while the unpaid and unfed troops became progressively more restless and angry. On 25 May 1366 the Archpriest was murdered in the course of an altercation with some of his men. The whole venture then collapsed and the eastern group dispersed. As for the western group, they remained in dangerous idleness until they too began to disperse. In June the Duke's officers were ordered to arrest and execute those who remained behind, and a small army was assembled to back them up. By the autumn of 1366 Burgundy was virtually clear of the companies. Most of the Gascons returned to Gascony, where fresh opportunities for soldiering were now opening up. Their leaders are found amongst the retainers of the Prince of Wales later in the year. The rest merged with the population and vanished from sight.[42]

On New Year's Day 1366 Peter IV of Aragon gave a great feast for the leaders of the *routier* army in the hall of the royal palace of Barcelona. Bertrand du Guesclin sat in the place of honour beside the King. Hugh Calveley and Arnoul d'Audrehem sat side by side at the high table. Assorted bandits were distributed about the hall. During the following days the troops began to make their way west into the valley of the River Ebro. As they passed, they left regular reminders of the casual violence for which they were notorious. Peter IV received daily reports of their 'great and irreparable destructions', ranging from petty theft from rural barns to incidents as serious as the sack of Barbastro in Upper Aragon, in which 200 of the inhabitants were burned alive in the tower of the church to which they had fled for safety.[43] It was the largest army that had been seen in the Iberian peninsula since the great crusades against the Moors more than a century before, and probably larger than the combined military strength of both Aragon and Castile. They became known, like the White Company arriving in Italy in 1362, as the 'Gente Blanca', and their equipment, organisation and tactics provoked the same awe among the inhabitants. Their battle tactics were quite new to the peninsula, whose heavily armed knights took the same disdainful view of the notion of fighting on foot as the French had done in the early fourteenth century, in spite of the warnings of those who had followed the course of the war in France. 'It is their way of crushing their enemy,' Peter IV told his son when advising him not on any account to risk a battle.[44]

The leaders of the army had not forgotten why they had come to Spain, and quickly fell to menacing debate with their hosts about money. Peter IV had already paid the 100,000 florins which was due to them, which he had collected together with much difficulty from the early receipts of the special taxes voted by the Cortes, and from borrowing. But the captains were not satisfied. They came before the King at Tarragona to demand more. The sums already received had been distributed to the army, they explained. But fresh companies were still arriving across the Pyrenees. Another 20,000 florins would be required for them. Peter paid half of this sum down and promised the rest later. He had to sell land to do it. Then came another demand for an additional sum representing three months' wages in advance, which had not been mentioned before. Individual captains added their own personal requirements. Bertrand du Guesclin had already shown the way. He obtained extensive grants of land and castles and the title of count. Hugh Calveley extracted a pension of 2,000 florins a year and grants of land on the Aragonese march. As for the spoil of Castile, du Guesclin and Calveley reached an agreement about that shortly after their arrival in the peninsula, which was designed to prevent competition for loot between the English and French divisions of the army. In addition to being paid the wages of his army (which du Guesclin guaranteed) Calveley was to have a quarter of all the spoil of Castile and du Guesclin the other three quarters. In return for Calveley's agreement to this unequal division, du Guesclin was to cede everything that he received in grants from Henry of Trastámara. On 13 February 1366 the King arrived at Sarragossa, the ancient capital of Aragon which had been appointed as the forward assembly point of the army. He declared himself overjoyed by the spectacle of the great mass of foreign soldiers 'which the divine majesty has sent to aid us against our notorious enemy', and looked forward to their destruction of the King of Castile. The truth was that he and his subjects were prisoners of these terrible allies.[45]

Pedro I of Castile had established his headquarters in the city of Burgos. His plan of campaign was based on the assumption that the enemy would strike directly west from Sarragossa. The main natural defence of his kingdom was a chain of mountains extending from the Sierra de la Demanda in the north, south-east towards the Mediterranean at Valencia which any invader approaching from this direction would have to cross. It was difficult terrain, liable to unseasonable extremes of climate. The bulk of the Castilian forces were concentrated around the

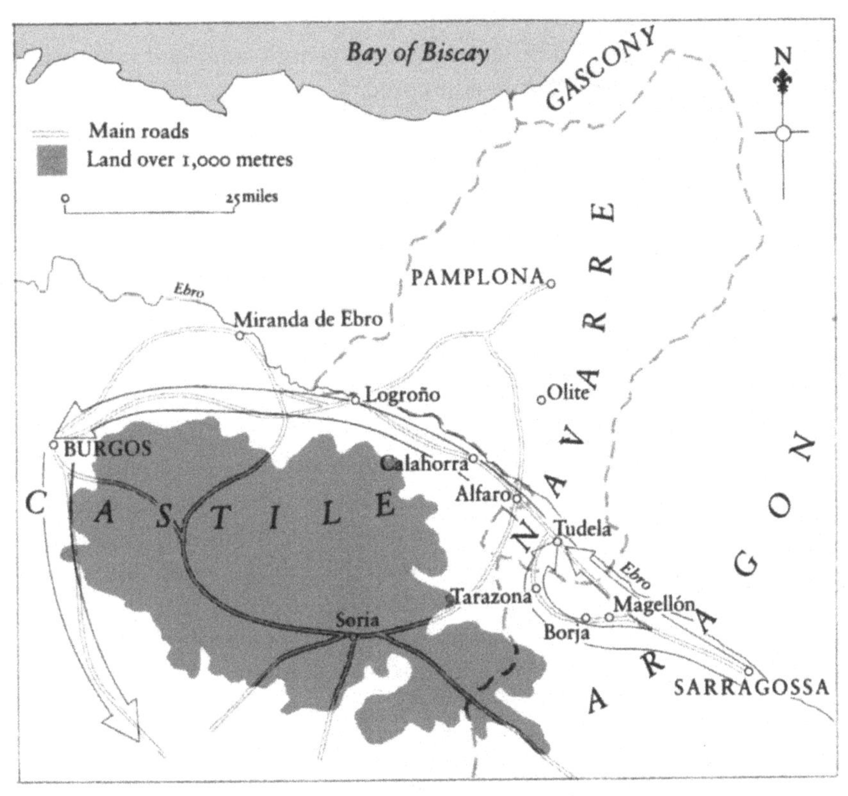

38 Du Guesclin in Spain, January–May 1366

approaches to Soria, an important walled town some eighty miles west of Sarragossa, which was the hub of the road system of the region. However, the easiest route for the invaders lay not this way but along the fertile, low-lying valley of the Ebro, which passed through the southern salient of the kingdom of Navarre before emerging into the plain north of the Sierra de la Demanda. Don Pedro's plans depended on the Navarrese closing their frontier to the King of Aragon and his allies and blocking this route. This was not a wise assumption. Charles of Navarre was ostensibly Don Pedro's ally, and he had no desire to see the richest part of his kingdom invaded by the hordes of Bertrand du Guesclin and Hugh Calveley. But he did not have the strength to stop them and was unwilling to provoke such dangerous enemies. He had therefore, unbeknown to Don Pedro, concluded a secret agreement with the King of Aragon before Christmas. By this document, he had promised to join the invasion of Castile himself, with 600 armed men, provided that they left his territory alone. Then he ignored his engagements to both sides and manned his borders against them all as best he could.[46]

The campaign began in the last week of February 1365 and lasted barely a month. The van of the invading army was led by the English companies of Hugh Calveley. At first they struck west as the Castilians had expected, towards Magellón and Borja, which were abandoned by their garrisons as they approached. Within a few days they had entered the Castilian city of Tarazona. But then Calveley suddenly turned north and invaded Navarre. By the end of the first week of March the English were beneath the walls of Tudela, the chief Navarrese fortress of the Ebro. Bertrand du Guesclin, with the main body of the army, came straight up the Ebro from Sarragossa and followed Calveley's march west at about a day's distance. The King of Navarre skulked in the fortress of Olite, a well defended place about 30 miles north of Tudela. He had no choice but to reach a new accommodation with the invaders, paying their leaders a large sum to keep the damage to a minimum. On about 10 March 1366 Calveley's division passed across the western frontier of Navarre into Castile. On the following day they arrived outside the cathedral city of Calahorra. The inhabitants of Calahorra were ready to resist, in spite of the strength of the enemy. But the garrison commanders were not. They felt no loyalty to Don Pedro and had no stomach for the fight. So they arrested the dissenters in the city and delivered it up to Henry of Trastámara. On 16 March 1366 the usurper was acclaimed by the assembled English, Gascon and French soldiers as King of Castile. Henry made lavish use of his newly won prerogatives, showering his mercenaries with grants and favours. Calveley received much of the credit. 'A great knight, renowned in arms', was what the King of Aragon later said about him; 'he was our servant and, thank God, the chief cause of the reconquest of our realm from Pedro King of Castile.' Burgos was little more than 100 miles away.[47]

In the following days Don Pedro's cause collapsed about his ears. The effect of the flanking movement executed by Calveley and du Guesclin was to place the invading army between Don Pedro and the bulk of his troops, who were spread about the march of Aragon. In Burgos the Castilian King had only a personal bodyguard of 600 Moorish calvary and the retinues of his principal officials and courtiers. Pedro was a competent general and did not lack courage, but he recognised that the game was up. On the night of 28 March 1366, when the companies had come within 25 miles of Burgos, he abandoned the city and fled south.

On the following day Henry of Trastámara reached Burgos and was crowned King 'by election and consent of the lords and captains of the army' at the great royal monastery at Las Huelgas outside the walls. Once more, largesse was showered on the captains who had brought him here with hardly a blow struck in anger. Bertrand du Guesclin received Henry's county of Trastámara, which was transformed into a duchy for his benefit. Hugh Calveley became Count of Carrión. Their followers, deprived by the swift surrender of Pedro's subjects of the chance of sack and spoil, were allowed to help themselves to the property of the Jewish and Moslem communities of Burgos. In an imaginative passage of his poem the Chandos Herald describes Henry's wife mocking her own fate when her time of troubles came a year later. 'And men will ever say', she cried; 'behold the Queen of Castile, whom the Great Company crowned'. Within a few days of the coronation the whole of northern Castile had submitted to the usurper, except for the region of Galicia in the north-western corner, and six isolated frontier garrisons in the east.[48]

Don Pedro's plan was to assemble the dispersed packets of his army from the eastern marches of his kingdom and make a fresh stand at Toledo. But by the time he reached the city, his support was rapidly fading away. For the nobility this was the moment of revenge for years of assertive centralised government. For the towns, whose relations with the Crown had traditionally been better, the chief motive was fear. In Toledo itself the citizens rose in rebellion as their King approached. The captain of the citadel and most of his garrison declared for the usurper. Henry of Trastámara entered the city in triumph on 11 May 1366, while Don Pedro took refuge in Seville with a handful of companions. Here, in his favourite city, he had built his famous Moorish palace, held his court and lodged his family. But it was impossible for him to stay. There were already mutterings of rebellion in the city's streets as he arrived. Within a few days mobs were attacking the Alcázar where he was sheltering. At the end of May Don Pedro fled north with his family, a few attendants and his personal jewellery, and escaped into Portugal. The King's great treasury of coin and plate, which was kept in the castle of Almodóvar near Córdova, was loaded onto a galley on the River Guadalquivir under the supervision of Pedro's treasurer. He was ordered to sail at once into the Atlantic and rejoin his master in Portugal. But the galley was seized by Gil Boccanegra, the Genoese Admiral of Castile. Like the rest of Don Pedro's retainers he could see that the cause was lost and resolved to ingratiate himself as best he could with the usurper. A few days after Pedro's departure, Henry entered Seville with his army. Much of Pedro's treasure was promptly distributed to the foreigners. This enabled him to see them off his territory before they completed its destruction. Henry kept du Guesclin and Calveley with him at Seville with a select few of their companies. The rest were allowed to leave with their wages, and advances for the return journey to France.[49]

For the companies, and especially their leaders, the whole venture had been effortlessly profitable. We cannot know how much du Guesclin's gains were worth, but we have some idea of Calveley's because they were the subject of years of litigation in the courts of the King of Aragon. He and his companies earned 63,108 francs (about £12,800) in war wages up to the beginning of May 1366. Most of this appears to have been paid from the looted treasury of Don Pedro when the companies entered Seville. At the beginning of July 1366 another 26,257 florins (about £3,700) was due, most of which must have represented further wages accruing since May. According to the agreement between the two principal captains, this sum was the personal liability of Bertrand du Guesclin. In addition Bertrand owed him a quarter of his own vast spoils. Calveley's outstanding claims at the end of the campaign came to 55,000 florins (about £7,800). Unfortunately, before the two men were able to settle their accounts they found themselves on opposite sides again. Calveley therefore had to sue du Guesclin in the courts of Aragon. He obtained judgment in August 1368, and over a number of years was able to enforce it against various properties, rent charges and ships in Aragon which belonged to the great French captain. Even so, he did not get the last of his money until 1388. Some of the proceeds must have been paid out to his men. Some of it was claimed by his partner-in-arms Matthew Gournay, in another bitterly contested lawsuit. But Calveley himself retained the lion's share of the spoil of Castile in addition to the largesse poured upon him by a grateful King of Aragon. He ended his days a rich man.[50]

As for Don Pedro, he made his way across Portugal, and in early June 1366 reached the Castilian province of Galicia, the only part of his kingdom which still remained loyal to him. There he set about planning his counter-attack. He had just 200 cavalry with him. His advisers reckoned that he could raise another 500 in the region, as well as 2,000 infantry. In addition, there were the distant and isolated garrisons still holding out at Soria and Logroño on the Aragonese march, perhaps 500 men in all. It was obvious that the only hope of recovery lay in finding allies of his own outside Castile. The prevailing view among the King's companions was that he should make for Logroño, which was close to the Navarrese border. From there he would be able to open negotiations with Charles of Navarre and the Prince of Wales. But Pedro resolved upon a riskier plan. He decided to go to La Coruña and there take ship for Gascony. He intended to re-invade his kingdom from beyond the Pyrenees. At about the beginning of July 1366 a Gascon knight of the Prince's court arrived at La Coruña with an invitation and a message of goodwill. The Prince, he told the Castilian monarch, was already resolved to restore him by force to his throne. 'And now', sang the Chandos Herald, 'begins a noble tale of pity, love and justice made'.[51]

CHAPTER XII

Nájera: the Disastrous Victory 1366–1369

In the summer of 1366, the Prince of Wales was at the height of his fame: victor of Poitiers, captor of a King of France, arbiter of disputes among the nobility of western Europe, broker of peace between Montfort and Blois, Armagnac and Foix. The chronicler Froissart, who passed several months at the Prince's court in 1366, captured the mood well: the lavish entertainments at Bordeaux, Angoulême and Poitiers; the clattering escorts of men-at-arms and maids of honour wherever the Prince and his wife went; the jousts and tournaments at which 'small men grew great'; the extravagant formulae of courtesy, largesse and flattery. 'And they all loved and honoured him as their lord, and proclaimed his realm to be the greatest in the world, and the richest in valiant men-at-arms.' In Aquitaine he possessed for the first time in his life a domain in which he could cut a great figure.[1]

Yet the Prince's estate, for all its grandeur, was built on sand. Gascony, the heart of the principality around Bordeaux and Bayonne and the lower reaches of the Garonne and the Adour, had never been rich. It is true that the region had suffered little war damage since the early 1340s and virtually none after 1355. But it suffered economic difficulties of its own which were only partly attributable to the war. The epidemics of bubonic plague in 1348 and 1362 did more damage here than in any other region of France with the possible exception of the Mediterranean coast. The best estimates that can be made suggest that it may have lost as much as two thirds of its population in the course of the fourteenth century. The main pillars of the local economy were wine and war, both of which suffered not only from the general economic depression but from their own problems. The export of wine and was running at less than half the level of activity recorded before the war, in spite of a persistent increase in prices and a certain amount of replanting. As for war, that had briefly become a major export trade in the 1350s displacing even wine, statistically unquantifiable but generating great wealth for the leading Gascon captains, much of which must have found its way back to the region. Important ancillary trades had grown up, such as the famous armourers of Bordeaux, the iron-founders of Bayonne and the bankers and intermediaries who dealt in loot and ransoms. The scale of these activities inevitably diminished after the peace even if the presence of the Prince of Wales and the continued fighting in the French provinces ensured that there was still work for them to do. In these respects the economic fortunes of Gascony proved very different from those of the rest of France.[2]

Beyond Gascony lay the new provinces ceded to the English dynasty at Brétigny, a domain about five times as extensive as the duchy which Edward III had inherited in 1327, parts of which had once counted among the most prosperous regions of France. But integrating them with the older territories required time, and perhaps greater administrative talent than the Prince had. Most of the new provinces had been continuously wasted by soldiers for more than a decade. In Saintonge the fragmentary records of the Prince's administration show that many parts of his personal domain were still uninhabited in the 1360s as a result of the war. Much of the rest produced nothing owing to war damage, usurpation and the profligate assignments made by John II before the treaty. These problems were aggravated by the administrative confusion associated with the handover of the territories to Edward III. In many places it was found impossible to discover what revenues there should be or to identify officials to account for them. Yet the situation in Saintonge was by no means untypical. On the eastern march of the principality, it must have been worse.[3]

The financial implications of all this were only dimly appreciated at Westminster when the Prince was invested with the duchy of Aquitaine in 1362. The much smaller duchy of Edward II had usually been self-sufficient in peacetime and in good years had even generated surpluses. After thirteen years in which the government of Gascony had been financed with the aid of large subventions from England, it became the policy of the English government that the principality should once more be self-sufficient. The Prince received a large subsidy from the Exchequer of England in order to defray his initial expenses. But otherwise there was no significant receipt from England until the peace failed at the end of the 1360s. This policy made altogether unrealistic assumptions about the Prince's local revenues. War damage and grants had decimated the Prince's domain. By far the largest source of revenue was the Great Custom levied at Bordeaux on exports of wine, which fluctuated with the prosperity of the trade and produced historically low receipts in the 1360s. During the war, the seneschals had been able to bridge the gap from confiscations of the property of enemies and traitors, which dried up after the peace. There were also difficulties on the expenditure side. A sharp fall in the cost of paying war wages and maintaining garrisoned fortresses must have been anticipated. What was not anticipated was the effect on expenditure of sending to Aquitaine a viceroy who was not only the heir to the English throne but a man of European stature in his own right. The seneschals who had previously governed the duchy had generally been English household knights who lived in dignified, but not magnificent style. Their personal retinues had rarely exceeded fifty men. The Prince's household was a very different affair. He and the English noblemen whom he retained came to Aquitaine with several hundred soldiers and officials. Many more were retained after his arrival from the nobility of the south-west and the crowded ranks of the existing civil service. The Prince's splendid court in Bordeaux and Angoulême called for expenditure on a great scale: on average about £10,000 sterling per year including the wages of his personal military retinue. This provoked some criticism in England. The Prince, said an English chronicler, lived 'on such a scale and at such outrageous expense that no living King could have borne it.' It was true that the Prince had extravagant ways. But he would have had to maintain a great household with the largesse proper to his status even if he had not. His court was a major source of patronage and an important instrument of government in a region controlled by an ambitious, powerful and warlike aristocracy.[4]

To some extent the Prince was able to make up the deficiency by drawing on his English domains, particularly in Cheshire and North Wales. To a quite remarkable degree, these domains were governed together with Aquitaine as a single lordship. The Prince levied taxes on his subjects in England to finance his expenditure in south-eastern France. He mortgaged his ordinary revenues there by selling annuities on a large scale. He recruited Cheshire men to serve in Aquitaine as administrators, men-at-arms and above all as mounted archers, paying the initial cost and sometimes the daily wages out of his English receipts. Within the duchy of Aquitaine, the Prince's officials did what they could to increase his local revenues. A new gold coinage must have generated profit as well as prestige. The wartime cycle of devaluations of the silver coinage continued. The non-coinage revenues of the domain rose dramatically, albeit from a low base: five-fold in Saintonge, almost as much in Poitou. Much of this was achieved by intensive administration of a kind which was itself expensive as well as unfamiliar and unpopular with the inhabitants of Aquitaine. Froissart was no doubt mouthing the prejudices of his aristocratic hosts when he remarked on the crowd of 'seneschals, bailiffs, mayors, treasurers, intendants, sergeants and every other kind of public officer' whom the Prince's subjects had learned to associate with his government.[5]

The most significant new resource, however, was taxation. Even at the height of the military crisis of the 1340s, the English government in Aquitaine had never been able to institute a system of regular taxation. The Prince was bolder. He summoned more or less annual assemblies to grant *fouages* (hearth taxes) in spite of the fact that the principality was at peace and that the money was required to pay for the ordinary expenses of his household and administration, not usually regarded as a proper purpose of extraordinary revenue. The first *fouage* was conceded by an assembly meeting at Périgueux at the end of June 1364 at the very high rate of 3s 4d sterling per hearth. Another, at half that rate, was authorised by an assembly meeting at Périgueux in September of the following year. In the first eight years after the Prince's arrival in Aquitaine, direct taxation accounted for about 36 per cent of his local receipts. These taxes generated surprisingly little opposition. Yet the acquiescence of the Prince's subjects probably concealed wide differences of attitude among them. The Estates of the principality were dominated by the new provinces, which had grown used to regular taxation at high rates in the time of the Valois, as the Gascons never had. It also seems likely that, as in much of southern France, the grant of subsidies was controlled by the towns, whereas the natural opponents of taxation were generally to be found among the nobility who wanted to preserve the taxable capacity of their domains for themselves. In the absence of records, all this is necessarily conjecture. What is clear is that even without allowing for war expenditure, by 1366 the Prince was reaching the outer limits of what could be extracted from his subjects without provoking serious political difficulties.[6]

The Prince had been the main promoter of the Anglo-Castilian treaty of 1362, but to all outward appearances he was indifferent to the fate of Don Pedro. He did nothing to stop his subjects invading Castile. Froissart recorded much hostility to the King of Castile among the Prince's entourage, many of whom regarded him as a tyrant, a murderer and a friend of infidels who deserved to lose his crown.[7] It would have been in keeping with the Prince's mental outlook if he had shared this view. England's relations with the Iberian kingdoms had traditionally been left to the government in Bordeaux, but in the mid-1360s the strategic dangers of a French client state in Castile seemed to have been better understood at Westminster. The order of events certainly suggests that English policy was being made there. In the autumn of 1365 Don Pedro had sent one of his councillors, the Master of the Order of Calatrava, to England to call for Edward III's assistance under the treaty. Pedro evidently understood the difficulties posed by his unsavoury reputation abroad, and a large part of the ambassador's instructions was taken up with the various ways in which the record might be put straight. Edward III was either convinced or unconcerned. Bypassing his son's authority he appointed the Constable of Aquitaine, Sir John Chandos, and two other commissioners (one of whom was Hugh Calveley himself) to stop his English and Gascon subjects invading Castile with Bertrand du Guesclin. By the time that this order reached Gascony it was already too late: most of them were on the road to Sarragossa. But a gesture had been made, and another followed. In February 1366 Arnaud-Amanieu lord of Albret arrived in Burgos to reinforce Don Pedro with some companies of Gascons. He did not stay there long. He thought that the Castilian King's plans to fight off the companies were doomed, and said so. He suggested that the companies could be suborned if they were paid enough, and that this might be cheaper as well as better than fighting them. Don Pedro rejected this idea and Albret returned in high dudgeon to Gascony just as the campaign was beginning.[8]

It seems to have been shortly after Don Pedro's flight from Burgos that the English government instructed the Prince to proceed to more determined measures. The actual process of decision is obscure. The Prince's chamberlain, Sir Neil Loring, came to England in the spring of 1366. In the middle of April letters from the Prince reached Westminster. The sequel suggests that both events had to do with the developing crisis in Castile. By chance Parliament was due to meet on 4 May 1366. And, although the official roll records no discussion of Pedro's fate, the decision to come to his rescue was probably made in the course of the opening sessions. On 8 May 1366 the Prince's stepson Sir Thomas Holland was ordered urgently to Gascony, accompanied by Loring, a company of troops and some sappers. A month later, on 8 June, orders were given to requisition shipping for a much larger force which was to follow them. The Prince had already begun recruiting soldiers among the Gascon nobility. Reports reaching Barcelona suggested that a large army was to be mustered in Gascony in the middle of July.[9]

By the time July came these preparations had been overtaken by the collapse of Don Pedro's cause in Castile. The news of this disaster forced the Prince to delay his expedition and to increase its scale. At Westminster the government stepped up its recruitment in the counties. They signified the importance which they attached to the expedition by appointing the King's son John of Gaunt to lead it to Gascony. In Bordeaux the Prince opened negotiations with Charles of Navarre to secure the passage of the army across the Pyrenean passes. In the last week of July the Navarrese King was in Bordeaux and his councillors were locked in debate with the Prince's. It was while they were there that the news arrived that a large carrack had entered Bayonne bearing the King of Castile with his daughters, a few intimate advisers and some chests of personal jewellery, the only disposable wealth which he still possessed.[10]

The three men met early in August 1366 at the small fishing port of Capbreton, north of Bayonne. They agreed in principle that the Prince would gather a great army to invade Castile in Pedro's name in January of the following year. The terms, however, proved more controversial. They were only drawn up and sealed at Libourne on 23 September 1366, after several weeks of haggling between the councillors of the three principals. As his reward for opening the mountain passes to the invaders, Charles of Navarre was to have the Castilian provinces of Guipuzcoa and Alava, which would carry the borders of his landlocked kingdom to the sea, as well as a string of major fortresses along the eastern march of Castile and a lump sum of 200,000 florins in cash. The Prince was to have the whole of the Basque country of Viscaya, around Bilbao, which was to be annexed to the duchy of Aquitaine. In addition, Don Pedro was required to reimburse the Prince the entire cost of the expedition. These were formidable undertakings, which Don Pedro could take lightly. He had nothing to lose. But the Prince could not. His personal expenses were expected to come to 250,000 florins (about £35,400) even before the expeditionary army set out. The mobilisation expenses of the Gascon lords, for which he would be personally responsible, were expected to add another 300,000 florins (about £42,500). In addition he was obliged to advance to the Castilian King part of the lump sum which the latter had undertaken to pay to Charles of Navarre. The Prince was therefore committing himself to expenditure many times the income of his domains on the assumption not only that

Castile would be swiftly reconquered and its revenues unlocked, but that its notoriously fickle King could be relied upon to honour his promises. His only security was the Castilian King's personal jewellery, which was handed over to the prince's treasurer and sold onto a glutted market in Bordeaux for 52,447 *l.b.* (about £10,500).

For the Gascons, who were to supply the bulk of the troops, the matter was altogether simpler. They saw the expedition as a straightforward business venture just as Bertrand du Guesclin and his followers had done the year before. It was an opportunity to earn war wages and to plunder the wealth of Castile. They were readily convinced of the justice of the cause, being 'grandement convoiteux' as Froissart remarked in a rare moment of cynicism. The lord of Albret put their motives very clearly when, at a late stage of the planning process, the Prince asked him to reduce the size of his contingent. Albret was indignant and refused. His men were professional soldiers of fortune. They had turned away other opportunities for profit, he said, which they would certainly have found in Prussia or the east if the Prince had not promised to lead them into Spain.[11]

The army which gathered in Gascony during the autumn of 1366 was even more heterogeneous than du Guesclin's army of 1365. The kernel of it comprised the personal retinues of the Prince of Wales and the leading noblemen of Aquitaine. Around them gathered much of the great diaspora of Gascon, Breton and English soldiers of fortune hitherto spread across France and Spain. Sir John Chandos had approached the leaders of the Gascon companies which were still operating, in increasingly difficult conditions, in the Saône valley and Auvergne. In August there was a great armed migration across southern France as these men marched to join their new paymaster. It included some of the most notorious *routier* captains of the past decade: Bertucat d'Albret, their loosely acknowledged leader; Séguin de Badefol's old lieutenant Garciot du Châtel; le Bourc Camus, the notorious Navarrese gang leader from the Bourbonnais. Louis of Anjou, who was at this stage desperately trying to shore up Henry of Trastámara's position in Castile, did his best to stop them reaching their destination. He sent du Guesclin's cousin and former lieutenant Olivier de Mauny to hold the Tarn against them, south of Montauban. The result was a military fiasco and an embarrassing diplomatic incident. Mauny succeeded in dispersing the first column to reach the river, but on the following day, 14 August 1366, Bertucat d'Albret fell upon him with the main body near the village of Villedieu-du-Temple and captured most of his army.

Two hundred Gascons on Mauny's side, reasoning that the enemy were of the 'same alliance and allegiance' as themselves, changed sides at the critical moment and completed the rout. Louis of Anjou later claimed that this incident had cost him 3,000,000 francs in ransoms.[12]

By this time the Prince was also receiving large accessions of troops who had served under du Guesclin in Castile. They were now streaming back across the Pyrenees into Gascony. They had earned a great deal of money putting Henry of Trastámara on the throne, and were quite happy to earn more by putting him down again. Most of them were Gascons. But there were also northerners among them, such as the Anglo-Breton companies of John Cresswell and Robert Briquet and the Bretons and Hainaulters of Eustache d'Aubricourt. In addition there was a miscellaneous group of Spanish exiles, dissidents and malcontents thrown up by two decades of civil strife: a few hundred Castilians loyal to Don Pedro; friends and retainers of the Count of Osona, son of the disgraced Aragonese minister Bernardo de Cabrera, who had thrown in his lot with Don Pedro; another band of Aragonese gathered round the exiled King James of Majorca. The last important contingent to arrive was John of Gaunt's. He sailed from Plymouth to Cherbourg early in December 1366 with an army which was probably between 400 and 500 strong, most of them archers. In Brittany, Gaunt was joined by a large company of English and Breton soldiers recruited by Sir Robert Knolles. They marched south together, the first time that an English army had made use of the coastal corridor which Edward III now controlled from Dinan to Bayonne. The whole mass of men assembled at Dax in the foothills of the Pyrenees during January 1367. French spies in Bordeaux and Bayonne reported that it was the largest army that either the Prince or his father had ever commanded in France. This was an exaggeration. But it was a large army, probably numbering between 8,000 and 10,000 men, about the number which the Prince had commanded at the battle of Poitiers.[13]

Henry of Trastámara was now extremely vulnerable. He had paid off the companies, keeping only some retainers of Bertrand du Guesclin, about 1,000 men, mostly Bretons; and Hugh Calveley with about 400 English men-at-arms and some archers who could certainly not be relied upon to fight against the Prince of Wales. In addition, the large Breton company of Olivier de Mauny had come to join them from Languedoc in September when the Prince's plans first became known. It was nothing like enough. The fear which had made the Castilians submit to the usurper waned once most of his terrible auxiliaries had left. The towns in particular were reassessing their interests now that Don Pedro seemed likely to return. The exiled King's agents came down the mountains from Gascony to fan the embers. Writing at the beginning of February 1367 an Aragonese in Henry's retinue gave it as his opinion that almost every one of them would rise in rebellion when Pedro crossed the Pyrenees. Another doubted whether Henry would even retain the loyalty of his household troops once he had exhausted his predecessor's treasure.[14]

In the new year, Henry's position was gravely weakened as a result of what had at first seemed to be a great diplomatic coup. Shortly after Christmas 1366 he had met the King of Navarre in the small village of Santa Cruz de Campezo on the Navarrese border. Charles was terrified that if the prince's enterprise was abandoned or failed, he would be left to face the combined wrath of Castile and Aragon alone. So he sold himself to Henry in return for the cession of the border town of Logroño and a modest cash payment of 60,000 *doblas* (about £11,600). Since the Pyrenean passes could be closed against the Prince by a quite small number of men, Henry believed that by this deal he had stopped the invasion in its tracks. This view was widely shared in the peninsula when the news got out. There were even reports that the Prince's army was being disbanded. In the second half of January 1367, Henry, confident that the crisis was over and worried about the continuing drain of money, dispensed with the services not only of Hugh Calveley's Englishmen but also of the larger and more reliable Breton companies of du Guesclin and Mauny. They departed into Aragon and took service with Peter IV.[15]

As soon as the Prince learnt of the happenings at Santa Cruz he ordered Calveley, whose company was then in northern Castile, to invade Navarre from the south and remind Charles of his obligations. Hugh performed this function with efficiency and despatch. He crossed the River Ebro and marched on Pamplona, capturing all the principal towns in his path. When he had come within 20 miles of the Navarrese capital Charles performed a fresh volte-face. He sent his principal captain, Martin Henriquez de Lacarra, to meet the Prince at Dax. Martin was a reliable friend of the English who had fought with them for several years in France. He assured the Prince that his master had never been sincere in his dealings with Henry of Trastámara, which may have been true. He promised that he would open the Pyrenean passes after all. On 14 February 1367 the Prince's army began to move out of

Saint-Jean-Pied-de-Port into the narrow defile leading to the pass of Roncevalles. Ten days later they were encamped in the plain around Pamplona. The King of Navarre had been as good as his last word. He had accompanied them across the mountains. He also supplied 300 men-at-arms to reinforce the army. But he did not care to take part in the campaign personally. So he made a collusive arrangement with Olivier de Mauny, who was commanding the garrison at Borja on the Aragonese frontier. Mauny agreed to stage an ambush in which Charles would be captured and held until the fighting had ended. The stratagem deceived no one and made Charles a laughing-stock throughout western Europe.[16]

In the last few days of February 1367 Henry of Trastámara received a letter of advice from the King of France, in which the King gave him the benefit of his father's and grandfather's bitter experience of facing English armies. Its main purpose was to persuade Henry not to run the risk of a pitched battle against an army which comprised the 'flower of the chivalry of the world'. Better to harass their scouts and foragers, to keep them moving and force them to withdraw through hunger and exhaustion. Much of this must have been obvious to an experienced soldier like Henry of Trastámara who had fought against the English in France. To begin with he followed the prescriptions scrupulously. He set up his headquarters near Santo Domingo de la Calzada on the west side of the Rio Oja. Here he gathered what forces he could find to reinforce his demoralised army. Bertrand du Guesclin was summoned urgently from Sarragossa in eastern Aragon. With him came the leading captains who had served Henry the year before: the Marshal Arnoul d'Audrehem; Jean de Neuville, captain of the fleet which had destroyed Rye in 1360; and a miscellaneous group of *routier* captains including Perrin de Savoie, Arnaud du Solier ('le Limousin') and Petit Meschin. But they came with only a part of their former strength. Most of their men had to stay behind to defend the march of Aragon. The combined forces of the French contingent numbered only about 1,000 men-at-arms. They were joined shortly afterwards by a small corps of Aragonese noblemen, including Peter IV's mayordomo and his cousin the Count of Denia.[17]

The Prince's objective, like Henry of Trastámara's the year before, was the great city of Burgos, the historic capital of the kingdom of the old county of Castile, from which the kingdom had sprung. Henry of Trastámara assumed that he would approach it from the east, after crossing the Ebro at Logroño. The garrison of Logroño was still holding out for Don Pedro, and the road west of it passed through relatively

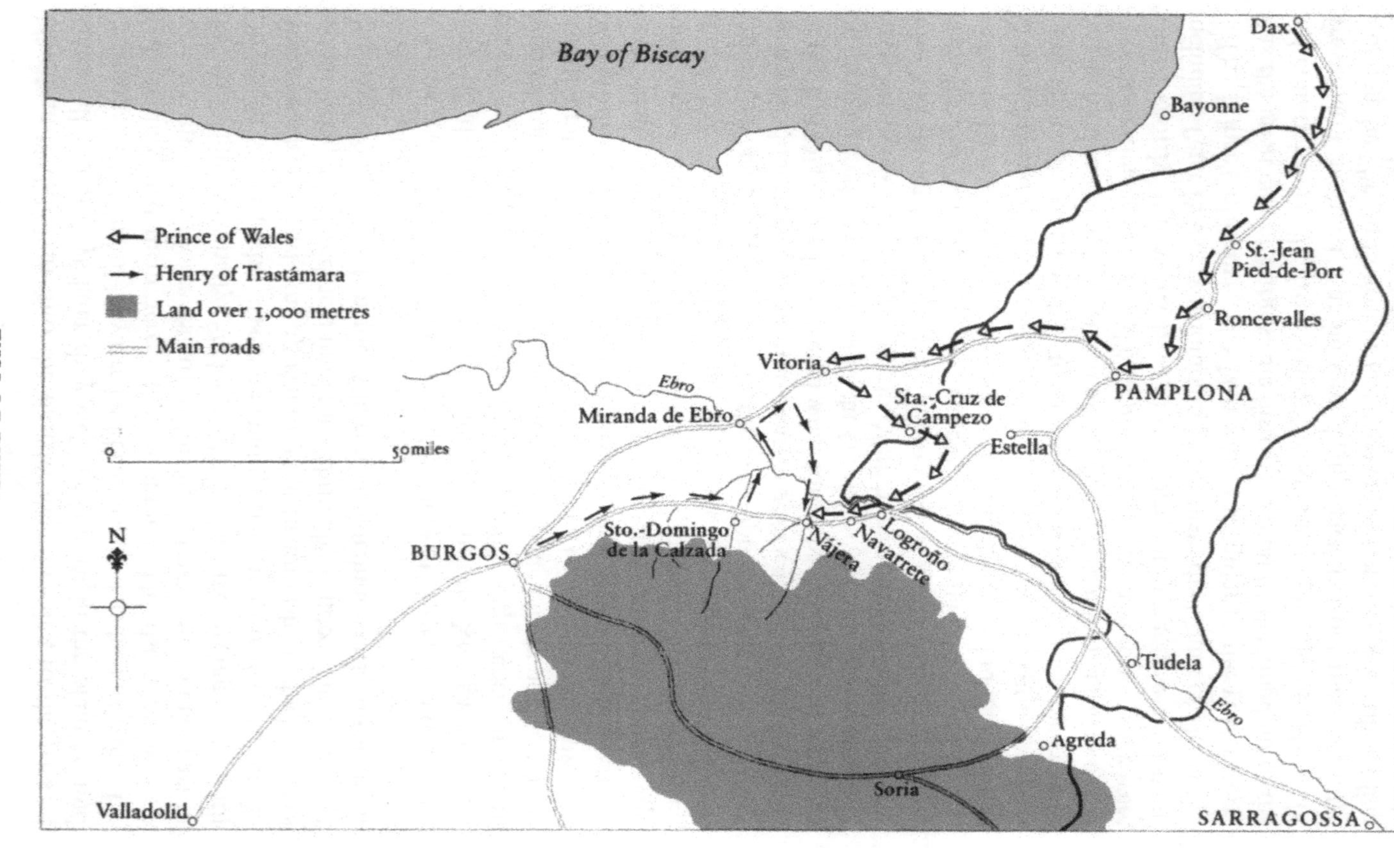

39 The Prince of Wales in Spain, February–September 1367

easy country, low lying and fertile. But it was interrupted by a succession of rivers flowing north from the Sierra de la Demanda, all swollen by spring floods and offering excellent natural lines of defence to the Castilian army. The Prince's first instinct was to outflank the defence by the north, via Vitoria and the bridge-town of Miranda de Ebro. Better staff work and a fuller knowledge of the geography of the country would have spared him this false start. The march took him through extremely inhospitable territory, much of it mountainous, sparsely populated and uncultivated, where fodder was hard to obtain and freezing winds swept down from the north. By the time the Prince reached Vitoria Henry of Trastámara had brought his army across to occupy the river gorges between Vitoria and Miranda. The invaders' route was blocked. There was a stalemate. The Prince's army encamped in the torrential rain on the plain south of Vitoria. From time to time Henry's men came down without warning from the mountains to attack isolated detachments. The Prince drew up his army in battle order in the plain. He made them stand in line from dawn to sunset. He dubbed 200 new knights from the ranks of his army, including Don Pedro himself. But Henry and du Guesclin would not be drawn into a general engagement. At the end of March 1367 the Prince was forced to retreat. He turned south-east across the rugged hills of the Sierra de Cantabria to find the route which geography should perhaps have suggested to him in the first place. On 1 April 1367 his army encamped among the orchards and olive groves around the fortress-town of Logroño. Henry of Trastámara shadowed him from the west. He took up a position not far from Logroño on the west bank of the River Najerilla, by the small town of Nájera.[18]

It was at this stage that Henry abandoned the defensive strategy that had served him so well so far. The decision was much debated within his camp. The French captains, who knew their enemy well, urged him to starve out the Prince rather than fight him. Foremost among the advocates of caution was Arnoul d'Audrehem, who had urged John II to attack the Prince's army at Poitiers eleven years before with such disastrous consequences. Here was a man who had learned wisdom from experience. But Henry was in no position to take his advice for the same reason as John II had refused to listen to the voices of caution in 1356. His political position was too weak. Every town on the Prince's path had opened its gates to Don Pedro. Others, further from his line of march, had risen in rebellion. Even some of Henry's traditional allies were now wavering. A force of 600 men sent to recapture the rebellious town of

Agreda on the Aragonese frontier had mutinied and gone over in a body to the legitimate King. Henry's Castilian advisers, who understood politics quite as well as Arnoul d'Audrehem understood war, advised him to fight. Unless he was seen to meet the Prince's challenge, his support would melt away as Don Pedro's had done when he had turned his back on the enemy the year before. The Prince skilfully fed these fears. He sent a herald into Henry's lines with a letter, the terms of which were widely publicised. Addressing Henry as 'Count of Trastámara', the Prince recited the claims of Pedro I to succeed his father and the homage done to him on his accession by the Castilians, including Henry himself. He called upon the usurper to surrender the domains which he had conquered and submit himself to the justice of his half-brother. Henry was advised to return a polite answer. 'Even between enemies,' Ayala wrote, 'there should be reason and courtesy.' Instead, with an eye to wider opinion, he addressed a bad-tempered and patronising response to the Prince 'who calls himself eldest son of the King of England and Prince of Aquitaine'. Then, abandoning the protection of the River Najerilla, he ordered his army to cross the bridge and take up stations on the open ground beyond. They stood in their battle lines across the main road, on gently sloping ground falling away to a stream called the Yalde. It was, as the Prince acknowledged, 'a good place to await us'.[19]

On 2 April 1367 the Prince's army crossed the great stone bridge over the Ebro at Logroño and advanced to the village of Navarrete. Here they formed up in battle order. The first line included most of the English and Breton men-at-arms, with English archers at their wings. The nominal commander of this division was the young John of Gaunt. Real control lay with Sir John Chandos and the two marshals of the army, the Englishman Steven Cusington and the Poitevin Guichard d'Angle. Behind them stood the main body, which consisted mainly of Gascons: on the right Albret and Armagnac, on the left the Captal de Buch, in the centre the Prince himself with the *routiers* of the Great Company and the various contingents of exiled Castilians and Aragonese. About 10 miles of broad treeless plain separated them from the army of the pretender.[20]

Although a great battle had been expected by both sides for several days, the Prince achieved complete tactical surprise. His army advanced silently out of Navarrete well before dawn on 3 April 1367. Instead of moving along the main road, as the Castilians had expected, they approached around the far side of a long steep ridge which bounded the plain on the north. As dawn broke, the cross of St. George appeared without warning on the left flank of Henry of Trastámara's army only a

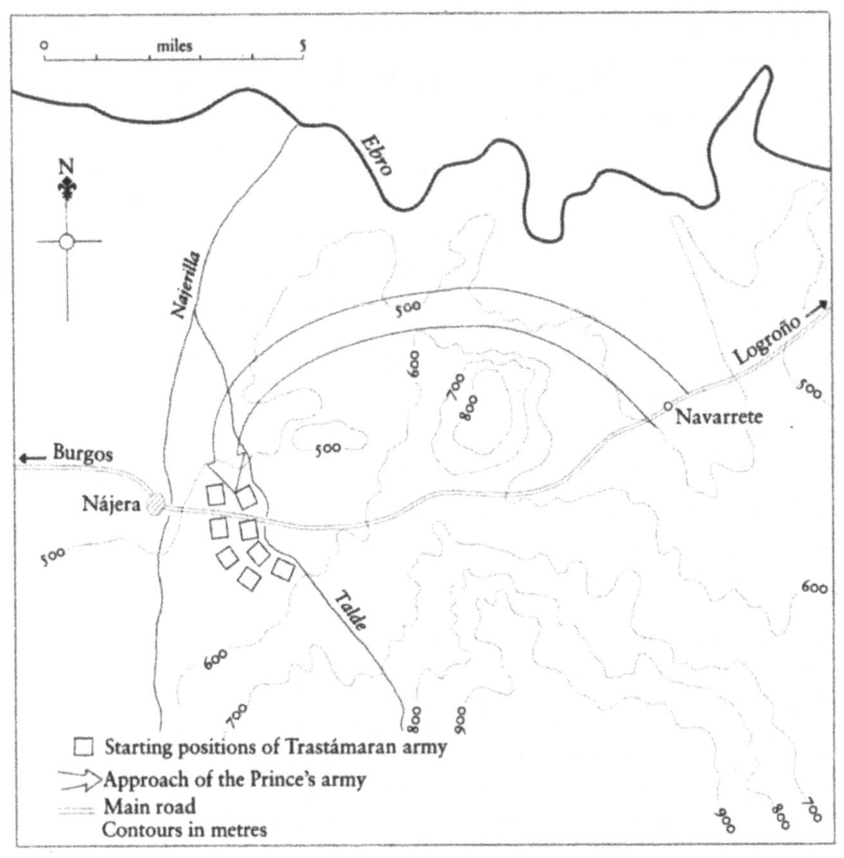

40 The battle of Nájera, 3 April 1367

few hundred yards away. As the English and Gascon troops dismounted to fight, Bertrand du Guesclin was obliged to wheel the whole army round to face this unexpected line of attack. The first division executed the manoeuvre with great skill and speed. But the second began to break up in confusion and panic. Some of the Castilian light horse deserted to the enemy. They were followed by a rather larger number of infantrymen. Bertrand, sensing the situation getting out of hand, decided that he could not wait in line until the English attacked. Abandoning the advantage of the defensive, he ordered his front line, comprising the French men-at-arms and the best of the Castilians, to charge the English van.

The chronicler Ayala, a former minister of Don Pedro who had bought his place in this battle by betraying him, carried the standard of the Knights of La Banda in this famous, doomed charge. The main impact of the attack was borne by the troops of John of Gaunt and Sir John Chandos in the centre of the English line. They recoiled, then found their footing and stopped du Guesclin's charge. The two wings of the Prince's army, the elite of the Gascon troops, advanced to outflank and surround the French from each side. The rest of the Castilian army were impotent spectators. Henry of Trastámara's brother Don Tello, who commanded the light cavalry on the left wing of the Castilian army, tried to advance to their aid. But he was met by a rain of arrows. The lightly protected men and horses suffered terrible casualties before they finally turned and fled. Henry himself tried to relieve the French by charging around the flank of the Anglo-Gascons and engaging the Prince in the centre of the second line. He encountered the same fate. The heavy Castilian cavalry who were with him declined to demean themselves by fighting on foot. Their horses fell in dozens beneath the dense mass of arrows. So the French companies were left isolated in the middle of the fighting. They were efficiently crushed.

The main body of the Castilian army, most of which had so far taken no part in the battle, found itself attacked from two directions at once, from the front by the Prince and from the side by the victorious troops of Gaunt and Chandos. It was all over in minutes. The Castilians broke their ranks and fled in disorder towards Nájera as the pretender vainly tried to rally them. The Prince's reserve, which consisted mainly of the Aragonese cavalry of James of Majorca, was ordered to pursue the fleeing mass of men. Most of them were trapped and killed on the banks of the fast-flowing river or cut down as they tried to force their way across the narrow bridge. Some were caught hiding in the houses of the town or trying to escape over the walls. When on the following morning the heralds went through the field to identify the fallen they found more than 5,000 bodies. At least half of Henry of Trastámara's army had perished, almost all of them in the final minutes of the battle when the outcome was already decided. On the Prince's side, the casualties were negligible.

The Prince spent the night on the field of battle surrounded by the carnage, as tradition required. Don Pedro's joy, however, was marred by the escape of his rival. Henry of Trastámara's horse was found and sent to England to be presented as a trophy to Edward III. But the heralds were unable to find his body, and he was certainly not among the prisoners. He had in fact escaped unharmed on the mount of one of his squires in the closing moments of the battle. Within two days he was in Aragon. From there he escaped to France.[21]

The haul of prisoners was immense. All of the principal captains, French, Castilian and Aragonese, who had fought on Henry's side were captured. There could hardly have been a better illustration of how developed the hunt for prisoners had become in fourteenth-century warfare than the scale of the slaughter at Nájera combined with the almost complete survival of the rich and ransomable. Their treatment gave rise to a number of problems which revealed much about contemporary attitudes to prisoners of war. The first and most delicate concerned those French prisoners who had been captured before and whose ransoms were still unpaid. They included Arnoul d'Audrehem, who still owed part of the ransom of Poitiers. The Prince singled him out as the prisoners filed past him, calling him a false traitor and accusing him of breaking the terms of his parole. Arnoul defended himself. He had not armed himself against the Prince, he said, but against Don Pedro. The cause was Pedro's, even if the army was the Prince's. The jury of twelve knights (four English, four Gascon and four Breton) who had been appointed to try the case agreed and acquitted him. There was in fact much sympathy for the gallant old Marshal, now more than sixty years old. Even the Prince professed himself 'glad that so valiant a knight had found good reasons to defend himself.' This was fortunate for Bertrand du Guesclin, who still owed most of the ransom of Auray and faced exactly the same accusation from Sir John Chandos. There would probably have been less sympathy for him.[22]

More remarkable in some ways and certainly more venomous was the dispute between Don Pedro and the Prince about the fate of the Castilian prisoners. According to the treaty of Libourne, all prisoners were to belong to their captors, with the single exception of Henry of Trastámara himself. To Pedro, however, these men were not articles of commerce but rebels. After the battle he had recognised among them a famous military engineer who had deserted his cause the year before. He fell on him and killed him with his own hands. The engineer's captor, a Gascon knight, was furious at the loss of the ransom and dishonoured by the breach of the protection which every captor owed to his prisoners by the laws of war. He complained to the Prince, who remonstrated with the Castilian King. On the following day Pedro demanded the surrender of all Castilian prisoners, offering to pay their value personally. In the event Pedro was permitted by the Prince to order the execution of one of the captives, Henry of Trastámara's chamberlain Gomez Carillo de Quintana, against whom he felt particular animosity. He was drawn from a hurdle and then had his throat slit. According to Ayala, who was himself among the prisoners, the Castilian King also succeeded in executing three other prominent Castilian noblemen, whether with or without the Prince's approval it is difficult to say. But the Prince refused to allow the wholesale slaughter which Don Pedro conceived to be necessary to the security of his throne. The men-at-arms of his army, he said, had 'fought for honour and the prisoners were theirs.' He may also have reflected that Don Pedro could not afford to pay for them whatever his promises. Chivalry was a code of conduct for regulating the private legal relations of men engaged in war. Politics hardly entered into it.[23]

The prisoners of Nájera made fortunes for their captors. Some of the prisoners were to be traded and fought over for years to come. Bertrand du Guesclin was appropriated by the Prince, and his ransom was eventually fixed at 100,000 Castilian *doblas* (about £19,200). The Prince challenged him to fix his own ransom, wondering whether he would discredit himself by fixing it too low or ruin himself by fixing it too high. Du Guesclin was generally thought to have got it just right. However, he was not released until the end of the year, after the King of France had guaranteed almost a third of the agreed sum. A man of du Guesclin's stature could be counted on to pay his ransom sooner or later. His place in the comradeship of arms mattered to him. Moreover, he could expect to encounter his captors again. The Castilians and Aragonese had a different calculation to make and some of them could not afford the vast sums which they had promised to pay under the pressure of defeat and captivity. The cousin of Peter IV of Aragon, Alfonso Count of Denia, had been captured by two English squires, Robert Hawley and Richard Chamberlain and then taken over by the Prince in return for the promise of compensation. His ransom was fixed at 150,000 *doblas* (about £28,800), the largest recorded ransom of any of the prisoners of Nájera. Denia was shortly afterwards released on delivering up his two sons as hostages and producing a guarantee from the Count of Foix. When the ransom proved difficult to collect, the Prince sold his rights at a discount to that great trader in prisoners, Edward III. He in turn sold them at an even greater discount to Hawley and the heirs of Chamberlain in settlement of their claims for compensation. There followed thirty years of litigation between the Crown, the captors and various other creditors of the prisoner, punctuated by diplomatic incidents, physical violence and a murder. The hostages were the main victims of this process. One of Denia's sons had been delivered up to the Count of Foix, who kept him for years in a dungeon loaded with chains. The other appears to have been kept more suitably in England, but was not released until the accounts of the ransom were finally settled in 1390, twenty-three years after the battle. The story of Muñiz Godoy, Master of the Order of Calatrava in Aragon, was in some ways rather similar. Godoy was captured by a squire of the Prince called John Kempton and released on parole shortly after the battle. He refused to pay a penny of his ransom. Kempton was advised to pursue him in the courts of Aragon, first to prove his rights, and then, when these had been established in his favour, to collect the money. Since the Order of Calatrava was in financial difficulty and the King of Aragon depended on them for the defence of an important sector of his frontier, this was a delicate and drawn out matter. Kempton was to pass most of the rest of his life pursuing his fortune, travelling frequently to Barcelona, instructing a succession of attorneys, and eventually settling permanently in Sarragossa as a naturalised Aragonese. He finally recovered the last of what was due to him in the year 1400. He had spent most of his life in pursuit of this fortune.[24]

The invasion of Castile was the Prince's greatest military victory and his worst political failure. Don Pedro entered Burgos to a rapturous reception on 7 April 1367 almost exactly a year after he had last left it. But when the Prince tried to enforce the promises which had been made to him at Libourne, he found his client argumentative and obstructive. The Prince demanded the immediate cession of the Basque provinces. Don Pedro could not contemplate weakening his kingdom and discrediting himself at such a moment. So he pretended to agree, but arranged with the communities of the region to refuse their co-operation. When the lord of Poyanne came to take possession in the Prince's name, the Basques would not recognise Pedro's charters. They were entitled by custom to choose their own lord, they said. The Castilian King was no more forthcoming about money. The expedition had been extremely expensive. The Prince's claims for mobilisation costs and wages of war came to no less than 2,720,000 florins (about £385,000). This prodigious sum was roughly comparable to the cost of Edward III's two-year campaign in the Low Countries between 1338 and 1340. It was about two thirds of the ransom of John II of France, which a much richer country than Castile was having the utmost difficulty collecting. The Prince demanded immediate payment. If that was impossible, then he wanted twenty castles ceded to him as security. Don Pedro, whose treasury had been squandered by the usurper, was quite unable to pay at once. As for the castles, he would not cede them 'in any circumstances'. There was an ill-humoured debate between the councillors on each side, at the end of which the Prince reluctantly accepted that he would get neither money nor security. All that Don Pedro would do was swear a mighty oath before the high altar of the great cathedral of Burgos that he would perform his undertakings in due course. A first instalment was promised in four months time.[25]

In order to maintain the pressure on his fickle ally, the Prince was obliged to remain with his army in Castile throughout that time. Their wages mounted up. They soon exhausted the supplies of northern Castile and were compelled to move south and encamp around the city of Valladolid. The summer heat intensified. The men began to suffer from hunger, then dysentery. Don Pedro pressed his subjects for loans and taxes. 'I cannot meet these demands from my own resources,' he told them; 'I have no treasure, and no revenues.' At the end of August 1367, when the four months allowed for the payment of the first instalment had passed, Don Pedro sent the Prince a cool letter thanking him for his assistance, expressing his pleasure that the great mercenary army would no longer be required, and informing him that his subjects would pay nothing while it remained on Castilian soil. If the Prince would care to leave the country and nominate agents to handle his financial affairs in his absence, they would be paid in due course. There was nothing that the Prince could do. His men were at the end of their endurance. So he turned north and returned empty-handed to Gascony.[26]

For the next two years, the Prince's anger at the way in which he had been treated dominated Anglo-Castilian relations, displacing all the strategic and political considerations which had caused him to cross the Pyrenees in the first place. As a result he lost not only his money but whatever political advantage might otherwise have been extracted from the Spanish crisis. He began to resort to desperate schemes to enforce his rights and obtain his revenge against Don Pedro. He authorised Hugh Calveley to open secret discussions about the possibility of waging war upon the Castilian King in alliance with Aragon and Navarre. The King of Aragon, who had fallen out with the French and was terrified that the Prince's military strength might next be turned against him, was willing enough to encourage these fantasies. Charles of Navarre, whose hopes of extending the frontiers of his kingdom to the sea had been dashed, may even have believed in them. In November 1367 there was a long conference between the representatives of the three princes at Tarbes in southern Gascony. A memorandum was drawn up, in which it was suggested that Don Pedro should be called upon to make proposals not later than April 1368 for meeting the financial and territorial claims of the participants. Failing that, they intended to invite Henry of Trastámara to perform the treaty of Libourne himself, in return for their promise that they would leave Pedro to his fate. There was never the least prospect that either of the half-brothers would accept these terms.[27]

French policy was conducted on more realistic lines. Charles V made it his business to reverse the effects of the battle of Nájera as soon as the outcome was reported to him. He never imagined that this could be done without spending money. Once again Louis of Anjou was the prime mover. Within a month of the battle Louis had met Henry of Trastámara in the fortress of St. André on the bank of the Rhone at Villeneuve-lès-Avignon. Louis promised to persuade his brother to support another attempt to reconquer Castile. The King, cautious at first, became bolder as the scale of the Prince's misjudgments became clear. He instructed Louis to give Henry of Trastámara as much support as he could without, at this stage, overtly implicating him or repudiating the treaties with England. So Louis installed the Castilian pretender in the vast cliff-top fortress of Peyrepertuse on the march of Roussillon and gave him a war-chest of 100,000 francs. Henry sent agents to buy arms in Avignon, then a major centre of the arms trade, and others to recruit men-at-arms among his sympathisers in Castile.[28]

Charles V's thoughts are difficult to reconstruct. His brother certainly saw these measures as steps towards challenging the English position in south-western France. Louis allowed Henry of Trastámara to employ the companies under his control in needling raids over the eastern border of the Prince's domain. During the summer, le Limousin and Perrin Bouvetault were both active on his behalf in Bigorre and then in Rouergue. On 13 August 1367, acting in his private capacity and accompanied only by his most 'intimate and discreet' councillors, Louis secretly met Henry of Trastámara again, this time in the citadel of the port of Aigues-Mortes at the mouth of the Rhone. One of these councillors was Francisco Perellós, who had become for all practical purposes one of Anjou's ministers. He was probably the main author of the treaty which the two princes now made. Its prolix and violent language was plainly not drafted by the chancery clerks ordinarily entrusted with the preparation of diplomatic documents. The agreement provided for Louis to give Henry every possible assistance in the deposition of his rival. But their main target was expressed to be those 'latter day Nimrods' the King of England, his sons the Prince of Wales and John of Gaunt, and the King of Navarre.

These arrogant, presumptuous and audacious men resemble nothing so much as the fallen angels. They have dared to invade the kingdoms of France and Castile. They have unleashed and sustained terrible wars, despoiling churches, sanctuaries and other places in both kingdoms, but especially in France. Like Satan and his accomplices they have attacked, corrupted, polluted, violated and despoiled them, murdering men, women and children at the breast, and not even sparing young girls and holy nuns.

Once Castile had been reconquered the parties proposed to turn against these vipers and to make perpetual war against them. Henry of Trastámara expected to be master of his kingdom within six months. The combined assault on Aquitaine would then begin in March 1368.[29]

Henry did not recover Castile within six months, but he came closer to it than any one could have anticipated. In about the middle of September 1367 he crossed the Pyrenees through the county of Foix with about 500 men-at-arms and entered the kingdom of Aragon. Peter IV, who would have nothing to do with this enterprise after the disaster of Nájera, refused to let him pass through his dominions. But Henry crossed the western provinces of Aragon without Peter's consent and evaded every attempt to stop him. On 27 September 1367 he entered the kingdom of Castile, less than a month after the Prince had left it. The discontented nobility of the kingdom, who had always resented Don Pedro's rough hand, flocked to his standard. With them came many fresh enemies whom Pedro had made in the orgy of revenge that had followed the recovery of his kingdom in the spring. 'If you rule your kingdom now as you did before, you will risk losing it and your life as well,' the Prince had warned him in the course of their heated exchanges back in May; 'neither I, nor my father the King of England will be able to save you then, even should we wish to.' On 8 October 1367 Henry of Trastámara entered Burgos. He was joined there by some of the Breton bands who had fought for him in 1366, and even by a few English and Gascons who had been with the Prince at Nájera and now felt free to switch sides again. In the following months Henry recovered most of León and Old Castile, except for Galicia and the regions of the east bordering on Aragon. At the end of April 1368 he laid siege to Toledo.[30]

In England Edward III's ministers were transfixed by the rapidly deteriorating state of his relations with France. They stood by as the work of 1367 was undone in Spain. The extraordinary scheme devised by the Prince's agents at Tarbes required the endorsement of Edward III. But no decision was made at all until the beginning of 1369 when, pressed by the ambassadors of the King of Aragon, he eventually authorised the Prince to proceed. Edward declined to do anything about the 'rancour and hatred' which Don Pedro quite correctly conceived that the Prince bore him. The Castilian King's ambassadors, who were in England at about the same time as those of Aragon, were told in effect that the policy of the English government was to leave Pedro to his fate. By then it hardly mattered what their policy was.[31]

The first great reflux of *routiers* to return from Spain comprised the followers of Bertrand du Guesclin and Olivier de Mauny. Most of them were survivors of Nájera, defeated and disappointed men. Many were paroled prisoners of war. They trekked home through Aragon and began to arrive in Languedoc in the late summer and autumn of 1367, where they immediately began to cause serious disorder. The Duke of Anjou was still struggling to persuade the Estates of Languedoc to pay for a standing force of 600 men-at-arms to contain them. They did not finally agree until November 1367 by which time the *routiers* were beyond containment. Louis was at his wits' end to find work for them. Some served in garrisons around Languedoc or found cities to pay them for protection against other companies. The presence of a large number of Marshal Boucicaut's troops in Auvergne may well have made the situation worse by preventing them from dispersing northward out of the province.[32]

The solution eventually found was to export them across the Rhone into Provence. The decision seems to have been hastily made for no better reason than that Provence was the nearest available void beyond the frontiers of France. The Duke of Anjou had his own territorial ambitions in the Queen of Naples' territory and found it easy enough to pick a quarrel there. Early in 1368 Anjou made a treaty with Bertrand du Guesclin. The great captain was promised a substantial fee for mounting an invasion of Provence. The costs were eventually underwritten by the Estates of Languedoc. In February 1368 Bertrand reunited all the Bretons and most of the Gascon and Provençal companies whom he had commanded in Spain and led them across the Rhone. The official campaign was brief. It ended inconclusively in May after the army had passed nearly three months in reducing the town of Tarascon on the

Rhone and in failing to capture the much more important city of Arles. But the companies remained in Provence for their own account for several months longer. It was the fourth time in a decade that this rich Mediterranean principality had been overrun by *routier* armies expelled from France. This time it was barely defended. The small army which the officers of the Queen of Naples eventually succeeded in assembling was cut to pieces with heavy losses. The Papacy, which had taken the leading role in buying off the Great Companies of 1357, 1361 and 1365, had recently abandoned Avignon and returned to Rome. The papal rector in the territory paid protection money to Bertrand du Guesclin without result. No major town fell to them, but the *plat pays* was completely devastated. 'The Provençals are enemies of my lord of Anjou and all the damage that we can inflict on them we shall, whether you like it or not,' Bertrand wrote to a Frenchman who had ventured to complain about the brutality of his men. In July 1368 the Archbishop of Embrun reported that Bertrand's companies had spread over the whole of Provence and the Dauphiné and that the roads were impassable in both provinces.[33]

Worse was expected when eventually the Prince of Wales returned from Castile with the companies which had previously operated in Normandy and in the provinces of the Saône. Preparations to ward them off were in hand throughout the summer. The Estates-General of Languedoil met at Compiègne in June, at Chartres in July, and at Sens two months later. At these assemblies the King's ministers had produced a series of comprehensive ordinances for the defence of the provinces against the returning Gascons. The main priority was the control of fortifications. In each *baillage*, commissioners were appointed to inspect all fortifications and to repair and supply those which were defensible at the expense of their owners. Any that were not defensible or could not be repaired were to be demolished unless they were vital to the defence of the region, in which case they might be put in order at the expense of the King. This was not the first attempt to deal with the rash of fortifications which covered the French provinces, but it was much the most effective to date. Walled towns were allowed to apply a quarter of the aids collected within their jurisdiction to repair and reconstruction. The ordinances of the Estates-General provided for men-at-arms to be raised to defend these places. Their wages were to be paid out of the receipts of the aids levied in the region. Special measures were to be taken to guard bridge-towns in order to stop the companies from crossing rivers or supplying themselves over long distances. Everywhere, the population were required to withdraw to the nearest walled places as the invaders approached, taking with them everything that could be eaten or sold. The councillors of the Duke of Burgundy devised their own even more elaborate plan of defence in September 1367, which envisaged not only the withdrawal of people and victuals but the dismantling and removal of mill machinery and forges. In addition to these comprehensive measures of static defence, the officers of the Crown were required to make estimates of the number of men in their districts available for field service against the companies. One army was raised for mobile operations in Lower Normandy. Another operated under the command of Marshal Boucicaut and Louis of Sancerre in the provinces of the middle and upper Loire. These arrangements, particularly the reservation of part of the local yield of the aids to fortification, were the clearest demonstration so far of the King's changing strategic priorities, which attached much greater importance to emptying the countryside and defending the cities than to confronting the enemy in battle. They were undoubtedly more perfect on paper than on the ground, as all such plans are. But they gave the defence the advantage over the Great Companies for the first time since the latter's creation in the early 1360s, and served as the dress rehearsal for the greater conflict with the English in the following decade.[34]

The Prince's army was disbanded at Saint-Jean Pied-de-Port in the foothills of the Pyrenees at the beginning of September 1367. Almost at once several thousand discarded soldiers formed themselves into a new Great Company. Their purpose was to re-invade the provinces of eastern and central France where many of them had operated profitably before 1366. Their leaders were Bertucat d'Albret and Bernard de la Salle, both of whom had commanded important Gascon companies at Nájera. Bertucat was already a notorious figure in France, and Bernard de la Salle would soon become just as famous. We have it on the uncertain authority of Froissart that he had made his name as the man who scaled the walls of Clermont-en-Beauvasis and was first into la Charité-Sur-Loire: 'fort et subtil echelleur, ainsi comme un chat.' The great majority of the new company were Gascons. But there was also a troop of about 800 English and Bretons, led by John Cresswell and Robert Briquet. They called themselves the 'route des Englès des Granz Compagnies'. They were an amalgamation of at least twenty English-led *routier* bands which had fought with the Prince at Nájera, and in some cases with Bertrand du Guesclin and Henry of Trastámara the year before.[35]

In October 1367, the whole horde began to move east. They burned their way up the valleys of the Lot and the Dordogne through Quercy and

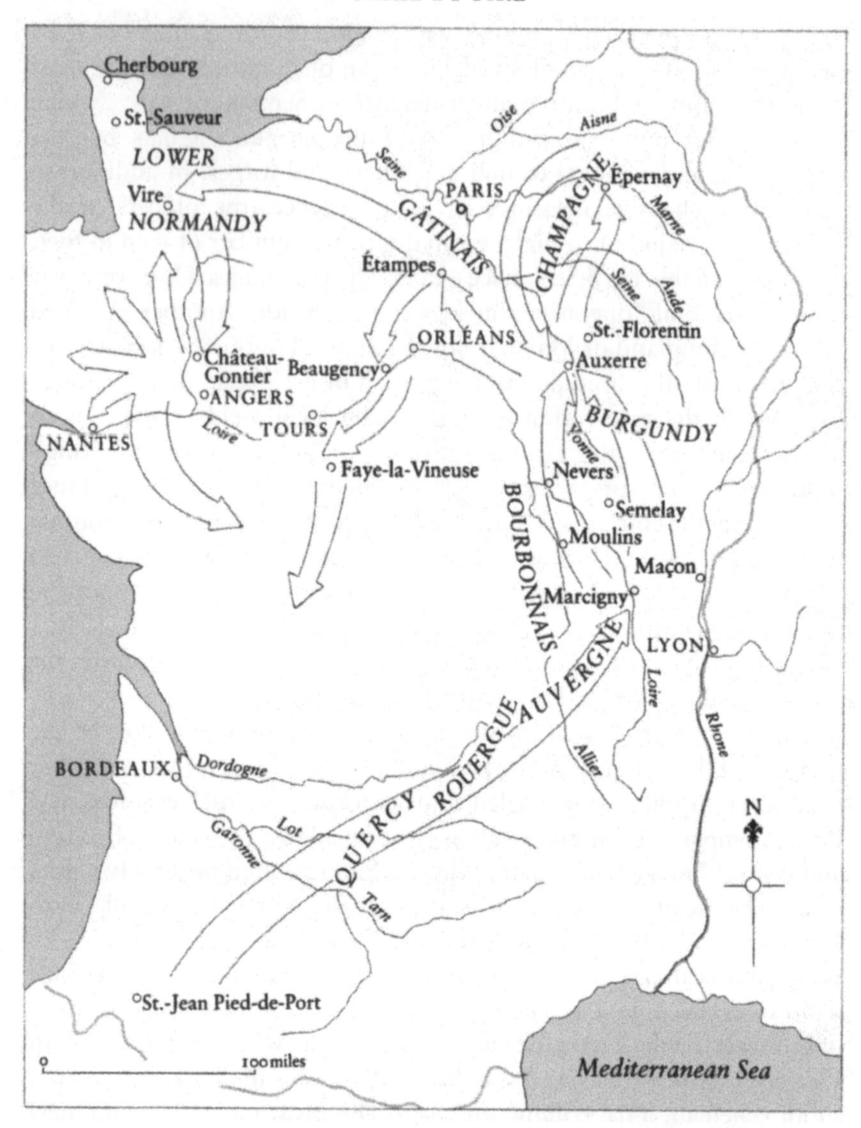

41 The Great Company of 1367, October 1367–January 1369

the Rouergue, the first time since the peace of 1360 that these provinces had been seriously damaged by *routiers*. The Count of Armagnac claimed that 600,000 florins of damage had been done in his domains alone. In Auvergne the French government made a determined attempt to stop them at the Loire. All the bridges over the river were defended. The fords were obstructed with sunken boats. The cavalry army of Marshal

Boucicaut and Louis of Sancerre hovered about the east bank. Some of the companies avoided the defences by marching up the west bank of the river into the Bourbonnais and the Nivernais. The main body eventually succeeded in forcing a crossing in February 1368 at the small bridge-town of Marcigny-les-Nonnains in the Charolais. It did them little good. Advancing through Burgundy, they found themselves in empty country, denuded of supplies and spoil, where they were continually harassed by the officers of the King and the Duke of Burgundy. The evidence, which is fragmentary, suggests that they did a great deal of localised damage in the places that they passed through, and captured a few poorly guarded places. But they were unable to supply themselves on their march or to establish themselves anywhere. They could not therefore pause long enough to conduct any significant operation. They passed through the whole length of the duchy of Burgundy in six or seven days, beating the air. The smaller group, which had invaded the Nivernais, fared little better. They passed barely six weeks there before leaving. In the first half of March 1368 the two wings joined up again in the Auxerrois.[36]

Here the companies were able to rest and resupply themselves at two inadequately fortified monasteries whose stores had been left in their barns. In the middle of March 1368 they resumed their march north. Crossing the Seine and the Aube, they entered the plain of Champagne. They captured Épernay, which was the only significant town without a royal garrison, and occupied a number of places around it. But this was their only success in the province. At the beginning of April they crossed the Marne in several places, apparently intending to make their way around Paris by the north. Criers passed through the northern Île de France and Upper Normandy ordering men to withdraw into fortified places with all their foodstuffs and movable goods. After a few days, the companies abandoned the attempt to penetrate further north and returned to the Marne valley. Here they split into small groups to ease their growing supply problem. As the enterprise declined from an organised military operation into an undisciplined mass of independent gangs, the leading captains tried to use what bargaining power they still had to negotiate a deal with the government. But they pitched their demands too high. They wanted 1,400,000 francs to leave France. Discussions were broken off at once. At this stage the Great Company began to break up. A number of companies separated from the main body and disbanded. In July 1368 the rest, a few thousand strong, moved south back into the Auxerrois. They were unable to enter Burgundy by the north. So they moved across the Gâtinais south of

Paris. On 4 July 1368 they encamped around Étampes and briefly threatened the capital. After five days, their supplies ran out.[37]

Misfortune sharpened tempers. At Étampes the English and Gascon companies fell out. The Gascons moved off south into the Loire valley on their own. Here they enjoyed some brief success. They captured the bridge-town of Beaugency and held it for three weeks. Then they abandoned it, moving south across the old stone bridge into the Sologne. This proved to be a mistake. Beaugency was promptly reoccupied by the government's troops. The rain began to fall heavily. The river swelled. The Gascons were unable to get back onto the north bank. They wandered westward searching in vain for a crossing. In Touraine they were challenged by a large force commanded by the army of the Marshal Louis of Sancerre. The Gascons, who had shed much of their strength in the course of their wanderings, did not care to fight a battle with these men. Instead they siezed the immense fortress of Faye-la-Vineuse on the southern march of Touraine, which belonged to the Marshal's brother. There was a desultory attempt to besiege this place. But the Gascons held out there for four months before they escaped into English territory and dispersed.[38]

The English wing of the Great Company survived for longer. They moved west from Étampes into Normandy. On 2 August 1368 they captured the town of Vire. About forty or sixty men entered the gates in daylight with their weapons concealed beneath their clothing. They killed the gatekeepers, seized the gate and called in the rest of the company hiding nearby. It was a famous coup. But the English were unable to sustain themselves for long in Vire. From Vincennes Charles V ordered the abandonment of the *plat pays* throughout Lower Normandy. Shortly, the invaders ran short of food. Four or five hundred of them, about half the strength, withdrew in the middle of August. A few days later they occupied Chateau-Gontier in Anjou. The rest were bought out in September and came south to join them there. In Anjou they spread themselves among a number of minor forts, wasting the region and gradually penetrating west towards the coast. With the harvest standing in the fields they enjoyed a brief respite from starvation.[39]

The French authorities responded to the new threat, potentially the most serious in Normandy since 1365, with a mixture of diplomacy, money and force. Sir John Chandos, who was then residing in his great fortress at Saint-Sauveur-le-Vicomte in the Cotentin, was recruited to negotiate with his fellow countrymen. He arranged the departure of the companies from Vire. He also did a certain amount to contain them around Chateau-Gontier. But when he returned to Gascony at the end of the year the long-distance raiding resumed. John IV, Duke of Brittany, was obliged to buy them off in return for a series of substantial payments. The Cotentin was repeatedly attacked. At one point the Englishmen came close to capturing Cherbourg. By the end of the year, however, conditions had become increasingly difficult for the English companies. They had exhausted the harvest of September. The government was concentrating larger forces in Lower Normandy to confront them. Isolated groups were ambushed as they looked for spoil and supplies. The Great Company began to suffer serious casualties. Robert Scot, one of the most famous of its captains, was cornered in the buildings of a priory near Chateau-Gontier and killed. Robert Briquet was killed shortly afterwards in another encounter with the government's forces. Early in 1369 Sir John Chandos returned briefly to the Cotentin and negotiated a fresh deal. The invaders agreed to leave in return for 3,000 francs, not a large sum. It was raised from local tax receipts and carefully counted out in the presence of the English captain. When the coin was found to be undervalue, the receiver of le Mans, who had delivered it, was made to leave his horses behind to make up the difference. He returned home on foot.[40]

There were many lessons to be learned from the story of the Great Company of 1367, which for all its internal weaknesses was the most sustained and disciplined enterprise of its kind in the 1360s. The traditional device of buying off the companies or paying them to fight for a brief period in some foreign war was discredited. Louis of Anjou's experience illustrated most of the vices of this expensive and unprofitable method of dealing with the invaders. In the autumn of 1368, when Bertrand du Guesclin's companies returned from Provence into Languedoc, he was once more having to find work for them in his own service or bribe them to go to other parts of France. Outside Languedoc the French government employed the methods which they were to use with success for the remainder of the fourteenth century, essentially the ones which Charles V had recommended to Henry of Trastámara before the battle of Nájera. The companies were forced to move in large numbers through country which had been cleared of every edible or stealable thing. Conditions became exceptionally difficult for the *routiers* even in summer and autumn, but almost impossible in winter. Those who remained behind in the hope of establishing themselves somewhere were generally wiped out. In the Bourbonnais the last remaining *routier* garrisons were cleared late in 1368. Le Bourc Camus returned from Spain to Monteschot and Beauvoir, but he was rooted out of both places and taken off in irons to the Duke of Bourbon's prisons at Moulins. Several factions of the Great Company tried to maintain themselves in the Auxerrois when the rest of the horde had moved into Champagne. Some of these men even succeeded in occupying Saint-Florentin in June 1368. But they were dislodged within weeks. In the autumn they were compelled to abandon their bases and withdraw south. They wandered aimlessly through Forez, Beaujolais and the Nivernais pursued by the Duke's officers. The remnants were eventually cornered and defeated at Semelay in the Nivernais in November. A large number of prisoners was found in their hands whom they had been unable to lodge anywhere in safety.[41]

Not long after the Prince's return to Gascony a sycophant preached a sermon before him at Périgueux in which he compared him to the son of God. 'No one should flatter even the greatest Prince to his face like that,' the Prince later remarked to a friend; 'fortune may strike him down at any moment, and all his famous deeds will then be forgotten and reduced to nothing.'[42] This fate was soon to befall the Prince of Wales.

Don Pedro's repudiation of his promises had left him bankrupt. To set against the enormous bill for mobilisation costs and war wages, he had only the sums realised from the sale of Don Pedro's jewellery and the initial instalments of the ransoms of Bertrand du Guesclin, Arnoul d'Audrehem and the Count of Denia.[43] There were no reserves, and no question of a subsidy from the English Exchequer. The only resource available to him was taxation. The solution eventually proposed was a permanent *fouage* of ten sous of Guienne (2s sterling) per year until the debt was paid. Initially it was proposed to ask the Estates of Aquitaine to authorise this imposition for a period of five years. Since the nominal yield of the tax was only 27,000 *l.b.* (£5,400) per year and some of that would have been needed to pay the continuing cost of the household, the Prince must have expected to make a drastic composition with his creditors as well. The only evidence about the origin of the scheme comes from Froissart, a doubtful authority at the best of times, who had by now left the Prince's court. According to him, it was devised by the Prince's Chancellor, John Harewell, Bishop of Bath and Wells. It is perfectly possible. Harewell, who had previously been the Constable of Bordeaux, understood the principality's finances as well as any one. The Estates first met at Niort in the autumn of 1367, but failed to agree. The new provinces were prepared to concede the point in return for a promise to abandon the unpopular practice of devaluing the silver coinage and some other reforms; but the nobility of Gascony and Rouergue, and the Count of Périgord would not agree to the tax in any circumstances. The assembly had to be adjourned. When it reconvened, in January 1368, the dissentients refused to appear, and the tax was voted in their absence. Froissart also tells us that the tax was opposed by some of the Prince's own councillors, including Sir John Chandos, who fell out with the Prince on the issue and shortly afterwards withdrew to his estates in Normandy. This account is consistent with fragments of information derived from other sources, and may well be correct.[44]

The Count of Armagnac refused to allow the *fouage* to be collected in his domains, and almost immediately emerged as the chief dissentient. Armagnac's problems were not at all typical, either in scale or in origin. Unlike the rest of the Gascon nobility he had fought on the losing side in the war with France and had enjoyed few opportunities for booty and ransoms. Indeed he had incurred large debts. The heavy personal expenditure which he had incurred in Provence in 1357 had still not all been reimbursed by the Queen of Naples. His capture at the battle of Launac had resulted in his imprisonment for two years and a ransom of 300,000 florins (about £42,500). In order to raise this sum he had had to pledge his personal jewellery, sell part of his domain and borrow heavily. Even then he was well short. Armagnac had opposed the very first *fouage* to be awarded after the Prince's arrival in the principality, the only notable figure to do so. On this occasion, the Prince had bought him off by lending him the money needed for his ransom. When Armagnac returned from Spain, he still owed the Prince 25,000 nobles (about £8,300) of this loan, but the Prince owed him (by his own account) more than 200,000 florins (about £28,300) in war wages for himself and his retainers. Armagnac was also untypical in another respect. He had never really been reconciled to the transfer of his domains to English sovereignty. The reason is plain enough. Before the peace he had been a great figure in southern France. Although he was admitted to the Prince's council in 1364 when he did homage, this could hardly disguise the fact that he now belonged to a political community in which his own role was marginal. It was not just a matter of pride, although that was no doubt part of it. Armagnac needed the power of the state to maintain his family against its enemies. He could not count on the Prince as he had counted on the house of Valois.[45]

Armagnac was in one sense an outsider in Gascon politics. But the *fouage* of 1368 gave him a grievance which was shared by much of the native nobility of the old duchy, and particularly strongly by two significant noble clans with whom Armagnac was connected by marriage, the lords of Albret and the Counts of Périgord. The grievances of these three men all illustrated, in their different ways, the problems of governing the English principality in the aftermath of the war.

Money was the root of the lord of Albret's difficulties just at it was of Armagnac's. Arnaud Amanieu d'Albret had done well out of the war. But he too had been captured at Launac and assessed for a heavy ransom, in his case 100,000 florins (about £14,000). The last instalment of this sum had been paid only in the spring of 1367. In addition he had had to contribute to the ransoms of two younger brothers and a cousin, who had been captured with him. These demands on Albret's purse came at a difficult time for him. During the 1350s he and his clan had been among the most successful military entrepreneurs of the south-west, drawing large profits from the operations of garrisons and companies spread across much of central France. These profits had been much reduced after the peace, as the Albrets gradually sold out of their strongholds in Auvergne and the Bourbonnais, and conditions became more difficult for them elsewhere. Many years later, at a banquet in Paris, Albret was overheard by Froissart complaining that he had never had as much money since the days when every passing merchant was at his mercy. The words were said in jest, but they were truer than the chronicler knew. The Spanish campaign might have repaired Albret's fortunes. Instead he had lost face and money, and gained nothing. He was also, like Armagnac, sensitive to his waning influence in the enlarged duchy which had emerged from the peace of 1360, where power had to be shared not only with the magnates of other, formerly French provinces, but with Englishmen such as Chandos and Harewell, Streatley, Felton and Stafford, who now dominated the affairs of Aquitaine and were themselves surrounded by greedy and ambitious clients. Albret was a dangerous antagonist. His huge domains were concentrated in the Landes and the lower reaches of the Dordogne close to Bordeaux. His kinship extended through most of the south-west. His family had a long history of unstable alliances, discarded as their interests required. Arnaud-Amanieu's grandfather had fought for Edward I and against Edward II. His father had fought against Edward III for the first three years of the war and for him for the next twenty. Arnaud-Amanieu himself had supplied troops to fight for Charles V at Cocherel, only to become the King of Navarre's lieutenant in France in the following year. In Bordeaux cathedral in July 1363, he had been the first baron of Aquitaine to do homage to the Prince. But like his forebears Albret was essentially a superior freebooter, fond of money and willing to sell his support to whoever seemed likely over the longer term to offer him most.[46]

Archambaud Count of Périgord was a very different sort of individual, an impulsive young man who had recently inherited the county from his father at the age of twenty-one. He had fought with the Prince in Spain and presumably accumulated debts. But his motives for joining the opposition were probably political rather than financial. The Counts of Périgord had been trying for generations to create a consolidated fief in Périgord which would stand comparison with the princely appanages of France. This ambition had brought them up against the main towns, in particular Périgueux, and some powerful noble houses in the southern part of the province. The incorporation of Périgord in the principality of Aquitaine might have been a great opportunity for him. As soon as it had happened he made a large number of claims to recover property, most of it in the valleys of the Vezère and the Dordogne, which had belonged to his father and had been regranted to others after the English had conquered the area in 1345. Since he was now a subject of the King of England, he said, he should be restored to them. Sir John Chandos, who had had to deal with some of these claims before the Prince's arrival, accepted the principle. But the Prince did not. He had a good deal less sympathy for aristocratic empire-builders, and was a personal friend of one of some of the Count's rivals. When, early in 1368, Archambaud raised a small army to attack one of those rivals, the lord of Mussidan, he was arrested by the Prince's Seneschal in Périgord and briefly imprisoned at Périgueux, a humiliation which rankled with him for many years.[47]

The Prince had once been able to resolve such tensions. He had made adroit gifts and loans to potential enemies. He had flattered them with his friendship and with the life of his court and council. But political manoeuvre had never been the Prince's strong point. His capacity to draw men by his charm diminished after the Spanish campaign, and his natural generosity was stifled by his financial difficulties. Gascon noblemen who attended his court complained that they were stiffly, even coldly received. These changes in the Prince's manner were aggravated by illness. Like much of his army he had suffered in the summer heat of the Castilian plain, and he returned with a debilitating illness, possibly malaria, from which he was to suffer on and off for the rest of his life. There were intermittent phases of lassitude and long periods when he was bedridden. The Prince's declining health, together with his resentment and frustration as the fruits of the battle of Nájera vanished before his eyes, affected not only his appetite for business, but his temper and his judgment. He became intolerant of opposition. We have only Armagnac's account of his dealings with the Prince, which is no doubt coloured by bitterness and an instinct for propaganda. But it is credible. According to this version, Armagnac sent two of his retained knights to the Prince to plead for an exemption from the *fouage*. They explained his financial difficulties. They declared that the Counts of Armagnac were free men who had never been bound to pay taxes to the Kings of either France or England. The Prince might have treated this as the opening bid in a difficult bargaining process, instead of an insult to his authority. His answer was that he would have the count's money in the teeth of his objections, or destroy him so completely that his family would never again hold a corner of land in Aquitaine.[48]

At the beginning of 1368, when the Prince's quarrel with the Count of Armagnac began, Anglo-French relations were in a state of stagnant calm. Nothing had come of the hypocritical professions of mutual respect which followed Charles V's accession. The ransom of John II was still being paid, late and in small amounts. Edward III had shown little interest in resolving the minor territorial disputes which had served as the excuse for postponing the renunciations of sovereignty. Two bones of contention, concerning the terre de Belleville and some minor fiefs said to belong to the counties of Ponthieu and Montreuil, had been referred to joint commissions of jurists, whose work quickly lost itself in interminable preliminaries and administrative confusion. A curious lethargy overtook English policy. At one important meeting, the English did not even bother to turn up. It is difficult to escape the conclusion that Edward III did not want to perfect the peace, preferring to keep his claim to the French Crown in reserve in case it should become useful again.[49]

In April 1368 the King of England's second son Lionel Duke of Clarence passed through Paris with a magnificent cavalcade on his way to marry a daughter of Galeazzo Visconti, Duke of Milan. The Dukes of Berry and Burgundy met him on the road at Saint-Denis. Charles V received him splendidly at the Louvre. He was entertained for three nights in the principal palaces of the capital and sent on his way loaded with precious gifts.[50] On the surface, relations were correct, even warm. Such courtesies concealed from Edward III the degree to which the

French government too had come to regard the treaties as provisional. He never understood how empty the peace appeared to most Frenchmen after eight years of intermittent brigandage by large armies most of whose leaders were English or Gascon. The English King had done what he conceived that he had to do about the activities of his subjects in France, but no more. He had co-operated in the attempts to clear the surviving garrisons in the course of 1361. He had denounced the Anglo-Gascon companies when the French King had made an issue of them. Occasionally he had taken steps to enforce his will by arresting notorious offenders or sequestering their property in England. But he did not touch those, such as the Captal de Buch, Robert Knolles or Eustache d'Aubricourt, who were his friends. The Prince's approach was even more equivocal. He never overtly patronised the operations of the companies, but he showed no sign of objecting to them, even for form. He allowed the armies of the King of Navarre to cross his territory to make war in France in 1364 and his agents to hire ships in Gascon ports. The independent companies moved freely through the river valleys between Auvergne and the coast. Bordeaux was a major centre for the trade in armour, artillery and prisoners of war. The Prince turned a blind eye to all of this. He enjoyed the company of professional soldiers and did not distinguish between public and private war, any more than the *routiers* themselves did. Several well known captains and patrons of the Great Companies were welcome guests at Bordeaux and Angoulême, where they enjoyed the reflected light of the most lavish court of Europe, as the French government did not fail to notice. All that was wanting to destroy the treaties in their eyes was the occasion.[51]

Charles V had never concealed from his intimates his ambition to recover at least the major part of the English dominions in France. The limiting factors were his conscience, which required at least a plausible juridical ground for repudiating treaties which he had sworn to observe, and the resources of his shrunken and damaged kingdom, which would not necessarily bear the strain of another war. He was also conscious of the need to manage public opinion. Several elements of this calculation were changing in the late 1360s. The successful containment of the Great Company of 1367, the bankruptcy of the Prince and the divisions among the Prince's subjects, the distant lethargy of Edward III were all significant factors. The government's tax revenues were buoyant. In the summer of 1367 the King had felt able to placate the Estates-General of Languedoil by halving the rates at which the aids and the *fouage* were levied, as well as cutting the regulated prices on which the *gabelle* was charged. In spite of heavy expenditure on containing the companies and on maintaining a resplendent court and indulging his extravagant appetite for building, Charles V had accumulated a contingency reserve in coin at the Louvre, the Hotel St.-Pol and the royal castles of Melun and Vincennes, much as Edward III was doing in England. By 1368 it amounted to some 400,000 francs.[52]

As for the juridical excuse, this was providentially furnished by the complaints of the Gascon lords against the *fouage*. Charles had carefully cultivated his relations with them, ever since his accession. He had employed their companies in his armies. He had entertained and flattered them at his court. He had released the Captal de Buch without ransom. He had lent the Count of Armagnac money when he fell out with the Prince of Wales. On 4 May 1368, Arnaud-Amanieu d'Albret was married to the Charles V's sister-in-law, Marguerite de Bourbon, in the chapel of the King's private residence at the Hotel St.-Pol in Paris. Charles had not only arranged the marriage but contributed a lump sum of 30,000 francs and an income of 4,000 francs a year to the bride's dowry. A large number of prominent Gascon noblemen attended the celebrations. It is difficult to believe that Charles had not planned what happened next. Among the guests in Paris was the Count of Armagnac. While he was there, he secretly lodged papers for an appeal against the *fouage* on behalf of himself and his son. The appeal was addressed to the King of France 'in his capacity as the sovereign lord of the Duke and the whole duchy of Aquitaine'.[53]

By the treaty of Calais, the King of France had undertaken in the clearest terms not to exercise any sovereign powers in Aquitaine pending their complete renunciation in due course. If Charles entertained the appeal, he would be repudiating the treaty. War would be bound to follow, as he knew. The delay in reacting to Armagnac's document was due mainly to the need to cultivate support for such a bold move among his family and councillors, and to prepare the management of opinion outside. The legal issues involved were unusual and difficult. Could a sovereign Prince renounce his sovereignty? If the King of France was still nominally sovereign in the south-west, was he entitled to refuse to hear an appeal from a subject? Had the promise not to exercise sovereign powers lapsed when the time for making the renunciations had passed? Could Edward III and the Prince invoke the treaty when their subjects were still making war in France in breach of it? There was to be much learned debate on all these questions over the following year, and in due course the law schools of the leading universities of Europe would be asked to pronounce upon them.[54] But Charles V's decision never depended on the answers. His was a political calculation. If the appeal was rejected as incompetent, he would be acknowledging the loss of his Crown's powers in the principality. It would be more difficult to repudiate the treaty later. He would also lose the chance to confront the Prince of Wales with the support of some of some the Prince's most powerful subjects. The Prince's problems in Aquitaine were not of Charles V's own making, but he could not afford to turn aside from them.

Six weeks passed, as the pressure on Armagnac increased. Reports arrived of the Prince's plans to enforce payment of the *fouage*. He was said to be recruiting men-at-arms to march against recalcitrant noblemen. There was a persistent rumour that he had offered the Count of Armagnac's lands to Olivier de Clisson. In Paris, Armagnac pressed the French King for an answer. On 30 June 1368, as the Great Company was marching through the Gâtinais towards Paris and men-at-arms were gathering across the Île de France to defend the capital, an important meeting of the royal Council was held to 'reassure the King's conscience' as Charles later put it. It was attended by all the principal civil and military officers of the realm, and many of the leading members of the royal family and the nobility. They resolved that the King should receive the appeals. Immediately after the Council meeting the King entered into a secret agreement with Armagnac, his son John, Arnaud-Amanieu and Bérard d'Albret, and Archambaud Count of Périgord. This document went far beyond the role of disinterested justiciar which Charles V proposed to project in public. He promised to receive the appeal of Armagnac and his son, and any similar appeals which might be lodged by the others. He promised that he would not make the renunciations of sovereignty required by the treaty of Calais without the consent of the appellants. And they for their part agreed not to abandon their appeals or settle with Edward III and the Prince without the consent of the King of France. Turning to the war which they all knew would follow, the appellants agreed to fight for the King of France in the provinces bordering on Aquitaine. Within the duchy the King bound himself to defend them by force of arms if the Prince attacked them or their domains. 'Because they have appealed they are in the King's obedience,' as Charles later informed the King of England. When the agreement had been sealed Charles V granted to the Count of Armagnac an enormous pension of 100,000 gold francs per year. He also made him generous grants of land in the south-west, most of which would have to be conquered from the Prince of Wales and his subjects.[55]

The decision to receive the Gascon appeals was followed by an intense round of diplomatic activity as Charles V set about securing his frontiers in preparation for war. Within a few days of the fateful Council meeting of 30 June Charles' ambassadors left for Castile with offers of money and men to enable Henry of Trastámara to complete the destruction of Pedro I. On 21 November 1368 a formal treaty of alliance was sealed in the pretender's camp at Toledo, where he was still engaged in the prolonged siege at Pedro's principal garrison in central Castile. The treaty provided for the creation of a joint Atlantic war fleet comprising ten French sailing ships and twenty Castilian galleys which were to operate against the English possessions in south-western France in the year 1369. In return Charles proposed to send Bertrand du Guesclin back to Castile with a small army of men-at-arms to complete the work of 1366. Bertrand, who had already begun to recruit men in Languedoc, arrived with some 600 cavalry early in February 1369. He was present at the battle of Montiel on 14 March 1369, when Don Pedro's army was defeated and scattered as it tried to relieve Toledo; and again a few days later at the famous encounter in his tents, when Henry of Trastámara wrestled with Don Pedro on the ground and killed him with his own hands.

O noble, O worthy Pedro, glorie of Spayne,
Whom fortune held so hy in magestee
Well oughten men thy pitous death complayne!

sang Chaucer's monk. Behind the personal tragedy lay a grave political reverse for Edward III and the Prince, who now found a permanently hostile power installed on the southern flank of Aquitaine and the largest war fleet of the Atlantic seaboard committed to the service of their enemies. Only a few weeks before Pedro's death Edward's ministers at Westminster had declined to intervene in the Castilian King's dispute with the Prince of Wales and washed their hands of their sometime ally.[56]

Edward III was destined to suffer a worse humiliation in Flanders, a territory much more important to him, in which he had once held most of the cards. In spite of the nominal allegiance of the Count, Louis de Mâle, to the house of Valois, Edward III had retained the support of the towns and much of the nobility of Flanders for a generation. In October 1364, perhaps the high point of Edward III's prestige on the European continent, Louis de Mâle had agreed in the course of a long conference with the English King in Dover Castle to marry Margaret, his only child, to Edward's fifth son Edmund Langley, Earl of Cambridge. Margaret was the most valuable bride of western Europe, the heiress not only of her father's territories in Flanders, but also of Artois and the imperial county of Burgundy, which belonged to her grandmother. The marriage would have made Edward the greatest prince of northern Europe and created a ring of English-controlled territories around France's northern and eastern borders. But it was not to be. The couple were, like almost all princely personages, related within the prohibited degrees of affinity. A papal dispensation was therefore required. This would normally have been a formality. But in spite of intense lobbying by successive English agents, Urban V refused it. Professing to find in the match 'a danger to their souls, a pernicious example to others and a scandal to many', he eventually annulled the couple's betrothal and declared them to be at liberty to find spouses elsewhere. One of the Pope's earliest biographers wrote of this decision that the Pope could perfectly properly refuse to Edward III what he had granted to others with no better spiritual justification, because the power to give dispensations for marriage was a matter of 'grace and not of justice'. Then, perhaps sensing that a better reason was required, he added that 'if the English dynasty, already so powerful, had succeeded in this, they would have surrounded most of the French kingdom. Either France would have been absorbed by them, or else there would have been unending tribulations, turbulence, war and dissension.' Once again it seemed natural, as it had been before Edward III's victories, to regard France as the cornerstone of western Europe, whose interests could be identified with those of Christendom. Edward III nursed his disappointment and went for the next best thing, which was a political alliance with Louis de Mâle. But the treaty, which was concluded in May 1367, conferred little of value on the English King apart from Louis' undertaking, for what it was worth, not to allow the county to be used as a base for military operations against England.[57]

It was not, in the event, worth very much. The alliance of the Count and the hand of his daughter were eventually to go to Charles V's brother, Philip, Duke of Burgundy. This marriage, first broached with a reluctant Count in 1364, was pressed with growing vigour once Charles V had sealed his pact with the Count of Armagnac. After prolonged and difficult negotiations agreement was finally reached on 12 April 1369. Margaret was even more closely related to Philip than she was to

Edmund Langley, but the necessary papal dispensation was granted at once. It was the beginning of the long eclipse of English influence in Flanders, which had been the main source of tension in the region for more than a century and a half and had three times opened France's northern frontier to English armies. It was also a good indication of the way that intelligent observers with their own interests to protect perceived that things were going.[58]

The Prince of Wales understood the implications of the Count of Armagnac's appeal as soon as he heard that Charles V intended to receive it. Throughout August 1368, his agents were busy recruiting men-at-arms and archers in his domains in Cheshire and North Wales and among his retainers in the English counties. Nearly 800 of these men mustered at Northampton in September. Others were being raised on his behalf by the Prince's brother Edmund Langley and the ambitious young Earl of Pembroke. Edward III's ministers at Westminster took much longer to appreciate the direction of events. They observed the developing crisis in paralysed disbelief. Early in September 1368, an embassy led by John Neville lord of Raby and the former constable of Bordeaux John Streatley left urgently for Paris to find out what was happening. The French King, who had no desire to bring matters prematurely to a head, put off his answer. In due course, he said, he would send the Count of Tancarville to Westminster with a considered statement of his position. The only result of Neville's embassy was to enable the lord of Albret to bend the ambassadors' ears to his cause and to create friction between Westminster and Bordeaux. Albret, who had lodged his own appeal a few days before the ambassadors reached Paris, presented them with a document summarising his grievances in language which made a great impression among his many friends at Westminster. When Edward III wrote to his son asking for an explanation, he received a furious response from the Prince threatening to challenge anyone who took Albret's word against his. In the meantime the English government stuck to its policy that Aquitaine must finance its own defence. They paid for the retinues of the Earls of Cambridge and Pembroke, but otherwise made no contribution to the prince's preparations.[59]

As the autumn advanced the French worked hard to turn the appeals of Armagnac and Albret into a general rebellion against the Prince's authority in the south-west. Charles V and Louis of Anjou wrote letters to the larger towns and the more prominent noblemen of the principality, rehearsing all the reasons why the King was entitled to act as he had in spite of the treaties, and inviting them to join their own names to the appeals. They promised grants and favours, and protection from the Prince's revenge. Except in regions dominated by the Count of Armagnac, which produced a rash of appellants during September and October, the initial reactions were incomprehension and fear. The Count of Périgord was offered 40,000 francs to join the appeals, but refused to move for several months until the direction of events had become clear. The consuls of the small town of Cajarc in Quercy had no idea what to do. They sent two of their number to Figeac to find out what others were doing. They consulted the lord of Cardaillac and the Bishop of Cahors. They put off making any decision at all for as long as they could. The town of Millau in Rouergue, which received letters from the King and his brother, as well as from Sir John Chandos, consulted the Bishops of Lodève and Vabres. They asked for the views of the lord of Arpajon. They sent agents to Avignon to consult the most learned men to be found there. Rather later, they sent for the opinions of the doctors of the University of Bologna. Such scruples were uncommon, and in Millau's case may have owed something to the presence of an English garrison in the town. Once momentum had gathered, fresh appellants appeared in hundreds, mainly from the regions of Aquitaine bordering on Languedoc. 'We have already received the appeals of counts, viscounts, barons, noblemen and the governing bodies of towns, communes and universities,' Anjou wrote to those who were still wavering in December. The motives of the appellants were very varied. Patriotic sentiment certainly played its part. But in general once men understood what was happening they consulted their interests. The *fouage* was now no more than a symbol. Some appellants had long-standing disputes with the Prince or his local officials, and saw themselves as victims of an intrusive style of government. Some had been unsuccessful litigants in one of the innumerable squabbles over land which had followed the upheavals of the war, and welcomed the possibility of a fresh avenue of appeal. 'You must be well aware of the losses which I have suffered at the hands of the Prince's officers, who have disinherited me of my castle,' one of these men wrote to explain why he had joined the appeals. Others were simply bribed. Few documents are more evocative than the long shopping list of grants and favours which the viscount of Castelbon presented to Louis of Anjou as his price for adhering to the appeals.[60]

On 16 November 1368 Charles V issued the formal summons which initiated the appeals. The Prince was commanded to answer them before the Parlement of Paris on 2 May 1369. The King was anxious to delay the onset of hostilities for as long as possible, partly for logistical reasons and partly for legal ones. 'We have no intention of making war on our brother the King of England or our nephew the Prince of Wales,' he was later to tell the Count of Armagnac; 'we shall deal with them by way of judicial proceedings as we have done so far, simply defending ourselves if they should choose to attack us'. This was hardly realistic, as Charles knew. Appellants in French royal courts were entitled to temporary immunity from the jurisdiction of their adversary and to protection from his officers. This protection was intrusive and very visible. The French King's standard flew from the appellants' towers, and posts bearing his arms were planted at the bounds of their property. Some of them were given small forces of French soldiers to protect them. Even this level of military intervention was not enough for the Duke of Anjou, who lacked his brother's patience and obsession with legal forms. He may also have been concerned to strike quickly before substantial reinforcements could reach Gascony from England. In one way or another he intended to precipitate matters well before 2 May 1369. In October 1368 Anjou presided over the Estates of Languedoc at Toulouse. Painting an arresting picture of the dangers faced by Languedoc from the 'enemies of France', he obtained large new subsidies for war purposes. As the year drew to its close he was recruiting among the nobility and towns of Languedoc. A series of troop musters was held around Toulouse in the course of December. Several of the larger *routier* companies still operating in the south were hired for service against the English.[61]

These events happened at the worst possible time for the Prince. At the beginning of November 1368 his illness suddenly deteriorated. He retired to bed in 'tresgrant malencolie et disease de cuer' and remained there for several months, unable to control events and following them only with difficulty. Within the administration all was confusion and the breath of treachery. 'The head is sick, the limbs suffer,' an official wrote home to friends in England. Sir John Chandos, the Prince's ablest general and probably his wisest adviser, was recalled urgently from Normandy to take charge. With many of the traditional recruiting areas for Gascon troops under the control of the Albrets and their clients, the Prince's officers cannot have found it easy to raise an army locally. Apart from an advance party of some 250 men, which left Southampton in November, no soldiers and no news arrived from England. In their absence the government was obliged to adopt a system of static defence,

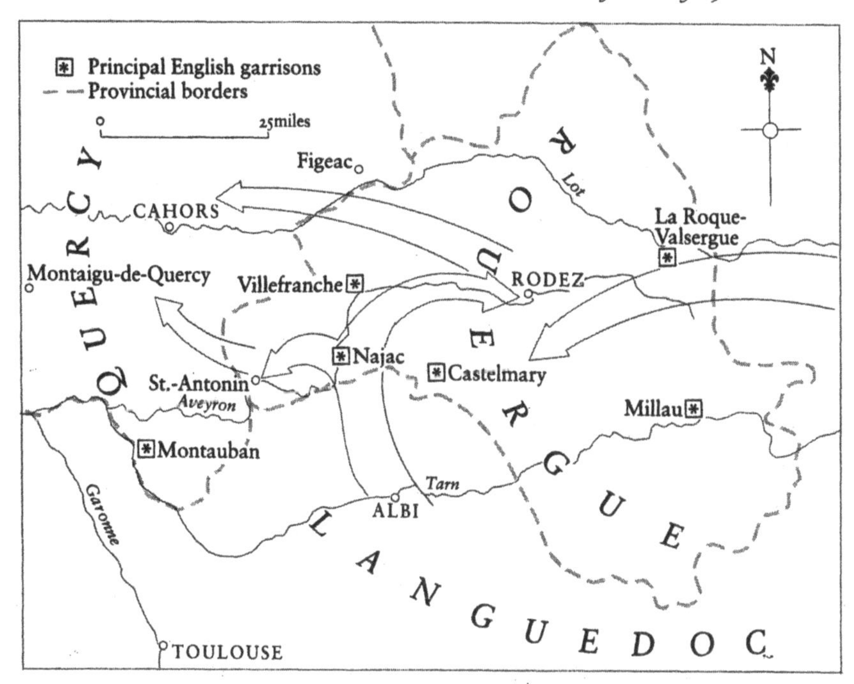

42 The French invasion of Rouergue and Quercy, January–March 1369

all available troops being shut into the principal towns and castles. In the midst of the confusion, two emissaries of the Seneschal of Toulouse arrived in the new year to serve the French King's summons. According to the Chandos Herald, when the Prince heard of its terms, 'lifting himself from his bed' he declared that if God would but give him life and health he would answer Charles V's summons with his helmet on his head and an army at his back. As the emissaries passed through the Agenais on their way back to Toulouse, they were arrested by the local English Seneschal and thrown into prison in the great fortress of Penne overlooking the river Lot. There they died some time afterwards in obscure and perhaps discreditable circumstances.[62]

The first blows in the coming war had already been struck. At the beginning of January 1369 small groups of French soldiers began to penetrate into Rouergue. The province was dominated by the house of Armagnac and its clients and dependants. The prince had few friends here. When Louis of Anjou's men appeared outside the walls of Najac, the fortress-town guarding the gorges of the Aveyron, the inhabitants rose up in a body and attacked their garrison, seventeen of whom were killed. Then they opened the gates. John of Armagnac, the eldest son of the Count, invaded Rouergue by the east along the valley of the Lot from the Gevaudan. On about 9 January 1369 he captured the great border fortress of la Roque-Valsergue by storm. From here he marched across the province burning villages and taking prisoners. The defence was paralysed. As in other sensitive parts of the march the original Gascon officers installed by Sir John Chandos had been replaced over the years by English retainers of the Prince. Rouergue in 1369 was administered by a trio of Cheshire men, the Seneschal of the province Sir Thomas Wetenhall, his deputy David Craddock and James Mascy, the castellan of Millau. Wetenhall was a vigorous administrator with a good deal of experience of Gascon affairs. But he had been in England when the crisis of the appeals began, and had only got back to his province just before Christmas 1368. With only a few garrison troops at his disposal, he could do nothing except shut himself in the town of Villefranche, the seat of the administration, and appeal to the dwindling number of loyal towns to hold out until help could arrive. Mascy took refuge in the citadel at Millau. He seems to have got on well with the inhabitants, who remained loyal to the Prince for many months. Craddock withdrew to the castle of Castelmary, a border fortress in the valley of the river Viaur on the southern march of the province, where he was promptly blockaded by troops of John of Armagnac. The *plat pays* around was effortlessly taken over by the invaders.[63]

The main body of the French army moved slowly north from Toulouse in the course of January 1369 and concentrated around Albi at the end of the month. The English estimated their strength at about 4,000 men. The command of this force was given to the Seneschal of Toulouse, Raymond de Rabastens, a veteran of royal service in Languedoc, who bore the title of special commissioner and captain-general of the Crown in Rouergue and Quercy. Raymond's orders were to visit all the principal places in the region, charging them to recognise Charles V as their sovereign. Objectors, he was told, were to be constrained by force. At the beginning of February 1369 he marched out of Albi into the valley of the Aveyron, the Count of Armagnac at his side. On about 19 February 1369 Rodez, the provincial capital, opened its gates to him. Here he set up his headquarters and received the surrenders of much of the rest of the province, while Armagnac issued an inflammatory manifesto to his subjects vindicating his conduct over the past year.[64]

In Quercy the pattern was very similar. Bands of armed men in the service of Louis of Anjou began to enter the province in the middle of

January from Rouergue. On 16 January 1369, one of them ambushed a column of troops commanded by the English Seneschal of Quercy near Montaigu-de-Quercy. In the rout which followed the Seneschal was captured, together with the captain of Montauban, the main English garrison town of the province. This incident left the English administration in Quercy rudderless for two months, while much of the east and south of the province defected to the French. The cathedral city, Cahors, which had never cared for the English administration, was among the first to adhere to the appeal. They received a small guard of French troops sent from Toulouse in the middle of January. This was in due course reinforced by some 200 *routiers* sent by Raymond de Rabastens from Rouergue. Early in February 1369 the Archbishop of Toulouse arrived in the city to undertake a great preaching tour through the province, instructing the inhabitants in the legal rights and prerogatives of the King of France. A team of lawyers followed behind with forms of adherence to the Gascon appeals.[65]

By the middle of March 1369 the English position had collapsed in Rouergue and most of Quercy, and the French were making good progress in the neighbouring provinces. By 18 March 1369, a total of 921 communities and noblemen had subscribed to the appeal. Of these, about a third were in the domains of the Count of Armagnac in Rouergue and Armagnac-Fezensac. The rest were distributed across Aquitaine, but came mostly from the regions of the eastern march where the war had been fought out in 1350s: Rouergue, Quercy and Agenais. In Rouergue, the only substantial places holding out for the Prince were the garrisoned towns of Villefranche and Millau. Only four significant places in Quercy were still loyal. According to one report all the noblemen of the Agenais had adhered to the appeals save one. Writing to a friend at home an English official in the province remarked that he heard more bad news in a day than good news in all the years before. 'The French have struck a blow against the principality from which it will not recover for a long time.'[66]

The long-promised embassy of the Count of Tancarville arrived in England towards the end of January 1369. Tancarville knew England, and understood Edward III as well as any of Charles V's councillors. But his instructions left little room for manoeuvre. They had been settled in the course of a full session of Charles V's Council a few days before his departure, at which it had been agreed on all sides that the Gascon appeals should proceed come what may. Tancarville's message was simple: the King of France had never ceded his sovereignty and it was too late to cede it now. To this was added a great catalogue of the French government's grievances against Edward III and his subjects, in particular their support for Charles of Navarre and the companies, which the King blamed for the continuing destruction of the French countryside and for his inability to pay the rest of his father's ransom. Edward III's answer was contained in a curt memorandum or 'bill' delivered to Tancarville at Westminster. The essence of it was that he was willing to consider marginal compromises in the various territorial squabbles that had remained unresolved since the treaties had been made in 1360. But he expressed himself astonished and outraged by the decision to entertain the Gascon appeals, which was a breach of faith and a repudiation of the treaties that could lead only to war.[67] Beyond the walls of the Palace of Westminster the first signs of the approaching conflict were already noticeable: fear, insecurity, rumours. In London there were threats of violence against the French hostages. Men were departing for service in Calais and Ponthieu. The Earls of Cambridge and Pembroke finally left for Gascony in February 1369. There were persistent reports of an imminent descent by French ships on the Channel coast. In the south and east coast ports shipping was being requisitioned for war service and men were mustering to guard the coasts.[68]

On 29 April 1369 French troops commanded by Hugh de Châtillon, the Master of the Royal Archers, entered Abbeville, the capital of Edward III's county of Ponthieu on the Somme. The move was probably a pre-emptive strike. Ponthieu, which had been virtually ungarrisoned the year before, was being rapidly reinforced by troops from England. They included Nicholas Tamworth, the famous knight who had terrorised northern Burgundy on behalf of Edward III in the winter of 1359–60, and a number of other captains known to be close to the English King's service. The French overran the whole county within a week, surprising Edward's garrisons before they had had time to prepare or supply themselves. In Abbeville the English governor and receiver were arrested and their houses ransacked for papers. These were sent off to Paris to be scrutinised by the King's lawyers looking for grounds on which to justify this necessary but unjudicial act.[69]

In the event it was only slightly premature. On 2 May 1369, the day appointed for the first hearing of the Gascon appeals, the attorneys of the leading appellants appeared in the Parlement de Paris to hear the Prince's name called. There was no answer. A week later, on 9 May, the King and Queen of France appeared in person in the chamber of the

Parlement, taking their seats on the ceremonial bench of blue velvet sewn with golden *fleurs de lys*. They were accompanied by the Chancellor, most of the princes of the royal blood, the leading prelates and noblemen of the realm, and a crowd of lawyers, officials and representatives of the towns who had been specially summoned for the occasion. The deliberations, which continued over three days, served to make the King's position public and to commit his subjects to supporting it. Charles asked those present whether he had done anything contrary to the law. No, they answered with one voice. He 'took it to be plain that the war had been forced on him by the wrongs of his enemies and that the law was on his side.' Now, he said, it was his intention to throw his 'body, wealth and lands into the fight.' He called on all those present to commit their loyalty. All of them promised.[70] There were very similar scenes at Westminster three weeks later, when Edward III presided over the opening of the English Parliament. The events of the past few months were recounted to the peers by the Chancellor, William of Wyckham. Was the King not justified in resuming the title of King of France? They all replied that he was. On 11 June 1369 Edward III altered his seals to add the arms of France to those of England.[71]

On 19 June 1369 the marriage of Philip of Burgundy and Margaret of Flanders was celebrated in the abbey of St. Bavo outside Ghent, where John of Gaunt had been born. A few hundred yards away there were revellers in the narrow lanes where men had once rioted in the cause of the English alliance and in the Friday Market where Edward III had first proclaimed himself King of France.

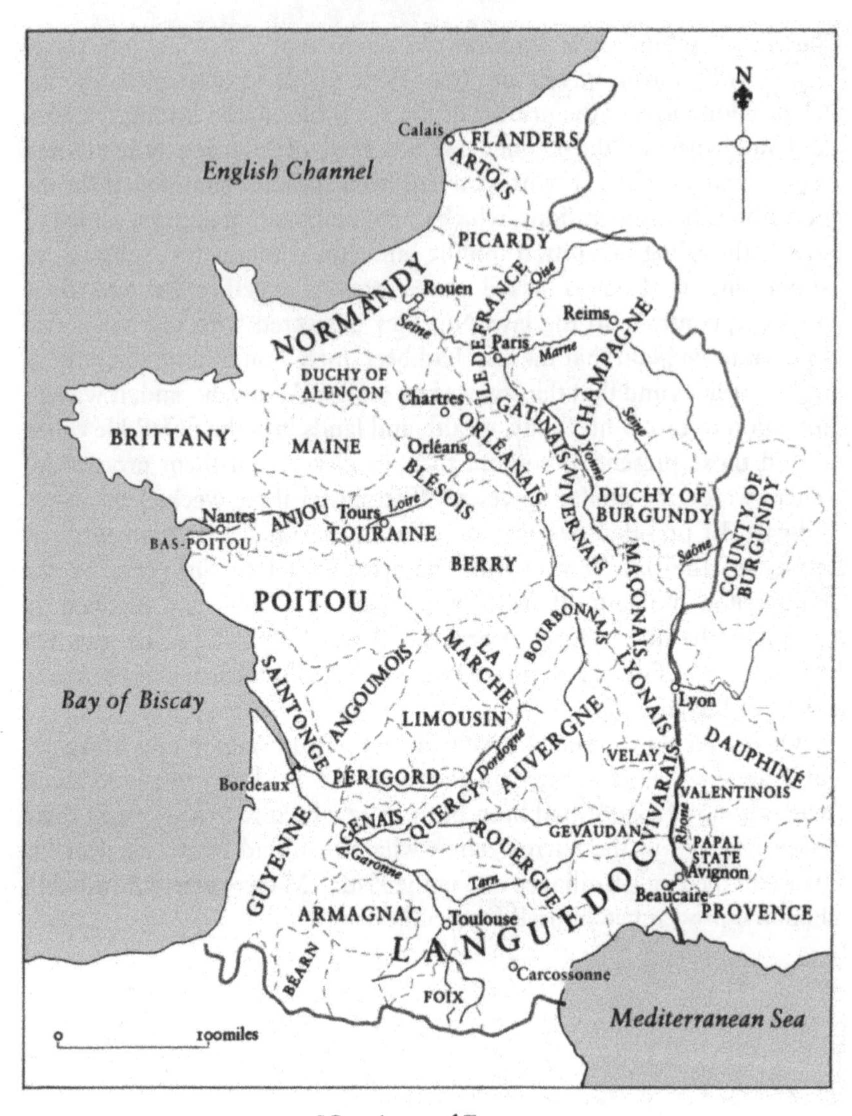

I Provinces of France

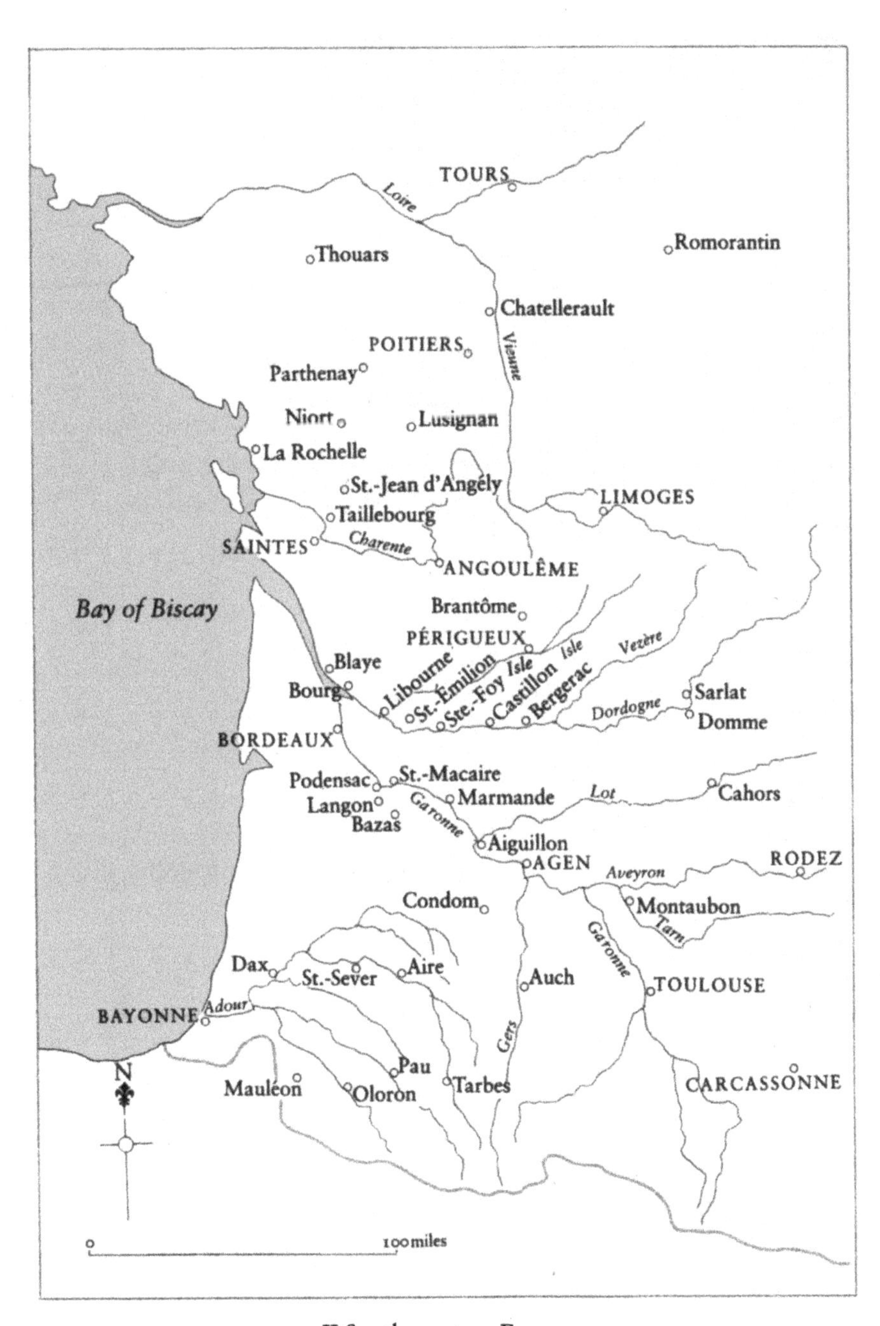

II South-western France

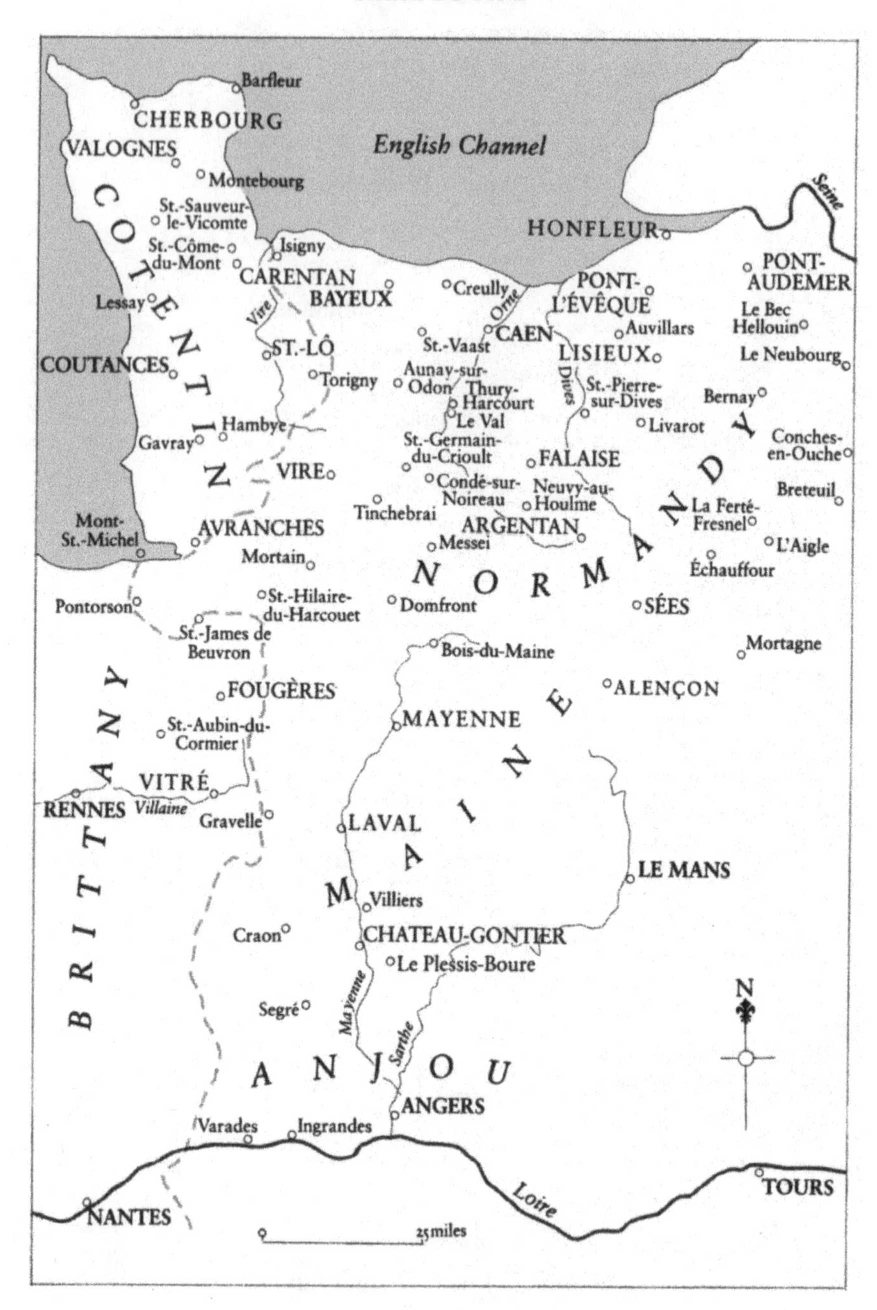

III Eastern Brittany and Lower Normandy

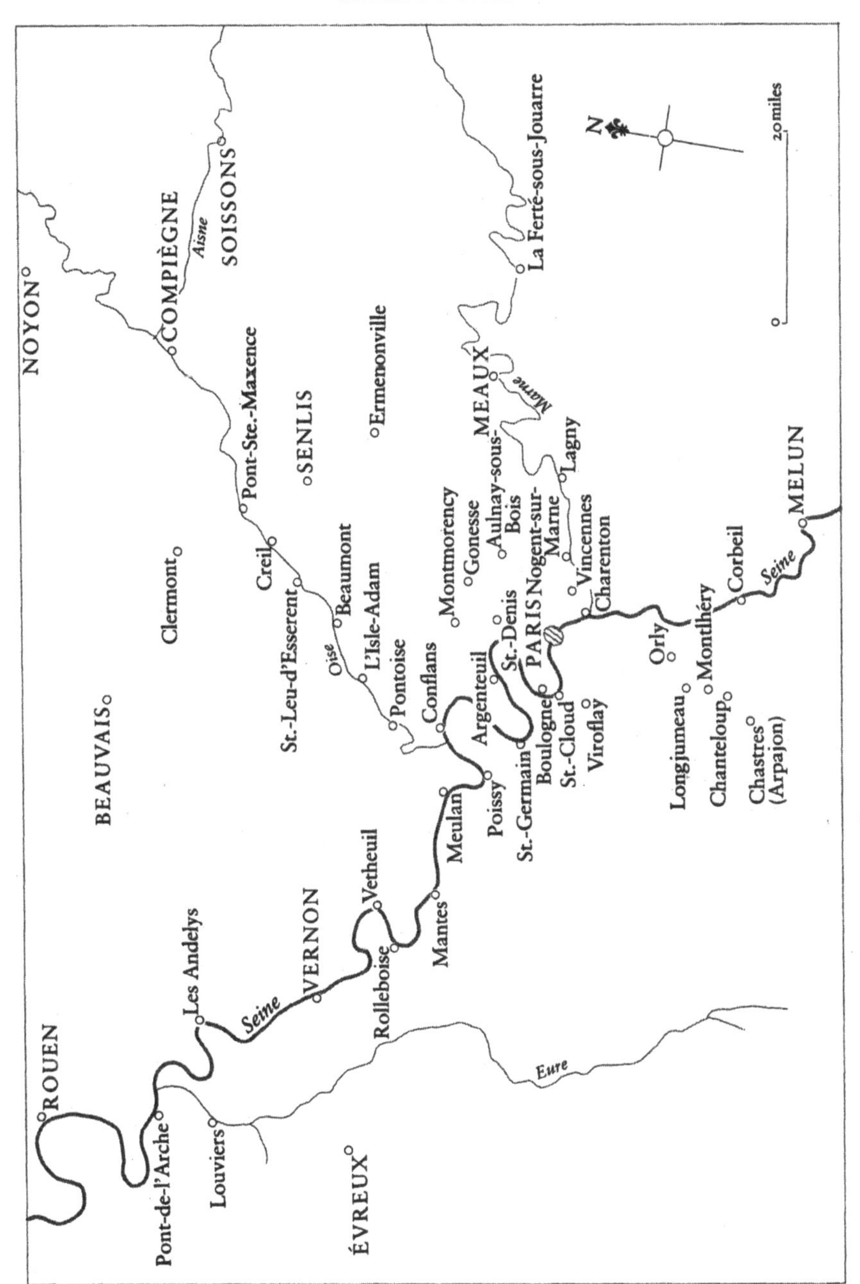

IV Île de France and the Seine valley

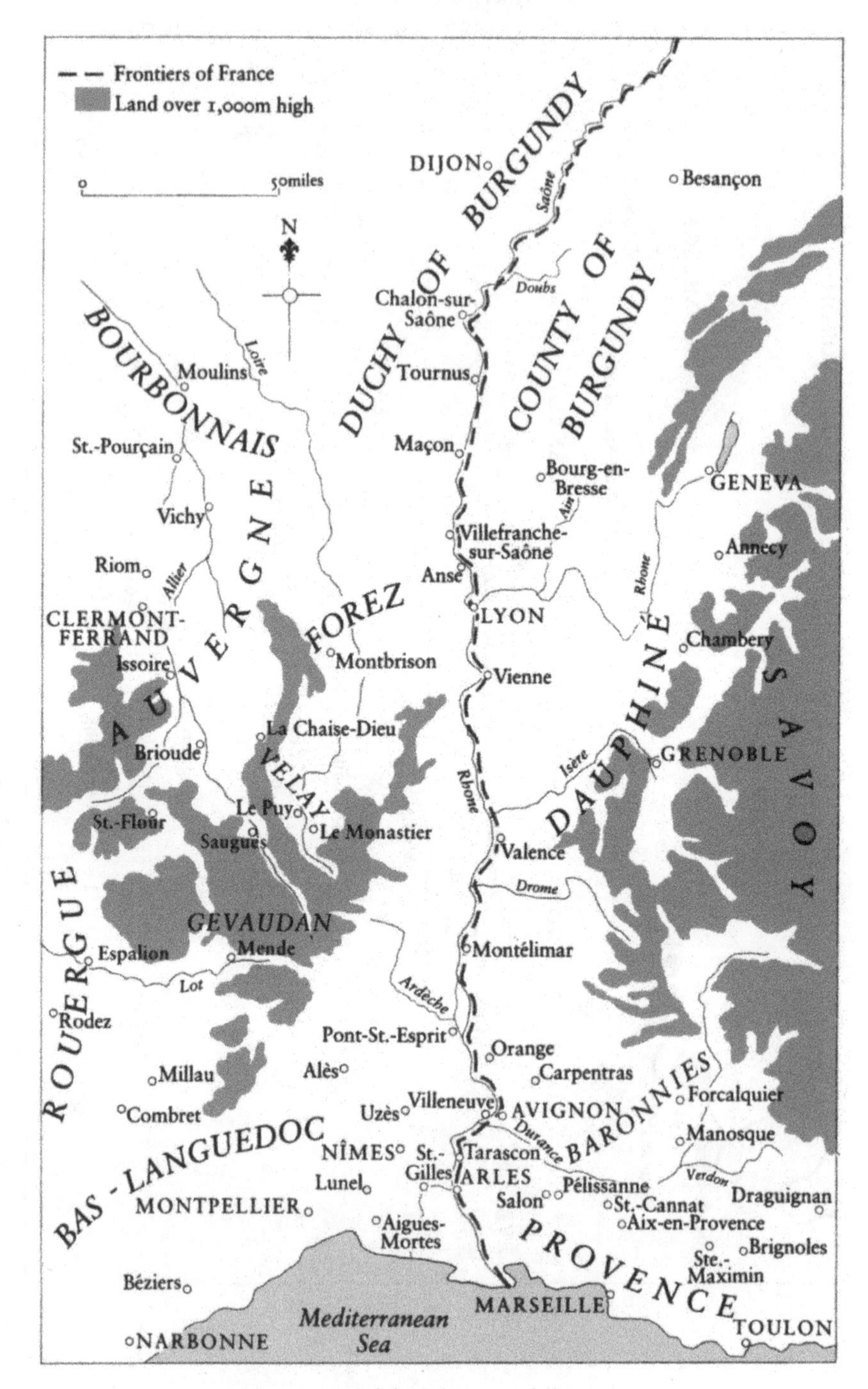

V Provinces of the Rhone and the Saône

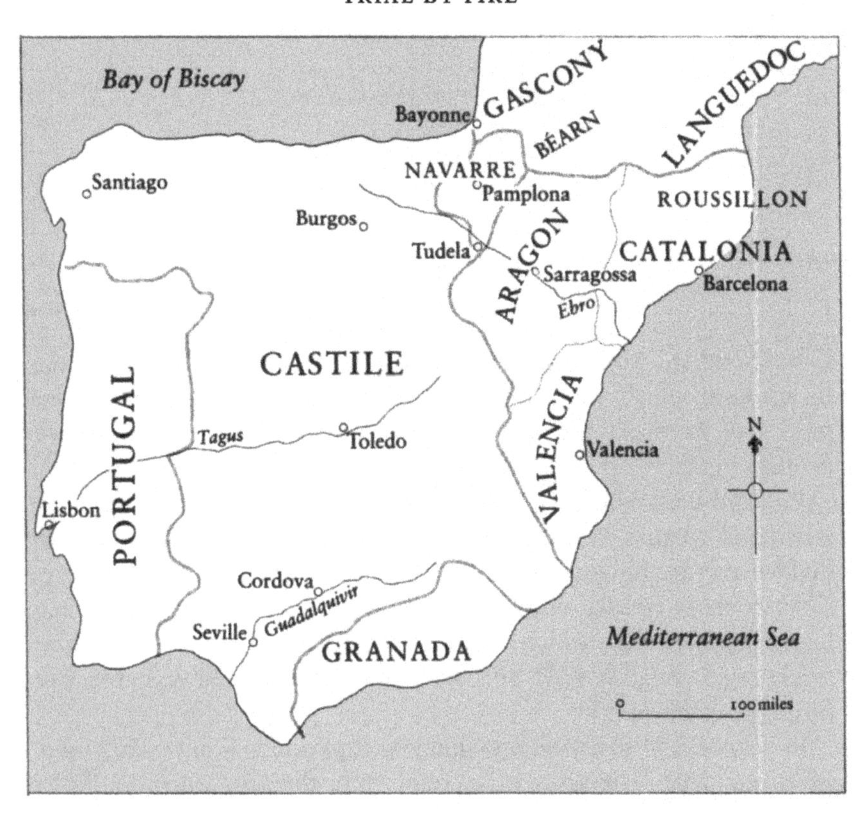

VI Kingdoms of Spain

Note on Money

In both England and France it is necessary to distinguish between money of account, which was simply a conventional measure of value, and money of payment, that is to say the coins in which payments were actually made.

England used a silver standard. The unit of account was the pound sterling (£), equal to one and a half marks of silver. The pound was divided into 20 shillings (s), each of 12 pennies (d). There was a variety of silver coins in circulation. There was also, from 1344, a gold coinage based on the noble, which was conventionally worth 6s 8d, but was rarely used. English gold and silver coin maintained a stable value throughout this period.

In France, the situation was more complicated. France also used a silver standard. The units of account were the *livre tournois* (*l.t.*) or pound of Tours, the *livre parisis* (*l.p.*) or pound of Paris, and the *livre bordelais* (*l.b.*) or pound of Bordeaux, which was used in the duchy of Aquitaine. Like the pound sterling, they were divided into 20 shillings (*sous*), each of 12 pennies (*deniers*). The pound sterling was worth five *l.t.*, five *l.b.*, and four *l.p.* Soldiers were usually paid in coins of silver or base metal whose quality and value varied considerably. Larger sums were commonly reckoned in gold coin, which although far from immutable was a good deal more reliable. There were four French gold coins in common use in this period. The *écu*, or *florin à l'écu* or *à la chaise*, was minted between 1337 and 1355. It was so-called because the King was shown on the obverse side seated on a throne (*chaise*) and holding a heraldic shield (*écu*). It was initially worth about 4s od sterling, but after 1348 the quality was progressively reduced and its value fell to about 2s 10d sterling. It became common to stipulate for 'old' *écus* or *écus* of Philip, which meant coin of the original quality. The *mouton*, or *florin au mouton* (first minted in 1355) was so called after the paschal lamb on the obverse side. It was worth half as much again as the last issue of *écus* to be minted, about 4s 10d sterling, and was the most highly prized French gold coin of the period. The *royal* was a short-lived coin first minted in 1358, which was worth about 3s 10d sterling at the first issue, but rather less thereafter. The *franc* (first minted in 1360) was the first coin for many years to retain a stable value. It was worth about 4s 0d sterling.

The gold florin of Florence circulated quite widely in both countries. This famous coin, first minted in 1252, was the nearest thing to an international standard of value in fourteenth-century Europe, but it was becoming discredited by imitations and forgeries. The genuine article was worth 2s 10d sterling.

The campaign of the Prince of Wales in Castile in 1367 gave rise to a number of transactions reckoned in Castilian *doblas*. The *dobla* was a gold coin based on the double dinar of the Almoravid rulers of Andalusia and Morocco, which was struck in quantity from the reign of Alfonso XI (1312–1350) onward. It had an intrinsic value of a little less than 4s sterling.

In the text, sterling equivalents are generally given for sums reckoned in French, Italian or Spanish coin. Modern equivalents of fourteenth century values are notoriously elusive. A gallon (4.5 litres) of good ale cost about a penny in an average year. An English building craftsman could expect to earn about three or four pence per day in the 1350s. One pound sterling represented five days' wages at standard rates for an English man-at-arms with his own horse, page and equipment. Ten pounds bought an adequate but unremarkable war-horse for such a man, probably his most valuable movable property.

Abbreviations

AC Archives Communales
AD Archives Départmentales
AGN *Catalogo del Archivo General de Navarra*
AGN Archivo General de Navarra (Pamplona)
AHG *Archives historiques . . . de la Gironde*
AHP *Archives historiques du Poitou*
AHSA *Archives historiques de la Saintonge*
AHVF *Atlas historique des villes de France*
AN Archives Nationales (Paris)
ASV Archivio Segreto Vaticano (Rome, Cittá del Vaticano)
BEC *Bibliothèque de l'École des Chartes*
BL British Library (London)
BN Bibliothèque Nationale (Paris)
BPH *Bulletin philologique et historique du Comité des Travaux Historiques et Scientifiques*
CCF *Corpus chronicorum Flandriae*
CCR *Calendar of Close Rolls*
CFR *Calendar of Fine Rolls*
CIM *Calendar of Inquisitions Miscellaneous*
CPR *Calendar of Patent Rolls*
DCO Duchy of Cornwall Office (London)
EHR *English Historical Review*
GEC *Complete Peerage*
HGL Vic, C. de and Vaissete, J., *Histoire générale de Languedoc*
KOF Froissart, *Chroniques*, ed. Kervyn de Lettenhove [All references are to the documentary notes and appendices]
MSHP *Mémoires de la Société de l'Histoire de Paris et de l'Île de France*
PRO Public Record Office (London)
RDP *Reports from the Lords Committees touching the Dignity of a Peer*

RIS(1)	*Rerum Italicarum scriptores*, ed. L.A. Muratori, 25 vols (1723–51)
RIS(2)	*Rerum Italicarum Scriptores*, n.e., 34 vols. (1900–79)

References

Printed sources (Bibliography, Sections B and C) are cited by title or by author/editor and title. Secondary works (Bibliography, Section D) are cited without title by author alone or are identified as [D].

References marked with an asterisk * are to the documentary notes or appendices of the work cited.

CHAPTER I

1 Walsingham, *Hist. Angl.*, i, 272; Knighton, *Chron.*, 94 (quotation). Lichfield: PRO E372/207, m. 50 [John de Colonia].

2 Baker, *Chron.*, 101. Garter: J. Vale, 76–91.

3 Petrarch, *Fam.*, iv, 138. Germany: *Trautz, 431–2; *Foed.*, iii, 161; Baker, *Chron.*, 98; Knighton, *Chron.*, 90–2. Castile: *Foed.*, iii, 73–5, 147–8, 150, 151, 155; *Daumet, 152–3; Baker, *Chron.*, 97. Disputes: *Foed.*, iii, 199, 205, 219; *CCR 1349–54*, 366–7.

4 *Rot. Parl.*, ii, 166–72, 200–1, 237–8; Fryde (1959), 12–6; Fryde (1962), 26–7; Fryde (1966), 18–9; Harriss, 331–3, 335–40.

5 *Wynnere and Wastoure*, 8, 9 (ll. 194, 230). Resistance: *CCR 1346–9*, 374; *CPR 1345–8*, 454, 461, 463, 465; *CPR 1348–50*, 235–6, 320, 383–4, 389, 519, 526.

6 *Arch. admin. Reims*, ii, 1161–2; Guesnon, 'Documents', 242–4.

7 *Gr. chron.*, ix, 276.

8 Invasion: *Gr. chron.*, ix, 312. Tax: Henneman (1971), 230–4. Fleet: *Doc. Clos des Galées*, nos. 463–71. Assessment: *Arch. admin. Reims*, ii, 1167; *Boudet (1900)(2), 62–3. Intelligence: *Foed.*, iii, 151; *RDP*, iv, 575–7; *Rot. Parl.*, ii, 200 (2).

9 Muisit, *Chron.*, 196–8; 'Breve chron. cler. anon.', *CCF*, iii, 14–8; Venette, *Chron.*, ii, 210–14; *Gr. chron.*, ix, 314–6; Lescot, *Chron.*, 83; Machaut, *Oeuvres*, i, 149 (*Le jugement du roi de Navarre*, l. 355). Rouen: Cheruel, ii, 34–5. Burgundy: G. Gras, 'Le régistre paroissale de Givry', *BEC*, c (1939), 295–308. Provence: Baratier, 82, 127–9. Bordeaux: Boutruche, 199–200; *Foed.*, iii, 171. Perpignan: R.W. Emery, 'The Black Death of 1348 in Perpignan', *Speculum*, xlii (1967), 611–23. Paris: M. Mollat, 'Notes sur la mortalité à Paris au temps de la peste noire', *Le Moyen age*, lxix (1963), 506–27; Cazelles (1972), 149–53. Reims: Desportes, 544–9.

10 *Eulogium*, iii, 213–4; Baker, *Chron.*, 99–100; Avesbury, *G. Edwardi*, 406–8; Knighton, *Chron.*, 98–100; *Foed.*, iii, 180, 182. Mortality: Hatcher, J., *Plague, Population and the English Economy, 1348–1530* (1977), 21–6; Z. Razi, *Life, Marriage and Death in a Medieval Parish* (1980) 99–109.

11 Negotiations: *Foed.*, iii, 145, 161; *Rot. Parl.*, ii, 200 (2); Clement VI, *Lettres*, no. 3890. Tax: Henneman (1971), 235–7.

12 *Foed.*, iii, 191.

13 Class: [Simon of Couvin], 'Opuscule relatif à la peste de 1348', ed. E. Littré, *BEC*, ii, 204; cf. Gui de Chauliac, *La grande chirurgie*, ed. E. Nicaise (1890), 167 and Bower, *Chron.*, vii, 272; Hatcher, 22; Booth, 89–91, 97. Age: Cazelles (1962), 303; Russell, *British medieval population* (1948), 216–7; Razi, *Life, marriage and death in a medieval parish* (1980), 107–9.
14 Ormrod (1986), 178, 180–1, 182, 183–5.
15 'Chron. com. Fland.', 224–5.
16 *Foed.*, iii, 166.
17 *Inv. AD Pas-de-Calais*, i, 117; Muisit, *Chron.*, 191–2; *Gr. chron.*, ix, 316–7; *Journ. Trés.*, no. 331. Charny: Baker, *Chron.*, 103; Muisit, *Ann.*, 260; Cazelles (1958), 217. Amiens: *Actes normands*, 371, 372; *Arch. admin. Reims*, ii, 1210. Eu's truce: *Foed.*, iii, 170–1, 172–3, 173; on his activities in England, Deck, 8.
18 'Brev. chron. Fland.', 19–21; Muisit, *Chron.*, 199–205; 'Chron. com. Fland.', 22 225.
19 PRO E372/193, mm. 34 [Lancaster], 45 [Mauny]; E101/312/33; *Foed.*, iii, 174; *CPR 1348–50*, 281; 'Brev. chron. Fland.', 21.
20 Conference: Baker, *Chron.*, 98; Muisit, *Chron.*, 205–6. Edward's expedition: *Foed.*, iii, 175–6, 176–7. Delegation: Muisit, *Chron.*, 194–5.
21 *Foed.*, iii, 177–8; *Gr. chron.*, ix, 317.
22 Muisit, *Chron.*, 203.
23 Negotiations: 'Brev. chron.', 21; Muisit, *Chron.*, 206; 'Chron. com. Fland.', 225; PRO E372/193, mm. 34 [Lancaster], 45 [Mauny]; **KOF*, xviii, 324–7. King's arrival: *Foed.*, iii, 176–7; PRO C81/334/19888–9. Public treaty: *Foed.*, iii, 178–9, 181; *Inv. AD Nord*, i, 109–10. Secret treaty: **KOF*, xviii, 319–24; Chaplais, 'Chartes en déficit', 193.
24 **KOF*, xviii, 318–9.
25 Muisit, *Chron.*, 207–11.
26 PRO C76/127, m. 11 (1440).
27 Sumption, i, 239, 497. Although the fleet which carried Lancaster's expedition to Normandy in 1356 included 26 royal ships of well over 60 tons burden (PRO C76/34, m. 17), the average capacity was only 13 men per ship with horses and 18.5 without: Avesbury, *G. Edwardi*, 462.
28 Picardy: PRO E403/378, m. 5 (requisitions), mm. 41, 42 (Lancaster's ships, presumably the survivors of the fleet originally assembled for Normandy in June and July). Gascony: Hewitt (1958), 20–1; Avesbury, *G. Edwardi*, 425.
29 *Foed.*, iii, 138–9, 142–4, 201; *CPR 1345–8*, 561–8.
30 Baker, *Chron.*, 92; *Foed.*, iii, 150; PRO E372/194, mm. 45, 47 [Salop], E372/195, m. 45 [Tatton]; Brown, Colvin and Taylor, 454–6.
31 Organisation: *Foed.*, iii, 138–9, 142, 186, 193, 222, 226. Numbers: *Foed.*, iii, 324 (1356); PRO E101/170/16 (1351–2), E101/171/1 (1352–3), E101/171/3 (1353–5), E101/173/7 (1356–8), E101/174/7 (1359–60), E101/35/28 (1359–61).
32 *Foed.*, iii, 158, 413; Lennel, iii, 58–9; Brown, Colvin and Taylor, 427–8.
33 Burley, 'Victualling'; *Foed.*, iii, 185 (horses, carts); PRO E101/171/1, fol. 14vo (distribution); Brown, Colvin and Taylor, 426–7 (building materials). Black Prince: *Reg. Black Prince*, iv, 9–10. Protest: *Rot. Parl.*, ii, 227 (11). Gaunt: *An English chronicle of the reigns of Richard II, Henry IV, Henry V and Henry VI*, ed. J.S. Davies (1856), 7.
34 *Foed.*, iii, 158, 178.
35 PRO E372/194, m. 45, 47 [Salop]; E372/195, m. 45 [Tatton]; E372/196, mm. 47 [Baddeby]; E372/198, m. 43, E372/201, mm. 36, 38, E372/203, m. 39, E372/206, mm. 43, 44 [Ecceshale]; the proportion is 92 per cent if coinage profit (*avantagia auri*) is treated as part of the Exchequer receipt. Tolls: *Lettres de rois*, ii, 101. Mint: *Foed.*, iii, 150. Aquitaine: Fowler (1964), 83 (Table II).
36 PRO E372/194, mm. 45, 47 [Salop]; *Foed.*, iii, 165.
37 PRO E372/209, m. 47 [Clewere]; E101/24/7; C76/22, m. 14; C76/26, m. 14. Sovereignty:

Foed., iii, 165; *CPR 1348–50*, 281.

38 *Foed.*, 165; Clement VI, *Lettres*, nos. 3485, 3494; Pocquet, i, 301–3.
39 Morice, *Preuves*, i, 1478.
40 Court of appeal: *Foed.*, iii, 226. Brest: Jones (1970), 144–6.
41 *Foed.*, iii, 169, 204, 307, 403.
42 Dagworth forces: PRO E101/25/19; Avesbury, *G. Edwardi*, *389*. Le Caours: *Foed.*, 100, 101–2, 168; *Jones (1987), 8. Recruitment, foreigners: Avesbury, loc. cit.; Lescot, *Chron.*, 80n. Criminals: *CPR 1345–8*, 481; *CPR 1348–50*, 24, 186; *CPR 1350–4*, 224, 259–60, 264–5, 300–1; *CPR 1354–8*, 11, 22, 24, 27, 33, 53, 107; **KOF*, xviii, 340–1.
43 *Brefs*: *Foed.*, ii, 1241; PRO C61/56, mm. 7, 5d; C81/297/16125, 329/19324. Lands: PRO E372/198, m. 41 [Charnels].
44 **KOF*, xviii, 339–40.
45 Bel, *Chron.*, ii, 175–6; Froissart, *Chron.*, iv, 302.
46 *Gr. chron.*, ix, 299.
47 Timbal, *Rég. Parl.*, 456; Keen (1965), 137–9, 251–3. Lesneven: *CPR 1345–8*, 440.
48 Spinefort: *Jones (1980), 638–9. Bentley: **KOF*, xviii, 339–43; *Foed.*, iii, 242.
49 Origins: PRO E101/35/3; *Wardrobe Book of W. de Norwell*, 318, 321; *CPR 1343–5*, 109; *CCR 1346–9*, 493. Conquests, PRO C81/332/19691.
50 PRO E101/25/18; E30/1495; C76/30, m. 6; C76/32, m.7; *Foed.*, iii, 276, 307. Wiltshire: *CPR 1354–8*, 27. On Jeanne: Anselme, iv, 54 (but she married before 28 Feb. 1352, see PRO E30/1495).
51 T. Bentley: *Foed.*, iii, 190. N. David: *CPR 1354–8*, 27. Calveley: *Reg. Black Prince*, iii, 173; Bennett, 17, 165; *Chron. norm.*, 99, 107 (Bécherel); *Diplomatic correspondence of Richard II*, ed. E. Perroy (1933), 233 (princess).
52 Chandos Herald, *Vie*, 112 (ll. 2331–2); Walsingham, *Hist. Angl.*, i, 286; John of Malvern, *Chron.*, 372; Bel, *Chron.*, ii, 251; Bennett, 175, 182. Castles: PRO C76/30, m. 12 (Fougeray, Gravelle); *Foed.*, iii, 307 (Chateaublanc).
53 Fougeray: Cuvelier, *Chron. B. du Guesclin*, i, 33–40. Thirty: Bel, *Chron.*, ii, 194–7; *Chron. norm.*, 100; Lescot, *Chron.*, 86; 'Bataille'. Berwick: Wyntoun, *Oryg. Chron.*, ii, 440–6. Gascony: Knighton, *Chron.*, 124. Froissart: *Chron.*, iv, 115, 341.
54 Bock, 'Documents', 95–6 (1354); PRO E403/388, m. 23 (1356).
55 PRO E372/207, m. 52 [Stretle].
56 Fowler (1964), 59–60; Fowler (1969), 73–4; Capra (1975), 274–99. The best documented examples are PRO E101/167/10, fols. 20–22 (operations in April-May 1348); PRO E101/170/20, fols. 51–52, 54, 55, 64vo, 81 (relief of Moncuq, July 1352); Capra (1962), 204–10 (relief of Aiguillon, June 1354); PRO E101/168/12 (76, 78, 84), E101/169/1 (14, 16, 21–2, 27, 29, 30, 33, 38, 49, 55, 59, 77), E101/169/2 (14, 60), E101/169/3 (7, 8, 12, 13, 19) (operations against Count of Armagnac and Marshal de Clermont, summer 1355).
57 PRO E372/197, m. 38 [Richard Stafford].
58 PRO E101/167/10, esp. fol. 24 (Bergerac); E101/168/3, esp. fols. 8, 13 (Mauléon), fol. 14 (Rochefort); E101/170/20, esp. fol. 60vo (Bergerac). On Rochefort, see also PRO E403/359, m. 22; E403/378, m. 37; E403/378, m.37; E101/169/2(5); E43/82.
59 Lands: PRO E101/167/10, fol. 7vo; E101/171/5 (8). Revenues: PRO E372/198, m. 40 [Charnels]; E372/207, m. 52 [Stretle]. Exchequer contribution: Fowler (1964), 83 (Table II).
60 PRO C61/70, m. 14; *AHP*, iv, 424. On its original capture, Sumption, i, 402–3.
61 Froissart, *Chron.*, xii, 205.
62 Bergerac: PRO E101/167/10, fol. 24; E101/170/20, fol. 60vo. Darampton arrived there in aut. 1347: PRO C81/320/18410. His conquests: PRO E101/168/3, fol. 6, E101/170/20, fol. 84 (Fouleix); *ibid.* and PRO C61/61, m. 6, C61/63, m. 5 (Clermont-de-Beauregard); PRO C61/61, m. 10. Augier: PRO C61/54, m. 29; E101/168/3, fol. 12; E101/170/20, fol. 84vo.

63 *Inv. AC Périgueux*, 79–82. St.-Astier regained: PRO E372/207, m. 52 [Stretle].
64 PRO C61/60, mm. 34, 31d; E372/207, m. 53 [Stretle]. Recruitment: *Rec. doc. Poitou*, ii, 394, 412–4, iii, 1–3, 150; AN X2a 5, fol. 213; AN JJ 78/35, 79A/46.
65 'Chron. Maillezais', 167; *Rec. doc. Poitou*, iii, 150 (Faye). Poitiers: *Ord.*, iv, 168–70. Niort: *Journ. Trés.*, no. 1890. St.-Maixent: AN J400/54; *Rec. doc. Poitou*, ii, 392–3. Parthenay: 'Lettres d'état', nos. 428, 528. Montreuil-Bonnin: BN Fr. n.a. 7413, fols. 533–533vo. Trade: *Rec. doc. Poitou*, iii, 7–8, 150–1. Ambush: Oxford, MS Bodley 462, fol. 33vo.
66 Périgueux: *Inv. AC Périgueux*, 80. Thibault: BN PO 187 [Barbazan 5, 6, 10]; BN Fr. 32510, fols. 225–225vo. Bertrand: BN Clair. 43/3239, 3241, 3243.
67 BN Coll. Languedoc 84, fols. 381–385vo.
68 Law: Chaplais (1951), 278–9. Seneschal: *Rot. Parl.*, ii, 209 (16); PRO C61/61, m. 4; E101/167/10, fols. 10, 10vo, 11, 11vo, 13; E101/167/12, fols. 8, 9vo. Private truces: *Foed.*, iii, 149–50, 157.
69 Bordeaux, Toulouse: PRO E101/167/10, fols. 20–22; E101/167/12, fol. 10. Saintonge: *Journ. Trés.*, nos. 2598–2600. Poitou: *Gall. Reg.*, iv, no. 17549; BN Fr. 20684, p. 356; *Rec. doc. Poitou*, ii, 414.
70 Oxford, MS Bodley 462, fol. 33vo; AC Martel BB5, fols. 30vo, 31, 34; *Ord.*, xv, 442.
71 Bel, *Chron.*, ii, 174. March 1349: PRO E101/169/2 (283).
72 Nontron: AN JJ68/187, 428, 78/148; *Bertrandy, 50n; Murimuth, *Chron.*, 217 (siege); *Molinier, 212–3 and BN Doat 243, fol. 218 (buy-out). Montbrun: AN X2a 5, fols. 113, 130vo. Aixe: AN JJ68/238, 78/151.
73 Origin, pseudonym: BN Clair. 111, p. 7859; BN Fr. 32510, fol. 216 ('dis le Gascon de Mareuil'). Mareuil: BN PO 1849 [Mareuil, 2, 4]; AN JJ82/196. Showy: Bel, *Chron.*, ii, 175; *Inv. sceaux Coll. Clair.*, no. 8427. 'Party': PRO C61/81, m. 3. Comborn: Bel, *Chron.*, ii, 174–5; Innocent VI, *Lettres*, nos. 64, 203. Its lord: 'Lettres d'état', no. 342; *Journ. Trés.*, no. 2182.
74 *Molinier, 207–11, 214. Other castles in Limousin occupied between 1348 and 1353: Molinier, 214 (Maisonnais, St.-Amand-de-Coly); BN Fr. n.a. 7607, fols. 283vo-284; Bel, *Chron.*, ii, 174, AC Martel CC3–4, fols. 33, 34 (Donzenac); AN JJ84/35 (Montrocher); BN Fr. 32510, fol. 216 (Saillant); BN Clair. 69, p. 5357 (St.- Auvent); AC Martel BB5, fol. 36vo; AN JJ 81/65 (St.-Rabier).
75 Paralysis: Bautier, 357–60. Truce: PRO E101/312/33, 37, 38, 39; *Journ. Trés.*, nos. 1218, 1223–4; *Foed.*, iii, 182, 184–5. Tonneins: PRO E101/167/12, fol. 8 (English garrison, 1348); AN 68/399 (recaptured by English, before April 1349). Port-Ste.-Marie: AN JJ68/399, 84/23–4.
76 Montcuq: *Jurades d'Agen*, 161–2; AC Martel BB5, fol. 43. St.-Astier: PRO E372/207, m. 52 [Stretle]; AN JJ 78/35, 40; *Journ. Trés.*, no. 3171. Bergerac: PRO E372/207, m. 52 [Stretle]. Lusignan, Limalonges: Gray, *Scalacr.*, 181; *Chron. norm.*, 94–5; BN PO 1926 [de Mar, 3]. On Cook: Fowler (1969), 184. Boucicaut: *Livre des faits*, 11 (quotation).
77 Taillebourg: *Foed.*, iii, 397–8; PRO C61/62, m. 4. Saintes: BN Fr. 25998/538–9; AN K44/15. English reinforcements: E403/347, mm. 12, 13, 15, 18. Truce: BN PO 1555 [d'Igny, 5].

CHAPTER II

1 *Comptes du Trésor*, ed. R. Fawtier (1930), p. lxiv, based on *Journ. Trés.*, 329–632; Cazelles (1966), 97–8; Henneman (1971), 340. Poilevillain: Cazelles (1966), 98–100; Braque: Valois, 101–2.
2 AN JJ68/356, 78/99.
3 Cange, C. du, *Glossarium mediae et infimae latinitatis*, ed. G.A.L. Henschel and L. Favre, ii (1883), 134 (*s.v.* 'capitaneus generalis'); AN JJ78/87. Guy's career: Anselme, vi, 49–50,

723–4; *Journ. Trés.*, no. 2015. Army: BN Fr. 20684, pp. 315–28, 339–51.

4 Vendetta settled: *Foed.*, iii, 152, 166; *CPR 1348–50*, 247. Revived: PRO C61/61, m. 6; *CPR 1348–50*, 387–8. July 1349: *Journ. Trés.*, nos. 1981–3, 4239–40.

5 *Foed.*, iii, 188–9.

6 Charny: *Journ. Trés.*, no. 1048; Philip VI, 'Lettres Closes', no.209. Simultaneous English embassy: *Foed.*, iii, 181; PRO E101/312/40. Autumn messages: *Foed.*, iii, 189–90; PRO E101/312/36.

7 *Reg. Black Prince*, iv, 144, reflecting previous arrangements, see PRO E372/207, m. 53 [Stretle] (Rochefort); PRO C61/60, m. 41 (Soubise); PRO E403/377, m.11, C81/332/19665 (Tonnay-Charente). For St.-Jean-d'Angély, see below.

8 Tonnay-Boutonne: PRO C61/60, m. 17 (in English hands, July 1348); BN Clair. 72, pp. 5601, 5605, 5609 (French garrison from Oct. 1349). As distribution centre: PRO E101/169/2 (56); E43/293. Cf. E101/167/10, fol. 23, E101/170/12, fol. 63vo; E101/170/20, fols. 77–77vo; E372/197, m. 38 [Richard Stafford]. Siege: BN Fr. n.a. 7413, fol. 551vo; BN Clair. 40/304; 47, p. 3517; 54, p. 4069; 80, p. 6301; PRO E43/293 (2); E372/207, m. 53 [Stretle].

9 Salines: Touchard, 5–26; Bridbury, 55–61. Strategic value: Avesbury, *G. Edwardi*, 340. Prigny: Jones (1987), 8. Retz, Fulk: *Cart. sires de Rays*, i, pp. xcviii-xcix; *Journ. Trés.*, nos. 2115, 2826, 2923, 4138; 'Lettres d'état', no. 595; La Tour Landry, *Livre*, 239–40. Belleville castles: *Foed.*, iii, 190; *Bel, *Chron.*, ii, 355; *CPR 1348–50*, 532.

10 PRO C76/27, m. 6; *Rec. doc. Poitou*, iii, 29–31; *Foed.*, iii, 190; *Bel, *Chron.*, ii, 355–6.

11 *Chron. norm.*, 95; *Journ. Trés.*, no. 4129; 'Lettres d'état', no. 563. Ships: *Journ. Trés.*, no.4647; Baker, *Chron.*, 109; Avesbury, *G. Edwardi*, 412; Muisit, *Ann.*, 271. Islands: 'Lettres d'état', no. 633; they are later recorded as being in French hands: *Rec. doc. Poitou*, iii, 30, 105. Belleville: *CPR 1348–50*, 532; 'Lettres d'état', no. 561.

12 Ambush: *Gr. chron.*, ix, 326; Baker, *Chron.*, 101–2; Avesbury, *G. Edwardi*, 411. Sequel: **KOF*, xviii, 334–5; *Rec. doc. Poitou*, iii, 102, 105–7, 137–9, 157.

13 Baker, *Chron.*, 108; PRO E43/293 (2); E372/195, m. 46 [Lancaster].

14 Knighton, *Chron.*, 106–8; *Chron. norm.*, 92–3. Agen: *Jurades d'Agen*, 187–92. Lancaster's purpose: see PRO C61/61, m. 3.

15 *Actes normands*, 409–13. Flavacourt: *Gall. Reg.*, iii, no. 13669; *Ord.*, vii, 152.

16 *Inv. AC Toulouse*, 463 (AA 35/76); *HGL*, ix, 617; Knighton, *Chron.*, 108; *Jurades d'Agen*, 192. Toulouse: Wolff, 96–8.

17 *Journ. Trés.*, nos. 3379, 3551; *HGL*, ix, 617. 30 Dec.: PRO C61/67, m. 15.

18 Beaumont: *Chron. norm.*, 92. Bourbon: *HGL*, ix, 618n^{2}.

19 Main accounts: Avesbury, *G. Edwardi*, 408–10; Reading, *Chron.*, 107; Muisit, *Chron.*, 260–3; *Gr. chron.*, ix, 321–2. Baker, *Chron.*, 103–8 and Bel, *Chron.*, ii, 176–82 are embellished and inaccurate. Also: *Chronographia*, ii, 247–8; Lescot, *Chron.*, 85; *Recits d'un b. de Valenciennes*, 264–6. Edward's sortie: PRO E372/194, m. 47 [Salop]; *Foed.*, iii, 195. 'Covetous': Froissart, *Chron.*, iv, 71.

20 Ribbemont: Muisit, *Chron.*, 263; *CCR 1349–54*, 155–6. Charny: *Issues of Exch.*, 156, 158; *Foed.*, iii, 212; PRO C76/29, m. 14; BN Clair. 41, p. 3109; Anselme, viii, 201. Aimeric: PRO E101/170/16, fol. 10; Muisit, *Chron.*, 261–2 (son).

21 Truce: *HGL*, ix, 618n^{2}, *x, 1061; Clement VI, *Lettres*, nos. 4317, 4399, 4401, 4403–4, 4426, 4481. Dispersal: PRO E372/195, m.46 [Lancaster]; BN Fr. 20684, p. 314 (Nesle). Conference: Clement VI, *Lettres*, nos. 4442–6; *Foed.*, iii, 196; PRO E101/313/1; *Journ. Trés.*, no. 4824; *Gr. chron.*, ix, 325.

22 *RDP*, iv, 587; *Foed.*, iii, 192, 193–4. Requisitioning: PRO E372/204, m. 37 [Causton].

23 Instructions: **HGL*, x, 1061. Spanish ships: *Journ. Trés.*, nos. 4239, 4415; PRO E372/204, m. 37 [Causton]; cf. Baker, *Chron.*, 109. French: *Doc. clos des galées*, nos. 474–5; *Actes normands*, no. 250; BN Fr. 20684, p. 246vo, 250; *Lescot, *Chron.*, 232–3. Amiens: BN Fr. 20684, p. 295; BN Fr. n.a. 7413, fols. 535–536; 'Lettres d'état', no. 618.

24 'Lettres d'état', no. 607; *Chron. norm.* 92–4; *Jurades d'Agen*, 206–7. Tax: **HGL*, x, 1061–5; Henneman (1971), 242. Crossbowmen: BN Coll. Languedoc, 159, fol. 59vo.
25 *Foed.*, iii, 197–8.
26 Joy: Muisit, *Ann.*, 270. Messengers: PRO E101/313/1; Clement VI, *Lettres*, nos. 4639–40, 4813. Copies: BN PO, 1065 [Espagne, 2]; BN Fr. n.a. 7607, fols. 238vo-239.
27 Domme: BN PO 1065 [Espagne-Montespan, 8]. Ste.-Foy: *ibid.*; PRO C61/65, m. 4, E101/170/12, fol. 56vo. Villefranche: BN Fr. n.a. 7607, fols. 230vo-231, 231vo-235; BN Fr. 32510, fols, 224vo, 228 (in French hands, June 1352).
28 *Chron. norm.*, 99; *Gr. chron.*, ix, 326; *Rec. doc. Poitou*, iii, 50–1. Germans, Lusignan: Timbal, *Reg. Parl.*, 332.
29 Loudun: BN Fr. 32510, fol. 198vo; BN Coll. Languedoc, 159, fol. 59vo; BN Clair. 71, p. 5555; 72, p. 5601; *Chron. norm.*, 99. Lusignan: BN PO 106 [Ars, 3, 8]; 1324 [Giliers, 3]; 1107 [Fauré, 2]; 2061 [Mortemer, 3, 5, 6]; *Chron. norm.*, 100; Gray, *Scalacr.*, 182. The Seneschal of Poitou's authority to recruit troops extended to Touraine: *Gall. Reg.*, iv, 17552, 17585; vi, 22108.
30 *Foed.*, iii, 200–1, 201–2; PRO C76/28, m. 7; *Letter Books*, F, 217.
31 Avesbury, *G. Edwardi*, 412; Baker, *Chron.*, 109–11; Muisit, *Ann.*, 271, 275–8; Reading, *Chron.*, 111; Froissart, *Chron.*, iv, 94.
32 *CFR 1347–58*, 252; *Foed.*, iii, 206, 210. Wine fleets: PRO C61/62, m. 2; Delpit, *Coll. gen.*, 76; James, 20. Offord: PRO E101/313/7.
33 Froissart, *Chron.*, iv, 176.
34 Bucy: Valois (1885), 66–7; F. Aubert, *Le Parlement de Paris de Philippe le Bel à Charles VII. Son organisation* (1887), 78–80. Lorris: Cazelles (1958), 242–4; Cazelles (1982), 77–80.
35 Cazelles (1958), 113, 223–4, 231–4, 235–9, 355; Cazelles (1962), 288; Cazelles (1982), 77–80, 137–8, 160. Charles (quotations): Villani, *Hist.*, 219; 'Acte d'accusation', 366.
36 'Acte d'accusation', 381.
37 Celebrations: *Gr. chron.*, i, 27–8; *Les entrées royales francaises de 1328 à 1515*, ed. B. Guenée and F. Lehoux (1968), 48–50; *Chron. premiers Valois*, 19.
38 *Cité* Palace: Guérout, ii, 69–72. Rebuke: Lescot, *Chron.*, 106–7.
39 *Gr. chron.*, i, 28–31; Muisit, *Ann.*, 279–82; *Chron. norm.*, 96–7; Bel, *Chron.*, ii, 198–201. Explanation: Villani, *Hist.*, cols. 138–9.
40 Grants: *Rec. doc. Poitou*, iii, 40–4, 41n1.
41 *Ord.*, iv, 67; Contamine (1972), 622–4.
42 Coinage: Henneman (1971), 340; Muisit, *Ann.*, 302–3. Tenths: Causse, 303–7; AN JJ80/380. Taxes: Henneman (1971), 244–63; *HGL*, ix, 624 (Languedoc); *Ord.*, ii, 391–6, 400–10, 557 (Languedoil).
43 Pont-Audemer: *Ord.*, ii, 405. Rouen: Cheruel, ii, 165–8; *Coville (1894), 369–70; AN JJ87/267.
44 Appointments: *Gall. Reg.*, iii, nos. 13681, 13995–6, iv, no. 17557. Joan: Sumption, i, 556.
45 *Foed.*, iii, 207, 214; PRO C76/28, m. 2; PRO E372/198, m. 38 [Richard Stafford]; *CFR 1347–56*, 273–7.
46 Depopulation, walls: *Foed.*, iii, 138; *Reg. St.-Jean d'Angély*, i, 136–40. Garrison, recruitment: PRO E43/298; E403/347, mm. 12, 13, 15, 18; Baker, *Chron.*, 115 (Rous). Pay, supplies: PRO E101/25/35; E372/207, m. 52 [Stretle]; E43/293, 298; C61/61, m. 5.
47 *Chron. norm.*, 97; Bel, *Chron.*, ii, 187, 192.
48 Avesbury, *G. Edwardi*, 413; Gray, *Scalacr.*, 181–2; *Chron. norm.*, 97–8, 99; *Gr. chron.*, i, 31; Bel, *Chron.*, ii, 189–92; PRO E101/169/2 (270) (Caupenne). Date: BN Fr. n.a. 7608, fols. 118–9. Place: *ibid.*; PRO E101/170/12, fol. 52vo; *Titres Bourbon*, no. 2602. Ransoms: Anselme, vi, 723 (Nesle); AN JJ84/224 (Audrehem).
49 *Chron. norm.*, 99; BN Fr. n.a. 7607, fols. 285vo-286vo (fixes latest date); *Chérest (1879), 363. Garrison: AN JJ81/43; BN Fr. 26000/309.

50 Fronsac: AN JJ80/208, 552; *KOF, xviii, 345–50; 'Extraits journ. Trés.', no. 171. Durfort: *AHG*, xxvi, 356–8; *Doc. Durfort*, nos. 990, 1000–7, 1012, 1030–44. Bazas: PRO E101/170/12, fol. 48.
51 Melun: Morice, *Preuves*, i, 1469–74; BN Clair. 32, p. 2417; 73, p. 5703; 80, p. 6305; *Mandements*, no. 262. Bentley diversion: *Luce (1876), 515–8; BN Clair. 73, p. 5685.
52 PRO E101/313/7; Muisit, *Ann.*, 283.
53 L. de Mâle: 'Chron. com. Fland.', 227–8 (*entrée*); PRO E101/313/7; *Foed.*, iii, 224; BN PO 1916 [Melun, 188] (French embassy). Raids: Baker, *Chron.*, 114–5; Knighton, *Chron.*, 110.
54 Baker, *Chron.*, 115–6; *Chron. norm.*, 101–2; Muisit, *Ann.*, 294–5; Knighton, *Chron.*, 110; *Istore*, ii, 75; *Recits d'un b. de Valenciennes*, 268–9. Beauchamp: PRO C76/29, m. 11. Compiègne: BN Coll. Picardie 238/36; BN Fr. 20684, p. 903.
55 *Foed.*, iii, 221–2; PRO E101/26/15–16, 18; E101/313/8. L. de Mâle: *Foed.*, iii, 224.
56 Bateman: *Foed.*, iii, 225, 227; PRO E101/26/15. L. de Mâle: A. Gallard, *Preuves de Mémoires pour l'histoire de Navarre et de Flandre* (1648), 156–8; *KOF, xviii, 329–34; *Foed.*, iii, 232.
57 *Reg. St.-Jean d'Angély*, i, 130–4.
58 Surrender: *Reg. St.-Jean d'Angély*, i, 134–6; PRO E101/169/2 (270), E101/168/3, fol. 3; AN JJ81/917 (John's presence). Truce: *Foed.*, iii, 230, 232. Lancaster: Fowler (1969), 105–6. Bankruptcy: *Ord.*, ii, 449.
59 PRO E101/170/12, fols. 52vo, 53, 63, 63vo.
60 A. de Cervole: *Chérest (1879), 363. Friquet: *Gall. Reg.*, i, no. 1093. Ste.-Foy: *Chron. norm.*, 98–9; PRO C61/63, m. 1; *Foed.*, iii, 251; date from PRO E101/170/12 and E372/198, m. 40 [Charnels].
61 Belaye: AN JJ76/303; *Doc. Durfort*, nos. 943–6, 959–60. Belcastel: AC Martel BB5, fols. 33vo, 36vo, 38vo, 43; AN JJ78/287; Clement VI, *Lettres*, no. 4136. Montcuq: *Jurades d'Agen*, 161–2; AC Martel BB5, fol. 42vo, 43; *Journ. Trés.*, no. 3316 (Lauzerte garrisoned, Dec. 1348–July 1349). Pestillac: AN JJ80/421, 84/667: cf. AN JJ68/194, 75/43, 542; *Actes du Parl.*, nos. 6683, 6699; Clement VI, *Lettres*, nos. 1283–4, 1657–9, 1735, 2484. Souillac: AN JJ80/454.
62 Mascaro, 'Libre', 45; **HGL*, 1099, 1101. On the Captal: Froissart, *Chron.*, viii, 69–70 (quotation); AD Pyr.-Atl. E36 (marriage).
63 Souillac: AC Martel BB5, fols. 71vo, 72, 72vo, 73, 77vo, 94vo, 105vo; CC3–4, fol. 41vo, 45, 45vo; Innocent VI, *Lettres*, no. 457. Martel: AC Martel, BB5, fols. 67–73; CC3–4, fols. 38vo-45vo. Rest of Quercy: *Denifle, 823–4 (papal enquiry).
64 *Ord.*, ii, 465–6, iv, 116–7, 161–2; *Pannier, 63–74; Lescot, *Chron.*, 90–1.
65 Baker, *Chron.*, 116–8; Avesbury, *G. Edwardi*, 414–5; *Gr. chron.*, i, 34. On Dancaster: PRO E101/170/16, fol. 12vo; *CPR 1350–4*, 220, 238, 349; *CCR 1349–54*, 558; *CCR 1354–60*, 22, 124, 281. Parliament: *Rot. Parl.*, ii, 236–8 (1, 6–10). Occupation: PRO E101/170/16, fol. 19.
66 Muisit, *Ann.*, 302; *Chron. norm.*, 102; *Gr. chron.*, i, 34–5; BN PO 683 [Charny, 9].
67 *Rec. doc. mon.*, i, 300–3; *Ord.*, ii, 472–5, 484–94; Muisit, *Ann.*, 302–3; Henneman (1971), 340.
68 *Foed.*, iii, 230, 241; *Mon. proc. canonisation*, 28; PRO C76/30, m. 10; E101/313/10; E403/362, m. 4.
69 Redon: Morice, *Preuves*, i, 1485; in English hands, aut. 1351, *Luce (1876), 516. Breton army: Morice, *Preuves*, i, 1475, 1478; Avesbury, *G. Edwardi*, 416. Saintonge: BN PO 42 [Aloigny, 5]; 77 [Antoign, 6]; 526 [la Broie, 3]; 1487 [Harponville]; 2086 [Muzant, 2]; 2119 [Noillettes, 2]; 2763 [St.-Martin, 4], etc.; PRO E372/197, m. 41d [Ralph Stafford]; PRO E101/170/20, fol. 67vo; Anselme, vi, 752 (local commanders). Guines: BN Fr. 32510, fol. 197vo; Baker, *Chron.*, 119; Villani, *Hist.*, 176.
70 Stafford: PRO C61/64, mm. 6, 5, 4; *RDP*, v, 46; *Foed.*, iii, 239–40. Bentley: PRO C76/30,

mm. 11, 6; E403/362, m. 2. Enemy ships: PRO C61/64, m. 9d (Flemish); PRO C76/30, mm. 13, 12, 12d (French). Fowey: PRO C76/30, m. 11. Counter-raid: PRO C76/30, m. 13; C61/64, m. 9; E403/362, m. 1; Baker, *Chron.*, 121.

71 PRO E101/170/16, fols. 19vo-21. On Hogshaw: *CPR 1348–50*, 543.

72 *Chron. norm.*, 102–3; Baker, *Chron.*, 119; Villani, *Hist.*, 176; BN Fr. 32510, fols. 202vo-203vo; BN PO 274 [Belleferière, 3]; 385 [Bois, 295]; 683 [Charny, 6, 11]; 1507 [Houdetot, 9]; 2061 [Mortier, 2]; BN Clair. 9, p. 499; 12, p. 794; 37, p. 2752; 60, p. 4625, etc. Planned expedition: *Foed.*, iii, 243–6; PRO C76/30, mm. 11, 10.

73 *Chron. norm.*, 104; PRO E101/170/16, fol. 18vo (fixes date).

74 Morice, *Preuves*, i, 1478–9, 1481; Avesbury, *G. Edwardi*, 416.

75 PRO E403/362, mm. 2, 7, 9; C76/30, mm. 11, 7, 6.

76 Morice, *Preuves*, i, 155 (place), 1482–3 (French movements); Avesbury, *G. Edwardi*, 415–7; *Chron. norm.*, 105–6; Baker, *Chron.*, 120; Bel, *Chron.*, ii, 206–7. Drafts: PRO C76/30, m. 4. Alain, vic. de Rohan (d. 1352) was the eldest son of Alain VIII, vic. de Rohan (d. 1347). He is missing from the genealogies of Anselme and Lobineau.

77 PRO E372/197, m. 38d [Richard Stafford], m. 41d [Ralph Stafford].

78 BN Fr. 32510, fols. 218–218vo, 223vo-224vo, 229vo; BN Coll. Languedoc, 159, fol. 27; BN PO 922 [Craon, 8, 9]; 622 [Caumont, 22]; PRO E101/170/12, fol. 59vo; *Jurades d'Agen*, 289–90.

79 *Jurades d'Agen*, 291–4, 308; Baker, *Chron.*, 121. Numbers, supply ships: PRO E372/197, m. 38 [Richard Stafford]. Marmande: BN Fr. 32510, fol. 229; BN PO 2297 [Plantier, 2, 3, 4]. Boucicaut: *Issues of Exch.*, 159; *Foed.*, iii, 271; Innocent VI, *Lettres*, nos. 1349–50. Stafford was in Bordeaux on 7 September: *Doc. Durfort*, no. 1018.

80 *Jurades de Bergerac*, 16–8, 30, 31; PRO E101/170/20, fol. 51.

81 Blaye: PRO E101/170/19; E101/170/20, fols. 44, 48vo. Bergerac, Moncuq: PRO E101/170/20, fols. 51–52, 54–54vo, 55, 64vo, 81. Taillebourg: PRO 372/197, m. 41 (Ralph Stafford).

82 Stafford: PRO SC1/40/179. Craon: BN PO 622 [Caumont, 2]; BN Fr. 32510, fol. 218.

83 *Arch. Montpellier*, ii, no. 645; BN Doat 93, fols. 196–199vo; **HGL*, x, 1065–6.

84 *Arch. admin. Reims*, iii, 21n; *Musée des Archives Départmentales* (1878), 289; BN Fr. 32510, fol. 205; BN Clair. 1021, pp. 73–4.

85 BN 32510, fols. 194–197, 197vo-198, 199, 203vo-204.

86 *Mon. proc. canonisation*, 90 (resignation); Morice, *Preuves*, i, 1486–7; *Foed.*, iii, 250; Bock, 'Documents', 84–91.

CHAPTER III

1 *Arch. admin. Reims*, iii, 53–8.

2 'The Bad': Honoré-Duverger (1951).

3 Cazelles (1958), 48–50, 205–7.

4 M. Berthe, *Famines et épidémies dans les campagnes navarraises à la fin du moyen age* (1984), 165–96, 327–41.

5 *AGN Comptos*, ii, nos. 310, 325 and *passim* to no. 441.

6 Lieutenant: *HGL*, ix, 627–8. Port-Ste.-Marie: see above. Picardy: BN Fr. n.a. 20258, p. 11. Obituary: *Chron. du réligieux de St.-Denis*, ed. L. Belaguet, i (1839), 468. Marriage, financial arrangements: Secousse, *Preuves*, 23–7; *Nouv. rec. comptes argenterie*, pp. xx-xxi (date); F. Piponnier, *Costume et vie sociale* (1970), 25.

7 Angoulême: Secousse, *Preuves*, 29–31; 'Acte d'accusation', 367 (14) ('disinherited'); AN JJ 81/464 (confirmation). Further grants: AN JJ81/452, 767; J166/28. Précigny: AN X^{1a} 16, fol. 372.

8 Cazelles (1982), 77–80, 88–9, 122, 142–3, 148, 158; Honoré-Duvergé (1947–8).

9 'Acte d'accusation', 365–7; Cazelles (1958), 255–61; Cazelles (1982), 46, 154–5.

10 Innocent VI, *Lettres*, no. 84 (quotation). Character, health: Guillemain, 115, 140–1; **Vitae paparum*, ii, 439–40, 487. Legation: Clement VI, *Lettres*, nos. 2168, 2173, 2694–5, 2792, 2844; *Foed.*, iii, 88, 92; Sumption, i, 512, 513–4, 579–80.

11 *Vitae paparum*, i, 296. He was in Paris by July: PRO E403/388, m. 23.

12 Jugie, 115–6.

13 Duel: Fowler (1969), 106–9. Conference: 'Quatre lettres', 161, 162–3 (2nd doc. misdated, see Jugie, 125–7); Innocent VI, *Lettres*, nos. 61, 83–4, 433.

14 Surgères: Barbot, i, 157; BN Fr. 32510, fol. 210; BN PO 616 [des Champs, 2]; 2063 [la Mote, 4], etc.; *AHP*, xx, 275–6. Lafrancaise: BN Coll. Languedoc 159, fol. 27 (subsidy); *Inv. AC Toulouse*, i, 465 (98), 470 (27), 534 (29). Date of siege, see dates of occupation of French forward base at Labastide-du-Temple: BN Fr. 32510, fols. 225, 226; BN Clair. 158/39, 192/119, 193/30. Fall: AN JJ81/549; BN Clair. 17, p. 1135.

15 *HGL*, ix, 595–8, 640; *Gall. Reg.*, iii, no. 13675.

16 Bertrand: Henneman (1971), 156n, 186, 214–5, 242, 246; *HGL*, ix, 619–20, 622; *x, 1060–5; Bishop of Vabres (Gard) from 1352. Appointment: *Ord.*, ii, 521–3. Conditions: *Ord.*, ii, 522 (6). G. de Cantobre: Débat, 73–7; Clement VI, *Lettres*, nos. 3870, 4006. Mints: *Rec. doc. mon.*, i, 315.

17 Mascaro, 'Libre', 46; *HGL*, ix, 640–1, 641n[3].

18 *Foed.*, iii, 254–5; 'Quatre lettres', 162; *Ord.*, iv, 277–8. Knight: PRO E101/171/1, fol. 15.

19 *HGL*, ix, 641n[3], 642–3, *x, 1067–9, 1094–6. Reinforcements: BN PO 1957 [Mez, 2].

20 *Ord.*, iv, 277–9, 285; AD Hérault, A231/58A. Lancaster: PRO E101/313/12, 17, 19, , 41.

21 'Quatre lettres', 162. This letter refers to an agreement to adjourn the Guines conference to a date before 24 June. It cannot refer to the conference of March-April 1354 (as Jugie, 125 proposes) because that was adjourned at its conclusion to October. *Arrière-ban*: BL Add. Chart. 14.

22 Council: Cazelles (1982), 158; Jugie, 115. Whitsun: AN KK8, fols. 170–171. Navarrese: *AGN Comptos*, ii, nos. 529, 555–63, 565, 584–6, 588, 590–5, 598, 600–6.

23 *Rot. Parl.*, ii, 251–2 (32).

24 *Rot. Parl.*, ii, 251–2 (32); Innocent VI, *Lettres*, nos. 433, 466. On Woodruff: *CPR 1350–4*, 209; *CPR 1361–4*, 319. On Pelegrini: *CCR 1349–54*, 186. On Whittleseye: *Cal. Pap. R. Petitions*, i, 208.

25 Surgères: Secousse, *Preuves*, 50; BN PO 1573 [Jaubert, 3]; BN Clair. 32, p. 2359. Subsidies, recruitment: BN Coll. Languedoc 159, fol. 27vo; AD Hérault, A5/4; *Doc. Millau*, no 204. St.-Antonin: BN PO 956 [Cusaguet, 3]; BN Clair. 10, p. 611; 62, p. 4811; 61, p. 5109; 71, p. 5541. Feneyrols: BN Clair. 76, p. 5927.

26 1352: *Molinier, 213–4. Comborn: **ibid.*, 218–21; *Chron. norm.*, 100–1; BN Fr. 32510, fol. 216; Bel, *Chron.*, ii, 175.

27 Excideuil: AN JJ84/117. Uzerche: 'Chron. Uzerche', 414–5.

28 Agen: *Jurades d'Agen*, 251, 254, 260, 262, 271, 294, 295–6, 297, 301–2, 323, 325–6. Périgueux: *Rec. titres Périgueux*, 258–60, 262, 292–4; *Inv. AC Périgueux*, 54, 82; Higounet-Nadal (1978), 146–7, Graph I (end) (population).

29 *Chron. norm.*, 100–1. Élie: PRO C61/66, m. 9; *Foed.*, iii, 278.

30 Truce: *Foed.*, iii, 261–2 (July); AN J637/8 (Dec.). St.-Antonin: Mascaro, 'Libre', 46. Saintonge: Secousse, *Preuves*, 50. Frequent quittances in BN PO and BN Clair. for the siege of Surgères continue until late Oct.; last reference to siege as continuing is 25 Nov.: BN PO 529 [Brouard, 3]. Local cease-fires: *Jurades d'Agen*, 328–9.

31 Bascon, candour: Secousse, *Preuves*, 51–2. Dury: *Chron. prem. Valois*, 28. His origins: Bel, *Chron.*, ii, 278; Froissart, *Chron.*, v, 136–7. Navarrese: see above. Messengers: *AGN Comptos*, ii, no. 564. Lancaster: **KOF*, xviii, 352. Burgundy: *Inv. AD Côte d'Or*, ii, 109 (B4392). Council: Cazelles (1982), 155.

32 *Chron. prem. Valois*, 25–8; Secousse, *Preuves*, 52; *Lehoux, i, 41n[3]; Venette, *Chron.*, 227–8; *Gr. chron.*, i, 37–8. AN JJ82/183, 226, 278, 445–7, 463–9, 474–6, 510

25 Ayton, 96–120, 127–37. Regards: Prince (1933), 293–4. Chandos, 1359: PRO E101/393/11, fol. 80. Stafford: Morgan (1987), 55 (an outstanding study).
26 Harriss, 344–5.
27 Collection: Ormrod (1986), 185. Edington: Reading, *Chron.*, 113.
28 Career: Emden, i, 629–30. Administration: Tout (1920–37), iv, 281–311. Debt liquidation: Fryde (1988), 192–6. Staple, customs: *Rot. Parl.*, ii, 246(4)-251(30), 252(32), 253(42); Lloyd, 205–9; Ormrod (1987), 27, 28–34, 39; Avesbury, G. *Edwardi*, 431.
29 Summons: *Gr. chron.*, i, 49. Fleet: *Doc. Clos des Galées*, nos. 503, 505–7, 510–3, XXXVI, XXVII; Anselme, iv, 490; *Doc. Monaco*, i, 408. Subsidy: *Cat. comptes royaux*, no. 494; *Gr. chron.*, i, 50–1; *Doc. Clos des Galées*, no. 509.
30 Dauphin: Delachenal (1909–31), i, 94–5. Subsidy: *Cat. comptes royaux*, no. 494; Secousse, *Preuves*, 577–8. Entourage: 'Inv. coll. Villevieille', no. 12; Secousse, *Preuves*, 583–6.
31 Guines: *Foed.*, iii, 308. Clermont: PRO E101/168/12(78), E101/169/1(38). Armagnac: PRO E101/168/12(84), E101/169/1(21, 27, 29, 49), E101/169/2(14, 51–2, 58, 60).
32 Fordun, *Chron.*, 370–1; *Rot. Scot.*, i, 777–8, 778, 779–80, 781.
33 *AGN Comptos*, nos. 657, 659, 690; *Doc. ch. comptes Navarre*, xxvii-xxix, 56–9; AGN Comptos 12/90 (perfunctory summary in *AGN Comptos*, ii, no. 706). Cortes: Yanguas, ii, 338–9, 358, 644, 645. Henriquez: Yanguas, ii, 157–63; *AGN Comptos*, nos. 558, 590, 597; *Frag. chron. B-Normandie*, 4.
34 Secousse, *Preuves*, 55.
35 Secousse, *Preuves*, 55, 565–6, 567; Innocent VI, *Lettres*, no. 1442; Bel, *Chron.*, ii, 210.
36 AN K47/35.
37 Secousse, *Preuves*, 568–73; **KOF*, xiii, 337–8.
38 AGN Comptos 12/90 (perfunctory summary in *AGN Comptos*, ii, no. 706); *Foed.*, iii, 308–9; cf. Innocent VI, *Lettres*, no. 1613.
39 *Lescot, *Chron.*, 239–40; BN PO 2300 [Plessis, 5], 2373 [Préaux], cf. 493 [Braque, 9], 525 [Brocheroude, 7, 9], 875 [Coucorp, 2], 1814 [Malet, 4], 1892 [Maucourt, 6], 2130 [Noyers, 5], 2760 [St.-Laurent, 2], 2780 [St.-Yon, 9], etc.; BN Fr. 26000, nos. 361–74, 376, 382–93, etc. Commission: 'Lettre à Ch. le Mauvais'; Secousse, *Preuves*, 575–6.
40 Rouen, Bibl. Mun. Ms. 3408, fol. 159; Secousse, *Preuves*, 55; **KOF*, xiii, 339–40.
41 Avesbury, G. *Edwardi*, 425–6; Knighton, *Chron.*, 130.
42 **KOF*, xiii, 339–40; Secousse, *Preuves*, 576–81; *Gr. chron.*, i, 51.
43 *Foed.*, iii, 305, 308; *CCR 1354–60*, 164–5; PRO E372/200, m. 40 [Northburgh]. The English retained the *bastide*.
44 BN Fr. 26001/490 (two ships); *Lettres de rois*, ii, 111; Secousse, *Preuves*, 55; Avesbury, G. *Edwardi*, 426.
45 *Rot. Parl.*, ii, 264(7, 8); Avesbury, G. *Edwardi*, 426–7; Bel, *Chron.*, ii, 211; Baker, *Chron.*, 125.
46 Secousse, *Preuves*, 582–95. Vaudreuil: Delachenal (1909–31), i, 112–5. Louvre: *Gr. chron.*, i, 51–2.
47 Baker, *Chron.*, 127
48 Pillaging: *Gr. chron.*, i, 51. Navarrese: PRO E403/377, m. 37, E403/380, mm. 6, 18, 20, 24, E403/384, m. 1. Lancaster: *Foed.*, iii, 312; PRO E403/377, 37, E403/378, mm. 41, 42.
49 Avesbury, G. *Edwardi*, 427–8.
50 Bel, *Chron.*, ii, 211–2; BN Fr. n.a. 9241, fols. 162–192vo; **Gr. chron.*, iii, 67–8. *Oriflamme*: Contamine (1975), 25.
51 Lancaster: PRO C76/33, m. 3. Scottish border: *Rot. Scot.*, i, 782; *CPR 1358–61*, 18; Avesbury, G. *Edwardi*, 427.
52 Funds: BN Clair. 60/6, 109/141. Campaign: Fordun, *Chron.*, 371–2; Gray, *Scalacr.* [tr. 2]; *Chron. norm.*, 108.
53 *Rot. Scot.*, i, 782; PRO 76/33, m. 4; *RDP*, iv, 606–8. Ed's itin.: PRO C81/22917–8.

54 English army: Avesbury, *G. Edwardi*, 427–8; *Rot. Parl.*, ii, 264(9). French: BN Fr. n.a. 9241, fol. 162–192vo; *Ord.*, iii, 34(26); *Arch admin. Reims*, iii, 73n^{1}, 73–4; 'Rep. doc. Lenoir', no. 6; AN JJ84/456; *Recits d'un b. de Valenciennes*, 278. Garrisons: Bel, *Chron.*, ii, 212. Campaign: *Rot. Parl.*, ii, 264(9); Avesbury, *G. Edwardi*, 428–31; Bel, *Chron.*, ii, 212–6; *Gr. chron.*, i, 53–4; *Recits d'un b. de Valenciennes*, 279–80; Venette, *Chron.*, 229; and other sources cited below. John's itin.: AN JJ84/335, 352, 445

55 PRO C81/22919.

56 BN Fr. n.a. 9241, fol. 164.

57 *Rot. Parl.*, ii, 264–5(10); Gray, *Scalacr.*, 303; Fordun, *Chron.*, 372; *Anonimalle Chron.*, 33; Avesbury, *G. Edwardi*, 431. Angus: *Scots Peerage* [D], i, 170. Defences: Brown, Colvin and Taylor, 567. Greystoke: *CPR 1358–61*, 18.

58 Bower, *Chron.*, vii, 282; *Rot. Scot.*, i, 783. Mines: PRO E101/482/16. Castle: Brown, Colvin and Taylor, 564–6.

59 **Gr. chron.*, iii, 67–8.

60 Ceremony: *Arch. mun. Bordeaux*, v, 439–44. Council: Baker, *Chron.*, 127–8; Black Prince, Letter (i), 434. Armagnac's raids: PRO E101/169/1(21, 49), E101/168/12(73), E101/169/1(36, 37, 51, 57), E101/169/3(20); BN Fr. 26000/469.

61 Baker, *Chron.*, 128–30; Black Prince, Letter (i), 434; Wingfield, Letter (i), 440. St.-Macaire: DCO Henxteworth, fols. 3vo, 8. Numbers: Knighton, *Chron.*, 128.

62 Baker, *Chron.*, 130–1; Black Prince, Letter (i), 434; Wingfield, Letter (i), 440.

63 *HGL*, ix, 653; Black Prince, Letter (i), 434; Wingfield, Letter (i), 440. Strength: **Gr. chron.*, iii, 69.

64 Baker, *Chron.*, 131–2; Black Prince, Letter (i) 434.

65 Baker, *Chron.*, 132; Black Prince, Letter (i) 434–5. Froissart: *Chron.*, iv, 164, 165.

66 Baker, *Chron.*, 132–3; Black Prince, Letter (i), 435; Wingfield, Letter (i), 440.

67 Baker, *Chron.*, 133–4; Black Prince, Letter (i), 435; Wingfield, Letter (i), 441–2. Walls: BN Doat 53, fols. 140–6, 215–21. Emissaries' appointment: Innocent VI, *Lettres*, nos. 1800–7.

68 Baker, *Chron.*, 134; Black Prince, Letter (i), 435; *Petit Thalamus*, 351; Mascaro, 'Libre', 48; Bel, *Chron.*, ii, 221–2.

69 Baker, *Chron.*, 134–5; Denifle, 91–2.

70 *Tucoo-Chala (1961), 160–1; Tucoo-Chala (1959), 64–5, 67, *384 (no. 141); Innocent VI, *Lettres*, nos. 162, 184–7.

71 Arnaud-Guilhem: PRO E403/377, m. 19; on him, Tucoo-Chala (1959), 123n^{26}. Tacit arrangements: Baker, *Chron.*, 135, 138.

72 Baker, *Chron.*, 135–7.

73 Baker, *Chron.*, 136–8; Black Prince, Letter (i), 436; Villani, *Hist.*, 353.

74 Villani, *Hist.*, 353; Bel, *Chron.*, ii, 222.

75 Wingfield, Letter (i), 442. Walls: *Doc. Millau*, 93; *L. Menard, ii, 169–70, 179–81; *HGL*, ix, 654, x, *1125–6. Exemptions: *Ord.*, iii, 73–83, 177–8; Jeanjean, 50–4.

76 *HGL*, ix, 653–4; Avesbury, *G. Edwardi*, 433; Villani, *Hist.*, 353.

77 Lescot, *Chron.*, 98; **Gr. chron.*, iii, 67–70.

78 Avesbury, *G. Edwardi*, 432; Black Prince, Letter (i), 436–7. Coast: *Foed.*, iii, 315, 316–7; PRO C76/33, m. 1.

79 *Anonimalle Chron.*, 33–4; *Foed.*, iii, 314; *Rot. Scot.*, i, 783, 784, 786; PRO E372/203, m. 39d [Haddon]. King's itin.: PRO C81/22955, 22958.

80 *Anonimalle Chron.*, 34; Avesbury, *G. Edwardi*, 450–1; Fordun, *Chron.*, 373. Garencières: BL Add. Chart. 4162; BN Fr. n.a. 7413, fol. 561vo.

81 *Rot. Scot.*, i, 799–800; Fordun, *Chron.*, 373–4; *Cal. Doc. Scot.*, iii, nos. 1622, 1626; Balfour-Melville (1954), 17.

82 Avesbury, *G. Edwardi*, 454–6; *Anonimalle Chron.*, 34; Knighton, *Chron.*, 136–8; Fordun, *Chron.*, 374–5.

83 Bower, *Chron.*, vii, 296; *Liber Pluscardensis*, i, 298; Wyntoun, *Oryg. Cron.*, ii, 487; *Rot. Scot.*, i, 761.
84 Truce: *Foed.*, iii, 325, 327. Douglas: Fordun, *Chron.*, 376, 377n^{3}; Gray, *Scalacr.*, 175; Baker, *Chron.*, 143.
85 Baker, *Chron.*, 138–9; Chandos Herald, *Vie*, 66 (ll. 666–75); Wingfield, Letter (i), 442.
86 Wingfield, Letter (ii), 446, 447; Chandos Herald, *Vie*, 66–7 (ll. 676–88). Port-Ste.-Marie: BN Fr. 32510, fols. 228, 228vo, 229; AN JJ84/426, 475. Souillac: AC Martel BB5, fols. 94vo, 99; CC3–4, fols. 64, 73vo, 79; AC Gourdon, CC18, fol. 104vo. Beaulieu: AC Martel BB5, fol. 93; CC3–4, fol. 73vo; *Comptes Rodez*, i, 223–4; *Cartulaire de l'abbaye de Beaulieu*, ed. M. Deloche (1859), pp. xli-xlii. Martel: AC Martel BB5, fols. 93, 93vo. Banditry: *Rec. titres Périgueux*, 300.
87 Wingfield, Letter (ii), 446–7; Avesbury, *G. Edwardi*, 457; Chandos Herald, *Vie*, 67 (ll. 691–702). Garrisons: DCO Henxteworth, fols. 18, 20vo (English); *Villepelet, 233 (French).
88 Wingfield, Letter (ii), 446–7.
89 Avesbury, *G. Edwardi*, 449–50; *Doc. Durfort*, nos. 1093–5; *Doc. Galard*, i, 500–4, 506–21, 522–3; *Foed.*, iii, 399–400 (Caumont, cf. Sumption, i, 334, 422–3).
90 Lancaster: PRO C76/34, m. 17. Prince: *Reg. Black Prince*, iii, 223–5; *Foed.*, iii, 323, 325–6; PRO C61/68, mm. 6, 4.

CHAPTER V

1 *Ord.*, iii, 15–6.
2 Henneman (1971), 288.
3 Henneman (1971), 341; Oresme, *De moneta*, ed. C. Johnson (1956), 24, 30–1, 34.
4 *Rec. doc. mon.*, i, 348–9.
5 *Delachenal (1909–31), i, 121n^{1}; *Gr. chron.*, i, 55–6, 57–8; *Ord.*, iii, 21–37. Venue, layout: Guerout, ii, 145–52; Hervieu, 57–60.
6 Cazelles (1982), 206–8, 209.
7 Cazelles (1960), 847–62. Harcourt: Secousse, *Preuves*, 57. Le Coq: 'Acte d'accusation', 367–8 (16–20).
8 'Acte d'accusation', 368 (20–2); Secousse, *Preuves*, 45–9, 55–7, 60; *Gr. chron.*, i, 56–7; *Delachenal (1909–31), i, 119n^{5}.
9 *Chron. premiers Valois*, 33–4; cf. *Chron. des abbés de St.-Ouen*, ed. F. Michel (1840), 89. Date: *Delachenal (1909–31), i, 135n^{4}.
10 Secousse, *Preuves*, 57; 'Acte d'accusation', 368–9 (23–9). Denials: BN Fr. 26001/541.
11 Flanders: *Doc. Clos de galées*, no. XXXIX. Aragon: A. de Capmany y de Monpalau, *Memorias históricas sobre la marina. . . de Barcelona*, n.e., i (1962), 258–60. Dauphin: *Delachenal (1909–31), ii, 372–3.
12 Beaujolais: *Guigue, 6n^{1}; *Titres Bourbon*, i, 475–9. Burgundy: Petit (1885–1905), ix, 44–8, 51–5. Normandy: *Gr. chron.*, i, 64; Henneman (1971), 293–4.
13 *Gr. chron.*, i, 58–61; Innocent VI, *Lettres*, no. 2349, 2351; *Inv. AC Montferrand*, i, 391; *Ord.*, iii, 24n, iv, 171–5. Arras: *Inv. chartes Arras*, 103; *Rec. doc. droit. mun.*, i, 346–8, 364–6; *Gr. chron.*, i, 62; Avesbury, *G. Edwardi*, 457–8.
14 Tax: Henneman (1971), 297–8. Recruitment: *Delachenal (1909–31), ii, 373–4.
15 **HGL*, x, 1112–20.
16 Rumours: *Foed.*, iii, 329; cf. Villani, *Hist.*, 369–70. Beaupré: Secousse, *Preuves*, 60; Noyal, 'Chron.', 156; *Chron. norm.*, 111; Delachenal (1909–31), 142–3.
17 **KOF*, v, 522; *Chron. premiers Valois*, 34–5, 36–7; *Gr. chron.*, i, 62–5; Venette, *Chron.*, 230–1; Bel, *Chron.*, ii, 224; Lescot, *Chron.*, 99; Villani, *Hist.*, 369. Doublet: Froissart, *Chron.*, iv, 178. Executioner: *Delachenal (1909–31), ii, 377–8.
18 Secousse, *Preuves*, 49–60, 59, 76–7.

19 *Gr. chron.*, i, 65; Venette, *Chron.*, 231; *Chron. premiers Valois*, 37. Châtelet: BN PO 632 [Celier, 2]. Chateau-Gaillard: AN JJ 90/69; *Doc. Ch. Comptes Navarre*, 64–6. Crèvecoeur, Arleux: Secousse, *Preuves*, 65.
20 *Foed.*, iii, 329 (documents); BN Fr. 26001/541 (statement of case); 'Journal des États', 445; Machaut, 'Le confort d'ami', ll.1805–7, *Oeuvres*, iii, 65.
21 Harcourt: BN Fr. 26001/497. Troops: *Chron. premiers Valois*, 37; BN PO 1266 [Gal, 7].
22 Secousse, *Preuves*, 62; *Chron. premiers Valois*, 37–8; Venette, *Chron.*, 232; *Recits d'un b. de Valenciennes*, 286. Dauphin, engines: Delachenal (1909–31), i, 171. Topography: A. and S. Plaisse, 21–40; AHVF Evreux.
23 **KOF*, v, 378, 522; *Frag. chron. B-Normandie*, 5; Avesbury, *G. Edwardi*, 462. Froissart, *Chron.*, iv, 183–4 (Louis).
24 *Foed.*, iii, 330; *AGN Comptos*, ii, nos. 799, 806, 822–3, 834–5.
25 PRO C76/34, m. 17; E403/380, mm. 1, 2, 5.
26 **KOF*, v, 521–3, xviii, 378–81; *Foed.* iii, 328, 329; Avesbury, *G. Edwardi*, 461. Lancaster: PRO E403/380, m. 1. Brittany: Avesbury, *G. Edwardi*, 462–3. Gascony: *Foed.*, iii, 330; *AGN Comptos*, ii, no. 849.
27 Sea: *Doc. Clos des galées*, nos. 523–4, 529–30; Pere III, 'Cron.', 1124–6. Land: BN Fr. 26001/656.
28 Lehoux, i, 56–62.
29 Quercy: AC Martel BB5, fols. 96, 97; Lacoste, iii, 153–4. Fons: Alauzier (2), 168–70; BN Clair. 23/1687; AC Martel EE1/18, CC3–4, fol. 81vo; *Comptes Rodez*, i, 220; Innocent VI, *Lettres*, nos. 2340–2. Rouergue: *Comptes Rodez*, i, 224, 225–6, 227, 255–6, 259, 337; *Doc. Millau*, no. 208; **HGL*, x, 1120–2. Limousin: AC Martel BB5, fol. 99. Poitou: *AHP*, xx, 282–6; BN PO 1349 [Gaillons, 4] (walls); *Rec. doc. Poitou*, iii, p. xxxviiin[3].
30 *Ord.*, iii, 53–5.
31 Coville (1894), 80–1, *361, *363.
32 *Rec. doc. mon.*, i, 357–9; cf. *Ord.*, iii, 89–90. Poilevilain, Braque: Cazelles (1982), 223–4.
33 Bel, *Chron.*, ii, 65; Contamine (1972), 114–5; 'Journal', 435.
34 Contamine (1972), 38–46, 78–9.
35 *Ord.*, v, 67–8; Contamine (1972), 82–3, 106–7, 605–9.
36 La Tour Landry, *Livre*, 225; *Livre des fais*, 12.
37 Charny, 'Livre de chevalerie', 513, 515–6; Galard: AN JJ82/601.
38 *Ord.*, iii, 231–2(24).
39 Contamine (1972), 17–9, 655–6; Ayton, 43–8.
40 Lances: Villani, *Hist.*, cols. 747–8; Azario, *Liber gestorum*, 128; Froissart, *Chron.*, v, 168.
41 Avesbury, *G. Edwardi*, 462–3.
42 Venette, *Chron.*, 232–3; *Chron. premiers Valois*, 38; *Recits d'un b. de Valenciennes*, 286–7; *Gr. chron.*, i, 68; Secousse, *Preuves*, 61; Date: AN JJ84/638.
43 Avesbury, *G. Edwardi*, 463; *Chron. premiers Valois*, 39–40; *Gr. chron.*, i, 67–8; Secousse, *Preuves*, 62.
44 Army: Avesbury, *G. Edwardi*, 464; *Chron. premiers Valois*, 40–1; *Chron. norm.*, 110. Ct. of Poitiers: **HGL*, x, 1122–3; *Lehoux, i, 66n[3]. John's itin.: *Froissart, *Chron.*, iv, p. lxxn[2]; Fowler (1969), 149, 152. Seine: BN Fr. 26001/596.
45 Avesbury, *G. Edwardi*, 463–5; *Gr. chron.*, i, 68–9; *Chron. premiers Valois*, 41–2; Lescot, *Chron.*, 101. Conches: BN PO 90 [Argeville, 3–5], 1814 [Malet, 19].
46 Black Prince, Letters (ii), (iii), 382. Stafford: *Reg. Black Prince*, iii, 224–5; PRO C61/68, m.4, E403/378, m. 42, E403/380, mm. 6, 7, 12; DCO Henxteworth, fol. 24vo (date).
47 Prince's movements: Baker, *Chron.*, 139–40; Black Prince, Letter (ii). Languedoc: BN Doat 53, fols. 271–276; *L. Menard, ii, 172, 173, 180; BN Coll. Languedoc 159, fols. 82–82vo. Quotation: Froissart, *Chron.*, iv, 393, 396.
48 *Recits d'un b. de Valenciennes*, 289; *Chron. premiers Valois*, 43–4; *Arch. Montpellier*, ii,

no. 743. Date: Petit, 'Séjours', 612. Quotation: Froissart, *Chron.*, iv, 194. Participants: **ibid.*, iv, p. lxxn[2]. Mines: BN Fr. 26001/656.

49 Prince: Baker, *Chron.* 140; AC Martel, BB5, fol. 100vo. Coinage: *Ord.*, iii, 71–2.

50 Edward's Council: PRO E403/380, m. 3. His orders: PRO C76/34, mm. 14, 12, 11. French reaction: *Ord.*, iii, 72–3; *Rec. doc. mon.*, i, 359–60.

51 Baker, *Chron.*, 140; Black Prince, Letters (ii), (iii), 382; *Eulogium*, iii, 215–6.

52 *Eulogium*, iii, 216–8. Countess: PRO C81/339/20390. On her lands, J.R.S. Phillips, *Aymer de Valence, Earl of Pembroke* (1972), 2–3. Issoudun: Raynal, ii, 296.

53 PRO C76/34, m. 8; *Foed.*, iii, 377–8.

54 Black Prince, Letter (iii), 383.

55 Lehoux, i, *70n[2], 70–1; *Arch. Montpellier*, ii, no. 686.

56 *Arch. Montpellier*, ii, no. 743; *Chron. premiers Valois*, 46; *Gr. chron.*, i, 69. Last document dated at siege was 18 August, BN Fr. 25701/89.

57 *Arch. Montpellier*, ii, no. 686; BN Fr. 26001/656; Black Prince, Letter (iii), 382.

58 Infantry: *Chron. premiers Valois*, 46; Lescot, *Chron.*, 101–2; *Arch. admin. Reims*, iii, 79–81; Machaut, 'Le confort d'ami', *Oeuvres*, iii, 117. Summonses: *Gr. chron.*, i, 69; BN Fr. 26001, nos. 656, 687.

59 *Eulogium*, iii, 218–9; Baker, *Chron.*, 142. Vierzon: AN JJ84/803, 90/406.

60 *Eulogium*, iii, 219–20; Baker, *Chron.*, 141–2; Black Prince, Letter (iii), 382, 383. John's itin.: Petit, 'Séjours', 612.

61 Baker, *Chron.*, 142n; 'Mirac. S. Gatiani', 613–4; *Eulogium*, iii, 220–1. Topography: Chevalier (1975), 44–5, 54–61, 176–7; *Ord.*, v, 457–8.

62 Baker, *Chron.*, 142; Bel, *Chron.*, ii, 231; *Eulogium*, iii, 221; Lehoux, i, 75.

63 Innocent VI, *Lettres*, nos. 2022–85, 2197–8, 2202–4, 2267; *Vitae paparum*, i, 334, 344–5; *Foed.*, iii, 333–4, 338; *Delachenal (1909–31), ii, 380–1. Montbazon: Black Prince, Letter (iii), 383. On Talleyrand: Zacour, 7–31; *Rot. Parl.*, ii, 144 (59). On Capocci: *Vitae paparum*, i, 367–8; Innocent VI, *Lettres*, no. 2404.

64 *Eulogium*, iii, 221; Petit, 'Séjours', 612. Lancaster: *Anonimalle Chron.*, 36; *Chron. premiers Valois*, 45–6; 'Chron. Briocense', 43; 'Chron. Brittanicum', 8, 113.

65 Black Prince, Letter (iii), 383; Gray, *Scalacr.*, 173; *Eulogium*, iii, 221–2; *Gr. chron.*, i, 70–1; Lescot, *Chron.*, 102. La Chaboterie: Burghersh, Letter; this place was in the parish of Nouaillé, *Chartes et documents du xiiie siècle en langue vulgaire*, ed. M.S. la Du, i (1960), 66–7, 146; it is probably the hamlet shown in the eighteenth century Casini map as 'La Chabossière'; this accords with the Prince's report that the fight occurred 3 (English) leagues from Chauvigny. Gascons: PRO E403/388, mm. 1, 17, 27, E403/394, m. 35, E30/1506 (ransom payments).

66 Black Prince, Letter (iii), 383; *Eulogium*, iii, 222; *Anonimalle Chron.*, 37. French army: *Petite chron. fr.*, 27–8; Baker, *Chron.*, 143; Burghersh, Letter (numbers).

67 Baker, *Chron.*, 143, 146–7, 148, 150; *Eulogium*, iii, 224; *Gr. chron.*, i, 72; *Chron. norm.*, 114; Burghersh, Letter (numbers).

68 Black Prince, Letter (iii), 383–4; *Eulogium*, iii, 222–3; Baker, *Chron.*, 143–4; Villani, *Hist.*, cols. 411–3.

69 Baker, *Chron.*, 144. Entourage: Froissart, *Chron.*, v, 39–40.

70 *Eulogium*, iii, 224; *Gr. chron.*, i, 72, 73; Villani, *Hist.*, 415.

71 Baker, *Chron.*, 143, 144; Froissart, *Chron.*, v, 21–3; *Chron. premiers Valois*, 51.

72 Black Prince, Letter (iii), 384; Fordun, *Chron.*, 376; *Anonimalle Chron.*, 38; Chandos Herald, *Vie*, 77–8 (ll. 1061–99). Ordinances: *Reg. Black Prince*, iv, 338.

73 Baker, *Chron.*, 147–8; *Anonimalle Chron.*, 38. Douglas: Fordun, *Chron.*, 376.

74 Baker, *Chron.*, 148–9; *Eulogium*, iii, 224. Noise: Chandos Herald, *Vie*, 83 (ll. 1157–8); *Chron. premier Valois*, 54.

75 Baker, *Chron.*, 149–50; *Chron. norm.*, 114, 115, 116n[1]; *Gr. chron.*, i, 74; Villani, *Hist.*, 416; *L. Menard, ii, 181.

76 Baker, *Chron.*, 150–3; *Chron. premiers Valois,* 56. Audley: Chandos Herald, *Vie*, 83 (ll. 1283–1302); Walsingham, *Hist. Angl.*, i, 282. Champ d'A: *Petite chron. fr.*, 28; *Rec. doc. Poitiers,* ii, 168. Citizens: Froissart, *Chron.*, v, 53, 65.

77 *Reg. Black Prince,* iv, 338–9; cf. **HGL*, x, 113 2.

78 Froissart, *Chron.*, v, 54–5, 57–8, 280; *Foed.*, iii, 385, 467; PRO E403/387, m. 28, E403/395, m. 31, E403/396, mm. 13, 26.

79 Villani, *Hist.*, 419; *Foed.*, iii, 341;

80 Dead: Black Prince, Letter (iv). Quotations: Baker, *Chron.*, 153–4; Guesnon, 'Documents', 245.

81 *Eulogium,* iii, 225; Black Prince, Letter (ii); Avesbury, G. *Edwardi,* 469. Charny: Lescot, *Chron.*, 103; *Chron. premiers Valois,* 55. Burials: *Rec. doc. Poitiers,* ii, 164–75.

82 Prisoners: *Eulogium,* iii, 225; Black Prince, Letter (ii); Avesbury, G. *Edwardi,* 470–1; Bel, *Chron.*, ii, 237–8; PRO E403/388, m. 17 (Bourbon), m. 22 (Eu), m. 17 (Audrehem); cf. m. 16 (lord of Derval), m. 17 (Count of Auxerre), mm. 17, 32 (Count of Joigny), m. 23 (Count of Nassau) Given-Wilson and Bériac, *EHR* cxvi (2001), 814–7. Spoil: *Petit (1874), 172n[3]; *Reg. Black Prince,* iv, 254, 333; BL Roy. D II (Bible); Froissart, *Chron.*, v, 61 (quotation).

83 *Eulogium,* iii, 225–6.

84 *Issues of Exch.*, 165; **KOF*, xviii, 388; *Foed.*, iii, 340, 341; Villani, *Hist.*, 419.

CHAPTER VI

1 Chartres: BN Clair. 8, p. 409; 32, p. 2383; 59, 4507; 75, p. 5835; 77, p. 6017; 82, p. 6419; 107, pp. 72, 135, etc. Paris: Venette, *Chron.*, 245–6; Sauval, i, 38–9.

2 *Mon. proc. canonisation,* 63, 71, 72; *Chron. Brittanicum,* 8,113; *Chron. Briocense,* 43. Ransom treaty: Déprez (1926), 50–2, *Foed.*, iii, 335, 336–7.

3 **Gallia Christiana,* i 1715), 12; *Gr. chron.*, i, 74–5; 'Journal', 429.

4 'Complainte', ll. 5–11, 25–8, 41–7, 81–4, 94–5; Lescot, *Chron.*, 101–2; Monte-Belluna, 'Tragicum argumentum', 150; AN JJ84/715.

5 Cazelles (1982), 197–203; Delachenal (1909–31), i, 288–9.

6 'Journal', 429–31; *Gr. chron.*, i, 75–7; 'Acte d'accusation', 371 (42–4).

7 'Acte d'accusation', 382–3. Marcel, Toussac: Cazelles (1982), 280–1.

8 'Journal', 431–7; *Gr. chron.*, i, 77–81; 'Acte d'accusation', 373–5 (52–64).

9 *Gr. chron.*, i, 81–3; 'Journal', 437–8; 'Acte d'accusation', 372 (72).

10 *Gr. chron.*, i, 83–6, 87–9; 'Journal', 438–9; 'Acte d'accusation', 377, 379 (74–7, 87).

11 'Journal', 440–59; 'Acte d'accusation', 377–9 (78–85); *Gr. chron.*, i, 89.

12 *Arch. St.-Quentin,* ii, no. 669.

13 *Gr. chron.*, i, 89; Guesnon, 'Documents', 245–6; 'Acte d'accusation', 379 (88).

14 Languedoc: *Ord.*, iii, 101–10; *Gr. chron.*, i, 86–7. Auvergne: *Ord.*, iii, i, pp. lv-lx; Ledos (1895).

15 AN JJ90/185; *Ord.*, iii, 143 (52)

16 Armagnac: *HGL,* ix, 666. On G. de Melun, B. de Ventadour: Cazelles (1982), 190–4, 402–10.

17 Mourning: *Gr. chron.*, i, 86–7. Quotation: Guesnon, 'Documents', 245–6.

18 Bock, 'Documents',98.

19 Innocent VI, *Lettres,* nos. 2404, 2481–2, 2509; PRO E403/383, mm. 2, 7; *Foed.*, iii, 341–2.

20 Innocent VI, *Lettres,* nos. 2138, 2149, 2407, 2414, 2508; *Lescot, *Chron.*, 240–1; *Foed.*, iii, 343; PRO E403/383, m. 11, 403/384, m. 1. Thorns: Delachenal (1909–31), i, 274.

21 Bock, 'Documents', 97–9.

22 *Gr. chron.*, i, 91; Lescot, *Chron.*, 106–7; Venette, *Chron.*, 244; *Chroniques de Metz,* 98–9; Delachenal (1909–31), i, 276–9. Treaty, loan: *Luce (1876), 524–6 (misdated); *Regesta Bohemiae et Moraviae,* vi.2 (1929), 279.

23 *Ord.*, iii, 72–3, 84–5, 87–8, 89–91, 94–5; *Doc. mon.*, i, 366; *Gr. chron.*, i, 92–3.
24 *Gr. chron.*, i, 93–4. Provinces: *Doc. mon.*, i, 368; AN JJ85/52.
25 English: figures based on numbers participating in campaign of June-July 1356: see above. Navarrese: figures based on numbers offered to Edward III in Sept. 1355: see above; reinforcements, *AGN Comptos*, nos. 838, 849.
26 *Frag. chron. B-Normandie*, 6; Secousse, *Preuves*, 63; AN JJ85/15; Timbal, *Reg. Parl.*, 121. Messengers: BN Fr. 26001/688.
27 Lescot, *Chron.*, 110–11; Knighton, *Chron.*, 148.
28 Timbal, *Reg. Parl.*, 456–7; AN X^{2a} 7, fols. 217–227.
29 *Doc. Maine*, 93–6; *Rec. doc. Poitou*, iii, 251–4; AN JJ89/127; Martin de Bois-Gautier, 'Vita Mariae de Malliaco', 738.
30 *Foed.*, iii, 347; BL Cotton Caligula D III, fol. 59.
31 Pont-Audemer: *Chron. norm.*, 118; BN Clair. 93, p. 7193; 107, p. 8376; *Gr. chron.*, i, 90–1. Revenue: Henneman (1976), 39–40; Coville (1894), 84. Numbers: *Chron. norm.* 112, 119. Harcourt: *Frag. chron. B-Normandie*, 6; *Chron. premiers Valois*, 66–7; *Gr. chron.*, i, 89–90; *Chron. norm.*, 119–20; Noyal, 'Chron.', 256.
32 Rochefort: Morice, *Preuves*, 1503–7, 1512–4, 1522. His career: *Foed.*, iii, 165; Morice, *Preuves*, 1466, 1482, 1486. Craon/Laval: *Rec. doc. Poitou*, iii, 252–3; Morice, *Preuves*, 1501–2; *Mon. proc. canonisation*, 63.
33 Lescot, *Chron.*, 110–3; *Chron. norm.*, 159; *Luce (1891).
34 *Gr. chron.*, i, 100; *Frag. chron. B-Normandie*, 6; Guesnon, 'Documents', 246–7; Villani, *Hist.*, col. 435. English recruits: PRO E403/383, mm. 5, 6, 8, 9, 11; *Foed.*, iii, 339.
35 *Foed.*, iii, 306–7, 312, 403–4; PRO E101/174/4 (list of castellanies at farm). Conquests: PRO C76/33, mm. 14, 3 (grants to John Maitland). Example of indenture for garrison service in France: PRO E101/27/34 (Saint-Sauveur, Feb. 1360).
36 PRO E101/174/4, 5; Jones (1970), 164–6.
37 *Frag. chron. B-Normandie*, 6; Timbal, *Reg. Parl.*, 456–7; *Foed.*, iii, 421.
38 *Foed.*, iii, 333, 340, 342, 345.
39 *Chevauché*: BL Cotton Caligula D III, fol. 47; *Foed.*, iii, 363; AN X^{2a} 7, fols. 217–217vo. Avranches: *Frag. chron. B-Normandie*, 6; AN JJ89/181. On Scholl, PRO C76/33, m. 9; C76/38, m. 16. On Tutbury: *Cal. Pap. R. Petitions*, i, 275.
40 BL Cotton Caligula D III, fol. 54; PRO E403/384, mm. 11, 16; *Foed.*, iii, 351; Chaplais, *Dipl. Practice*, 75–6. Permanent captain (Simon Newington): *Foed.*, iii, 346, 357. Newington had been Lancaster's captain at St.-Germain de Crioult, PRO C76/35, m. 11, *Foed.*, iii, 421.
41 *Gr. chron.*, i, 95–9. Poilevillain: Valois (1885), 81 and n^3. Lorris: *Foed.*, iii, 348.
42 *Ord.*, iii, 128 (5), 345–6; *Gr. chron.*, i, 100–6.
43 Ord., iii, 121–46.
44 *Gr. chron.*, i, 106–7, *iii, 76–81.
45 Ch. of Blois: Cazelles (1982), 253–8; Pocquet (1928), i, 327–8. Council: Cazelles (1982), 265–70.
46 Baker, *Chron.*, 155; *Anonimalle Chron.*, 40; *Gr. chron.*, i, 98–9.
47 *Gr. chron.*, i, 107; *L. Menard, ii, 185; *Foed.*, iii, 348–51, 356.
48 *Gr. chron.*, i, 108; Lescot, *Chron.*, 109; *Delachenal (1909–31), $312n^5$.
49 *Gr. chron.*, i, 108–10; Lescot, *Chron.*, 109; *Coville (1893), $61n^3$.
50 *Reg. Black Prince*, iv, 253; Reading, *Chron.*, 126.
51 Estates-Gen.: Coville (1893), 61–2. Revenues: *Gr. chron.*, i, 111; *Cat. comptes royaux*, nos. 510–11. Forez: *La Mure, iii, 123–7; *Guigue, 246–53. Languedoc: *HGL*, x, 1129–31; *Inv. AC Toulouse*, 535; *Doc. Millau*, 94; *Vitae paparum*, i, 319–20. Moratorium: *Ord.*, iii, 161–2.
52 *Foed.*, iii, 349.
53 *Foed.*, iii, 353, 359; *Anonimalle Chron.*, 40; Knighton, *Chron.*, 152–4. Totesham: PRO

E372/202, m. 34 [Totesham]. Dauphin's representatives: BN PO 1280 [Garencières, 13].

54 Knolles, Pipe: Knighton, *Chron.*, ii, 99. Gascons: *Chron. premiers Valois*, 63. Bascon: *AGN Comptos*, iii, no. 684; *Luce (1876), 538–9. English: *Foed.*, iii, 381; Knighton, *Chron.*, 160; Gray, *Scalacr.* 177–8, 180. Fogg: PRO C76/35, m. 11. Vaudry: AN X^{2a} 7, fols. 217, 222vo-223. Vire: AN JJ87/248, 331. Bayeux-Caen: Delisle (1876), 115–6; *Chron. norm.*, 120 (Rots, Cairon). Abandoned settlements: AN JJ87/107, 92/272, 112/323. Refugees: Bois (1976), 267–9. 'All Normandy. . .': *Chron. norm.*, 121.

55 Knighton, *Chron.*, 154; *Chron. premiers Valois*, 62. Supply: *CPR 1358–61*, 126, 312.

56 Caen, Vire: AN JJ87/248, 331; *Delisle (1876), 115–6. Honfleur: *Doc. clos des galées*, no. XLIII; *La Roque (1662), iv, 1880–4; *Chron. premiers Valois*, 62–4; Knighton, *Chron.*, 154.

57 Bel, *Chron.*, ii, 249–50.

58 Cost: *Letter Book*, G, 85. War contractors: *Foed.*, iii, 303–4. Financiers: Fryde (1959), 5–6, 14–6; Fryde (1988), 191–6. Lancaster: Knighton, *Chron.*, 188. Mauny: W. St. John Hope, *History of the London Charterhouse* (1925), 3–18. Calais: *CPR 1345–8*, 561–8.

59 *Anonimalle Chron.*, 41; *Chron. anon. Cant.*, 204–6; Knighton, *Chron.*, 150. Quotation: Chandos Herald, *Vie*, 89 (ll. 1513–5).

60 *Cal. Pap. R. Letters*, iii, 625; *Gr. chron.*, i, 110; *Foed.*, iii, 355, 356, 358–9, 362.

61 *Gr. chron.*, i, 110–11; *Chron. anon. Cant.*, 206–7; Knighton, *Chron.*, 152; *Foed.*, iii, 357, 358, 369; PRO C76/35, m. 13 (Paris).

62 David II, *Acts*, no. 141; *Foed.*, iii, 329, 344, 352, 354, 369, 371–9; *Cal. Doc. Scot.*, iii, no. 1629; 'Papers rel. captivity and release of David II', 17, 22.

63 Coville (1893), 61–2.

64 *Gr. chron.*, i, 111–3; Lescot, *Chron.*, 113. Councillors: Cazelles (1982), 279–80, 284–6; *Réformateurs*: AN X^{2a} 6, 328vo; Valois (1885), $104n^7$.

65 *Coville (1894), 361–4; *Gr. chron.*, i, 112–3; *Doc. mon.*, i, 375–6; *Ord.*, iii, 180–1.

66 *Gr. chron.*, i, 114–5; *Inv. arch. Poitiers*, no. 773.

CHAPTER VII

1 'Acte d'accusation', 383; Secousse, *Preuves*, 97, 98. Walls: Calonne, i, 271–3 and plate VII.

2 *Gr. chron.*, i, 115–7; Lescot, *Chron.*, 114; Venette, *Chron.*, 250; *Chron. premiers Valois*, 61; *Chron. norm.*, 125; Secousse, *Preuves*, 98, 154; Guesnon, 'Documents', 247–8; Guichenon, iv, 202–3. On J. de Picquigny, Honoré-Duverger (1947–8).

3 *Gr. chron.*, i, 117–8, 123–4, 125–6.

4 *Gr. chron.*, i, 118–20; Lescot, *Chron.*, 114; Venette, *Chron.*, 250–1; Bel. *Chron.*, ii, 253.

5 *Gr. chron.*, i, 120–6, 144–5; Lescot, *Chron.*, 115; Secousse, *Preuves*, 65–8, 70–1.

6 ASV Reg. Vat. 239, fol. 217vo; *Foed.*, iii, 384.

7 BL Cotton Caligula D III, fol. 45; *Doc. Ch. Comptes Navarre*, 61–2.

8 *Delachenal (1909–31), ii, 402–11.

9 *Delachenal (1909–31), ii, 393–4, 396–8; Lehoux, i, 91–4.

10 *AGN Comptos*, ii, nos. 1048, 1062, 1067, 1074; iii, nos. 38–40; *Doc. Ch. comptes Navarre*, 64–7.

11 Stafford: PRO SC1/41/101; *Cal. Pap. R. Petitions*, i, 233; PRO C76/33, m. 8. Scotland: *Rot, Scot.*, i, 637. Calais: *CPR 1345–8*, 551. Blaye: PRO E101/170/20, fol. 81; *CCR 1354–60*, 7. Seneschal: PRO C61/66, mm. 5, 3; E101/168/3, fol. 5. Lancaster: PRO C76/34, m. 14; Knighton, *Chron.*, 160.

12 Neubourg: *Chron. norm.*, 121, 121–2. Pont-Audemer: AN JJ87/166; *Chron. premiers Valois*, 61–2; *Chron. norm.*, 122.

13 *Gr. chron.*, i, 127–8. Champagne: BN Fr. 25701/121. Refugees: Venette, *Chron.*, 246–7.

14 Secousse, *Preuves*, 64–7, 68–70; *Guichenon, iv, 202–3; *Gr. chron.*, i, 126–7.

15 R. le Coq: *Gr. chron.*, i, 129; Secousse, *Preuves*, 130. Marshals: Cazelles (1982), 294–7.
16 Summons: *Gr. chron.*, i, 128–9, 141; **KOF*, vi, 462; BN Clair. 165/15. Captains: *Gr. chron.*, i, 130; Lescot, *Chron.*, 116; Venette, *Chron.*, 252–3.
17 *Gr. chron.*, 128, 129–30; Venette, *Chron.*, 252–3. Marlborough: *Eulogium*, iii, 227.
18 *Gr. chron.*, i, 131–4; *Chron. norm.*, 126. 'Without ceremony': Secousse, *Preuves*, 67.
19 *Gr. chron.*, i, 141, 142, 159, 160–1, 175–6.
20 *Luce (1894), 193.
21 *Delachenal (1909–31), ii, 397; *Foed.*, iii, 381, 387, 388; PRO E372/202, m. 34 [Totesham]; BN PO 2608 [Saintré, 2]; *Gr. chron.*, i, 158–9.
22 *Gr. chron.*, i, 128; *Luce (1876), 533. On Villiers: Cazelles (1982), 292–3.
23 *Gr. chron.*, i, 129, 130, 141; Venette, *Chron.*, 248; *Ord.*, iv, 346–7.
24 *Gr. chron.*, i, 134–9; Lescot, *Chron.*, 117–8.
25 Estates: *Gr. chron.*, i, 139–40; Lescot, *Chron.*, 118; *Ord.*, iii, 193–7. Incident: *Gr. chron.*, i, 142–3; *Chron. premiers Valois*, 68; Villani, *Hist.*, cols. 484–5.
26 *Gr. chron.*, i, 143–4; *Delachenal (1909–31), ii, 396–7; *Foed.*, iii, 386. Secrecy: *Chron. norm.*, 123.
27 *Gr. chron.*, i, 137, 144–7; Lescot, *Chron.*, 119. Messenger: PRO C76/36, m. 15.
28 Walsingham, *Hist. Angl.*, i, 285; *Delachenal (1909–31), ii, 400–1.
29 *Gr. chron.*, i, 156–7; *Delachenal (1909–31), ii, 400–2; *Notes et doc. rél. Jean II*, 73–81.
30 *Gr. chron.*, i, 154.
31 *Viollet, 'États', 273–92, esp. clauses 1, 3–7, 11, 15–6, 18 (for date, *ibid.*, 281n[4]); *Gr. chron.*, i, 147.
32 Lescot, *Chron.*, 119; *Gr. chron.*, i, 148; *Chron. premiers Valois*, 68; *Delachenal (1909–31), ii, 427, 428.
33 Venette, *Chron.*, 248–9; *Gr. chron.*, i, 149–50. Topography of palace: Guerout, ii, 87–93.
34 Venette, *Chron.*, 249; *Gr. chron.*, i, 148–9. On Regnaut: Autrand (1981), 253–5; Delachenal (1885), 333.
35 *Gr. chron.*, i, 150–3, 158.
36 *Gr. chron.*, i, 153–5, 157–8, 161–2. Council: Cazelles (1982), 309–13. Seal: *Ord.*, iii, 212–3. His first known act as Regent was sealed on 1 March 1358: *Delachenal (1909–31), ii, 399.
37 *Gr. chron.*, i, 153. Confessions: *Delachenal (1909–31), ii, 428.
38 *Gr. chron.*, i, 155–6, 159–60; Secousse, *Preuves*, 73–6; *Delachenal (1909–31), ii, 399–400.
39 Pipe: *Gr. chron.*, i, 159. Truce: BN PO 1668 [Laval, 18]. Villiers: *Luce (1876), 533. Le Bègue: *Gr. chron.*, i, 162–3, 164; Lescot, *Chron.*, 122; Venette, *Chron.*, 260; *Chron. norm.*, 124.
40 *Gr. chron.*, i, 162–3.
41 Coville (1894), 365–6; *Gr. chron.*, i, 163–4. Councillors: Cazelles (1982), 316.
42 *Gr. chron.*, i, 164–8.
43 *Gr. chron.*, i, 168–9.
44 Garrisons, etc.:**KOF*, vi, 462, 463. Recruitment: *Chron. norm.*, 127; *Chron. premiers Valois*, 80; *Gr. chron.*, i, 180–1; Venette, *Chron.*, 258. Estates: *Gr. chron.*, i, 173. Proscribed: Cazelles (1982), 316–7.
45 Venette, *Chron.*, 258–9; *Gr. chron.*, i, 170–1, 175–6; Lescot, *Chron.*, 124–5; *Chron. norm.*, 127; AN X^{1a} 19, fol. 503vo (blockade at Montereau). Quotation: **KOF*, vi, 463.
46 *Gr. chron.*, i, 170; **KOF*, vi, 462–4; *Ord.*, iii, 347; *Delachenal (1909–31), i, 385n[2].
47 *Gr. chron.*, i, 173–4; Lescot, *Chron.*, 125–6.
48 Vertus: *Gr. chron.*, i, 172–3. Compiègne: Venette, *Chron.*, 254–5; *Gr. chron.*, i, 174–5; *Ord.*, iii, 221–32, 221n, 692–3.
49 University: Venette, *Chron.*, 255. Notre-Dame: 'Doc. nouv. E. Marcel', 320–1; *Frémaux (1903), 242. Mint: *Ord.*, iii, 257–8; iv, 347. Defences: Venette, *Chron.*, 256–8; Lescot,

Chron., 125; *Arch. admin. Reims*, iii, 213n. Avignon: Secousse, *Preuves*, 142.

50 *Ord.*, iv, 347; 'Doc. nouv. E. Marcel', 321–3; *Gr. chron.*, i, 178–80; AN JJ86/233 (secretary).

51 Meaux: *Gr. chron.*, i, 169. Amiens: *Doc. Amiens*, i, 69–70, 71, 85–6, 108–10; *Rec. mon. tiers état*, i, 587; *Gr. chron.*, i, 171. Laon: Secousse, *Preuves*, 103–4; AN JJ86/446, 514, 559; JJ90/14, 35, 212, 475.

52 *Delachenal (1909–31), ii, 21n, 416, 419.

53 Rouen: Secousse, *Preuves*, 95; *Chron. premiers Valois*, 77–80; Cheruel, ii, 199–200; BN Fr. 26002/806. Reims: Desportes, 554–6. Évreux: *Gr. chron.*, i, 175.

54 Villani, *Hist.*, col. 497; Knighton, *Chron.*, 158; Reading, *Chron.*, 130; Gray, *Scalacr.*, 176–7; *L. Menard, ii, 204.

55 *L. Menard, ii, 204; **KOF*, xviii, 397; Villani, *Hist.*, col. 499; *Chron. anon. Cant.*, 208.

56 South: *Delachenal (1909–31), ii, 412–3; *L. Menard, ii, 204; **HGL*, x, 1143; *Arch. Montpellier*, ii, no. 653. Paris: *Gr. chron.*, i, 176–7.

57 *Gr. chron.*, i, 177–8; *Luce (1894), 276.

58 *Luce (1894), 300–1; *Gr. chron.*, i, 178; Lescot, *Chron.*, 127; Bel, *Chron.*, ii, 256–7; *Chron. premiers Valois*, 71–2; Venette, *Chron.*, 263–4. Corvées: *Chron. norm.*, 127–8.

59 Venette, *Chron.*, 263, 264; *Chron. premiers Valois*, 71; *Luce (1894), 297–9.

60 *Luce (1894), 188, 192, 261–2, 276–7; *Gr. chron.*, i, 180.

61 *Chron. premiers Valois*, 72; *Gr. chron.*, i, 181. Senlis: Flammermont, 136–7.

62 Montmorency: *Gr. chron.*, i, 180; *Luce (1894), 206–7, 254–6, cf. 188 (Cormeilles), 191 (Deuil). Champagne: *Luce (1894), 194 (Fère), 256–7, 264–72, 281–5, 293–4, 306–9; Bel, *Chron.*, ii, 257–8.

63 *Chron. norm.*, 129; Secousse, *Preuves*, 98; Beauvillé (1875), i, 110, *514–7; *Luce (1894), 207, 296, 335–8.

64 *Chron. premiers Valois*, 72; *Luce (1894), 255.

65 South of Seine: *Luce (1894), 253–5; Fourquin (1964), 233–4. Army: *Luce (1894), 181 (Boissy), 200 (Jaux), 223 (Villiers), 234. Trappes, Palaiseau: *Chron. norm.*, 128; *Luce (1894), 209, 220. Bucy: *Luce (1894), 304–6. Orgemont, la Vache: *Luce (1894), 313–7, 320–2. Lorris: *Luce (1894), 192–3, 261; *Chron. norm.* 130.

66 *Chron. premiers Valois*, 72, 73, 73–4.

67 *Gr. chron.*, i, 181–2.

68 *Chron. premiers Valois*, 73, 74–5. Senlis: *ibid.*, 76–7; Venette, *Chron.*, 267–8; *Luce (1894), 288–9.

69 *Luce (1894), 230–1, 234, 240–4, 258–9; *Gr. chron.*, i, 182–4; Venette, *Chron.*, 265–7; Bel, *Chron.*, ii, 260–2. Crusaders: Froissart, *Chron.*, v, 103, xii, 97; Tucoo-Chala (1959), 77–8. Topography: Secousse, 243–8.

70 *Chron. premiers Valois*, 75–6; *Luce (1894), 189, 210.

71 *Delachenal (1909–31), ii, 417–8, 420; *Luce (1894); *Luce (1894), 182 (Bordeaux), 247–8, 268–70, 283–5, 293–4; AN JJ86/380; Bel, *Chron.*, ii, 259–60; *Chron. norm.*, 132.

72 *Gr. chron.*, i, 181, 186–7. Gestures: *Delachenal (1909–31), ii, 419.

73 *Gr. chron.*, i, 184–6; Venette, *Chron.*, 259.

74 *Gr. chron.*, i, 187–8; *Chron. norm.*, 131–2; *Chron. premiers Valois*, 80–1; *Luce (1894), 263–4; Luce (1875), 115, 121–2, 123; *Delachenal (1909–31), ii, 422 (Poissy). On Standon: *CPR 1354–8*, 22; *CPR 1358–61*, 398; *Foed.*, iii, 391. On Jewel: *Chron. premiers Valois*, 62. Circular: Secousse, *Preuves*, 98; Vandenpeereboom, vii, 430–1. Senlis: Secousse, *Preuves*, 99–100; AN JJ86/171.

75 *Gr. chron.*, i, 189–90; Bel, *Chron.*, ii, 263–4.

76 *Gr. chron.*, i, 188, 191; Bel, *Chron.*, ii, 264.

77 *Gr. chron.*, i, 190–3, 195; *Delachenal (1909–31), ii, 425; *Chartularium universitatis Parisiensis*, ed. H. Denifle and E. Chatellain, iii (1894), 55.

78 Venette, *Chron.*, 261; *Gr. chron.*, i, 193; *Chron. premiers Valois*, 80–1, 82; *Delachenal (1909–31), ii, 414–21, esp. 420–1, 425–6.
79 Venette, *Chron.*, 261; *Chron. premiers Valois*, 82; *Gr. chron.*, i, 201, 202; *Luce (1875), 122–8.
80 *Gr. chron.*, i, 195, 196–8; *Chron. premiers Valois*, 81; *Luce (1875), 124.
81 *Gr. chron.*, i, 198–9; *Delachenal (1909–31), ii, 425. On Belot: *Ord.*, iii, 47; Sauval, i, 38–9; *Félibien, i, pp. cxvi-cxvii.
82 *Gr. chron.*, i, 199; *Delachenal (1909–31), ii, 425–6.
83 *Gr. chron.*, i, 200–1; *Chron. norm.*, 133.
84 *Chron. premiers Valois*, 81–2, 83; *Delachenal (1909–31), ii, 421. Captal: Froissart, *Chron.*, xii, 97. On Fotheringhay: AN JJ91/319. On Chastelleyn: *CPR 1354–8*, 451, 492, 626, 628; *Foed.*, iii, 348, 393. On Cusington: *Foed.*, iii, 393, 408; PRO E372/202, m. 34 [Totesham]; E372/203, m. 41 [Cusington]. His career: *Foed.*, iii, 181; *Reg. Black Prince*, iv, 178–9, 269.
85 *Gr. chron.*, i, 201–4; *Chron. premiers Valois*, 81–3; *Chron. norm.*, 133.
86 *Gr. chron.*, i, 204; *Chron. norm.*, 133–4.
87 *Chron. premiers Valois*, 83–5; *Chron. norm.*, 134; Secousse, *Preuves*, 79; *Luce (1857), 422–3; Cazelles (1982), 336–7.
88 Prisoners: *Gr. chron.*, i, 204–5. Plot: Venette, *Chron.*, 269–70; *Chron. norm.*, 134; *Gr. chron.*, i, 212; *Chron. premiers Valois*, 84; *Delachenal (1909–31), ii, 421, 426.
89 *Gr. chron.*, i, 205–9, 210; Lescot, *Chron.*, 132–3; Venette, *Chron.*, 270–2; Secousse, *Preuves*, 296–7; *Delachenal (1909–31), ii, 426–7.
90 *Gr. chron.*, i, 209–10, 211; Venette, *Chron.*, 272–3.
91 *Delachenal (1909–31), ii, 421–3.
92 Lescot, *Chron.*, 133–4; *Chron. premiers Valois*, 86; *Chron. norm.*, 136; *Chronographia*, ii, 281.
93 *Gr. chron.*, i, 210, 211–2; *Delachenal (1909–31), ii, 427; Secousse, *Preuves*, 80–1, 101–2, 112–4, 119–20; Valois (1883), 105–11, *115–26; 'Pièces inédites rél. à E. Marcel', 81–3; AN JJ86/185, 193, 197, 198, 203, 210, 213, 328, 233, 238, 350, 429, 464, 474, 502, 512, 543, 565, JJ89/325.
94 Amnesty: *Ord.*, iv, 346–8. Ladit: *Delachenal (1909–31), ii, 427–9; *Gr. chron.*, i, 215–6; Lescot, *Chron.*, 136.

CHAPTER VIII

1 Marmande: PRO E101/172/1(78–9). Finances: PRO E372/207, m. 54 [Stretle].
2 Pommiers: AC Martel CC3–4, fols. 87vo, 88. Bétaille: AC Martel BB5, fols. 105vo, 109vo, 111vo; CC3–4, fols., 86vo, 88, 89vo; *Foed.*, iii, 368–9. Fons: AC Cajarc CC Supp., 42; *Foed.*, iii, 368–9. Nadaillac: AC Gourdon CC19, fols. 34, 38–38vo, 39; EE6/5; II5; *Foed.*, iii, 390. Cheverston: AC Martel BB5, fols. 115vo-116, 117; Lacoste, iii, 155.
3 Estates: *Ord.*, iii, 101, iv, 188; **HGL*, x, 1150. Agenais was summoned once, in April 1359, before it was ceded to Edward III: **HGL*, x, 1158.
4 Patria: Dognon, 214–5.
5 **HGL*, x, 1145–50 (Arts. I, VIII, XIV, XV). Fortification: BN Doat 60, fols. 106–8. Cavalry: Lehoux, i, 116–7, 124.
6 Gilles le Bouvier, *Le livre de la description des pays*, ed. E.-T. Hamy (1908), 39.
7 Boudet (1908), 35–7, 39; Boudet (1893), 340. Felletin: *Inv. AC Montferrand*, i, 392–3; AC Martel CC3–4, fol. 71. St.-Pourçain: *Rec. doc. mon.*, i, 358.
8 Felletin: *Arch. Montpellier*, ii, no. 743; *Titres Bourbon*, i, no. 2921. La Chapelle: ASV Reg. Vat. 232, fol. 266vo. Beaumont: *Inv. AC Montferrand*, i, 394. Arnaud's ransoms were payable at Beaumont or la Chapelle: *Titres Bourbon*, i, no. 2810. Volvic, Sermur: *Inv. AC Riom*, 58. Bourbonnais: *Chron. Bourbon*, 16; Leguai, 188–90, 192n[17], 193.

9 Lehoux, i, 97–8, 98n[3], 120n[5]; Ledos (1895).
10 Lehoux, i, 98–9; BN Fr. 26002/760, 764; BN PO 1675 [de Laye, 10], 1471 [Hames, 8]. Conservators: *Foed.*, iii, 350.
11 Sermur: *A. Tardieu, *Histoire de la ville de Clermont-Ferrand*, ii (1870), 349–51. Montbrun: *Boudet (1900), 283–5. Fresh men: BN Fr. 26001/698; AC Martel CC3–4, fol. 98vo.
12 *Vitae paparum*, i, 345; Villani, *Hist.*, col. 456. Background: Léonard, ii, 52–74, iii, 134–54; *Encycl. B-du-R* [D], ii, 391–5.
13 *Vitae paparum*, ii, 461; Chérest (1879), 7–8, 26–8, *363–4, *366–9, *396; *Denifle, 190n[1], 191n[4]; *Recits d'un b. de Valenciennes*, 289; Froissart, *Chron.*, v, 23, 47; *Foed.*, iii, 350.
14 *Vitae paparum*, i, 345–6; *Denifle, 193–4; *Ausgaben Innocenz VI*, 456, 648. Numbers: Villani, *Hist.*, col. 645.
15 Y. Renouard, *Les relations des papes d'Avignon et les compagnies commerciales et bancaires* (1941), 32–3, Table A.
16 *Vitae paparum*, i, 346; Denifle, 199–201, *208n[5]; *Inv. chartes des Baux*, nos. 1357, 1360, 1376; Villani, *Hist.*, col. 457.
17 *Ausgaben Innocenz VI*, 645, 648; Léonard, iii, 287; *L. Menard, ii, 186, 190.
18 Villani, *Hist.*, cols. 456–7.
19 Denifle, 196–8, 202n[5]; Léonard, iii, 287; Guichenon, iv, 201–2.
20 Albanès, 'Chartes', 208–10; *Inv. Marseille*, no. 343; BN Doat 195, fols. 116–146vo; *L. Menard, ii, 191; Léonard, iii, 305–6, 310, *621–2, *627–8, *672; *Petit Thalamus*, 352.
21 *Léonard, iii, 618–25, 628–9. Armagnac: *ibid.*, iii, 310 and n[3]. Relics: Denifle, 204.
22 Léonard, iii, 313–6; *Inv. chartes des Baux*, no. 1370; *Vitae paparum*, i, 321.
23 Villani, *Hist.*, cols. 500, 526; *Petit Thalamus*, 352; *Denifle, 208n[2], 209n[1]; *Prou (1887), 143.
24 Léonard, iii, 318–20; *Inv. chartes des Baux*, nos. 1378, 1380.
25 *Delachenal (1909–31), ii, 429; Secousse, *Preuves*, 88–9, 102–3, 117, 124; Le Grand, 288–90, 290–1; *Gr. chron.*, i, 212–3, 215; Venette, *Chron.*, 277.
26 AN JJ91/319; *Gr. chron.*, i, 214; Bel, *Chron.*, ii, 282; Secousse, *Preuves*, 148; *Delachenal (1909–31), ii, 429. Description: Boursier, 2–5, 19. Beatrice: *Titres Bourbon*, nos. 2067, 2070.
27 *Chron. norm.*, 136–7; Venette, *Chron.*, 276, 278–9; *Gr. chron.*, i, 214–5; *Chron. premiers Valois*, 87; Bel, *Chron.*, ii, 268.
28 Amiens: *Gr. chron.*, i, 216–7, 225; *Chron. norm.*, 138–9; Venette, *Chron.*, ii, 274–6; Bel, *Chron.*, ii, 271; *Rec. mon. tiers état*, i, 599–601. Abbeville: AN JJ86/473, 90/386. Mauconseil: *Chron. norm.*, 137; Bel, *Chron.*, ii, 268–9; Gray, *Scalacronica*, 180; *Foed.*, iii, 512. Poix: Timbal, *Rég. Parl.*, 286–7. St.-Valéry: *Chron. Norm.*, 121; *Chron. premiers Valois*, 87; AN JJ86/473.
29 AN JJ86/484, 505, 586; Secousse, *Preuves*, 124–5. Creil: AN JJ90/82, 385, 388, 91/319, 100/708.
30 Fees: Froissart, *Chron.*, v, 121. Argenteuil: *Luce (1875), 126–7; Venette, *Chron.*, 281–2.
31 Venette, *Chron.*, 280–2. Islands: AN JJ90/127, 610; Secousse, Preuves, 167–8. Longueil: *ibid.*, 288–93; *Chron. norm.*, 147–8; Lescot, *Chron.*, 140–1; Gray, *Scalacronica*, 184. St.-Leu, Royaumont: Secousse, *Preuves*, 148; AN JJ90/301. St.-Eloi: AN JJ90/137. Beauvais: *Denifle, 222n[2].
32 Froissart, *Chron.*, v, 121–2, 125–6; PRO C76/40, m. 7, E101/175/5, 6(9).
33 Venette, *Chron.*, 276–9; Bel, *Chron.*, ii, 272; *Gr. chron.*, i, 218; AN JJ86/612, 90/209, 218, 237, 240–1, 567. Convoys: *Ord.*, iii, 298–9; Roncière, i, 518. Plots: *Gr. chron.*, i, 220–4; Secousse, *Preuves*, 104–8, 110–2, 120–1.
34 *Delachenal (1909–31), ii, 429.
35 Coville (1894), 92, *367–9, *371–3; Fourquin, 257.

36 *Ord.*, iii, 243–5, 252, 265–6, 301; Gazelles (1982), 363–4.
37 Secousse, *Preuves*, 149–50; Gr. *chron.*, i, 225; Venette, *Chron.*, 280.
38 AN JJ89/532, 90/194, 440, 567; cf. JJ90/429, 489, 501, 527.
39 AN JJ90/532; Secousse, *Preuves*, 126–7. Cf. Luce (1876), 340nn[2, 3]; AN JJ86/478–9, 486, 505, 533, 538–9, 550, 576.
40 Lehoux, i, 111n[1], 114nn[1, 3]; *Arch. Montpellier*, ii, no. 653; **HGL*, x, 1139, 1143–4; *Ord.*, iii, 337–8, iv, 188–9, 191–2.
41 *Foed.*, iii, 405; *Moisant, 257–8.
42 *Foed.*, iii, 414; Villani, *Hist.*, cols. 529–30; Knighton, *Chron.*, 160–2; Walsingham, *Hist. Angl.*, ii, 284. Quote: **KOF*, xviii, 396–7.
43 *Foed.*, iii, 412–3, 414, 415–6, 416; PRO C76/36, m. 5; *Lit. Cant.*, ii, 374; *Reg. Black Prince*, iii, 331. Cardinals: *Gr. chron.*, i, 224.
44 Perroy, 'Select documents', 153; PRO E372/203, m. 41 [Cusington], E403/394, m. 9, E101/313/36. 20 Dec.: PRO E101/313/32, 37.
45 *Chérest (1879), 72,* 370–1; *Lehoux, i, 182n[3]; AN JJ98/491; Inv. AD Cote d'Or, ii, 112; Froissart, *Chron.*, xii, 100.
46 AN JJ103/214; Ledru, ix, 229–31.
47 Lescot, *Chron.*, 127; Venette, *Chron.*, 262; AN JJ97/512. Headquarters: BN Clair. 4/157, 23/1621, 53/3981, 55/4199, 56/5075, etc.
48 The French estimate of 2,200 at Orléans (Timbal, *Reg. Pari*, 191) is consistent with other information. About 240 were lost at Troyes in January 1359 and 1,000 took part in the capture of Auxerre in March 1359: *Gr. chron.*, i, 225–6, 227. Garrisons left at Chateauneuf and Malicorne must have accounted for about 200 more, and some companies withdrew from the army on their own adventures. Their origins: Gray, *Scalacronica*, 183; *Gr. chron.*, i, 227; *Plancher, ii, no. 300; AN JJ 107/167.
49 *CPR 1361–4*, 16; *Chérest (1879), 394; Froissart, *Chron.*, v, 351.
50 Knighton, *Chron.*, 164; *Gr. chron.*, i, 218–9, 231; Denifle, 230–2; Timbal, *Reg. Parl.*, 191, 194, 197; AN JJ90/48, 380, 100/299; *Morin, ii, 729–31; Petit (1885–1905), ix, 116n[2].
51 'Choix de pieces', 359–60.
52 *Gr. chron.*, i, 219; Chérest (1879), 371, 379; Petit (1885–1909), ix, 116n[3]; Gray, *Scalacronica*, 182.
53 Regennes: Lebeuf (1851–5), iii, 232; AN JJ86/566. Ligny: AN JJ86/566, and cf. JJ86/553, 90/110–12. Heton: CPR 1358–61, 395, 526; CPR 1361–4, 85, 88, 170; PRO E30/1499; BN PO 9 [Ades, 2]. Dalton: G. Wrottesley, *Crécy and Calais* (1897), 110; Fowler (1969), 287n[115]. Starkey: *Reg. Black Prince*, iii, 154–5; Petit (1885–1905), ix, 119nn[2, 3], 120nn[1–4]; Chaplais, 'Doc. Brétigny', 45.
54 *Plancher, ii, 313–24; Petit (1885–1905), ix, 142–3; Cox, 134.
55 *Gr. chron.*, i, 225–6; Venette, *Chron.*, 281. Troyes: Timbal, *Reg. Parl*, 179–84; Boutiot, ii, 114–6, 119–21, 122–3, 173–4.
56 Petit (1885–1905), ix, 120–1, 151–2; *Luce (1894), 222; *Chérest (1863–8), ii, 234–8; Chérest (1879), 122n[2]; *Lebeuf (1851–5), iv, 182–4.
57 Lebeuf (1851–5), i, 528, iii, 234; *Gr. chron.*, i, 226–8; Lescot, *Chron.*, 137.
58 *Gr. chron.*, i, 229, 230–1; Lebeuf (1851–5), iii, 234–7, *iv, 190, 191–2, 194 (misdated), 239–40 (corrected by Chérest (1863–8), ii, 226); *Denifle, 507n[4].
59 *Gr. chron.*, i, 224; Petit (1885–1905), ix, 144–5; *Ausgahen Innocenz VI*, 740.
60 Agenais: Gardelles, 18. Montferrand: Fournier and Charbonnier, 275–6. Caen: 'Relation de visite'. Gâtinais: 'Procès-verbal de visite'. I de France: Venette, *Chron.*, 280, 302–3.
61 *Forestié, 203–10.
62 Timbal, *Reg. Parl.*, 153–65. Burgundy: Pegeot, 247–8.
63 Ledos (1890), 48–50; Timbal, *Reg. Parl*, 190–8; *Chron. du Bee*, ed. C. Porée (1883), 61–2.

64 BN Doat 110, fols. 96vo-101vo (Monastiés); 'Docs. Maçon', 167–8; AN JJ82/196 (R. de Mareuil)
65 Timbal, *Reg. Parl.*, 106n^{2}, 107n^{7}; *HGL*, ix, 655; Keen (1965), 79 (quotation).
66 Faye: *AHP*, xlii, 97–110. Abbeville: AN JJ89/351, 353. Orléans: Timbal, *Reg. Parl.*, 190–8. Tours: *Comptes Tours*, i, nos. 415–23. Estates: *Viollet, 279–80; *Ord.*, iii, 224 (cl. 5); **HGL*, x, 1148 (cl. 8). Commissioners: Timbal, *Reg. Parl.*, 107, 109–11, 190–1; AN JJ90/563 (Beauvaisis); *Cart. Montier-la-Celle*, p. xxxv (Champagne). Verdey: *ibid.* Azay: *Comptes Tours*, i, nos. 382, 397, 419–20; ii, nos. 131, 133.
67 Chains: Venette, *Chron.*, 245; AC Martel BB5, fol. 25; *Comptes Rodez*, i, 174.
68 'Le livre messire Geoffroy de Charny', 403; Froissart, *Chron.*, v, 222. Mine countermeasures: Forestié, 215–6.
69 12 palms: BN Doat 53, fols. 227–297vo; 60, fols. 106–108; Arch. *Montpellier*, xii, 6–7.
70 Cahors: F. Lot, *Recherches sur la population et superficie des cités*, ii (1950), 234. Avignon: André-Michel (1910). Reims: Desportes, 526–9. Montpellier: *Arch. Montpellier*, xi, 20; xii, 13.
71 St.-Maixent: *Rec. doc. Poitou*, iii, 119–22. Crossbowmen: *Ord.*, iii, 297–8, 360–2, 668–72. Poitiers: *Ord.*, iv, 169–70. Rodez: *Comptes Rodez*, i, 255–6. Picardy: Froissart, *Chron.*, v, 202; *Arch. St.-Quentin*, ii, 239–41. Captains: *Forestié, 213; *Comptes Rodez*, i, 239.
72 Poitiers: *Ord.*, iv, 169–70. Nîmes: *Menard, ii, 225–30. Rodez: Miquel, i, 197, 198. Lyon: *Inv. AC Lyon*, ii, 180–1. Paris: *Ord.*, iii, 304. St.-Quentin: Froissart, *Chron.*, v, 150–1.
73 Martel: AC Martel BB5, fols. 70vo-72. Tours: *Ord.*, v, 457–8; Chevalier (1975), 79–80, 89–90.Orléans: Timbal, *Reg. Parl.*, 190–8.
74 *Ressort*: Timbal, *Reg. Parl.*, 248–9, 254–7. St.-Lô: AN JJ87/25. Auxerre: AN JJ89/65. Martel: AC Martel BB5, fol. 70vo. Rouen: AN JJ87/239. For problems of refugees, see, e.g., BN Doat 145, fols. 145–146vo (Millau, 1364); AN X^{1a} 22, fols. 80–80vo.
75 Orléans: Timbal, *Reg. Parl.*, 190–8. Sens: AN JJ89/615.
76 Nîmes: *Menard, ii, 219. Poitiers: *Ord.*, iv, 169. Montauban: *Forestié, 213–4. Bourges: AN JJ90/776. Martel: AN BB5, fol. 71. Guards: see, e.g. *Ord.*, iv, 169; AN JJ90/503.
77 Perroy, 'Select documents', 153; *Foed.*, iii, 421; PRO E403/394, m.34; E101/313/39. Somerton: *Foed.*, iii, 411, 414; Aumale, *Notes et docs*, 101–2, 102, 132.
78 Cosneau, *Traités*, 3–31; Villani, *Hist.*, cols. 544–5. Postponement: *Foed.*, iii, 422–3; PRO C76/37, m. 16; *Lit. Cant.*, ii, 378–80. Emissaries: Aumale, *Notes et docs.*, 114; *Delachenal (1909–31), ii, 434; **KOF*, xviii, 433–4.
79 Germain, 'Projet', 247–9.
80 *Gr. chron.*, i, 232–6; Bel, *Chron.*, ii, 288–9; Lescot, *Chron.*, 137–8.
81 *Gr. chron.*, i, 237–8; Lescot, *Chron.*, 138; Germain, 'Projet', 428; *Delachenal (1909–31), ii, 435–6.
82 Languedoc: Germain, 'Projet', 429–30; *Comptes St.-Antonin*, 43–4; *Comptes cons. Albi*, nos. 510–1, 514, 520. Scots: *Exch. R. Scot.*, ii, 50, 77; AN J677–8.
83 PRO C76/37, m. 16; *Foed.*, iii, 427–8, 428; *Reg. Black Prince*, iii, 347–8, 349, 350; *Arch. admin. Reims*, iii, 140–1. Audrehem: Aumale, *Notes et docs.*, 138, 139.

CHAPTER IX

1 *Chron. premiers Valois*, 27–8, 73, 101; Froissart, *Chron.*, v, 121, 136–7; *Chron. norm.*, 144.
2 Bel, *Chron.*, ii, 278–9, 284; AN JJ90/484; *Arch. admin. Reims*, iii, 234; Noyal, 'Chron.', 257.
3 Aubricourt: Beltz, 92; *Chron. norm.*, 113; Froissart, *Chron.*, iv, 136, 166, v, 16, 35–6. Albrecht: AN JJ93/14; Petit (1885–1905), ix, 119, 145; Froissart, *Chron.*, 175; for the identification with Sterz, see below, Chap. X. Audley: Froissart, *Chron.*, iv, 135, v, 31, 135. Gyé, Beaufort: Roserot, ii, 675, 958.

4 Bel, *Chron.*, 276–7, 280–1, 283; *Chron. norm.*, 140; Venette, *Chron.*, 281.
5 Noyal, 'Chron.', 259; Bel, *Chron.*, i, 278–9.
6 Delaborde, 200; Bel, *Chron.*, ii, 280; AN JJ92/251.
7 Bel, *Chron.*, 280–1; Lescot, *Chron.*, 136–7; *Chron. norm.*, 139–40; Delaborde, Cat. no. 957. Date: Froissart, *Chron.*, v, 173.
8 Noyal, 'Chron.', 258–9; Bel, *Chron.*, ii, 279, 283–4; *Arch. admin. Reims*, iii, 144–7; AN JJ90/297.
9 Aubricourt: Froissart, *Chron.*, v, 172–3, 183. Scot: *Chron. premiers Valois*, 101; *Chron. norm.*, 144. Albrecht: Froissart, *Chron.*, v, 175. Audley: Bel, *Chron.*, ii, 281; Gray, *Scalacr.*, 188–9; Froissart, *Chron.*, 153–7, 182. Pont: *Reg. Parl.*, 302–3. Brocard: Bel, *Chron.*, ii, 285–6; *Ord.*, iii, 365–6; AN J514/3; Delaborde, Cat. nos. 964–5.
10 Knolles: *Gr. chron.*, i, 231–2. Waldboef: **HGL*, x, 1291–2; *Reg. Black Prince*, iii, 323; Gray, *Scalacr.*, 182–3. Wyn: *Doc. Millau*, no. 230; *Foed.*, iii, 545. Calveley: *Boudet (1900), 272.
11 Guigue, 33–4; *Boudet (1900), 260, 270–1; *Doc. Millau*, no. 230.
12 Boudet (1900), 18–31, 58–66, 254–8, 257n[2], *267, *270–1; Moranvillé (1905); Lehoux, i, 135.
13 Boudet (1900), 111, *271, *259, *267–71; *Petit Thalamus*, 356.
14 *Boudet (1900), 273–4; *Doc. Millau*, no. 230; *L. Menard, ii, 190, 219, 234; *Petit Thalamus*, 356; Gray, *Scalacr.*, 185; Bel, *Chron.*, ii, 286.
15 *Denifle, 261nn[1, 2].
16 **HGL*, x, 1158–9; *Actes royaux*, no. 597; *Comptes Albi*, nos. 494–5; *HGL*, ix, 697, 702–3, *x, 1162–3.
17 *L. Menard, ii, 190, 208, 219, 234; *Actes royaux*, no. 606; *Petit Thalamus*, 356. Thomas: *Boudet (1900), 271, 273; *Lehoux, i, 144n[8], 145n[6].
18 Waldboef, Wyn: Guigue, 36–7, *221–2 (refers to 1359, not 1357); La Mure, i, 434–5.
19 Route: Route: *Boudet (1900), 274 (Knolles' was presumably the second cavalcade). Le Puy: Knighton, *Chron.*, 164: 'Amisi' is Anicium, i.e. le Puy (not Auxerre), see *Gall. Christ.*, ii, 685.
20 Knighton, *Chron.*, 164; *L. Menard, ii, 235; Bel, *Chron.*, ii, 286.
21 Gray, *Scalacr.*, 185; *Petit Thalamus*, 356.
22 Calveley: AN JJ97/459. Wyn: Petit (1885–1905), ix, 194–6; *Foed.*, iii, 545–6, Chaplais, 'Doc. Brétigny', 44. Mercenaries: Lehoux, i, 144–8, *144nn[3, 8].
23 AN JJ93/212, 100/708; Knighton, *Chron.*, 164.
24 Picquigny: Bel, *Chron.*, ii, 282; AN JJ90/554. St.-Valéry: *Chron. premiers Valois*, 89–93; *Chron. norm.*, 121, 142; *Chronographia*, ii, 285; Froissart, *Chron.*, v, p. xlivn[6] (date). Mauconseil: Venette, *Chron.*, ii, 283.
25 Venette, *Chron.*, ii, 283–4; *Chron. premiers Valois*, 93–4; Gray, *Scalacr.*, 185; *Chron. norm.*, 143–4; Noyal, 'Chron.', 258.
26 Cazelles (1982), 362–3; *Gr. chron.*, i, 236–7; *Ord.*, iii, 345–59.
27 Delachenal (1909–31), ii, 111nn[2, 3]; Secousse, *Preuves*, 149–50, 151–2; *Lacabane (1844), 52; Lescot, *Chron.*, 139; *Gr. chron.*, i, 238; *Chron. premiers Valois*, 96–7.
28 Preparations: *Foed.*, iii, 417, 427–8; PRO C76/37, mm. 16, 15, 14; E101/174/7, fols. 11[vo], 13, 14[vo]-16; Knighton, *Chron.*, 168; Bel, *Chron.*, ii, 290. Prisoners: Delpit, *Doc. fr.*, 82–3; *Foed.*, iii, 436, 437–9, 477, 478; Bel, *Chron.*, ii, 297; *Comptes argenterie*, 210–1, 213, 232–3; **HGL*, x, 1199. Household: Aumale, *Notes et docs.*, 123–4, 137. Spies: *Foed.*, iii, 442; *Arch. admin. Reims*, iii, 142–3.
29 *Arch. admin. Reims*, iii, 142–3.
30 *Gr. chron.*, i, 238–47; *Delachenal (1909–31), ii, 437; Venette, *Chron.*, 285–7; Villani, *Hist.*, col. 554.
31 *Frag. chron. B-Normandie*, 6–7; Gray, *Scalacr.*, 186; PRO C76/38, m. 6; *Foed.*, iii, 452–3.
32 *Gr. chron.*, i, 243–4; *Chron. premiers Valois*, 100; *Luce (1876), 543–4. Poix: *Arch. St.-*

Quentin, ii, no. 675; Timbal, *Reg. Parl.*, 283–302. Épernon: Gray, *Scalacr.*, 191; AN X[1a] 17, fol. 17. Melun: *Gr. chron.*, i, 247; *Gall. Reg.*, iv, no. 15499.

33 *Gr. chron.*, i, 247–8, 250; Gray, *Scalacr.*, 187–8; Venette, *Chron.*, 295; Lescot, *Chron.*, 141; Chaplais, 'Doc. Brétigny', 44; *Arch. St.-Quentin*, ii, no. 683; Froissart, *Chron.*, xii, 97.

34 Descalat: *Cart. Cormery*, 236–40 (misdated); *Comptes Tours*, nos. 434, 437, 465; Chaplais, 'Doc. Brétigny', 43 (name). Langeais: *ibid.*, 42; *Comptes Tours*, nos. 304, 380, 424–7. Montbazon: *Comptes Tours*, no. 438; AN JJ97/49.

35 Timbal, *Reg. Parl.*, 121–7; Martin.

36 Tax: *Ord.*, iii, 358–9; Henneman (1976), 91, 97; Coville (1894), 97–8.

37 *Gr. chron.*, i, 248–9; *Rec. doc. mon.*, i, 400, 406, 411–2, 412, 413, 413–4, 414, 421, 429; *Ord.*, iii, 400.

38 Numbers: PRO E101/393/11, fols. 79–116[vo]. Logistics: PRO E101/392/14; E101/174/7, fols. 14[vo]-16; E101/174/8, fols. 2–8; *CCR 1354–60*, 574; *CPR 1358–61*, 323; *Reg. Black Prince*, iii, 379; Bel, *Chron.*, ii, 312–3. Ships: Walsingham, *Hist. Angl.*, ii, 287.

39 Bel, *Chron.*, ii, 298.

40 Harriss, 346–7.

41 *Foed.*, iii, 440–1

42 Bel, *Chron.*, ii, 290, 291–2; Knighton, *Chron.*, 168; Gray, *Scalacr.*, 186–7; *Delachenal (1909–31), ii, 438; *Doc. Amiens*, i, 130.

43 *Foed.*, iii, 452; Gray, *Scalacr.*, 187–8; Knighton, *Chron.*, 170; *Controversy*, 178; Walsingham, *Hist. Angl.*, i, 287; *Anonimalle chron.*, 44–5; Bel., *Chron.*, ii, 299–300; *Gr. chron.*, i, 253; *Arch. admin. Reims*, iii, 156n[1]. Germans: PRO E101/393/11, fols. 87, 91–97[vo]; Bel, *Chron.*, ii, 294–6.

44 Desportes, 526–9, 540–4, 552–3, 557; *Arch. admin. Reims*, iii, 229–30; *Delachenal (1909–31), ii, 155n[1].

45 *Arch. admin. Reims*, iii, 117–8, 136–9, 147–50, 168–9, 191–4, 210n, 212–3n, 217–8n, 218–9, 231, 233–7, 246–7; Desportes, 558–60; Machaut, *Oeuvres*, i, p. xxiiin[1].

46 *Gr. chron.*, i, 251–2; Knighton, *Chron.*, 170; Villani, *Hist.*, 587–8; *Arch. admin. Reims*, iii, 156–9.

47 Boucicaut: *Rec. doc. mon.*, i, 414, 419, 423, 427, 428; *Rec. doc. Poitou*, iii, 279–84. Normans: Coville (1894), 97–8; *Chron. premiers Valois*, 103, 110; *Doc. Clos des galées*, no. 565.

48 *Chron. de S. Marien*, ed. Lebeuf, *Mémoires concernant l'histoire. . . d'Auxerre*, ii (1743), 262; Gray, *Scalacr.*, 189; *Foed.*, iii, 461–2; *Arch. admin. Reims*, iii, 156–9; N JJ89/671.

49 *Luce (1876), 547–8; *Chron. premiers Valois*, 110–11. Neuville: Cazelles (1982), 248–9.

50 *Chron. premiers Valois*, 105–6.

51 Knighton, *Chron.*, 170–2; Bel, *Chron.*, ii, 301; Gray, *Scalacr.*, 188; *Gr. chron.*, i, 253. Christmas: PRO E101/393/11, fol. 59. Argonne: AD Nord B1596, fol. 174[vo]; AN JJ88/11.

52 PRO C76/38, m. 2; C76/40, m. 14; E101/393/11, fol. 63; E101/531/36.

53 Gray, *Scalacr.*, 191; *Gr. chron.*, i, 254; *Anonimalle chron.*, 45–6; Bel, *Chron.*, ii, 306; Petrarch, *Fam.* XXII.14, iv, 138–9. Chaucer: PRO E101/393/11, fol. 72. French looters: AN JJ90/537–9.

54 Courcelles: AN X1[a] 21, fol. 230. Flavigny: Petit (1885–1905), ix, Cat. no. 9114; Gray, *Scalacr.*, 189–90 (for 'Dagworth' read 'Tamworth'). Other Regennes companies: *CPR 1358–61*, 395, 523, 526, 551; *CPR 1361–4*, 85, 88, 170. Treaty: *Plancher, ii, p. cçli; *Foed.*, iii, 473; AN X1[a] 21, fol. 230; Venette, *Chron.*, 297–8. Bar: *Anonimalle Chron.*, 45.

55 *Gr. chron.*, i, 254–5; Lescot, *Chron.*, 143; Bel, *Chron.*, 306–7.

56 *Foed.*, iii, 449–50, 455–8, 459–60; *RDP*, iv, 618–9; *Rot. Scot.*, i, 844.

57 PRO C76/38, mm. 16, 3; *Foed.*, iii, 468–9; *CPR 1358–61*, 404–8, 414–5; CCR *1360–4*, 308–9.

58 *Chronographia*, ii, 291; *Foed.*, iii, 470–2, 476.

59 *Foed.*, iii, 477; *Chronographia*, ii, 291–3; *Chron. premiers Valois*, 111–3; *Wigmore Chron.*, 291; *Chron. norm.*, 150; Gray, *Scalacr.*, 190–1; Knighton, *Chron.*, 174. Winchelsea: M. Beresford, *New towns of the middle ages* (1983), 14–28; H.L. Turner, *Town defences in England and Wales* (1971), 176–9.

60 *CCR 1360–4*, 36, 55–6, 101–2, 104–5, 170–1, 308–9; *CPR 1358–61*, 349, 411, 413–4, 415–6, 452; *Foed.*, iii, 476, 478, 479–80; Knighton, *Chron.*, 174; *Chron. premiers Valois*, 117.

61 Venette, *Chron.*, 300, 302; Gray, *Scalacr.*, 192; *Gr. chron.*, i, 256; *Anonimalle Chron.*, 46. Manor: Lebeuf (1883–93), iv, 151–2.

62 *Foed.*, iii, 425, Aumale, *Notes et docs.*, 138; *Comptes argenterie*, 238, 270; Cazelles (1982), 370–6.

63 *Recits d'un b. de Valenciennes*, 302; *Foed.*, iii, 455, 472; *Gr. chron.*, i, 257; *CPR Letters*, iii, 629–30; *Denifle, 355–6; *Ausgaben Innocenz VI*, 745. Simon: Cazelles (1982), 302; *Gr. chron.*, i, 145–7. Lynn: Emden, ii, 1195; *Foed.*, iii, 285, 348. Androin: Villani, *Hist.*, col. 532; *Recits d'un b. de Valenciennes*, 302; *Vitae paparum*, ii, 474. Hugh: Sumption, i, 322–4, 381–2, 422.

64 PRO E101/393/11, fol. 64vo; *Foed.*, iii, 484; *CPR Letters*, iii, 630. Burton was regularly employed on diplomatic business: see *Foed.*, iii, 348, 518, 531; PRO E101/314/11.

65 *Foed.*, iii, 475–6; *Comptes argenterie*, 237, 247; *KOF*, xviii, 433–4; Cazelles (1982), 374.

66 Lescot, *Chron.*, 143–4; *Gr. chron.*, i, 256–7.

67 Venette, *Chron.*, 302–6; Lescot, *Chron.*, 143; AN JJ89/458.

68 *Gr. chron.*, i, 256–9; Venette, *Chron.*, 299–304; Chron. norm. 141–2; *Recits d'un b. de Valenciennes*, 304; Lescot, *Chron.*, 144. La Ferté: *Foed.*, iii, 443, 444; Gray, *Scalacr.*, 188–9; BN Clair., 39/2905. Devaluations: *Ord.*, iii, 401.

69 *Gr. chron.*, i, 257–8; Lescot, *Chron.*, 144–5; Knighton, *Chron.*, 176; Gray, *Scalacr.*, 193; *Arch. admin. Reims*, iii, 159–60; Villani, *Hist.*, col. 599.

70 Gray, *Scalacr.*, 193; *Gr. chron.*, i, 258; *Chron. premiers Valois*, 115–6; Walsingham, *Hist. Angl.*, i, 288–9.

71 PRO E101/531/36; *CCR 1360–4*, 83–4, 85–6, 186; Gray, *Scalacr.*, 190, 193–4; *Chron. premiers Valois*, 107–10, 155; *Chron. norm.*, 150–2. Cope: AN JJ90/510.

72 *Gr. chron.*, i, 259; *Anonimalle Chron.*, 46; Venette, *Chron.*, 307–8.

73 *Anonimalle Chron.*, 46; Gray, *Scalacr.*, 193–4; Knighton, *Chron.*, 178; Walsingham, *Chron.*, i, 289; Lescot, *Chron.*, 145; Froissart, *Chron.*, vi, 2, 4–5; *Chronicles of London*, ed. C.L. Kingsford (1905), 13 (quotation).

74 PRO E101/531/36 (supplies); Venette, *Chron.*, 306–7; Lescot, *Chron.*, 143; *Gr. chron.*, i, 259; *Chron. norm.*, 152; Gray, *Scalacr.*, 194; *Anonimalle Chron.*, 46–7; Bel, *Chron.*, ii, 313; Timbal, *Reg. parl.*, 270–2; AN JJ89/440. Nids: *Lescot, *Chron.*, 209.

75 Froissart, *Chron.*, vi, 4; *Gr. chron.*, i, 259–62; Gray, *Scalacr.*, 194; *Lescot, *Chron.*, 209.

76 *Foed.*, iii, 485; Knighton, *Chron.*, 176; *Chron. premiers Valois*, 117–8; Gray, *Scalacr.*, 194–5.

77 *Gr. chron.*, i, 260–2, 298; BN PO 2031 [Montmorency, 10]; BN Clair. 106/167.

78 *Foed.*, iii, 486–94. Virgin: Venette, *Chron.*, 310.

79 *Chron. premiers Valois*, 116–7; Gray, *Scalacr.*, 195–6; *Gr. chron.*, i, 300–1, 314–6; Venette, *Chron.*, 310–2; Walsingham, *Hist. Angl.*, i, 289.

80 Knighton, *Chron.*, 178; Bel, *Chron.*, 317–8; *Gr. chron.*, i, 317–8; *Chron. premiers Valois*, 118–9; Gray, *Scalacr.*, 196; *Anonimalle Chron.*, 49–50.

81 *Comptes argenterie*, 248–9, 249–50, 251, 253, 255–63, 270–5; *Foed.*, iii, 485; *Lettres de rois*, ii, 120; Chaplais, *Dipl. practice*, 363; **HGL*, x, 1199; *Lecoy, ii, 367.

82 AN P2294, pp. 47–9; BN Fr. 20412/12; Richard, 'Instructions', 86 (Art. XXI); *Delachenal (1909–31), ii, 440–4; *Arch. admin. Reims*, iii, 163–5, 165–6; *Arch. St.-Quentin*, ii, n. 680; Timbal, *Reg. parl.*, 382. Paris: *Gr. chron.*, i, 320. Rouen: AN JJ87/

325; BN Clair. 214/6, 11. Normandy: Henneman (1976), 114–5.

83 *Gr. chron.*, i, 319–20; Bel, *Chron.*, ii, 319.

84 AN P2294, p. 41; Villani, *Hist.*, cols. 617–8; Froissart, *Chron.*, vi, 23–4; Delachenal (1909–31), ii, 231–7.

85 Denifle, 364–5; *Foed.*, iii, 505, 508; PRO E101/314/2–5, 7–12; *Doc. Brétigny, 7n[1].

86 *Gr. chron.*, i, 320–2; Secousse, *Preuves*, 172–3; *Foed.*, iii, 499, 508.

87 Cosneau, *Traités*, 46–7 (Arts. XI, XII); *Foed.*, iii, 522–5, 532, 535–7, 538.

88 La Rochelle: *Thes. nov. anecd.*, i, 1427–9; Molinier, 80–2; *Foed.*, iii, 504, 512–4, 540–1. Charles: Secousse, *Preuves*, 172–6. Hostages: Bel, *Chron.*, ii, 320; BN Doat 193, fols. 47–8.

89 *Foed.*, iii, 533; *Delachenal (1909–31), ii, 444–5.

90 *Gr. chron.*, i, 322; *Foed.*, iii, 520–1; AN J638/4; Chaplais, *Dipl. practice*, 825. Guines: PRO E372/206, m. 43 [Roka]; C61/74, m. 7.

CHAPTER X

1 *Recits d'un b. de Valenciennes*, 308.

2 Incomplete lists as at Oct. 1360 in *Foed.*, iii, 535–6, 646, and Chaplais, 'Doc. Brétigny', 42–4, supplemented from many other sources.

3 *Luce (1876), 543–5, 585–6; Chaplais, 'Doc. Brétigny', 44; *Arch. S. Quentin*, no. 683. Fotheringhay: PRO C76/40, m. 10; E101/175/5. Bagworth: *Luce* (1876), 589; BN Clair. 39/2905.

4 Timbal, *Reg. Parl.*, 462; *Coville (1894), 376–7; 'Procès-verbal de délivrance', 127–8; BN Fr. 26004/1148; BN PO 9 [Ades, 2], 384 [Bois, 9], 447 [Boulay, 28], 669 [Chandos, 3], 1909 [Mazuyer, 5], 1931 [Mercier, 9], 2229 [Peluquet, 3], 3055 [Windesomme, 2]. Cost: Chaplais, 'Doc. Brétigny', 18; *Coville (1894), 376–9; *Cat. comptes royaux*, nos. 527–32; BN PO 1438 [Guichard, 2, 3]; BN Fr. 26004/1186–9. Honfleur: BN Clair. 167/41, 144; *Moranvillé (1888), 203; Chaplais, 'Doc. Brétigny', 18.

5 Chaplais, 'Doc. Brétigny', 15; Timbal, *Reg. Parl.*, 456–60.

6 Champagne: *Arch. admin. Reims*, iii, 177–8; Chaplais, 'Doc. Brétigny', 19, 42, 44; Delaborde, Cat. nos. 964–5, 967; AN J514/3, 4; Froissart, *Chron.*, v, p. lxviiin[8]. Touraine: *Comptes Tours*, nos. 971, 1181–4 and pp. 177n1, 179n1, *229n[1]; Chaplais, 'Doc. Brétigny', 18, 19, 42, 43; Timbal, *Reg. Parl.*, 439–40. Albrets: *Foed.*, iii, 546–7; *Titres Bourbon*, nos. 2812, 2864, 2921–2, 2924, 2945, 2960–1. Camus: *Chron. Louis de Bourbon*, 16, 20–1.

7 Bell: AN JJ89/619. Welles: *Mandements*, no. 121. Lucas: *Chron. premiers Valois*, 154. Poupon: Itin PB, 465–7. Warin: Petit (1909), 149. Marshall: Chaplais, 'Doc. Brétigny', 18, 43; BN Clair., 70/5449, 5451. Wyn: AN X^{1a} 21, fols. 230, 253vo; Petit (1909), x, 208, 213n[1]; *Gr. chron.*, ii, 137; *Mandements*, nos. 1462, 1830; AN JJ122/128.

8 *Foed.*, iii, 658, 664, 678; Jones (1970), 39–40, 41–2, 45, 48–51.

9 Froissart, *Chron.*, vi, 51. Calais: *Foed.*, iii, 713. Scot: PRO C76/40, m. 3. Fogg: John IV, *Actes*, i, 84–5, 143. Tyldesley: *ibid.*, i, 142; Chaplais, 'Doc. Brétigny', 43. Knolles: *Prou, 148–50; Chaplais, 'Doc. Brétigny', 19; *CPR 1361–4*, 16. Calveley: *Chron. norm.*, 158–9; *Luce (1876), 551–3; Ledru, viii, 70–3. Gournay: Jones (1970), 146, *205–7; *CPR 1360–4*, 296, 299–300; *CIM*, iii, no. 545; his early career was described in the inscription on his tombstone at Stoke, now lost but recorded in 1542 in Leland's *Itinerary*, ed. L. Toulmin Smith, i (1907), 159.

10 Péronne: Venette, *Chron.*, 313–4; Albigeois: **HGL.* x, 1332–5, 1349–50. Hutin: JJ91/215; *Chartes Albret*, i, 724–5, 726; Timbal, *Reg. Parl.*, 482–4.

11 Charles: Moranvillé (1907), 436–44. Pipe, Marshall: Delisle, 124n[1], 125n[3]; BN Clair. 214/9521; BN Fr. 26004/1309, 1318; PRO E36/79, p. 474; PRO C76/45, m. 14; *Foed.*, iii, 685; *Luce (1876), 371n[1]; *Chron. norm.*, 160.

12 Albrecht: Chaplais, 'Doc. Brétigny', 19. Trésiguidi: Borderie, iii, 517. Auvergne: Boudet (1900), 101–3; AN X[2a] 7, fols. 68vo-70. Limousin: 'Procès-verbal de délivrance', 192, 262; PRO C61/75, m. 23.
13 Guigue, 45–8; Petit (1885–1905), ix, 199–200. Quotation: Froissart, *Chron.*, xii, 98. Germans: Bel, *Chron.*, ii, 231–2. Albrecht: Chaplais, 'Doc. Brétigny', 19; Delaborde, Cat., no. 967. Starkey: AN JJ93/130. Hawkwood: Froissart, *Chron.*, ix, 155–6. Verney: Innocent VI, 'Reg. Epp. MCCCLXI', cols. 924–5. Walter: *ibid.*, cols 882–3; *Cal. Pap. R. Petitions*, i, 368; L. Menard, ii, 283. Leslie had fought with the Teutonic knights in Prussia and later fought with the companies in Italy: *Rot. Scot.*, i, 797; Temple Leader, 31; for his arrival in France with his brother Norman: *Rot. Scot.*, i, 830. After their mission was completed, Norman, and probably Walter, fought for the Queen in Burgundy: Gray, *Scalacr.*, 190.
14 Organisation: *Denifle, 381n[1]; Innocent VI, 'Reg. Epp. MCCCLXI', cols. 882–3; Ledos (1890), 51 ('chancellor').
15 Finot, 10n[1]. For illustrations of their origins, see AN JJ89/634, 92/278, 93/130, 246, 98/70.
16 *Ausgaben Innocenz VI*, 751; Innocent VI, 'Reg. Epp. MCCCLXI', cols. 848–9, 880–2, 925; *HGL*, ix, 719, 721; *Petit Thalamus*, 357; Villani, *Hist.*, cols. 642–3; Bel, *Chron.*, ii, 316, 322–3; Denifle, 391–6, *399n[1]; Guigue, 49–55. Coin: *HGL, x, 1254–5.
17 Villani, *Hist.*, col. 647; Denifle, 386, *398n[3]; Innocent VI, 'Reg. Epp. MCCCLXI', cols. 888–9, 910.
18 Denifle, 395, *397n[2]; Innocent VI, 'Reg. Epp. MCCCLXI', cols. 848–6, 867–8, 872–4; Bel, *Chron.*, ii, 323; *Petit Thalamus*, 357; Froissart, *Chron.*, vi, 73–4; *Vitae paparum*, i, 340.
19 Appeals: Molinier, 89–90; Innocent VI, 'Reg. Epp. MCCCLXI', 882–3; **HGL*, x, 1339. Negotiations: Denifle, *398n[4]; Innocent VI, 'Reg. Epp. MCCCLXI', cols. 882–3; *Molinier, 98n[1].
20 Villani, *Hist.*, cols. 647, 651–2, 656–7; Bel, *Chron.*, ii, 324; Denifle, 398n[5, 6]; Froissart, *Chron.*, vi, p. xxxiiin[3]; Innocent VI, 'Reg. Epp. MCCCLXI', cols. 909, 985, 1000; *Filippini, xii, 307. Sterz: Azario, *Liber gestorum*, 128; Villani, *Hist.*, col. 680.
21 Azario, *Liber gestorum*, 110–2, 128; Villani, *Hist.*, cols. 747–8.
22 The main accounts are Azario, *Liber gestorum*, 110–12, 128–33, 157, 159–61, 163; and Villani, *Hist.*, cols. 663, 680. English strength (summer 1364): *Cron. Pisa*, *RIS(1)*, xv, 1045 (one of the few sources to distinguish between English and Germans of the White Company). The company's total strength at this stage was about 4,000: Donato di Neri, *Cron. Senese*, 606.
23 Azario, *Liber gestorum*, 164, 166; Donato di Neri, *Cron. Senese*, 606; Giovanni Sercambi, *Chroniche*, ed. S. Bongi, i (1892), 121.
24 Temple Leader, 6–7; Villani, *Hist.*, cols. 746–7; Higden, *Polychronicon*, viii, 371; Froissart, *Chron.*, ix, 155–6; xii, 99.
25 Villani, *Hist.*, cols. 750–1; *Cron. Pisa*, 1047; Temple Leader, 31.
26 A. Theiner, *Codex diplomaticus dominii temporalis S. Sedis*, ii (1862), 419–26; Donato di Neri, *Cron. Senese*, 609, 613; *Chron. Placentinum*, *RIS(1)*, xv, 508; *Ephemerides Urbevetanae*, ed. L. Fumi, *RIS(2)*, xv.5 (1902–29), i, 88; *Cal. Pap. R. Letters*, iv, 28. Mortimer ('dominus de Lasuchia') was described in May 1366 as being abroad by the King's license: *CPR 1364–7*, 236. On Hawkwood's later career: see Temple Leader.
27 Froissart, *Chron.*, vi, p. xxn[3]; AD Pyr.-Atl. E40 (retaining fees owed by lord of Albret, Feb. 1365); **HGL*, x, 1488–9.
28 AN JJ93/75, 82; *Petit Thalamus*, 357–8, 359; **HGL*, x, 1488–9.
29 Denifle, 400n[4]; ASV Reg. Aven. Inn. VI, no 26, fol. 582; *Doc. Millau*, no. 242 and p. 120n[1].
30 *Petit Thalamus*, 358–9; *Doc. Millau*, nos. 248–9; *Arch. Montpellier*, i, no. 750. Bérard in Bourbonnais: *Titres Bourbon*, no. 2812.

31 'Procès-verbal de délivrance' (quotation at 133). Arms: *Doc. Millau*, nos. 255, 260; PRO E101/176/7, fol. 23.
32 Guichard: *Gall. Reg.*, v, no. 20066, 20069, 20077; Froissart, *Chron.*, iv, 105, 107; v, 20; Avesbury, *G. Edwardi*, 470; 'Procès-verbal de délivrance', 173, 250; *GEC*, vi, 650–3. Harcourt: Chandos Herald, *Vie*, 112 (l. 2321).
33 *Foed.*, iii, 660–1. Bretons: PRO C61/75, m. 23. Blois: 'Procès-verbal de délivrance', 262. Doc. Brétigny, 42.
34 Rouergue: *Doc. Millau*, no. 253; **Comptes Rodez*, 412–5; *Rouquette, 466. Gourdon: 'Procès-verbal de délivrance', 203–4. Cahors: *ibid.*, 205, 206–9; Calvet, 177.
35 Limousin: 'Procès-verbal de délivrance', 190–1, 262; PRO C61/75, m. 23; Gray, *Scalacr.*, 201.
36 *Doc. Millau*, no. 250; Molinier, 98–9, 100, 101–2; *Petit Thalamus*, 360. Strength: *HGL*, ix, 730–2; *x, 1263.
37 AN JJ91/313; Guigue, 61–3, *222; *Comptes Louppy*, 17. Name: *AGN Comptos*, v, no. 271. Career: *KOF*, xviii, 349; **HGL*, x, 1339; *Petit Thalamus*, 358; Villani, *Hist.*, cols. 679, 681.
38 Petit (1885–1905), ix, 237–52, 271, 275–6; Chérest (1879), 137–42.
39 BN Coll. Bourgogne 72, fol. 93; Petit (1885–1905), ix, 284–83; Chérest (1879), 164, 197–8; **KOF*, xviii, 470–1; *Guigue, 64n[3], 68n[3]; *Gr. chron.*, i, 336; Villani, *Hist.*, cols. 680, 681; Froissart, *Chron.*, vi, 63, 260.
40 Villani, *Hist.*, cols. 680–1; *Petit Thalamus*, 360; Froissart, *Chron.*, vi, 261. On Meschin's army, see also Guigue, 61–3, 66, *222. Many participants can be identified from their signature of the treaty of Clermont in July: *Hay du Chastelet, 313. On Tallebard, see AN JJ115/70.
41 BN Coll. Bourgogne, 21, fol. 4vo; *Chérest (1879), 189n[1].
42 *Petit Thalamus*, 360–1; Chérest (1879), 193–8.
43 Ayala, *Cron.*, i, 357.
44 Pere, 'Crón.', p. 1131; Russell, 24.
45 *Lecoy, ii, 372 (quotation); Daumet, 22–5; Hillgarth, 376–7.
46 *Foed.*, iii, 656–8; *AGN Comptos*, iv, no. 183; Russell, 26.
47 Ayala, *Cron.*, 326–7; BN Coll. Languedoc 159, fol. 104vo; Russell, 25–6; Villani, *Hist.*, cols. 657, 669, 674, 677; *Petit Thalamus*, 360–1; *L. Menard, ii, 242.
48 BN Coll. Bourgogne 21, fol. 3; *Luce (1876), 563.
49 *Hay du Chastelet, 313–6; **HGL*, x, 1224, 1232, 1241; Chérest, 196–7.
50 Rouquette, 52; *L. Menard, ii, 245, 246, 247–8; *Petit Thalamus*, 361; **HGL*, x, 1231–3.
51 Money: Molinier, 114–5; BN Coll. Languedoc 159, fol. 106; **HGL*, x, 1232, 1241. Withdrawals: *L. Menard, ii, 249, 250; *Petit Thalamus*, 361; *Preuves Polignac*, ii, 31–2; Rouquette, 52–3.
52 Tucoo-Chala (1959), 82–4; **HGL*, x, 1183–91, 1242.
53 BN Doat 190, fols. 326–326[vo]; **HGL*, x, 1231–2, 1339–40; *Petit Thalamus*, 362.
54 Esquerrier, 55–7. Prisoners: BN Doat 195, fols. 26–114[vo]; Froissart, *Chron.*, xii, 28, 45; Tucoo-Chala (1959–61), 90–2, 144–8, 155–61.
55 **HGL*, x, 124, 1226–7, 1231, 1233, 1234, 1242, 1248; BN Coll. Languedoc 159, fols. 105, 106, 107; Molinier, 153–6.
56 Monastier: *Preuves Polignac*, ii, 31–2; *L. Menard, ii, 250, 251, 252, 283–4; *HGL*, ix, 755; x, 1306–8; *Cat. comptes royaux*, no. 535. Combret: Rouquette, 52–4; Urban V, *Lettres*, no. 230; *Petit Thalamus*, 362.
57 *Comptes St.-Antonin*, 59; *Arch. Montpellier*, xiii, nos. 737–8; *Petit Thalamus*, 363, 364, 366; Mascaro, *Libre*, 55, 56; *HGL*, ix, 760–1, 763–4; *Petit (1909), x, 115–6.
58 *Arch. Montpellier*, xiii, nos. 714; *Menard, ii, 272; *Petit Thalamus*, 363, 364; *Petit (1909), 55–6. Loot: N JJ97/107, 98/279; *Moisant, 267–8. Rabaud: *Preuves Polignac*, ii, 41–2; Froissart, *Chron.*, xii, 109–10. Castilians: *Inv. AC Montferrand*, ii, 2.

59 Velay: *L. Menard, ii, 275, 283–4. Auvergne: 'Inv. le Puy', 687–8; *Spic. Briv.*, 405–10; AN JJ98/70 (Clermont); Ledos (1890), 43. Rouergue: *Doc. Millau*, no. 283. Rhone: *Comptes Louppy*, 52; Urban V, *Lettres*, no. 1522.
60 *Petit (1909), 55–6; *Guigue, 222. *Videment*: Spic. Briv. 361–8; BN Coll. Périgord 10, fols. 15–15vo.
61 Francois, 151–2; Venette, *Chron.*, ii, 329; Denifle, 473n[3].
62 Île de Fr.: AN JJ92/258, 279. Orléans: Venette, *Chron.*, 323. Burgundy: Chérest (1879), 213–6, 218, 229–30; Venette, *Chron.*, ii, 329–30; Petit (1885–1905), ix, 310–9.
63 *Chron. norm.*, 161–2; AN JJ108/276; *Chron. Brioc.*, 43; Morice, *Preuves*, i, 1565–6; John IV, *Actes*, i, 142 (no. 101).
64 *Hunger (1932), 8–10 and *passim*; *Chron. norm.*, 162–4; *Frag. chron. B-Normandie*, 7; *Chron. premiers Valois*, 131–2. Death of Philip: *ibid.*, 132; Anselme, i, 283.
65 *Chron. premiers Valois*, 129, 131, 135; On Jewel: ibid., 81, 89, 95. On Strael: Secousse, *Preuves*, 295–6. On Rolleboise: Lescot, *Chron.*, 159; Venette, *Chron.*, 358. Date: *Doc. Clos des Galées*, i, no. 578.
66 Murs: Venette, *Chron.*, 327–8, 331. La Charité: AN JJ97/638; *Itin. Phil. le Hardi*, 457, 458.
67 *Chron. premiers Valois*, 136–7. Rolleboise: BN Fr. 26005/1506–9; *Doc. Clos des Galées*, i, 579–99. Murs: BN Fr. 7414, fols. 16–16vo; Venette, *Chron.*, 331; Lescot, *Chron.*, 157.
68 Tallebard: *Petit (1885–1905), ix, 324; Petit (1909), 72–3, 79; Chérest (1879), 235; Charmasse (1880), 501–2; *Itin. Phil. le Hardi*, 549. Guiot: *ibid.*; *Rec. doc. Poitou*, iii, 328–30; AN JJ115/70. Cervole: Chérest (1879), 399; Timbal, *Reg. Parl.*, 486–7; Ledos(1890), 51. Gascons: Petit (1909), 56, 57, 61, 79–80; Chérest (1879), 234; *Itin. Phil. le Hardi*, 459.
69 *Foed.*, iii, 665, 667–70; Reading, *Chron.*, 153; *Eulogium*, iii, 231; Chandos Herald, *Vie*, 92 (ll. 1609–19).
70 Chaplais, 'Doc. Brétigny', 45–6.
71 PRO E101/314/18–19; *Foed.*, iii, 629; Chaplais, 'Doc. Brétigny', 14, 42–5; *Delachenal (1909–31), ii, 338n[1].
72 Chaplais, 'Doc. Brétigny', 12, 30–1, 36–7, 39, 41, 42, 45; AN J641/9 (Gaure); AN J654/1–5 (Belleville); Tucoo-Chala (1959), 94.
73 Compiègne: *Ord.*, iii, 433–9. Languedoc: Henneman (1976), 148–50, 153, 162; **HGL*, x, 1230–1. Languedoil: Rey, 505; Henneman (1976), 209.
74 *Plancher, ii, *Preuves*, nos. 308, 310; *Gr. chron.*, iii, 132.
75 Terms: *Foed.*, iii, 539–40, 611, 618, 621, 697. Attendants: *Foed.*, iii, 597, 598, 599, 617. Amusements: Froissart, *Chron.*, vi, 56; *Chron. Bourbon*, 5; *Mandements*, no. 163; Machaut, 'Dit de la fontaine amoureuse', ll. 1439–1500, 2246–54, *Oeuvres*, iii, 194–6, 223. Finance: *Chron. Bourbon, 5*; *ibid.*, nos. 85, 289, 409; *CCR 1364–8*, 384, 408; Timbal, *Reg. Parl.*, 405, 407; *Gr. chron.*, iii, 132.
76 Agreements: *Arch. admin. Reims*, iii, 169–74; Guigue, 40–1; Arbois de J., *Voy. pal.*, 137–9; 'Doc. Maçon', 170. Dishonoured: Timbal, *Reg. Parl.*, 428–30. London, plague: *Foed.*, iii, 618; Chaplais, 'Doc. Brétigny', 11.
77 *Foed.*, iii, 538.
78 *Foed.*, iii, 651, 654; Chaplais, 'Doc. Brétigny', 48–50; AN J641/9; Broome, 'Ransom', 13, 16–8. 'Beau parleur': la Tour Landry, *Livre*, 51.
79 *Foed.*, iii, 681–2, 685, 694, 699, 700–1.
80 Driffield: *Foed.*, iii, 701–2; PRO E101/29/3. Anjou: *Chronographia*, ii, 298–9; Noyal, 'Chron.', 262; Venette, *Chron.*, 332.
81 Venette, *Chron.*, 331, 333; Lescot, *Chron.*, 159–60, 162; *Gr. chron.*, i, 339–41; *Anon. Cant.*, 215–6. Payment: Broome, 'Ransom', 11–12; *Comptes Louppy*, 50–1. Agreement: *Perroy (1928), 265; *Recits d'un b. de Valenciennes*, 318.
82 *Anon. Cant.*, 216–7; Venette, *Chron.*, 339; *Lescot, *Chron.*, 244–5; *Perroy (1928), 264–5.

83 Ormrod, 37, 39; Harriss, 479, 477–8, 483–7, 492, 494–5; *Rot. Parl.*, ii, 273.
84 *Broome and Tout, 'Balance sheet'; *Harriss, 527–30; *Rot.Parl.*, ii, 285.
85 Doc. Brétigny, 15.
86 Brown, Colvin & Taylor, 662–6, 793–802.

CHAPTER XI

1 *AGN Comptos*, iii, nos. 625 (misdated), 752, 1100, 1106–7, 1136, iv, nos. 22–3; Secousse, *Preuves*, 200–2. Philip: *Plancher, ii, nos. 313–4, *Foed.*, iii, 708–9.
2 Secousse, *Preuves*, 202–3, 205–6; *Doc. Ch. Comptes Navarre*, 85; *AGN Comptos*, iv, no. 244.
3 Secousse, *Preuves*, 202–3, 203–4, 206–7; *AGN Comptos*, iv, nos. 1703, 1708, v, 365, 547, 576, 804; 'Anglo-French negotiations', 83. Betrothal: *Chron. premiers Valois*, 144–5; Retainers: Pamplona, AGN Comptos, Reg. 111, fol. 90.
4 Secousse, *Preuves*, 203, 204; *Mandements*, no. 1. Rolleboise: *Chron. premiers Valois*, 137–8; *Chron. norm.*, 170–1; *Luce (1876), 592.
5 *Chron. premiers Valois*, 139–42, 143–4; Lescot, *Chron.*, 163–5; *Chron. norm.*, 169; Venette, *Chron.*, 336–7; *Chron. R. Charles V*, i, 342; *Luce (1876), 593–7; *Mandements*, no. 2; *Delachenal (1909–31), iii, 543–5.
6 *Chron. premiers Valois*, 144; Lescot, *Chron.*, 167; Venette, *Chron.*, 341; *Compte R. Navarre*, 228; *Chronographia*, ii, 306; Froissart, *Chron.*, xii, 100–1. Brittany: BN Fr. 26006/12.
7 Lescot, *Chron.*, 168; Froissart, *Chron.*, vi, 106–7, 111–2, 124–5, 292, 296, 306–7; *313; Recits d'un b. de Valenciennes*, 321–2. Gascon retainers: *Mandements*, nos. 45, 480; AN J622/75.
8 Early uniforms: M. Prestwich, *War, politics and finance under Edward I* (1972), 101; J.E. Morris, *The Welsh wars of Edward I* (1901), 97; Morgan (1987), 104–5; Hewitt (1958), 15–6; J.F. Willard and W.A. Morris, *The English Government at work, 1327–36*, i (1940), 362–3; Avesbury, 428. G. Wrottesley, *Crécy and Calais* (1898), 148. 1355: Baker, 128; *HGL*, ix, 649. Arms: *Controversy*, i, 110–11. War-cry: Froissart, *Chron.*, vi, 117–9.
9 *Chron. norm.*, 171–3; Lescot, *Chron.*, 167–72; *Chron. premiers Valois*, 145–8; *Chronographia*, ii, 307–8; Froissart, *Chron.*, xii, 101; Secousse, *Preuves*, 211. Ordinal: *The coronation book of Charles V of France*, ed. R.S. Dewick (1899), 10.
10 Health: Christine de Pisan, *Livre des fais*, i, 48–9, 132; Froissart, *Chron.*, ix, 280–1; Brachet, 527–60. Tancarville: *Perroy (1928)(2), 266. Gontier: *Delachenal (1909–31), iii, 551–3.
11 *Plancher, ii, nos. 314–5; *Chron. R. Charles V*, ii, 4.
12 *Chron. norm.*, 174–5; *Chron. premiers Valois*, 150–4; *Itin. Phil. le Hardi*, 11–2; *Recits d'un b. de Valenciennes*, 327–8; BN Fr. 26006/94 (Barfleur); BN Fr. 26006/72(3) (Échauffour).
13 *Mandements*, no. 562 (p. 277); *Arch. admin. Reims*, iii, 273–6; Cazelles (1982), 532–4.
14 Moulineaux: *Chron. premiers Valois*, 154–5; *Mandements*, 225A (pp. 106–7). Seaborne expedn.: *AGN Comptos*, v, nos. 341, 348, 356, 358–9, 365, 367, 370, 383, 402, 404–5, 409, 413–20, 432, 434–9, 447–51, 463–9, 476, 480, 483, 958, 1101. Aubricourt: *ibid.*, nos. 313, 721; cf. *CPR 1361–2*, 312; *CCR 1360–4*, 450, 455; *GEC*, vii, 149.
15 Companies: *AGN Comptos*, v, 228, 269–71, 297–9, 327, 330, 340, 342, 368, 372, 374, 441, 499; *Chron. R. Charles V*, ii, 300–1; Secousse, *Preuves*, 203, 206. March north: *Petit (1909), 115–7; 'Anglo-French negotiations', 83; *AC Montferrand*, i, 395. La Charité: *Itin. Phil. le Hardi*, 13; *Chron. norm.*, 175; *Chron. premiers Valois*, 156–8; *Petit (1909), 122–3; *Mandements*, nos. 84, 93.
16 Morice, *Preuves*, i, 1565–6, 1567–8, 1581; 'Chron. Brioc.', col. 43; John IV, *Actes*, nos. 30, 32, 34; Borderie, iii, 578.

17 *Chron. norm.*, 175; *Anonimalle chron.*, 50–1; *Chron. premiers Valois*, 159; *Recits d'un b. de Valenciennes*, 334–5; Froissart, *Chron.*, vi, 150 (Chandos). Charles V: BN Fr. 26006/62; *Mandements*, no. 117.

18 *Chron. premiers Valois*, 159–63; *Chron. norm.*, 175–6; Venette, *Chron.*, 350–2; *Anonimalle Chron.*, 51; *Recits d'un b. de Valenciennes*, 335–8, 340; Froissart, *Chron.*, vi, 162–3, xii, 105. Ransoms: *Cart. Rays*, i, 32–6.

19 *Recits d'un b. de Valenciennes*, 339–40; *Chron. premiers Valois*, 162–3; *Chron. R. Charles V*, ii, 6; Noyal, 'Chron.', 264; John IV, *Actes*, i, nos. 37–9, 41; Borderie, iv, 6–7.

20 Froissart, *Chron.*, vi, 346.

21 *Recits d'un b. de Valenciennes*, 341–2; Morice, *Preuves*, i, 1584, 1588–9; *Mandements*, nos. 96–8, 114–5; *Foed.*, iii, 753; John IV, *Actes*, i, nos. 43–4.

22 *Petit Thalamus*, 367; *Petit (1909), 135; Guigue, 107–14, *332; Froissart, *Chron.*, xii, 109–10. Fortifications: *Guigue, 218–9, 314–5, 320–1. Blot: *AC Montferrand*, i, 397, 399. Pope: Urban V, *Lettres*, nos. 1514, 1519; *Denifle, 425n[7].

23 La Charité: *Gall. Christ.*, xii, 410. Albret: AD Pyr.-Atl. E40; *AGN Comptos*, v, 856; *Doc. Ch. Comptes Navarre*, 100–3. Clerk: AD Pyr.-Atl. E520. Treaty and sequel: Urban V, *Lettres*, nos. 1191, 1394–7, 1456, 1521, 1529; Prou, 43–5; Secousse, *Preuves*, 214–24; *AGN Comptos*, v, 984, 1194; *Mandements*, no. 218–219A, 225A (pp. 105–10); BN Fr. 26006/151.

24 Urban V, *Lettres*, nos. 1822, 1849; *Chron. R. Charles V*, ii, 19; Venette, *Chron.*, 359–60.

25 Guigue, *114n[2], 116, *120–1, 128n[2] *323–8, 336–44; Urban V, *Lettres*, no. 1880; *Petit (1909), 167–8. Bertucat: *Guigue, 333; BN Fr. 20412/24; BN PO 3005 [Villebeuf, 8]. Money: *HGL*, x, 1343–4; *Arch. Montpellier*, i, no. 191, xiii, no. 1125; Guigue, 123–6; Prou, 54; 'Doc. Maçon', 178–80.

26 Venette, *Chron.*, 359; *Vitae paparum*, i, 356; Chérest (1879), 314–24, 337–9; Petit (1909), 180–1.

27 Cox, 208–10; Guigue, 152, *333–4; Cordey, 180; Petit (1909), 179–82.

28 *Chron. R. Charles V*, ii, 300–1; Secousse, *Preuves*, 381.

29 Hillgarth, 383–4.

30 Anselme, vii, 758; *Delachenal (1909–31), iii, 268n[1].

31 *HGL*, ix, 767–8. On Louis: *Chron. du réligieux de Saint-Denis*, ed. L. Belaquet, i (1839), 328–30; Christine de P, *Livre des fais*, i, 135, 136; *Foed.*, iii, 756, 757; *Delachenal (1909–31), iii, 553.

32 *Delachenal (1909–31), iii, 268n[1], 270n[1], 272nn[1,2]; Zurita, Lib. IX, cap. 98.

33 See agreement of Calveley and Du Guesclin, 2 Jan. 1366: Gutierrez de Velasco, 309–10.

34 Pere III, 'Crón', 1150; *Cortes de Cataluña*, ii, 360, 369–70. Bordeaux: Urban V, *Lettres*, nos. 1762–4.

35 Urban V, *Lettres*, nos. 1884–5, 2039–40; *Cortes de Cataluña*, ii, 360, 369–71.

36 Du Guesclin: *Cuvelier, *Chron.*, ii, 393; Urban V, *Lettres*, nos. 1762–3; AN J381/4; *Mandements*, no. 851. Others: *Petit Thalamus*, 369–70; Ayala, *Crón.*, i, 399–400; Pere, 'Crón.', 1150. Partnership: Gutierrez de Velasco, 310. Cresswell: Froissart, *Chron.*, xii, 102, 105; Chandos Herald, *Vie*, 103 (ll. 1987–90). Rolleboise: Venette, *Chron.*, 357–8; *Mandements*, no. 213. Moulineaux: BN Fr. 26006/249; *Mandements*, no. 250. Burgundy/Lyonnais: **Itin. Phil. le Hardi*, 462; *Molinier, 320. Quotation: Cuvelier, *Chron.*, i, 263 (ll. 7225–6).

37 Rouergue: *Doc. Millau*, no. 293. Pope: Labande (1904), 14–6; *Denifle, 486n[2], 487n[1]; *Prou, 140–4; *Molinier, 320; Cuvelier, *Chron.*, i, 271–80. Strength: Ayala, *Crón.*, i, 394; *Chron. R. Charles V*, ii, 15. Perpignan: AN K49/5; *Molinier, 320.

38 Chamerolles: *Recits d'un b. de Valenciennes*, 327–8. Rabaud: *Spic. Briv.*, 391–2; *Petit Thalamus*, 368; *Arch. Montpellier*, xiii, 1125; Froissart, *Chron.*, xii, 110–15.

39 Morville/Wilston: *Chron. norm.*, 165–6; BN Fr. 26006/191. St.-Sever: *Mandements*, no. 266; *Coville (1894), 385–6; BN Fr. 26007/269, 271. Le Hommet: *Mandements*, nos.

308–10; *Chron. premiers Valois*, 169–70; *Chron. norm.*, 167–8; Delisle (1867), i, 143–4.

40 Lehoux, i, 190–1; *Chron. Bourbon*, 14–5.

41 Petit (1909), 128–30, 142, 161–2, *211.

42 Petit (1909), 183–91, 200–9, 212–3; Chérest (1879), 345–6; **Itin. Phil. le Hardi*, 470–1.

43 Pere, 'Crón.', 1150; *Delachenal (1909–31), iii, 314n[1], 325–6, 330n[1].

44 Awe: Ayala, *Crón.*, i, 399n; *Miret y Sans (1905), 128.

45 Miret y Sans, 80–1; Pere, 'Crón.', 1151;*Delachenal (1909–31), iii, 320n[1]; Russell, 42; Gutierrez de Velasco, 309–10. Quotation: *Delachenal (1909–31), iii, 315n[1].

46 Ayala, *Crón.*, i, 400; *Miret y Sans, 78–9; *Doc. Ch. Comptes Navarre*, 122–4, 127–30, 134–5, 138.

47 Pere, 'Crón.', 1151; Ayala, *Crón.*, i, 399n, 400, 402–4; *Miret y Sans, 81–2; *Delachenal (1909–31), iii, 335n[2]; *Doc. Ch. Comptes Navarre*, 147–8. Date of acclamation: Russell, 47. Quotation: Fowler (1988), 33–4.

48 Miret y Sans, 85; Ayala, *Crón.*, i, 405–6, 406–10; Pere, 'Crón.', 1151; *Delachenal (1909–31), iii, 433n[1]; *Chron. R. Charles V*, ii, 15; *Molinier, 320. Quotation: Chandos Herald, *Vie*, 146 (ll. 3584–6).

49 Ayala, *Crón.*, i, 410–12, 421–3; *Molinier, 320.

50 Gutierrez de Velasco, 309–17.

51 Ayala, *Crón.*, i, 414–7, 419; Miret y Sans, 87–8. Quotation: Chandos Herald, *Vie*, 98 (ll. 1817–21).

CHAPTER XII

1 Froissart, *Chron.*, vi, 80.

2 Population: compare *Rôles Gascons*, iv, ed. Y. Renouard (1964), 568–74 (fiscal survey of 1315–6) and *Archives Municipales de Bordeaux*, iv, *Registres de la Jurade. Délibérations de 1414 à 1416 et de 1420 à 1422* (1883), 88 (estimate of taxable capacity of a slightly smaller area in 1414). Wine: James, 20–4, 32–6. Armour: Renouard, 420–1.

3 PRO E101/176/2; Delpit, *Coll. gen.*, 134–68; *Foed.*, iii, 679

4 Subsidy: *Foed.*, iii, 671; Chaplais, *Dipl. practice*; Delpit, *Coll. gen.*, 136–7 (no. 48), 175 (nos. 19, 22). War damage: see note 3 above. Grants: Delpit, *Coll. gen.*, 134–68 (nos. 4, 9, 12, 14, 19, etc.). Custom: Delpit, *Coll. gen.*, 136–7 (nos. 49, 55). Expenditure: *ibid.*, 176 (nos. 53, 55, 56); *Anonimalle chron.*, 53.

5 Froissart, *Chron.*, vii, 305. English revenues: Booth, 135–6; Morgan, 126–35. Local domain: Delpit, *Coll. gen.*, 169, 171. Coinage: Boutruche, 266–7.

6 1364: Rouquette, 78; *AHG*, xxxiv, 190. 1365: AD Pyr.-Atl. E40; Doat 244, fols. 4–4vo; Higounet (1973), plate; *Doc. Millau*, no. 289. Receipts (less John's ransom and Exchequer subsidy): Delpit, *Coll. gen.*, 173–6.

7 Froissart, *Chron.*, vi, 201

8 Russell, 37–8; *Foed.*, iii, 779; Ayala, *Crón.*, i, 397–8.

9 Ayala, *Crón.*, i, 397–8. Loring: PRO C61/79, m. 14; *CCR 1364–6*, 269; cf. Froissart, *Chron.*, vi, 205. Letter: PRO E403/427, m. 1. Holland: PRO C61/79, mm. 15, 14, 13. Ships: *Foed.*, iii, 791. July: Miret y Sans, 87–8.

10 *Foed.*, iii, 797, 799; Chandos Herald, *Vie*, 100–1 (ll. 1910–18); *AGN Comptos*, vi, nos. 489, 493; Ayala, *Crón.*, i, 420, 430.

11 Ayala, *Crón.*, i, 430–1; Miret y Sans, 89, *90–1; *Foed.*, iii, 799–807. Jewels: Delpit, 175 (no. 24); *Russell, 556. Gascons: Froissart, *Chron.*, vi, 203, 233.

12 Chandos Herald, *Vie*, 102 (ll. 1972–4); Petit (1909), 206; *Petit Thalamus*, 372; *Foed.*, iii, 808; *Chron. R. Charles V*, ii, 111–2; *Delachenal (1909–31), iii, 363n[2].

13 From Castile: *Molinier, 322, 327; Chandos Herald, *Vie*, 102–3 (ll. 1975–95); *Delachenal (1909–31), iii, 358nn[2–5]; *AGN Comptos*, vi, nos. 609, 737, 773. Castilians: Ayala, *Crón.*, i, 443. Aragonese: Russell, 79. Gaunt: Chandos Herald, *Vie*, 106–7 (ll.

2119–56); PRO C61/79, mm. 8, 5, 4, 3, 2, 1. Gaunt's force was carried in 20 ships, which could have carried up to 20 men each, without horses or baggage (both sent in advance): *Foed.*, iii, 809–10. Spies: 'Lettres closes', 84.

14 Ayala, *Crón.*, i, 422–3, 437; Miret y Sans, *88–9, 89. Du Guesclin's strength: *ibid.*, *104, 109; Garcia y Lopez, i, 365n[2], 373n[2]. Agents: *Cortes de Cataluña*, ii, 147.

15 Ayala, *Crón.*, i, 434–5, 437; Miret y Sans, 104–9, 111, 113.

16 Chandos Herald, *Vie*, 108–9, 111–2, 113 (ll. 2189–2206, 2291–2314, 2383–6); *AGN Comptos*, vi, no. 764; Ayala, *Crón.*, i, 435–6.

17 Ayala, *Crón.*, i, 438–9, 443–4; *Petit Thalamus*, 381, 382; list of captives in Black Prince, Letter (v). French strength: Miret y Sans, 104; Ayala, *Crón.*, i, 441.

18 Chandos Herald, *Vie*, 117–28; Ayala, *Crón.*, i, 444–8.

19 Ayala, *Crón.*, i, 439, 444, 450–4; *Delachenal (1909–31), iii, 555–6; Black Prince, Letter (v).

20 Ayala, *Crón.*, i, 442–3.

21 Ayala, *Crón.*, i, 454–6, 461–2, 578; Chandos Herald, *Vie*, 132–43; Black Prince, Campaign letter (v); *Chron. premiers Valois*, 180; *Foed.*, iii, 825.

22 Ayala, *Crón.*, i, 458–60; *Chron. premiers Valois*, 180–1.

23 Ayala, *Crón.*, i, 458, 471–3; Chandos Herald, *Vie*, 145 (ll. 3521–33, 3536–45).

24 Guesclin: *Cuvelier, *Chron.*, ii, 401–4; Ayala, *Crón.*, i, 467–9. Denia: Perroy (1951); Gutierrez de Velasco, 288–9, 291–305. Godoy: *ibid.*, 291–305.

25 Ayala, *Crón.*, i, 473–83, 494–5. Cost: PRO E30/1085, 1225.

26 Chandos Herald, *Vie*, 148, 149 (ll. 3639–43, 3677–92); Knighton, *Chron.*, 194; Ayala, *Crón.*, i, 506–7; *Chron. R. Charles V*, ii, 35.

27 Russell, 123–5, 134–6.

28 Ayala, *Crón.*, i, 462–3, 503–5, 506, 507, 508, 509.

29 *Delachenal (1909–31), iii, 557–62. Raids: *HGL*, ix, 788; *Doc. Millau*, no. 303; Rouquette, 111–5.

30 *Miret y Sans, 126–9; Ayala, *Crón.*, i, 509–13, 516–9, 521–3; *Chron. R. Charles V*, ii, 36.

31 Russell, 137, 142, *555–6.

32 *Petit Thalamus*, 381, 382; *HGL*, ix, 790–; BN Doat 92, fols. 511–9. Subsidy: *Inv. AM Toulouse*, AA45/60; **HGL*, x, 1378–9. Boucicaut: see below, note 34.

33 *Petit Thalamus*, 382; *Die Chronik des Garoscus Veteri und Bertrand Boysset (1365–1415)*, ed. F. Ehrle, *Archiv für Literatur und Kirchengeschichte des Mittelalters*, vii (1900), 323; *Prou, 161–3; 'Lettre de B du Guesclin au sire de la Voute', ed. L. Delisle, *BEC*, lxv (1884), 302–3; Ameilh, *Corr.*, nos. 372–3, 375, 386–7, 389–93, 416; *HGL*, ix, 791–3; Denifle, 509–21, *778–87; *Encycl. B-du-R* [D], ii, 404–6; Labande (1904), esp. 31, 64–5, 75–6, 79–80.

34 *Arch. admin. Reims*, iii, 319–20; *Ord.*, v, 15–8, 20–1; 'Instructions pour la défence. . . de Bourgogne'; *Plancher, iii, no. 35. Field forces: *Chron. premiers Valois*, 192–3; BN Clair. 31/2255, 2299, 47/3525, 52/3913, 65/5037, 89/7009, etc.

35 *Chron. R. Charles V*, ii, 38–9. La Salle: Froissart, *Chron.*, v, 350, vi, 138. For composition of English corps, see quittances for *pâtis* given to D. of Brittany in Dec. 1368: *Borderie, iv, 113. Cresswell, Briquet: *Samaran (1951), 642; AN JJ104/164; Jones (1970), 216.

36 Quercy: *Denifle, 821–2; Lacoste, iii, 192–5. Rouergue: Rouquette, 188. Thereafter: *Titres Bourbon*, no. 3025; Arbois de J., *Voy. pal.*, 140 (misdated); *Petit (1909), 225–6, 232–3, 237–8; *Chron. R. Charles V*, ii, 37–8.

37 *Chron. R. Charles V*, 38–40, 42–4; Arbois de J, *Voy. pal.*, 141–2 (misdated); *Mandements*, no. 441.

38 *Chron. R. Charles V*, ii, 44–5, 60–1, 110–1; *Comptes Tours*, ii, 29–32.

39 *Chron. R. Charles V*, ii, 44–5, 60; *Chron. premiers Valois*, 196; BN PO 3046 [Wargnies, 19]; Hunger, *Actes*, ii, 4–8; Fréville, 276–8; *Mon. hist.*, no. 1468; *Mandements*, no. 465. Anjou: AN JJ100/155, 104/164.

40 *Borderie, iv, 113; Jones (1970), 216; *Frag. chron. B-Normandie*, 8; *Chron. premiers Valois*, 196–7; *Comptes R. Navarre*, 100, 219. Chandos: *Delisle (1867), ii, 166–7; *Mon. hist.*, no. 1466; *Samaran (1951), 641–2; *Comptes R. Navarre*, 219. Horse: AN JJ100/84. Govt. forces: BN Clair. 13/853, 26/1912, 47/3489, 56/4295vo, 4271, etc.
41 *Chron. Bourbon*, 19–21; *Chron. R. Charles V*, ii, 61; **Itin. Phil. le Hardi*, 476.
42 *Vitae paparum*, i, 412.
43 Delpit, *Coll. gen.*, 175–6 (nos. 30–3, 36).
44 Froissart, *Chron.*, vii, 66–9, 308–9; *Arch. Bordeaux, Bouillons*, 173–7; AD Pyr.-Atl. E40. Cf. Rouquette, 188 (absence of the dissentients at Angoulême suggested by Armagnac's later complaint that the *fouage* had been granted to the prince by 'plusieurs de ses gens'); *Compte R. Navarre*, 351 (departure of Chandos). Yield calculated from Delpit, *Coll. gen.*, 173–4.
45 Rouquette, 186–92. Provence: BN Doat 195, fols 116–146vo. Ransom: AD Pyr.-Atl. E237 (175), 301; *Tucoo-Chala (1959–61), 351–2.
46 Ransoms: AD Pyr.-Atl. E40, 41. War profits: *Titres Bourbon*, nos. 2812, 2864, 2921–2, 2924, 2945, 2960–1; Froissart, *Chron.*, xii, 205. Homage: *Livre des hommages*, no. 528.
47 AD Pyr.-Atl. E627; BN Coll. Périgord 9, fols. 208vo, 211–211vo, 214vo; BN Doat 243, fols. 272–273vo, 276–277vo; *Livre des hommages*, nos. 546, 548.
48 Rouquette, 189. Stiffness: Froissart, *Chron.*, vii, 306. Illness: Chandos Herald, *Vie*, 153 (ll. 3815–21); Walsingham, *Chron. Angl.*, 88–9.
49 Broome, 'Ransom', 37; *Foed.*, iii, 781–2, 793, 826–7, 836; Perroy (1928), 260–1, *277–8.
50 *Foed.*, iii, 842, 845; *Chron. R. Charles V*, ii, 40–1.
51 'Anglo-French negotiations', 83; **Chron. R. Charles V*, iii, 203–4.
52 *Arch. admin. Reims*, iii, 319–20; *Ord.*, v, 17; Cazelles (1982), 532–4.
53 Loan: AN J293/15. Dowry: *Titres Bourbon*, nos. 3047–8; AN J477/3; *AHG*, i, 158–9.
54 *Chron. R. Charles V*, ii, 253–4.
55 **Chron. R. Charles V*, iii, 135–6, 137, 138–9; *KOF*, xviii, 485–8; *Ord.*, vi, 104. Pressure: **HGL*, x, 1387; Rouquette, 190.
56 Treaty: *Mandements*, nos. 457–8; *Foed.*, iii, 850–2, 869–70; *Daumet, 163–8. Guesclin: Ayala, i, *Crón.*, 552, 548–9, 551–6; Chaucer, *Complete Works*, iv (1894), 256. Edward III: *Russell, 554.
57 *Foed.*, iii, 750–1, 826; Urban V, *Lettres*, nos. 1455, 1510, 2016–7; AN J558/7; *Vitae paparum*, i, 358.
58 *Chron. R. Charles V*, ii, 58–9, 70–1, 119–31.
59 Recruitment: PRO E101/29/24; C61/81, m. 3; *Foed.*, iii, 857, 862. Embassy: PRO E101/315/27–9; *Perroy (1948–9), 302–3. Tancarville's safe-conduct was issued at Westminster 3 days after Neville's return: *Foed.*, iii, 850.
60 *Delachenal (1909–31), iv, 102–5; **HGL*, x, 1404–6, 1420–1; *Mandements*, no. 478; *HGL*, x, 1405; *Doc. Millau*, no. 319. Cajarc: Alauzier (1957)(1), 96–7. Millau: *ibid.*, nos. 316, 318, 322–5; Artières, 278; *Rouquette, 193–4; Chaplais, 'Doc. Brétigny', 58.
61 *Loirette (1913), 334–5; BN Doat 193, fols. 79–80vo (quotation). Estates: **HGL*, x, 1396–9; Dognon, 610–1. Recruitment: BN PO 159 [Azay, 3], 235 [Baynac, 25], 292 [Berail, 12], 625 [Caussade, 4], 1999 [Mons, 10], 2004 [Montagut, 4], 2230 [Penne, 7], 7603 [Karelleu, 2], etc.; *Doc. Durfort*, nos.1198–1200; *HGL* 9/799–800, 802–3.*Routiers*: *Doc. Millau*, no. 320; *Douze comptes Albi*, nos. 1657, 1664.
62 *Anglo-Norman Letters*, 198, 200; *Foed.*, iii, 848–9. Emissaries: Chandos Herald, *Vie*, 155 (ll. 3889–96); BN PO 676 [Chaponval, 5]; *Chron. R. Charles V*, ii, 99, 254; Froissart, *Chron.*, vii, 97–8.
63 Najac: BN Doat 146, fols. 81–82; AN JJ100/537, 102/101, 202; BN PO 292 [Berail, 24]. Armagnac: *Comptes Rodez*, ii, 61; *Doc. Millau*, no. 317; *Rouquette, 184–5. Officers: *Doc. Millau*, nos. 289–90, 293, 303, 313, 360. Wettenhall's absence: PRO E101/29/24. Defence: Rouquette, 178; *Anglo-Norman Letters*, 199. Castelmary: *ibid.*; *Comptes*

Rodez, 80.

64 BN Doat 196, fols. 319[vo]-322 (Rabastens' commission); *Anglo-Norman Letters*, 201; *Doc. Millau*, no. 320; *Douze Comptes Albi*, nos. 1586–7, 1591–2, 1595. Rodez: *Comptes Rodez*, ii, 62, 73; *Ord.*, v, 255–7; BN Doat 149, fols. 106–15; 196, fols. 322–328vo.

65 *Doc. Millau*, no. 319; BN PO 1577 [Jean, 8]. Cahors: BN Fr. 26008/623; *Anglo-Norman Letters*, 198, 199–200; BN PO 146 [Auriolla, 4], 1891 [Maubuisson, 4], 2135 [Odin, 2]; Lacoste, iii, 202–3, 205–6, 206n[1].

66 AN J655/18 (lost: summary in 18th cent. catalogue of Trésor des Chartes); *Anglo-Norman Letters*, 198, 199; 200; *Doc. Millau*, no. 319.

67 *Mandements*, no. 485; *Foed.*, iii, 850; **Chron. R. Charles V*, iii, 123–43.

68 *Foed.*, iii, 858, 861–4.

69 *Chron. R. Charles V*, ii, 71–2; *Chronographia*, ii, 337–9; Storey-Challenger, 201–2, *310–1. Garrison: Storey-Challenger, 185, 197–9, 205; PRO E36/79, pp. 485, 542, 549, 553.

70 *Chron. R. Charles V*, ii, 72–6; AN X[1a] 1469, fol. 342.

71 *Rot. Parl.*, ii, 299–300.

Bibliography

A MANUSCRIPTS

Cahors: Archives départmentales du Lot

Archives communales de Martel:
BB 5: Consuls and councillors, proceedings [1344–60]
CC 3–4: Accounts [1341–3, 1349–62]
EE 1: War (correspondence)

Archives communales de Cajarc
CC: Accounts

Gourdon: Archives communales

BB 3–4: Consuls, proceedings and accounts [1350–1, 1353–4]
CC 17–9: Accounts [1350–1, 1355–6, 1357–8]
CC40: Miscellaneous instruments
EE6: War (correspondence)
II5: Miscellaneous (15th-century extracts)

Lille: Archives départmentales du Nord

Série B: Chambre des Comptes de Lille

London: British Library

Additional Charters
  1–208: Collection Courcelles
  232–505, 1397–1516, 2028–4578: Collection Joursanvault
Cotton Manuscripts
  Caligula DIII: Diplomatic documents

London: Duchy of Cornwall Office

Account of John Henxteworth [1355–6]

London: Public Record Office

Chancery
C49/46 Council and Parliamentary proceedings
C61/59–82 Gascon rolls [1347–69]
C76/25–52 Treaty (formerly French) rolls [1347–69]
C81/325–413 Chancery warrants [1347–69]

Exchequer
E30 Diplomatic documents
E36/79 Treasury books (Ponthieu)
E43 Ancient deeds, W.S. series [Wardrobe debentures]
E101 Accounts various
  E101/25/29–101/29/40, 101/35/1–30, 101/531/36: Army, navy and ordnance [1347–1370]
  E101/167/10–101/178/20: English possessions in France [1347–70]
  E101/312/27–101/315/40: *Nuncii* [messengers and diplomatic agents] [1348–70]
  E101/393/11: Wardrobe account (Richard Farley) [1359–60]
  E101/482/16–30: Works (Scottish Marches) [1344–68]
E364/2–5 Pipe rolls [enrolled accounts] [1368–72]
E372/193–212 Pipe rolls [enrolled accounts] [1347–68]
E403/341–438 Issue rolls [1348–70]

Special Collections
SC1 Ancient Correspondence

Montpellier: Archives départmentales de l'Hérault

Série A: Administrative orders (seneschalsies of Beaucaire and Toulouse)

Oxford: Bodleian Library

Ms. Bodley 462, fols. 21–34
  Fragments of a Latin chronicle of England, 1339–47

Pamplona: Archivo General de Navarra

Sección de comptos
Cajones: 11–20, 31, 38 [1349–65]
Registros: 111

Paris: Archives nationales

Série J Trésor des Chartes, Layettes
  514: Brocard de Fénétrange
  636–42, 654–5: Angleterre
  677: Écosse
Série JJ Trésor des Chartes, Régistres
  76–117 [1345–80]
Série K Monuments historiques
  44–51: Cartons des Rois [1344–80]
Série KK Monuments historiques
  648: Corps politiques (États provinciaux)
Série P Chambre des Comptes
  2292–5: Mémoriaux C, D [1346–81]
Série X Parlement de Paris
  X^{1a}: Parlement civil
    13–29: Régistres de jugés, lettres et arrêts [1350–80]
    1469–72: Régistres du Conseil et des Plaidoiries [1364–80]
    9182: Grands Jours de Troyes, arrêts [1367, 1374, 1376]
  X^{2a}: Parlement criminel
    5–8: Régistres [1345–75]

Paris: Bibliothèque nationale

Collection Clairambault, 1–227: Titres scellés
Collection Doat (Languedoc):
53: Narbonne
60: Béziers
64: Carcassonne
87: Montauban
92: Castelsarrasin
93: Pamiers
96: Foix (town)
110: Albi
117: Guyenne
119: Cahors
127: Moissac
132: Rodez
145: Millau
146: Najac, St.-Antonin
147: Villefranche de Rouergue
149: St.-Affrique
157: Languedoc (general)
190–7: Houses of Foix, Armagnac and Albret
243–4: Counts of Périgord
Collection de Languedoc (Bénédictins), 84–6, 159
Collection du Périgord:
9–10: Counts of Périgord
46–7: Towns
Collection de Touraine, 8
Manuscrits français
20026: Chambre des Comptes, miscellaneous
20590: Chambre des Comptes, travel expenses
20684, pp. 293–363: War Treasurers' accounts, Barthélémy du Drach, 1348–50 (transcribed extracts)
20692, pp. 167–172: War Treasurers' accounts, Barthélémy du Drach, 1355 (extracts)
25764: Montres [1347–80]
25998–26009: Quittances et pièces diverses
26485–29545: Pièces originales [cited as PO, 1–3061]
32510: Chambre des Comptes, war accounts, musters (transcribed extracts)
n.a. 7413–4: Chambre des Comptes, war accounts, musters (transcibed extracts)
n.a. 7606–15: Portefeuilles de Fontanieu (miscellaneous transcriptions) [1345–80]
n.a. 9241, fols. 162–192vo: War Treasurers' accounts, Barthélémy du Drach, 1355
n.a. 20528, pp. 1–20: War Treasurers' accounts, Jean Chauvel, 1351–4 (extracts)

Pau: Archives départmentales des Pyrenées-Atlantiques

Série E
13–236: Albret
237–287: Armagnac
288–367: Béarn
368–390 Bigorre
391–484: Foix
513–593: Navarre
600–881: Périgord, Limousin

Rodez: Archives départmentales de l'Aveyron

G31: Diocese of Rodez, ecclesiastical taxation

Archives communales de Najac
2E178/8: Accounts [1350–83]

Archives communales de Saint-Affrique
2E216/BB2: Councillors, proceedings [1358–60]

Rome, Cittá del Vaticano: Archivio Segreto Vaticano

Regesta Avinionensia 134–49, 167 [Curial letters, 1357–62]
Regesta Vaticana 232–4, 239–41 [Curial letters, 1357–60]
Regesta Vaticana 244K [Drafts, 1358]

Rouen: Bibliothèque municipale

Ms 3398–3413
Collection Leber, Extraits de Menant (Chambre des Comptes, transcribed extracts)

B PRINTED RECORD SOURCES

'Acte d'accusation contre Robert le Coq, évêque de Laon', ed. L. Douet d'Arcq, *BEC*, ii (1840–1), 350–387

Actes normands de la Chambre des Comptes sous Philippe de Valois, ed. L. Delisle (1871)

Actes du Parlement de Paris, 2e série, *de l'an 1328 à l'an 1350*, ed. H. Furgeot, 3 vols (1920–75)

Actes du Parlement de Paris. Parlement criminel, règne de Philippe VI de Valois, ed. B. Labat-Poussin, M. Langlois, and Y. Lanhers (1987)

Actes royaux des Archives de l'Hérault, i, *1151–1422*, ed. A. Caramel (1980)

Acts of the Parliament of Scotland, ed. T. Thomson and C. Innes 12 vols (1814–75)

Albanès, J.H., 'Chartes provençales des Archives départmentales des Bouches-du-Rhone', *Revue des sociétés savantes des départements*, 6e série, v (1877), 195–216

Ameilh, Pierre, *La correspondance de Pierre Ameilh, archevêque de Naples puis d'Embrun (1363–1369)*, ed. H. Bresc (1972)

'Anglo-French negotiations at Bruges, 1374–1377', ed. E. Perroy, *Camden Miscellany*, xix (*Camden Third Series*, lxxx) (1952), 83.

Anglo-Norman Letters and Petitions, ed. M.D. Legge (1941)

Arbois de Jubainville, H., *Voyage paléographique dans le département de l'Aube* (1855)

Archives administratives de la ville de Reims, ed. P. Varin, 5 vols (1839–48)

Archives anciennes de la ville de Saint-Quentin, ed. E. Lemaire, 2 vols (1888–1910)

Archives historiques de la Saintonge et de l'Aunis, 50 vols (1874–1967)

Archives historiques du Département de la Gironde, 58 vols (1859–1932)

Archives historiques du Poitou, 61 vols (1872–1982)

Archives municipales de Bordeaux, i, *Livre des Bouillons* (1867); v, *Livre des Coutumes*, ed. H. Barckhausen (1890)

Archives de la ville de Montpellier, ed. J. Berthelé and M. Oudot de Dainville, 13 vols (1895–1984)

Aumale, H., duc d', *Notes et documents relatifs à Jean, roi de France, et à sa captivité en Angleterre, Miscellanies of the Philobiblon Society*, ii (1855–6)

Ausgaben der apostolischen Kammer unter Benedikt XII, Klemens VI, und Innocenz VI, ed. K.H. Schäfer (1914)

Ausgaben der apostolischen Kammer unter den Päpsten Urban V und Gregor XI, ed. K.H. Schäfer (1914)

Balfour-Melville, E.W.M., 'Papers relating to the Captivity and Release of David II', *Miscellany of the Scottish History Society*, ix (1958), 1–56

Beaurepaire, F. de (ed.), 'Les sources de l'histoire du moyen age à la Bibliothèque de la Ville de Rouen', *Cahiers Léopold Delisle*, xiii (1964), fasc. 2

Black Prince: see Edward, Prince of Wales

Blois, Charles of, Duke of Brittany, *Recueil des Actes de Charles de Blois et Jeanne de Penthièvre, Duc et Duchesse de Bretagne (1341–1364)*, ed. M. Jones (1996)

Bock, F. (ed.), 'An Unknown English Register of the Reign of Edward III', *EHR*, xlv (1930), 353–72

Bock, F. (ed.), 'Some New Documents Illustrating the Early Years of the Hundred Years War (1353–1356)', *Bull. John Rylands Lib.*, xv (1931), 60–99

Broome, D.M. (ed.), 'The Ransom of John II, King of France', *Camden Miscellany*, xiv (Royal Historical Society, Camden Third Series, xxxvii) (1926)

Broome, D.M., and Tout, T.F., 'A national balance sheet for 1362–3', *EHR* xxxv (1920), 26–54
Broussillon, B. de, *La Maison de Craon, 1050–1480. Étude historique accompagné du cartulaire de Craon*, 2 vols (1893)
Burghersh, Bartholemew, Letter to John Beauchamp, in Chandos Herald, *The Black Prince. An Historical Poem*, ed. H.O Coxe (1842), 36
Calendar of Close Rolls, 45 vols (1892–1954)
Calendar of Documents relating to Scotland, ed. J. Bain, 5 vols (1881–1988)
Calendar of Entries in the Papal Registers relating to Great Britain and Ireland. Petitions to the Pope, i *(1342–1419)*, ed. W.H. Bliss (1896)
Calendar of Entries in the Papal Registers relating to Great Britain and Ireland. Papal letters, ed. W.H. Bliss and C. Johnson, 14 vols (1894–1961)
Calendar of Fine Rolls, 22 vols (1911–63)
Calendar of Inquisitions Miscellaneous, 7 vols (1916–69)
Calendar of Letter Books of the City of London, ed. R.R. Sharpe, 11 vols (1899–1912)
Calendar of Letters from the Mayor and Corporation of the City of London, circa 1350–1370, ed. R.R. Sharpe (1885)
Calendar of Patent Rolls, 70 vols (1891–1982)
Cartulaire de Cormery, ed. J.-J. Bourassé (1861)
Cartulaire de Montier-la-Celle, ed. C. Lalore (1882)
Cartulaire des sires de Rays (1160–1449), ed. R. Blanchard, 2 vols, *AHP*, xxviii, xxx (1898–9)
Carus-Wilson, E.M., and Coleman, O. (ed.), *England's Export Trade* (1963)
Catalogo del Archivo General de Navarra, Catalogo de la Seccion de Comptos, ed. J. Ramon Castro and F. Idoate, 52 vols (1952–74)
Catalogue de comptes royaux des règnes de Philippe VI et de Jean II, 1328–1364, 1ère partie, ed. R. Cazelles (1984)
Catalogue des rolles Gascons, Normans et Francois conservés dans les archives de la Tour de Londres, ed. T. Carte, 2 vols (1743)
Chaplais, P., 'Chartes en déficit dans les cartons "Angleterre" du Tresor des Chartes', *BEC*, cix (1951), 96–103
Chaplais, P., 'Documents concernant l'Angleterre et l'Écosse anciennement conservés à la Chambre des Comptes de Lille', *Revue du Nord*, xxxviii (1956), 185–210
Chaplais, P., 'Some documents regarding the fulfillment and interpretation of the treaty of Bretigny (1361–1369)', *Camden Miscellany*, xix (Royal Historical Society, Camden Third Series, lxxx) (1952)
Chaplais, P., *English Medieval Diplomatic Practise*, i: *Documents and Interpretation* (1982)
Chartulary of Winchester Cathedral, ed. A.W. Goodman (1927)
'Choix de pièces inédites', ed. J. Quicherat, *BEC*, xviii (1857), 352–69
Clement VI, *Lettres closes, patentes et curiales se rapportant à la France*, ed. E. Deprez, J. Glenisson and G. Mollat (1901–61)
Combarieu, L., 'Analyse de quelques actes concernant Cajarc', *Bull. Soc. Études du Lot*, xxxix (1914), 167–82
Compte de Raoul de Louppy, gouverneur du Dauphiné, de 1361 à 1369, ed. U. Chevalier (1886) [for corrections, see Prou (1886)]
Compte des recettes et dépenses du roi de Navarre en France et en Normandie de 1367 à 1370, ed. E. Izarn (1885)
'Compte de transport de métal précieux de Londres à Bordeaux en 1357', ed. P.-J. Capra, *Bull. Soc. Fr. Numism.*, 2e année (1957), 136–7
*Comptes de l'argenterie des rois de France au xiv*e *siècle*, ed. L. Douet d'Arcq (1851)
Comptes consulaires d'Albi (1359–1360), ed. A. Vidal (1900)
Comptes consulaires de la Cité et du Bourg de Rodez, 1ere partie: *Cité*, ed. H. Bousquet, 2 vols (1926–43)

Comptes consulaires de Saint-Antonin du XIVe siècle, ed. R. Latouche (1923)
Controversy between Sir Richard Scrope and Sir Robert Grosvenor in the Court of Chivalry, 2 vols, ed. N.H. Nicolas (1832)
Cortes de los antiguos reinos de Aragon, y de Valencia y pricipiado de Cataluña. Cortes de Cataluña, 26 vols (1896–1922)
Cosneau, E., *Grands traités de la guerre de Cent ans* (1889)
David II, *The Acts of David II, King of Scots*, ed. B. Webster (1982)
Delpit, J., *Collection générale des documents français qui se trouvent en Angleterre* (1847)
Documents sur l'ancien hopital d'Aubrac, ed. J.-L. Rigal and P.-A. Verlaguet, 2 vols (1913–34)
Documents des archives de la Chambre des Comptes de Navarre (1196–1384), ed. J.-A. Brutails (1890)
'Documents comptables des Archives Générales de Navarre concernant la Normandie durant les règnes de Philippe Ie d'Evreux (1328–1345) et Charles le Mauvais (1349–1387), rois de Navarre', ed. M. Baudot, *Cahiers Léopold Delisle*, xiv (1965), fasc. 1, 75–118
Documents pour l'histoire de St.-Hilaire de Poitiers, ed. L. Rédet, *Mems. Soc. Antiq. Ouest*, 1ère série, xiv (1847), xix (1852)
Documents historiques sur la maison de Galard, ed. J. Noulens, 4 vols (1871–6)
Documents historiques. . . relatifs a la seigneurie de Monaco, ed. G. Saige, i (1905)
Documents inédits concernant la ville et le siège du baillage d'Amiens extraits des régistres du Parlement de Paris et du Trésor des Chartes, i, *xiv*e *siècle (1296–1412)*, ed. E. Maugis (1908)
*Documents inédits pour servir à l'histoire du Maine au xiv*e *siècle*, ed. B. de Broussillon (1905)
Documents linguistiques de la France (série francoprovencale). Documents linguistiques du Lyonnais, ed. P. Durdilly (1975)
Documents sur la maison de Durfort, ed. N. de la Peña (1977)
'Documents nouveaux sur Étienne Marcel', ed. S. Luce, *MSHP*, vi (1879), 304–24
Documents relatifs au clos des galées de Rouen et aux armées de la mer des rois de France de 1293 à 1418, ed. A. Chazelas, 2 vols (1977–8)
'Documents relatifs à l'histoire de la ville de Mâcon (1362–1367)', ed. L. Michon, *Rev. soc. savantes*, 5e série, i (1870), 161–83
Documents sur la ville de Millau, ed J. Artières (1930)
*Douze comptes consulaires d'Albi du xiv*e *siècle*, ed. A. Vidal, 2 vols (1906–11)
Edward, Prince of Wales, Campaign letters (i) 25 December 1355, to the Bishop of Winchester, in Avesbury, *G. Edwardi*, 434–7; (ii) 20 October 1356, to the Bishop of Worcester, ed. C. Lyttelton, *Archaeologia*, i (1754), 212–5; (iii) 22 October 1356, to the Corporation of London, in Delachenal, *Histoire de Charles V*, ii, 381–4; (iv) undated (ca. October 1356) to prior of Winchester, in *Chartulary of Winchester Cathedral*, 162–3; (v) 5 April 1367, to Joan of Kent, ed. A.E. Prince, 'A letter of Edward the Black Prince describing the battle of Nájera in 1367', EHR, xli (1926), 415–7
Exchequer rolls of Scotland, ed. J. Stuart et al., 23 vols (1878–1908)
'Extraits de journaux du Trésor (1345–1419)', ed. H. Moranvillé, *BEC*, xlix (1888), 149–214, 368–452
Faucon, M., 'Prêts faits aux rois de France par Clement VI, Innocent VI et le comte de Beaufort (1345–1360)', *BEC*, xl (1879), 570–8
Foedera, conventiones, literae et acta publica, ed. T. Rymer, n.e. A. Clark et al., 7 vols (1816–69); *Appendices to the Report on Rymer's Foedera*, E, *A Chronological Catalogue of Materials Transcribed for the New Edition of the Foedera* (1869)
Gallia Christiana, 16 vols, ed. D. de Sainte-Marthe, F. Hodin, et al. (1716–1865)
Gallia Regia, ou état des officiers royaux des baillages et des sénéchaussés de 1328 à 1515, ed. G. Dupont-Ferrier, 7 vols (1942–65)
Gascogne dans les régistres du Trésor des Chartes, ed. C. Samaran (1966)
Guesnon, A.-H., 'Documents inédits sur l'invasion anglaise et les états au temps de Philippe VI et Jean le Bon', *BPH* (1897), 208–59

Historical Papers and Letters from the Northern Registers, ed. J. Raine (1873)
Hunger, V., *Quelques actes normands des XIVe, XVe et XVIe siècles*, 3 vols (1909–11)
Innocent VI, *Lettres secrètes et curiales*, ed. P. Gasnault, M.H. Laurent, and N. Gotteri, 4 vols (1959–in progress)
Innocent VI, 'Registrum epistolarum anni MCCCLXI', ed. E. Martène and U. Durand, *Thesaurus novus anecdotorum*, ii (1717), 843–1072
'Instructions pour la défense du duché de Bourgogne contre les Grandes Compagnies (20 septembre 1367)', ed. Mirot, L., *Annales de Bourgogne*, xiv (1942), 308–11
Inventaire des archives communales de la ville d'Aurillac antérieures à 1790, ed. G. Esquier, 2 vols 1906–11
Inventaire des archives de la ville de Poitiers, ed. L. Redet, *Mems. Soc. Antiq. Ouest*, 2e serie, v (1882)
Inventaire chronologique et analytique des chartes de la maison des Baux, ed. L. Barthélémy (1882).
Inventaire chronologique des chartes de la ville d'Arras. Documents, ed. A.-H. Guesnon (1862)
Inventaire chronologique des documents relatifs a l'histoire d'Ecosse conservés aux Archives du Royaume à Paris, ed. A. Teulet (1839)
'Inventaire qui contient les titres et privilèges de la maison consulaire de la ville du Puy', ed. A. Aymard, *Ann. Soc. agric., sci., arts et commerce du Puy*, xv (1850), 601–778
'Inventaire des documents normands de la collection Villevieille de la Bibliothèque Nationale', ed. M. Nortier, Société Parisienne d'Histoire et d'Archéologie Normande, *Répertoire périodique de documentation normande*, 2e série, no. 2 (1987)
'Inventaire raisonné et analytique des archives municipales de Cahors. 2e partie, xive)^', ed. E. Albe, *Bull. Soc. Études du Lot*, xli (1920), 1–48, xliii (1922), 1–28, xlv (1924), 29–99
Inventaire des sceaux de la Collection Clairambault à la Bibliothèque Nationale, ed. G. Demay, 2 vols (1885–6)
Inventaire des sceaux de la Collection des Pièces Originales du Cabinet des Titres à la Bibliothèque Nationale, J. Roman, i (1909)
Inventaire-sommaire des Archives Communales antérieures à 1790.
Ville d'Amiens, ed. G. Durand, 7 vols (1891–1925)
Ville de Clermont-Ferrand. Fonds de Montferrand, ed. E. Teilhard de Chardin, 2 vols (1922)
Ville de Lyon, Séries AA-CC, ed. F. Rolle, M.-C. Guigue, J. Vaësen, et al., 5 vols (1865–1962)
Ville de Périgueux, ed. M. Hardy (1897)
Ville de Riom, ed. F. Boyer (1892)
Ville de Toulouse, i, ed E. Roschach (1891)
Inventaire-sommaire des Archives Départmentales antérieures à 1790.
Basses-Pyrennées, ed. P. Raymond, 6 vols (1863–76)
Côte d'Or. Archives civiles. Série B: Chambre des Comptes de Bourgogne, ed. C. Rossignol and J. Garnier, 5 vols (1863–78)
Doubs. Archives civiles, Série B: Chambre des Comptes de Franche Comté, ed. J. Gauthier, 3 vols (1883–95)
Nord. Archives civiles, Série B: Chambre des Comptes de Lille, ed. Dehaisnes, J. Finot, A. Desplanque, et al., 9 vols (1899–1913)
Pas-de-Calais. Archives Civiles, Série A, ed. J.-M. Richard, 2 vols (1878–87)
'Inventaires de comptes royaux particuliers de 1328 à 1351', ed. R.-H. Bautier, *BPH* (1960), 773–837
Issues of the Exchequer, ed. F. Devon (1837)
Itinéraires de Philippe le Hardi et de Jean sans Peur, ed. E. Petit (1888)
John IV, Duke of Brittany, *Recueil des actes de Jean IV, duc de Bretagne*, ed. M. Jones (1980–3)
Johnson, C. (ed.), 'Negotiations for the Ransom of David Bruce in 1349', *EHR*, xxxvi (1921), 57–8

Johnson, C. (ed.), 'An Early Admiralty case', *Camden Miscellany*, xv (Royal Historical Society, Camden Third Series, xli) (1929)
'Journal des États Généraux réunis à Paris au mois d'Octobre 1356', ed. R. Delachenal, *Revue historique de droit français et étranger*, 3e série, xxiv (1900), 415–65
Journaux du Trésor de Philippe VI de Valois, ed. J. Viard (1899)
Jurades de la ville d'Agen (1345–1355), ed. A. Magen (1894)
Jurades de la ville de Bergerac, 14 vols, ed. G. Charrier (1892–1941)
Langlois, C.-V., 'Instructions remises aux deputés de la commune de Montpellier qui furent envoyées au roi pendant sa captivité en Angleterre (1358–1359)', *Mems. Soc. archéol. Montpellier*, viii (1892), 437–52
Languedoc et le Rouergue dans le Trésor des Chartes, ed. Y. Dossat, A.-M. Lemasson and P. Wolff (1983)
Larson, A., 'English Embassies during the Hundred Years War', *EHR*, lv (1940), 423–31
'Lettre à Charles le Mauvais', ed. H. Moranvillé, *BEC*, xlix (1888), 91–4
'Lettre originale d'Étienne Marcel et autres documents parisiens', ed. L. Delisle, *MSHP*, xxiv (1897), 51–60
'Lettres closes des premiers Valois', ed. J. Miret y Sans, *Le moyen age*, xx (1917–8), 53–88
'Lettres d'état enregistrées au Parlement de Paris sous le règne de Philippe de Valois', ed. J. Viard, *Bull. Soc. Hist. Fr.* (1897), 193–267, (1898), 177–249
Lettres de rois, reines et autres personnages des cours de France et d'Angleterre, ed. L.-A. Champollion-Figeac, 2 vols (1839–43)
Literae Cantuarienses, ed. J.B. Sheppard, 3 vols. (1887–9)
Livre des hommages d'Aquitaine. Resitution du second livre noir de la connétablie de Bordeaux, ed. J.-P. Trabut-Cussac (1959)
Livre Noir et les établissements de Dax, ed. F. Abadie, *AHG*, xxxvii (1902)
Mandements et actes divers de Charles V (1364–1380), ed. L. Delisle (1874)
Mirot, L. and Deprez, E., 'Les ambassades anglaises pendant la guerre de Cent ans. Catalogue chronologique (1327–1450)', *BEC*, lix (1898), 530–77, lx (1899), 177–214, lxi (1900), 20–58 [for corrections, see Larson, A.]
Monuments historiques. Cartons des rois, ed. J. Tardif (1866)
Monuments du procès de canonisation du bienheureux Charles de Blois duc de Bretagne, 1320–64, ed. F. Plaine (1921)
Morice, P.-H., *Mémoires pour servir de preuves à l'histoire ecclesiastique et civile de Bretagne*, 3 vols (1742–6)
Notices et extraits des documents manuscrits conservés dans les depôts publics de Paris et relatifs à l'histoire de la Picardie, ed. H. Cocheris, 2 vols (1854–8)
Ordonnances des rois de France de la troisième race, ed. D. Secousse et al., 21 vols (1729–1849)
Parliamentary Records of Scotland in the General Register House, Edinburgh, i, ed. W. Robertson (1804)
Pays de la Loire moyenne dans le Trésor des chartes. Berry, Blésois, Chartrain, Orléa-nais, Touraine, 1350–1502 (Archives nationales, JJ 80–235), ed. B. Chevalier (1993)
Perroy, E., 'Select Documents. France, England and Navarre from 1354 to 1364', *Bull. Institute of Historical Research*, xiii (1936), 151–4
Perroy, E., 'Quatre lettres du cardinal Guy de Boulogne', *Rev. du Nord*, xxxvi (1954), 159–64
Petit, E., 'Séjours de Jean II (1350–1356)', *BPH* (1896), 587–612
Petrarca, Francesco, *Le familiari*, ed. V. Rossi, 4 vols (1933–42)
Philip VI, King of France, 'Lettres closes, lettres "de par le roi" de Philippe de Valois', ed. R. Cazelles, *Bull. Soc. Hist. Fr.* (1956–1957), 61–225
'Pièces inédites relatives à Étienne Marcel et à quelques uns de ses principaux adhérents', ed. S. Luce, *BEC*, xxi.1 (1860), 73–92
Preuves de la maison de Polignac. Recueil de documents pour servir à l'histoire des anciennes

provinces de Velay, Auvergne, Gévaudan, Vivarais, Forez, etc., ixe-xviiie siècle, ed. A. Jacotin, 5 vols (1898–1906)

'Procès-verbal de délivrance à Jean Chandos commissaire du roi d'Angleterre des places françaises abandonnées par le traité de Brétigny', ed. A. Bardonnet, *Mems. Soc. stat. sci. et arts dep. Deux-Sèvres*, 2e série, vi (1866), 2e partie, 119–282

'Procès-verbal de visite des places fortifiées du baillage de Melun en 1367', ed. H. Moranvillé, *Annales de la Société historique et archéologique du Gâtinais*, xxi (1903), 304–19

Recueil de documents concernant la commune et la ville de Poitiers, 2 vols, ed. E. Audouin, *AHP*, xliv, xlvi (1926–8)

Recueil des documents concernant le Poitou contenus dans les registres de la Chancellerie de France, ed. P. Guerin and L. Célier, 14 vols, *AHP*, xi, xiii, xvii, xix, xxi, xxiv, xxvi, xxix, xxxii, xxxv, xxxviii, xli, l, lvi (1881–1958)

Recueil de documents relatifs à l'histoire du droit municipal en France des origines à la Révolution, ed. G. Espinas, 3 vols (1934–43)

Recueil de documents relatifs à l'histoire des monnaies frappées par les rois de France, ed. L.F.J.C. de Saulcy, 4 vols (1879–92)

Recueil des monuments inédits de l'histoire du tiers état, ed. A. Thiery, 4 vols (1850–70)

Recueil de titres et autres pièces justificatives employées dans le Mémoire sur la constitution politique de la ville de Périgueux (1775)

Register of Edward the Black Prince, 4 vols (1930–33)

Régistres des comptes municipaux de la ville de Tours, ed. J. Delaville le Roulx, 2 vols (1878–81)

Régistres de l'échevinage de Saint-Jean d'Angély, 3 vols, ed. D. d'Aussy, *AHSA*, xxiv, xxvi, xxxii (1895–1902)

Régistres du Trésor des Chartes. Inventaire analytique, iii, *Règne de Philippe de Valois*, ed. J. Viard and A. Vallée, 3 vols (1978–84)

'Relation de la visite des forteresses du baillage de Caen en 1371', ed. A de Caumont, *Mems. Soc. antiq. Normandie*, xi (1840), 185–204

'Répertoire analytique des actes de Charles de Blois', ed. L. Maitre, *Bull. Soc. Arch. Nantes*, xlv (1904), 247–73

'Répertoire des documents copiés ou analysés par dom Lenoir concernant la région de Vire et ses principaux familles, 1271–1724', ed. E. Taverson, Société Parisienne d'Histoire et d'Archéologie Normande, *Répertoire périodique de documentation normande*, 2e série, no.1 (1984)

Reports from the Lords Committees. . . touching the Dignity of a Peer, 5 vols (1820–9)

Richard, J.-M., 'Instructions données aux commissaires chargés de lever la rançon du roi Jean (1360)', J.-M. Richard, *BEC*, xxxvi (1875), 81–90

Rotuli Parliamentorum, et J. Strachey et al., 7 vols (1767–1832)

Rotuli Parliamentorum Angliae hactenus inediti, ed. H.G. Richardson and G.O. Sayles (1935)

Rotuli Scotiae, ed. D. Macpherson et al., 2 vols (1814)

Sceaux Gascons du moyen age, ed. P. La Plagne Barris (1888–92)

Secousse, D., *Recueil de pièces servant de preuves au Mémoires sur les troubles excités par Charles II, dit le Mauvais, roi de Navarre et comte d'Evreux* (1755)

'Sources de l'histoire de la Normandie aux Archives Nationales. Serie KK: Actes concernant les états provinciaux', ed. F. Blanchet, *Cahiers Léopold Delisle*, xv, fascs. 3–4 (1966), 21–32

Spicilegium Brivatense. Recueil de documents historiques relatifs au Brivadois et à l'Auvergne, ed. A. Chassaing (1886)

*Timbal, P-C., *La guerre de Cent ans vue à travers les régistres du Parlement (1337–1369)* (1961)

Titres de la maison ducale de Bourbon, ed. A. Huillard-Bréholles, 2 vols (1867–74)

Trésor des Chartes d'Albret, i, *Les archives de Vayres*, ed. J. Marquette (1973)

Urban V, *Lettres secrètes et curiales du pape Urbain V (1362–1370) se rapportant à la France*, ed. P. Lecacheux and G. Mollat (1902–55)

Vandenpeereboom, A. (ed.), *Ypriana. Notices, études, notes et documents sur Ypres*, vii (1883)
Viard, J., 'Itinéraire de Philippe VI de Valois', *BEC*, lxxiv (1913), 74–128, 524–619, lxxxiv (1923), 166–70
Wardrobe Book of William de Norwell, 12 July 1338 to 27 May 1340, ed M. Lyon, B. Lyon and H.S. Lucas (1983)
Wingfield, Sir John, Letters (i) 23 December 1355, to the Bishop of Winchester, in Avesbury, *G. Edwardi*, 439–43; (ii) 22 January 1356, to Sir Richard Stafford, in *ibid.*, 445–7

C NARRATIVE AND LITERARY SOURCES

Asterisks * mark editions having important documentary notes or appendices

Anonimalle chronicle, 1333–1381, ed. V.H. Galbraith (1927)
Avesbury, Robert of, *De gestis mirabilibus regis Edwardi tertii*, ed. E.M. Thompson (1889)
Ayala, Pedro Lopez de, *Crónicas de los reyes de Castilla. Don Pedro, Don Enrique II, Don Juan I, Don Enrique III*, ed. E. de Llaguno Amirola, 2 vols (1779–80)
Azario, Pietro, *Liber gestorum in Lombardia*, ed. F. Cognasso, *RIS(2)*, xvi.4 (1925–39)
Baker, Geoffrey le, *Chronicon*, ed. E.M. Thompson (1889)
'Bataille de trente', ed. H.R. Brush, *Modern philology*, ix (1911–2), 511–44, x (1912–3), 82–136
*Bel, Jean le, *Chronique*, ed. J. Viard and E. Déprez, 2 vols (1904–5)
Bower, Walter, *Scotichronicon*, ed. D.E.R. Watt, 9 vols (1989–98)
'Breve chronicon Flandriae', *CCF*, iii, 1–30
Brut, or the Chronicles of England, ed. F.W.D. Brie (1906–8)
Chandos Herald, *La vie du Prince Noir*, ed. D.B. Tyson (1975)
Charny, Geoffroy de, 'Le Livre messire Geoffroy de Charny', ed. A. Piaget, *Romania*, xxvi (1897), 394–411
Charny, Geoffroy de, 'Le livre de chevalerie', *KOF*, i.3, 462–533
Christine de Pisan, *Le livre des fais et bonnes meurs du sage roy Charles V*, ed. S. Solente, 2 vols (1936–40)
Chronicon anonymi Cantuariensis: see Reading, John of
'Chronicon Briocense', ed. Morice, *Preuves*, i, 7–102
'Chronicon Britannicum', ed. Morice, *Preuves*, i, 1–7, 102–17
'Chronicon Comitum Flandrensium', *CCF*, i, 34–257
'Chronique de Bazas', *AHG*, xv (1874), 1–67
Chronique du bon duc Loys de Bourbon, ed. A-M. Chazaud (1876)
'Chronique de Maillezais', ed. P. Marchegay, *BEC*, ii (1840–1), 148–68
**Chronique normande du xiv*^e^ *siècle*, ed. A and E. Molinier (1882)
Chronique des quatre premiers Valois (1327–1393), ed. S. Luce (1862)
'Chronique d'Uzerche, La suite de la', ed. G. de Manteyer, *Mélanges Paul Fabre. Études d'histoire du moyen age* (1902)
Chroniques de la ville de Metz, ed. J.-F. Huguenin (1838)
Chronographia regum Francorum, ed. H. Moranvillé, 3 vols (1891–7)
'Complainte sur la bataille de Poitiers', ed. C. de Beaurepaire, *BEC*, 3e série, ii (1851), 257–63
Corpus chronicorum Flandriae, ed. J.J. de Smet, 4 vols (1837–65)
*Cuvelier, *Chronique de Bertrand du Guesclin*, ed. E. Charrière, 2 vols (1839)
Donato di Neri, *Cronica Senese*, ed. A. Lisini and F. Jacometti, *RIS(2)*, xv.6 (1939)
Esquerrier et Miègeville, Arnaud, *Chroniques romanes des comtes de Foix composées au xv*^e^ *siècle*, ed. H. Courteault and F. Pasquier (1893)
Eulogium historiarum, ed. F.S. Haydon, 3 vols (1858–63)
Fordun, John, *Chronica gentis Scotorum*, ed. W.F. Skene (1871)
'Fragment d'une chronique latine', ed. Secousse, *Preuves*, 599–630

Fragments d'une chronique inédite relatifs aux événements militaires arrivés en Basse-Normandie, de 1353 à 1389, ed. L. Delisle (1895)
Froissart, Jean, *Chroniques de J. Froissart*, ed. S. Luce, G. Raynaud, L. and Mirot, A., 15 vols (1869–in progress) [all citations of the text are in this edition]
*Froissart, Jean, *Oeuvres de Froissart. Chroniques*, ed. Kervyn de Lettenhove, 25 vols (1867–77) [cited as *KOF*; all references are to the documentary notes and appendices]
Grandes chroniques de France, ed. J. Viard, 10 vols (1920–53) [to the death of Philip VI: all references are to vols. ix and x]
**Grandes chroniques de France. Chronique des règnes de Jean II et de Charles V*, ed. R. Delachenal, 4 vols (1910–20)
Gray, Sir Thomas of Heton, *Scalacronica*, ed. J. Stevenson (1836)
Higden, Ranulph, *Polychronicon*, Continuations (i) 1352–1376, ed. J.R. Lumby, Higden, Ranulph, *Polychronicon* (Appendix), viii (1882), 407–28; (ii) 1348–1381, by John of Malvern, ed. J.R. Lumby, *ibid.*, 355–406; (iii) 1337–77, ed. T. Hog in Murimuth, Adam, *Chronica* (1846), 171–227; (iv) 1355–77, ed. J. Taylor, 'A Wigmore Chronicle, 1355–1377', *English Historical Literature in the Fourteenth Century* (1987), 284–300
Istore et croniques de Flandres, ed. Kervyn de Lettenhove, 2 vols (1879–80)
Knighton, Henry, *Chronicle, 1337–1376*, ed. G.H. Martin (1995)
Langland, William, *The vision of William concerning Piers the Plowman*, 2 vols (1886)
La Tour Landry, *Le livre du chevalier de La Tour Landry*, ed. A. de Montaiglon (1854)
*Lescot, R., *Chronique*, ed. J. Lemoine (1896)
Liber Pluscardensis, ed. F.J.H. Skene, 2 vols (1877–80)
Livre des fais du bon messire Jehan le Maingre, dit Boucicaut, ed. D. Lalande (1985)
Machaut, Guillaume de, *Oeuvres*, ed E. Hoepffner, 3 vols (1908–31)
Malvern, John of: see Higden
Martin de Bois-Gautier, 'Vita Mariae de Malliaco', *Acta Sanctorum*, March, iii (1736), 737–47
Mascaro, Jacme, 'Le Libre de memorias', ed. C. Barbier, *Revue des langues romanes*, 4e série, iv (1890), 36–100
'Miracula S. Gatiani', ed. C. Chevalier, 'Les origines de l'église de Tours', *Mems. Soc. archéol. Touraine*, xxi (1871), 610–17
Monte-Belluna, Francois de, 'Le Tragicum argumentum de miserabili statu regni Francie (1357)', ed. M.A. Vernet, *Bull. Soc. Hist. Fr.* (1962–3), 101–163
Muisit, Gilles li, *Chronique et annales*, ed. H. Lemaître (1906)
Noyal, Jean de, 'Fragments inédits de la chronique de Jean de Noyal', *Bull. Soc. Hist. Fr.* (1883), 246–75
Pere III el Ceremoniós, 'Crónica', ed. F. Soldevila, *Les Quatre Grans Cróniques* (1971)
Petit Thalamus de Montpellier, La chronique romane, ed. F. Pegat, E. Thomas, and E. Alicot (1840),
Petite chronique francoise de l'an 1270 à l'an 1356, ed. L. Douet d'Arcq, *Mélanges de litterature et d'histoire receuillis et publiés par la Société des bibiophiles français*, 2e partie (1867)
Political Poems and Songs, ed. T. Wright, 2 vols (1859–61)
Reading, John of, *Chronica Johannis de Reading et Anonymi Cantuariensis, 1346–1367*, ed. J. Tait (1914)
Récits d'un bourgeois de Valenciennes (xive siècle), ed. Kervyn de Lettenhove (1877)
Venette, Jean de, 'Continuatio Chronici Guillelmi de Nangiaco', ed. H. Géraud, *Chronique latine de Guillaume de Nangis*, ii (1843), 178–378
Villani, Matteo and Filippo, *Historia universalis*, ed. L.A. Muratori, *RIS(1)*, xiv (1729), 1–770
Vitae paparum Avenionensium, ed. E. Baluze, n.e., G. Mollat, 4 vols (1916–22)
Walsingham, Thomas, *Historia Anglicana*, ed. H.T. Riley, 2 vols (1863–4)
Wigmore Chronicle: see Higden

Wynnere and Wastoure, ed. S. Trigg (1990)
Wyntoun, Andrew of, *Orygynale Cronykil of Scotland*, ed. D. Laing, 3 vols (1872–9)

D SELECTED SECONDARY WORKS

Asterisks * mark works having important documentary appendices

Alauzier, L. d', 'Comptes consulaires de Cajarc (Lot) au xive siècle', *BPH* (1957)(1), 89–103
Alauzier, L. d', 'Trois prises de Fons par les Anglais au xive siècle', *Bull. Soc. Études du Lot*, lxxviii (1957)(2), 168–74
Allmand, C., *The Hundred Years War. England and France at War, c.1300–c.1450* (1988)
André-Michel, R., 'La construction des remparts d'Avignon au xive siècle', *Société française d'archéologie, Congrès archéologique de France, LXXVIe session tenu à Avignon en 1909* (1910), ii, 341–60
André-Michel, R., 'Anglais, bretons et routiers à Carpentras sous Jean le Bon et Charles V', *Mélanges d'histoire offerts à M. Charles Bémont* (1913), 341–52
André-Michel, R., 'Les défenseurs des chateaux et des villes fortes dans le Comtat-Venaissin au xive siècle', *BEC*, lxxvi (1915), 315–30
Anselme, Le P., *Histoire généalogique et chronologique de la maison royale de France*, 3rd ed., 9 vols. (1726–33)
Armitage-Smith, S., *John of Gaunt* (1904)
*Artières, J., 'Notice historique sur les libertés, privilèges, coutumes et franchises de la ville de Millau en Rouergue, suivi de nouveaux documents inédits concernant la ville de Millau', *Méms. Soc. L. Sci. et Arts de l'Aveyron*, xvi (1900–5), 171–312.
Atlas historique des villes de France (1982–in progress)
Autrand, F., *Naissance d'un grand corps de l'état. Les gens du Parlement de Paris* (1981)
Autrand, F., 'La déconfiture. La bataille de Poitiers (1356) à travers quelques textes français des xive et xve siecles', *Guerre et société en France, en Angleterre et en Bourgogne, xive-xve siecles*, ed. P. Contamine, C. Giry-Deloison and M. Keen (1991), 93–121
Avout, J. d', *Le meurtre d'Etienne Marcel* (1960)
Ayton, A., *Knights and warhorses. Military service and the English aristocracy under Edward III* (1994)
*Balasque, J. and Dulaurens, E., *Études historiques sur la ville de Bayonne*, 3 vols. (1862–75)
Balfour-Melville, E.W.M., *Edward III and David II* (1954)
Balfour-Melville, E.W.M., 'David II's Appeal to the Pope', *Scottish Historical Review*, xli (1962), 86
*Baluze, E., *Histoire généalogique de la maison d'Auvergne*, 2 vols (1708)
Baratier, E., *La démographie provençale du XIIIe au XVIe siècle* (1961)
Barber, R., *Edward Prince of Wales and Aquitaine* (1978)
Barbot, A., *Histoire de la Rochelle*, ed. D. d'Aussy, 3 vols, *AHSA* xiv, xvii, xviii (1886–90)
Barker, J.R.V., *The tournament in England, 1100–1400* (1986)
Barnes, J., *The history of that Most Victorious Monarch Edward III* (1688)
Barnie, J., *War in Medieval English Society. Social Values in the Hundred Years War, 1377–99* (1974)
Bautier, R.H., 'Recherches sur la chancellerie royale au temps de Philippe VI', *BEC*, cxxii (1964), 89–176; cxxiii (1965), 313–459
*Beauvillé, V. de, *Histoire de la ville de Montdidier*, 3 vols (1875)
Bennett, M. J., *Community, Class and Careerism. Cheshire and Lancashire Society in the age of Sir Gawain and the Green Knight* (1983)
*Bertrandy, M., *Étude sur les chroniques de Froissart. Guerre de Guienne, 1345–1346* (1870)
Billot, C., *Chartres à la fin du moyen age* (1987)
Bois, G., *Crise du feodalisme* (1976)

Booth, P.H.W., *The Financial Administration of the Lordship and County of Chester, 1272–1377* (1981)
Borderie, A. le Moyne de la, *Histoire de Bretagne*, 6 vols (1905–14)
Boudet, M., 'Assauts, sièges et blocus de Saint-Flour par les anglais pendant la guerre de cent ans, 1356–1391', *Revue d'Auvergne*, x (1893), 337–67
*Boudet, M., 'Les états d'Issoire de 1355 et leurs commissaires royaux', *Annales du midi*, xii (1900)(1), 33–66
Boudet, M., *Thomas de la Marche, bâtard de France et ses aventures (1318–1361)* (1900)(2)
Boudet, M., *Les baillis royaux et ducaux de la Haute-Auvergne* (1906)
Boudet, M., 'Note sur le commencement de l'invasion anglaise en Auvergne pendant la guerre de cent ans', *Bull. hist. et sci. de l'Auvergne*, 2e série (1908), 21–48
Boursier, A., *Histoire de la ville et chatellenie de Creil* (1883)
Boutiot, T., *Histoire de la ville de Troyes et de la Champagne méridionale*, 5 vols (1870–80)
Bouton, A., *Le Maine. Histoire économique et sociale, XIVe, XVe et XVIe siècles* (1970)
Boutruche, R., *La crise d'une société. Seigneurs et paysans du Bordelais pendant la guerre de Cent ans* (1963)
Brachet, A., *Pathologie mentale des rois de France* (1903)
Breuils, A., 'Jean I, Comte d'Armagnac et le mouvement national dans le midi au temps du Prince Noir', *Revue des Questions Historiques*, lix (1896), 44–102
Bridbury, A.R., *England and the Salt Trade in the Later Middle Ages* (1955)
Brief Note upon the battles of Saintes and Mauron, 1351 and 1352 (1918)
British Atlas of Historic Towns, iii, *The City of London from Prehistoric Times to c. 1520*, ed. M.C. Lobel (1989)
Brown, R.A., Colvin, H.M., and Taylor, A.J., *The History of the King's Works*, i-ii, *The Middle Ages* (1963)
Burley, S.J., 'The victualling of Calais, 1347–65', *Bull. Institute of Historical Research*, xxxi (1958), 49–57
Burne, A.H., *The Crécy War* (1955)
Calonne, A. de, *Histoire de la ville d'Amiens*, 3 vols (1899–1906)
Calvet, 'Prise de possession par le roi d'Angleterre de la ville de Cahors', *Rec. trav. Soc. ag., sci. et arts d'Agen*, v (1850), 167–209
Campbell, J., 'Scotland and the Hundred Years War in the 14th century', *Europe in the Late Middle Ages*, ed. J. Hale, R. Highfield and B. Smalley (1965), 184–216
Capra, P.-J., 'Recherches sur la valeur des monnaies dans le Bordelais au temps de la lieutenance du Prince Noir (1354–1357)', *BPH* (1957), 471–563
Capra, P.-J., 'Le séjour du Prince Noir, lieutenant du roi, à l'archevêché de Bordeaux', *Rev. hist. de Bordeaux et du dép. Gironde* (1958), 241–52
Capra, P.-J., 'Le siège d'Aiguillon en juin 1354', *Fédération historique du sud-ouest, Fédération des sociétés académiques et savantes Languedoc-Pyrenées-Gascogne. Actes des XIVe et XIVe Congrès d'etudes régionales* (1962), 201–12
Capra, P.-J., 'Les bases sociales du pouvoir anglo-gascon au milieu du XIVe siècle', *Le moyen age*, lxxxi (1975), 273–99, 447–73
Carr, A.D., 'Welshmen and the Hundred Years War', *Welsh History Review*, iv (1968), 21–46
Causse, B., *Église, finance et royauté. La floraison des décimes dans la France du moyen age* (1988)
Cazelles, R., *La société politique et la crise de la royauté sous Philippe de Valois* (1958)
Cazelles, R., 'Le parti navarrais jusqu'à la mort d'Étienne Marcel', *BPH* (1960), 839– 69
Cazelles, R., 'Les mouvements révolutionnaires du milieu di XIVe siècle et le cycle de l'action politique', *Rev. hist.*, ccxxviii.2 (1962)(1), 279–312
Cazelles, R., 'La peste de 1348–1349 en langue d'oil: épidemie prolétarienne et enfantine', *BPH* (1962)(2), 293–305
Cazelles, R., 'Quelques réflexions à propos des mutations de la monnaie royale française

(1295–1360)', *Le moyen age*, lxxii (1966), 83–105, 251–78
Cazelles, R., *Nouvelle histoire de Paris de la fin du règne de Philippe Auguste à la mort de Charles V, 1223–1380* (1972)
Cazelles, R., 'La stabilisation de la monnaie par la création du franc (decembre 1360)-blocage d'une société', *Traditio*, xxxii (1976), 293–311
Cazelles, R., *Société politique, noblesse et couronne sous Jean le Bon et Charles V* (1982)
Chaplais, P., 'The Court of Sovereignty of Guyenne (Edward III-Henry VI) and its antecedents', *Documenting the Past. Essays in Medieval History Presented to George Peddy Cuttino*, ed. J.S. Hamilton and P.J. Bradley (1989), 137–53
Charmasse, A. de, 'L'église d'Autun pendant la guerre de cent ans (1358–1373)', *Mems. Soc. Éduenne*, n.s., xxvi (1898), 1–135
Charmasse, A. de, 'Note sur le passage et le séjour des Grandes Compagnies dans le prévôté de Baigneux-les-juifs en 1364 et 1365', *Mems. Soc. Éduenne*, n.s., ix (1880), 499–507
*Chérest, A., *Vézélay. Étude historique*, 3 vols (1863–8)
*Chérest, A., *L'archiprêtre. Épisodes de la guerre de Cent ans au xive siècle* (1879)
Chéruel, A., *Histoire de Rouen pendant l'époque communale, 1150–1382*, 2 vols (1844)
Chevalier, B., *Tours. Ville royale, 1356–1520* (1975)
Chevalier, B., *Les bonnes villes de France du XIVe au XVIe siècle* (1982)
Clément-Simon, G., 'Notice de quelques manuscrits d'une bibliothèque limousine, iii, xive siècle. Livres de raison d'un homme d'affaires limousin', *Bull. soc. sci. hist. et archéol. de la Corrèze*, xvi (1894), 147–63
Combarieu, L., *Une ville de Quercy pendant la guerre de Cent ans* (1881)
*Compayré, C., *Études historiques et documents inédits sur l'Albigeois, le Castrais et l'ancien diocèse de Lavaur* (1841)
Cokayne, G.E., *The Complete Peerage*, ed. V. Gibbs et al., 12 vols (1910–59)
Contamine, P., 'The French nobility and the war', *The Hundred Years War*, ed. K. Fowler (1971), 135–62
Contamine, P., *Guerre, état et société à la fin du moyen age. Étude sur les armées des rois de France, 1337–1494* (1972)
Contamine, P., *L'Oriflamme de St.-Denis aux xive et xve siècles* (1975)
Contamine, P., *La vie quotidienne pendant la guerre de Cent ans* (1976)
Contamine, P., 'Les fortifications urbaines en France à la fin du moyen age: aspects financiers et économiques', *Revue historique*, cclx (1978), 23–47
Contamine, P., *La guerre au moyen age* (1980)
*Cordey, J., *Les comtes de Savoie et les rois de France pendant la guerre de Cent ans* (1911)
Coville, A., 'Les États-Généraux de 1332 et 1357', *Le moyen age*, vi (1893), 57–63
*Coville, A., *Les états de Normandie. Leurs origines et leur developpement au xive siècle* (1894)
Coville, A., 'Écrits contemporains sur la peste de 1348 à 1350', *Histoire littéraire de la France*, xxxvii (1938), 325–90
Coville, A., 'Poèmes historiques de l'avènement de Philippe VI de Valois au traité de Calais (1328–1360)', *Histoire littéraire de la France*, xxxviii (1949), 259–333
Cox, E.L., *The Green Count of Savoy. Amadeus VI and Transalpine Savoy in the Fourteenth Century* (1967)
Cuttler, S.H., *The Law of Treason and Treason Trials in Later Medieval France* (1981)
*Daumet, G., *Étude sur l'alliance de la France et la Castille au xive et au xve siècles* (1898)
Débat, A., 'Trois lettres de Gilbert de Cantobre pour la défence du Rouergue, 18 et 20 avril 1347', *Proc-verb. Soc. lettres, sci. et arts de l'Aveyron*, xliv (1983), 66–77
Deck, S., *La ville d'Eu. Son histoire, ses institutions (1151–1475)* (1924)
*Delaborde, H.-F., *Jean de Joinville et les seigneurs de Joinville* (1894)
*Delachenal, R., *Histoire des avocats au Parlement de Paris*, 1300–1600 (1885)
*Delachenal, R., 'Premières négociations de Charles le Mauvais avec les Anglais

(1354–1355)', *BEC*, lxi (1900), 253–82
*Delachenal, R., *Histoire de Charles V*, 5 vols (1909–31)
*Delisle, L., *Histoire du château et des sires de Saint-Sauveur-le-Vicomte* (1867)
Denholm-Young, N., *The Country Gentry in the Fourteenth Century* (1969)
*Denifle, H., *La guerre de Cent ans et les désolations des églises, monastères et hopitaux en France*, i, *Jusqu'à la mort de Charles V (1380)* (1899)
Déprez, E., 'La querelle de Bretagne de la captivite de Charles de Blois à la majorité de Jean IV de Montfort (1347–1362)', *Mems. Soc. hist. et archéol. de Bretagne*, vii (1926), 25–60
Desportes, P., *Reims et les Remois aux xiii*[e] *et xiv*[e] *siècles* (1979)
Dessalles, L., *Périgueux et les deux derniers comtes de Périgord* (1847)
Dessalles, L., *Histoire du Périgord*, 3 vols (1883–5)
Diller, G.T., *Attitudes chevaleresques et réalités politiques chez Froissart* (1984)
Dion, R., *Le Val de Loire* (1934)
Dognon, P., *Les institutions politiques et administratives du pays de Languedoc du XIII*[e] *siècle aux guerres de religion* (1895)
Drouyn, L., *La Guyenne militaire*, 3 vols (1865)
Dubois, H., *Les foires de Chalon et le commerce dans la vallée de la Saône à la fin du moyen age (vers 1280–vers 1430)* (1976)
*Duhamel, L., 'Une ligue au XIVe siècle. Épisode du passage des grandes compagnies en France', *Bull. hist. et arch. de Vaucluse*, ii (1880), 102–15
Dupaquier, J. (ed.), *Histoire de la population française*, i, *Des origines a la renaissance* (1988)
Emden, A.B., *A Biographical Register of the University of Oxford to A.D. 1500*, 3 vols (1957)
Encyclopédie départmentale des Bouches-du-Rhône, ed. P. Masson, 16 vols (1913–37)
Faral, E., 'Robert le Coq et les États Généraux d'Octobre 1356', *Revue historique de droit français et étranger*, 4e série, xxiii (1945), 171–214
Fauré, C., *Étude sur l'administration et l'histoire du Comtat-Venaissin du XIII*[e] *au XV*[e] *siècle (1229–1417)* (1909)
Favreau, R., *La ville de Poitiers à la fin du moyen age* (1978)
Favreau, R., *La commanderie du Breuil-du-Pas et la guerre de Cent ans dans la Saintonge méridionale* (1986)
Favreau, R., 'La cession de La Rochelle à l'Angleterre en 1360', *La "France Anglaise" au moyen age. Actes du III*[e] *congrès nationale des sociétés savantes (Poitiers, 1986), Section d'histoire médiévale et de philologie*, i (1988), 217–31
*Filippini, F., 'La seconda legazione del cardinal Albornoz in Italia (1358–1367', *Studi storici*, xii (1903), 263–337; xiii (1904), 1–52; xiv (1905), 28–68
Fino, J.-F., *Forteresses de la France médiévale*, 3e ed. (1977)
Finot, J., *Recherches sur les incursions des anglais et des grandes compagnies dans le duché et le comté de Bourgogne à la fin du xiv*[e] *siècle* (1874)
Flammermont, J., 'La Jacquerie en Beauvaisis', *Rev. hist.*, ix (1879), 123–43
*Forestié, E., 'Hughes de Cardaillac et la poudre à canon', *Bull. Soc. archéol. Tarn-et-Garonne*, xxix (1901), 93–132, 185–222, 297–312
Fournier, G., *Le chateau dans la France médiévale* (1978)
Fournier, G. and Charbonnier, P., 'La maison forte en Auvergne', *La maison forte au moyen age*, ed. M. Bur (1986), 271–88
Fournier, P., *Le royaume d'Arles et de Vienne (1138–1378)* (1891)
Fourquin, G., *Les campagnes de la région Parisienne à la fin du moyen age* (1964)
Fowler, K., 'Les finances et la discipline dans les armées anglaises en France au xive siècle', *Actes du Colloque internationale de Cocherel, 16, 17 et 18 mai 1964, Les Cahiers Vernonnais*, no. 4 (1964), 55–84
*Fowler, K., *The King's Lieutenant. Henry of Grosmont Duke of Lancaster, 1310–1361* (1969)
Fowler, K., 'Truces', *The Hundred Years War*, ed. K. Fowler (1971), 184–215
Fowler, K., 'L'emploi des mercenaires par les pouvoirs ibériques et l'intervention militaire

anglaise en Espagne (vers 1361–vers 1379)', *Realidad e imagenes del poder. España a fines de la edad media*, ed. A. Rucquoi (1988), 23–55
*Frémaux, H., 'La famille d'Etienne Marcel, 1250–1397', *MSHP*, xxx (1903), 175–242
Fréville, E. de, 'Des Grandes Compagnies au quatorzième siècle', *BEC*, iii (1841–2), 258–81, v (1843–4), 232–53
Fryde, E.B., 'The English Farmers of the Customs', *Trans. Roy. Hist. Soc.*, 5th series, ix (1959), 1–17
Fryde, E.B., 'The Last Trials of Sir William de la Pole', *Econ. Hist. Rev.*, xv (1962), 17–30
Fryde, E.B., 'Some Business Transactions of York Merchants', *St. Anthony's Hall Publications*, xxix (1966), 3–27
Fryde, E.B., 'The Financial Policies of the Royal Government and Popular Resistance to them in France and England, c.1270–c.1420', *Revue Belge de philologie et d'histoire*, lvii (1979), 824–60
Fryde, E.B., *William de la Pole, Merchant and King's Banker (d. 1366)* (1988)
Garcia y Lopez, J. Catalina, *Castilla y León durante los reinados de Pedro I, Enrique II, Juan I y Enrique III*, 2 vols (1893)
Gardelles, J., *Les chateaux du moyen age dans la France du sud-ouest* (1972)
Garnier, E., 'Notice sur Robert de Fiennes, Connétable de France (1320–1384)', *BEC*, 3e série, iii (1852), 23–52
Gauvard, *'De grace especial'. Crime, état et société en France à la fin du moyen age* (1991)
*Germain, A., 'Projet de descente en Angleterre concerte entre le gouvernement français et le roi de Danemark Valdemar III pour la délivrance du roi Jean', *Mems. Soc. archéol. Montpellier*, iv (1855), 409–34
Goyheneche, M.E., 'Bayonne, port d'embarquement des Navarrais vers la Normandie', *Actes du Colloque internationale de Cocherel, 16, 17 et 18 mai 1964, Les Cahiers Vernonnais*, no. 4 (1964), 107–17
Gresser, P., *La Franche-Comté au temps de la guerre de Cent ans* (1989)
Guerout, J., 'Le Palais de la Cité à Paris des origines à 1417. Essai topographique et archéologique', *Mems. Féd. Socs. hist. et archéol. de Paris et de l'Île-de-France*, i (1949), 57–212, ii (1950), 21–204, iii (1951), 7–101
*Guigue, G., *Les tard-venus en Lyonnais, Forez et Beaujolais, 1356–1369* (1886)
*Guichenon, S., *Histoire généalogique de la maison de Savoie*, n.e., 4 vols (1778–80)
Guillemain, B., *La cour pontificale d'Avignon, 1309–1376* (1966)
Gutierrez de Velasco, A., 'Los ingleses en España', *Estudios de Edad Media de la Corona de Aragon*, iv (1951), 215–319
Harriss, G.L., *King, Parliament and Public Finance in Medieval England, to 1369* (1975)
*Hay du Chastelet, P., *Histoire de Bertrand du Guesclin* (1660)
Hébert, M., 'L'armée provençale en 1374', *Annales du Midi*, xci (1979), 5–27
Henneman, J.B., *Royal Taxation in Fourteenth Century France. The Development of War Financing, 1322–1356* (1971)
Henneman, J.B., *Royal Taxation in Fourteenth Century France. The Captivity and Ransom of John II, 1356–1370* (1976)
Hewitt, H.J., *The Black Prince's Expedition of 1355–1357* (1958)
Hewitt, H.J., *The Organisation of War under Edward III, 1338–62* (1966)
Higounet, C., *Le comté de Comminges de ses origines à son annexion à la couronne* (1949)
*Higounet, C., 'Un mandement du sénéchal d'Aquitaine sur le fouage de 1366', *Économies et sociétés au moyen age. Mélanges offerts à Édouard Perroy* (1973), 462–4
*Higounet-Nadal, A., 'Un dénombrement des paroisses et des feux de la sénéchaussé de Périgord en 1365', *BPH* (1962), 307–45
Higounet-Nadal, A., *Les comptes de la taille et les sources de l'histoire démographique de Périgueux au xive siècle* (1965)
Higounet-Nadal, A., *Périgueux aux xive et xve siècles. Étude de démographie historique* (1978)

Hillgarth, J.N., *The Spanish Kingdoms, 1250–1516*, i (1976)
Histoire générale de Paris. Atlas des anciens plans de Paris (1880)
Holmes, G.A., *The Estates of the Higher Nobility in Fourteenth Century England* (1957)
Honoré-Duvergé, S., 'Les partisans de Charles le Mauvais: les Picquigny', *BEC*, cvii (1947–8), 82–92
Honoré-Duvergé, S., 'L'origine du surnom de Charles le Mauvais', *Mélanges d'histoire du moyen age dediés à la mémoire de Louis Halphen* (1951), 345–50
Honoré-Duvergé, S., 'Notes sur la politique économique de Charles le Mauvais', *Actas del Primer Congreso Internacional de Estudios Pirenaicos. San Sebastian, 1950* (1952), 95–107
Honoré-Duvergé, S., 'Participation Navarraise à la bataille de Cocherel', *Actes du Colloque internationale de Cocherel, 16, 17 et 18 mai 1964, Les Cahiers Vernonnais*, no. 4 (1964), 99–106
Humbert, F., *Les finances municipales de Dijon du milieu du xive siècle à 1477* (1961)
*Hunger, V., 'Le rachat du fort d'Aunay-sur-Odon (Calvados) en 1363', *Bull. Soc. Antiq. Normandie*, xl (1932), 326–36
James, M.K., *Studies in the Medieval Wine Trade* (1971)
Jones, M., *Ducal Brittany, 1364–1399* (1970)
*Jones, M., 'Sir Thomas Dagworth et la guerre civile en Bretagne au xive siècle: quelques documents inédits', *Annales de Bretagne*, lxxxvii (1980), 621–39
Jones, M., 'La mort de Walter Huet (1373)', *Bull. Soc. d'études et de recherches historiques du pays de Retz*, iv (1984), 28–34
*Jones, M., 'Raoul de Caours', *Bull. Soc. d'études et de recherches historiques du pays de Retz*, vii (1987), 5–10
Jones, M., 'Les capitaines anglo-bretons et les marches entre la Bretagne et le Poitou de 1342 à 1373', *La "France Anglaise" au moyen age. Actes du IIIe congrès nationale des sociétés savantes (Poitiers, 1986), Section d'histoire médiévale et de philologie*, i (1988), 357–75
*Jones, M., 'Guillaume, sire de Latimer, et la Bretagne: un nouveau témoignage (1365)', *Charpiana. Mélanges offerts par ses amis à Jacques Charpy* (1991), 257–65
Jugie, P., 'L'activité diplomatique du Cardinal Gui de Boulogne en France au milieu du xive siècle', *BEC*, cxlv (1987), 99–127
Keen, M., *The Laws of War in the Late Middle Ages* (1965)
Keen, M., *Chivalry* (1984)
*Kervyn de Lettenhove, *Histoire de Flandre*, 6 vols (1847–50)
King, D.J.C., *Castellarium Anglicanum*, 2 vols (1983)
Labande, L.-H., 'Bertrand du Guesclin et les États Pontificaux de France. Passage des routiers en Languedoc (1365–1367). Guerre de Provence (1368)', *Mems. Acad. Vaucluse*, n.s., iv (1904), 43–80
Lacabane, L., 'Mémoire sur la mort d'Etienne Marcel, 1358', *BEC*, i (1839–40), 79–98
*Lacabane, L., 'De la poudre à canon et de son introduction en France', *BEC*, vi (1844), 28–57
*Lacabane, L., 'Mémoire sur les deux prétendues délivrances de Condom en 1369 et 1374', *BEC*, 3e série, ii (1851), 97–130
Lacoste, G., *Histoire générale de la province de Quercy*, ed. L. Combarieu and F. Cangardel, 4 vols (1883–6)
Lacour, R., *Le gouvernement de l'apanage de Jean, duc de Berry, 1360–1416* (1934)
*La Mure, J.-M. de, *Histoire des ducs de Bourbon et des comtes de Forez*, ed R. Chantelauze, 4 vols in 3 (1860–8)
Landry, A., *Essai économique sur les mutations des monnaies dans l'ancien France, de Philippe le Bel à Charles VII* (1969)
*La Roque, G.-A. de, *Histoire généalogique de la maison de Harcourt*, 4 vols (1662)
*La Roque, G.-A. de, *Traité du ban et arrière-ban* (1734)
Larrayoz-Zarranz, M., 'Reaccion de Carlos el Malo rey de Navarra a la noticia de la derrota

de Cocherel', *Actes du Colloque internationale de Cocherel, 16, 17 et 18 mai 1964, Les Cahiers Vernonnais*, no. 4 (1964), 119–141
*Latouche, R., 'Saint-Antonin de Rouergue et la domination anglaise au xive siècle (1358–1369)', *Mélanges d'histoire offerts a M. Charles Bémont* (1913), 305–315
*Lebeuf, J., *Mémoires concernant l'histoire civile et ecclesiastique d'Auxerre et de son ancien diocèse*, 4 vols (1851–5)
Lebeuf, J., *Histoire de la ville et de tout le diocèse de Paris*, ed. F. Bournon, 7 vols (1883–93)
Le Breton, C., *L'Avranchin pendant la guerre de Cent ans* (1879)
*Lecoy de la Marche, *Les relations politiques de la France avec le royaume de majorque*, 2 vols (1892)
*Ledos, G., 'Deux documents rélatifs aux Compagnies en Auvergne après 1360', *Revue de l'Auvergne*, vii (1890), 40–53
*Ledos, E., 'L'imposition d'Auvergne en janvier 1357', *Mélanges Julien Havet* (1895), 429–50
*Ledru, A., 'Le Maine sous le règne de Jean le Bon, 1350–1364', *Province du Maine*, vii (1899), 17–29, 66–74, 177–87, 218–26, 273–87, 322–32, 357–65, viii (1900), 70–5, 122–8, 203–6, 228–33, 267–71, 365–7, 384–9, ix (1901), 34–7, 164–71, 227–32, 254–63
*Le Grand, L., 'Episode de l'occupation de Melun par l'armée du roi de Navarre', *Ann. Soc. hist. archéol. Gâtinais*, vii (1889), 285–92
Leguai, A., *De la seigneurie à l'état. Le Bourbonnais pendant la guerre de Cent ans* (1969)
Leguay, J-P., *Un réseau urbain au moyen age: les villes du duché de Bretagne aux xive et xve siècles* (1981)
*Lehoux, F., *Jean de France, duc de Berri. Sa vie, son action politique*, 4 vols (1966–8)
Lennel, F., *Histoire de Calais*, 3 vols (1908–1913)
*Léonard, E.-G., *Histoire de Jeanne Ire, reine de Naples, comtesse de Provence (1343–1382)*, 3 vols (1932–6)
Leroy, B., 'Le royaume de Navarre en 1365–1366', *Revue de Pau et du Béarn*, viii (1980), 3–17
*Leroy, B., 'La Navarre au XIVe siècle sous la dynastie d'Evreux (1328–1327)', *Les communications dans la péninsule iberique au moyen age. Actes du Colloque de Pau, 1980. Collection de la Maison des Pays Iberiques*, no. 4 (1981), 79–109
Leroy, B., 'Autour de Charles "le Mauvais": groupes et personnalités', *Revue historique*, cclxxiii(1) (1985), 3–17
Lewis, N.B., 'The Organisation of Indentured Retinues in Fourteenth Century England', *Trans. Roy. Hist. Soc.*, 4th series, xxvii (1945), 29–39
Llobet, C. de, 'Absolutions accordées en 1349 à deux Limousins collaborateurs des Anglais', *La "France Anglaise" au moyen age. Actes du IIIe congrès nationale des sociétés savantes (Poitiers, 1986), Section d'histoire médiévale et de philologie*, i (1988), 315–22
Lloyd, T.H., *The English Wool Trade in the Middle Ages* (1977)
*Lobineau, G.A., *Histoire de Bretagne*, 2 vols (1707)
Lodge, E.C., 'The Constables of Bordeau in the reign of Edward III', *EHR*, l (1935), 225–41
*Loirette, G., 'Arnaud Amanieu sire d'Albret et l'appel des seigneurs gascons en 1368', *Mélanges d'histoire offerts à M. Charles Bémont* (1913), 317–40
Loirette, 'Armand Amanieu d'Albret, 1364–80', *Annales du Midi* 43 (1931), 5–39
Loisne, A.M. de, *Dictionnaire topographique du département du Pas-de-Calais* (1907)
*Luce, S., 'Du role politique de Jean Maillart en 1358', *BEC*, xviii (1857), 415–26
*Luce, S., 'Négociations des Anglais avec le Roi de Navarre pendant la revolution Parisienne de 1358', *MSHP*, i (1875), 113–31
*Luce, S., *Histoire de Bertrand du Guesclin et de son époque* (1876)
*Luce, S., 'Du Guesclin au siège de Rennes', *BEC*, lii (1891), 615–8
Luce, S., 'Du Guesclin en Normandie. Le siège et la prise de Valognes', *Revue des Questions Historiques*, liii (1893), 372–411
*Luce, S., *Histoire de la Jacquerie*, 2e ed. (1894)

Marquette, J-B., *Les Albrets* (1975–9)
Martin, H., 'Enguerrand d'Eudin, capitaine royal de Loches, sénéchal de Beaucaire, gouverneur du Dauphiné', *Bull. Soc. archéol. Touraine*, xxxii (1958), 131–59
Masson d'Autume, M. de, *Cherbourg pendant la guerre de Cent ans* (1948)
Maubourguet, J.-M., *Le Périgord méridional des origines à l'an 1370. Étude d'histoire politique et religieuse* (1926)
McFarlane, K.B., *The Nobility of Later Medieval England* (1973)
*Menard, L., *Histoire civile, ecclesiastique et littéraire de la ville de Nismes*, 7 vols (1744–58)
*Menard, V., *Histoire réligieuse, civile et militaire de Saint-James de Beuvron* (1897)
*Mendl, B. and Quicke, F., 'Les relations politiques entre l'empereur et le roi de France de 1355 à 1356', *Revue belge de philologie et d'histoire*, viii (1929), 469–512
*Mesqui, J., *Provins. La fortification d'une ville au moyen age* (1979)
Mesqui, J., *Châteaux et enceintes de la France médiévale*, 2 vols (1991–3)
Miller, E., *War in the North. The Anglo-Scottish Wars of the Middle Ages* (1960)
Miquel, J., *L'architecture militaire dans le Rouergue au moyen age et l'organisation de la défence*, 2 vols (1981)
*Miret y Sans, J., 'Négociations de Pierre IV d'Aragon avec la cour de France', *Bull. Hisp.*, xiii (1905), 76–135
*Moisant, J., *Le Prince Noir en Aquitaine, 1355–1356, 1362–1370* (1894)
*Molinier, E., *Étude sur la vie d'Arnoul d'Audrehem, maréchal de France, 130.-1370*, *Mems. Acad. Inscr. et Belles-Lettres*, 2e sér., vi, 1ere partie (1883)
Mollat, G. 'Innocent VI et les tentatives de paix entre la France et l'Angleterre (1353–1355)', *Rev. hist. eccl.*, x (1909), 729–43
Mollat, M. (ed.), *Histoire de Rouen* (1979)
*Monicat, J., *Les Grandes Compagnies en Velay, 1358–1392*, 2e ed. (1928)
*Moranvillé, H., *Étude sur la vie de Jean le Mercier* (1888)
Moranvillé, H., 'Le siège de Reims, 1359–1360', *BEC*, lvi (1895), 90–98
Moranvillé, H., 'De l'origine de Thomas de la Marche', *BEC*, lxvi (1905), 281–6
Moranvillé, H., 'Charles d'Artois', *BEC*, lxviii (1907), 433–80
Morin, G., *Histoire du Gastinois*, n.e., 3 vols (1883–9)
Morgan, P., 'Cheshire and the defence of Aquitaine', *Trans of the Hist. Soc. of Lancashire and Cheshire*, 128 (1979), 139–60
Morgan, P., *War and Society in Medieval Cheshire, 1277–1403* (1987)
Myers, A.R., *London in the Age of Chaucer* (1972)
Nicholson, R., *Scotland. The Later Middle Ages* (1974)
*Nicolas, N.H., 'Observations on the institution of the Most Noble Order of the Garter', *Archaeologia*, xxxi (1846), 1–163
*Nicolas, N.H., *A History of the Royal Navy*, 2 vols (1847)
Ormrod, W.M., 'The English government and the Black Death of 1348–49', *England in the Fourteenth Century. Proceedings of the 1985 Harlaxton Symposium*, ed. W.M. Ormrod (1986)
Ormrod, W.M., 'The English Crown and the Customs, 1349–63', *Econ. Hist. Rev.*, 2nd series, xl (1987), 27–40
Ormrod, W.M., *The Reign of Edward III. Crown and Political Society in England, 1327–1377* (1990)
Ormrod, W.M., 'The Crown and the English Economy, 1290–1348', *Before the Black Death. Studies in the "Crisis" of the early fourteenth century*, ed. B.M.S. Campbell (1991), 149–83
*Pannier, L., *La noble-maison de Saint-Ouen* (1872)
Pataki, T., 'Notes sur Aurillac et ses glacis défensifs au début de la guerre de cent ans (1345–1362)', *Revue de la Haute-Auvergne*, Oct-Dec 1967, 3–16
Patourel, J. Le, 'L'occupation anglaise de Calais', *Revue du Nord*, xxxiii (1951), 228–41

Patourel, J. Le, 'Edward III and the kingdom of France', *History*, xliii (1958), 173–89
Patourel, J. Le, 'The Treaty of Brétigny, 1360', *Trans. Roy. Hist. Soc.*, 5th series, x (1960), 19–39
Patourel, J. Le, 'The King and the Princes in Fourteenth Century France', *Europe in the Late Middle Ages*, ed. J. Hale, R. Highfield and B. Smalley (1965), 155–83
Pegeot, P., 'Les destinées des maisons fortes à la fin du moyen age: exemples franc-comtois, *La maison forte au moyen age*, ed. M. Bur (1986), 243–51
Perroy, E., 'La fiscalité royale en Beaujolais aux xive et xve siècles', *Le moyen age*, 2e ser., xxix (1928), 5–47
*Perroy, E., 'Charles V et le traite de Brétigny', *Le moyen age*, 2e ser., xxix (1928), 255–81
Perroy, E., *The Hundred Years War*, tr. W.B. Wells (1945)
*Perroy, E., 'Édouard III et les seigneurs gascons en 1368', *Annales du Midi*, lxi (1948–9), 91–6
Perroy, E., 'L'administration de Calais en 1371–1372', *Rev. du Nord*, xxxiii (1951), 218–227
*Petit, E., *Les sires de Noyers* (1874)
*Petit, E., *Histoire des ducs de Bourgogne de la race Capétienne*, 9 vols (1885–1905)
*Petit, E., *Ducs de Bourgogne de la Maison de Valois*, i, *Philippe le Hardi*, 1ère partie (1909)
Petit-Dutaillis, C., and Collier, P., 'La diplomatie francaise et le traite de Bretigny', *Moyen Age*, 2e serie, i (1897), 1–35.
Pirenne, H., *Histoire de Belgique*, 4th ed, 6 vols (1947)
Plaisse, A. and S., *La vie municipale à Évreux pendant la guerre de Cent ans* (1978)
*Plancher, U., *Histoire générale et particulière de Bourgogne*, 4 vols (1739–81)
Pocquet du Haut-Jussé, B.A., *Les papes et les ducs de Bretagne*, 2 vols (1928)
Port, C., *Dictionnaire historique, géographique et biographique de Maine et Loire et de l'ancienne province d'Anjou*, n.e., 4 vols (1965–96
Prentout, H., *Les états provinciaux de Normandie*, 3 vols (1925–7)
Prestwich, M., *Armies and Warfare in the Middle Ages. The English Experience* (1996)
Prince, A.E., 'The Strength of English Armies in the Reign of Edward III', *EHR*, xlvi (1931), 353–71
Prince, A.E., 'The Indenture System under Edward III', *Historical Essays in Honour of James Tait* (1933), 283–97
Prince, A.E., 'The payment of army wages in Edward III's reign', *Speculum*, xix (1944), 137–60.
*Prou, M., 'Compte de Raoul de Louppy, gouverneur du Dauphiné de 1361 à 1369', *BEC*, xlvii (1886), 567–73
*Prou, M., *Étude sur les relations politiques du pape Urbain V avec les rois de France Jean II et Charles V* (1887)
Quicke, F., *Les Pays-Bas à la veille de la période bourguignonne, 1356–1384* (1947)
*Regné, J., 'La levée du capage et l'émeute toulousaine du 9 mai 1357', *Annales du Midi*, xxx (1918), 421–8
Reid, R.C., 'Edward de Balliol', *Dumfriesshire and Galloway Nat. Hist. and Antiq. Soc., Transactions*, 3rd ser., xxxv (1956–7), 38–63
Reid, R.R., 'The office of Warden of the Marches; its origin and early history', *EHR*, xxxii (1917), 479–96
Renouard, Y., *Bordeaux sous les rois d'Angleterre* (1965)
Reuss, R., 'La première invasion des "anglais" en Alsace. Épisode de l'histoire du quatorzième siècle', *Mélanges d'histoire offerts a M. Charles Bémont* (1913), 281–303
Rey, M., 'Aux origines de l'impôt: Les premiers comptes des aides dans l'éléction de Langres', *Économies et sociétés. Mélanges offerts à Édouard Perroy* (1973), 498–517
Rigaudière, A., 'Le financement des fortifications urbaines en France du milieu du xive siècle à la fin du xve siècle', *Revue historique*, cclxxiii (1985), 19–95
Roncière, C. de la, *Histoire de la marine française*, 6 vols (1899–1932)

Rouquette, J., *Le Rouergue sous les Anglais* (1887)
Russell, P.E., *The English Intervention in Spain and Portugal in the Time of Edward III and Richard II* (1955)
*Samaran, C., 'Pour l'histoire des Grandes Compagnies. Le "vuidement" de Chateau-Gontier par les anglais', *Mélanges d'histoire du moyen age dédiés à la mémoire de Louis Halphen* (1951), 641–4
Samaran, C., 'Les comptes consulaires d'Escazeaux (Tarn-et-Garonne), 1358–1464', *Annales du Midi*, lxviii (1956), 263–83
Saul, A., 'Great Yarmouth and the Hundred Years War in the Fourteenth Century', *Bull. Institute of Historical Research*, lii (1979), 105–115
Saul, N., *Knights and Esquires. The Gloucester Gentry in the Fourteenth Century* (1981)
Sauval, H., *Histoire et recherche des antiquités de la ville de Paris*, 3 vols (1724)
Scots peerage (The), ed. J. Balfour Paul, 9 vols (1904–14)
Storey-Challenger, S., *L'administration anglaise du Ponthieu apres le traité de Brétigny, 1361–1369* (1975)
Sturler, J. de, *Les relations politiques et les échanges commerciaux entre le duché de Brabant et l'Angleterre au moyen age* (1936)
Sumption, J., *The Hundred Years War*, i, *Trial by Battle* (1990)
*Temple-Leader, J., and Marcotti, G.O., *Sir John Hawkwood (l'Acuto). Story of a Condottiere*, tr. L. Scott (1889)
Thomas, A., 'Le comté de La Marche et le traité de Brétigny', *Revue historique*, lxxvi (1901), 79–97
Touchard, H., *Le commerce maritime Breton à la fin du moyen age* (1967)
Tourneur-Aumont, J.M., *La bataille de Poitiers et la construction de la France* (1940)
Tout, T.F., *Chapters in the Administrative History of Medieval England*, 6 vols (1920–37)
Tout, T.F., 'Some Neglected Fights between Crécy and Poitiers', *Collected Papers*, ii (1934)(1), 227–31
Tout, T.F., 'Firearms in England in the Fourteenth Century', *Collected Papers*, ii (1934)(2), 233–75
*Trautz, F., *Die Könige von England und das Reich, 1272–1377* (1961)
Tuck, J.A., 'War and Society in the Medieval North', *Northern History*, xxi (1985), 33–52
*Tucoo-Chala, P., *Gaston Fébus et la vicomté de Béarn* (1959)
*Tucoo-Chala, P., *La vicomté de Béarn et le problème de la souveraineté* (1961)
Vale, J., *Edward III and Chivalry* (1982)
*Valois, N., 'Notes sur la revolution parisienne de 1356–58. La revanche des frères Braque', *MSHP*, x (1883), 100–26
Valois, N., 'Le gouvernement représentatif en France au xive siècle. Étude sur le conseil du roi pendant la captivité de Jean le Bon', *Rev. des quest. hist.*, xxxvii (1885), 63–115
*Varenbergh, E., *Histoire des relations diplomatiques entre le comté de Flandre et l'Angleterre au moyen age* (1874)
Vaultier, R., *Le folklore pendant la guerre de Cent ans d'après les lettres de rémission du Trésor des Chartes* (1965)
*Viard, J., 'Documents français remis au gouvernement anglais à la suite du traité de Brétigny', *BEC*, lviii (1897), 155–61
*Vic, C. de and Vaissète, J., *Histoire générale de Languedoc*, n.e., 16 vols (1874–1905)
Villepelet, R., *Histoire de la ville de Périgueux et de ses institutions municipales jusqu'au traité de Brétigny (1360)* (1908)
*Viollet, P., 'Les états de Paris en février 1358', *Mems. Acad. Inscr. et Belles-Lettres*, xxxiv (1892), 261–92
Vuitry, A., *Études sur les institutions financières de la France avant la Révolution de 1789*, n.s., 2 vols (1878–83)
Watt, D.E.R., *A Biographical Dictionary of Scottish Graduates to A.D. 1410* (1977)

Webster, B., 'The English Occupations of Dumfriesshire in the Fourteenth Century', *Dumfriesshire and Galloway Nat. Hist. and Antiq. Soc., Transactions*, 3rd ser., xxxv (1956–7), 64–80
Wolff, P., *Commerces et marchands de Toulouse (vers 1350–vers 1450)* (1954)
Yanguas y Miranda, J., *Diccionario de antiguedades del reino de Navarra*, 3 vols (1840)
Zacour, N.P., *Talleyrand: the Cardinal of Périgord (1301–1364)* (1960)
Zurita y Castro, G, *Anales de la Corona de Aragón* (1610)

Index